Criminal Law Textbook

University Centre at
Blackburn
College

Telephone: 01254 292165

Please return this book on or before the last date shown

13/10/14	

Criminal Law Textbook

SECOND EDITION

Russell Heaton, LLB

Former Principal Lecturer in Law,
Department of Academic Legal Studies,
Nottingham Trent University

OXFORD

UNIVERSITY PRESS

OXFORD
UNIVERSITY PRESS

Great Clarendon Street, Oxford OX2 6DP

Oxford University Press is a department of the University of Oxford.
It furthers the University's objective of excellence in research, scholarship,
and education by publishing worldwide in

Oxford New York

Auckland Cape Town Dar es Salaam Hong Kong Karachi
Kuala Lumpur Madrid Melbourne Mexico City Nairobi
New Delhi Shanghai Taipei Toronto

With offices in

Argentina Austria Brazil Chile Czech Republic France Greece
Guatemala Hungary Italy Japan Poland Portugal Singapore
South Korea Switzerland Thailand Turkey Ukraine Vietnam

Oxford is a registered trade mark of Oxford University Press
in the UK and in certain other countries

Published in the United States
by Oxford University Press Inc., New York

© Russell Heaton 2006

British Library Cataloguing in Publication Data

Data available

Library of Congress Cataloging in Publication Data

Data available

Typeset by Newgen Imaging Systems (P) Ltd., Chennai, India
Printed in Great Britain
on acid-free paper by
Ashford Colour Press Ltd., Gosport, Hampshire

ISBN 0-19-928705-8   978-0-19-928705-5

10 9 8 7 6 5 4 3 2

To Kane and Lorraine

■ PREFACE

The aim of this book is to provide students with a clear, understandable and readable exposition of the general principles of criminal law and of the major offences commonly studied in degree and professional courses. Originally written for distance learning students who are without ready access to tutorial guidance, I believe that the approach is well suited to students attending university courses, where increasing resource problems mean that the availability of tutorial guidance and advice reduces by the year.

I have endeavoured to pass on the benefits of many years' experience (I am not prepared to reveal how many!) of teaching criminal law to law degree and non-law graduate conversion students embracing full-time, part-time and sandwich attendance modes as well as distance learning modes. I know what students find difficult and the common misunderstandings and mistakes which occur and I have tried particularly hard to enable readers to avoid them. Indeed one five-star review of a previous edition on the Amazon web site felt 'a deep sense of communication' from the author to the reader. That has certainly been my aim and it is good to know that it succeeded for at least one person!

I have included lots of examples to illustrate my explanations, along with some flow charts and diagrams and comprehensive summaries at the end of each chapter to enable students to maintain or regain their bearings amidst the inevitable detail of the subject. More than most law subjects, criminal law bristles with inconsistencies, uncertainties, illogicalities and anachronisms. I have attempted to face these and avoid a superficial treatment which can only mislead students.

The book can function quite satisfactorily as a stand-alone text but its utility will be considerably increased when used in conjunction with the Online Resource Centre, specially designed to complement it and featuring a fairly comprehensive collection of cases and materials cross-referenced from the book. The sources include not only extracts from legislation and the important cases but also passages from Law Commission reports and academic writings where I feel that these aid understanding rather than obscure it! Effectively the web site functions as an electronic casebook. It will also be used to update readers on important future developments in the law.

For this edition, I have acceded to popular demand and added a chapter on sexual offences which covers the major offences in the Sexual Offences Act 2003. The major legislative development since the last edition is the projected Fraud Act 2006 which sweeps away much of the old law on deception and replaces it with a generalised fraud offence. At the time of writing, the Fraud Bill had reached the Committee stage in the House of Lords and it appeared very likely that it would be enacted without significant amendment. I therefore took the decision (or should I say the gamble!) to re-write Chapter 11 on the basis that the new law was in place. Absent any unforeseen delays, the Bill is expected to become law in April when this book is likely to be published but readers are warned to check that there have been no changes from the original Bill which forms the basis of my account. I will produce an update for the Online Resource Centre as soon as the Bill is enacted detailing any changes affecting the accuracy of the text.

Of the usual deluge of case law, I would highlight the House of Lords' decision in *Hasan* which aims to curtail the scope of the defence of duress and the Privy Council's decision in *Attorney General for Jersey* v *Holley*, which overturns *Smith* (*Morgan*) in the law of provocation. A five judge Court of Appeal has just confirmed that *Holley* represents the law in *James*; *Karimi* (2006), a decision which came too late to incorporate in the text. There have been a number of other important Court of Appeal decisions on complicity (*Bryce, Kennedy* (*No 2*), *Attorney-General's Reference* (*No 3 of 2004*) and *D*), intoxicated mistake and self-defence (*Hatton*), necessity and duress of circumstances (*Quayle* and, too late for the text, *Altham* (2006)), manslaughter (*Rogers, Finlay, Kennedy* (*No 2*), Misra, *Willoughby*), conspiracy (*Sakavickas, Harmer, Ali*), and consent in non-fatal offences of violence (*Dica, Barnes, Konzani*).

Apart from the anticipatory Chapter 11 on fraud (see explanation above), the text is based on the law as I understood it at 31 October 2005.

Finally, I should like to thank colleagues and students who, over the years, have unknowingly assisted in the work, Hussain Hadi and the team at Oxford University Press for their friendly, reliable and efficient support and the excellence of the book's design and, most of all, my wife Lorraine for her selfless love and support.

Russell Heaton
January 2006

■ OUTLINE TABLE OF CONTENTS

TABLE OF CASES   xix

TABLE OF STATUTES   xxxix

1   **Introduction**   1

2   ***Actus reus***   17

3   ***Mens rea* and fault**   47

4   **Non-fatal offences against the person**   87

5   **Sexual offences**   121

6   **Homicide**   139

7   **General defences I: Age and insanity**   193

8   **General defences II: Automatism, intoxication, mistake and self-defence**   207

9   **General defences III: Duress, necessity and marital coercion**   247

10   **Offences against property I: Theft**   275

11   **Offences against property II: Fraud**   325

12   **Offences against property III**   355

13   **Strict liability**   403

14   **Secondary participation in crime**   419

15   **Vicarious and corporate liability**   459

16   **Inchoate offences**   477

APPENDIX: ASSESSMENT QUESTIONS AND ANSWERS   519

INDEX   557

■ CONTENTS

SOURCE ACKNOWLEDGEMENTS		xvii
TABLE OF CASES		xix
TABLE OF STATUTES		xxxix
GLOSSARY OF JOURNAL AND OTHER REFERENCES		xlv
HOW TO USE THIS BOOK		xlvii

1	**Introduction**	1
1.1	What is a crime?	2
1.2	The role of the substantive criminal law	2
1.3	Classification of offences	4
1.4	Appeals and the role of the trial judge	5
1.5	Burden of proof	8
1.6	Reform of the criminal law	12
	Further reading	14
	Summary	15

2	***Actus reus***	17
2.1	Objectives	17
2.2	Introduction	17
2.3	*Actus reus*	18
2.4	The elements of *actus reus*	19
2.5	Consequences	19
2.6	Circumstances	20
2.7	Conduct	21
2.8	Causation	30
2.9	Coincidence of *mens rea* and *actus reus*	43
	Further reading	44
	Summary	45

3	***Mens rea* and fault**	47
3.1	Objectives	47
3.2	Introduction	47
3.3	Intention	50
3.4	Recklessness	63
3.5	Negligence	72
3.6	*Mens rea* as to circumstances	74
3.7	Fault element variable	79

3.8	Some other *mens rea* words	79
3.9	Mistake and *mens rea*	80
3.10	Transferred malice	82
	Further reading	83
	Summary	84

4 Non-fatal offences against the person | | 87 |
4.1	Objectives	87
4.2	Introduction	87
4.3	The less serious offences	88
4.4	The more serious offences	106
4.5	Reform	117
	Further reading	118
	Summary	118
	Assessment exercise	120

5 Sexual offences | | 121 |
5.1	Objectives	121
5.2	Introduction	121
5.3	Rape	122
5.4	Assault by penetration	129
5.5	Sexual assault	130
5.6	Causing a person to engage in sexual activity without consent	133
5.7	Child victims under 13	134
5.8	Sexual offences protecting children under 16	134
	Further reading	135
	Summary	135

6 Homicide | | 139 |
6.1	Objectives	139
6.2	Introduction	139
6.3	*Actus reus*	140
6.4	Murder	142
6.5	Manslaughter	149
	Further reading	189
	Summary	189
	Assessment exercise	192

7 General defences I: Age and insanity | | 193 |
7.1	Objectives	193
7.2	Introduction to and overview of general defences	193
7.3	Age and criminal responsibility	195
7.4	Insanity	196
	Further reading	205
	Summary	205

8   **General defences II: Automatism, intoxication, mistake and self-defence**   207

   8.1   Objectives   207

   8.2   Introduction   208

   8.3   Automatism   208

   8.4   Intoxication   215

   8.5   Mistake   226

   8.6   Self-defence, prevention of crime and defence of property   234

       Further reading   242

       Summary   242

       Assessment exercise   245

9   **General defences III: Duress, necessity and marital coercion**   247

   9.1   Objectives   247

   9.2   Introduction   247

   9.3   Duress by threats   249

   9.4   Duress of circumstances   259

   9.5   Necessity   263

   9.6   Marital coercion   269

   9.7   Superior orders   270

       Further reading   270

       Summary   271

       Assessment exercise   274

10   **Offences against property I: Theft**   275

   10.1   Objectives   275

   10.2   Introduction   275

   10.3   Theft   276

   10.4   Definition   277

       Further reading   321

       Summary   322

       Assessment exercise   324

11   **Offences against property II: Fraud**   325

   11.1   Objectives   325

   11.2   Introduction   325

   11.3   A brief summary of the old law of deception   326

   11.4   The new offence of fraud   331

       Further reading   351

       Summary   351

12   **Offences against property III**   355

   12.1   Objectives   355

   12.2   Introduction   355

   12.3   Robbery   355

12.4	Offences of temporary deprivation	357
12.5	Abstracting electricity	364
12.6	Burglary	364
12.7	Aggravated burglary	371
12.8	Blackmail	373
12.9	Handling stolen goods	378
12.10	Criminal damage	388
	Further reading	398
	Summary	399
	Assessment exercise	402

13   Strict liability 403

13.1	Objectives	403
13.2	Introduction	403
13.3	The development of strict liability	405
13.4	How do the courts decide on strict liability?	406
13.5	Is the imposition of strict liability justified?	416
	Further reading	417
	Summary	417

14   Secondary participation in crime 419

14.1	Objectives	419
14.2	Introduction	419
14.3	Perpetrators	420
14.4	Accessories	423
	Further reading	456
	Summary	456
	Assessment exercise	458

15   Vicarious and corporate liability 459

15.1	Objectives	459
15.2	Vicarious liability	459
15.3	Corporate liability	464
	Further reading	475
	Summary	476
	Assessment exercise	476

16   Inchoate offences 477

16.1	Objectives	477
16.2	Introduction	477
16.3	Attempt	479
16.4	Conspiracy	491

16.5	Incitement	511
	Further reading	515
	Summary	515
	Assessment exercise	518

| APPENDIX: ASSESSMENT QUESTIONS AND ANSWERS | 519 |
| INDEX | 557 |

■ SOURCE ACKNOWLEDGEMENTS

Grateful acknowledgement is made to all the authors and publishers of copyright material which appears on the accompanying Online Resource Centre, and in particular to the following for permission to reprint material from the sources indicated:

Extracts from *Law Commission Reports* (LCR) 276 & 290, *House of Lords Reports* (UKHL) 10 & 51, and Home Office consultation papers are Crown copyright material and are reproduced under Class Licence Number C01P0000148 with the permission of the Controller of HMSO and the Queen's Printer for Scotland.

Cambridge Law Journal and the authors: extracts from *Cambridge Law Journal*: P R Glazebrook: Commentary on *B v DPP*, 'How Old Do *You* Think She Was?', *CLJ* 26 (2001); A T H Smith: Commentary on *R v Hinks*, 'Theft or Sharp Practice: Who Cares Now?', *CLJ* 21 (2001); G Williams: '*Finis for Novus Actus*', *CLJ* 391 (1989) and 'Oblique intention', 46 *CLJ* 417 (1987).

Cambridge University Press: extract from J Finnis: 'Intention and Side Effects', in R G Frey & C W Morris: *Liability and Responsibility: Essays in Law and Morals* (Cambridge University Press, 1991).

Columbia Law Review: extract from P Robinson: 'Criminal Law Defences: A Systematic Analysis', 82 *Col LR* 199 (1982).

George Fletcher: extracts from G P Fletcher: *Rethinking Criminal Law* (Little, Brown & Co., 1978).

Incorporated Council of Law Reporting for England and Wales, Megarry House, 119 Chancery Lane, London WC2A IPP: extracts from *King's Bench Reports* (KB), *Queen's Bench Reports* (QB), *Appeal Court Reports* (AC) and *Weekly Law Reports;* www.lawreports.co.uk.

LexisNexis UK: extracts from J C Smith: *The Law of Theft* (7th edn., Butterworths, 1973); *New Law Journal:* J C Smith: 'Secondary participation in crime—can we do without it?', 144 *NLJ* 679 (1994); and from *All England Law Reports, England and Wales Court of Appeal Criminal Division, Northern Ireland Law Reports, Road Traffic Reports*, and *Criminal Law Review* Lexis transcripts.

News International Newspapers Ltd: extracts from case reports *R v Wilson (Alan Thomas)* in (1996) *The Times* 5 March (Court of Appeal) and *Roper* v *Taylor's Central Garage (Exeter) Ltd* (1951) from 2 *Times Law Reports* 284 (King's Bench Division) copyright © The Times 2003.

Oxford University Press: extracts from H L A Hart and T Honoré: *Causation in Law* (2nd edn., OUP, 1985); and Jeremy Horder: *Provocation and Responsibility* (OUP, 1992); www.oup.com.

Sweet & Maxwell: extracts from A T H Smith: 'On *Actus Reus* and *Mens Rea*', and D A Thomas: 'Form and Function in Criminal Law', in P R Glazebrook (ed), *Reshaping the Criminal Law* (Stevens, 1978); Glanville Williams: *Textbook of Criminal Law* (2nd edn., Stevens, 1983); Glanville Williams: *Criminal Law: The General Part* (2nd edn., Stevens, 1961); and L H Leigh: *Strict and Vicarious Liability* (Sweet & Maxwell, 1983); extracts from *Law Quarterly Review*: N L A Barlow: 'Drug Intoxication and the Principle of *Capacitas Rationalis*', 100 *LQR* 639 (1984); and from *Criminal Law Review*: Criminal Law Case Reports, and extracts from articles by N Bamforth: 'Sado Masochism and Consent', *Crim LR* 661 (1994); R A Duff: 'Recklessness', *Crim LR* 282 (1980); J Gobert: 'Corporate Criminality: New Crimes for the Times', *Crim LR* 722 (1994); J Horder: (2) 'Occupying the moral high ground? The Law Commission on Duress', *Crim LR* 334 (1994); Sir Bernard McKenna: 'Blackmail: a Criticism', *Crim LR* 466 (1966); E Paton: 'Reformulating the Intoxication Rules: The Law Commission's Report', *Crim LR* 382 (1995); A T H Smith: 'The Idea of Criminal Deception', *Crim LR* 721 (1982); and from Published Reports: *Discrimination Law Reports* and *Criminal Appeal Reports*.

Every effort has been made to trace and contact copyright holders prior to going to press but this has not been possible in every case. Although we are continuing to seek the necessary permissions up to publication, if notified, the publisher will undertake to rectify any errors or omissions at the earliest opportunity.

TABLE OF CASES

A (Children), Re [2001] 2
WLR 480... 57, 141, 148, 249,
251, 264, 266, 272

A v Hayden (No. 2) (1984) 156 CLR
532... 270

A v R [1978] Crim LR 689... 389

A v UK [1998] Crim LR 892... 94

Abbott v R [1977] AC 755... 258

Abdul-Hussain et al. [1999] Crim
LR 570, CA... 255, 256, 261,
262, 263, 272

Acott [1997] 1 All ER 706... 154, 190

Adams v R [1995] 1WLR 52... 504

Adesanya [1983] Crim LR 720... 102

Adomako [1994] 3 All ER 79,
HL... 72, 173, 174, 175,
177, 178, 180, 191

Ahlers [1915] 1KB 616... 53, 62, 84

Ahluwalia [1992] 4 All
ER 889... 153, 154, 165, 168, 190

Ahmad (1986) 84 Cr App R 64... 24

Airedale NHS Trust v Bland [1993] 1 All
ER 821... 27, 142, 248, 264

Airedale Trust v Bland; Re T [1992] 4 All
ER 649, CA... 28, 45

Aitken [1992] 1 WLR 1006, Courts
Martial Appeal Court... 104

Ali [1995] Crim LR 303... 250, 257, 271

Ali [2005] EWCA Crim 87... 499

Allchorn v Hopkins (1905) 69 JP
355... 463

Allen [1985] 2 All ER 641... 346,
350, 354

Allen [1988] Crim LR 698, CA... 223

Allen v Whitehead [1930] 1KB 211... 463

Allied Domecq Leisure Ltd v Cooper
[1999] Crim LR 230, DC... 461

Allsop (1976) 64 Cr App R 29, CA... 337,
338, 504, 506, 507, 517

Alphacell Ltd v Woodward [1972] 2 All ER
475, HL... 408, 411, 413, 462

Ambler [1979] RTR 217... 359

AMK (Property Management) Ltd [1985]
Crim LR 600, CA... 58

Anderson [1985] 2 All ER 961, HL... 496,
497, 498

Anderson [1995] Crim LR 430, CA... 234

Anderson and Morris [1966] 2 All ER 644,
CA... 449

Anderton v Ryan [1985] 2 All ER 355...
490

Andrews [2003] Crim LR 477... 183

Andrews v DPP [1937] AC 576, [1937] 2
All ER 552, HL... 72, 85, 173,
182, 191

Antar [2004] EWCA Crim 2708,
CA... 252

Antoine [2000] 2 All ER 208,
HL... 167, 203

Ardalan [1972] 2 All ER 257, CA... 493

Arnold [1997] 4 All ER 1... 299, 310, 320

Arrowsmith v Jenkins [1963] 2 All ER 210,
DC... 80

Arthur v Anker [1997] QB 564... 377

Associated Octel Co. Ltd [1996] 4 All ER
846, HL... 415, 465

Atakpu [1993] 4 All ER 215, CA... 283,
284, 285, 286, 322, 357, 385

Atkinson [1985] Crim LR 314 CA... 168

Atkinson [2004] Crim LR 226... 315

Attorney-General for Hong Kong v Nai
Keung [1987] 1 WLR 1339, PC... 292

Attorney-General for Jersey v Holley
[2005] UKPC 23... 150, 155, 161, 162,
163, 164, 190, 252, 253

Attorney-General for Northern Ireland v
Gallagher [1963] AC 349,
HL... 216, 218

Attorney-General v Able [1984]
QB 795 ... 427

Attorney-General's Reference
(No. 1 of 1974) [1974] 2 All ER 899,
CA ... 380

Attorney-General's Reference
(No. 1 of 1975) [1975] 2 All ER 684,
CA ... 423, 424, 426, 427, 436, 456

Attorney-General's References (Nos. 1
and 2 of 1979) [1979] 3 All ER 143,
CA ... 371, 489

Attorney-General's Reference (No. 4 of
1979) [1981] 1 All ER 1193, CA ... 381

Attorney-General's Reference (No. 6 of
1980) [1981] 2 All ER 1057 CA ... 100,
101, 102

Attorney-General's Reference (No. 1 of
1982) [1983] 2 All ER 721, CA ... 505,
507

Attorney-General's Reference (No. 1 of
1983) [1984] 3 All ER 369 ... 301

Attorney-General's Reference (No. 2 of
1983) [1984] 1 All ER 988, CA ... 237,
238, 245

Attorney-General's Reference (No. 1 of
1985) [1986] 2 All ER 219, CA ... 296,
322, 308

Attorney-General's Reference (No. 1 of
1992) [1993] 2 All ER 190 ... 484

Attorney-General's Reference (No. 2 of
1992) [1993] 4 All ER 683 ... 209

Attorney-General's Reference (No. 3 of
1992) [1994] 2 All ER 121, CA ... 398,
486, 487, 516

Attorney-General's Reference (No. 3 of
1994) [1997] 3 All ER 936, HL ... 82, 83,
85, 86, 141, 184, 188, 191

Attorney-General's Reference (No. 1 of
1995) [1996] 1 WLR 970, CA ... 233

Attorney-General's Reference (No. 3 of
1998) [1999] 3 All ER 40, CA ... 203, 206

Attorney-General's Reference (No. 2 of
1999) [2000] 2 Cr App R 207, CA ... 468,
469, 475, 476

Attorney-General's Reference (No. 2 of
1999) [2000] 3 All ER 182 CA ... 177,
468, 469

Attorney-General's Reference (No.4 of
2002); Sheldrake v DPP [2004] UKHL
43 ... 11

Attorney-General's Reference (No. 2 of
2003) [2004] EWCA Crim 785 ... 461

Attorney-General's Reference (No. 3 of
2003) [2004] 3 WLR 451 ... 24

Attorney-General's Reference
(No.1 of 2004) [2004] EWCA Crim
1025, CA ... 11

Attorney-General's Reference (No. 3 of
2004) [2005] EWCA Crim 1882 ... 445,
449, 458

Austin [1981] 1 All ER 374, CA ... 431

Ayres [1984] 1 All ER 619 ... 492

Aziz [1993] Crim LR 708,
CA ... 349, 354

B [2005] Crim LR 486 ... 361

B & S v Leathley [1979] Crim
LR 314 ... 369

B v DPP [2000] 2 WLR 452; [2000] 1 All
ER 833, HL ... 47, 78, 79, 82, 96, 105,
226, 228, 230, 231, 244, 340, 406, 407,
410, 411, 412, 416, 488

Bailey (1800) Russ & Ry 1 ... 233

Bailey [1983] 2 All ER 503 ... 213, 214,
224, 243

Baille [1995] Crim LR 739 ... 153

Bainbridge [1959] 3 All ER 200,
CCA ... 437, 440

Baker and Ward [1999] 2 Cr App R 335,
CA ... 255, 257

Baker and Wilkins [1997] Crim LR 497,
CA ... 260

Baldessare (1930) 22 Cr App R 70,
CCA ... 449

Ball [1989] Crim LR 730, CA ... 185, 191

Barker v R (1983) 7 ALJR 426 ... 368

Barnes [2005] 2 All ER 113, CA ... 96, 101,
103, 113, 119

Barnet London Borough Council v Eastern Electricity Board [1973] 2 All ER 319, DC... 388

Barnfather v Islington Education Authority [2003] 1 WLR 2318, DC... 14, 405

Barr [1978] Crim LR 244... 363

Bastian [1958] 1 WLR 413... 204

Bateman (1925) 19 Cr App R 8; (1925) 94 LJKB 791... 173–4

Baxter [1971] 2 All ER 359, CA... 374

Beasley (1981) 73 Cr App R 44... 112

Becerra (1975) 62 Cr App R 212, CA... 452

Beck [1985] 1 All ER 571, CA... 424

Beckford v R [1987] 3 All ER 425; [1988] AC 130, PC... 220, 228, 231, 234, 237, 240, 244, 245

Bedder v DPP [1954] 2 All ER 801, HL... 156, 157

Belfon [1976] 1 WLR 741... 116

Bell [1984] 3 All ER 842, CA... 22, 203, 210

Belleni [1980] Crim LR 437, CA... 387, 401

Benge (1865) 4 F & F 504... 32

Benham v UK (1996) 22 EHRR 293... 2

Bennett [1995] Crim LR 877, CA... 218

Bentham [2005] UKHL 18, HL... 372

Billinghurst [1978] Crim LR 553... 104

Bird [1985] 2 All ER 513, CA... 237, 245

Birtles (1969) 53 Cr App R 469... 455, 458

Blackburn v Bowering [1994] 3 All ER 380, CA... 109

Blackshall [1999] 1 Cr App R 35... 268

Blake [1997] 1 All ER 963... 409, 415

Blake v Barnard (1840) 9 C & P 626... 91

Blake v DPP [1993] Crim LR 586, DC... 391

Blakely, Sutton v DPP [1991] Crim LR 763, DC... 427, 436, 438, 457

Blaue [1975] 3 All ER 446... 39, 40, 45

Bloxham [1982] 1 All ER 582, HL... 382, 383, 385, 401

Board of Trade v Owen [1957] AC 602... 504, 505

Bogacki [1973] 2 All ER 864... 358

Boggeln v Williams [1978] 2 All ER 1061... 314

Boldsizsar v Knight [1980] Crim LR 653... 361

Bollom [2004] Cr App R 6... 110, 112

Bonner [1970] 2 All ER 97, CA... 295

Booth [1999] Crim LR 144, CA... 398

Bourne [1938] 3 All ER 615, CCA... 268

Bourne (1952) 36 Cr App R 125, CCA... 432, 457

Bow (1976) 64 Cr App R 54, CA... 359

Bowen [1996] 2 Cr App R 157, CA... 252, 253, 271

Boyea [1992] Crim LR 574... 101

Bradshaw (1878) 14 Cox CC 83... 104

Brain (1834) 6 C & P 349... 141

Bratty v Attorney-General for Northern Ireland [1961] 3 All ER 523; [1963] AC 386, HL... 22, 198, 204, 208

Bravery v Bravery [1954] 3 All ER 59, CA... 103

Breckenridge (1984) 79 Cr App R 244, CA... 78

Briggs [1987] Crim LR 708, CA... 360

Briggs [2003] EWCA Crim 3662... 288, 289

British Steel plc [1995] Crim LR 654, CA... 465

Brockley (1994) 99 Cr App R 385, CA... 411

Brook [1993] Crim LR 455... 387, 401

Brooks and Brooks (1982) 76 Cr App R 66... 348

Broome v Perkins [1987] Crim LR 272... 209, 215

Brown [1969] 3 All ER 198, CA... 384

Brown [1972] 2 All ER 1328, CA... 163, 190

Brown [1985] Crim LR 212... 365

Brown [1993] 2 All ER 75, HL... 96, 100, 101, 102, 103, 105, 108, 112, 113, 119, 190

Brutus v Cozens [1972] 2 All ER 1297, HL... 313

Bryce [2004] EWCA Crim 1231, CA... 434, 435, 437, 439, 443

Bryson [1985] Crim LR 669, CA... 58, 116

Bullock [1955] 1 All ER 15, CCA... 428

Burgess [1991] 2 All ER 769, CA... 198, 200, 201, 206, 208

Burgess and McLean [1995] Crim LR 425... 154

Burke [1988] Crim LR 841, CA... 58

Burns (1984) 79 Cr App R 173, CA... 494, 516

Burns v Bidder [1966] 3 All ER 29... 208, 209

Burrell v Harmer [1967] Crim LR 169... 97

Burstow [1997] 3 WLR 534, HL... 93, 110, 111, 112, 115, 116, 119, 260

Bush v Commonwealth 78 Ky 268 (1880)... 37

Byrne [1960] 3 All ER 1... 167, 168, 169, 191

C v DPP [1994] 3 All ER 190; [1995] 2 All ER 43, HL... 195

C v DPP [2002] Crim LR 322, DC... 373

Cahill [1993] Crim LR 141, CA... 318

Cairns [2003] 1 Cr App R 662... 269

Caldwell, see Metropolitan Police Commissioner v Caldwell

Calhaem [1985] 2 All ER 266, CA... 424, 427

Callow v Tillstone (1900) 83 LT 411... 244, 404, 416, 437, 462

Cambridge [1994] 2 All ER 760, CA... 154

Campbell (1987) 84 Cr App R 255, CA... 171

Campbell [1991] Crim LR 268, CA... 483, 515

Campbell [1997] Crim LR 495, CA... 167

Carter v Richardson [1974] RTR 314, DC... 438

Cartledge v Allen [1973] Crim LR 530... 110

Cash [1985] QB 801, CA... 385, 401

Cato [1976] 1 All ER 260, CA... 183, 185

Chamberlain v Lindon [1998] 2 All ER 538... 393

Champ [1982] Crim LR 108... 407

Chan- Fook [1994] 2 All ER 552... 108

Chan Man-sin v R [1988] 1 All ER 1, PC... 287, 290

Chan Wing-siu v R [1984] 3 All ER 877... 442, 443

Chandler v DPP [1962] 3 All ER 314, HL... 61, 62

Charge Card Services Ltd, Re [1988] 3 All ER 702... 349

Charlson [1955] 1 All ER 859... 208

Chase Manhattan Bank NA v Israel-British Bank (London) Ltd [1979] 3 All ER 1025... 296

Cheshire [1991] 3 All ER 670, CA... 31, 32, 41, 46

Chief Constable of Avon v Shimmen (1986) 84 Cr App R 7, DC... 66, 70, 85, 394

Chief Constable of Norfolk v Fisher [1992] RTR 6, DC... 414

Chief Metropolitan Stipendiary Magistrate, ex parte Choudhury [1991] 1 All ER 306, DC... 405

Choi [1999] All ER (D)... 509

Chrastny [1992] 1 All ER 189, CA... 493

Church [1965] 2 All ER 72, CCA... 43, 184, 191

Cichon v DPP [1994] Crim LR 918, DC... 267, 268

Clarence (1888) 22 QBD 23... 98, 110, 112

Clark (Brian) [2001] Crim LR 572... 320

Clarke (1984) 80 Cr App R 344... 455, 458

Clarke [1972] 1 All ER 219, CA... 201

Clarke [1990] Crim LR 383, CA... 164

Clarkson [1971] 1 WLR 1402; [1971] 3 All ER 344, CA... 427, 428, 429, 430, 457

Clarkson [2005] Crim LR 677... 472

Clarkson and Allan [1963] 2 All ER 897, CCA... 429

Clear [1968] 1 All ER 74... 375

Clegg [1995] 1 All ER 334... 239, 240, 245

Clode v Barnes [1974] 1 All ER 1166, DC... 460, 462

Clouden [1987] Crim LR 56... 356, 399

Clucas [1949] 2 All ER 40, CCA... 327

Coady [1996] Crim LR 518, CA... 327, 351

Cobb v Williams [1973] Crim LR 243... 460

Cocker [1989] Crim LR 740... 152

Codère (1916) 12 Cr App R 21... 202

Cogan and Leak [1975] 2 All ER 1059; [1976] 2 QB 217, CA... 123, 422, 432

Cole [1994] Crim LR 582, CA... 250, 255, 256, 261, 262, 263, 271, 272

Coleman [1986] Crim LR 56, CA... 384

Coles (1980) 144 JPN 528... 168

Coles [1995] 1 Cr App R 157, CA... 69

Collins [1972] 2 All ER 1105, CA... 124, 365, 399, 400

Collins v Wilcock [1984] 3 All ER 374... 97

Collister and Warhurst (1955) 39 Cr App R 100... 374, 376

Comer v Bloomfield (1970) 55 Cr App R 305... 481

Concannon [2002] Crim LR 213, CA... 444

Coney (1882) 8 QBD 534... 429, 430, 457

Constanza [1997] 2 Cr App R 492... 90

Conway [1988] 3 All ER 1025, CA... 254, 260, 261, 271

Cooke [1986] 2 All ER 985, HL... 327, 492, 506, 517

Cooper [2004] EWCA Crim 1382... 394

Coppen v Moore (No. 2) [1898] 2 QB 306... 460, 462

Corbett [1996] Crim LR 594... 38

Corcoran v Anderton (1980) 71 Cr App R 10... 356

Cort [2004] 4 All ER 137, CA... 96

Cory Bros Ltd [1927] 1 KB 810... 469

Court [1989] AC 28... 131

Cox [1993] 12 BMLR 38... 57

Cox [1995] Crim LR 741, CA... 154

Cox v Riley (1986) 83 Cr App R 54... 389

Crédit Lyonnais Nederland NV v Export Credits Guarantee Department [1998] 1 Lloyd's Rep 19... 451

Cunningham [1957] 2 All ER 412... 65

Curr [1967] 1 All ER 478... 514, 517

D [2005] EWCA Crim 1981... 442, 449, 453

D & C Builders Ltd v Rees [1955] 3 All ER 837, CA... 378

Dalby [1982] 1 All ER 916; (1982) 74 Cr App R 348, CA... 34, 185, 187, 191

Dalloway (1847) 2 Cox 273... 33

Data Protection Registrar v Amnesty International [1995] Crim LR 633, DC... 64

Davies [1975] 1 All ER 890, CA... 151

Davies v DPP [1954] 1 All ER 507; [1994] Crim LR 604, HL... 362, 442

Davies v Leighton (1978) 68 Cr App R 4, DC... 298, 302

Dawson [1976] Crim LR 692, CA... 356, 399

Dawson (1985) 81 Cr App R 150... 185, 191

Day (1841) 9 C & P 722... 97

Day (1845) 1 Cox CC 207... 92

Day [2001] Crim LR 984, CA... 449, 458

Dear [1996] Crim LR 595, CA... 40

Deller (1952) 36 Cr App R 184... 21

Denton [1982] 1 All ER 65, CA... 391

Dias [2002] Cr App R 96, CA... 34, 183, 186

Dica [2004] EWCA Crim 1103, CA... 96, 98, 101, 102, 103, 112, 113, 114, 119, 125

Dietschmann [2003] UKHL 10... 168, 169, 191

Diggin (1980) 72 Cr App R 204, CA... 361

Director-General of Fair Trading v Pioneer Concrete (UK) Ltd [1994] 3 WLR 1249, HL... 474

Dix (1981) 74 Cr App R 306... 170

Dobson v General Accident Insurance Corporation plc [1989] 3 All ER 927, CA... 302, 303

Donovan [1934] 2 KB 498, CA... 102

Doring [2002] Crim LR 817, CA... 411

Doughty (1986) 83 Cr App R 319, CA... 151, 190

Doukas [1978] 1 All ER 1061, CA... 327, 333

DPP for Northern Ireland v Lynch [1975] 1 All ER 913... 428, 435, 457

DPP for Northern Ireland v Maxwell [1978] 3 All ER 1140... 437, 440, 457

DPP v A [2001] Crim LR 140, DC... 66, 115

DPP v Armstrong [2000] Crim LR 379... 511, 514, 517

DPP v Bell [1992] Crim LR 176, DC... 255, 262

DPP v Camplin [1978] 2 All ER 168, HL... 155, 156, 157, 158, 159, 163, 190, 251

DPP v Doot [1973] 1 All ER 940, HL... 492, 493, 502, 516

DPP v H [1997] 1 WLR 1406, DC... 203, 404

DPP v Harris [1995] 1 Cr App R 170... 268

DPP v Jones [1990] RTR 33, DC... 255, 262

DPP v K and B [1997] 1 Cr App R 36, DC... 422, 432, 433, 457

DPP v K [1990] 1 All ER 331, DC... 92, 94

DPP v Kent and Sussex Contractors Ltd [1944] 1 All ER 119, DC... 465

DPP v Lavender [1994] Crim LR 297... 318

DPP v Little [1992] 1 All ER 299... 88

DPP v Lynch [1975] AC 653... 253, 258

DPP v Majewski [1976] 2 All ER 142, HL... 212, 214, 216, 217, 219, 223, 224, 225, 231, 243, 244

DPP v Morgan [1975] 2 All ER 347... 211, 226, 227, 244

DPP v Newbury [1976] 2 All ER 365, HL... 181, 183, 184, 187, 191

DPP v Nock [1978] AC 979; [1978] 2 All ER 654, HL... 501, 514, 515, 517

DPP v P & O European Ferries (Dover) Ltd (1991) 93 Cr App R 72... 67, 468, 469, 476

DPP v Ray [1973] 3 All ER 131, HL... 333, 334, 347

DPP v Rogers [1998] Crim LR 202... 260, 261

DPP v Santana-Bermudez [2003] EWHC Admin 2908; [2004] Crim LR 471... 29, 94

DPP v Smith [1961] AC 290... 110, 144

DPP v Spriggs [1993] Crim LR 622... 361

DPP v Stonehouse [1978] AC 55; [1977] 2 All ER 909, HL... 5, 480, 481, 482, 515

DPP v Withers [1974] 3 All ER 984, HL... 505, 517

Drake v DPP [1994] Crim LR 855, DC... 389

Drameh [1983] Crim LR 322... 349

Drummond [2002] Crim LR 666, CA... 11

Du Cros v Lambourne [1907] 1 KB 40... 429

Dubar [1995] 1 All ER 781... 307

Dudley [1989] Crim LR 57, CA... 397, 402

Dudley and Stephens (1884) 14 QBD 273... 265, 266, 272

Duffy [1949] 1 All ER 932... 151

Duguid (1906) 21 Cox CC 200... 494

Dunbar [1957] 2 All ER 737, CCA... 170

Dunbar [1988] Crim LR 693, CA... 447

Duru [1973] 3 All ER 715, CA... 320

Dyke and Munro [2002] Crim LR 153; [2002] 1 Cr App R 404, CA... 306, 308

Dytham [1979] 3 All ER 641, CA... 24

Easom [1971] 2 All ER 945, CA... 321

Eaton v Cobb [1950] 1 All ER 1016, DC... 80

Edgington v Fitzmaurice (1885) 29 ChD 459, CA... 335

Edwards v Ddin [1976] 3 All ER 705, DC... 298, 347

Edwards v R [1973] 1 All ER 152, PC... 152

Egan [1992] 4 All ER 470, CA... 168, 170, 191

Elbekkay [1995] Crim LR 163, CA... 100

El-Faisal [2004] EWCA Crim 456... 512, 514

Elliott v C [1983] 2 All ER 1005, DC... 68

Emery (1993) 14 Cr App R (S) 394, CA... 253

Emmett (1999) The Times, 15 October 1999... 101, 102, 103

Empress Car Co. (Abertillery) Ltd v National Rivers Authority [1998] 1 All ER 481, HL... 32, 34, 35, 42, 45, 413

English [1997] 4 All ER 545... 419, 421, 442, 445, 446, 451, 457

Enoch (1833) 5 C & P 539... 141

Esop (1836) 7 C & P 456... 233

Evans and Co. Ltd v LCC [1914] 3 KB 315... 465

F v West Berkshire Health Authority [1989] 2 All ER 545, HL... 96, 97, 248, 249, 259, 264, 267, 272

Fagan v MPC [1968] 3 All ER 442, DC... 29, 93, 94

Feely [1973] 1 All ER 341, CA... 313, 364, 385

Fenton (1975) 61 Cr App R 261, CA... 168, 216

Ferguson v Weaving [1951] 1 All ER 412, DC... 464

Fernandes [1996] 1 Cr App R 175, CA... 317

Fiak [2005] EWCA Crim 2381... 389

Finlay [2003] EWCA 3868... 35, 183, 186

Firth (1990) 91 Cr App R 217, CA... 334

Fitzmaurice [1983] 1 All ER 189, CA... 514, 515

Fitzpatrick [1977] NILR 200... 257

Flatt [1996] Crim LR 576, CA... 253

Flattery (1877) 2 QBD 410, CCR... 125

Floyd v DPP [2000] Crim LR 411, DC... 307

Forbes (Giles) [2001] UKHL 40... 228

Forman and Ford [1988] Crim LR 677... 429

Forrester [1992] Crim LR 793... 355

Forsyth [1997] 2 Cr App R 299, CA... 76, 381, 384, 387, 401

Francis [1982] Crim LR 363, CA... 372

Franklin (1883) 15 Cox CC 163... 182

Frenchay Healthcare NHS Trust v S [1994] 2 All ER 403... 27

Fretwell (1862) Le & Ca 161... 435

Fussell [1997] Crim LR 812, CA... 504

G [2003] UKHL 50... 64, 66, 71, 77, 83, 84, 109, 218, 394, 396

G and Another ([2004] 1 AC 1034, HL... 177

Gallasso [1993] Crim LR 459... 281

Gamble [1989] NI 268... 445, 457

Gammon (Hong Kong) Ltd v Attorney-General of Hong Kong [1984] 2 All ER 503... 407, 416

Gardner v Akeroyd [1952] 2 All ER 306, DC... 464

Garwood [1987] 1 All ER 1032, CA... 375, 400

Gateway Foodmarkets Ltd [1997] 2 Cr App R 40, CA... 415, 465

Gaughan [1990] Crim LR 880, CA... 421

Geddes (1996) 160 JP 697, CA... 484

Gemmell and Richards [2002] Crim LR 926, CA... 69

George [1956] Crim LR 52... 132, 136

Ghosh [1982] 2 All ER 689, CA... 313, 314, 323, 328, 344, 351, 354, 364, 376, 385, 393, 506

Giannetto [1997] 1 Cr App R 1, CA... 421

Gibbins and Proctor (1918) 13 Cr App R 134, CCA... 25

Gibson [1991] 1 All ER 439, CA... 405, 457, 508, 509

Gibson and Gibson (1984) 80 Cr App R 24, CA... 429, 456

Gilks [1972] 3 All ER 280, CA... 304, 305, 314

Gill [1963] 2 All ER 688, CCA... 255

Gillick v West Norfolk Area Health Authority [1985] 3 All ER 402... 53, 57, 62, 84, 97, 124, 265, 435, 436

Gilmour [2000] 2 Cr App R 407... 437, 439, 448, 458

Gittens [1984] 3 All ER 252; [1984] Crim LR 554... 168

Goldman [2001] Crim LR 894... 511, 512

Gomez [1993] 1 All ER 1, HL... 277, 278, 280, 282, 284, 290, 299, 302, 304, 306, 309, 328, 385, 385

Goodfellow (1986) 83 Cr App R 23, CA... 183, 187, 191

Goodfellow v Johnson [1965] 1 All ER 941... 461, 463

Gotts [1992] 1 All ER 832... 258, 271

Gould [1968] 1 All ER 849, CA... 229

Graham [1982] 1 All ER 801, CA... 221, 230, 244, 250, 252, 271

Graham [1997] 1 Cr App R 302... 320

Gray v Barr [1971] 2 All ER 949, CA... 184

Grayson [2002] Crim LR 659, CA... 410

Greatrex [1999] 1 Cr App R 126, CA... 446

Green v Burnett [1954] 3 All ER 273, DC... 462

Gregory (1982) 77 Cr App R 41... 284, 372, 385, 400

Gresham [2003] EWCA Crim 2070... 285, 301, 304

Griffiths (1974) 60 Cr App R 14, CA... 387, 401

Griffiths v Studebakers Ltd [1924] 1 KB 102... 461, 464

Grimshaw [1984] Crim LR 108... 115

Groombridge (1836) 7 C & P 582... 196

Gross (1913) 23 Cox CC 455... 83, 85, 86

Grundy [1977] Crim LR 543, CA... 451

Gullefer [1990] 3 All ER 882, CA... 481, 482, 483, 515

H [2002] 1 Cr App R 59... 95

H [2005] 2 All ER 859, CA... 130, 131, 132

H v UK (App. No. 150... 23/89), unreported, 4 April 1990... 10

Hale (1978) 68 Cr App R 415, CA... 284, 322, 357, 385, 400

Hall [1972] 2 All ER 1009, CA... 307

Hall (1985) 81 Cr App R 260, CA... 76, 387

Hallam and Blackburn [1995] Crim LR 323, CA... 307, 309, 323

Hammond [1982] Crim LR 611... 348, 354

Hancock and Shankland [1986] 1 All ER 641, CA; [1986] 1 All ER 646, HL... 54, 55, 56, 58, 84, 116, 143, 144, 145, 146, 443

Hanson (1849) 4 Cox CC 138... 92

Hardie [1984] 3 All ER 848, CA... 214, 215, 216, 219, 224

Hardman v Chief Constable of Avon [1986] Crim LR 330... 388

Harmer (Roy) [2005] EWCA Crim 1, CA... 498, 516

Harmer [2002] Crim LR 401... 257

Harris [1964] Crim LR 54, CCA... 450

Harris (1975) 62 Cr App R 28... 333

Harris (1998) The Times, 4 March 1998... 357

Harrow London Borough Council v Shah [1999] 3 All ER 302, DC... 408, 409, 412, 461

Harry [1974] Crim LR 32... 375

Harvey (1980) 72 Cr App R 139, CA... 376, 401

Harvey [1999] Crim LR 70... 498

Hasan [2005] UKHL 22... 221, 231, 244, 248, 250, 253, 254, 255, 256, 261, 271

Hashman and Harrup v UK [2000] Crim LR 185... 315

Hatton (Jonathan Alan) [2005] EWCA Crim 377... 216, 221, 231, 241, 244, 245

Hatton (Jonathan) [2005] EWCA Crim 2951... 216, 221, 231, 241, 244, 245

Haughton v Smith [1975] AC 476; [1973] 2 All ER 896, CA; [1973] 3 All ER 1109... 481, 489, 501, 514, 517

Hayes (1976) 64 Cr App R, CA... 307

Haystead v Chief Constable of Derbyshire [2000] 3 All ER 890... 88, 93

Hayward (1833) 6 C & P 157... 153

Hayward (1908) 21 Cox CC 692... 39

Heath [2000] Crim LR 109... 257

Hegarty [1994] Crim LR 353, CA... 252, 253

Hennessy [1989] 2 All ER 9, CA... 198, 199, 200, 201, 203

Herbert (1960) 25 Crim LJ 163... 292

Hibbert (1869) LR 1 CCR 184... 79, 404

Hibbert v McKiernan [1948] 1 All ER 860, DC... 294, 295

Hill (1988) 89 Cr App R 74, CA... 392

Hill v Baxter [1958] 1 QB 277... 209

Hilton [1997] 2 Cr App R 445, CA... 287, 289, 290, 322

Hinks [2000] 4 All ER 833... 277, 283, 299, 303, 315, 322, 323, 328, 339, 340, 380

HL Bolton (Engineering) Co. Ltd v P. J. Graham & Sons Ltd [1956] 3 All ER 624... 466

Hobson [1997] Crim LR 759, CA... 168

Hogden [1962] Crim LR 563... 359

Holden [1991] Crim LR 480... 222, 311

Hollinshead [1985] 2 All ER 769, HL... 505

Holmes v DPP [1946] 2 All ER 124, HL... 151

Hopley (1860) 2 F & F 202... 94

Horne [1994] Crim LR 584, CA... 252, 271

Horrex [1999] Crim LR 500, CA... 163, 190

Horseferry Road Magistrates' Court, ex parte K [1997] QB 23, DC... 203

Horsman [1998] Crim LR 128, CA... 309

Howe [1987] 1 AC 417; [1987] 1 All ER 771, HL... 221, 250, 251, 258, 266, 271, 431, 435

Howells [1977] 2 All ER 417, CA... 415, 416

Howker v Robinson [1972] 2 All ER 786, DC... 464

Hudson and Taylor [1971] 2 QB 202... 253, 255, 256, 271

Hughes [1995] Crim LR 956, CA... 241

Hui Chi-ming v R [1991] 3 All ER 897... 431, 442

Humphreys [1977] Crim LR 225... 373

Humphreys [1995] 4 All ER 1008, CA... 153

Humphreys and Turner [1965] 3 All ER 689... 430

Hunt (1977) 66 Cr App R 105... 392

Hurst [1995] 1 Cr App R 82, CA... 253, 255

Hussey (1924) 18 Cr App R 160, CCA... 238

Hyam v DPP [1974] 2 All ER 41, HL... 52, 54, 55, 143, 144, 145, 146, 148, 181, 212

Hyde [1990] 3 All ER 892, CA... 443

ICR Haulage Ltd [1944] 1 All ER 691, CCA... 465, 469, 493

Inseal [1992] Crim LR 35, CA... 169

Instan [1893] 1 QB 450... 25, 28

Invicta Plastics Ltd v Clare [1976] RTR 251, DC... 511

Ireland [1997] 3 WLR 534... 89, 90, 92, 107, 111, 119, 260

Isitt (1977) 67 Cr App R 44, CA... 209

Ismail [2005] EWCA Crim 397... 123

J. F. Alford Transport Ltd [1997] 2 Cr App R 326, CA... 429, 434, 437, 438, 457

Jackson [1985] Crim LR 442, CA... 499, 501

Jaggard v Dickinson [1980] 3 All ER 716, DC... 222, 223, 244, 391

James & Son Ltd v Smee [1954] 3 All ER 273, DC... 414, 416

James (1837) 8 C & P 131... 270

James [1997] Crim LR 598... 357

Janjua [1999] 1 Cr App R 91, CA... 110

JJC v Eisenhower [1983] 3 All ER 230, DC... 112

John Henshall Quarries Ltd v Harvey [1965] 1 All ER 725, DC... 467

Johnson (1986) 8 Cr App R (S) 343... 104

Johnson [1989] 2 All ER 839... 152

Johnson v DPP [1994] Crim LR 673, DC... 393

Johnson v Phillips [1975] 3 All ER 682, DC... 267, 272

Johnson v Youden [1950] 1 All ER 300, DC... 437

Johnstone [2003] UKHL 28... 10, 11

Jones (1986) 83 Cr App R 375, CA... 104

Jones (1993) The Times, 15 February, CA... 334

Jones [1987] Crim LR 123, CA... 105

Jones [1990] 1 WLR 1057, CA... 483, 515

Jones [2004] EWCA Crim 1981... 235

Jones and Smith [1976] 3 All ER 54... 368, 369

Jones v Gloucestershire Crown Prosecution Service [2004] EWCA Crim 1981... 249, 264, 392, 400

Jordan (1956) 40 Cr App R 152, CA... 41

Julien [1969] 2 All ER 856... 237

K [2001] Crim LR 134, CA; [2002] 1 Cr App R 121, HL... 229, 230, 412

K [2002] 1 AC 462; [2001] UKHL 41... 78, 79, 105, 407, 409, 410

Kanwar (1982) 2 All ER 528, CA... 384, 401

Kara [1988] Crim LR 42, CA... 269

Kay v Butterworth (1947) 173 LT 191... 215

Kearns [2003] 1 Cr App R 7, CA... 411

Kelly (1992) 97 Cr App R 245... 373

Kelly [1998] 3 All ER 741, CA... 292

Kelt [1977] 1 WLR 1365, CA... 373

Kemp [1956] 3 All ER 249... 199, 206, 208

Kendrick and Hopkins [1997] 2 Cr App R 524, CA... 282

Kennedy [1999] Crim LR 65... 34, 185

Kennedy (No. 2) [2005] EWCA Crim 685... 35, 183, 186, 420, 421, 451

Khan [1990] 2 All ER 783... 487

Khan and Khan [1998] Crim LR 830, CA... 24, 176, 177

Kimber [1983] 1 WLR 1118; [1983] 3 All ER 316; (1983) 77 Cr App R 225, CA... 78, 227, 231, 244

Kimsey [1996] Crim LR 35... 32

King and Stockwell [1987] 1 All ER 547... 327, 351

Kingston [1994] 3 All ER 353, HL... 215, 216, 217, 223, 244

Kirk; Russell [2002] Crim LR 756, CA... 410

Kirkland v Robinson [1987] Crim LR 643... 415

Klass [1998] 1 Cr App R 453, CA... 366, 373

Kleinwort Benson Ltd v Lincoln City Council [1998] 4 All ER 513, HL... 296

Klineberg and Marsden [1999] 1 Cr App R 427, CA... 307

Knuller v DPP [1972] 2 All ER 898, HL... 508, 509, 517

Kohn (1979) 69 Cr App R 395, CA... 287, 290, 291, 310, 322

Konzani [2005] 2 Cr App R 198, CA... 102, 113, 114, 115, 119

Kumar, Re [2000] Crim LR 504, DC... 307, 407

L v DPP [2002] Crim LR 320, DC... 10

Laing [1995] Crim LR 395, CA... 366

Lamb [1967] 2 QB 981; [1967] 2 All ER 1282, CA... 69, 89, 183

Lambert; Ali; Jordan [2001] 1 All ER 1014... 10, 11, 170, 413

Lambie [1981] 2 All ER 776, HL... 333, 339

Land [1998] 1 All ER 403, CA... 409

Lane (1986) 82 Cr App R 5... 421

Larkin [1943] 1 All ER 217, CA... 184, 191

Larsonneur (1933) 24 Cr App R 74... 29, 403

Latif and Shahzad [1996] 2 Cr App R 92, HL... 420, 454, 455, 458

Latimer (1886) 17 QBD 359... 82, 85, 86

Lawrence [1981] 1 All ER 974, HL... 67, 69, 85, 174, 178

Lawrence and Pomroy (1971) 57 Cr App R 64... 337, 378, 401

Lawrence v MPC [1971] 2 All ER 1253, HL... 278, 279, 280, 299, 303, 305, 311, 315, 323

Le Brun [1991] 4 All ER 673, CA... 44, 46

Lee Chun-Chuen v R [1963] 1 All ER 73, PC... 12

Leicester v Pearson [1952] 2 All ER 71, DC... 22

Leigh v Gladstone (1909) 26 TLR 139... 264

Lemon [1979] 1 All ER 898... 405

Lennard's Carrying Co. Ltd v Azeatic Petroleum Co. Ltd [1915] AC 705, HL... 467

Lesbini [1914] 3KB 1116, CCA... 156

Letenock (1917) 12 Cr App R 221, CCA... 152, 221

Lewin v Barratt Homes Ltd [2000] Crim LR 323, DC... 335, 336

Lewin v Bland [1985] RTR 171, DC... 474

Lewis [1970] Crim LR 647... 110

Lewis v Averay [1971] 3 All ER 907, CA... 301, 302, 303

Lewis v Cox [1985] QB 509... 80

Lewis v Lethbridge [1987] Crim LR 59, DC... 305

Liangsiriprasert v US Government (1991) 92 Cr App R 77, PC... 479, 517

Light (1857) [1843–60] All ER Rep 934... 91

Lillienfield (1985) The Times, 17 October... 208

Lim Chin Aik v R [1963] 1 All ER 223, PC... 416

Linekar (Gareth) [1995] Crim LR 320, CA... 98, 100, 125

Linnet v Metropolitan Police Commissioner [1946] 1 All ER 380... 463

Lipman [1969] 3 All ER 410, CA... 213, 215

Lloyd [1967] 1 All ER 107... 169

Lloyd [1989] Crim LR 513... 104

Lloyd [1991] Crim LR 904, DC... 389

Lloyd v DPP [1992] 1 All ER 982... 393

Lockley [1995] Crim LR 656, CA... 357

Logdon v DPP [1976] Crim LR 121, DC... 89, 91

Lomas (1913) 110 LT 239, CCA... 428

Loosely [2001] UKHL 53... 453, 454

Loukes [1996] 1 Cr App R 444, CA... 430, 433, 434

Low v Blease (1975) 119 SJ 695... 292

Lowe [1973] 1 All ER 805, CA... 182

Luc Thiet Thuan v R [1996] 2 All ER 1033... 157, 161, 162

Lynsey [1995] 3 All ER 654... 88, 117

Magna Plant Ltd v Mitchell [1966] Crim LR 394, DC... 467

Mainwaring (1981) 74 Cr App R 99, CA... 307

Malcherek and Steel [1981] 2 All ER 422, CA... 40, 42, 142, 189

Malone [1998] 2 Cr App R 447, CA... 123

Mancini v DPP [1941] 3 All ER 272, HL... 8, 163

Mandair [1994] 2 All ER 715, HL... 110

Manning [1998] 2 Cr App R 461, CA... 276

Marchant [2004] 1 WLR 442, CA... 33

Marjoram [2000] Crim LR 372, CA... 38

Marlow [1997] Crim LR 897, CA... 512

Marsh [1997] 1 Cr App R 67, CA... 361

Marshall [1998] 2 Cr App R 282, CA... 318

Martin (Anthony) [2002] Crim LR 137... 231, 240

Martin (David) [2000] 2 Cr App R 42... 231, 251

Martin [1989] 1 All ER 652, CA... 221, 230, 261, 272

Matthews and Alleyne [2003] EWCA Crim 192... 57, 84, 147, 149

Matudi [2003] EWCA Crim 697... 408, 409, 411, 415, 416

Maughan (1934) 24 Cr App R 130, CCA... 409

Mawji v R [1957] 1 All ER 385, PC... 493

Mayling [1963] 1 All ER 687, CCA... 509

Mazo [1997] 2 Cr App R 518... 282

McAllister [1997] Crim LR 233... 98

McAuliffe v R (1995) 130 ALR 26... 442

McCalla (1988) 87 Cr App R 372... 373, 400

McCarthy [1954] 2 All ER 262, CCA... 152, 156, 160

McCullum (1973) 57 Cr App R 645, CA... 81, 387, 401

McDavitt [1981] Crim LR 843... 348

McDonagh [1974] QB 448... 358

McDonnell [1966] 1 All ER 193... 493

McDonough (1962) 47 Cr App R 37... 514

McHugh (1976) 64 Cr App R 92, CA... 298

McHugh (1993) 97 Cr App R 335, CA... 307

McInnes [1971] 3 All ER 295... 234, 240

McIvor [1982] 1 All ER 491, CA... 314

McKechnie (1991) 94 Cr App R 51, CA... 42

McKnight v Davies [1974] RTR 4, DC... 358

MD [2004] EWCA Crim 1391... 58, 144

Meech [1973] 3 All ER 939, CA... 307

Melias Ltd v Preston [1957] 2 QB 380... 461

Melwani [1989] Crim LR 565, CA... 328

Meridian Global Funds Management Asia Ltd v Securities Commission [1995] 3 All ER 918, PC... 467

Merrick [1996] 1 Cr App R 130, CA... 70

Metropolitan Police Commissioner v Caldwell [1981] 1 All ER 961... 64, 66, 67, 68, 69, 70, 74, 84, 85, 115, 174, 178, 208, 216, 217, 218, 396, 438

Metropolitan Police Commissioner v Charles [1977] AC 177, HL... 328, 333, 339, 351

Michael (1840) 9 C & P 356... 37

Miller [1954] 2 QB 282... 107, 176

Miller (1972) The Times, 16 May... 168

Miller [1976] Crim LR 147, CA... 361

Miller [1983] 1 All ER 978, HL... 18, 28, 29, 44, 45, 94, 398

Millward [1994] Crim LR 527, CA... 433, 434, 436, 450, 456

Misra [2004] EWCA Crim 2375 CA... 177, 178, 180

Mitchell [1993] Crim LR 788, CA... 309, 320

Mitchell [1995] Crim LR 506, CA... 170

Mitchell [2004] Crim LR 139 CA... 393

Mitchell and King [1999] Crim LR 496... 452, 458

Moberly v Alsop [1991] TLR 576, DC... 349

Mohammed (Faqir) [2005] EWCA Crim 1880, CA... 153, 162, 163, 190

Mohan [1976] QB 1; [1975] 2 All ER 193, CA... 51, 84, 485

Mohan v R [1967] 2 AC 187, PC... 421

Moloney [1985] 1 All ER 1025... 54, 55, 58, 84, 116, 143, 144, 145, 146, 147, 149, 181, 212, 443

Montila [2004] UKHL 50... 76, 498, 499

Moon [2004] All ER (D) 167... 454

Moore (1898) 14 TLR 229... 104

Moore v I Bresler Ltd [1944] 2 All ER 515, DC... 465

Morhall [1995] 3 All ER 659, HL... 155, 156, 157, 158, 159, 160, 163, 190

Morphitis v Salmon [1990] Crim LR 48, DC... 389

Morris (Clarence) [1998] 1 Cr App R 386, CA... 108

Morris [1983] 3 All ER 288, HL... 277, 278

Morrison (1988) 89 Cr App R 17, CA... 117

Morrow v DPP [1994] Crim LR 58, DC... 240

Moses v Winder [1980] Crim LR 232... 215

Most (1881) 7 QBD 244... 512

Mousell Bros Ltd v London and North Western Railway Company [1917] 2 KB 836... 465

Mowatt [1967] 3 All ER 47, CA... 115, 116, 117, 119

Muhamad [2003] 2 WLR 1050... 408, 411, 412, 415, 416

National Rivers Authority v Alfred McAlpine Homes East Ltd [1994] 4 All ER 286, DC... 461

National Rivers Authority v Yorkshire Water Services [1995] 1 All ER 225, HL... 413

Naviede [1997] Crim LR 662, CA... 288, 345

Navvabi [1986] 3 All ER 102, CA... 291

NCB v Gamble [1958] 3 All ER 203, DC... 424, 428, 434, 437

Neal v Gribble [1978] RTR 409... 358

Nedrick [1986] 3 All ER 1... 55, 56, 58, 84, 144, 146, 147, 148, 485

Ngan [1998] 1 Cr App R 331... 289, 290, 301, 304

NHS Trust v S [1998] 3 All ER 673, CA... 264

Nicholls (1874) 13 Cox CC 75... 25

Nicklin [1977] 2 All ER 444, CA... 382

Norfolk Constabulary v Seekings & Gould [1986] Crim LR 167... 369

Nottingham City Council v Amin [2000] 2 All ER 946, DC... 454, 455

Nottingham City Council v Wolverhampton and Dudley Breweries [2004] 2 WLR 820... 461

O'Brien [1995] 2 Cr App R 649, CA... 443

O'Connell [1997] Crim LR 683, CA... 168

O'Connor [1991] Crim LR 135, CA... 216, 221

O'Driscoll (1977) 65 Cr App R 50, CA... 184, 191

O'Flaherty [2004] EWCA Crim 526... 453, 458

O'Grady [1987] 3 All ER 420, CA... 152, 216, 221, 231, 241, 244, 245

O'Hadhmaill [1996] Crim LR 509, CA... 499

O'Leary (1986) 82 Cr App R 341... 372

O'Toole [1987] Crim LR 759... 486, 515

Ofori and Tackie (1994) 99 Cr App R 223, CA... 379

Ohlson v Hylton [1975] 2 All ER 490, DC... 373

OLL Ltd and Kite (1994) 144 NLJ 1735... 470

Osland v R (1998) 73 ALJR 173... 451

Owino [1996] 2 Cr App R 128, CA... 236

Oxford v Moss (1978) 68 Cr App R 183... 292, 322

P & O European Ferries (Dover) Ltd, see DPP v P & O European Ferries (Dover) Ltd

Page [1953] 2 All ER 1355... 140

Pagett (1983) 76 Cr App R 279, CA... 30, 33, 36, 38

Palmer v R [1971] AC 814, PC... 236, 240, 245

Park (1988) 87 Cr App R 164, CA... 382

Parker [1977] 2 All ER 37... 72

Parker [1993] Crim LR 856, CA... 396

Parkes [1973] Crim LR 358 . . . 337, 378, 401

Parmenter [1991] 4 All ER 698, HL; [1991] 2 All ER 225, CA . . . 66, 79, 85, 91, 104, 107, 108, 109, 115, 119

Pattni and Others [2001] Crim LR 570 . . . 315

Pearce [1973] Crim LR 321 . . . 358

Pearman (1984) 80 Cr App R 259, CA . . . 485, 515

Pearson [1992] Crim LR 193 . . . 151, 152, 190

Peart [1970] 2 All ER 823, CA . . . 360, 399

Pembliton (1874) LR 2 CCR 119 . . . 83, 85, 86

Perman [1996] 1 Cr App R 24 . . . 452

Petters and Parfitt [1995] Crim LR 501, CA . . . 441, 444, 457

Pharmaceutical Society of Great Britain v Storkwain Ltd [1985] 3 All ER 4 . . . 412, 415

Phipps and McGill (1970) 54 Cr App R 300 . . . 359, 360, 399

Pitchley (1972) 57 Cr App R 30, CA . . . 383, 384

Pitham and Hehl (1976) 65 Cr App R 45, CA . . . 286, 287, 322, 385

Pittwood (1902) 19 TLR 37 . . . 28

Pommell [1995] 2 Cr App R 607, CA . . . 254, 259, 262

Pordage [1975] Crim LR 575 . . . 218

Poulton (1832) 5 C & P 329 . . . 141

Powell [1997] 4 All ER 545, HL . . . 437, 441, 442, 446, 447

Powell v MacRae [1977] Crim LR 571, DC . . . 296, 308

Pownall (1994) The Times, 19 February . . . 238

Preddy [1996] 3 All ER 735, HL . . . 288, 309, 310, 320, 328, 329, 331, 339, 381

Prentice and Sullman [1993] 4 All ER 935, CA . . . 173, 175, 178

Price (1971) The Times, 22 December . . . 167

Price [2004] 1 Cr App R 12, CA . . . 132, 136

Prince (1875) LR 2 CCR 154 . . . 79, 244, 488

Prince [1874–80] All ER Rep 881 . . . 229, 404, 407, 416

Purdy (1945) 10 JCL 182 . . . 259

Quality Dairies Ltd v Pedley [1952] 1 All ER 380, DC . . . 463

Quayle [2005] EWCA Crim 1415 . . . 248, 249, 260, 263, 265, 267, 268, 269, 272

Quick [1973] 3 All ER 347 . . . 199, 200, 201, 206, 208, 213

R (McCann) v Crown Court at Manchester [2003] 1 AC 787 . . . 3

R (On the application of O) v Coventry Magistrates' Court [2004] Crim LR 948; [2004] EWHC 905 . . . 511, 513

R [1991] 4 All ER 481 . . . 233

R v Bournewood Community and Mental Health NHS Trust, ex parte L [1998] 3 All ER 289 . . . 248, 264, 265, 268, 272

R v Governor of Brixton Prison, ex parte Levin [1997] 1 Cr App R 335, DC . . . 284, 289, 296

R v Governor of Pentonville Prison, ex parte Osman [1989] 3 All ER 701, DC . . . 289

R v HM Coroner for East Kent, ex parte Spooner (1989) 88 Cr App R 10 . . . 468

R v Horseferry Road Magistrates' Court, ex parte Bennett [1993] WLR 90, HL . . . 453, 454

R v Redfern and Dunlop Ltd (Aircraft Division) [1993] Crim LR 43, CA . . . 467

R, Re [1991] 4 All ER 177, CA . . . 264

Rabey (1978) 79 DLR 435 . . . 201

Race Relations Board v Applin [1973] 1 QB 815, CA . . . 511

Rai [2000] 1 Cr App R 242, CA . . . 335

Ransford (1874) 13 Cox CC 9 . . . 512

Read v Coker (1853) 13 CB 850 . . . 91

Reader (1977) 66 Cr App R 33, CA... 387, 401

Reardon [1999] Crim LR 392, CA... 439, 443

Reed [1982] Crim LR 819, CA... 500

Reed v Wastie [1972] Crim LR 221... 94

Reid (1975) 62 Cr App R 109, CA... 431, 448

Reid [1992] 3 All ER 673... 64, 67, 68, 70

Revill v Newbery [1996] 1 All ER 291, CA... 238

Reynolds [1988] Crim LR 679... 167

Reynolds [2004] EWCA Crim 1834... 167

Richardson (1834) 6 C & P 335... 382

Richardson [1998] 2 Cr App R 200, CA... 99, 125

Richardson and Brown [1998] 2 Cr App R (S) 87... 366

Richardson and Irwin [1999] 1 Cr App R 392, CA... 104, 105, 221

Richens [1993] 4 All ER 877, CA... 153

Roach [2001] EWCA Crim 2698... 210

Robert Millar (Contractors) Ltd [1970] 1 All ER 577, CA... 469

Roberts (1971) 56 Cr App R 95... 107, 108, 109

Roberts (1987) 84 Cr App R 117, CA... 386, 401

Roberts and George [1997] Crim LR 209, CA... 430, 433, 434, 438

Robinson [1915] 2 KB 342, CCA... 481

Robinson [1977] Crim LR 173... 356

Rodger and Rose [1998] 1 Cr App R 143, CA... 260

Roe v Kingerlee [1986] Crim LR 735, DC... 388

Rogers [2003] 2 Cr App R 10, CA... 35, 183, 186, 420, 421

Rook [1993] 2 All ER 955, CA... 444, 452, 457

Roper v Taylor's Central Garages [1951] 2 TLR 284... 76, 77

Ross v Moss [1965] 3 All ER 145... 464

Rossiter [1994] 2 All ER 752, CA... 154

Rostron [2003] EWCA Crim 2206... 294

Rothery [1976] RTR 550... 292

Rowley [1991] 4 All ER 649, CA... 508

Royle [1971] 3 All ER 1363... 329

Ruffel [2003] EWCA Crim 122... 26

Ruse v Read [1949] 1 All ER 398, DC... 222

Russell and Russell [1987] Crim LR 494, CA... 429

Ryan [1996] Crim LR 320... 366

Ryan v DPP [1994] Crim LR 457... 385

Safi [2003] Crim LR 721, CA... 251

Sakavickas [2004] ECWA Crim 2686... 499, 516

Salabiaku v France (1988) 13 EHRR 379... 405

Salisbury [1976] VR 452... 111

Samchai Liangsiriprasert v United States Government (1990) 92 Cr App R 77... 502

Sanderson (1994) 98 Cr App R 325, CA... 168

Sang [1979] 2 All ER 1222, HL... 455, 458

Sangha [1988] 2 All ER 385, CA... 396

Sansom (1991) 92 Cr App R 115... 502

Sargeant [1997] Crim LR 50, CA... 133

Satnam and Kewal Singh (1984) 78 Cr App R 149, CA... 78, 79

Saunders [1985] Crim LR 230... 110

Savage [1991] 4 All ER 698, HL... 66, 79, 85, 91, 107, 108, 112, 115, 119

Scarlett [1993] 4 All ER 629, CA... 173, 184, 191, 233, 236, 238, 240

Scott (1979) 68 Cr App R 164, CA... 493, 517

Scott v Metropolitan Police Commissioner [1974] 3 All ER 1032, HL... 503, 504

Secretary of State for the Home Department v Robb [1995] 1 All ER 677... 264

Secretary of State for Trade and Industry v Hart [1982] 1 WLR 481, DC... 233

Senior [1899] 1 QB 283... 61

Seymour [1983] 2 All ER 1058... 173, 174

Shadrokh-Cigari [1988] Crim LR 465, CA... 296, 304, 322, 323

Shankland [1986] 1 All ER 641, CA; [1986] 1 All ER 646, HL... 54, 55, 56, 58, 84, 116, 143, 144, 145, 443

Shannon (1980) 71 Cr App R 192, CA... 236

Sharp [1987] 3 All ER 103, CA... 257

Shaw [1994] Crim LR 365... 514, 517

Shaw v DPP [1961] 2 All ER 446... 508, 509, 517

Shaw v R [2002] Crim LR 140... 241

Shayler [2001] Crim LR 986, CA; [2002] UKHL 11, HL... 249, 253, 254, 256, 259, 261, 262, 263, 267, 269, 272

Sheehan [1975] 1 WLR 739, CA... 218

Shendley [1970] Crim LR 49, CA... 357, 399

Shepherd (1987) 86 Cr App R 47, CA... 257

Sheppard [1980] 3 All ER 399, HL... 80, 86

Sherras v De Rutzen [1895] 1 QB 918... 408

Sherriff [1969] Crim LR 260... 92

Shivpuri [1986] 2 All ER 334... 379, 490, 516

Shortland [1996] 1 Cr App R 116, CA... 269

Silverman (1986) 86 Cr App R 213, CA... 333, 334

Simcox [1964] Crim LR 402... 170

Singh [1999] Crim LR 582, CA... 175, 178

Siracusa (1990) 90 Cr App R 340, CA... 495, 498

Slingsby [1995] Crim LR 570... 101

Small (1988) 86 Cr App R 170, CA... 311

Smedleys Ltd v Breed [1974] 2 All ER 21, HL... 413

Smith (Morgan) [2001] 1 AC 146, HL... 71, 155, 157, 158, 161, 165, 253

Smith (Wallace) [1996] 2 Cr App R 1, CA... 276

Smith [1959] 2 All ER 193... 40, 45

Smith [1960] 1 All ER 256, CCA... 60, 455

Smith [1974] QB 354; [1974] 1 All ER 632, CA... 226, 229, 232, 394, 400

Smith [1979] Crim LR 251... 26

Smith [1982] Crim LR 531... 167, 190

Smith [1985] Crim LR 42... 94

Smith v Chief Superintendent, Woking Police Station (1983) 76 Cr App R 234... 89

Smith v Mellors and Soar [1987] RTR 210... 421

Smith v Reynolds [1986] Crim LR 559, DC... 429

Sockett (1908) 1 Cr App R 101, CCA... 451

Sodeman v R [1936] 2 All ER 203... 203, 204

Sofroniou [2003] EWCA Crim 3681... 344

Sood [1998] 2 Cr App R 355, CA... 61

Sopp v Long [1969] 1 All ER 855... 463

Southwark v Williams [1971] 2 All ER 175, CA... 247

Spratt [1991] 2 All ER 210, CA... 91, 104, 108, 109

St Q [2002] Cr App R (2) 40... 377

Steane [1947] KB 997; [1947] 1 All ER 813, CCA... 53, 62, 84, 259

Steer [1987] 2 All ER 833, HL... 396, 397, 402

Stephen Malcolm R (1984) 79 Cr App R 334, CA... 68

Stephenson [1979] 2 All ER 1198... 65

Stewart [1995] 4 All ER 999, CA... 154, 155

Stewart and Schofield [1995] 3 All ER 159; [1995] Crim LR 420... 444, 447, 451, 457, 458

Stokes [1983] RTR 59, CA... 359

Stone and Dobinson [1977] 2 All ER 341... 25, 173, 191

Strutt v Clift [1911] 1 KB 1... 461

Sullivan [1981] Crim LR 46... 115

Sullivan [1983] 2 All ER 673, HL... 197, 198, 199, 206, 208

Sullivan and Ballion [2002] Crim LR 758... 295

Sweet v Parsley [1969] 1 All ER 347... 406, 408, 416

Swindall and Osborne (1846) 2 Car & Kir 230... 32

T [1990] Crim LR 256... 200, 208

T, Re [1992] 4 All ER 649, CA... 28, 264

T v Calgarth [1926] P 93... 368

Tabassum [2000] Crim LR 686... 99, 125, 131

Tacey (1821) Russ & Ry 452; Fisher (1865) LR 1 CCR 7, DC... 389

Tandy (1988) 87 Cr App R 45... 169, 191

Taylor (1869) 11 Cox CC 261... 112

Taylor (1985) 80 Cr App R 327, CA... 78

Teixeira de Castro v Portugal (1998) 28 EHRR 101... 454

Tesco Stores Ltd v Brent London Borough Council [1993] 2 All ER 718, DC... 474

Tesco Supermarkets Ltd v Nattrass [1970] 3 All ER 357, HL... 461, 466, 467, 476

Thabo Meli [1954] 1 All ER 373, PC... 43, 44, 46

Thambiah v R [1965] 3 All ER 661, PC... 428

Thomas (1985) 81 Cr App R 33, CA... 92

Thomson (1965) 50 Cr App R 1... 497

Thorne v Motor Trade Association [1937] 3 All ER 157, HL... 375, 400

Thornton [1992] 1 All ER 306, CA... 153, 165

Thornton (No. 2) [1996] 2 All ER 1023, CA... 153

Thornton v Mitchell [1940] 1 All ER 339, DC... 430, 457

Tolson (1889) 23 QBD 168... 226, 230, 244

Tomsett [1985] Crim LR 369, CA... 290

Toothill [1998] Crim LR 876, CA... 484, 489

Tosti [1997] Crim LR 746, CA... 484

Trainer (1864) 4 F & F 105... 270

Treacy v DPP [1971] 1 All ER 110, HL... 374, 375, 400

Troughton v Metropolitan Police [1987] Crim LR 138, DC... 349, 354

Tuberville v Savage (1669) 1 Mod Rep 3... 91

Tuck v Robson [1970] 1 All ER 1171, DC... 429

Turner (No. 2) [1971] 2 All ER 441, CA... 297, 303, 322

Tyrrell [1894] 1 QB 710... 451, 513

Uddin [1998] 2 All ER 744... 446, 448, 457

Valderrama-Vega [1985] Crim LR 220... 253, 254, 271

Van Dongen [2005] EWCA Crim 1728... 155

Vane v Yiannopoullos [1964] 2 All ER 820, HL... 460, 463, 464, 476

Vann and Davis [1996] Crim LR 52, CA... 415

Vehicle Inspectorate v Nuttall [1999] 3 All ER 833... 414

Velumyl [1989] Crim LR 29, CA... 317

Venna [1975] 3 All ER 788... 91, 219

Vinagre (1979) 69 Cr App R 104, CA... 168

Vincent [2001] Crim LR 488, CA... 349

W v Dolbey [1983] Crim LR 681... 115

W, Re [1992] 4 All ER 177, CA... 264

Wacker [2003] 1 Cr App R 22; [2003] Crim LR 108... 26, 29, 100, 176, 295

Wai Yu-tsang v R [1992] 1 AC 269, PC... 337, 338, 507, 517, 504, 505

Wain [1995] 2 Cr App R 660... 305

Waite [1892] 2 QB 600... 196

Walkden (1845) 1 Cox CC 282... 92

Walker [1996] 1 Cr App R 111... 509

Walker and Hayles (1990) 90 Cr App R 226, CA... 58

Walkington [1979] 2 All ER 716, CA... 369, 399, 400

Wan and Chan [1995] Crim LR 296... 444, 447, 457, 458

Wang [2005] UKHL 9... 5

Warner v MPC [1968] 2 All ER 356, HL... 415

Watson [1989] 2 All ER 865, CA... 185, 187

Waverley Borough Council v Fletcher [1995] 4 All ER 756, CA... 294, 322

Webster; Warwick [1995] 2 All ER 168, CA... 396, 397

Welham v DPP [1961] AC 103, HL... 504, 505

Weller [2003] EWCA Crim 815, CA... 160

Wells [2004] EWCA Crim 79... 385

Welsh [1974] RTR 478... 292

Westdeutsche Landesbank Girozentrale v Islington London Borough Council [1996] 2 All ER 961, HL... 296, 304, 322, 323

Westminster City Council v Croyalgrange Ltd [1986] 2 All ER 353, HL... 76, 85

Wheeler (1991) 92 Cr App R 279... 286

Wheelhouse [1994] Crim LR 756, CA... 366, 433, 457

Whitchurch (1890) 24 QBD 420... 494, 516

White [1910] 2 KB 124... 31

Whitefield (1983) 79 Cr App R 36, CA... 451

Whitehouse [1977] 3 All ER 737, CA... 451, 513

Whiteley (1991) 93 Cr App R 25, CA... 389, 390

Whittaker v Campbell [1983] 3 All ER 582, DC... 360, 399

Whybrow (1951) 35 Cr App R 141, CCA... 485

Wibberley [1965] 3 All ER 718... 358

Wilcox v Jeffrey [1951] 1 All ER 464, DC... 428, 429, 457

Wiley (1850) 2 Den 37... 382

Willer (1986) 83 Cr App R 225, CA... 260, 261, 262

Williams (1984) 78 Cr App R 276, CA... 105, 220, 228, 231

Williams (1986) 84 Cr App R 299, CA... 59

Williams (Roy) [2001] Crim LR 253, CA... 309, 334

Williams [1923] 1 KB 340, CCA... 125

Williams [1980] Crim LR 589, CA... 334

Williams [1987] 3 All ER 411, CA... 236, 240, 245

Williams [1992] 2 All ER 183, CA... 38, 119

Williams [1994] Crim LR 934, CA... 387, 401

Williams [2001] Crim LR 253... 287, 289

Williams v Phillips (1957) 41 Cr App R 5... 295, 322

Williamson v Secretary of State for Education and Employment [2003] 1 All ER 385, CA... 95

Willoughby [2004] EWCA Crim 3365, CA... 176, 177

Wilson (Alan Thomas) [1996] 3 WLR 125, CA... 102

Wilson [1983] 3 All ER 448, HL... 93, 110

Windle [1952] 2 All ER 1, CCA... 202, 206

Winzar v Chief Constable of Kent (1983) The Times, 28 March... 29, 404

Woodman [1974] 2 All ER 955, CA... 295

Woods [1982] Crim LR 42... 212

Woollin [1998] 4 All ER 103... 51, 54, 57, 58, 62, 65, 84, 115, 144, 146, 147, 148, 149, 181, 267, 338, 485

Woolmington v DPP [1935] All ER Rep 1,
    HL... 8, 9, 12
Woolven (1983) 73 Cr App R 231,
    CA... 328
Worthy v Gordon Plant (Services) Ltd
    [1985] CLY 624, DC... 467
Wright [1992] Crim LR 596... 373, 400

Wright [2000] Crim LR 510,
    CA... 254

Yip Chiu-Cheung v R [1994] 2 All ER
    924... 61, 270, 497, 498, 516

Z [2003] 2 Cr App R 173... 257

■ TABLE OF STATUTES

Where sections are reproduced in full, the page number is shown in **bold**

Abortion Act 1967 ... 140
Accessories and Abettors Act 1861
   s.8 ... 419, **423**, 456
Aggravated Vehicle Taking Act
   1992 ... 357, 361
Anti-Terrorism, Crime and Security
   Act 2001 ... 62

Banking Act 1987 ... 233

Child Abduction Act 1984
   s.2 ... 79, 404
Children Act 1989
   s.31 ... 195
Children Act 2004
   s.58 ... 95
Children and Young Persons Act 1933
   s.1 ... 95
   s.50 ... 195
Companies Act 1985
   s.458 ... 343
Company Director's Disqualification
   Act 1986
   s.11(1) ... 411
Computer Misuse Act 1990 ... 292, 389
Contempt of Court Act 1981
   s.1 ... 406
Crime and Disorder Act 1998 ... 62
   s.1 ... 3
   s.30 ... 394
   s.34 ... 195, 205
   s.36 ... 141
Criminal Appeal Act 1968
   s.2 ... 6
   s.8 ... 15
Criminal Appeal Act 1995 ... 7
   s.1 ... 6

Criminal Attempts Act 1981 ... 24, 321,
   480, 481, 489
   s.1(1) ... 479, 482, 515
   s.1(1)(b) ... 501
   s.1(2) ... 490
   s.1(3) ... 488, 490
   s.1(4) ... 479
   s.4(3) ... 482
Criminal Damage Act 1971 ... 64,
   66, 67, 71, 275, 388, 389
   s.1 ... 371
   s.1(1) ... 222, 274
   s.1(2) ... 217, 218, **395**, 486
   s.1(3) ... 274
   s.5(2) ... 222
   s.5(2)(a) ... 222
   s.5(2)(b) ... 239, 268, 272
   s.5(3) ... 222
Criminal Justice Act 1925
   s.47 ... 269
Criminal Justice Act 1967 ... 4
   s.4(1) ... 427
   s.8 ... 9, 219, 243
Criminal Justice Act 1972
   s.36 ... 5
Criminal Justice Act 1987
   s.12 ... 492, 503, 516
Criminal Justice Act 1988
   s.37(1) ... 358
   s.39 ... 88
Criminal Justice Act 1993
   Pt I ... 276, 480
   s.2(3) ... **276**
   s.3 ... 276, 479, 480, 502,
     515, 517
   s.4 ... 480
   s.4(b)(1) ... 276

s.5 ... 479, 480, 502, 515, 517
s.5(3) ... 507
Criminal Justice Act 2003
  s.269 ... 143
Criminal Justice and Public Order
  Act 1994 ... 227
ss 32–7 ... 8
s.142 ... 233
Criminal Law Act 1967 ... 491
  s.3 ... 94, 234, 235, 239, 240, 244
  s.3(1) ... **234**
  s.3(2) ... 234
  s.4(1) ... 427
Criminal Law Act 1977 ... 419
  s.1 ... 495, 516
  s.1(2) ... 496, 498, 499
  s.1(4) ... 502, 517
  s.1A(3) ... 507
  s.2(2) ... 493
  s.5(1) ... 508
  s.5(2) ... 491, 492, 503
  s.5(3) ... 491, 492, 508, 509
  s.5(8) ... 494
  s.54 ... 513
Criminal Procedure (Insanity) Act 1964
  s.5 ... 196
  s.5(3) ... 196
  s.6 ... 204
Criminal Procedure (Insanity and
  Unfitness to Plead) Act 1991 ... 196
  s.1 ... 197, 204
Customs and Excise Management
  Act 1979
  s.170(2) ... 228

Dangerous Dogs Act 1991
  s.1(2)(d) ... 267
Data Protection Act 1984
  s.5 ... 64
  s.5(5) ... 64
Domestic Violence, Crimes and Victims
  Act 2004
  s.5 ... 73, 421
  s.6 ... 421

s.10 ... 4
s.24 ... 196

Education Act 1996
  s.444 ... 405
  s.548 ... 95
Enterprise Act 2002 ... 275

Female Genitals Mutilation
  Act 2003 ... 103
Financial Services and Markets
  Act 2000 ... 275
Firearms Act 1968 ... 262, 415
  s.1(3) ... 58
  s.16 ... 58
Food Safety Act 1990 ... 473
  s.21 ... 74, 415
Football (Disorder) Act 1991 ... 3
Forgery and Counterfeiting Act
  1981 ... 276, 479
Fraud Act 2006 ... 13, 275, 276, 310,
  325, 502, 503, 507, 510
  s.1 ... 379, 381, 491
  s.2 ... 281, **332**, 338, 342
  s.2(2) ... 336
  s.3 ... 332, 335, **339**, 342
  s.4 ... 332, **340**, 342
  s.5 ... 336, 337
  s.6 ... 342
  s.7 ... 342
  s.11 ... **343, 344**

Gambling Act 2005
  s.63 ... 10
Genocide Act 1969 ... 139

Health and Safety at Work etc.
  Act 1974 ... 74
  s.3(1) ... 465
Homicide Act 1957
  s.2 ... 10, 140, 160, 161, **166**, 167,
  169, 171, 190
  s.2(2) ... 170
  s.2(4) ... 431

s.3... 150, 151, 152, 153, 155, 156, 158, 159, 160, 161, 162, 163, 166, 190
Human Fertilisation and Embryology Act 1990
  s.37... 140
Human Rights Act 1998... 14, 15
  s.3(1)... 10

Indecency with Children Act 1960... 230
  s.1(1)... 407, 413
Infant Life (Preservation) Act 1929
  s.1... 139, 268
Infanticide Act 1938
  s.1... 139
Insolvency Act 1986
  s.362(1)... 411

Law Reform (Year and a Day Rule) Act 1996
  s.2... 142
Licensing Act 1872
  s.12... 29,404
Licensing Act 1964
  s.59(1)... 460
Licensing Act 2003... 460

Magistrates' Courts Act 1980
  s.17... 511
  s.32... 511
  s.44... 419, 423, 456
  s.45... 511
Malicious Damage Act 1861
  ss 1–3... 388
Medicines Act 1968
  s.58(2)(a)... 412
  s.67... 183
Metropolitan Police Act 1839... 463
Misuse of Drugs Act 1971... 265
  s.4... 183
  s.4(2)... 512
  s.5... 18, 29
  s.8... 406
Murder (Abolition of Death Penalty) Act 1965... 142

Obscene Publications Act 1959... 509
Offences Against the Person Act 1861... 79
  s.4... 511, 513
  s.18... 23, 58, 87, 88, 92, 100, 110, 111, 112, 116, 117, 118, 119, 120, 142, 150, 212, 213, 218, 220, 259, 274, 431, 447, 448
  s.20... 66, 87, 88, 92, 96, 98, 100, 109, 110, 111, 112, 113, 114, 116, 118, 119, 120, 213, 213, 218, 220, 221, 371, 431, 448, 485, 486
  s.23... 92, 118, 183, 185, 186, 420, 430
  s.24... 92, 118
  s.47... 87, 88, 95, 100, 104, **106**, 107, 108, 110, 112, 113, 114, 118, 119, 120, 213, 274, 447
  s.56... 431
  s.58... 140, 268
  s.59... 140
Official Secrets Act 1911... 61

Patents Act 1977
  s.30... 292
Perjury Act 1911
  s.5... 61
Police and Criminal Evidence Act 1984
  s.24(1)... 4
  s.24(2)... 4
  s.78... 454, 458
Prevention of Crime Act 1953... 373
Proceeds of Crime Act 2002... 498
Prohibition of Female Circumcision Act 1985... 103
Protection of Children Act 1978
  s.1... 409
  s.1(1)... 410
Protection from Eviction Act 1977
  s.1(3)... 24, 58, 62
Protection from Harassment Act 1997
  s.4... 90

Regulation of Investigatory Powers
    Act 2000... 454
Road Traffic Act 1988
  s.3A... 139
  s.4(2)... 29
Road Traffic Offenders Act 1988
  s.15... 11

Sale of Goods Act 1979
  s.18... 298
  s.18(1)... 302
School Standards and Framework
    Act 1998
  s.131... 95
Sexual Offences Act 1956... 513
  s.5... 265
  s.6... 410, 436
  s.12... 407
  s.14... 230, 410, 412
  s.14(2)... 412, 413
  s.14(4)... 413
  s.20... 229, 404
Sexual Offences Act 1993
  s.1... 196
Sexual Offences Act 2003... 3, 4, 13,
    15, 49, 71, 78, 81, 82, 98, 229, 370,
    487, 488
  s.1... 23, 79, **122**, 129, 135, 227, 233,
    433
  s.1(2)... 79, **128**, 129
  s.1(3)... 79
  ss 1–3... 123, 124
  s.2... 122, 123, **129**, 130
  s.3... 122, **130**, 136, 412
  s.4... **133**, 136
  s.5... 134
  ss 5–7... 123
  ss 5–10... 410
  s.6... 134
  s.7... 20, 122, 134
  s.8... 511
  s.9... 124, 134, 230, 410, 436
  ss 9–12... 124
  s.10... 134, 230, 407, 511

  s.11... 134
  s.12... 134
  s.13... 121
  s.14... 134
  s.15... 134
  s.16... 413
  s.17... 511
  s.25... 134
  s.26... 134, 511, 513
  ss 32–42... 134
  s.45... 410
  s.63... 365
  s.66... 121, 365
  s.67... 121, 365
  s.73... 53
  s.74... 97, 123, 127, 135, 136
  s.75... 100, 122, 123, 126, 128, 130,
    133, 135, 136
  s.75(1)(c)... 126
  s.75(2)... **126**
  s.76... 100, 122, 123, 124, 126, 128,
    130, 133, 135, 136
  s.76(2)(a)... 125
  s.76(2)(b)... 124
  s.78... 131, 132, 136
  s.79(2)... 123
  s.79(3)... 123
  s.79(8)... 130
  s.79(9)... 123
Sexual Offences (Amendment)
    Act 1976... 227
Sexual Offences (Conspiracy and
    Incitement) Act 1996... 502
Shops Act 1912... 465
Suicide Act 1961
  s.1... 172
  s.2... 172
  s.3... 413
  s.4... 172

Tattooing of Minors Act 1969... 97
Terrorism Act 2000
  s.11... 12
  s.19... 23

Theft Act 1968... 275, 279, 325, 355, 510
  s.1... 371
  s.1(1)... 276, **277**, 322, 390, 394,
    395, 402
  s.1(2)... 310, 396
  s.1(3)... 277, 328, **398**
  s.2... 310, 328, 364
  s.2(1)... 310, 311, 312, 323
  s.2(1)(a)... 311, 315
  s.2(1)(b)... 283, 311, 312, 315
  s.2(1)(c)... 285, 311, 312
  s.2(2)... 312, 323
  ss 2–6... 276, 277
  s.3... 277, 299
  s.3(1)... 277, 278, 284, 285, 286,
    322, 386
  s.3(2)... 286, 386
  s.4... 277, 291, 364, 395
  s.4(1)... 290, 291, 293, 322
  s.4(2)... 322
  s.4(2)(a)–(c)... 293
  s.4(3)... 322
  s.4(4)... 294, 322
  s.5... 277, **294**, 322, 390, 402
  s.5(1)... 297, 299, 300, 303, 304, 305,
    306, 307, 308, 323, 390, 395
  s.5(2)... 299, 306, 308
  s.5(2)(a)... 391
  s.5(2)(b)... 392, 393
  s.5(3)... 298, 299, 305, 306, 307, 323
  s.5(4)... 298, **299**, 300, 301, 303, 304,
    305, 307, 323
  s.5(5)... 390
  s.6... 316, **317**, 320, 323, 324
  s.6(1)... 318, 319, 324, 357, 362
  s.6(2)... 318, 319, 324
  s.8... 399
  s.8(1)... **355**
  s.8(2)... 355
  s.9... **364**, 399, 400
  s.9(1)(a)... 370, 372
  s.9(1)(b)... 365, 372
  s.9(2)... 368
  s.9(3)... 369

  s.9(4)... 369
  s.10... 371, 373
  s.10(1)... **371**
  s.10(2)... 390
  s.11... 316
  s.11(1)... **362**
  s.11(2)... 363
  s.11(3)... **363**
  s.12... 316, 357, 358, 399
  s.12(5)... 358
  s.12(6)... **360**
  s.12(7)(a)... 358
  s.12A... 357, 361, 399
  s.12A(2)(b)... 361
  s.12A(3)... **362**
  s.13... 292, **364**
  s.15... 287, 326, 329, 351, 352, 380,
    480, 481, 491
  s.15(1)... 328
  s.15(4)... 333
  s.15A... 326, 329, 351, 352
  s.16... 326, 329, 351, 352
  s.16(2)... 352
  s.16(2)(a)... 330
  s.17... 276, 343
  ss 17–20... 343
  s.19... 276, 343
  s.20(1)... 343
  s.20(2)... 326, 331
  s.20(3)... 331
  s.21... 373
  s.21(1)... **374**, 376
  s.21(2)... 375
  s.22... 379, 385
  s.22(1)... **379**, 382, 383
  s.24(1)... 379
  s.24(2)... 401
  s.24(3)... 379, 380, 381, 401
  s.24A... 381
  s.24A(2A)... 381
  s.24A(5)... 381
  s.24A(8)... 381
  s.25... 342
  s.34(2)... 336, 401

s.34(2)(a)... 377, 378
Theft Act 1978... 62, 510
s.1... 325, 326, 329, 344, 351, 352
s.1(1)... 20, 329
s.2... 326, 330, 351, 352
s.2(1)... **330**
s.2(1)(a)... 222
s.3... 4, 346, **347**, 349, 350, 354
s.3(2)... 348
s.3(3)... 350
s.3(4)... 349
s.9(1)(a)... 63, 84
s.22... 20
Theft (Amendment) Act 1996... 310, 326
s.1... 329
s.2... 381

Trade Descriptions Act 1968... 460, 473
s.24... 415
Trade Marks Act 1994
s.92... 10
s.92(5)... 10
Transport Act 1968
s.96(11)... 414
Treasure Act 1996... 295
Trial of Lunatics Act 1883
s.2(1)... 203

Water Resources Act 1991
s.85... 461
s.85(1)... 35
Wireless Telegraphy Act 1949
s.1(1)... 409

■ GLOSSARY OF JOURNAL AND OTHER REFERENCES

CLJ	Cambridge Law Journal
CLRC	Criminal Law Revision Committee
Crim LR	Criminal Law Review
J Crim L	Journal of Criminal Law
Law Com	Law Commission
LQR	Law Quarterly Review
LS	Legal Studies
MLR	Modern Law Review
NLJ	New Law Journal
OJLS	Oxford Journal of Legal Studies

■ HOW TO USE THIS BOOK

This book will give students of criminal law a good, clear, and accurate introduction to the subject. Our aim has been to make the material as accessible as possible for those students coming to the subject for the first time. To this end we have included a number of features throughout the text to allow for interactive use of the book by students, in testing their knowledge and checking their understanding.

Special features of the book include:

Cases and Materials

The cases and materials referred to in the textbook can be found in the book's accompanying Online Resource Centre. To access the online cases and materials, go to www.oxfordtextbooks.co.uk/orc/heaton2e/, click on the 'Cases and Materials' link and login using the following details: username: heaton2e; password: materials. Wherever the case is cited on the web site, the Online Resource Centre symbol appears in the margin of the textbook. This allows the student access to extended extracts directly relevant to the discussion in the textbook. The Online Resource Centre effectively functions as an electronic casebook with extracts from all the major sources and will also be used to update the text in the event of major developments during the life of this edition.

Chapter Objectives

Each chapter opens with a set of objectives to help students identify the areas they should understand by the end of the chapter.

Question Boxes

A major innovation of the book is the incorporation into the text of frequent questions and exercises which are designed to encourage the reader to become more involved in the learning process by thinking about the material presented, and applying it. The questions posed vary considerably in the level of difficulty and you should not be worried if you find some of them impossible to answer or even understand on a first reading! The answers to them are embedded in the text that follows them. Most of you will find that they are particularly useful on a second reading of the chapter or to test your knowledge and understanding once you have read a topic or chapter. In other words, they would prove useful aids to revision. Sometimes the questions look forward to issues yet to be discussed and sometimes they look back at matters already discussed, maybe in a previous chapter. The latter form part of our strategy to reinforce earlier learning where we can, even at the expense of occasional duplication.

Exercises

Exercises are included throughout the text for students to test their understanding of the issues raised by key cases, and to encourage deeper reading and analysis of cases. The cases referred to in the exercises are included in the Online Resource Centre.

Chapter Summaries

Each chapter ends with a comprehensive summary of the main issues discussed in the chapter. This is not intended as a substitute for reading the chapter, but rather as a section to refresh the student's memory on the key issues discussed.

Assessment Exercise

Chapters end with an 'Assessment Exercise' that asks a question or sets up a scenario for the student to assess and answer using the knowledge gained through the reading of the chapter. A full specimen answer to each Assessment Exercise incorporating hints on technique is given at the end of the book.

Further Reading

A list of periodical articles and other materials useful for a deeper understanding is provided at the end of each chapter.

1 Introduction

Most law students think that they will find criminal law the most appealing of all the law subjects they have to study. Your own decision to study law may have been taken as a result of coverage of criminal cases in newspapers or on television, or interest generated by fictional portrayals of criminal proceedings. If so, what has attracted you is the criminal justice system, of which criminal law is only one element. As traditionally studied in law schools and treated in this book, criminal law means the substantive criminal law, concerning itself largely with the issue of criminal liability. We examine the extent to which there are any general principles governing criminal liability as a whole, e.g., are there any defences such as mental disorder applicable to offences generally? What are the rules on attempted crime or people who only assist in the commission of a crime? In addition, we choose some of the more important and well-known specific offences, such as murder, manslaughter, non-fatal offences of violence and offences against property, such as theft and criminal damage, and explore their detailed requirements as to liability. There are literally thousands of criminal offences in our law (and the present Government has added to them at a seemingly exponential rate!) and it is impossible for us to consider specifically in detail more than a few of the major ones. That is why the search for principles which can be applied generally is such a major focus of any criminal law course.

Generally speaking, we are not concerned with other aspects of the criminal justice system except in so far as they impinge on criminal liability, even though these, far more than the substantive law, are the stuff of the criminal law in practice. We do not deal with sentencing issues (the punishments available upon conviction and how the judges arrive at their sentencing decisions), which are an important part of criminology courses. Our consideration focuses on guilt or innocence. Criminal procedure is another matter largely outside our remit. The basic mechanics of the criminal process tend to form part of legal system courses, with a more critical review reserved for criminology courses and more practical detail in the Legal Practice Course. Similarly, the law of criminal evidence is taught normally as part of a separate subject. By and large, we are not concerned with methods of proving facts and the surrounding law, e.g., admissibility of evidence. We are concerned only whether, on given facts, D (the accused) is liable for any offence and, if so, which. You will probably appreciate that, in practice, most contested cases involve disputes about the facts, not about the law (D denies that he was the person who robbed the bank, that he turned right without signalling, or whatever). Thus, even though academic criminal law may not be quite what you expected, we hope and believe that you will find it interesting and enjoyable. You will certainly find it a challenge to understand its complexities and must be prepared to work hard to overcome its undoubted difficulties.

1.1 **What is a crime?**

Academics have long quested for the Holy Grail of a general definition of a 'crime' which identifies the quality of an act or omission which makes it an offence ('crime' and 'offence' are synonymous). However, crimes are so many and varied and embrace such widely differing kinds of conduct that all attempts to illuminate the essential characteristics of a crime, whether based on moral criteria or otherwise, have proved fruitless. Writers have been forced to abandon the search for the 'nature' of a crime and to fall back on rather lame definitions based on the type of legal proceedings which may follow from the act. In other words, an act is a crime if it 'is capable of being followed by criminal proceedings, having one of the types of outcome (punishment, etc.) known to follow these proceedings' (Professor Glanville Williams, 8 CLP 107, p. 123). Thus, although there are some crimes, such as murder and theft, which are instantly recognisable as crimes, if you wish to know definitively whether particular conduct is a crime, you must have recourse to statutes and case law to see whether criminal proceedings and punishment can follow such an act. As Dine and Gobert point out (*Cases and Materials on Criminal Law*, 3rd ed., p. 43), this definition 'puts the cart before the horse'. Furthermore, it is clear that the European Court of Human Rights is free to reject a domestic law classification as non-criminal if the nature of the proceedings is characteristic of criminal offence proceedings (general enforcement by a public authority with punitive elements based on fault) with a significant penalty attached (see *Benham* v *UK* (1996) 22 EHRR 293 (imprisonment for failure to pay the community charge)). There is no 'magic' definition.

It is a case of the State deciding that certain conduct ought to be criminal because it is too important to leave it to the private citizen wronged to bring civil proceedings. The State takes it upon itself to discourage such conduct. Of course, the wheels of change run slowly and it is inevitable that conduct that is no longer considered to be in this category remains criminal, whilst conduct which is now considered worthy of criminal sanctions may not yet be criminal.

1.2 **The role of the substantive criminal law**

The rules governing criminal liability define what is and what is not, criminal conduct and should therefore be clear and certain to enable people to ascertain in advance and with reasonable confidence whether any conduct will or will not involve criminal liability. Unfortunately, as we shall see, this is often far from the case and is one of the reasons for the growing pressure towards codification of the criminal law.

More importantly, the substantive rules on criminal liability define the playing field upon which the apparatus of the criminal justice system can be brought to bear. The coercive powers of the police (search, arrest, etc.) and the courts (to convict and sentence) are based on conduct defined as 'criminal' by the substantive law. The social control mechanism which is the criminal justice system is founded upon the rules prescribing what is and what is not, a crime.

The Wolfenden Committee on Homosexual Offences and Prostitution ((1957) Cmnd 247) viewed the purpose of the criminal law (at para. 13) as:

> ... to preserve public order and decency, to protect the citizen from what is offensive or injurious, and to provide sufficient safeguards against exploitation and corruption of others, particularly those who are especially vulnerable ... It is not ... the function of the law to intervene in the private lives of citizens, or to seek to enforce any particular pattern of behaviour, further than is necessary to carry out the purposes we have outlined.

The Committee concluded that the criminal law should not be used to impose society's current moral standards on non-conformist individuals (even assuming these standards are readily ascertainable). This probably represents the prevailing view of the judiciary now (but *cf. Brown* discussed under 4.3.3.1 below). The truth is that whilst there might be a large measure of agreement about the central core of any criminal law, the issue of whether conduct on the periphery should be criminal often involves balancing a number of competing considerations and interests, and is ultimately a matter of social, economic and political judgement.

? QUESTION 1.1

Is there any conduct (a) which is not criminal which you would like to see made criminal and (b) which is criminal which you think should be de-criminalised?

We can at this point note one development which the current Government seems increasingly keen to use which threatens to undercut the substantive criminal law and the procedural safeguards surrounding it. There is a trend towards legislation which lays down what might be called 'civil' offences which do not attract criminal sanctions as such but merely allow the courts to impose an order on D to refrain from doing something. However, they are then indirectly criminalised by providing that breach of the 'civil' order **is** a criminal offence which attracts penal sanctions. This kind of procedure enables avoidance of traditional criminal safeguards in respect of standards of proof and admissibility of evidence in the initial proceedings imposing the relevant order. You will have heard of ASBOs (Anti-Social Behaviour Orders—see s.1 of the Crime and Disorder Act 1998). Other examples include Foreign Travel Orders, Sexual Offence Prevention Orders and Risk of Sexual Harm Orders under the Sexual Offences Act 2003 and Football Banning Orders under the Football (Disorder) Act 1991. In *R (McCann)* v *Crown Court at Manchester* [2003] 1 AC 787, the House of Lords has held that ASBO proceedings are not subject to the protections conferred by Art. 6 of the European Convention on Human Rights (see 1.6 below).

In addition to this, the Government seems wedded to a marked extension of the reach of criminal liability based on a populist agenda fuelled by the tabloid press. The quantity of criminal offences has certainly grown but, more importantly, the tentacles of the criminal law are expanding into arguably inappropriate areas. In short, there is an anti-libertarian overkill in important pieces of legislation pouring out of Westminster. Offences are over-inclusive and rely on vague relativist notions such as 'anti-social', 'offensive' and 'insulting'. Furthermore, it appears that over-expansive legislation aimed at particular mischiefs, notably the anti-terrorist laws, is being hijacked for unrelated and arguably inappropriate purposes such as the stifling of legitimate protest. We may instance offences proposed in new anti-terrorism legislation such as 'glorification' of acts of terrorism (though, at the time of writing, it appears that the Government has decided to rein in the worst excesses in the proposals), and the overbroad offences under the Sexual Offences Act 2003.

1.3 Classification of offences

Offences are classified for procedural purposes as summary, indictable or triable either way. Summary offences are the less serious crimes which can only be tried in the magistrates' court without a jury. Examples include common assault and battery, assaulting a police officer in the execution of his duty, drink-driving offences, and taking a vehicle without the owner's consent. Indictable offences are more serious offences which can be tried in the Crown Court with a judge and jury. Some indictable offences such as murder, manslaughter and robbery can only be tried on indictment and this is the sense in which we use the term 'indictable' above. Strictly speaking, however, any offence which is capable of being tried on indictment is an indictable offence, which term therefore includes all offences which are triable either way.

The latter are offences where the seriousness varies enormously depending on the particular circumstances of the individual case. Thus, theft can range from petty pilfering to the Great Train Robbery (if you remember that) and is triable either way—summarily before magistrates in the first case, but on indictment before the Crown Court in the second case. Other such offences include handling stolen goods and obtaining property by deception. Where an offence is triable either way, the magistrates decide whether it should be tried summarily or on indictment, although the accused may elect to be tried on indictment before a jury where the magistrates rule in favour of summary trial.

Offences are also classified by reference to powers of arrest. Arrestable offences are generally more serious and, as such, are indictable offences for which it is possible to arrest without a warrant. Section 24(1) of the Police and Criminal Evidence Act 1984 designates offences carrying a maximum sentence of at least five years' imprisonment as arrestable offences, whilst s. 24(2) adds to the list a number of offences which fail to meet this criterion. It is also open to the legislature, when creating any new offence, specifically to make it an arrestable offence. For example, s. 3 of the Theft Act 1978 makes the offence of making off without payment 'arrestable' even though it is an offence triable either way with a maximum sentence of two years' imprisonment on indictment. Even the relatively minor offence of common assault (carrying a maximum of six months' imprisonment) has recently been made an arrestable offence (s. 10 of the Domestic Violence, Crimes and Victims Act 2004).

The old distinction between felonies (serious offences) and misdemeanours (less serious offences) was abolished by the Criminal Justice Act 1967, but you will still occasionally come across those terms.

1.4 Appeals and the role of the trial judge

Figures 1.1 and 1.2 set out briefly the system of criminal appeals and the grounds of appeal respectively for summary trials and trials on indictment.

Apart from legislative provision, the rules of substantive law are largely set by appeal cases and much of this text will be devoted to analysing such cases. In the majority of decisions relevant to us, the appeal is at least partly on the ground that the trial judge has got the law wrong in his direction to the jury. If a conviction follows, D is likely to appeal. If D is acquitted at the initial trial, it is now possible for the Attorney-General to 'refer' the case to the Court of Appeal for a ruling on the point of law decided by the Crown Court against the prosecution (Criminal Justice Act 1972, s. 36). Whatever the Court of Appeal's view on the point of law, D's acquittal cannot be overturned under this procedure. You will come across several of these 'Attorney-General's References' which have established important legal principles.

The House of Lords in *Wang* [2005] UKHL 9 (see *Cases and Materials* (1.4)) helpfully summarised the respective functions of the judge and jury in a criminal trial:

> The judge directs, or instructs, the jury on the law relevant to the counts in the indictment [i.e., the charges laid against D], and makes it clear that the jury must accept and follow his legal rulings. But he also directs the jury that the decision of all factual questions, including the application of the law as expounded to the facts as they find them to be, is a matter for them alone. And he makes it plain that, whatever views he may express or be thought to express, it is for them and not for him to decide whether, on each count in the indictment, the defendant is guilty or not guilty. [8]
>
> ...if a judge is satisfied that there is no evidence which could justify the jury in convicting the defendant and that it would be perverse for them to do so, it is the judge's duty to direct them to acquit (*DPP* v *Stonehouse* [1978] AC 55 at 70, 79–80 and 94)...a judge should withdraw a defence from the consideration of the jury if there is no evidence whatever to support it, and he need not direct the jury on an issue not raised by any evidence...in a case where, on applying the law as expounded by the judge to facts which have been agreed or not disputed at trial, the only reasonable course is to convict, the judge may comment in stronger terms than would otherwise be permissible. But even in such a case...the judge may not direct the jury to convict. [3]

Wang marks a welcome affirmation that the jury is ultimately the sole arbiter of guilt and that a trial judge cannot under any circumstances direct them to find a defendant guilty.

? QUESTION 1.2

If D appeals on a point of law, is it a case of the Court of Appeal simply deciding whether it would have convicted D of the offence? If not, what is its role?

When D appeals on a point of law, the Court of Appeal must decide whether the trial judge's explanation of the law to the jury was correct. It is exceptionally important to understand that it is not the appeal court's function to retry the case and substitute its verdict for that of the jury. As we have seen, the jury is the arbiter of guilt or innocence in trials on indictment, but if D may have been prejudiced by an error of the trial judge in explaining the law to the jury, the Court of Appeal must give D the benefit of any doubt and if the jury might have returned a different verdict, the court must quash the conviction. The Criminal Appeal Act 1995 reformed the grounds of appeal to the Court of Appeal by amending s. 2 of the Criminal Appeal Act 1968 (see *Cases and Materials* (1.4)). There is now only one ground of appeal—that the conviction is 'unsafe'. This will include cases where the trial judge misdirects the jury on the law, though now the leave of the Court of Appeal or the trial judge to appeal is a pre-requisite (Criminal Appeal Act 1995, s. 1).

There are two points we need to make about this. First, students often focus on the outcome of the appeal when what matters far more is the reasoning employed by the appeal court in affirming or quashing the conviction. This incorrect focus leads to bewilderment that an 'obviously guilty' villain goes free. Unfortunately, it is a fact of life that misdirections in law sometimes occur because the trial judge is straining too hard to ensure the conviction of an 'obviously guilty villain'. It is the appeal court's job to ensure that the jury has considered its verdict on the correct basis and that if there is even a small possibility of a different verdict had the jury been told correctly what constituted the ingredients of the crime or, maybe, the defence in issue, the conviction should be quashed as being 'unsafe'.

Paradoxically, the second point is the converse of the first. Sometimes the appeal court's overwhelming desire to ensure that an 'obviously guilty villain' is not acquitted because of

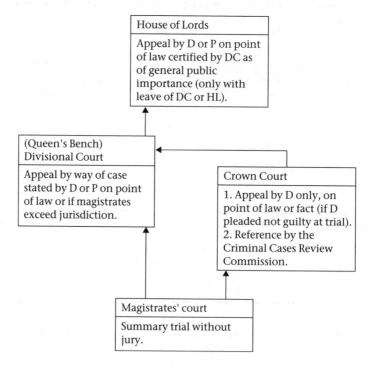

Figure 1.1 Appeals from summary trials

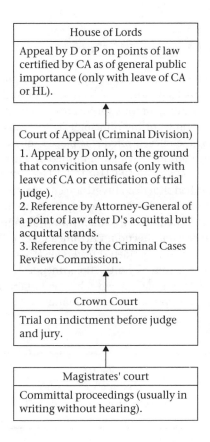

Figure 1.2 Appeals from trials on indictment

an unfortunate error by the trial judge, leads it to distort the applicable principle of law to enable it to hold that there has been no misdirection on the law. The court loses sight of its wider role of ensuring consistency and clarity in the law.

One other change made by the Criminal Appeal Act 1995 was to provide for the establishment of the Criminal Cases Review Commission. This body took over from the Home Secretary the role of investigating and referring to the Court of Appeal or, in the case of summary convictions, the Crown Court, convictions involving alleged miscarriages of justice, normally where standard appeals procedures have been exhausted and fresh evidence and/or arguments have come to light since. The Commission is constitutionally independent of the government though appointment of its members is by the Queen on the recommendation of the Prime Minister. Its Annual Report for 2004–2005 discloses that, since its establishment, it has referred to the courts only 4.4% of the 6,842 cases reviewed by it (seemingly a testimony to the general competence of the criminal courts). The Commission's referrals 'success rate' in terms of convictions quashed is around two-thirds and attests to the competence of its judgments.

1.5 **Burden of proof**

It is a fundamental principle of English law reinforced by Art. 6(2) of the European Convention on Human Rights, that a person is innocent until proved guilty (although inroads on the 'right of silence' by ss. 32–37 of the Criminal Justice and Public Order Act 1994 may be seen as a serious derogation from the principle). This means that the legal burden of proving that D committed the alleged offence is placed squarely on the prosecution. It must prove 'beyond reasonable doubt' that D committed the crime charged (*Woolmington v DPP* [1935] All ER Rep 1, HL; *Mancini v DPP* [1941] 3 All ER 272, HL). In *Woolmington* (see *Cases and Materials* (1.5)), D had shot dead his estranged wife. He claimed that the gun had gone off accidentally when he was showing it to her. The trial judge had directed the jury that it was up to D to satisfy them that the killing was not murder i.e., an accident. The House of Lords held this to be a misdirection, Viscount Sankey LC stating: 'Throughout the web of the English Criminal Law one golden thread is always to be seen, that is the duty of the prosecution to prove the prisoner's guilt . . . the principle . . . is part of the common law of England and no attempt to whittle it down can be entertained'. Thus, the prosecution had to establish that D killed with the requisite intention to kill or cause serious injury in order to secure a conviction for murder.

 QUESTION 1.3

How would the prosecution be able to prove what was going on in D's head when the gun went off?

At the trial, the prosecution will first present its case calling witnesses to the incident, scientific evidence (e.g., fingerprints or bloodstains), evidence as to D's motive and circumstantial evidence (e.g., linking D with the scene of the crime) and any statements he has made under police interrogation. Assuming the prosecution has made out a prima facie case, the defence presents its case calling its own witnesses (including, if it wishes, the accused himself) and evidence (e.g., alibi evidence supporting a claim to be miles from the scene of the crime). At the close of evidence, each side in turn makes a closing address to the court. The trial judge then has to sum up for the jury. He must review the evidence for them, summarising each side's case, pointing out discrepancies and weak points and focusing the jury on the crucial issues to be determined on the facts. He must also direct them on any relevant law. Thus, in a murder trial, he must explain the legal ingredients of murder and what the jury must be satisfied about before they can convict. If D is claiming a defence, e.g., that he acted in self-defence, the judge would have to explain the legal requirements of such a defence.

In serious crimes, one of the standard requirements for the prosecution is to prove that D had a particular state of mind at the time of performing the prohibited conduct. This is the *mens rea* for the crime and the definition of each crime will prescribe precisely what the requisite state of mind is. Usually it will be either an intention to do something (e.g., kill, injure) or a realisation that the conduct involves a risk of doing something (e.g., killing, injuring). This brings us to Question 1.3: how can it be proved beyond reasonable doubt what D was thinking at the time of the act? After all, we cannot look inside D's head and if he says he did not intend to fire the gun, have we not got to give him the benefit of the doubt and take his word for it? The first point is that it is clearly open to the jury to disbelieve D's evidence in the same way as that of any other witness. For example, that evidence may be contradicted by D's earlier confession to the police. Witnesses may have seen the incident or overheard D threatening P and their evidence may be inconsistent with D's version.

What the jury must do if they wish to convict in cases where D denies he had the requisite intention or foresight (realisation) is to infer that intention or foresight from proof of what actually happened, what D did and the surrounding circumstances. This rule of common sense is enshrined in s. 8 of the Criminal Justice Act 1967 (see *Cases and Materials* (1.5)) which contains instructions for how D's intention or foresight of a harmful consequence (e.g., death) must be proved if and when the definition of the offence charged requires it to be proved. It reads:

A court or jury, in determining whether a person has committed an offence—

(a) shall not be bound in law to infer that he intended or foresaw a result of his actions by reason only of its being a natural and probable consequence of those actions; but

(b) shall decide whether he did intend or foresee that result by reference to all the evidence, drawing such inferences from the evidence as appear proper in the circumstances.

Thus, the prosecution has the legal burden of proving beyond reasonable doubt the presence of all the ingredients of the crime and that D was the person who committed it. That is the position where, for example, D simply denies that he was the person who did it. However, the position is more complicated if he admits to performing the acts but claims they do not amount to the crime because he has a defence, e.g., he acted in self-defence or under duress or he was insane. It would be ridiculously onerous for the prosecution if, in every trial, it had to deal with and eliminate every possible defence which D might have raised and the law does not require it to do so. An evidential burden (termed by some 'the burden of going forward') is placed on D to put forward some credible evidence to support his claimed defence. Only if he does this will the prosecution then have the legal burden of disproving this defence. For example, in *Woolmington*, D claimed that the shooting of his wife was an accident and that, despite appearances, he did not intend to kill or injure. For this to become an issue in the trial compelling the prosecution to disprove it, D would have to provide some evidence to support it, e.g., by his own testimony at the trial, testimony from friends as to good relationship with wife, or that he had no reason to kill.

1.5.1 Reverse burdens of proof

There are some defences where D's burden is even higher. He bears the 'burden of persuasion'—persuading the court that, more probably than not, he satisfies the conditions for the claimed defence. There is only one instance at common law—the defence of insanity. Since the law presumes everyone sane unless the contrary is proved, if D claims to have been insane when acting, he must prove it on the balance of probabilities (accepted by the European Commission on Human Rights as not contrary to Art. 6(2) of the ECHR in *H* v *United Kingdom* Appn No 15023/89, 4 April 1990 (unreported)). This is the only exception to the rule developed by the common law, but it is always possible for the legislature to make exceptions to it expressly or impliedly by statute (*Hunt* [1987] 1 All ER 10, HL). This has been done on numerous occasions and is quite a favoured modern drafting technique (for a recent example see s. 63 of the Gambling Act 2005). It usually happens in the limited context of a specific statutory offence where the legislature defines the basic ingredients of the offence but then expressly excuses D from liability if he can 'prove' certain specified facts. For example, s. 2 of the Homicide Act 1957 enacts the statutory defence to murder of diminished responsibility (a form of mental disorder) and expressly imposes not just an evidential burden but the legal burden of proof on D. The Court of Appeal in the consolidated appeals of *Lambert; Ali; Jordan* [2001] 1 All ER 1014 refused to hold that reversing the burden of proof contravened the presumption of innocence enshrined in Art. 6(2) of the ECHR. That would not necessarily prevent imposing a burden of proof on D especially where the substance of what he had to prove was not 'an essential element' or 'ingredient' of the offence, but rather 'a special defence or exception' as in the case of diminished responsibility under s. 2.

The case of *Lambert*, though neither of the other consolidated appeals, was appealed to the House of Lords. The decision ([2001] UKHL 37) necessitates a fundamental reassessment of provisions which place a burden of proof on D whether couched in terms of a constituent element of the offence definition itself or a special defence or exception. The House's view was that placing a burden of proof on D was prima facie a contravention of the presumption of innocence guaranteed by Art. 6(2) of the ECHR. Although some inroads were permissible, they had to be confined within 'reasonable limits', be 'objectively justified' and comply with the 'principle of proportionality' (Lord Steyn). The majority's view was that a provision that made someone in possession of a controlled drug guilty unless he could 'prove' on the balance of probabilities that he did not know, suspect or have reason to suspect that the bag he possessed contained a controlled drug, did contravene Art. 6(2). The remarkable solution adopted by their Lordships (Lord Hutton dissenting) was to invoke s. 3(1) of the Human Rights Act 1998 to 'read down' the statutory provision so that when it said 'prove', it did not mean 'prove on the balance of probabilities' but only 'giving sufficient evidence'. Thus, an apparently clear imposition of a burden of proof on D is interpreted as a mere evidential burden so as to make the legislative provision comply with Art. 6(2). It seemed to follow that the numerous statutory provisions couched in terms of burden of proof might no longer mean what they say!

However, in *Johnstone* [2003] UKHL 28, the House of Lords, showing a much greater readiness to uphold reverse burdens of proof, seriously softened the *Lambert* approach where the starting point was a strong assumption that there was a contravention of Art. 6(2). D was convicted of possessing pirated recordings which infringed recording companies' trade marks contrary to s. 92 of the Trade Marks Act 1994. Section 92(5) gave D a defence if he could 'show' that he reasonably believed he was not infringing the trade mark. Their Lordships found the necessary 'compelling reasons' for upholding the provision's imposition of the reverse burden of proof. Emphasis was placed on the need to respect the will of Parliament and not to be too astute to find that the reverse burden was a disproportionate response to the mischief Parliament was trying to correct. Even before *Johnstone*, the lower courts had been quite ready to sidestep *Lambert* (whilst paying lip service to it, of course!). In *L* v *DPP* [2002] Crim LR 320 DC, D had in his possession a lock knife in a public place. This was an offence under s. 139 of the Criminal Justice Act 1988 unless D could 'prove that he had good reason or lawful authority for having' it with him. The Court distinguished *Lambert* holding that placing the onus of proving something that was essentially within his own knowledge was 'a proportionate measure, weighed by Parliament and well within reasonable limits'. A similar line was taken in *Drummond* [2002] Crim LR 666, CA in relation to drink-driving legislation. Section 15 of the Road Traffic Offenders Act 1988 allows a driver who tests positive a defence if he 'proves (a) that he consumed alcohol before he provided the specimen and...after the time of the alleged offence...and (b) that had he not done so the proportion of alcohol...would not have exceeded the prescribed limit...' Again this was held to impose a persuasive burden of proof and not just an evidential burden. The imposition of a reverse burden was a justifiable response to the evils of drink/driving and the problems posed by post-offence drinking (formerly called 'the hip-flask defence') and it was proportionate as it related to a matter peculiarly within D's own knowledge. Thus, it became far from inevitable that the word 'prove' would be read down in accordance with *Lambert* but there was an unfortunate air of unpredictability as to whether or not the word would be held to mean what it said.

In *Attorney-General's Reference (No. 1 of 2004)* [2004] EWCA Crim 1025, the Court of Appeal recognised the divergence of approach between *Lambert* and *Johnstone* and plumped for *Johnstone* with an instruction to trial judges and magistrates to ignore *Lambert*! The stage was set therefore for a final resolution by the House of Lords. Unfortunately the anticipated clarification did not materialise in the consolidated appeals of *Attorney-General's Reference (No. 4 of 2002); Sheldrake v DPP* [2004] UKHL 43 and we are still left a legacy of uncertainty and unpredictability. Certainly their Lordships disapproved of the Court of Appeal's sidelining of *Lambert* which 'should not be treated as superseded or implicitly overruled [by *Johnstone*].' In assessing whether the provision 'unjustifiably infringes the presumption of innocence', the courts must not be unduly influenced by the fact that Parliament has thought it necessary to enact the provision, otherwise there is a danger of giving too little weight to the presumption of innocence ([31]). 'The overriding concern is that a trial should be fair, and the presumption of innocence is a fundamental right directed to that end.... [any provision] must be reasonable. Relevant to any judgment on reasonableness or proportionality will be the opportunity given to the defendant to rebut the presumption, maintenance of the rights of the defence, flexibility in application of the presumption, retention by the court of a power to assess the evidence, the importance of what is at stake and the difficulty which a prosecutor may face in the absence of a presumption.... The justifiability of any infringement of the presumption of innocence cannot be resolved by any rule of thumb, but on examination of all the facts and circumstances of the particular provision as applied in the particular case.' [21]. In other words, play it by ear!

Essentially, in assessing whether the reverse burden is a proportionate response, the court has to balance the legitimacy and importance of countering the social (and economic) mischief against the accused's right to a fair trial. Key factors will be the seriousness of the offence in terms of both penalty and stigma, the potential for a person 'who is innocent of any blameworthy or properly criminal conduct' to be convicted and the respective difficulty for either party in proving the matter(s) subjected to the reverse burden (51). The preponderance of cases have upheld the imposition of a reverse burden, as the House did in respect of drink-driving legislation in the *Sheldrake* part of the appeal. However, on the other appeal concerning the offence of being or professing to be a member of a proscribed organisation contrary to s. 11 of the Terrorism Act 2000, the House read down a reverse burden of proof provision making it a defence for D to 'prove' *inter alia* that the organisation was not proscribed when he joined it and he has not taken part in its activities since it became proscribed. The importance of countering terrorism did not justify the use of this legislative means because of its potential to undermine the fairness of D's trial and to convict him unfairly of a very serious offence (up to 10 years' imprisonment).

1.5.2 Standard of proof

> **? QUESTION** 1.4
>
> Taking D's claim in *Woolmington* that the shooting was an accident, would it be true to say that, if he produced some evidence to support his claim, but the jury ultimately disbelieved his claim, the jury would be entitled to convict him?

We need to conclude this section with a little more about the standard of proof required. You will have noticed that, in those exceptional instances where the legal burden of proof is placed on D, it is of a lower standard than applies when the burden is on the prosecution. D need only establish his defence 'on the balance of probabilities'—his claim is more likely to be true than not (the same standard borne by the claimant in civil cases). Where D has only an evidential burden, the standard is even lower than this. D need only point to material which might cause the jury to have a reasonable doubt about his guilt (*Lee Chun-Chuen v R* [1963] 1 All ER 73, PC).

When the legal burden of proof is laid on the prosecution it is the more onerous one of proof 'beyond reasonable doubt' (*Woolmington*). This means that, even if on balance the jury thinks that D did commit the offence charged, it must acquit if it entertains any reasonable doubt that he may not have committed the offence. Therefore, in Question 1.4, the jury should not convict if it thinks D's claim might reasonably be true, even though, on balance, it thinks it is probably not true. The benefit of any reasonable doubt has to be given to D.

1.6 Reform of the criminal law

It will quickly become evident that the English criminal law is in many areas in something of a chaotic state. It is often incoherent, illogical and lacking in clarity. Even its most basic concepts are uncertain. There is therefore a good deal of pressure for reform in legal circles and there are signs that this is beginning to bear fruit in the political arena. Whilst technical reform of the criminal law has not been seen as a high priority in the allocation of scarce Parliamentary time (see, e.g., Brooke (then Chairman of the Law Commission)

[1995] Crim LR 911, 917–19), the Government in 2002 professed its intention to codify the general principles of criminal law (see below).

The Law Commission is at the forefront of the push for reform and its output of material on criminal law in recent years has been phenomenal. We will be referring to the Law Commission's proposals in its consultation papers and reports throughout this book, and so it is appropriate at this point to explain in general terms something about the work of the Commission.

At the heart of the Law Commission's endeavours is a proposal for a comprehensive criminal code to replace much of the existing law. This draft Criminal Code, as it is now generally known, was published by the Law Commission as *The Report and Draft Criminal Code Bill for England and Wales in 1989* (Law Com. No. 177). It was based on the work of a small team of distinguished academic lawyers comprising the late Professor Sir John Smith, the late Professor Griew and Professor Dennis. Volume I includes the Commission's recommendations, a draft Criminal Code Bill and Appendices. Part I of the Bill covers the general principles of liability and Part II deals with specific offences. Appendix B gives illustrations of how the Code might operate in particular fact situations. Volume II offers a commentary on some of the Code's provisions.

Although the Commission's long-term aim is that such a Code should be enacted, in deference to political realities and the amount of Parliamentary time which would be needed for an enactment of that magnitude, it produced a less ambitious scheme in 1993. The Report, *Legislating the Criminal Code: Offences Against the Person and General Principles* has abstracted what the Commission sees as key areas desperate for reform and a Criminal Law Bill has been drawn up which builds on the relevant provisions in the original draft Criminal Code Bill (Law Com. No. 218).

In addition to these more generalised reports, the Commission has produced a number of reports and consultation papers on more specific and discrete topics, such as the defence of intoxication (1995), involuntary manslaughter (1996), fraud (2002) and partial defences to murder (2004). (More examples are given in the ensuing pages.) The procedure is that the Commission in the first instance issues a consultation paper discussing the existing law, indicating its preliminary views on changes and inviting comments from readers. Following consideration of these comments, it issues a report containing its final recommendations, which can differ quite dramatically from the initial consultation paper (e.g., see the report on intoxication in **Chapter 8**). These reports and papers often contain most lucid expositions of the current law and its anomalies and it is extremely instructive to read these sections of them (see *Cases and Materials* (1.6)).

Some of the Commission's Reports have stirred the Home Office into action to the extent of formulating proposals for consultation in respect of offences of non-fatal violence (see **Chapter 4**), involuntary manslaughter (see **Chapters 6** and **15**), fraud (see **Chapter 11**) and sex offences (see **Chapter 5**). However, only two have resulted in legislation—the Sexual Offences Act 2003 and the Fraud Act 2006. In terms of codification in general, the White Paper, *Criminal Justice: The Way Ahead*, 2002, committed the Government to 'a key idea…of reform and codification of criminal law providing a consolidated, modernised core criminal code to improve public confidence and make for shorter, simpler trials.' It is alleged that the Home Office is 'urgently working on what a programme of codification might consist of and how it might be managed.' (See Editorial at [2003] Crim LR 431.) We will not be holding our breath but, as part of this programme, the Law Commission has agreed to update its previous work and produce a series of consultation papers in 2005 and 2006 on the following topics:

- External elements of offences, in particular causation (i.e., *actus reus*—see Ch. 2)
- Fault (see Ch. 3)
- Parties to offences (see Ch. 14)
- Incapacity and mental disorder (see Chs. 7, 8 and 9)
- Intoxication (see Ch. 8)
- Defences (see Chs. 7, 8 and 9)
- Preliminary Offences (see Ch. 16)
- Proof (see Ch. 1)

Finally, we must note one other development whose effect on the criminal law is unpredictable but likely to be of great significance. The Human Rights Act 1998, which came into force on 2 October 2000, in effect incorporates the provisions of the European Convention on Human Rights into domestic law, thus paving the way for accused persons to argue that current interpretations of penal laws contravene rights enshrined in the Convention. If the argument is accepted, the courts will have either to reinterpret existing principles and statutory provisions so as to accord with Convention rights or, in the case of statutory provisions, to precipitate legislative amendment by declaring them incompatible with the Convention.

The formulation of any future legislation will have to take account of the Convention's provisions. Whilst the greatest impact will be (and has already been) felt in the area of procedure and evidence, it seems inevitable that lawyers will increasingly use Convention rights to argue for particular interpretations of the definitions of substantive offences. To date, however, the courts have almost always rejected such arguments often on the basis that the applicable Article (usually it has been Art. 6) is designed to ensure a fair trial **procedure** and does not extend to requiring a fair **substantive** law (see, e.g., *Barnfather* v *Islington Education Authority* [2003] 1 WLR 2318 DC at 13.3 below).

It should also be noted that European Community Law enshrines certain general rights such as freedom of movement which automatically take precedence over domestic law and which could be used to overturn or circumscribe particular criminal offences. Though this has been the case since the United Kingdom joined the Community, the impact so far has been very limited and, in practice, the Human Rights Act will be much more significant. We reproduce in *Cases and Materials* those provisions of the European Convention which seem most likely to influence the substantive law.

■ FURTHER READING

Ashworth: *Is Criminal Law a Lost Cause?* [2000] 116 LQR 225.

Ashworth: *The Human Rights Act and the Substantive Criminal Law: A Non-Minimalist View* [2000] Crim LR 564.

Ashworth: *Social Control and Anti-Social Behaviour: The Subversion of Human Rights?* (2004) 120 LQR 263.

Buxton: *The Human Rights Act and the Substantive Criminal Law* [2000] Crim LR 311.

Devlin: *The Enforcement of Morals* (1968, Oxford University Press).

Hart: *Law, Liberty and Morality* (1963, Oxford University Press).

Williams: *The Definition of Crime* (1955) Current Legal Problems 107.

■ SUMMARY

Criminal law is the study of the substantive law of criminal liability looking at general principles of liability and some specific offences. It is not a study of procedure, evidence, or sentencing. There is no standard definition of a 'crime'—it is simply conduct allowing criminal proceedings and punishment. Substantive criminal law defines the parameters of the criminal justice system by defining what is and what is not criminal conduct.

- *Classification of offences by mode of trial*— summary only (by magistrates), indictable only (most serious) (by jury in Crown Court) or triable either way (magistrates' or Crown Court depending on circumstances). Arrestable offences allow arrest without warrant—generally carrying a maximum penalty of at least five years' imprisonment.

- *Appeals*—see diagrams. Often concerns whether trial judge has explained the law correctly to the jury.

- *Burden of proof*— prosecution has legal burden of proving D's guilt beyond reasonable doubt (*Woolmington*). Applies to most defences although D would have an (evidential) burden of adducing credible evidence to put the defence 'in play'. Exceptionally, D may have legal burden of proving 'on balance of probabilities', e.g., insanity, or where statute expressly or impliedly puts burden on D, e.g., diminished responsibility though called into question by the presumption of innocence in ECHR Art. 6(2) (see *Lambert; Sheldrake* v *DPP*). Proof of D's state of mind often required—in absence of D's admission state of mind must be inferred from circumstances (*cf.* s. 8 of the Criminal Justice Act 1967).

- *Reform*— Law Commission's consultation papers and reports on specific topics. Draft Criminal Law Bill 1993 covers non-fatal offences against the person and many general principles of liability. Draft Criminal Code Bill 1989 is similar but much more comprehensive and wide-ranging. Government now showing interest: (i) draft Offences Against the Person Bill; (ii) Sexual Offences Act 2003; (iii) Home Office Review of murder; (iv) Fresh review of General Principles via Law Commission; (v) Human Rights Act incorporating European Convention on Human Rights into domestic law.

2 Actus reus

2.1 Objectives

By the end of this chapter you should be able to:

1 Analyse the general concept of *actus reus* and its constituent elements

2 Identify the bases on which the law imposes criminal liability for omissions

3 Describe the principles governing causation in the criminal law and apply them to any given fact situation

2.2 Introduction

We can identify two basic building blocks needed to establish liability for most of the crimes which are considered in this book. The first is the conduct which the particular crime prohibits, e.g., killing someone, taking another's property or telling lies in the witness box. This is known to criminal lawyers as the *actus reus*, a Latin phrase literally meaning 'the guilty act', but which is more aptly translated as 'the forbidden conduct'. The second element, known as the *mens rea*, is whatever state of mind or fault is required on the part of D according to the definition of the crime in issue. Although literally translated as guilty mind, *mens rea* is often used loosely to encompass fault elements such as negligence which do not depend on the state of D's mind. It is also worth noting at this point that this second element is not a universal requirement of all crimes, since there is an extensive range of offences, known as strict liability offences, where there is no necessity to prove a fault element.

There is a third element which, in a negative sense, is necessary to ground liability, namely, the absence of a defence. In practice, this will be assumed unless some credible evidence suggests otherwise. The question at issue is whether, assuming he has performed the prohibited conduct with the appropriate state of mind, D falls within any of the general defences to criminal liability which would absolve him from that liability. For example, D may have intentionally injured someone, but only because he was acting in reasonable self-defence. We shall be dealing with general defences and, indeed, other issues mentioned here, such as strict liability offences, in later chapters.

Liability for most mainstream criminal offences requires that:

(a) D caused the prohibited conduct (*actus reus*);

(b) with the relevant state of mind or fault element (*mens rea*);

(c) in circumstances where no defence is available (absence of defence).

There is no **necessity** to divide up the ingredients of crimes into *actus reus* and *mens rea*. However, experience has shown that it is a useful aid to a clear analysis and understanding of the ingredients of criminal offences. In those instances where such division complicates the analysis, it is best disregarded, e.g., in some offences a mental element or state of mind is an intrinsic part of the *actus reus*. Thus, you cannot 'possess' a controlled drug (the *actus reus*) under s. 5 of the Misuse of Drugs Act 1971 unless you know of the existence of the thing which turns out to be the drug. The fact that *actus reus* and *mens rea* are merely labels designed for ease of analysis should certainly mean that the legal outcome in terms of liability should not be affected by which label is applied to which ingredient. Unfortunately, as we shall see later, the courts have blinded themselves to this point in the important area of the effect of a mistake on criminal liability. D's criminal liability can depend precisely on whether or not the matter about which he has made the mistake is classified as part of the *actus reus* of the crime.

Lord Diplock (*Miller* [1983] 1 All ER 978, HL) attempted to discourage the use of the terminology, but not the underlying concepts, of *actus reus* and *mens rea*:

> My Lords, it would I think be conducive to clarity of analysis of the ingredient of a crime that is created by statute, as are the great majority of criminal offences today, if we were to avoid bad Latin and instead to think and speak . . . about the conduct of the accused and the state of mind at the time of that conduct, instead of speaking of *actus reus* and *mens rea*.

However, the terms *actus reus* and *mens rea* continue to be universally used. The Law Commission in its draft Criminal Code Bill (Law Com. No. 177) prefers the terms 'external elements' for the *actus reus* and 'fault element' for *mens rea*.

2.3 *Actus reus*

In general, the law is not concerned with evil thoughts and intentions unless and until they manifest themselves in conduct. D must do something towards carrying out the intentions before criminal liability will ensue. The physical conduct which is prohibited by the crime is what we call its *actus reus*. Only when D has demonstrated his seriousness of purpose and therefore potential danger to society, do we need to think about imposing criminal liability. As we shall see later, for some offences, notably the so-called 'inchoate offences', this conduct need not amount to much—in conspiracy, for example, all that is needed is an **agreement** to commit a crime.

2.4 **The elements of** *actus reus*

We would define *actus reus* as being whatever act, omission or state of affairs is laid down in the definition of the particular crime charged **along with** any surrounding **circumstances** (apart from D's *mens rea* and any excusatory defence he may have) and any **consequences** of that act or omission required by that definition.

? QUESTION 2.1

- Is the *actus reus* of all crimes the same?
- Is the *actus reus* different for all crimes?

You will see from our definition that the underlying notion of *actus reus* is the harmful conduct which is prohibited from occurring by the crime. It is those elements of the crime which are 'external' to D's thoughts and intentions. What actually is prohibited is determined by the definition of each individual crime and therefore varies enormously from crime to crime. If the crime is statutory (which is likely), it is necessary to examine the statutory wording, including any case law interpreting it; whereas if it is a common law crime, the definition has to be gleaned from case law alone. The *actus reus* of most crimes comprises two or more of the following three elements:

(a) an act or an omission to act;

(b) occurring in defined surrounding circumstances;

(c) causing any requisite prohibited consequence.

? QUESTION 2.2

- Can you think of two crimes which require D's conduct to produce a particular result?
- Can you think of two crimes which do not require D's conduct to produce any result?

2.5 **Consequences**

Some of our most well-known crimes require that D causes a particular prohibited consequence or result. However, this is by no means a universal requirement and the majority of crimes are not defined so as to require that D's conduct produces a particular result.

Crimes which do require the production of a proscribed consequence are known as 'result crimes'. Murder is an obvious example because D must cause the death of another person. The offence does not define the nature of D's conduct required (it can be shooting, stabbing, poisoning or whatever), only that it must result in the death of another person. Similarly, in criminal damage, the consequence of D's act must be that another's property is damaged. In the former offence of obtaining property by deception, the cause of D's obtaining of the property had to be his deceit of P. In such cases, if D's conduct does not cause the relevant consequence, the crime is not committed (although as we shall see later, it may be an attempt to commit that crime).

Where a crime does not require the production of any particular consequence but is satisfied by proof of mere conduct, it is known as a 'conduct crime'. Examples include handling stolen goods, rape, engaging in sexual activity in the presence of a child, and perjury (telling lies in the witness box). For example, the offence of rape does not require that anything should result from the conduct of having non-consensual sexual intercourse (e.g., pregnancy, disease); for perjury, there is no need to show that the lies influenced the legal proceedings or were even believed.

2.6 Circumstances

Whether the crime is a result crime or a conduct crime, it will almost certainly require the presence of some defined surrounding circumstances. Again, what particular circumstances are required is governed by the definition of the particular crime in issue. For example, it is an offence under s. 7 of the Sexual Offences Act 2003 to intentionally touch in a sexual way a person under 13. The *actus reus* would be incomplete unless the essential circumstance that the girl victim is under 13 is present. Similarly, the offence of handling stolen goods under s. 22 of the Theft Act 1968 necessitates proof of the fact or circumstance that the goods are stolen.

? **QUESTION** 2.3

According to s. 1(1) of the Theft Act 1968, D commits theft if he 'dishonestly appropriates property belonging to another with the intention of permanently depriving the other of it'.

- Using the words of the statute, state the *actus reus* of the crime.
- Using the words of the statute, state the *mens rea* of the crime.
- Is this a conduct crime or a result crime?
- In respect of the *actus reus*, which words describe the conduct which is the central feature of the crime; which, if any, describe circumstances that must be present; and which, if any, describe consequences that must be produced?

When we talk about circumstances in relation to the *actus reus*, we mean only those which are legally relevant, i.e., those laid down in the offence's definition. Thus it may be that in order to commit a robbery, a man disguises himself with a false beard and glasses, but although this is a circumstance of the offence, it is not legally relevant to its definition.

Clearly, we do not say robbery is committed when a man with a false beard and glasses etc.... Paradoxically, a legally relevant circumstance forming part of the *actus reus* of some crimes is the **victim's state of mind**. For example, rape requires that the intercourse is with a person who does not consent.

The *actus reus* of theft is 'appropriates property belonging to another'; the *mens rea* (D's required state of mind) is 'dishonestly' and 'with the intention of permanently depriving the other of it'. The conduct which is the central feature of the crime is 'appropriates property' and an essential circumstance which must be present is that the property 'belongs to another'. Nothing needs to result from D's act of taking the property (e.g., the owner does not need actually to be deprived of his property) and therefore theft is a conduct crime.

It is clear that no crime can be committed unless **all** the elements of the *actus reus* are present, including any prescribed circumstances. If, having had your leather coat stolen at a party one week, you decide to steal a similar coat at another party, you would not commit theft if, unknown to you, the coat was in fact yours. Because the coat did not 'belong to another', an essential element of the *actus reus* is missing. *Deller* (1952) 36 Cr App R 184 is an example. D sold his car to P stating that it was 'free from encumbrances'. D believed his car was subject to a hire-purchase agreement but, unknown to him, for reasons which need not concern us, the hire purchase agreement was void. The car was therefore free from encumbrances and D had unwittingly told the truth. Since D had made no 'false pretence', an essential element of the *actus reus* of the offence with which he was charged, he could not be guilty of that offence.

2.7 **Conduct**

The core element of any *actus reus* is D's 'conduct'. Such conduct consists usually of some act or acts on the part of D which produce any necessary consequence and/or take place in any necessary circumstances. However, exceptionally the conduct can consist of a failure or omission to act by D, e.g., wilful neglect of a child. Even more exceptionally, the *actus reus* may not require **any** conduct by D at all. This is where the offence simply requires proof of a defined state of affairs, e.g., being in possession of a controlled drug. We shall explore each of these three concepts in turn shortly, but first we need to make the important point that D's conduct must be **voluntary**.

2.7.1 **Voluntary conduct**

Implicit in the law's concept of 'conduct' and 'acting' is that the muscular movements by D constituting the relevant conduct are under the control and direction of D's conscious mind, i.e., the movements are willed by D's conscious mind. If they are not, they are regarded as involuntary and, in the eyes of most writers, contrary to appearances, D does not perform the *actus reus*. We cannot stress too strongly that the notion of 'involuntariness' is exceedingly narrow and in practice such a claim will be difficult to substantiate. An expression which is often used to denote involuntary conduct in this sense is 'automatism'. D's actions are said to be 'automatic' or 'autonomic' and he is described as an 'automaton'.

> **?** **QUESTION** 2.4
>
> Can you think of any situations where D's action will not be 'willed'?

You might have thought of situations where D loses control whilst driving his car. Goff LJ in *Bell* [1984] 3 All ER 842, CA instances a driver attacked by 'a swarm of bees or a malevolent passenger, or…affected by a sudden blinding pain, or' becoming 'suddenly unconscious by reason of a blackout, or' suffering some vehicle 'failure, for example, through a blow-out or through the brakes failing'. Other examples given by Lord Denning in *Bratty* v *Attorney-General for Northern Ireland* [1961] 3 All ER 523, HL included 'a spasm, a reflex action or a convulsion; or an act done by a person who is not conscious of what he is doing, such as an act done whilst suffering from concussion or whilst sleep walking' (see *Cases and Materials* (2.7.1)). We could add the case where D is **physically** forced to 'perform' the conduct, such as where a stronger man forces D's hand to pull a lever with the result that his crane drops a steel girder on someone below. Another example is where D is waiting in his car at a pedestrian crossing when the car is knocked onto the crossing by another car crashing into its rear (see *Leicester* v *Pearson* [1952] 2 All ER 71, DC). This would be an example of an involuntary **omission** to act, since the offence in question is failing to accord precedence to a pedestrian on a pedestrian crossing. That offence is also one of strict liability, i.e., not requiring any *mens rea* on the part of D and the example illustrates how, nonetheless, the requirement of voluntariness applies in exactly the same way to such offences.

We should point out that if D is at fault in getting himself into the situation where he 'performs' the involuntary conduct, he will probably not escape liability. For example, if D falls asleep whilst driving, he can still be convicted of careless and dangerous driving, even though he is not conscious when the car goes out of control, because he ought to have stopped driving when he became drowsy.

We shall see later that the most frequent occasion giving rise to the issue of voluntariness is when D 'acts' whilst in a state of unconsciousness. This can arise from concussion due to a blow on the head, internal conditions like epilepsy, diseases like diabetes and arteriosclerosis and external influences such as hypnotism and some drugs. The matter will be considered in some detail in **Chapter 8** on defences and it is sufficient for now to say that if the unconsciousness results from an internal bodily disorder, it will be classed as insanity, whereas if it results from an external factor it may lead to a complete no-strings acquittal. However, if the unconsciousness is self-induced, i.e., D is in some way at fault in getting into that state, he will not in most cases be completely acquitted (see 8.1 below for a more detailed discussion on 'automatism').

2.7.2 Acts

Most crimes have an 'act' as their central feature. Sometimes these 'acts' are defined precisely, but often they are defined vaguely. They tend to be more vaguely defined in offences where the words describing the act also embrace the production of a particular result or consequence of it. For example, the central feature of the offence of criminal damage is to damage or destroy property. It follows that any act of D, whatever its nature, will satisfy the *actus reus* of criminal damage provided it causes the damage or destruction of another's property. The same is true of 'wound or cause grievous bodily harm' under s. 18 of the Offences Against the Person Act 1861. Conversely, the nature of the act is precisely defined in the offence of rape which requires penile penetration of the vagina, anus or mouth of the victim (s. 1 of the Sexual Offences Act 2003).

2.7.3 Omissions

It is possible to be criminally liable for a failure to act, but this is still far less common than liability for a positive act.

> **? QUESTION 2.5**
>
> Can you think of a crime based on the omission to do something? You will find a number of examples in the ensuing discussion.

However, with the ever-increasing complication of modern society and the proliferation of statutes and statutory regulations to police it, it would be wrong to say that criminal liability for omissions is uncommon. Clearly, it is easier for the law to focus on positive acts that cause harm and which are committed by identifiable individuals. The problem with omissions is that everyone is not doing an infinite number of things all of the time! As Professor Williams explains, 'If there is an act, someone acts; but if there is an omission, everyone (in a sense) omits. We omit to do everything in the world that is not done. Only those of us omit in law who are under a duty to act' (*Textbook of Criminal Law*, 2nd ed., 1983, Stevens, p. 148). In order to ascribe responsibility to an individual for failing to act, the law must define the situation as one where D was obliged to act. D will only be liable if the law imposes a duty on him to act.

2.7.4 When will liability for omissions arise?

2.7.4.1 Specific statutory provision

There are numerous statutory offences which specifically impose liability for not doing something. For example, the field of motoring is littered with such offences—failing to display a vehicle tax disc, failing to stop after or report an accident, failing to conform to a traffic signal, and failing to provide a blood, breath or urine specimen in suspected drink-driving cases. Examples outside the motoring area include wilful neglect of a child and failing to disclose information about terrorism in certain circumstances under s. 19 of the Terrorism Act 2000. Of course, it is often a matter of chance or mere semantics as to whether such offences turn out to involve mere omissions. For example, failing to conform to a traffic signal could equally be regarded as the positive act of driving through a red light. Similarly, wilful neglect of a child is often failing to look after a child properly (rather than at all), which might be regarded as looking after a child badly!

As well as expressly **imposing** liability for omissions, the phrasing of a statutory offence may expressly **preclude** liability for omissions. For example, the offence of attempt under the Criminal Attempts Act 1981 is committed by one who 'does an act which is more than merely preparatory to the commission of the offence . . . ' so that an omission to act would not satisfy the definition. Section 1(3) of the Protection from Eviction Act 1977 is to the same effect (see *Ahmad* (1986) 84 Cr App R 64).

Characteristically, provisions imposing liability for omissions are conduct crimes which penalise the failure to act itself as opposed to requiring the omission to have produced any particular harm or other result. On the other hand, the situations arising at common law which are considered below are largely cases involving result crimes where D is penalised for causing harm through his failure to intervene to prevent it. There are, however, a couple of common law cases which focus on the failure to act itself rather than the resultant harm. In *Dytham* [1979] 3 All ER 641, CA, D, a uniformed police officer, was convicted of the common law offence of misconduct in a public office by failing to intervene when he saw a man being kicked to death 30 yards away by a night club bouncer. The same offence was charged in *Attorney-General's Reference (No. 3 of 2003)* [2004] 3 WLR 451 where, after receiving clearance from a hospital doctor, the defendant police officers had taken into custody for questioning a victim who had been injured in a fight. V was put carefully in a semi face-down position and was observed to be breathing less and less. Eventually he stopped breathing and attempts to resuscitate him failed. The Court of Appeal endorsing the Ds' acquittal said that the offence required wilful neglect where there was no reasonable excuse or justification for the inaction (the *mens rea* requirement is considered in the next chapter at 3.4.2). Dytham was guilty of gross neglect and if it could have been proved that this neglect caused V's death, he would have been guilty of manslaughter. In that event, the case would have fallen within the situations we turn to consider now.

2.7.4.2 Common law duty

In general terms, the common law does not impose any requirement on citizens to act to prevent physical harm, or, *a fortiori,* a non-physical harm, to their fellows. The law traditionally takes a laissez-faire, individualist stance which emphasises personal autonomy and freedom at the expense of a wider view of social responsibility. The law fixes liability only on those who have a duty to act and confines the scope of liability by a narrow interpretation of the notion of duty in this context. Thus, the stranger is free to watch a blind man walk over a cliff without shouting a warning or to watch a child drowning in a few inches of water without rescuing it or to leave a victim trapped by fire without alerting the fire brigade. In *Khan and Khan* [1998] Crim LR 830, the Court of Appeal was prepared to contemplate the possibility that a drug dealer who supplied heroin snorted by the victim in the dealer's flat, would owe a duty to summon medical assistance when she lapsed into a coma. The Court viewed this as requiring an extension of the current law but, arguably, it would fall within the *Miller* principle examined below—D must take reasonable steps to rectify a dangerous situation which he has helped to create. The law must decide as a matter of policy when there is a good reason to depart from this general principle that we are all free to mind our own business, no matter how socially irresponsible this may be.

? **QUESTION** 2.6

Can you think of any general situations where the law might want to impose a duty to act?

Let us examine what circumstances will lead the law to impose a duty to act.

Dependency

The first situation arises out of the fact that the circumstances are such that V's well-being can be said to be dependent on action by D. This may be an ongoing feature of their relationship where, for example, V is a young child or bedridden or it may arise in a one-off way where an apparently healthy V has a sudden heart attack. However, the law requires some further reason to regard D as responsible for V's safety and that may be found in the existence of a close relationship which automatically predicates responsibility or the fact that D has assumed responsibility for V by previous actions.

(a) Blood or other close relationship

An obvious situation where the law imposes a duty to act is where there is a relationship of parent or guardian and dependant child. Failing to feed or get medical assistance for a child who consequently dies could be either murder or manslaughter depending on whether the parent intended the child to die (see *Gibbins and Proctor* (1918) 13 Cr App R 134, CCA where a father was convicted of the murder of his child by omission as was his live-in lover who had assumed a caring responsibility). There is a dearth of authority on what other relationships would be covered but it is thought that spouses would be caught, where one partner is in the situation helplessly dependant on the other. Whether it would extend to 'live-in lovers' and the like remains to be seen. It is questionable whether the duty should be based on blood relationship or marriage as such (e.g., what of spouses who are separated or children who are independent adults?). A more convincing reason would be the interdependence and reliance that comes from living together.

(b) Assumption of responsibility

What is clear, however, is that even if a duty does not arise from the fact of relationship itself, it can very easily be expressly or impliedly assumed by D's conduct towards the victim. If D takes it upon himself to look after a person unable to care for themselves, whether by reason of age or infirmity, then he will be under a duty to continue to act—at least to the extent of alerting the relevant authorities. For example, in *Nicholls* (1874) 13 Cox CC 75, D took in her grandchild after her daughter's death and, having expressly assumed a duty to care, was liable when the grandchild died of neglect. A similar line was taken in *Instan* [1893] 1 QB 450 where D lived with her 73-year-old aunt who was healthy until shortly before her death. During the last 12 days of her life, she had gangrene in her leg which rendered her helpless. Only D knew of this condition and she did not give her aunt any food nor seek medical assistance. D was convicted of manslaughter on the basis that she had assumed a duty of care.

You will have noticed that these two cases are of some antiquity and certainly the most important case now is *Stone and Dobinson* [1977] 2 All ER 341, CA (*Cases and Materials* (2.7.4.2)). The case involved a very unfortunate household. S, who was 67, partially deaf, nearly blind and of low intelligence, lived with D, who was ineffectual and inadequate, as man and wife, together with S's mentally subnormal son. S's younger sister, Fanny, came to live with them in 1972 suffering from anorexia. She lived independently in her own room and latterly would have nothing to do with the others. She became increasingly infirm and helpless due to her failure to feed and look after herself. She died bedridden in a pool of her own excrement with horrendous bed sores. S and D made half-hearted, occasional and ineffectual attempts to care for her by washing her and leaving food out for her and to summon medical assistance, but the latter was some time before her death. They did not alert the social worker who visited S's son from time to time. Both S and D were held to be guilty of manslaughter and the court gave a number of reasons why a duty to act had arisen, which seemed to act cumulatively. First, Fanny was a blood relation to S; second, she was living in his house; and third, and most importantly, S and D had assumed a duty to act by their attempts, albeit pathetic, to care for her. The moral to be drawn from this sorry tale is rather unedifying: better to have done nothing at all, than to have tried and failed! We would, however, make the point that, it would have been comparatively easy to terminate the responsibility which had been assumed. Presumably the defendants could have discharged their responsibility by alerting the medical authorities or the local authority's social services department to Fanny's plight.

The principle was applied more recently in *Ruffel* [2003] EWCA Crim 122 where one February evening D invited his friend, V, to his house where they took a mixture of heroin and cocaine. V lapsed into unconsciousness and D took various actions to try to revive him. The following morning he put V outside on his doorstep. V was found three hours later but died in hospital of hypothermia and opiate intoxication. The Court of Appeal held that it was open to the jury to conclude that D had assumed a duty of care on the basis that he had tried to revive V and that V was his guest and friend.

Another illustration comes from the manslaughter case of *Wacker* [2003] 1 Cr App R 22. D, a Dutch lorry driver, transported 60 illegal immigrants in his container lorry. When he got near to the Belgian ferry port of Zeebrugge, he closed the air vent on the container to prevent noise emanating from the container. When the container was opened in Dover, it was discovered that all but two had suffocated from lack of oxygen. D had assumed responsibility for the immigrants who were obviously helplessly dependent on him.

? **QUESTION** 2.7

If a person has a duty to act, for whatever reason, do you think the law should release him from that duty if the person to whom the duty is owed, whilst in full possession of his faculties, specifically requests D not to do anything more, such as summoning medical assistance?

In *Smith* [1979] Crim LR 251, D was charged with the manslaughter of his wife, who had a phobia about doctors and medical treatment. She gave birth to a still-born child at home but refused to allow her husband to summon medical help. She subsequently relented and D called medical help but it was too late and she died. The trial judge instructed the jury to consider the wife's 'capacity to make rational decisions. If she does not appear too ill it may be reasonable to abide by her wishes. On the other hand, if she appeared desperately ill then whatever she may say it may be right to override.' In the event, the jury failed to agree on a verdict and were discharged. The judge's direction implies that a carer can be released from his duty to act by an explicit decision by V when having full capacity to make such a decision. This issue and a number of others were explored in depth by the House of Lords in *Airedale NHS Trust* v *Bland* which we will analyse under the next heading.

(c) Doctor–patient relationship

The responsibility of doctors towards their patients was explored at length by the House of Lords in *Airedale NHS Trust* v *Bland* [1993] 1 All ER 821 (*Cases and Materials* (2.7.4.2)). Although a civil case, it has implications for criminal law. The patient was a victim of the Hillsborough football stadium disaster which the writer was unfortunate enough to witness. He (the patient) had been in a persistent vegetative state for over three years due to the destruction of his cortex (a part of the brain governing higher functions at the conscious level), when the hospital authority applied for a declaration that it was lawful for the doctors to discontinue treatment and artificial feeding by nasal tube. Without this, the patient would (as subsequently happened) die within a relatively short time even though his brain stem, which controls reflexive functions at an unconscious level, enabled his heart and lungs to work unaided.

Although, in normal circumstances, doctors and medical staff would have a duty to act to treat and care for patients for whom they have assumed responsibility, they were not obliged to continue such treatment and care (or to institute it, in appropriate cases) where 'responsible and competent medical opinion' took the view that it was not in the patient's 'best interests' to continue the treatment and care. That was the situation in this case, where the atrophy of the patient's cortex meant that there was thought to be permanent sensory deprivation and no possibility of any further conscious existence. Therefore a declaration was granted allowing the discontinuance of treatment *and* the nasal feeding. Whilst the decision is understandable as a practical matter, we may question their Lordships' designation of nasal feeding as 'treatment'. Although their Lordships indicated that, for the moment, doctors should not, as a matter of practice, withdraw treatment without obtaining a declaration from the court, this cannot be mandatory and it is possible, if imprudent, for doctors to risk withdrawal without prior court approval. If this is in the best interests of the patient, presumably it cannot be unlawful to omit to continue treatment. The Court of Appeal in *Frenchay Healthcare NHS Trust* v *S* [1994] 2 All ER 403 recognised that there would be emergency situations where it would be impracticable to require prior court approval. Nonetheless, a Practice Note issued by the Official Solicitor ([1994] 2 All ER 413) emphasises that:

> the termination of artificial feeding and hydration for patients in persistent vegetative state will *in virtually all cases* require the prior sanction of a High Court judge. (Our emphasis.)

It is important to understand that this discussion concerns **omitting** to treat/care. It is certainly unlawful to take **active** steps, such as administering an overdose, or lethal injection, even to someone in Bland's condition and even if it was in the patient's 'best interests'. However, it must be said that both the *Bland* and *Frenchay Trust* cases allow doctors to discontinue treatment and feeding by active steps, e.g., removal of feeding tube, disconnection of a ventilator.

The courts have also made it clear that if the patient has validly refused treatment, e.g., for religious reasons, not only is the doctor permitted to omit to treat, he is **required** by the law to omit to treat. This is so even if the non-treatment, e.g., no blood transfusion, will result in the patient's death (*Airedale Trust* v *Bland; Re T* [1992] 4 All ER 649, CA). We consider this in more detail at 9.5.1 below.

Contract

Where D is under a contractual duty to act even though this is a private duty owed to the other party to the contract, it can be used by the criminal law as the basis for a duty owed to the public generally, certainly where its non-performance is likely to endanger the public. In *Pittwood* (1902) 19 TLR 37, D was employed by a railway company to operate a level crossing. He omitted to shut the gate before a train was due with the result that V was killed by a train on the crossing. D was convicted of manslaughter, his contractual obligation to close the gate to safeguard the public having spawned a criminal law duty to the public. We might also note *Instan* (above), where the aunt gave her niece money to look after her and buy her food, which the niece neglected to do. Whether a particular doctor has a duty to care for a particular patient may also depend on contractual matters. A passing doctor would have no duty to care for a road accident victim unless he assumed such a responsibility by getting involved. On the other hand, a GP would have a duty towards his own patients and similarly a hospital doctor in respect of patients falling within the scope of his contractual duties.

It could be argued that these cases are merely instances of an assumption of responsibility by D and the contract is merely evidence of that assumption of responsibility, helping to define its scope.

Where D creates a dangerous situation

 QUESTION 2.8

In *Miller* [1983] 1 All ER 978, HL (*Cases and Materials* (2.7.4.2)), D, a squatter, fell asleep smoking in his squat and his cigarette set fire to a mattress. He woke up to find the mattress smouldering but simply went to another room and resumed his sleep. The house caught fire. Should D be liable for arson (causing criminal damage by fire)? If so, on what basis?

The House of Lords in *Miller* held that D had a duty to take steps reasonably available to him to prevent further damage and was therefore guilty of arson (i.e., causing criminal damage by fire). D only has to do what is reasonable, e.g. calling the fire brigade; no heroism is expected. It would be up to the court to decide what steps are reasonable in any given situation, but they would certainly not include any actions putting himself at significant risk.

We can formulate the principle applied thus: where D inadvertently, without fault, creates by his own conduct a dangerous situation, he will be liable if, on becoming aware of what has happened, he fails to take reasonable steps to eliminate or minimise the danger he has created.

Another example might be the situation in *Fagan* v *MPC* [1968] 3 All ER 442, DC. D was directed by a police officer not to park his car in a particular spot but to park it in another position. He parked it on the officer's foot! When the officer politely or otherwise requested him to remove the car from his foot, D refused. It was accepted that the initial parking on the foot was accidental. D was convicted of battery. Because of doubts over whether it was possible to assault or batter someone by an omission to act, the court took the view that driving the car onto the foot and leaving it there was a continuous act. On learning of the situation, D continued to apply force intentionally, by leaving the car on V's foot. The Court of Appeal in *Miller* also adopted the 'continuous' act analysis. However, the House of Lords preferred to regard the failure to act as distinct from the inadvertent initial act, and as a separate omission. This seems to be the most realistic and sensible view. It follows that *Fagan* should have been convicted on the basis that he had, albeit inadvertently, created the dangerous situation and he was therefore under a duty to act to counteract it when he realised what had happened. His omission to do so with the appropriate *mens rea* therefore made him liable. D's duty in *Wacker* could also be based on this principle. He created the danger to the immigrants by closing the air vent and thereby came under a duty to avert it.

The Divisional Court in *DPP* v *Santana-Bermudez* [2003] EWHC Admin 2908; [2004] Crim LR 471 applied the *Miller* principle in upholding a conviction for assault occasioning actual bodily harm. V, a police officer, asked D to turn out his pockets. He produced a number of syringes. He then lied in assuring V that there were no more syringes in his pockets. V pricked herself on a syringe needle when lawfully searching his pockets. It was held that D's acts and words had created a dangerous situation exposing V to a reasonably foreseeable risk of injury and therefore he owed a duty to safeguard V. His failure to inform her of the danger resulting in the injury constituted the *actus reus* of the assault and he would be guilty if he had the *mens rea*, i.e., he intended V to prick herself or foresaw that she might.

The draft Offences Against the Person Bill recently issued by the Government for consultation produces a statutory replacement for the *Miller* principle which would be applicable only to the offences in the Bill (cl. 16—see *Cases and Materials* (2.7.4.2)). You will read a lot more about this Bill in **Chapter 4**.

2.7.5 State of affairs offences

Occasionally the *actus reus* simply requires the existence of a particular state of affairs to be proved, rather than any act or omission on the part of the accused. For example, being in possession of a controlled drug is an offence under s. 5 of the Misuse of Drugs Act 1971. The law is not interested in D's conduct in coming to have the drug but simply the fact of possession. Other examples are being in charge of a vehicle while unfit through drink or drugs contrary to s. 4(2) of the Road Traffic Act 1988 and being found drunk on the highway contrary to s. 12 of the Licensing Act 1872. (See *Winzar* v *Chief Constable of Kent, The Times*, 28 March 1983—we shall be considering this case and a similar one, *Larsonneur* (1933) 24 Cr App R 74, in detail in **Chapter 13**.)

2.8 **Causation**

2.8.1 **Introduction**

In the case of result crimes, it must be proved that D's acts or omissions **caused** the consequence prohibited by the crime charged. In murder and manslaughter, D's conduct must cause another's death. In the case of assault occasioning actual bodily harm, D's assault must cause actual bodily harm. In the case of criminal damage, D's conduct must cause the damage or destruction of another's property. In some pollution offences, D's conduct must cause polluting matter to enter a river or stream. There are many other examples where causation is a crucial element of the *actus reus*.

Events and consequences are never the result of a single cause but require the coincidence of multiple factors. If D wires up the electrics on a central heating system wrongly so that V is electrocuted when he touches a live radiator, many things apart from D's act, must happen before V's death is produced. V must touch the radiator, must not be wearing rubber gloves or rubber-soled shoes, the electricity must be switched on, the electricity company must be transmitting power down the lines, and so on. Naturally, the law focuses on whether the act performed by D is a cause of the death. In the case postulated, the law would regard D as causing the death. It is D's acts which ' "make the difference" between disaster and normal functioning' (Hart and Honoré, *Causation in the Law*, Oxford University Press, 1985). The law proceeds on the individualist assumption that people are independent actors who are the authors of their own effects in the world. They are viewed as autonomous individuals operating in isolation from their social context (see Norrie, *Crime, Reason and History*, 2nd ed., 2001, Butterworths, Ch. 7).

In practice, it is usually obvious that D's acts have caused the prohibited consequence and no issue of causation arises. However, where it does, it is the jury's decision as to whether the prosecution has established the necessary causal link between D's conduct and the proscribed result, although it is the trial judge's duty to direct the jury on any applicable legal principles (*Pagett* (1983) 76 Cr App R 279, CA). Let us then seek out these 'legal principles'.

2.8.2 **Legal principles**

It must be said that helpful legal principles are in short supply in this area and those which exist tend to be vague and of little concrete assistance.

The test for causation has two limbs:

(a) D's conduct must **in fact** cause the prohibited consequence; and

(b) D's conduct must **in law** cause that consequence.

Both must be satisfied before the harmful consequence will legally be attributed to D's act.

2.8.2.1 Factual causation

This is normally very obvious and simply requires that the prosecution proves that, as a matter of fact, D's acts played a role (in accordance with the ordinary laws of physics, cause and effect) in bringing about the prohibited consequence. In relation to murder or manslaughter, since everyone dies sooner or later, the concept of causing death here is simply causing an acceleration, or bringing forward, of death and it does not matter therefore that V is already terminally ill or mortally wounded.

The test which is often used is called the 'but for' test. If the result would not have occurred at the time and in the way it did but for D's conduct, then D has **in fact** caused that result. For an example of how it works we can look at *White* [1910] 2 KB 124.

D put potassium cyanide into his mother's drink intending to kill her. She suffered a heart attack and died having drunk only a quarter of the liquid. Medical evidence established that her death resulted not from poisoning but from unconnected heart failure. Thus D's acts were not a factual cause of death—his mother would have died in the same way whether he had acted or not. The lack of an *actus reus* prevented D's conviction for murder itself though he was convicted of attempted murder.

The 'but for' test can be problematic where D's conduct is only one of the causes of V's death. However, there is no doubt that as long as D's conduct is a 'significant' cause, it does not need to be the only cause or even the main cause (see *Cheshire* [1991] 3 All ER 670, CA). 'Significant' seems to mean simply 'more than minimal'. Thus, if another cause is more important and itself capable of causing death, V may have died in the same way without the contribution of D's conduct. The 'but for' test would not be satisfied, but if D's conduct was contributing more than minimally to the death, he will be held to have factually caused it.

2.8.2.2 Legal causation

Cause in fact is only the first stage. If D's act was not a cause in fact, there is no question of D's having caused the prohibited consequence. On the other hand, if D's act did in fact set in train or play a part in the events leading to the prohibited consequence, D will be held to have caused that consequence *only* if the court finds that his conduct was also a cause in law.

? **QUESTION** 2.9

Why do you think this second stage is necessary? Why does the law not treat proof of factual causation as establishing that D caused the consequence?

As Professor Williams explains (*Textbook of Criminal Law*, 2nd ed., p. 381 (our emphasis)):

> When one has settled the question of but-for causation, the further test to be applied to the but-for cause in order to qualify it for legal recognition is not a test of causation but **a moral reaction**. The question is whether the result can fairly be said to be imputable to the defendant...If the term 'cause' must be used, it can best be distinguished in this meaning as the 'imputable' or 'responsible' or 'blameable' cause, to indicate the value-judgement involved.

Essentially, the court here has to make a policy decision as to whether or not it is right to ascribe that consequence to D's act. The point is that any action a person performs may have infinite consequences and there comes a point where the law will say that it is not fair to legally attribute the harmful consequences to D's acts. For example, if D pushes V over so that he injures his back and has to give up his present job, it will hardly be fair to hold that he caused V's death when V is killed in a road accident whilst on his way to an interview for a lighter job.

How do the courts decide whether D's act is or is not a legal cause of the relevant consequence?

Unfortunately, there is no hard-and-fast principle, although there are a number of guidelines and some more specific rules to help. In many ways, the decision is largely common sense and, as we have seen, relegated to being a question of fact for the jury. As Lord Hoffmann put it in *Empress Car Co. (Abertillery) Ltd v National Rivers Authority* [1998] 1 All ER 481, HL:

> I doubt whether the use of abstract metaphysical theory has ever had much serious support and I certainly agree that the notion of causation should not be overcomplicated. Neither, however, should it be oversimplified.

Substantial cause

The courts often say that D's acts must have been a substantial cause of the consequence (see, e.g., *Cheshire; Smith* [1959] 2 All ER 193, CMAC). All this means is that it must be a significant cause or more than minimal cause of the consequence. Indeed in *Kimsey* [1996] Crim LR 35, a case of causing death by dangerous driving, the Court of Appeal held that there was no misdirection where the recorder told the jury that it was unnecessary that D's driving was a substantial cause of death as long as it was 'a cause and that there was something more than a slight or a trifling link'. This seems to be pitching it at an unacceptably low level and must be open to doubt. However, D's conduct certainly does not have to be the only cause or even the most important cause of it. It is not even necessary to prove that D's acts alone would have been themselves sufficient to cause it. Therefore, the fact that the victim himself also contributes to it is no defence. In *Swindall and Osborne* (1846) 2 Car & Kir 230 the defendants, while racing each other with horses and carts, ran over and killed an old man. The judge, directing the jury, said that if the defendants 'contributed to the victim's death by their negligence and improper conduct, it matters not whether P was deaf or drunk or in part contributed to his own death'.

Similarly, the fact that third parties also contributed to the consequence, will not absolve D where his act is also still a substantial cause. In *Benge* (1865) 4 F & F 504, D, a foreman platelayer lifted up a section of track when a train was due. He had misread the timetable and this train was on time! It was held that the fact that the accident was also partly caused by the train driver who failed to keep a proper look out, and the warning 'flag man' who failed to go the regulation distance, did not absolve D from responsibility for the ensuing deaths.

? **QUESTION** 2.10

Suppose D stabs V. V is taken to hospital and treated in a grossly negligent manner by X, a hospital doctor. V dies partly as a result of D's wound and partly from X's medical treatment. Who has legally caused V's death?

More than one person may, in appropriate circumstances, be held to have caused the death, and both D and X would have legally caused the death. D would be guilty of murder if he intended to kill or cause grievous bodily harm, whereas X would be guilty only of manslaughter.

We would also point out that the harmful consequence must be caused not just by D's act but by the particular feature of D's act which is regarded as culpable. In *Dalloway* (1847) 2 Cox 273, D was driving a horse and cart without reins when he ran over and killed a child who had suddenly jumped into the road. The jury could only convict of manslaughter if it was satisfied that D could have stopped if he was using the reins and driving properly. More recently in *Marchant* [2004] 1 WLR 442, CA, the driver of a tractor with a grab unit on the front was found not guilty of causing the death by dangerous driving of a motor cyclist who had been impaled on one of the unit's unguarded, metre-long spikes. The Court's view was that he would have died even if the dangerous spike had been guarded because the collision would still have occurred with probably fatal results.

Acts or events intervening between D's conduct and prohibited result

One of the most frequent problems the courts encounter is the effect on D's responsibility of some act or event occurring between D's initial act and the ultimate consequence (e.g., death or injury to V) which the prosecution claims that D has caused. Lord Hoffmann stated in the *Empress Car Co.* case, '. . . it is of course the causal significance of acts of third parties . . . or natural forces that gives rise to almost all the problems about the notion of "causing" and drives judges to take refuge in metaphor or Latin.' Sometimes the courts will hold that the intervening act breaks the chain of causation between D's act and the result, so that D has not *legally* caused that result.

The acts or events most likely to break the chain of causation are (i) the 'free, deliberate and informed intervention' of a third party or (ii) an abnormal act or event coinciding with or supervening after D's conduct (Hart and Honoré (above)). The former proposition was considered to be 'broadly correct' in *Pagett* (1983) 76 Cr App R 279, CA and Lord Hoffmann in the *Empress Car Co.* case commented, '. . . both the law and common sense normally attach great significance to deliberate human acts and extraordinary natural events', thus endorsing both ideas.

Of course, these concepts are of limited utility because of the elasticity and vagueness of the terms 'abnormal' and 'voluntary'. Norrie observes (*Crime, Reason and History*, 2nd ed., 2001, p. 140):

> Thus individuals are held to be the causes until something abnormal intervenes, but what is abnormal depends upon social perception, and therefore upon a socio-political label being stuck upon it. Similarly, causation stretches as far as the new voluntary act of a third party, but what is meant by

voluntary can be as narrow or as broad as one likes, depending upon how much one is prepared to recognise the social character of the lives of individuals.

Natural events

If D knocks V unconscious and leaves him on the beach below the high water mark so that V is drowned by the incoming tide, D has legally caused V's death. The natural event of the tide coming in is not abnormal or 'extraordinary' but exactly what could be expected and foreseen. It does not break the chain of causation. If, on the other hand, V dies through a lightning strike, the courts might well say that this was 'extraordinary' and not reasonably foreseeable so superseding D's conduct as the legal cause of death. Another example is given by Hart and Honoré: D knocks down V and, while V is on the floor, an old tree crashes down without warning killing V. D would have caused in law only the initial 'knock-down' injuries, if any, and not V's death.

Interventions by a third party

One of the most powerful notions informing causal responsibility in the criminal law is the individual's autonomy. He can choose whether to act and, if he does, he bears responsibility for the normal consequences of his conduct. A corollary to this is that any such 'free, deliberate and informed' action by another person occurring between D's initial conduct and the prohibited result should mark the limit of the causal reach of D's conduct and supersede it as the immediate and therefore legal cause of the prohibited result. Responsibility would be ascribed to the last voluntary human agency. D mortally wounds V. X shoots V dead. X legally causes V's death not D. As Professor Williams puts it (*Textbook of Criminal Law*, 2nd ed., Sweet & Maxwell, p. 39):

> What a person does (if he has reached adult years, is of sound mind and is not acting under a mistake, intimidation or other similar pressure) is his own responsibility and is not regarded as having been caused by other people.

Some recent appellate decisions in cases involving deaths caused by heroin overdose (building on the fallacious reasoning the *Empress Car* case—see exception 1 below) undermine this fundamental principle and must be regarded as unacceptable departures from it. The trend started with *Kennedy* [1999] Crim LR 65 where, at V's request, D sold some heroin to V, made up a syringe of it and handed it to V who injected himself with it. D left and V died about an hour later from the effects of the injection. The general principle would suggest that V's voluntary action in choosing to inject himself ('free and deliberate') knowing of the syringe's contents ('informed') was the sole legal cause of his death. D did not cause V's death but merely provided the opportunity for V to cause his own death. Surprisingly the Court held that D's actions did legally cause V's death on the basis that, by making up the syringe, he encouraged V to inject (distinguishing *Dalby* (1982) 74 Cr App R 348 which held that a **mere** supplier of heroin did not cause the user's death—surely any supplier by the fact of supply encourages the user to take the drug?). A possible argument not advanced in the case is that, if V was known to D to be an **addict**, his injection of the drug might not be seen as 'free'.

A similar fact situation arose in *Dias* [2002] Cr App R 96, CA where D's conviction for manslaughter was quashed (see 6.5.3.4 below). *Kennedy* was distinguished on the ground that the question of whether D's act had caused death had properly been left to the jury whereas in this case, it had not. Notice that the Court did not rule out legal causation in this kind of case holding that it was a 'question of fact and degree' to be left to the jury to decide. However, its view seemed to be that, in the ordinary way, chosen self-injection would break the chain of causation between D's acts and the death. It would require 'somewhat different facts' from the present case in order for the chain not to be broken. Unfortunately, no inkling is given as to what differences are needed but we may surmise that it would include situations where the victim's self-injection was not 'free and informed'. Thus, if he were forced to inject, deceived as to the contents of the syringe or under incapacity due to age or mental condition, his self-injection would **not** break the chain of causation. However, absent any such circumstances, we think the judge should rule that there is no evidence to establish causation in self-injection cases. The Court of Appeal continued its sidelining of *Kennedy* in *Rogers* [2003] 2 Cr App R 10, CA which followed the *Dias* line.

However in *Finlay* [2003] EWCA 3868, the Court of Appeal held that where D, at V's request, supplied, prepared and handed to V a syringe of heroin for immediate injection, he caused the heroin to be administered to V when V injected herself. In other words, the free, deliberate and informed act of V did not necessarily break the chain of causation. 'All that was necessary . . . is that the circumstances should be such that it could properly be said to fall within the ambit of possible and ordinary events that she [V] will take the opportunity given her [by D's acts].' This perpetuates the heresy propounded in the *Empress Car* case which mistakenly applies the rule applicable to abnormal natural events to voluntary human actions (see immediately below for a fuller explanation). The most recent case, *Kennedy (No. 2)* [2005] EWCA Crim 685, a further appeal following a reference by the Criminal Cases Review Commission, whilst not disputing the finding on causation, thought that it was an unnecessary complication because D 'administered' the heroin rather than caused it to be administered because he was 'acting in concert' with V (see 6.5.3.4 and 14.3 for a more detailed explanation and criticism. For a sustained (and deserved) roasting of the Court of Appeal, see Allen (a Commissioner at the Criminal Cases Review Commission): *Textbook of Criminal Law*, 8th ed., 2005, 42–46!).

Notwithstanding these aberrations, the general principle is, then, that a subsequent, voluntary act of another will absolve D from any further causal responsibility. However, we must now examine the many restrictions and exceptions which qualify this general rule of thumb.

Exception 1: Purpose and scope of offence

Whilst the general principle may be applicable in traditional offences involving causing death or injury, the courts are quite willing to depart from it where they judge that the 'purpose and scope' of the offence charged shows an intention to make D responsible for deliberate acts of third parties (or natural events) (*Empress Car Co. (Abertillery) Ltd v National Rivers Authority* [1998] 1 All ER 481, HL). They are likely to do this for regulatory offences (see **Chapter 13**) framed in terms of 'causing' something to happen or be done.

In the *Empress Car Co.* case (*Cases and Materials* (2.8.2.2)), an unknown person, who could have been an employee or a complete stranger, had turned on the unlocked tap of a tank containing oil which was maintained by D on its premises. As a result, the oil flowed into a storm drain and thence into a river and D was charged with causing polluting matter to enter controlled waters contrary to s. 85(1) of the Water Resources Act 1991. D was held to have caused the pollution to enter the river. For the House of Lords, the issue turned on whether the third party's act:

> ...should be regarded as a normal fact of life or something extraordinary. If it was in the general run of things a matter of ordinary occurrence, it will not negative the causal effect of the defendant's acts, even if it was not foreseeable that it would happen to that particular defendant or take that particular form. If it can be regarded as something extraordinary, it will be open to the justices to hold that the defendant did not cause the pollution....The distinction between ordinary and extraordinary is one of fact and degree to which the justices must apply their common sense and knowledge of what happens in the area.

Since, on the evidence, it was open to the magistrates to conclude that D had caused the pollution, D's appeal against conviction was dismissed.

Lord Hoffmann held that the same principles applied in the case of a natural event, e.g., a storm damaging the tank as opposed to an act of another. He considered that a lightning strike would be 'extraordinary' and so absolve D from causal responsibility.

The fallacy in Lord Hoffmann's argument is the equation of voluntary human acts with natural events. It has never been necessary for the free, deliberate and informed acts of a human third party to be 'extraordinary' or unforeseeable in order to break the chain of causation. Clearly the acts of the third party (almost certainly malicious) were foreseeable here. The entire edifice of criminal responsibility is constructed on the notion of the personal autonomy of each individual and their causal responsibility for the results of their own, freely chosen actions. No matter how predictable and 'unextraordinary' the third party's intervention, if it is free, deliberate and informed, it acts as a barrier to D's causal responsibility. 'Otherwise, D's criminal liability for causing an actus reus would not be under his own control, but would instead be subject to the autonomous choice of someone else' (Simester and Sullivan, *Criminal Law: Theory and Doctrine*, 2nd ed., 2003, Hart, p. 100).

One can understand why, as a practical and policy matter, their Lordships wanted to make the company liable for the pollution. They introduced the polluting matter and it was incumbent upon them to safeguard the nearby stream, e.g., by siting the tank in a suitable place and taking adequate precautions to prevent unauthorised interference. However, quite simply, the pollution was **caused** by the third party who opened the tap, not by the company whose defaults enabled it to occur. The House was, in effect, re-writing the offence to embrace not just 'causing' but also 'suffering' or 'allowing' polluting matter to enter the stream. The conclusion in terms of causation is: 'bad principle, bad law, bad reasoning' (Simester and Sullivan, p. 101). But, as we have seen above, it has infected the law of manslaughter in the area of drug overdose deaths.

Exception 2: Non-voluntary interventions by third parties

Of course, a third party's act would not be 'free' if it was brought about by intimidation, pressure or misapprehension created by D's conduct. In that kind of case, Lord Hoffmann's ordinary/extraordinary distinction might determine D's causal responsibility though we would prefer to follow Glanville Williams' idea that D would remain responsible so long as the death or injury was reasonably foreseeable as part of the general area of risk involved in D's conduct, notwithstanding the intervening event. *Pagett* (1983) 76 Cr App R 279, CA (*Cases and Materials* (2.8.2.2)) provides an example. In order to resist arrest, D used his girlfriend as a human shield and fired at armed police surrounding him. A policeman instinctively fired back in reasonable self-defence but killed the girl. It was held that D had caused the death on the ground that the policeman's 'reasonable act of self-preservation' (shooting in self-defence) did not break the chain of causation. It was not a 'free' act and was a reasonably foreseeable outcome of D's conduct—the kind of thing one might anticipate. In Lord Hoffmann's terms, it would not be an 'extraordinary' occurrence **in the given situation**.

Similarly, if the third party's act is not deliberate, D will remain responsible unless it was outside the range of reasonably foreseeable risks or 'something extraordinary'. Thus, in the US case of *Bush v Commonwealth* 78 Ky 268 (Ky CA, 1880), V died following an assault by D because the doctor treating him inadvertently infected him with scarlet fever. It was held that, because it was not reasonably foreseeable, D caused only the initial injury and not the death.

In exactly the same way, if the third party acts under mistake or misapprehension as to the nature of his conduct, his action will not be 'informed' and will not relieve D of causal responsibility. In *Michael* (1840) 9 C & P 356, D, intending the death of her child, handed a bottle of poison to its foster-mother saying it was medicine for the child. The foster-mother regarded it as unnecessary and put the 'medicine' on the mantelpiece. Her five-year-old daughter later picked it up and gave a lethal dose to D's child. D was held to have caused the death. Even though the precise turn of events might not have been reasonably foreseeable or 'ordinary', the outcome was within the general area of risk which was reasonably foreseeable.

Exception 3: Substantial and operating cause

This principle operates where there is no doubt that D has caused some initial injury, e.g., by a direct attack and the question is whether he is also responsible for the death (or more serious injury) which ultimately occurs, e.g., after bad medical treatment for the initial injury. The rule that D is responsible for the death if the initial injury is still a 'substantial and operating cause' at the moment of death illustrates the possibility of there being two or more persons acting independently (D and the doctor) who are both legal causers of the same death. It is explored below under the heading '*Direct infliction of injury*'.

Exception 4: Medical treatment

Intervention by doctors would seem generally to constitute 'free, deliberate and informed' conduct and should therefore break the chain of causation. However, as we shall see under '*Direct infliction of injury*' below, the courts rarely hold it to do so (sometimes but not always as a result of exception 3 above).

Exception 5: Actions of the victim

The principle and exceptions explained above in respect of third party intervention would apply equally to judge the effect of actions of the victim on the chain of causation. The 'escape' cases, where D's threatening conduct causes the victim to kill or injure himself whilst attempting to escape (e.g., by jumping out of a building or a moving car), exemplify situations where the victim's reaction is not a 'free' act but induced by pressure from D.

Do you think that if V kills himself in, say, jumping from a flat window to escape D's threatening conduct, D should be held to have caused V's death (a) in every case (b) in no case (c) in some cases (if so, which?)?

The rule is that, as long as V's reaction was understandable in the circumstances, i.e., not unexpected, D will be responsible. If, on the other hand, the reaction was not reasonably foreseeable, i.e., unexpected or 'daft', it will break the chain of causation and D will be held not to have caused the resulting death. As it was put in *Williams* [1992] 2 All ER 183, CA (*Cases and Materials* (2.8.2.2)), the question is 'whether the deceased's reaction in jumping from the moving car was within the range of responses which might be expected from a victim placed in the situation in which he was. The jury should bear in mind any particular characteristic of the victim and the fact that in the agony of the moment he may act without thought and deliberation.' Furthermore, if the victim is drunk or mentally ill, this must be taken into account in judging the range of responses to be expected to D's attack according to *Corbett* [1996] Crim LR 594. Presumably, this would only apply to characteristics which are either known to D or about which he ought to have known since only they would be reasonably foreseeable in the circumstances.

Marjoram [2000] Crim LR 372, CA confirms that the test of reasonable foresight is entirely objective and depends on whether a reasonable person 'finding himself in the circumstances in which the accused was' might have foreseen the victim's reaction. There is no question of the reasonable man being invested with any characteristics of the **defendant** so that, here, the fact that D was only 16 was irrelevant to the issue of causation.

It is clear that there must be some proportionality between the gravity of the threat to the deceased and the action he took in seeking to escape from it, otherwise the victim's act will break the chain of causation. As *Pagett* (above) confirms 'a reasonable act performed for the purpose of self-preservation' is not regarded as a 'voluntary' act and does not therefore break the chain of causation.

The 'take your victim as you find him' rule

This rule means that the fact that, owing to some pre-existing abnormality or condition, V suffers greater harm than would have been anticipated as a result of D's acts, will not prevent the finding that D's acts caused the full extent of the injuries, even though they were not reasonably foreseeable.

Can you think of an example of such an abnormality?

In *Hayward* (1908) 21 Cox CC 692, during the course of an argument with V, his wife, D chased her into the street. She suddenly collapsed and died due to a combination of the exertion and a pre-existing thyroid condition, of which D was unaware. It was held that D had caused her death because he had to take the victim's condition as he found it. Similarly, if D's victim has an eggshell skull or is a haemophiliac so that blows which even a reasonable person would foresee as causing no more than moderate injury, actually result in death, D will legally have caused that death.

The Court of Appeal in *Blaue* [1975] 3 All ER 446 (*Cases and Materials* (2.8.2.2)) extended this rule to include not only **physical** peculiarities of the victim, but also the mental outlook and beliefs of the victim. In that case it was D's misfortune that the victim he wounded turned out to be a Jehovah's Witness, who died after refusing a blood transfusion which would probably have saved her life. In fact, as we shall see shortly, this decision is probably better explained on another ground.

> ### ? QUESTION 2.13
>
> Would the result be the same if the victim refused the transfusion to ensure that he died so that D would be convicted of murder?

The 'eggshell skull' principle appears to contradict the second of Hart and Honoré's rules that an 'abnormal condition' will break the chain of causation. However, in their analysis, they except abnormal conditions existing at the time of D's acts on the ground that it is part of the 'stage already set' before D acts. Presumably, what they mean is abnormal conditions which are **pre-existing before** D's acts.

If we apply the *Blaue* rule that D must take his victim's psychological make-up as he finds it, we would have to say that if P refuses medical treatment it is irrelevant why he refuses it so that in our last Question D would be liable for the death.

> ### ? QUESTION 2.14
>
> Does the *Blaue* rule conflict with the escape cases like *Williams* where an 'unreasonable' or 'not reasonably foreseeable' reaction by the victim will break the chain of causation?

The short answer is yes. If D must take the victim's psychological condition as he finds it, then it is D's hard luck that he happens to have picked on an exceptionally nervous person who is prone to jump out of fourth floor windows or fast-moving cars at the drop of a hat. However, there are many cases applying the principle as stated in *Williams* and there is much to be said for limiting the 'take your victim' principle to pre-existing physical abnormalities, particularly as *Blaue* is explicable on other grounds. A possible distinction is to say that the 'take your victim' principle operates only where D has inflicted some harm but it turns out to be unexpectedly severe because of the eggshell skull or whatever. In the escape cases, V has not been injured at all until his own act in escaping causes it. Unfortunately, cases like *Hayward* are difficult to reconcile with the principle, unless it can be argued that the normal 'exertion' to be expected from chasing is an 'injury' made unexpectedly worse by the abnormal thyroid condition.

We have indicated that *Blaue* can be explained on other grounds and we can now look at the relevant principle.

Direct infliction of injury

It is convenient to consider separately the common case where there is no doubt that D's acts have caused some **initial** injury but there is a question as to whether he has caused the death which ultimately occurs. Certainly, in cases where D has committed a deliberate and wrongful attack, the courts lean strongly against finding a break in the chain of causation even where the ultimate death is avoidable and/or largely down to the subsequent actions of another.

Substantial and operating cause

The basic rule is very simple, but arguably harsh on D. If the initial wound is still 'a substantial and operating' cause at the time of death, then D has caused that death (*Smith* [1959] 2 All ER 193—*Cases and Materials* (2.8.2.2)). This is so whether or not the death was the reasonably foreseeable result of D's acts.

? **QUESTION** 2.15

How does this apply to *Blaue*?

Therefore if V, for whatever reason, refuses to undergo medical treatment which would have prevented the death, the wound will be a substantial and operating cause of death and D will have caused that death (e.g., the refusal of treatment on religious grounds in *Blaue*). Equally, the discontinuance of medical treatment which allows the initial wound to take its natural course and end in death, e.g., switching off a ventilator, will not break the chain of causation between D's acts and the death (*Malcherek* [1981] 2 All ER 422, CA). Even if V's wounds, having been properly treated, then re-open, whether accidentally or even by V's own, deliberate act, and V does nothing to staunch the blood, D will be held to have caused the death if the initial wounding is still a substantial and operating cause of death (*Dear* [1996] Crim LR 595, CA).

Even bad medical treatment which itself contributes to death will not break the chain of causation as long as the wound itself is still playing a significant (i.e., more than minimal) role in bringing about the death. In *Smith*, D died after being stabbed with a bayonet in a barrack-room brawl in Germany. The bayonet pierced his lung and caused a haemorrhage. Whilst being transported to the medical station, he was dropped—twice! The medical officer failed to realise the seriousness of the wound and gave the wrong treatment, described by the court as 'thoroughly bad'. In particular, if he had been given a blood transfusion, his chances of recovery would have been good (75%).

On these facts, how would you decide the case?

The Court of Appeal upheld D's conviction because the wound was still a substantial and operating cause of death. 'Only if it can be said that the original wound is merely the setting in which another cause operates can it be said that the death did not result from the wound. Putting it another way, only if the second cause is so overwhelming as to make the additional wound merely part of the history can it be said that the death does not flow from the wound.'

One case where the wound had become 'merely part of the history' so that D was held not to have caused the resultant death was *Jordan* (1956) 40 Cr App R 152, CA (*Cases and Materials* (2.8.2.2)). It was established that the original wound caused by D had almost healed when V died because the hospital had continued to administer an antibiotic to V to which he had already shown himself intolerant. Not surprisingly (in our view), D was acquitted, although a number of academics regard the decision as wrong. However, it must be emphasised that the initial wound need not be the *sole* cause of the death and that even quite serious negligence in the treatment of V will not absolve D from causal responsibility. The Court of Appeal in *Cheshire* [1991] 3 All ER 670 (*Cases and Materials* (2.8.2.2)) stated:

> ...the accused's acts did not need to be the sole or even the main cause of the death, it being sufficient that his acts contributed significantly to that result, and that even though negligence in the treatment of the victim was the immediate cause of his death, [the jury] should not regard it as excluding the responsibility of the accused unless the negligent treatment was so independent of his acts and in itself so potent in causing death that they regarded the contribution made by his acts as insignificant.

Does this mean that if D's initial wounding of V is no longer 'a substantial and operating cause' at the moment of death, D did not legally cause the death?

No longer a substantial and operating cause

Where the initial wound is no longer a substantial and **operating** cause at the moment of death, the principle enunciated in *Cheshire* preserves the chain of causation unless the intervening act was 'so independent of' D's acts and 'so potent in causing death' that D's acts became 'insignificant'. Unfortunately, little guidance is given as to the meaning of the crucial words 'independent' and 'potent' and where the line should be drawn between 'dependence' and 'independence'. We think that what the court probably had in mind but failed properly to articulate was a test based on reasonable foreseeability or the ordinary/extraordinary distinction in the *Empress Car Co.* case. Certainly a far more satisfactory test would be that D remains responsible where death was within the range of risks which were the reasonably foreseeable results of his acts. This would include ordinarily negligent treatment, but surely not outrageously (grossly) negligent treatment.

In *Cheshire*, it appeared that the initial bullet wounds which D inflicted on V had ceased to be life-threatening and that death was caused some time later by complications resulting from a tracheotomy necessitated by the initial injuries some days before death. Death was caused by a constriction of V's windpipe which was a complication known occasionally to follow tracheotomies. There was some evidence of negligence on the part of the doctors treating V. It is clear that the court viewed consequences flowing from the medical treatment of the victim as being directly caused by D's initial acts unless that treatment was 'so extraordinary as to be capable of being regarded as acts independent of the conduct of the accused but it is most unlikely that they will be.' As the court explained: 'Even if more experienced doctors than those who attended the deceased would have recognised the rare complication in time to have prevented the deceased's death, that complication was a direct consequence of D's acts.' In other words, the court would regard negligent medical treatment in the modern health service as within the range of normal (i.e., reasonably foreseeable) risks arising from hospitalisation.

D's responsibility is even clearer where V is killed not by the wound, but by an unexpected reaction whilst undergoing proper medical treatment for the wound, e.g., allergy to anaesthetic (see the '**take your victim**' rule above and also *Malcherek* [1981] 73 Cr App R 173, CA). In *McKechnie* (1991) 94 Cr App R 51, CA, D was held to have caused V's death where the injuries caused by D precluded a necessary operation for the duodenal ulcer which killed V. Since the operation would have saved V's life, D's acts in causing the injuries were held to have caused the death.

2.8.3 **Reform**

The Law Commission's Draft Criminal Code Bill 1989 does little to clarify the law, using the same elastic concepts as the case law. Clause 17 reads:

(1) Subject to subsections (2) and (3), a person causes a result which is an element of an offence when—
   (a) he does an act which makes a more than negligible contribution to its occurrence; or
   (b) he omits to do an act which might prevent its occurrence and which he is under a duty to do according to the law relating to the offence.

(2) A person does not cause a result where, after he does such an act or makes such an omission, an act or event occurs—
   (a) which is the immediate and sufficient cause of the result;
   (b) which he did not foresee; and
   (c) which could not in the circumstances reasonably have been foreseen.

2.9 Coincidence of *mens rea* and *actus reus*

It is a general rule of liability that the *mens rea* or fault element prescribed by the crime charged must coincide in time with the performance of the *actus reus*. This is usually inherent in the definition of the offence. Thus, theft is where D 'dishonestly appropriates property belonging to another with the intention of permanently depriving the other of it'. It is obvious that at the moment of appropriating (taking) another's property, D must (a) be dishonest and (b) intend to permanently deprive.

However, a number of cases have arisen in relation to unlawful homicides which are claimed to infringe this principle and necessitate the creation of an exception to it. In *Thabo Meli* [1954] 1 All ER 373, PC (*Cases and Materials* (2.9)), D1 and D2, in pursuance of a pre-arranged plan, lured V to a hut where they struck him over the head intending to kill him. They knocked him unconscious, but he was alive. D1 and D2 mistakenly believed he was dead and, in an effort to fake an accident, rolled him off a low cliff. V died only later of exposure at the bottom of the cliff. D1 and D2 were charged with V's murder.

> **? QUESTION** 2.18
>
> - Can you identify the problem?
> - Can you suggest a solution?

The defence argument was that D1 and D2 did not have the intention to kill when they rolled V over the cliff, which was the act which caused V's death. How could they if they thought he was already dead? Although they did have the intention to kill when they hit him over the head, this act did not cause the death. The Privy Council appeared to accept the underlying propositions in the argument, but brushed them aside by holding that 'it was impossible to divide up what was really one series of acts in this way. There is no doubt that the accused set out to do all these acts in order to achieve their plan, and as parts of their plan...' They were therefore held guilty of murder.

It is questionable whether there was any need to devise an apparent exception to the coincidence principle by holding that it is enough that D has the *mens rea* at any time during the 'series of acts' which led to death. The *mens rea* must accompany the *actus reus*. The *actus reus* of murder is conduct which causes death. Remembering that the conduct need not be the only cause of death, can we not say that the accused's act of knocking D unconscious, which was accompanied by the *mens rea* for murder, was a substantial and operating cause of death? The act of rolling D off the cliff could not be regarded as breaking the chain of causation.

The Privy Council regarded as important the fact that rolling the body over the cliff to fake an accident was part of a pre-arranged plan. What if D's disposal of the 'body' was not part of any plan but a panic reaction to D's belief that he had killed V? This was the situation in *Church* [1965] 2 All ER 72, CCA where D, with the *mens rea* for murder, beat a woman unconscious and, in a panic and thinking she was dead, threw her into a river. At the time she was alive but died from drowning. On normal causation principles, it could be argued that D's act in knocking her unconscious played a significant role in bringing about her death by drowning. However, the court again adopted the 'continuing transaction' analysis, holding that the jury could have convicted of murder 'if [it] regarded the appellant's behaviour from the moment he first struck her to the moment when he threw her into the river as a series of acts designed to cause death...' This seemed to extend the principle in *Thabo Meli* to a case where there was no planned series of acts and the disposal was thought of only after the initial attack.

More recently the principle was applied in *Le Brun* [1991] 4 All ER 673, CA (*Cases and Materials* (2.2)) to convict of manslaughter. D hit his wife on the chin knocking her unconscious. While he was trying to drag her body along the street to avoid detection, he lost his grip. Her head hit the pavement, fracturing her skull and causing her death. The court held that where the initial 'unlawful application of force and the eventual act causing death are parts of the same sequence of events, the same transaction, the fact that there is an appreciable interval of time between the two does not serve to exonerate the defendant from liability. That is certainly so where the appellant's subsequent actions which caused death, after the initial unlawful blow, are designed to conceal his commission of the original unlawful assault...' In this case, not only was there no pre-arranged plan but D knew that V was still alive at the time he dropped her.

The court recognised that an alternative way of solving the problem was the causation analysis we have explained above. In its view it could not 'be said that the actions of the appellant in dragging the victim away with the intention of evading liability broke the chain which linked the initial blow with the death.'

? QUESTION 2.19

What is the position in the converse case where, when D performs the initial act causing the harm, he does not have the *mens rea*, but when he learns of the true situation, he does have the *mens rea*? You have already encountered this situation earlier in the chapter. Refer back to check your answer.

Again, it is not necessary to create an exception to the coincidence principle, as long as we rely on the principle enunciated by the House of Lords in *Miller* (above) which founds liability on D's intentional omission to counteract the dangerous situation he has inadvertently created.

Clause 31 of the draft Criminal Law Bill 1993 prefers the idea of a 'continuing *actus reus*', but achieves much the same result as the *Miller* principle (Law Com. No. 218).

■ FURTHER READING

Ashworth: *The Scope of Criminal Liability for Omissions* (1989) 105 LQR 424.

Hart & Honoré: *Causation in the Law* (2nd ed., 1985, Oxford University Press).

Heaton: *Dealing in Death* [2003] Crim LR 497.

Heaton: *Principals? No Principles!* [2004] Crim LR 463.

Hogan: *Omissions and the Duty Myth* in P. Smith (ed.): *Criminal Law: Essays in Honour of J.C. Smith* (1986, Butterworths).

Norrie: *A Critique of Criminal Causation* (1991) 54 MLR 685.

Simester: *Why Omissions are Special* (1995) 1 Legal Theory 311.

Smith ATH: *On Actus Reus and Mens Rea* in Glazebrook (ed.): *Reshaping the Criminal Law* (1978, Sweet & Maxwell).

Smith JC: *Liability for Omissions in the Criminal Law* (1984) 4 LS 88.

Stannard: *Medical Treatment and the Chain of Causation* (1993) 57 JCL 88.

Williams: *Criminal Omissions—the Conventional View* (1991) 107 LQR 86.

■ SUMMARY

For purposes of analysis, the definition of a crime is usually divided into the *actus reus* and the *mens rea*. The *mens rea* is whatever state of mind (or, more loosely, fault element) is required for the crime charged. The *actus reus* is the physical conduct forbidden by the crime. All crimes require *actus reus*—some crimes (strict liability) have no *mens rea* or fault element. A third negative element is the absence of a defence excusing liability.

- *Actus reus*—(i) whatever act, omission or state of affairs is prohibited by the offence charged **plus** (ii) any surrounding **circumstances** prescribed (except D's *mens rea* or any excusatory defence) and (iii) any **consequences** of D's act/omission prescribed by the offence definition. **Result** crimes require D's conduct to cause a defined consequence, e.g., death for murder/manslaughter, damage to property for criminal damage. **Conduct** crimes require no particular consequence to follow D's conduct, e.g., perjury and rape. Almost all crimes require D's conduct to occur in defined **circumstances**, e.g., handling stolen goods (the goods handled must be stolen), rape (the victim must be not consenting). All required elements must come together for the *actus reus*.

- *Voluntary conduct*—D's conduct, i.e., muscular movements, must be performed under the control and direction of D's conscious mind (not, say, while unconscious). Conduct is usually **acts** but can be **omissions** or even state of affairs.

- *Omissions*—only liable where a specific statutory provision imposes it (e.g., wilful neglect of child, failing to report a motor accident) or where the common law imposes a duty to act. A duty can arise through: (i) blood or other close relationship, e.g., parent and dependant child, (ii) voluntary assumption of responsibility to care whether expressly, e.g., contractual agreement to care, or impliedly, e.g., doing acts of assistance (*Stone and Dobinson*). If 'dependant' of full capacity instructs D to cease caring this may absolve D (*Smith*; *Airedale NHS Trust v Bland*); (iii) doctor–patient relationship where doctor has assumed responsibility by contract or otherwise. But duty to treat/care may end if 'responsible and competent medical opinion' decided this would be in 'patient's best interests', e.g., persistent vegetative state (*Airedale NHS Trust v Bland*); (iv) contract—probably just an instance of assumption of responsibility (*Pittwood*—employed as level crossing keeper); (v) creation of dangerous situation—if D inadvertently creates danger by his conduct he is under a duty to take reasonable steps to nullify the danger when he becomes aware of it (*Miller*).

- *Causation*—for result crimes it must be proved D's conduct **caused** the prohibited result. Step 1—was D's conduct a cause **in fact**, i.e., played some part in bringing about the consequence (in terms of the physical laws of cause and effect)? Most cases can be solved by applying '**but for**' test. Step 2—D's conduct **must** also be a **legal** cause of death—essentially policy question as to when law should cease to ascribe to D's conduct responsibility for further consequences. Must be a **substantial** cause (seems to mean no more than 'significant' or 'more than minimal' (*Cheshire*)) but need not be the only cause or the most important or, by itself, capable of causing the prohibited result. Thus, the fact that V or others are partly to blame does not absolve D (*Swindall and Osborne; Benge*).

- *Intervening acts*—acts/events occurring after D's conduct, but before the prohibited result may break the chain of causation between D's conduct and that result. Normally will do if (i) 'free, deliberate and informed' intervention of third party or (ii) an **abnormal** act/event coinciding with or supervening after D's conduct. However, there are exceptions: (a) the purpose and scope of some offences (e.g., pollution and other regulatory offences) may show an intention to make D responsible for both natural events and the free, deliberate and informed acts of another unless they were 'something extraordinary' (*Empress Car Co.*). (b) The deliberate act of the other (whether third party or victim) may not be **free and voluntary**, e.g., reasonable act of self-preservation (*Pagett*); understandable act of victim in trying to escape a threat (*Williams; Marjoram*)—though will break the chain if 'extraordinary' or not 'reasonably foreseeable' or **informed**, e.g., mistake about the contents of a syringe (*cf. Michael*). (c) Despite the third party's or victim's deliberate act, D's act is still a substantial and operating cause. (d) Medical treatment of the injuries caused to the victim by D unless 'extraordinary' **and** (c) is inapplicable. D must take his victim as he finds him and therefore causes injuries (or death) which are unexpectedly and unforeseeably serious due to some unknown physical weakness of the victim (e.g., heart condition (*Hayward*); eggshell skull) or, according to *Blaue*, mental peculiarity. (The latter case appears to contradict the 'escape' cases which state that an **unreasonable** reaction by the victim will break the chain.)

- *Direct infliction of injury*—we assume D has caused an initial injury but query whether he has caused the ultimate death. Basic rule—D causes the death if the initial wound is still a 'substantial and operating cause' at the time of death (*Smith*). Thus, V's refusal of medical treatment for whatever reason (*Blaue*) or thoroughly bad medical treatment (*Smith*) or even V's deliberate re-opening of treated wounds (*Dear*) makes no difference. Even if initial wound **not** a substantial and operating cause of time of death, D responsible if intervening act responsible for death was within the range of risks which were the reasonably foreseeable results of his acts (e.g., normal or even negligent medical treatment (*Cheshire*) but **grossly** negligent probably not foreseeable (*Jordan*)).

- *Coincidence of actus reus and mens rea*—D must possess the requisite *mens rea* at the moment he performs the *actus reus*. But if D's conduct is a series of acts forming one transaction *mens rea* at any time in the sequence will suffice (*Thabo Meli*) whether or not they form part of a pre-arranged plan (*Le Brun*).

3 Mens rea and fault

3.1 Objectives

By the end of this chapter you should be able to:

1 Identify and describe the basic concepts of *mens rea* and fault in relation to both act/consequence and circumstance

2 Analyse the concept of intention and distinguish it from (a) motive and (b) subjective recklessness

3 Analyse the concept of recklessness distinguishing (a) subjective recklessness from objective recklessness and (b) recklessness from negligence

3.2 Introduction

Although *mens rea* is generally thought of as meaning 'guilty mind', it is important to realise that it actually means whatever state of mind D must be proved to have according to the definition of the crime charged. In fact, it is also used loosely to embrace fault elements such as negligence and objective recklessness which do not depend on the state of D's mind. Because the term *mens rea* used in its strict sense would exclude important indicators of blame such as negligence, the Law Commission prefers to use the term 'fault element' in place of '*mens rea*'. The House of Lords in *B* v *DPP* [2000] 2 WLR 452 interpreted *mens rea* in this strict sense (see 13.4.1 below).

In general, the presence of some fault element accompanying the *actus reus* is seen as an essential condition for imposing liability for serious criminal offences. It would be unfair to convict D of a serious crime, even though he caused the harmful consequence, if he was in no way at fault in causing it. However, there are many offences known as strict liability offences which do not require proof of *mens rea* or any fault element in relation to one or more parts of the *actus reus*. We will be examining these in detail in **Chapter 13**.

In its strict sense, *mens rea* is used to describe whatever state of mind D is **required** to have **according to the definition** of the crime charged. Normally, this will involve proving that D was at least aware that he might perform the *actus reus* of the crime charged if he went ahead with his planned conduct. Sometimes, it might involve more than that, for example, proving that he **intended** to perform the crime's *actus reus*. If we can say that

D realised he might commit the *actus reus* of the crime, we can see that in going ahead with his plan, he has chosen to commit the crime or, at least, **chosen** to take **the risk** of committing it. For this reason, the more serious crimes, such as offences of violence against the person, tend to require as a minimum that D be aware of the possibility of harm resulting to V from his conduct. However, lack of awareness, although not *mens rea* in the strict sense, will itself be blameworthy in a situation where the law says that D **ought to have been aware** of the possibility of committing the *actus reus* and guarded against it. Nonetheless, such fault would be rather less blameworthy than where D knows he might commit the *actus reus*.

? QUESTION 3.1

- What do you think might be the *mens rea* for (a) murder (b) rape and (c) criminal damage? The *actus reus* of these offences is (a) causing the death of another (b) having sexual intercourse with a woman without her consent (the most common form) and (c) destroying or damaging another's property.
- Do any of these offences have the same *mens rea*?

We will be considering what *mens rea* is actually required for these offences in due course, but it is necessary to appreciate that, just as the *actus reus* differs from crime to crime, so the *mens rea* will differ too. To ascertain the *mens rea* for any particular crime, it is necessary to examine the definition of that crime, whether statutory or common law, and any case law interpreting that definition. However, offence definitions tend to base their own particular *mens rea* requirements upon the generalised concepts which will be examined in this chapter. Thus, murder and rape both utilise the concept of 'intention' even though what must be intended is very different—the death of another in murder, and sexual intercourse in rape.

When students are asked what is the *mens rea* of murder, for example, there is a tendency to reply 'intention' or, in the case of criminal damage, 'recklessness'. However, such replies cannot define the *mens rea* required until they specify what it is that must be intended or in relation to which D must be reckless. In the real world of actual offences, definitions usually detail an act or consequence which must be intended or about which D must be reckless or negligent. Murder requires an intention to kill or cause grievous bodily harm, not, for example, an intention to steal. Criminal damage requires recklessness as to the damaging of another's property, not recklessness as to failing an examination. Please form the habit of always specifying what must be intended or what D must be aware might happen (subjective recklessness).

It is very important to understand the concept of *mens rea* and we make no apology for reiterating that the *mens rea* of an offence is simply what the definition of that offence says it is. If D intends to kill, he has the *mens rea* for murder whether or not he feels or would be regarded by people generally as having any moral guilt. Law and morals often coincide but by no means always. The person who sits down in the road in an effort to block the export of live animals will feel morally justified in refusing a police officer's request to move. There is no doubt that he is 'wilfully' obstructing the police officer in the execution of his duty.

?   **QUESTION** 3.2

- Suppose V is terminally ill and in agonising pain with cancer. He begs his doctor to put him out of his misery and give him a lethal injection. The doctor, realising that V has lost all quality of life, finally succumbs to V's pressure and deliberately kills V by administering a lethal injection. Would the doctor have the *mens rea* for murder?
- D has anal intercourse with a boy he knows to be 17 years old. He thought that the age of consent for such acts was 16, as indeed intercourse *per vaginam* is in relation to girls. He is a foreign national and, in his country, such acts are not against the law. Would he be guilty of the offence of buggery (recently replaced by the Sexual Offences Act 2003), the *actus reus* of which he has committed?

Equally, it is generally unnecessary to show that D knew he was committing a crime because such a state of mind will be no part of that required by the definition of the offence. If D knows he is or may be committing the *actus reus* of the crime, there is no need to prove that he realised that such conduct constituted a criminal offence. Hence, in Question 3.2, D would, prior to its repeal by the Sexual Offences Act 2003, have committed the crime of buggery. You will no doubt have heard of the maxim: ignorance of the law is no excuse.

Before we look at *mens rea* concepts in detail, it might be useful to have an overview of the most frequently used states of mind and fault elements as set out in **Figure 3.1**.

We would stress that the definitions given in the diagram are far from being comprehensive and are intended only to be indicative. You should find it a useful aide-mémoire and we would recommend you to refer back to it, whenever you become confused, as you surely will, about the basic *mens rea* concepts and the relationships between them.

You will notice that we have divided our diagram into two major sections, headed subjective and objective. If the test of culpability is subjective, it means that the outcome depends on proof of what D was **actually** thinking—what was **actually** going on in his mind—at the time he performed the prohibited conduct. In other words, it is concerned with *mens rea* in the strict sense—proving that D has the particular state of mind required by the offence's definition. If the test is objective, then the court is not interested in what D was actually thinking at the time, but rather what he **ought** to have been thinking and doing. D is blamed for failing to think and act in accordance with ordinary standards of conduct laid down by the courts.

You will have done well to notice that our diagram does not include *mens rea* in relation to **circumstances** forming part of the *actus reus* (see 2.6). For example, in rape an essential part of the *actus reus* is the presence of the circumstance that the victim does not consent. Although the concepts used have much in common with those used in respect of acts and consequences, there are some differences. However, it is best to postpone consideration of these until after we have examined the basic concepts in relation to acts and consequences.

In this regard, there are two subjective states of mind to consider—intention and subjective recklessness. In both cases, D is aware that the prohibited act or consequence may occur but, with intention, there is the added aggravating factor that D **aims** to do the prohibited act or cause the prohibited consequence. We will see in later chapters that many offences are satisfied by proof of intention or subjective recklessness so that the boundary line between intention and recklessness is not important. However, there are some crimes

Subjective (D's own view—depends on what the court finds D was thinking)		Objective (depends on the court's view of how D ought to have behaved in the situation **not** on D's state of mind)	
Intention	Subjective (*Cunningham*) **Recklessness**	Objective (*Caldwell*) **Recklessness** (effectively abolished by *G*)	**Negligence**
D's **aim** or **purpose** is to do the act or produce the consequence forbidden	D **consciously** takes the **risk** of the prohibited act or consequence, i.e., he realises it might happen	D gives **no thought** to an **obvious** risk of the prohibited act or consequence resulting *Gross negligence*	*Ordinary negligence*
	'Grey area' known as oblique intention	D falls **seriously** short of the standard expected of the ordinary, prudent person	D falls short of the standard expected of the ordinary, prudent person
		Extreme Carelessness	*Average Carelessness*

Figure 3.1 *Mens rea* in relation to doing an act or omitting to act and/or producing a consequence

which can be satisfied **only** by proof of intention, making it necessary to know where intention ends and recklessness begins. Unfortunately, this is a question which is not easily answered and takes up most of our discussion on the meaning of intention. In effect, the courts tend to stretch the concept of intention beyond its natural meaning, annexing for intention a small part of what is properly recklessness. We hope **Figure 3.2** will make the general idea clearer.

3.3 Intention

It might be thought that since the criminal law has been developing for centuries, the courts would long since have settled the meaning of the key *mens rea* concepts, foremost of which is intention. Regrettably, this is not the case. Although 'intention' seems a fairly straightforward concept in everyday language, the courts have struggled to define its limits, despite a number of recent attempts by the House of Lords. In a most significant decision

 Subjective recklessness
D is aware he might do the prohibited act/cause the prohibited result

Intention
D is aware he might do the prohibited act/cause the prohibited result **and** he aims to do it

The grey area sometimes called oblique intention which, in effect is intention even though D does not aim to do the prohibited act/cause the prohibited result

Figure 3.2 *Mens rea*

the House provided some much needed clarification and simplification though, as we shall see, difficulties remain (*Woollin* [1998] 4 All ER 103—see *Cases and Materials* (3.3)). Although their Lordships noted that the meaning of 'intent' may vary according to its context in the criminal law, the decision will undoubtedly be influential beyond the confines of the *mens rea* for murder with which they were dealing.

EXERCISE 3.1

Please write down any synonyms you can think of for 'intention'.

Although the concept of intention may be hazy at the edges, there is a large measure of agreement on the central core and almost everyone would agree that there is an intention to kill in the following cases: D desires to kill; wants to kill; aims to kill; decides to kill; D's purpose or object is to kill.

In fact, in *Mohan* [1975] 2 All ER 193, the Court of Appeal, in holding that intention was an essential ingredient on a charge of attempting to commit an offence, said that intention meant: 'a decision [by D] to bring about ... the commission of the offence which it is alleged D attempted to commit, no matter whether D desired that consequence of his act or not.'

It follows that D undoubtedly intends to kill, where he sets out to kill, i.e., it is his purpose or aim to kill. Referring back to **Figure 3.2**, this is the central core of intention and is known as 'direct intent' and is encapsulated in the Law Commission's latest definition in cl. 1 of the draft Criminal Law Bill: 'a person acts ... "intentionally" with respect to a result when ... it is his purpose to cause it ...'

If it is D's purpose to kill, it does not matter that his conduct is very unlikely to achieve it. He intends it nonetheless. If D takes a pot-shot at V aiming to kill him, he intends to kill even though he is a rotten shot and even though V is outside the normal range for D's gun.

The difficulties and uncertainties surrounding the definition of intention generally stem from the issue of how far, if at all, intention stretches beyond this core notion of purpose. Non-purpose intention has often been referred to as 'oblique intention' or 'indirect intention'.

3.3.1 Prohibited result known by D to be a condition of achieving his aim

> **? QUESTION** 3.3
>
> D is married to V who has his life insured for £1 million. D, who loves her husband, needs £1 million and, seeing no other way to get it, she decides to kill him. She does not want him to die; she wishes there were some other way but there is not. Does she intend to kill her husband when she shoots him, with tears streaming down her face?

The fact that, emotionally, D does not desire V's death or does not desire it for its own sake, will not prevent her having an intention to kill. You may recall that the quotation from *Mohan* says that a decision to kill is intention 'no matter whether D desired that consequence of his act or not'. The point is that D knows that, in order to achieve her ultimate objective (getting the insurance money), she **has to** kill V. Can it be doubted that, after weighing up the pros and cons, in deciding to go ahead and shoot, her **aim** is to kill V? It may be a subsidiary aim to her main purpose of obtaining the insurance money, but that does not make it any less her aim. As Lord Hailsham put it in *Hyam* v *DPP* [1974] 2 All ER 41, it includes 'the means as well as the end'. The law would focus on D's aim to produce the prohibited consequence—killing—and regard her ultimate aim as the **motive** or reason for acting and, as such, irrelevant to legal liability.

Let us look at another example commonly given in illustration. D decides to shoot V, his enemy, whom he sees sitting in his conservatory. He fires the gun at V and obviously intends to shoot V. Does he intend to break the conservatory glass? Once again he realises that, if he is to succeed in his main purpose, he **must** break the glass. We might again say that his subsidiary aim is to break the glass because he knows that this is the only way of achieving his main purpose in the circumstances. Again it does not matter that he is an appalling marksman and might miss the conservatory altogether. **If** he achieves his purpose, he knows that he will definitely break the window.

So obvious are these cases, that you might have thought that the courts would have no difficulty in regarding them as intention every time. Unfortunately, we cannot make even this limited assertion because, on odd occasions, the courts have bent the rule to allow acquittal in what they have regarded as deserving cases.

In *Ahlers* [1915] 1 KB 616, D was a German consul in Britain at the outbreak of World War I. He was charged with intentionally aiding the King's enemies (a form of treason) in that he helped German nationals to leave Britain after the declaration of war. It was held that he did not intend to aid the King's enemies, but rather he intended to do his duty as German consul (a case of 'Deutschland, Deutschland über Ahlers'?). World War II threw up a similar situation in *Steane* [1947] 1 All ER 813 where D was charged with the same offence. He broadcast enemy propaganda for the Germans during the war. He did it in order to save himself and his family from being sent to a concentration camp and being subjected to physical violence. Again, it was held that he lacked any intention to aid the King's enemies.

? QUESTION 3.4

Do you think that:

- Steane, when he decided to speak the propaganda into the microphone, intended to aid the King's enemies?
- the fact that Ahlers was intending to do his duty as German consul meant that he did not have the intent to aid the King's enemies when he was helping German nationals to flee Britain?

It seems that the courts in the two cases were confusing motive and desire with intention. We can accept that both defendants may have wished there were some other way of achieving their ultimate purpose (doing his duty or saving himself and his family), but both knew that, in order to achieve that purpose, they had to do acts which would certainly assist the King's enemies. Aiding the King's enemies was a pre-condition to achieving what they desired. What do you think the court would have said if Steane had argued that he did not intend to aid the King's enemies but only to obtain the £1,000 which the Germans had promised to pay him for the broadcasts? He intentionally broadcast, knowing this was necessarily aiding the King's enemies. His motive for acting, whether it be the laudable one of saving his family or the discreditable one of doing it for money, should have had no bearing on whether he intended to aid. In fact, the court could have acquitted Steane by utilising the defence of duress (see 9.3) rather than doing violence to the concept of intention. However, this would not have helped Ahlers, whose exposure to the death penalty probably explained the court's anxiety to acquit him.

More recently, some of the Law Lords in *Gillick* v *West Norfolk Area Health Authority* [1985] 3 All ER 402 adopted a similar line of reasoning in an interesting civil case. Their view, obiter, was that a doctor who gave contraceptive advice to a girl under 16, realising this would assist or encourage men to have sexual intercourse with her, would not be guilty of aiding and abetting any ensuing unlawful sexual intercourse. This was because his intention would be to prevent her pregnancy if she did have sex, not to encourage or assist another to have sexual intercourse with her. Again, the fallacy is that the two intentions are mutually exclusive. As in *Steane*, a better way of securing acquittal in such cases would be to utilise one of the general defences—in this case necessity (see 9.4 and 9.5). (This is now expressly provided for in s. 73 of the Sexual Offences Act 2003.)

Despite these exceptions, the general rule would be that if D knows or believes the prohibited consequence to be a condition, i.e., the certain result of achieving his ultimate objective, then he intends such prohibited consequence.

3.3.2 Results known by D to be virtually certain to accompany achievement of D's primary purpose

In this case, the prohibited consequence is again a by-product or side-effect of D's main aim, but it is not a condition of achieving that aim in the sense that it **has to** happen. D's primary purpose can, at least theoretically, be achieved without producing the forbidden result.

? QUESTION 3.5

In *Hyam* v *DPP* [1974] 2 All ER 41, HL, D had a rival for the affections of her man and, in the dead of night, after checking that he was not staying with her rival, she set fire to the rival's house pouring petrol through the letter box. Her aim was to frighten her rival into staying away from him, but two of her rival's children were asphyxiated in the blaze. It was found as a fact that she knew that death or serious injury was the highly probable result of her actions.

Do you think that she intended to kill or cause serious injury to any of the occupants?

The House of Lords in *Hyam* held that the *mens rea* for murder was satisfied where D knew that death or serious injury was highly probable. As we shall see in **Chapter 6**, that principle is no longer correct. The House of Lords never actually decided whether such a state of mind constituted intention, but it is now clear from the important subsequent House of Lords' cases of *Moloney* [1985] 1 All ER 1025, *Hancock and Shankland* [1986] 1 All ER 646 and now *Woollin* (*Cases and Materials* (3.3.2)) that it does not amount to intention. *Moloney* was absolutely categoric that foresight (i.e., knowledge, realisation) by D that the prohibited result is a highly probable consequence of his actions, is not in law 'equivalent or alternative to the necessary' intention. Whilst the House of Lords was clear that to foresee something as highly probable is not necessarily to intend it, it failed to give any positive definition of intention.

? QUESTION 3.6

Suppose that D wishes to perpetrate an insurance fraud. He sends by aeroplane a package, purporting to contain priceless jewels but which, instead, contains an explosive device timed to go off in mid-flight. He has insured the jewels for millions of pounds. Being a caring person, he fervently hopes that nobody will be killed, but he knows that there is little chance of this happening.

• Does he intend to kill any of those on board?
• Is there any difference between this case and *Hyam*?

In this situation, the risk of death is much higher than in *Hyam* and, more importantly, D **knows** it to be much higher. When Mrs Hyam set fire to her rival's house, it was by no means inevitable that someone would die or even be injured. She knew that the risk was high but well short of inevitability. With the bomb on the plane example, D knows that, for all practical purposes, death is the certain outcome of achieving his aim. D knows that it is a practical or moral certainty of achieving his aim of destroying his parcel in flight. It is not a pre-condition because, theoretically, it would be possible to destroy the parcel by an in-flight explosion without killing anyone. Miraculous escapes do sometimes occur! Most people would say, as a matter of policy, that if D is prepared deliberately to take a risk of that magnitude, he certainly ought to be guilty of murder when the deaths occur. Many people would also view D as intending to kill those on board whereas they would regard Mrs Hyam as not intending to cause death or harm. The draft Criminal Law Bill (and the draft Offences Against the Person Bill—see 4.4.3.3 below) reflects this approach: '. . . a person acts . . . "intentionally" with respect to a result when . . . although it is not his purpose to cause it, he knows that it would occur in the ordinary course of events if he were to succeed in his purpose of causing some other result.'

The key word is 'would'. It does not say 'might' or 'would be likely to' or 'would very probably'. D must know that it would definitely occur unless something extraordinary happened to prevent it (see Law Com. No. 218).

That is the Law Commission's **proposal**, but is it the current law? If D knows that the prohibited result is the virtually certain consequence of his actions, does he intend that prohibited result according to the law? The case of *Moloney* is ambiguous. Lord Bridge spoke for all the Law Lords, but his judgment is contradictory (see 6.4.1.1). However, the subsequent House of Lords' decision in *Hancock and Shankland* and the Court of Appeal's decision in *Nedrick* [1986] 3 All ER 1 both took the view that foresight of any degree, even foresight by D that the prohibited result is virtually certain, is not, in itself, intention. However, a high degree of foresight on the part of D, whilst not establishing intention per se, can give rise to an evidential inference that D not only foresaw it but actually intended it. According to *Hancock*, if the jury finds that D foresaw the prohibited consequence as likely, it **may** go on to 'infer'—it is proper for the jury, as a matter of evidence, to infer—that D actually intended the consequence as well. (Note that the jury is not **obliged** to infer—it is for the jury itself to decide whether or not to infer.) The greater the probability foreseen by D, the stronger the inference of intention will be. The Court of Appeal in *Nedrick*, whilst purporting to apply *Hancock*, took a much more restrictive view as to when it was permissible for the jury to draw the inference of intention from foresight:

> . . . the jury [is] not entitled to infer the necessary intention unless [it] feel[s] sure that death or serious bodily harm was a virtual certainty (barring some unforeseen intervention) as a result of the accused's actions and that the accused appreciated such was the case.
>
> Where a man realises that it is for all practical purposes inevitable that his actions will result in death or serious harm, the inference may be irresistible that he intended that result, however little he may have desired or wished it to happen. The decision is one for the jury to be reached upon a consideration of all the evidence.

Lord Lane CJ came tantalisingly close to saying that realisation by D that the harmful consequence is virtually certain is a species of intention—'the inference may be **irresistible**'. However, he could not say that it **was** intention because the House of Lords in *Hancock* had categorically stated that it was not intention.

These cases display a tendency which has bedevilled this area of the law for many years, namely, a confusion between what is the substantive law defining intention (and the *mens rea* of murder) and what are the rules of evidence governing how the intention required by the substantive law can be proved. These ghosts have to some extent been laid to rest by the House of Lords' decision in *Woollin*, though there is still an element of ambiguity.

In *Woollin*, D, in anger and frustration threw his three-month-old son across the room with considerable force. The baby's head struck a hard object causing serious brain damage from which he died. The prosecution accepted that D did not aim to kill or cause grievous bodily harm to his son, but the trial judge directed the jury that 'it would be open to' them to infer intention from the fact that D 'appreciated when he threw the child that there was a substantial risk that he would cause serious injury to it'. The House of Lords unanimously held this to be incorrect and quashed D's conviction for murder.

In a rather selective, but nonetheless welcome interpretation of the previous case law, the House initially appeared to take the step denied to the Court of Appeal in *Nedrick* and rule that where D foresees a consequence as virtually certain, he intends that consequence. On that view, intention extends beyond aim or purpose and would include foresight of virtual certainty (but nothing less than virtual certainty). Such foresight would no longer be merely evidence from which a jury might infer intention: it would **amount to** intention.

However, in the concluding part of the leading judgment, the House seemingly backtracked on its earlier recognition of foresight of virtual certainty as a species of intention and reverted to a slightly modified *Nedrick* test. The House warmly endorsed as the ideal direction to the jury in 'non-purpose' cases a modified form of the *Nedrick* direction quoted above. The jury would not be entitled to **find** (previously 'infer') the necessary intent unless they felt sure the prohibited consequence was virtually certain to result from D's actions and that D appreciated this was the case. In fact, given the House of Lords' earlier pronouncement that foresight of virtual certainty **is** a form of intention, this is a rather odd way of putting it. If it **is** a form of intention and the jury find that D did foresee the consequence as virtually certain to result, they **must** find intention and it is misleading to talk about 'being entitled to find' it. That implies a discretion which, according to the earlier part of the judgment, they do not have. The House appears to shy away from the logic of its earlier conclusions in implying that the jury, after all, would have a discretion. A chink of obscurity remains!

Another curiosity of the *Nedrick* approved formulation is that the prosecution has to establish that the risk of the consequence, e.g., death, was **in fact** virtually certain **as well as** that D **realised** it was virtually certain. Since we are talking about *mens rea*, there seems no reason why if D is prepared to go ahead thinking that death is virtually certain, intention should not be found even though, as it turns out, D is mistaken in his view of the magnitude of the risk, death **not being in fact** a virtually certain consequence.

? QUESTION 3.7

Can you think of any policy reason why the House of Lords did not *oblige* juries to find intention where they were satisfied that D, whilst not aiming to kill, foresaw death as virtually certain?

It may well be the case that the House wanted to give the jury an area of discretion in non-purpose cases so as to allow them **not** to find intention in 'deserving' cases. This is especially true of what some writers call 'double effect' cases where D has a legitimate primary purpose, but realises the virtual inevitability of the illegitimate side-effects of his actions. For example, the area of medical treatment can cause great difficulty and *Gillick* (3.3.1 above) provides one instance. Consider also the case of a doctor who gives treatment, e.g., powerful painkilling drugs to a terminally ill patient for the purpose of relieving pain, knowing that it is virtually certain that this will shorten the patient's life. The hard and fast rule suggested in the earlier parts of Lord Steyn's lead judgment in *Woollin* would establish an intention to kill. By allowing the jury a discretion where it is not D's **purpose** to kill, the ratio in *Woollin* enables them to exempt from murder morally deserving cases such as treatment which D believes to be proper medical treatment in the best interests of the patient (*cf. Moor*, 11 May 1999 (unreported) but discussed in [2000] Crim LR 31 and 41). We would stress that this discretion would not be available where D's **purpose** in administering the drugs is to kill even if the doctor's motive is the altruistic one of ending unnecessary suffering where the quality of life remaining is minimal (e.g., *Cox* [1993] 12 BMLR 38).

The difficulty with this approach is that it breeds uncertainty. Doctors would not know what was acceptable and what was not if it was dependent on how a particular jury exercised its discretion. It would surely be better to admit that the intention is present and to articulate a defence to liability based on necessity (see 9.5 below) or a special doctor's defence. This was the approach taken by the majority of the Court of Appeal in the tragic conjoined twins case, *Re A (Children)* [2001] 2 WLR 480. Doctors sought permission to operate to separate the twins who would probably both die within a matter of months if no such operation was performed. The doctors knew, as has proved to be the case, that the operation would give Jodie, the viable twin, every chance of a relatively normal life, but would almost certainly cause the death of Mary, the non-viable twin, within a few minutes. The majority held that *Woollin* meant that the doctors performing the operation in the light of such knowledge would intend to kill. The doctrine of double effect could not apply where the 'illegitimate' effect conferred no benefit on the person suffering it (Mary), the 'legitimate' effect being entirely for the benefit of another (Jodie). There was no suggestion that the jury would have a discretion whether or not to find intention in this case suggesting that the majority viewed foresight of virtual certainty as a form of intention not merely a permission to find intention. Such an interpretation of *Woollin* seems preferable (see more on *Woollin* at 6.4.1.1 below).

Subsequently, the Court of Appeal in *Matthews and Alleyne* [2003] EWCA Crim 192 (*Cases and Materials* (3.3)) (without referring to *Re A*) rejected the idea that the law had 'reached a *definition* of intent in murder in terms of appreciation of virtual certainty'. The Court did not 'regard *Woollin* as yet reaching or laying down a substantive rule of law' but thought that 'once what is required is an appreciation of virtual certainty of death, and not some lesser foresight of merely probable consequences, there is very little to choose between a rule of evidence and one of substantive law. It is probably this thought that led Lord Steyn [in *Woollin*] to say that a result foreseen as virtually certain is an intended result . . . Lord Lane had also spoken in *Nedrick* of an irresistible inference.' The defendants had killed the victim by throwing him from a bridge into the river below, knowing that he could not swim. In the Court's opinion, if the accused appreciated the virtual certainty of the victim's death and had no intention of saving him, 'it is impossible to see how the jury could **not** have found that the appellants intended [the victim] to die.'

It appears that the judges want to have their cake and eat it. In most cases, the jury would be mad not to find intention, but it is not to be made compulsory to allow for the odd 'deserving' case like *Re A*.

We would like to stress that, in this section, we have only been talking about **non-purpose** intention. You should at all costs avoid the common student mistake of thinking that in all cases of intention, the harmful consequence must have been virtually certain and seen as virtually certain to result. That is most certainly **not** required when D's **purpose** is to produce the prohibited consequence. It is only necessary when purpose is ruled out (see *MD* [2004] EWCA Crim 1391 at 6.4.1.1 below).

3.3.3 **Offences other than murder**

The major recent cases on intention—*Moloney, Hancock, Nedrick* and *Woollin*— have all been concerned with the offence of murder. However, it would appear that the comments in those cases also apply to intention in the law generally. *Walker and Hayles* (1990) 90 Cr App R 226, CA applied the cases to a charge of attempt (admittedly it was attempted murder) and they have also been applied to s. 18 of the Offences Against the Person Act 1861 in *Bryson* [1985] Crim LR 669, CA. In *AMK (Property Management) Ltd* [1985] Crim LR 600, CA the cases were applied to the offence under s. 1(3) of the Protection from Eviction Act 1977 (although *Burke* [1988] Crim LR 841, CA prefers the narrower concept of 'purpose' in relation to the same offence). *Jones & Ors* [1997] Crim LR 510, CA applies *Nedrick* and *Hancock* to s. 16 of the Firearms Act 1968 which requires an **intent** to enable another to endanger life.

It is true that the House of Lords in *Woollin* entered the caveat that 'intent' does not necessarily have 'precisely the same meaning in every context in the criminal law' (and their context was the offence of murder), but we would suggest that it will only be in exceptional situations that the courts will depart from the *Woollin* view of intent whatever the offence in question.

3.3.4 **Intention and motive**

It is a basic principle of English law that motive, good or bad, is generally irrelevant to criminal liability. A person may act from the best of motives and yet if he performs the defined *actus reus* with the prescribed *mens rea* or fault element, he will be guilty of that crime (e.g., mercy killing). To put it another way, crimes are generally defined in terms of the fact of harm (the *actus reus*) and that it was done intentionally (or at least with realisation of the risk of the harm—subjective recklessness) (the *mens rea*) as a way of excluding accidental harm. Conversely, if D has not performed the *actus reus* with the appropriate *mens rea*, he cannot be guilty of the crime, no matter how evil his motive.

Thus, the law makes a rudimentary assessment of what constitutes sufficient fault or blame to impose criminal liability. Any analysis of blame of any sophistication would inevitably require a careful consideration of D's motive and indeed the context of his actions. We could not pronounce on the **moral** wrongness of D's act unless we had investigated **why** he acted as he did, in addition to establishing that D intentionally caused the harm. The law does not normally concern itself with such matters. In general the court's judgment of the **legal** wrongness of the act is concerned only with the fact that D performed the *actus reus* intending to do so or realising he might.

There are two separate reasons why the law should want to exclude issues surrounding motive from the question of criminal liability. First and most important, it would undermine the law's claim to **define** what is legally wrong. Acceptance that a 'good' motive could avoid legal wrongness would enable alternative views of right and wrong to compete with the criminal law's conception of right and wrong. It would raise all sorts of difficult ethical questions which are now largely avoided (*cf.* deliberate 'mercy' killings, blocking a dangerous road to campaign for traffic-calming measures following fatal accidents, stopping-up a pipe discharging 'permitted' effluent into the sea). The law wishes to simplify and foreclose the debate about what is legally wrong.

The second reason is to preserve the law's individualist conception of responsibility. Each person is a distinct individual, acting in isolation from his social context and held accountable and responsible for his actions. To allow an examination of why D acted as he did in deciding whether he is blameworthy would introduce difficult considerations of the extent to which legal responsibility is negated by the social context and mores in which D lives and operates. It would open up questions like the influence of social deprivation such as unemployment, lack of housing and addiction to drugs or alcohol which might explain D's conduct. You will readily understand the law's desire to keep such intractable problems out of the legal definition of right and wrong.

> **?** **QUESTION** 3.8
>
> In fact the law does regularly take these issues surrounding motive into account. How?

Of course, that is not to say that these matters are totally ignored by the law. We shall see shortly that, despite the basic principle of irrelevance, the issue of motive manages to insinuate itself into questions of criminal liability in a number of ways. In addition, proof that D had a plausible motive is always useful evidence towards proving that D actually did what is alleged, since people do not usually act in a motiveless fashion (*Williams* (1986) 84 Cr App R 299, CA). However, even though the courts generally manage to keep it out of substantive liability issues, there is no doubt that motive always looms large when it comes to sentencing on conviction. Motive should not define what is and is not against the law, but justice requires that it be admitted when it comes to deciding D's punishment. The conviction states that the conduct is legally wrong and should not be performed despite the presence of a good motive or the excusing circumstances, but the judge's sentencing discretion enables suitable mitigation of punishment in most cases (though not on conviction of murder where the law mandates a penalty of life imprisonment whatever the circumstances).

3.3.4.1 What is 'motive'?

'Motive' is a word which is itself used loosely in this context. It can be used in its general sense of the **emotion** prompting D to act intentionally in the way he does. Thus, D might intentionally kill V out of jealousy, hatred, revenge, greed, anger, patriotism or even love. Such emotions might be termed the precipitating motive or motivating force which causes D to act as he does. However, the term 'motive' is also used to describe the specific means of satisfying the emotion. In this sense it is a **form** of intention but not a legally relevant intention because it is **ulterior** to the *actus reus* and the *mens rea*.

? **QUESTION** 3.9

If D intentionally shoots his wife V with the intention of killing her intending to obtain life insurance monies, which of those three intentions is legally relevant and which is not?

Which would *be described as* D's motive?

In a sense, we could describe any objective of D beyond his intention to do the initial act as his motive. Thus, we could say D intended to pull the trigger with the motive of shooting the gun with the motive of killing V with the motive of securing payment of the insurance monies. In legal terms only intentions to do things coming after or going beyond the causing of the *actus reus* and which are not part of the defined *mens rea* would be regarded as part of motive and therefore legally irrelevant. Clearly, intentions to do the acts and produce any consequences forming part of the *actus reus* would be legally relevant and not motive. Thus, the intention to fire the gun and the intention to thereby kill V are legally relevant. The intention to obtain the insurance money is not; it is 'ulterior' to the offence and falls outside or goes beyond what must be proved according to the definition of the offence. (As we shall see below it is possible for offences to be defined so as to **require** proof of an ulterior intent as part of the *mens rea*. Such an intention could not be regarded as motive and therefore irrelevant because, it is not ulterior to the **offence** (which includes any defined *mens rea*), but only to the *actus reus* (see 3.3.5).)

We have said that the general rule is that motive (D's reason for acting) is irrelevant to criminal liability. In fact, perhaps because the principle is perceived as so well entrenched that defendants rarely argue against it, there is surprisingly little case law providing direct authority for the proposition. In *Smith* [1960] 1 All ER 256, CCA, D was charged with corruptly offering a gift to the mayor of a borough to induce him to use his influence to secure the sale of some council-owned land to D. In fact D's intention was to expose what he believed was a corrupt council and he had no intention of going through with the purchase. It was held that since he intended that the mayor should be corrupted by his offer, his 'good' motive to expose the corruption did not negate the offence—it was ulterior to the definition of the offence. The Privy Council adopted the same line in *Yip Chiu-cheung v R* [1994] 2 All ER 924 in respect of a law enforcement officer importing illegal drugs to entrap members of a drugs ring. His creditable motive did not prevent commission of the offence (see 9.6 below). Similarly, in *Senior* [1899] 1 QB 283, D was convicted of manslaughter in neglecting to summon medical assistance for his child 'no matter what his motive' might be. D belonged to a religious sect known as the 'Peculiar People' and believed that God would take care of his child.

A useful modern statement came in *Sood* [1998] 2 Cr App R 355, CA. D was convicted of 'wilfully and knowingly' making a false declaration in a medical certificate of cause of death contrary to s. 5 of the Perjury Act 1911. He falsely certified that he had seen the deceased alive on the day of her death. He asserted that this was standard in the practice of which he was a junior partner where, as was the case here, (a) there were no suspicious circumstances, and (b) one of the other partners had seen the deceased alive. He argued that he could not be guilty because he acted in good faith believing the practice to be acceptable and having no intention to deceive anyone. It was held that:

> ... [this] argument confuses the requirement of *mens rea* in relation to the physical elements of a crime with the concepts of motive, blame and moral culpability which the criminal law has always been astute to keep distinct, the former going to the question of guilt, the latter to the question of punishment.

In common with the other offences under the Perjury Act 1911, the essence of the offence is the intentional making of a false statement. The reason or motive for making the false statement is irrelevant.

Finally, *Chandler v DPP* [1962] 3 All ER 314, HL illustrates how the courts' exclusion of motive can disengage them from allowing political debate into the courtroom. The defendants tried to enter an airfield to protest against nuclear weapons carried by aircraft flying from the base. They intended to prevent aircraft from taking off by obstructing the runway. The charge under the Official Secrets Act 1911 required proof that they acted for a 'purpose prejudicial to the safety or interest of the State'. Needless to say, the defendants sought to argue that their actions were intended not to prejudice the 'safety or interest of the State' but to enhance it. Such a contention would involve consideration of the political rights and wrongs of maintaining nuclear weapons. The response of their Lordships was to construe 'purpose' narrowly in the same fashion as intention in order to exclude motive. Since their immediate intention ('direct purpose') was to obstruct the airfield, their purpose was 'prejudicial'. Their ultimate aim ('indirect purpose') to get rid of nuclear weapons was motive and irrelevant. It was unnecessary to consider whether nuclear disarmament was 'prejudicial'.

Nonetheless, there are certainly cases where a good motive has led the courts to the view that the ingredients of the offence were not established where it is inconceivable that they would have so held had D's motive been bad.

? QUESTION 3.10

We have already examined two such cases in this chapter. Can you recall them and the arguments involved? Refer to 3.3.1 above to refresh your memory.

The courts restricted the normal meaning of intention to avoid the conviction of people who acted from honourable motives. It is difficult to resist the conclusion that the courts' willingness to stretch *mens rea* concepts in *Steane* and *Ahlers* whilst narrowing them in *Chandler* is based simply on the political and moral acceptability of the conduct to them (see also the discussion of *Woollin* at 3.3.2 above and *Gillick* in *Cases and Materials* (14.4.2)).

Occasionally, statutory definitions of offences compel the courts to take D's motive into account in certain situations. This can be expressed in and be obvious from the statutory wording, or be implicit and hidden in the concepts used by the offence definition. The former is illustrated by the creation of a number of 'racially or religiously aggravated' offences by the Crime and Disorder Act 1998 as amended by the Anti-Terrorism, Crime and Security Act 2001 (adding 'religiously'). These convert certain existing offences (such as assault and other offences of violence against the person) into more serious offences with increased penalties where, *inter alia*, 'the offence is motivated (wholly or partly) by hostility towards members of a racial or religious group, based on their membership of that group' (ss. 28–32). Examples of the latter are the concepts of 'unwarranted demand' in blackmail (see 12.8.1.2 below) and 'dishonesty' in theft and various other Theft Act offences (see 10.4.2.1).

Finally, motive is an essential consideration in the elements of a number of the general defences to criminal liability. Thus, D will avoid criminal liability for violence inflicted in using reasonable force in self-defence or the prevention of crime. His reason for acting (i.e., his motive) must be self-defence or the prevention of crime (see 8.6). Similarly, if D's motive for committing the 'crime' is threats of serious violence if he does not, this could give him the defence of duress by threats (see 9.3). A laudable motive may open the way for the defence of necessity (or, at least, duress of circumstances) to be invoked, although, as we shall see, the courts strive to keep the lid on this defence precisely because it provides a potential back entrance for wide-ranging considerations of motive (see 9.4 and 9.5).

3.3.5 **Further or ulterior intent**

'Further' or 'ulterior' intent are terms which are synonymous and can be used interchangeably. They are not difficult to understand with the help of a concrete illustration. They arise where a crime is so defined that the *mens rea* includes an intention to produce a consequence which **goes beyond (is ulterior to)** the physical conduct required by the *actus reus* of the crime. For example, s. 1(3) of the Protection from Eviction Act 1977 makes it an offence, *inter alia*, persistently to withdraw or withhold services reasonably required for the occupation of premises as a residence, 'with intent to cause the residential occupier of any premises...(a) to give up the occupation of the premises or any part thereof...'.

The *actus reus* is performed by withholding services, e.g., cutting off electricity and does not require that, as a result, the occupier actually gives up occupation of the premises. The offence simply requires D to **intend** to cause the occupier to give up occupation of the premises and this state of mind is the ulterior intent to produce a consequence going beyond the physical conduct needed for the *actus reus*.

EXERCISE 3.2

Read s. 9(1)(a) of the Theft Act 1968 (*Cases and Materials* (12.3.1)) for the classic example of ulterior intent.

3.3.6 **Specific and basic intent**

'Specific intent' is a misleading expression since it is used with variable meanings. The possible meanings are:

(a) as synonymous with ulterior intent;

(b) as synonymous with direct intent, i.e., aim or purpose intention; or

(c) the state of mind required in offences where voluntary intoxication which prevents D having that state of mind will be a defence.

The term 'specific intent' in this last sense is contrasted with an even more confusing term—'basic intent'. This expression is used by the courts to refer to offences to which, because they are not specific intent offences, voluntary intoxication can never be a defence. The confusing thing is that the offences to which voluntary intoxication can never be a defence are offences where no intent needs to be proved at all—offences where mere recklessness suffices for conviction. We will be examining these matters in detail when we come on to the defence of intoxication in **Chapter 8**.

3.4 **Recklessness**

Whilst for some crimes only intention and intention alone will suffice for the *mens rea*, for many crimes proof of either intention or recklessness will secure a conviction. Therefore if a person is reckless as to the prohibited consequence that will often be enough.

?   **QUESTION** 3.11

How would you discover whether recklessness does suffice?

The only way to find out if proof of recklessness is enough for a conviction in any particular case is to examine the definition of the offence charged.

In essence, recklessness means unjustifiable risk-taking, i.e., actions involve a risk of the prohibited conduct or consequence occurring and it is unreasonable in the circumstances to take that risk.

At one time the courts were moving towards confining the term reckless to subjective recklessness (some writers call it '*Cunningham*' recklessness after a significant Court of

Appeal case in 1957), but that trend was abruptly reversed by the House of Lords in *Metropolitan Police Commissioner* v *Caldwell* [1981] 1 All ER 961, which established objective recklessness (sometimes called '*Caldwell*' recklessness). The House of Lords in *Caldwell* indicated that wherever the term 'reckless', 'recklessly', etc. appeared in the statutory wording defining an offence it should be construed as including either type. If either one is proved the *mens rea* is established. As we shall see, the courts were never comfortable with *Caldwell* and there has been a growing trend to retreat from its supposed general application and to find reasons for not applying it to particular offences. The House of Lords' decision in *Reid* [1992] 3 All ER 673 was a milestone in this regard, indicating that the House itself was softening its stance and, perhaps, preparing the way for a fundamental change in the *Caldwell* formulation.

In the event, that change was even more radical than expected. Rather than simply modifying the test, the House of Lords in *G* [2003] UKHL 50 (*Cases and Materials* (3.4.2.2)) performed a complete about-turn and abolished it. Henceforth, *Caldwell* should no longer be followed. It is true that the House confined itself to the meaning of 'reckless' in the Criminal Damage Act 1971, but it is likely in practice to have consigned the concept of objective recklessness to general oblivion. Indeed, even before *G*, given that the offence of reckless driving had been abolished by the legislature, it was not easy to find offences other than criminal damage to which *Caldwell* had been applied. (One such offence might have been the now repealed s. 5(5) of the Data Protection Act 1984—'recklessly' contravening any of the provisions in s. 5 (*Data Protection Registrar* v *Amnesty International* [1995] Crim LR 633, DC).) **From now on, it appears that the concept of recklessness means only subjective recklessness and nothing else**.

3.4.1 Unjustifiable risk

In **both** types of recklessness, subjective or objective, the risk of the proscribed consequence which D is taking must be an **unjustifiable** risk. It must be unreasonable to run the risk of the harmful consequence.

> **? QUESTION** 3.12
>
> If V has been injured by D engaging in conduct which D had realised, before engaging in it, might cause injury to others, can you explain why we might not regard him as reckless in relation to causing injury?

Many of our everyday activities involve the risk of, say, injuring another or damaging property, e.g., driving. The risk involved in normal driving is usually acceptable to the courts and not unjustifiable. Similarly, surgeons performing routine operations, e.g., pinning a broken arm, know that this involves a small but clear risk of death; but it is socially acceptable.

How do you tell if the risk is unjustifiable? It is an objective not a subjective question. It is not whether D **thinks** that it is unjustifiable but whether the court decides that it is unacceptable. In making that judgment the court will balance the social utility of the activity against the probability of the harmful consequence occurring coupled with the seriousness or gravity of that consequence if it does ensue, e.g., an ambulance driver on his way to an emergency would receive more latitude than someone who is late for a Robbie Williams concert. Clearly, the court must engage in a value judgement about D's conduct and whether it is worthwhile from the community's point of view to permit that kind of activity despite the risks it generates.

Thus, the court is the sole arbiter of whether the risk was unreasonable, D's view being irrelevant. Reminding ourselves that the justifiability requirement is common to both types of recklessness, we must now examine what these types are.

3.4.2 Subjective recklessness

The key element in subjective recklessness is that D must **know** that he is taking a risk of the forbidden consequence occurring. He is **consciously** taking the risk. He is deliberately taking the risk. He realises that the consequence might occur. He recognises that there is a risk of it. He is aware of the chance of it happening. He foresees the possibility of it occurring. He knows it might happen but he carries on regardless deliberately taking the risk. If the court decides the risk was unjustifiable, D is subjectively reckless in regard to it (see *Cunningham* [1957] 2 All ER 412 and *Stephenson* [1979] 2 All ER 1198—*Cases and Materials* (3.4.2)).

Geoffrey Lane LJ explained in *Stephenson* that D is reckless in relation to damaging property 'when he carries out the deliberate act [in this case lighting a fire] appreciating that there is a risk that damage to property may result from his act. It is however not the taking of every risk which could properly be classed as reckless. The risk must be one which it is in all the circumstances unreasonable for him to take.'

? QUESTION 3.13

Suppose you see an old car tyre on top of a cliff and you decide to roll it over the cliff edge on to the beach below. If it strikes and injures someone on the beach, what would determine whether you:

(a) intended to injure; or

(b) were subjectively reckless as to injury?

If you were hoping (or aiming) to injure someone, you would intend it. Intention can also be found from the fact that D realised that injury was virtually certain (*Woollin*). If you knew that people were packed like sardines on the beach below, this might be feasible. In terms of subjective recklessness, the prosecution would have to show two things:

(a) that you were aware of the risk of injury; and

(b) that it was unreasonable in those circumstances for you to take that risk.

In regard to the first question, the test is your actual awareness. You would not need to know that injury was likely to result still less that it **would** result, but merely that it was a possibility, however slight (*Chief Constable of Avon* v *Shimmen* (1986) 84 Cr App R 7, DC; *DPP* v *A* [2001] Crim LR 140, DC). If, however, the possibility of injuring never occurred to you, **subjective** recklessness would be ruled out. The second question would be easily resolved against you. There would, in the court's eyes, be no social utility in your conduct so that it would be unreasonable to take the risk of causing injury even if that was an unlikely possibility, e.g., the weather was bad and there were few people on the beach.

Typical instances of crimes where only subjective recklessness suffices even in the days of *Caldwell* are those where the statute uses the word 'maliciously' to describe the *mens rea*, e.g., s. 20 of the Offences Against the Person Act 1861 and also it seems the offences of common assault and assault occasioning actual bodily harm (*Savage; Parmenter* [1991] 4 All ER 698, HL—see further 4.4.2.2). Of course, since *G* [2003] UKHL 50 (*Cases and Materials* (3.4.3.3)), 'reckless' in the Criminal Damage Act 1971 can only be satisfied by proof of subjective recklessness—D must be shown to have realised he was risking damage to property.

The House of Lords in *G* adopted the definition given by the Law Commission in its draft Criminal Code Bill (Law Com. No. 177, 1989):

A person acts recklessly . . . with respect to—

(i) a circumstance when he is aware of a risk that it exists or will exist;

(ii) a result, when he is aware of a risk that it will occur;

and it is, in the circumstances known to him, unreasonable to take the risk.

Although this was in relation to criminal damage, there seems little doubt that it will now form the accepted definition of recklessness throughout the criminal law.

3.4.3 **Objective recklessness**

It is likely that the House of Lords' decision in *G* not to follow *Caldwell* in relation to offences of criminal damage heralds the complete demise of the concept of objective recklessness. Probably most but certainly not all academic writers would welcome this development as eliminating the terminological confusion surrounding recklessness since *Caldwell*. As we shall see later, objective recklessness has much more in common with gross negligence than subjective recklessness and can be readily subsumed under that head of culpability. In order to understand the arguments in *G*, it is necessary to review the concepts introduced by *Caldwell* but, happily, we can now dispense with much of the detail.

The basic idea of objective recklessness is best explained by quoting Lord Diplock's model direction for the jury set out in *Caldwell* (*Cases and Materials* (3.4.3)) expounding the meaning of reckless in the offence of criminal damage:

A person is reckless as to whether or not any property would be destroyed or damaged if—

(1) he does an act which creates an obvious risk that property will be destroyed or damaged; **and**

(2) when he does the act he **either**

(a) has not given any thought to the possibility of there being any such risk; **or**

(b) has recognised that there was some risk involved and has nonetheless gone on to do it.

(We have supplied the numbering and lettering in an effort to make the ingredients of the definition clearer.)

This was endorsed by the House of Lords in *Lawrence* [1981] 1 All ER 974 (a case of reckless driving) except that the House held that the risk had to be both obvious and **serious**. However, the House of Lords in *Reid* [1992] 3 All ER 673 emphasised that Lord Diplock's direction is only a guideline and is not to be treated as carved in stone. Indeed, two of the Lords formulated an alternative model direction. (See *Cases and Materials* (3.4.3) for both cases.)

? QUESTION 3.14

Concentrating for the moment on element 2 of Lord Diplock's statement, in what way does this differ from *subjective* recklessness?

According to *Caldwell* and *Lawrence* therefore, the prosecution must in all cases prove element 1 and **either** element 2(a) **or** element 2(b). Disposing of element 2(b) first, this is in fact the type of recklessness we have described as subjective recklessness. D knows there is some risk; he has recognised it and gone ahead regardless. He is subjectively reckless. Nobody would quarrel with that amounting to recklessness.

The real criticism has been directed at the other alternative given in *Caldwell*—element 2(a). The first criticism is specific to the offence of criminal damage. It is clear from the Law Commission's Report (Law Com. No. 29) which led to the Criminal Damage Act 1971 that the word 'reckless' in criminal damage, meant **only** subjective recklessness and this is how it was understood by the Court of Appeal until *Caldwell* (see, e.g., *Stephenson*). The House of Lords simply ignored that. This is clearly demonstrated in *G*.

Secondly, and more importantly, *Caldwell* means that D can be convicted of offences of recklessness where he has no idea that his actions involve any risk at all of the prohibited consequence. Although Lord Diplock describes failing to think about a risk as the *mens rea*, it is really a misuse of language to so describe it because it is an absence of a state of mind, i.e., D is being convicted for **not** having a particular state of mind, for not thinking about the risk, for 'giving no thought to' the risk. This is particularly objectionable where, through no fault of his own, D does not have the ordinary person's capacity to perceive obvious risks, e.g., because of educational subnormality. This was the main reason why *Caldwell* was overturned in *G* where the House of Lords thought it 'capable of leading to obvious unfairness'.

Let us examine the elements of objective recklessness in more detail.

3.4.3.1 'Creates an obvious and serious risk'

Normally, whether a risk was 'obvious and serious' was decided by the jury, but it was permissible for the judge to rule that there was no evidence fit to go before the jury (as happened in the Channel Ferry disaster case, *P & O European Ferries (Dover) Ltd* (1990) 93 Cr App R 72, Cen. Crim. Ct).

What mattered was whether it would have been obvious immediately **before** D went ahead with his actions (not whether it was 'obvious' with **hindsight**). 'Obvious' seemed to refer solely to the probability of the risk, whereas 'serious' seemed to refer both to the likelihood of the risk occurring and to the gravity of the harm which might ensue if the risk eventuated (*cf.* Lord Goff in *Reid*). In so far as there were explanations in the cases, it seemed to require that the risk be 'not negligible', i.e., significant both in terms of probability of harm and seriousness of harm. Turner J in the Channel Ferry disaster case thought the words 'obvious and serious' 'convey a meaning that the defendant's perception of the existence of risk was seriously deficient when compared to that of a reasonably prudent person engaged in the same kind of activity as that of the defendant whose conduct is being called into question.'

You may recall that the model direction from *Caldwell* (see 3.4.3) seemed to require proof of element 1, i.e., that the risk was 'obvious' (and, *Lawrence* adds, 'serious') in every case including the subjective limb which we have termed element 2(b). However, this was called into question by the House of Lords' decision in *Reid*, where Lords Goff and Browne-Wilkinson expressed the view that, for the subjective limb (i.e., 2(b)) where D had recognised the risk, there was no need for that risk to have been 'obvious'. The point they were making is that if D **knows** he is taking the risk of causing the prohibited consequence, there is no reason why it should have to be shown to be 'obvious' to a reasonable person. On the other hand, where D has **not** seen the risk because he has not given thought to it (i.e., 2(a)), then it must be proved that the risk was objectively obvious in order to establish that D **ought** to have thought about it.

3.4.3.2 Obvious to whom?

There are two possibilities. One is to say that the risk must only be obvious to an ordinary prudent or reasonable person who stops to think. The other is to say that it would have to be obvious to D **if he** stopped to think. Although the two formulations appear similar, occasionally they would give a completely different result. That would happen where for some reason, e.g., extreme youth and inexperience, low intelligence or mental abnormality, D's own perceptions would be quite different from a normal person's so that he would not see a risk which would be patently obvious to all normal people.

Although there were ambiguities in *Caldwell*, the House of Lords made it clear in *Lawrence* that the risk need only be obvious to a reasonable person. It was immaterial that for some blameless reason, e.g., mental subnormality or lack of knowledge, experience and maturity due to youth, it would not have been seen as obvious by D even if D had stopped to think before acting. Furthermore, the reasonable person was normal in every way and the courts consistently refused to invest the reasonable, prudent person with any characteristics of D which might bear on his ability to foresee the risk, not even basic characteristics which are common to all, e.g., age and sex (see *Stephen Malcolm R* (1984) 79 Cr App R 334, CA).

Elliott v *C* [1983] 2 All ER 1005, DC (*Case and Materials* (3.4.3.2)) and *G* itself illustrate the sort of cases where the test could give rise to injustice. In *G*, the defendants, aged 11 and 12, were messing about in the backyard of the Co-op shop in Newport Pagnell with some bundles of newspapers they found there. They set light to some of the papers, threw them under a large plastic wheelie bin and left. The fire spread to the fascia of the overhanging eave and then into the roof space and eventually to adjoining buildings causing £1m worth of damage. The defendants could have been charged with damaging the wheelie bin since it was clear that they intended to damage the bin or, at the very least, realised that it might be damaged. However, they were charged with damaging the **buildings**. It was accepted that the boys expected the fire to go out itself on the concrete floor and that neither appreciated that there was any risk of the fire spreading to the buildings. Nonetheless because the risk to the buildings would have been obvious to any reasonable adult, they were objectively reckless and held guilty by the Court of Appeal. The House of Lords overturned the conviction because it was not prepared to stomach the 'obvious unfairness' (a view apparently shared by the trial judge and jury) in convicting 'a defendant (least of all a child) on the strength of what someone else would have apprehended' where 'the defendant himself had no such apprehension'.

One solution might have been to keep the basic test but to invest the reasonable person with those characteristics of D which, through no fault of his own, might reduce his ability to foresee what would be obvious to any normal person. There had been signs in *Reid* that the House of Lords might be willing to exclude from recklessness some cases where D's 'capacity to appreciate risks was adversely affected by some condition not involving fault on his part' (Lord Keith), but they were not taken up by the Court of Appeal which felt that only the House of Lords could modify the strict test laid down in *Caldwell* and *Lawrence* (see *Coles* [1995] 1 Cr App R 157, CA and *Gemmell and Richards* [2002] Crim LR 926, CA—the case which became *G* in the House of Lords). However, the House of Lords in *G*, perhaps mindful of the tortuous complications encountered in operating the reasonable man concept in the defence of provocation (see 7.6.2.2 below), opted to eliminate objective recklessness and the *Caldwell* formulation altogether rather than try to reformulate it in a more acceptable way.

3.4.3.3 The *Caldwell* lacuna or loophole—ruling out the risk

> **? QUESTION** 3.15
>
> Assuming that there was an obvious and serious risk in the prescribed sense, would it be the case that D would always be reckless if he took it, whether consciously or accidentally? After all under *Caldwell* he was reckless if he recognised the risk and he was reckless if he gave no thought to it.

There was a third possibility which was not covered by the *Caldwell* definition and which was therefore dubbed by some academics as a lacuna or loophole. Lacuna simply means 'gap'. This is where D **did** give thought to the risk but erroneously concluded that there was no risk. He ruled out the risk. He therefore did not recognise there was a risk when he acted and so was not subjectively reckless. Neither was it the case that he had given no thought to it and so was not objectively reckless under *Caldwell*. He had, however stupidly, formed the view that there was no danger. This is what our Question is driving at.

A perfect example would be supplied by the fact situation in *Lamb* [1967] 2 All ER 1282, CA, [1967] 2 QB 981. (This was a pre-*Caldwell* case on manslaughter and for that reason, there was of course no discussion of the *Caldwell* lacuna.) D was playing with a revolver. He checked to see that the bullet chamber opposite the firing pin was empty and then in jest pointed the gun at his friend, who was sharing the joke. He pulled the trigger and shot his friend who died laughing. D had failed to appreciate that on pulling the trigger the chamber revolved one space before the firing pin struck. There was a live bullet in the next chamber. D had given thought to the risk of the gun firing and had wrongly concluded there was **no** risk of it firing. Therefore D would not be reckless under either limb of *Caldwell*.

Although this situation is outside *Caldwell*, we know of no case where D was acquitted for that reason. The defence unsuccessfully pleaded the lacuna in *Chief Constable of Avon* v *Shimmen* (1986) 84 Cr App R 7, DC (*Cases and Materials* (3.4.3.3)), and in *Merrick* [1996] 1 Cr App R 130, CA (*Cases and Materials* (3.4.3.3)), and it might have been argued (but was not) in *Crossman* [1986] Crim LR 406. The House of Lords in *Reid* [1992] 3 All ER 673 recognised obiter the existence of the *Caldwell* lacuna.

3.4.4 **Why did the House of Lords in *G* reject *Caldwell*?**

Four reasons were advanced for this about-turn.

(1) As a matter of principle, conviction for a serious crime should require proof of a 'culpable' state of mind in the form of actual perception of the risk of the harmful consequence. Mere 'stupidity or lack of imagination' leading to failure to appreciate the risk should not expose someone 'to conviction of serious crime or the risk of punishment.' [32]

(2) The *Caldwell* 'direction is capable of leading to obvious unfairness . . . It is neither moral nor just to convict a defendant (least of all a child) on the strength of what someone else would have apprehended if the defendant himself had no such apprehension.' This reason elides with the first but its poorly articulated basis probably resides in the failure of *Caldwell* (or more accurately subsequent authorities) to give any concession where D's **capacity** to appreciate the risk (in this case, through the Ds' youth and inexperience) is impaired through no fault of his own. [33]

(3) 'Leading scholars of the day' had subjected *Caldwell* to 'reasoned and outspoken criticism' and judges and practitioners had expressed widespread reservations about it. [34]

(4) The framers of the Criminal Damage Act clearly intended 'reckless' to be limited to subjective recklessness and therefore Caldwell misinterpreted the statute. Because 'this misinterpretation is offensive to principle [ground 1 above] and is apt to cause injustice [ground 2 above] . . . the need to correct the misinterpretation is compelling.' [35]

Taking those reasons in reverse order, the fourth is incontrovertible and clearly demonstrated in Lord Bingham's historical review of the legislation. The third is also true but equally the zealous subjectivism espoused by Professors Smith and Williams has attracted considerable criticism from the current crop of academic commentators. Many of them would argue for *Caldwell* recklessness albeit in a modified form to cater for fault-free incapacity. Some judges, especially at Court of Appeal level, have certainly been hostile to unadulterated *Caldwell* recklessness although it is not clear that their hostility would extend to a suitably modified form.

This leads to the second reason—*Caldwell* recklessness 'is capable of leading to obvious unfairness'. The particular concern underlying this was probably the reduced ability of the defendant children to foresee the risk of the fire spreading owing to their age-based immaturity and inexperience. Obviously they could not help their immaturity and inex-perience and therefore their failure to foresee the obvious was not culpable. However, in the terms in which it is put, the reason is the broader one that 'it is neither moral nor just to convict a defendant (least of all a child) on the strength of what someone else would have apprehended if the defendant himself had no such apprehension.' That hard-core subjectivism surely goes too far and ignores the vast range of offences including manslaughter where inadvertence can found liability. Contrary to Lord Bingham's first reason that serious crime should as a matter of principle require proof of conscious risk-taking, there is nothing necessarily unjust or immoral about basing culpability on inadvertence. That will depend on the particular offence involved. The Sexual Offences Act 2003 utilises inadvertence-based culpability in a number of the revised sexual offences (see **Chapter 5**). This is neither unjust nor immoral but a perfectly tenable and rational response, made after due consideration, to resolve identified problems. Whilst one can accept that serious crimes ought to require serious culpability which would normally be a minimum of subjective recklessness, this should only be a starting point and not be elevated to the status of unswerving principle.

The House firmly rejected the idea of retaining the *Caldwell* principle in a modified form designed to take into account any blame-free reduced capacity of perception on the part of the accused at [37], [57] and [63]. The major reasons seemed to be that, although this might eliminate the worst of the injustices generated by *Caldwell*, it would perpetuate the misinterpretation of the Criminal Damage Act and would still offend Lord Bingham's point of principle that full *mens rea* should be required for serious offences. Perhaps more telling still, in practice, it would be difficult to devise such a modification and it would be bound to lead to 'difficult and contentious argument concerning the qualities and characteristics to be taken into account'. The House would be well aware of the convolutions and confusions reaped in *Smith (Morgan)* [2001] 1 AC 146, HL (6.6.2.2 below) in regard to similar problems in the law of provocation!

3.4.5 **Conclusion on recklessness**

As we have already indicated (see 3.4.2) the Law Commission wanted to confine the definition of recklessness to subjective recklessness so that there would again be a clear and simple dividing line between recklessness and negligence. Advertent or conscious risk-taking would be recklessness; inadvertent risk-taking could only be negligence. The introduction of the objective limb into recklessness by *Caldwell* blurred that sharp distinction with negligence. Happily the about-turn by the House of Lords in *G* has restored that simple and clear division. Although the House of Lords professed to confine itself to the meaning of 'reckless' in the Criminal Damage Act, it seems unlikely that its views would not be applied to the concept of recklessness wherever it appears in the criminal law unless there is a compelling reason in the statutory wording of the offence for a different construction. It looks like objective recklessness is effectively dead!

3.4.6 **Subjective recklessness—some remaining problems**

Although, by and large, the distinction between subjective recklessness and negligence is 'simple and clear', yet there are still some borderline situations which continue to give trouble.

The narrowness of fault based entirely on cognition—D's awareness of risk—has prompted the courts on occasion to enlarge their notion of **subjective** recklessness even where they have accepted that that is the minimum required to satisfy the *mens rea* of the offence before them. One case is where the accused acts in a fit of anger without thinking. In *Parker* [1977] 2 All ER 37, D broke a public telephone when he crashed it down in frustration after failing to make a call. D claimed to have acted without considering the risk of damaging the phone. The Court held that if he did not know of the risk, then he 'deliberately closed his mind to the obvious—the obvious being that damage in these circumstances was inevitable.' That sufficed for the subjective recklessness assumed, before *Caldwell*, to be necessary. Lord Bingham in *G* interprets closing the mind to risk as predicating actual realisation of risk (at [14]) but, if that is so, D must 'know' of the risk and there is no point in complicating things by adding a redundant alternative. The truth is that, if the alternative has any point, it does cover cases where, in reality, D was not aware of the risk at the time he acted because of his rage and frustration. However, it may be limited to cases where the risk is plainly inherent in and inextricably bound up with D's actions so that he can be assumed to be aware of the risk in the back of his mind even if he was not thinking about it at the time. It is a stretch but it can be regarded as a case where D must, however fleetingly, have been aware of the risk but his rage and frustration had despatched it to the inner recesses of his mind.

A second case which has exercised the courts especially in the offence of rape is where D 'could not care less' or is 'indifferent' about the risk and this is discussed at 3.6.5 below since it is likely to relate primarily to *mens rea* in respect of circumstances rather than consequences.

3.5 Negligence

Negligence is a failure by D to act in conformity with an objective standard decided on by the court looking back on what actually happened in the situation. Therefore, D's actual state of mind at the time of his actions is irrelevant. The yardstick used by the court in judging D's conduct is how it would expect a reasonable person to have behaved in those circumstances.

Negligence has two forms, which we can term **ordinary** negligence and **gross** negligence. Gross negligence can be regarded as extreme or serious negligence and very similar to the objective limb of *Caldwell* recklessness. Ordinary negligence is average carelessness. The dividing line between gross and ordinary negligence, is incapable of exact definition, being a matter of degree and dependent on individual judgments of the courts in particular cases. The distinction need not usually be made because most offences of negligence require proof only of ordinary negligence, e.g., driving without due care and attention. One major negligence offence where ordinary negligence is insufficient is manslaughter, for which gross negligence is needed (*Adomako* [1994] 3 All ER 79, HL).

In *Andrews* v *DPP* [1937] 2 All ER 552, HL, Lord Atkin said: 'Simple lack of care such as will constitute civil liability is not enough. For the purpose of the criminal law there are degrees of negligence, and a very high degree of negligence is required to be proved before the felony [manslaughter] is established.' Gross, culpable or criminal negligence are all terms which have been used for this serious form of negligence.

Lord Hewart CJ in *Bateman* (1925) 94 LJKB 791 described the distinction between gross negligence and civil negligence as follows:

> ... in order to establish criminal liability the facts must be such that, in the opinion of the jury, the negligence of the accused went beyond a mere matter of compensation between subjects and showed such disregard for the life and safety of others as to amount to a crime against the state and conduct deserving punishment.

Unfortunately this 'definition' is circular since it does not tell us what amount of 'disregard for the life and safety of others' constitutes 'a crime against the state'. It is therefore of little concrete assistance in resolving any particular fact situation.

If ordinary negligence is average carelessness where the standard the courts require to be observed is pitched at a fairly high level making it relatively difficult to comply with, then gross negligence is extreme or very serious negligence where the standard is pitched at a much lower level and is therefore very easy to comply with. In other words, the risk is so much more obvious and serious and the measures or precautions needed to prevent it occurring so much easier that it is difficult to see how anyone could fail to see the risk and/or take the precautions or modify his conduct to prevent it occurring. We will be exploring these matters further in **Chapter 6** when we examine involuntary manslaughter.

?   **QUESTION** 3.16

In judging whether D has been negligent, can we take into account any of D's characteristics which affect his ability to comply with the set standard of conduct?

In general terms, negligence imposes an objective standard which is the same for all. No account is normally taken of D's ability to conform to the norm. The standard of the ordinary prudent motorist applies just as much to a learner driver taking their first lesson as a driver of many years' experience. It is true that the standard expected may **increase** due to a characteristic of D in the sense that if D holds himself out as possessing a particular expertise or skill, e.g., a doctor or electrician, he will be judged against the standard of a reasonably competent person with that skill or expertise. But it is generally out of the question to lower the required standard of behaviour to take account of what we could reasonably expect of D given his weaknesses. This seems to be so even in the case of the serious offence of manslaughter as illustrated by a case we discussed at 2.7.4.2 above, *Stone and Dobinson*, where no concession was made to the limited intelligence and social inadequacy of the defendants.

Interestingly, the injustice of an absolutely objective stance is raised even more starkly by a new offence created by s. 5 of the Domestic Violence, Crime and Victims Act 2004. This offence is designed to cover the case where a child (or vulnerable adult) has been killed by the unlawful act of a member of its household but it cannot be proved which member caused the death, thus usually precluding a conviction for murder or manslaughter. Any member of the household who is 16 or over and had frequent contact with V may be convicted of 'causing or allowing' the death provided V was at significant risk of serious physical harm from such an unlawful act. For this serious offence carrying a maximum of 14 years' imprisonment, the fault element is simple (not even gross) negligence. It suffices that D 'ought to have been aware' (a) of the aforesaid risk of serious physical injury and (b) the possibility of the circumstances in which the killing occurred, arising. The final negligence requirement is that D 'failed to take such steps as he could reasonably have been expected to have taken to protect V from the risk'. Surely the courts must decide what D 'could reasonably have been expected to' do in the context of his own situation, intelligence, social adequacy and so forth.

3.5.1 **Negligence and recklessness**

The effective abolition of objective recklessness by the House of Lords in *G* means that the previously clear distinction between recklessness and negligence has been restored. Recklessness now means subjective recklessness and that requires deliberate or advertent, unjustifiable risk-taking, whereas negligence catches accidental or inadvertent, unjustifiable risk-taking. *Caldwell* had created a large overlap between recklessness and negligence since objective recklessness was also a species of inadvertent risk-taking. However, the elimination of objective recklessness ensures the quite distinct categories explained above and we need not concern ourselves with the nature of the previous overlap.

3.5.2 **Negligence and defences**

Although it is relatively uncommon to define the fault element of offences **positively** in terms of negligence, manslaughter and careless driving being notable exceptions (along with a number of offences under the occupational health and safety statutes such as the Health and Safety at Work etc. Act 1974), it is quite common for statutes which impose strict liability, i.e., liability without fault, to include no negligence defences (see further **Chapter 13**). For example, s. 21 of the Food Safety Act 1990 provides D with a defence to the strict liability offences created by the statute if he proves 'that he took all reasonable precautions and exercised all due diligence to avoid the commission of the offence . . .'—in other words, if he shows he acted without negligence.

3.6 *Mens rea* as to circumstances

The *actus reus* of offences very often requires the presence or existence of prescribed circumstances or facts, in addition to the act and/or consequence which is the central feature of the crime charged. Just as *mens rea* is usually required in relation to acts and consequences so it is required in relation to defined circumstances. However, although the *mens rea* concepts used are often similar, there are some differences, which can be seen in **Figure 3.3** below.

You will notice that most of the concepts utilised in respect of acts and consequences apply equally to circumstances. The main difference relates to subjective states of mind

Subjective			Objective	
Intention/ knowledge	*Wilful blindness*	*Subjective recklessness (suspicion)*	*Objective recklessness*	*Negligence*
Definite and correct belief that the circumstance exists (D has no substantial doubt)	D **is** aware of the possibility that the fact or circumstance exists but deliberately fails to enquire in order to avoid the unpalatable truth	D **is** aware of the possibility that the fact or circumstance exists but carries on regardless	D gives no thought to the possibility that an obvious fact or circumstance exists ---------------------- *Gross negligence* D is not aware of the possible existence of a blindingly obvious fact or circumstance	*Ordinary negligence* D is **not** aware of the possibility of a fact or circumstance where the ordinary prudent person would be (D **ought** to have been aware of it)

Figure 3.3 *Mens rea* in relation to circumstances forming part of the *actus reus*

where 'knowledge' tends to replace 'intention' and the concept of wilful blindness is utilised.

3.6.1 Intention

We do not know of any offence which requires the prosecution to prove that D, in the true sense, intended a particular circumstance to exist at the time of his acts. The reason is that if you intend a circumstance to exist, it means that you **hope** it exists or will exist when you perform your actions. For example, if such a state of mind was required in the offence of handling stolen goods, it would need to be proven that D hoped the goods were stolen. It would be extraordinarily difficult to prove this because every defendant could plausibly assert that he would have been delighted to discover that the goods he thought were stolen were not in fact stolen! In relation to circumstances, therefore, intention translates into 'knowledge'. If, therefore, the *mens rea* of rape was defined as an intention to have sexual intercourse without the victim's consent, this would require (a) an intention to have sexual intercourse and (b) knowing that the victim was not consenting.

3.6.2 Knowledge and belief

You may be forgiven for thinking that the word 'know' would be clear and straightforward, meaning **actual** knowledge by D that the circumstance does or will exist at the time of his acts. This is not so. We run into problems of degree. Very little is certain in human affairs and it may be very difficult to know with absolute certainty that the circumstance exists or will exist. According to *Hall* (1985) 81 Cr App R 260, CA a person would have actual knowledge that goods were stolen where he was 'told by someone with first-hand knowledge (someone such as the thief or burglar)'. That seems to translate into a requirement for a **definite and correct** belief that the circumstance exists (in that case, that the goods were stolen). As it was put by the House of Lords in *Montila* [2004] UKHL 50 at [27], 'A person cannot know something is A when in fact it is B. The proposition that a person knows something is A is based on the premise that it is true that it is A.'

In ordinary language, belief lies somewhere between actual knowledge and subjective recklessness. It can range from absolute conviction (certainty) to lukewarm (possibility). In legal terms, however, what seems to be the minimum required is that D must believe with a clear conviction or virtual certainty that the relevant fact or circumstance exists. D has no **significant** doubt about it. According to *Forsyth* [1997] 2 Cr App R 299, CA, 'belief is the mental acceptance of a fact as true or existing'. (See further 12.9.2.2 below.)

It seems that if D firmly believes (i.e., he has no substantial doubt) that the circumstance exists and he is correct in that belief, he will be taken to 'know' it. It is not enough to believe that it probably exists, still less that it might possibly exist but equally **absolute** certainty is not required.

3.6.3 **Wilful blindness and subjective recklessness**

If D is wilfully blind, he suspects that the fact or circumstance exists but deliberately refrains from enquiring further in case he learns the unpalatable truth. The person who buys goods at a knockdown price from a stranger in a pub asks no questions as to their origin because he does not want to have his suspicions confirmed. He thinks it better not to 'know'. He is aware that the goods might be stolen, but he deliberately turns a blind eye to it.

In the ordinary case, the courts will read 'knowingly' as embracing wilful blindness, which is sometimes referred to as knowledge of the second degree. (*Roper* v *Taylor's Central Garages* [1951] 2 TLR 284 (*Cases and Materials* (3.6.3).)

? QUESTION 3.17

In *Westminster City Council* v *Croyalgrange Ltd* [1986] 2 All ER 353, HL (see *Cases and Materials* (3.6.3)), D was charged with the offence of 'knowingly' permitting his premises to be used as a sex establishment without a licence. In the light of the discussion above, what do you think would suffice as the *mens rea* for this offence?

Where 'knowingly' appears, it will normally be construed as applying to all the elements necessary for the *actus reus*, not just one or some of them. Therefore, in the *Croyalgrange* case, D had to 'know' not only that the premises were being used as a sex establishment, but also that there was no licence. 'Know' was, as usual, construed to include not only actual knowledge of these two facts but also wilful blindness as to them, i.e., if D 'had deliberately shut his eyes to the obvious or refrained from enquiry because he suspected the truth but did not want to have his suspicions confirmed'.

Wilful blindness is a **form** of subjective recklessness and certainly anyone who is wilfully blind must realise that the fact or circumstance might exist, i.e., he 'suspects the truth'. However, it does contain an extra ingredient so that the converse is not true. It is not sufficient simply to be subjectively reckless. As well as realising that the circumstance might exist, D must deliberately refrain from enquiry where the means of knowledge might easily be available, in order to avoid the unpalatable answer. Although a species of recklessness and falling short of actual knowledge, wilful blindness is generally regarded as 'knowledge'.

Reflecting this, the Law Commission's draft Criminal Code (Law Com. No. 177) proposes the following:

> ...a person acts...'knowingly' with respect to a circumstance not only when he is aware that it exists or will exist, but also when he avoids taking steps that might confirm his belief that it exists or will exist.

The first part of the definition is a restatement of **actual** knowledge. D must know (be aware) that the circumstance **does** exist or **will** exist. Subjective recklessness would be satisfied if D knew that it **might** exist. The limited extension beyond actual knowledge predicates that he **believes** that the circumstance exists or will exist and presumably belief is intended to be understood in the sense explained above. Contrast this with the definition of 'recklessly' in the more recent draft Criminal Law Bill: '...a person acts... "recklessly" with respect to...a circumstance, when he is aware of a risk that it exists or will exist...' D need only be aware of a **risk** that the circumstance exists or will exist. To put it another way, it is sufficient if he knows that the circumstance **might** exist. That view of recklessness as to circumstance was endorsed by the House of Lords in *G*.

Needless to say, whether any particular crime is satisfied by mere subjective recklessness or requires 'knowledge' depends on the definition of that crime.

3.6.4 Objective recklessness and negligence

By and large, these concepts work in relation to circumstances in the same way as they apply to acts and consequences as discussed at 3.4.3 and 3.5. In his famous dictum in *Roper* v *Taylor's Central Garages*, Devlin J referred to a concept which he termed 'knowledge of the third degree'—sometimes called 'constructive knowledge'. By this he meant the fault element we are discussing under this head and it is a complete misnomer to refer to this as a species of 'knowledge'. It is, of course, the absence of knowledge because D does not **know** the fact or circumstance exists. He does not even realise or suspect that it may exist because he does not advert to or think about the possibility of it existing. Rather it is a case of the law saying he ought to have thought about and realised it and, for some offences, this will be sufficient to make him culpable. In other words, D has been negligent in failing to see what a reasonable man would have seen in the situation.

If D has made an incredibly stupid mistake in not seeing that the circumstance exists or will exist, we can regard him as being **grossly** negligent and, provided he had given no thought to the matter, he would be objectively reckless. Of course, since *G*, offences are unlikely to be construed as being based on a fault element of objective recklessness (though possible examples appear under the next heading). Clearly, the word 'knowingly' will never stretch to embrace a fault element of mere negligence or objective recklessness.

3.6.5 **Indifference**

On occasion, the courts have used the concept of indifference to convey the fault element required for some offences based on recklessness. By this they mean someone who 'could not care less'. The controversial question is the extent to which this imports a *mens rea* of objective recklessness. Thus, before the Sexual Offences Act 2003 re-wrote the law, the crime of rape (and other sex offences and offences of violence such as battery) required the prosecution to prove that D either knew the victim was not consenting or was reckless as to that fact. In a number of cases the courts have described the *mens rea* of recklessness as requiring that D was 'indifferent' or 'could not care less' whether the victim was consenting (e.g., *Kimber* (1983) 77 Cr App R 225, CA (indecent assault); *Satnam and Kewal Singh* (1984) 78 Cr App R 149, CA (rape)). Some writers argue that D cannot be indifferent **unless** he has **chosen** to disregard the risk that V is not consenting, i.e., he must be aware of the possibility. Thus indifference necessarily involves subjective recklessness. It is a type of subjective recklessness.

Others regard 'could not care less' as embracing a type of objective recklessness where D has given no thought to the risk **because** his general attitude is one of indifference to the wishes and feelings of his victim. But, of course, if D has not thought about the risk, it is a matter of speculation what his attitude to it would have been if he had thought about it. His hypothetical attitude to the risk is a dangerous basis for liability but was adopted in *Breckenridge* (1984) 79 Cr App R 244, CA and *Taylor* (1985) 80 Cr App R 327, CA. An alternative formulation by the Court of Appeal in *Satnam and Kewal Singh* (1984) 78 Cr App R 149 is contradictory. On the one hand, it holds that *Caldwell* objective recklessness has no application to rape which is based upon subjective recklessness. On the other hand, 'a practical definition of recklessness' is where D is indifferent or 'couldn't care less'. Far from viewing this as requiring that D must be aware that V might not be consenting (subjective recklessness), the court considered that D could not care less about consent unless he positively believed V **was** consenting. If D has to believe V was consenting to avoid being reckless, the conclusion must surely be that if he gave no thought to whether V was consenting or not (objective recklessness), he must be reckless. He could not believe V was consenting. Quite a muddle!

Nonetheless, the House of Lords in *B v DPP* [2000] 2 AC 428 and *K* [2002] 1 AC 462 has taken a similar view in respect of other sexual offences dependent on the victim being below a certain age. These have been interpreted as requiring recklessness on the part of D as to the victim being below the set age, such recklessness being satisfied by proving that D did not honestly believe that the victim was above the set age. There is no need to prove that D actually realised the victim might be under age. Whether *G* would have prompted a reconsideration of these three cases is speculative but the redefinition of the relevant offences by the Sexual Offences Act 2003 makes the speculation redundant.

Despite this endorsement from on high, our view is that the concepts of 'indifference' and 'could not care less' are apt to confuse rather than clarify and, if they must be used, should be taken to require subjective recklessness. That is how, rightly or wrongly, most text writers have interpreted *Satnam*. If subjective recklessness is thought to be inadequate as the *mens rea* of rape or other offences, it should be extended in a clear and explicit way without obscuring existing concepts. The definition of rape laid down by s. 1 of the Sexual Offences Act 2003 does just that. It requires a positive belief by D that the victim is consenting and even that may not be enough to acquit him (see s. 1(2) and 1(3)). A number of other offences in the Act adopt the same position.

3.7 **Fault element variable**

The *mens rea* or fault element varies from crime to crime. You should also be aware that it can also vary from element to element within the same crime. For example, before its repeal by the Sexual Offences Act 2003, it was an offence under s. 20 of the Sexual Offences Act 1956 'for a person acting without lawful authority or excuse to take an unmarried girl under the age of sixteen out of the possession of her parent or guardian against his will'. In *Prince* (1875) LR 2 CCR 154, it was held that no fault element whatsoever, not even negligence, was required to be proved by the prosecution in respect of the fact that the girl was under 16. (The correctness of this decision was seriously doubted by the House of Lords in *B* v *DPP* [2000] 2 WLR 452 and *K* [2001] UKHL 41 though it was not formally overruled—see 13.4.1 below.) On the other hand, in *Hibbert* (1869) LR 1 CCR 184, D met an unmarried girl under 16 on her way to Sunday School in Ashton and induced her to travel with him to Manchester where he had sexual intercourse with her and then returned her to Ashton. His appeal against conviction was allowed because there had been no finding by the lower court that he knew that the girl was in her father's care. Therefore knowledge was required in relation to the girl being in the possession of a parent or guardian. These two nineteenth-century cases were relevant to the 1956 Act because s. 20 used the same wording as was used by the replaced offence in the Offences Against the Person Act 1861. (The Sexual Offences Act 2003 contains no straightforward replacement offence but abductions would generally be caught by s. 2 of the Child Abduction Act 1984.)

3.8 **Some other *mens rea* words**

3.8.1 **Maliciously**

It is now settled that the term 'maliciously' imports a requirement of subjective recklessness and can be regarded as synonymous with that expression (*Savage; Parmenter* [1991] 4 All ER 698, HL and see 4.4.2.2).

3.8.2 **Wilfully**

The courts' interpretation of 'wilfully' has generated more than the usual amount of inconsistency, especially in relation to offences involving 'wilful obstruction'. In

Arrowsmith v *Jenkins* [1963] 2 All ER 210, DC 'wilful' was held to mean simply that D voluntarily did an act which **in fact** caused an obstruction of the highway. No fault element was required in relation to the causing of the obstruction. Since, as we have seen in **Chapter 2** (see 2.7.1), it is a general principle that all acts must be voluntary in the sense of being 'an exercise of free will', this interpretation makes 'wilful' superfluous. The section would mean the same if it had been omitted. Although a number of cases support such an alarmingly narrow interpretation, *Eaton* v *Cobb* [1950] 1 All ER 1016, DC held that the obstruction must be 'intentional'. D opened his car door into the path of a cyclist believing, after checking his mirror, that the road was clear. The court held that he did not intend to obstruct the highway when he intentionally opened his car door.

A similar view to *Eaton* v *Cobb* was taken in *Lewis* v *Cox* [1985] QB 509 where it was held that to be guilty of wilfully obstructing a police officer in the execution of his duty, D must have intended his 'conduct to prevent the police from carrying out their duty or to make it more difficult to do so'.

The leading authority is now *Sheppard* [1980] 3 All ER 399, HL where D was charged with wilfully neglecting a child 'in a manner likely to cause him unnecessary suffering or injury to health'. The child died from malnutrition and hypothermia after his parents had failed to summon medical assistance. Lord Diplock rejected the narrow view that 'wilfully' simply required a voluntary act, since this would render it nugatory. The term imported *mens rea*, namely, that either (a) D had thought about whether there was some risk to the child's' health and made a conscious decision not to seek medical help or (b) had not sought help because 'he did not care whether the child might be in need of medical treatment or not'. Thus it would seem that either subjective or objective recklessness in relation to the need for medical treatment will constitute 'wilful neglect' for the purposes of the offence. The House of Lords did not claim to be laying down a universal definition applicable in every offence, but its insistence that 'wilfully' imported *mens rea* suggests that those cases requiring simple voluntariness ought not to be followed.

3.8.3 Dishonestly

Dishonesty is an important constituent of many crimes against property such as theft, the new fraud offence and handling stolen goods. We shall therefore reserve our examination of it until we deal with theft in **Chapter 10**.

3.9 Mistake and *mens rea*

The question of whether D's liability is affected where he makes a mistake about the situation is interesting and complicated and is dealt with extensively in **Chapter 8**. The fact that D is labouring under a mistake **may** prevent him from having the *mens rea* required for the crime charged. For example, if D mistakenly believes that the stolen goods he is handling are not in fact stolen that will mean that he cannot have the requisite *mens rea* of 'knowing or believing the goods to be stolen'. On the other hand, if he believes the goods are stolen, even though he mistakenly believes they are stolen antiques rather than stolen rifles, the mistake will not negate his *mens rea* because he believes those goods are stolen (*McCullum* (1973) 57 Cr App R 645, CA). Whether a mistake does negate D's *mens rea* can only be ascertained by identifying the precise *mens rea* required for the crime charged. Where the crime charged requires proof of at least subjective recklessness in relation to that part of the *actus reus* about which the mistake has been made, there is no need for the mistake to be reasonable.

> **? QUESTION 3.18**
>
> Before the Sexual Offences Act 2003 re-defined it, the offence of rape required, among other things, proof that D knew or was subjectively reckless as to the fact that the victim was not consenting. If D had sexual intercourse with P, believing that she was consenting when she was not, would he have satisfied this *mens rea* requirement?

Because an unreasonable mistake would still have prevented D having the necessary subjective recklessness, D would have lacked the necessary *mens rea* and could not have been convicted of rape. Thus, in our Question a finding that D did genuinely make a mistake and believed that his victim was consenting is incompatible with a finding that he knew she might not be consenting. However incredulous you might be that D could make such a ridiculous mistake, if he did, he would not have had the requisite subjective recklessness as to the victim's lack of consent.

> **? QUESTION 3.19**
>
> • What kind of offences would require the mistake to be reasonable before it could possibly negative the fault element of the crime?
> • Are there any offences where even a reasonable mistake as to a component of the *actus reus* could not prevent liability?

Offences which can be satisfied by proof of an objective fault element such as negligence could not be defended by pleading an unreasonable (ordinary negligence) or grossly unreasonable (gross negligence) mistake. If the mistake is unreasonable then, far from negating *mens rea*, the mistake actually supplies it because it establishes the fault element of negligence. By definition it must be negligent to make an unreasonable mistake.

One final thought concerns offences of strict liability which we deal with in **Chapter 13**. This means that **no** fault element is required in relation to one or more elements of the *actus reus*. It follows that there is no *mens rea* or blameworthiness for the mistake to negate and so even the most reasonable mistake in the world will not avail the defendant. We have already mentioned *Prince* concerning the offence of taking an unmarried girl under 16 out of the possession of her parent or guardian against his will. D mistakenly believed the girl to be 16 or over, but the court held that this mistake was irrelevant because the prosecution did not need to prove knowledge, recklessness or even negligence in relation to her age. Once it was proved she was in fact under 16, the offence was satisfied in relation to that element. Even if the 'victim' had convinced a sceptical D that she was over 16 by producing an expertly forged birth certificate to that effect, D would still have been liable (Note the doubt about *Prince* in *B* v *DPP* [2000] 2 WLR 452, HL—see 8.5.2.2 and 13.4.1 below—and that the offence in question has been repealed by the Sexual Offences Act 2003.)

The issue of mistake is very much bound up with *mens rea*. There are, however, many more complex issues which it raises but these can be postponed until **Chapter 8**.

3.10 **Transferred malice**

Clearly, it is irrelevant to criminal liability that D, intending to burgle X's house, by mistake burgles Y's house. Nor does it matter that he thinks the man in front of him whom he intends to shoot and kill is X, when it is in fact Y.

In a case of 'transferred malice' the situation is that D aims to kill or injure X, but accidentally misses and kills or injures Y instead. Similarly, he might aim to destroy a police car by throwing a petrol bomb at it but miss and destroy a resident's car parked by the side of the road. In both cases, the law would allow his *mens rea* against the person who or the property which escapes to transfer and marry with the *actus reus* of causing the death of the unintended victim or damage to the unintended property respectively (*Latimer* (1886) 17 QBD 359). A novel application of the doctrine initially accepted by the Court of Appeal was overturned by the House of Lords in *Attorney-General's Reference (No. 3 of 1994)* [1997] 3 All ER 936 (*Cases and Materials* (3.10)). It was held that an intention to kill or cause serious injury to a pregnant woman could **not** be transferred from the mother to the foetus to make D guilty of murder where the foetus was born alive but died subsequently as a result of the injuries to its mother causing a premature birth (or, alternatively, as a result of pre-natal injuries to the foetus). Conviction would require 'a double "transfer" of intent: first from the mother to the foetus and then from the foetus to the child as yet unborn' and that was impermissible. Murder would only be possible if (a) D intended to kill or cause serious harm to the foetus itself or the child it would become after birth, and (b) the foetus was born alive and died subsequently as a result of the injuries inflicted by D on the foetus and/ or the mother (see further 6.3.2).

The judgments in the House of Lords imply (though do not clearly express) that the doctrine of transferred malice extends only to transferring a *mens rea* of intention and not, for example, one of subjective recklessness despite the fact that the latter falls within the concept of 'malice'. However, the proposed cl. 32 in the Law Commission's draft Criminal Law Bill would allow both intention and subjective recklessness to be transferred. Clause 17 of the draft Offences Against the Person Bill (see **Chapter 4**) would adopt substantially the same provision in respect of the offences in the Bill.

However, one may question whether the doctrine of transferred malice is needed as a separate doctrine at all. For example, if we say that the *mens rea* for murder is an intention to kill or cause grievous bodily harm to *a person* as opposed to the particular person killed, then proof that D caused the victim's death by conduct accompanied by the requisite *mens rea* towards any other person would automatically satisfy the definition of the crime charged. The 'transfer' of intention would not be an issue. Thus, in *Attorney-General's Reference (No. 3 of 1994)*, the facts accepted in argument were that D had stabbed the mother intending to cause her grievous bodily harm (the *mens rea* for murder) and had thereby caused the death of another human being—the child, after it was born alive. This should have made it murder (as the Court of Appeal had held). The irony is that, as we shall see in **Chapter 6**, the House of Lords used an analogous argument to hold that D's conduct did amount to manslaughter.

Taking the offence of criminal damage as another example, the *actus reus* is destroying or damaging another's property and the *mens rea* is intending to do so or being reckless thereto. There would seem to be no necessity that the property actually damaged should be the property D intended to damage or was reckless as to damaging. He commits the crime because whilst intending or being reckless as to the damaging of another's property, he did actually damage some (albeit not the same) property belonging to someone other than himself (whether the owner of the first property or someone else). Whether the foregoing is correct remains to be settled but it would make the doctrine of transferred malice redundant in the sphere of violence against the person or property. The point should have been debated in *G* (where the defendants intended or foresaw damage to the wheelie bin but not the buildings), but was overlooked.

? **QUESTION** 3.20

If you throw a stone at V intending to injure him, but he ducks and the stone breaks a window in the building behind him, will your intention to injure V supply the *mens rea* for a charge of criminal damage to the window?

The doctrine of transferred malice does not allow the prosecutor to mix and match the *actus reus* and *mens rea* of different crimes. You cannot therefore marry the *actus reus* of criminal damage (breaking the window) with the *mens rea* of an offence against the person (intention to injure V) (*Pembliton* (1874) LR 2 CCR 119). However, it will often be the case that D would have the *mens rea* in its own right without any necessity to worry about transferred malice. This is because many offences require only recklessness and that is certainly the case with criminal damage. Presumably, when D throws the stone, he may well realise that there is a risk of breaking the window (subjective recklessness).

If the doctrine of transferred malice operates, then any defence which D would have had in respect of the contemplated victim or thing, will also be transferred so as to be available in respect of the unintended victim or thing (*Gross* (1913) 23 Cox CC 455). The draft Criminal Law Bill adopts this position in cl. 32(2).

■ **FURTHER READING**

Heaton: *Reckless Abandon* (2004) 13(1) Nottingham Law Journal 35.

Heaton: *Murder Most Simple?* (1998) 7 Nottingham Law Journal 66.

Horder: *Gross Negligence and Criminal Culpability* (1997) 47 University of Toronto Law
   Journal 495.

Norrie: *After Woollin* [1999] Crim LR 532.

Pedain: *Intention and the Terrorist Example* [2003] Crim LR 579.

Simester: *Can Negligence be Culpable?* in Horder (ed.): *Oxford Essays in Jurisprudence* (2000, Oxford
   University Press).

Simester: *Moral Certainty and the Boundaries of Intention* (1996) 16 OJLS 445.

Sullivan: *Intent, Subjective Recklessness and Culpability* (1992) 12 OJLS 380.

Williams: *Oblique Intention* (1987) 46 CLJ 417.

■ SUMMARY

Mens rea is whatever subjective state of mind on the part of D must be proved according to the definition of the crime charged. This is normally intending to perform the *actus reus* or being aware that it might be performed. Other **objective** fault elements (not strictly *mens rea* because not dependent on proving particular state of mind on the part of D) include objective recklessness (doubtful since *G* [2003] HL) and negligence. D (for whatever reason) falls below a set external standard of conduct. Refer to **Figure 3.1**. **Subjective** tests depend on what actually is going on in D's mind, **objective** on what **ought** to be.

- *Intention*—core meaning is aim or purpose. D decides to do the act or bring about the prohibited consequence (*Mohan*). Distinct from 'desire' in the emotional sense. Includes express or implicit subsidiary aims—'the means as well as the end' (Lord Hailsham)—i.e., where D knows the prohibited consequence must **certainly** occur if he is to achieve his primary (legal) objective (*Ahlers* and *Steane* suspect). **Oblique or indirect intention**—where D does not aim to produce the prohibited consequence which is a very likely side effect of D's primary purpose, but not a *condition* of achieving it. It appears from *Woollin* (1998, HL) 'reinterpreting' *Moloney*, *Hancock* and *Nedrick*, that intention extends beyond aim/purpose and includes foresight by D of virtual certainty (but nothing less than virtual certainty)—**but only if** the jury, having complete discretion, chooses to 'find' intention (***Matthews & Alleyne***).

- *Intention and motive*—motive is any reason for acting which is **ulterior** to the *actus reus* and *mens rea* defined for the offence. Good or bad it is generally **irrelevant** to **liability** (*Smith*; *Senior*). However, courts sometimes influenced by a 'good' motive to distort ingredients of the crime to avoid liability (*Ahlers*; *Steane*; *Gillick*). Motive is an important ingredient in some general defences (e.g., self-defence, duress, necessity) and some offences due to the way they are defined (e.g., theft and blackmail).

- *Further/ulterior intent*—*mens rea* going beyond, i.e., ulterior to the *actus reus* (e.g., Theft Act 1968, s. 9(1)(a)).

- *Specific intent*—misleading expression with variable meaning best avoided. Basic intent likewise. Expressions only important for defence of intoxication.

- *Recklessness*—unjustifiable risk-taking. D's conduct involves a risk of prohibited consequence and, in the circumstances, it is unreasonable to go ahead and take that risk. Court decides whether risk is unjustifiable in D's situation by weighing the likelihood and gravity of the risk against any social merit in D's actions. Two types (i) subjective recklessness (ii) *Caldwell* objective recklessness (doubtful after *G*).

- *Subjective recklessness*—D **realises** he is taking a risk of causing the prohibited consequence. It is **deliberate** risk-taking. This is a minimum requirement for most offences of violence and, since *G*, criminal damage.

- *Objective recklessness*—inadvertent risk-taking—D must (i) have created an obvious and serious risk of the prohibited result and **either** (ii) have recognised that risk **or** (iii) have given no thought to the possibility of any such risk (*Caldwell*; *Lawrence*). Element (ii) is, in essence, subjective recklessness (see above). With objective recklessness D could be convicted of some serious offences where he had no idea his actions involved any risk, even where this was because he lacked, through no fault of his own, the ordinary person's **capacity** to perceive obvious risks (e.g., educational subnormality). Obvious and serious risk referred to the magnitude of the risk (how likely, how grave) viewed at the time D acted (not with hindsight—*Sangha*). **Obvious to whom?**—to a reasonable person not D (*Lawrence*; *Sangha*). Even if D, without fault, was **incapable** of seeing the risk, he was reckless (*Elliott* v *C*). Signs in *Reid* that courts would modify this harsh stance and would take into account D's capacity to appreciate risks (e.g., pre-existing mental conditions, age or temporary incapacitating conditions such as sudden illness). **Caldwell lacuna**—D not reckless under *Caldwell* if he did give thought to the possibility of the prohibited consequence occurring, but erroneously (even if stupidly) concluded there was in fact no such risk (*Chief Constable of Avon* v *Shimmen*). However, *Caldwell* objective recklessness was rejected in *G* so that in future a fault element of recklessness means only subjective recklessness.

- *Negligence*—again, **inadvertent** risk-taking. Not at all dependent on D's state of mind. Simply a failure to act in accordance with an external standard of conduct in the given situation set by the court looking back. Two forms—'ordinary' negligence is average carelessness; 'gross' negligence is extreme or serious carelessness. It is a question of degree incapable of exact definition (*Andrews* v *DPP*). 'No-negligence' defences are common in regulatory statutes, making D liable unless he proves he was not negligent.

- *Mens rea as to circumstances*—refer to **Figure 3.3**. Knowledge—can mean **actual** knowledge (knowledge of first degree where D firmly and correctly believes, i.e., has no substantial doubt (*Hall*)), but usually interpreted as including 'wilful blindness' (i.e., knowledge of the second degree—a form of subjective recklessness where D knows the circumstances **might** exist but deliberately shuts his eyes to the possibility and fails to avail himself of ready means to check) (*Westminster City Council* v *Croyalgrange Ltd*). Subjective recklessness is where D suspects that the circumstance might exist but carries on regardless, deliberately taking the risk. 'Constructive' knowledge (knowledge of the third degree)—**not** knowledge at all—D neither knows nor suspects, but he **ought** to. He is **negligent** in not knowing that the fact or circumstance does or might exist. 'Knowingly' can never embrace this fault element, which applies only if crime requires just negligence or objective recklessness. *Mens rea* or fault element not only varies from crime to crime, it can also vary from element to element in the **same** crime (*Prince*; cf. *Hibbert*).

- *Other mens rea words*—(i) 'maliciously' means intentionally **or** subjectively recklessly (*Savage*; *Parmenter*); (ii) 'wilfully'—meaning uncertain because of inconsistent decisions but probably imports a fault element of at least recklessness, although this seems to include objective recklessness (*Sheppard*); (iii) dishonestly—see **Chapter 10**.

- *Mistake and mens rea*—if D makes a mistake about an element of the *actus reus* and this prevents him having the *mens rea* for the offence, he is not guilty whether or not the mistake is a reasonable one. An unreasonable mistake will negate *mens rea* only if the crime requires intention/knowledge or subjective recklessness. A reasonable mistake will also negate a *mens rea* of negligence but not a strict liability offence—see **Chapter 8**.

- *Transferred malice*—intention against one person can be 'transferred' to marry with the *actus reus* against another (where D aims at X, misses and hits V) (*Attorney-General's Reference (No. 3 of 1994)*; *Latimer*). Only possible with *actus reus* and *mens rea* of same offence (*Pembliton*). Any defence can also be transferred (*Gross*).

4 Non-fatal offences against the person

4.1 Objectives

By the end of this chapter you should be able to:

1 Define and analyse assault and battery

2 Explain the concept of 'unlawful' force and how it affects the offence of battery

3 Define and analyse the offences created by ss. 18, 20 and 47 of the OAPA 1861

4 Identify the problems surrounding the *mens rea* of s. 47

5 Explain the differences between ss. 18 and 20 in terms of (a) *mens rea* and (b) *actus reus*

4.2 Introduction

This chapter is concerned with non-sexual offences of violence falling short of killing people. Like so much of the criminal law, it is an area where logic and consistency are in short supply and there is a serious need for reform. The necessity for modernisation is underscored by the fact that the principal statute defining these offences is the Offences Against the Person Act 1861 (hereafter the OAPA 1861). A number of proposals for change have been made by law reform agencies, culminating in a suggested Criminal Law Bill proposed by the Law Commission (Law Com. No. 218).

In 1998 the Government indicated its intention to introduce a comprehensive reform to rationalise but not 'to alter fundamentally the scope or operation of the law' by putting out a draft Offences Against the Person Bill for public consultation. The Home Office has since mid-1998 been evaluating the responses to the Bill which was based largely on the policies and principles adopted by the Law Commission, although it was structured rather differently from the Commission's own draft Criminal Law Bill. There is currently no sign of any Bill being brought to Parliament, which has given priority to the reform of sexual offences.

The OAPA 1861 contains a whole range of offences, some of which look very odd to modern eyes and are more or less obsolete. If you have access to a statute book, you would find it interesting and amusing to scan through them. We can select only the most common of these offences which, in ascending order of seriousness, are assault, battery, assault occasioning actual bodily harm, maliciously wounding/inflicting grievous bodily harm under s. 20 and wounding/causing grievous bodily harm with intent under s. 18.

4.3 The less serious offences

4.3.1 Common assault

The terms 'common assault', 'assault' and 'battery' are often used interchangeably by laymen and even lawyers and criminal law statutes. However, at common law there were two quite distinct offences of assault and battery. Professor Glanville Williams has suggested a new terminology which neatly expresses the difference between these two offences. He calls 'assault' 'psychic assault' and 'battery' 'physical assault'. Many writers refer to assault proper as 'technical' assault. These offences are not defined in any statutes and their ingredients must be gleaned from case law. However, the penalties are now prescribed by s. 39 of the Criminal Justice Act 1988.

The Divisional Court in the combined appeal of *DPP* v *Taylor* and *DPP* v *Little* [1992] 1 All ER 299 confirmed that there are two distinct offences and, more controversially, that these have been statutory offences since the enactment of s. 47 of the OAPA in 1861. Despite this, the better view (endorsed by the Divisional Court in *Haystead* v *Chief Constable of Derbyshire* [2000] 3 All ER 890) is that the offences are common law offences, the statute merely prescribing the penalty for their commission. The significance of the foregoing points relates to procedural matters which are outside the scope of this work.

The term 'common assault' is most often used to embrace both psychic assault and battery (physical assault). One exception is s. 39 of the Criminal Justice Act 1988 which expressly refers to 'common assault and battery'. Section 40 refers only to 'common assault'. The Court of Appeal in *Lynsey* [1995] 3 All ER 654 had to hold that 'common assault' means 'technical assault' only in s. 39, but technical assault or battery in s. 40! The latter usage also occurs in s. 47 of the OAPA 1861 (assault occasioning actual bodily harm).

4.3.2 'Technical' or 'psychic' assault

This offence is committed where D intentionally or subjectively recklessly causes the victim to apprehend immediate force to his person.

4.3.2.1 *Actus reus*

D's conduct must cause the victim to think that force is about to be applied there and then to his person. In most cases P will be frightened by this threat, but fear is not essential. It is unnecessary to prove any physical contact between the defendant and the victim, contact being the hallmark of battery (physical assault).

? **QUESTION** 4.1

List three ways in which you could commit a psychic assault on someone you dislike!

There are numerous possibilities including pointing a gun at V, waving your fist under V's nose, riding your bicycle at V, throwing a stone at V, making as if to set your pet puma on V! Of course, if in any of these cases you actually touch V, you could be committing battery as well as assault.

It is essential that V actually apprehends violence to himself so that if the threatening actions are unseen by V and done without his knowledge or if, say, V knows that the gun pointing at him is unloaded or an imitation, no psychic assault is committed.

? **QUESTION** 4.2

In *Lamb* [1967] 2 QB 981, D pointed a loaded gun at his friend V who thought it was a joke and that the gun would not fire. Do you think this was an assault? Give your reasons.

If V is in fear of immediate violence, it is irrelevant that, unknown to him, there is in fact no danger of the threat being carried out, e.g., where D points an unloaded or imitation gun at V (*Logdon* v *DPP* [1976] Crim LR 121, DC).

Immediate violence

The definition requires there to be an apprehension of **immediate** violence and this was recently confirmed by the House of Lords in *Ireland* [1997] 3 WLR 534 (*Cases and Materials* (4.3.2.1)). Thus a threat of future (non-immediate) force ('I will get you one dark night') does not constitute assault. Notice that it is the violence threatened which has to be immediate not the fear or apprehension of it. The Court of Appeal in *Ireland* fell into this trap for the unwary. Thus, if Julius Caesar had taken seriously the warning, 'Beware the Ides of March', he might have immediately apprehended the risk of violence to himself, but his fear would not have been of **immediate** violence but only of future violence—on 15 March.

But the crucial question is how immediate is immediate? The original concept was extremely narrow and confined to cases where V thought D was both on the point of applying force to him and in a position immediately to do so. By gradually expanding the concept of 'immediacy', the courts have in practice considerably widened the scope of the offence, taking it well beyond ordinary notions of assault. We can perhaps accept *Smith* v *Chief Superintendent, Woking Police Station* (1983) 76 Cr App R 234 (*Cases and Materials* (4.3.2.1)) where the Divisional Court held that the magistrates who tried the case were entitled to infer that V had apprehended the **immediate** application of force upon being frightened (as D intended she should be) by D's peering at her through her house window at 11.00 p.m. But the House of Lords went further in *Ireland* in holding that it was possible, 'as a matter of law', for someone to be guilty of assault by making persistent silent telephone calls to another. 'Whether he is or not will depend on the circumstance and in particular on the impact of the caller's potentially menacing call or calls on the victim' (*per* Lord Steyn). V would need to fear imminent violence, but this could be where a telephone caller threatens to be at the victim's door 'in a minute or two'. In the final analysis it is a question of fact for the jury as to whether V did fear immediate force.

Thus, we can see that whilst the House of Lords formally endorses the traditional 'immediacy' requirement, it leaves the way open for courts and juries to take an expansive view of it on the facts of their case. In *Constanza* [1997] 2 Cr App R 492 (*Cases and Materials* (4.3.2.1)), also a stalking case by, *inter alia*, persistent telephone calls and letters, the Court of Appeal, in a poorly expressed phrase, held that fear of violence in the immediate future would suffice. It appears from *Constanza* (decided before the House of Lords pronounced in *Ireland*) that an assault can be committed by means of letters alone provided they induce the requisite fear.

It seems that, in order to meet a new social evil, known fashionably as stalking, the courts have stretched the crime of assault towards a more general one of making threats of violence. The irony is that this occurred just at the time Parliament was enacting some new bespoke offences to deal with stalking and other forms of harassment in the Protection from Harassment Act 1997. Section 4 of the 1997 Act creates an offence carrying a maximum of five years' imprisonment of causing 'another to fear, on at least two occasions, that violence will be used against him . . .' No immediacy requirement here, but P has to fear not just that violence **may** be carried out (as for assault) but that it **will** be carried out.

Assaulting by words alone

The House of Lords in *Ireland* categorically rejected the proposition that an assault could never be committed by words alone unaccompanied by any threatening acts or gestures. For Lord Steyn, with whom the remaining judges concurred, 'A thing said is also a thing done. There is no reason why something said should be incapable of causing an apprehension of immediate personal violence, e.g., a man accosting a woman in a dark alley saying, "Come with me or I will stab you." ' This is surely correct as a matter of policy—blind people or persons in a pitch black room who cannot see any threatening actions may be terrified by threatening words. Presumably the same principle would apply to written words, thus opening up the possibility of assault by letter! Technically these pronouncements were obiter since D did not utter any words but made silent telephone calls which the House also held to be capable of constituting assault where the necessary fear was induced.

Earlier the Court of Appeal in *Constanza* [1997] 2 Cr App R 492 had upheld D's conviction for assault occasioning actual bodily harm based on threats contained in the last of a series of over 800 letters he sent to his 'stalking' victim. He had also persistently followed the victim and made numerous silent telephone calls and even unsolicited visits, but the indictment alleged that the assault charged was constituted by the last letter, which caused the victim to believe that D had 'flipped'. Strangely, although *Constanza* was cited in argument before the House of Lords in *Ireland*, it was not referred to in any of the judgments. However, as it accords with the general tenor of their Lordships' decision, it should be regarded as having settled the matter so that, in appropriate circumstances, it is possible to assault by written words alone (though the words will have to be read in the light of what has or has not gone on before).

Words negativing assault

Words accompanying an act or gesture, which would otherwise amount to an assault, can negative the assault. In *Tuberville* v *Savage* (1669) 1 Mod Rep 3, D put his hand to his sword (which would be prima facie assault) but said to V simultaneously, 'If it were not assize time, I would not take such language.' This clearly told V there was no danger of violence at that moment, because, in fact, the judges were in town—it was 'assize time'. However, the effect of the negativing words is always a question of fact as is shown by the case of *Light* (1857) [1843–60] All ER Rep 934. D raised a shovel over his wife's head and said, 'If it were not for the bloody policeman outside, I would split your head open.' Although the outcome of the case is not clear from the two contradictory reports of it, it seems clear that guilt turns on whether a reasonable woman in the wife's position might apprehend the use of violence. It could well be that, in this particular case, the actions were so threatening that the words would be insufficient to neutralise the victim's apprehension of immediate violence.

> **? QUESTION** 4.3
>
> Does this mean that the highwayman pointing his cocked pistol negatives any assault when he says, 'Your money or your life!'?

Conditional threats

It is probable that a conditional threat ('I will blow your brains out if you make any sound') would constitute an assault. Although the words clearly tell the victim that he has nothing to fear provided he does as he is told, D has no right to fetter V's freedom in this way and, if this fetter is the price of D's not inflicting the force, there will be an assault (*Read* v *Coker* (1853) 13 CB 850; *Logdon* v *DPP* [1976] Crim LR 121). It is probable that the incredible decision to the contrary in *Blake* v *Barnard* (1840) 9 C & P 626 would not be followed, and our highwayman would clearly be guilty of assault on the quiescent passenger who hands over his purse.

4.3.2.2 *Mens rea*

The prosecution must prove either an intention to create in V the expectation of the immediate application of force to his person or, alternatively, subjective recklessness as to that, i.e., a realisation by D that V may think that D is about to apply force to V's person (*Venna* [1975] 3 All ER 788) (see *Cases and Materials* (4.3.2.2)). The Court of Appeal took the view that *Caldwell*-type objective recklessness had no application here and was insufficient for liability (*Spratt* [1991] 2 All ER 210, CA and *Parmenter* [1991] 2 All ER 225, CA). Whilst most writers would regard this as correct, the House of Lords missed the opportunity to confirm it once and for all in *Savage* [1991] 4 All ER 698 though dicta in that case do support it. This issue is considered more fully under the *mens rea* for assault occasioning actual bodily harm.

The requirement that D must intend or foresee that V might apprehend an **immediate** application of force may prove a formidable obstacle in convicting silent telephone callers and obsessive letter writers. Is it likely, in the absence of specific threats designed to induce such a fear, that D will intend his victim to fear an **immediate** application of force (as opposed to a generalised fear of the future) or even realise that the victim might?

4.3.3 Battery or physical assault

Battery is committed where D intentionally or subjectively recklessly applies unlawful force to another. Battery is usually but not necessarily preceded by a psychic assault.

> **?** **QUESTION** 4.4
>
> Can you think of a situation where battery would *not* be preceded by an assault?

A blow from behind catching V completely unawares would be a battery, but not a psychic assault because V perceived no threat of violence before it occurred. Similarly where D kicks an unconscious V.

4.3.3.1 *Actus reus*

The House of Lords in *Ireland* confirmed that it is essential that there be an actual application of force by D to V so that there could be no battery where the activities of a stalker who did not touch the victim caused psychiatric harm. However, the notion of 'force' is extremely wide. It can include literally any contact with V's body or, even, his clothing (*Day* (1845) 1 Cox CC 207), whether or not V can feel the contact through the clothes (*Thomas* (1985) 81 Cr App R 33, CA—touching the hem of V's skirt). It follows that no particular violence is required and often, particularly in the offence of sexual assault, the merest touching suffices. According to *Sherriff* [1969] Crim LR 260, for D merely to pull away from someone attempting to hold him is not in itself a battery.

However, the necessity for force would exclude poisoning, gassing or drugging a person where there was no physical contact (*Walkden* (1845) 1 Cox CC 282; *Hanson* (1849) 4 Cox CC 138). There are separate offences in ss. 23 and 24 of the OAPA 1861 to cover such instances.

Indirect battery?

We must now consider the interesting but unresolved problem of whether an indirect application of force caused by D is sufficient. Suppose someone frightened you into jumping out of a window so that force was applied to your body when you hit the ground. Would this be the *actus reus* of battery? Although case law establishes that, if grievous bodily harm results, this can constitute an offence under ss. 20 or 18 of the OAPA 1861 (depending on D's *mens rea*), the courts have never clearly determined whether, if no injury resulted, it would constitute the offence of battery.

One modern case which holds that causing force to be applied indirectly can amount to battery is *DPP v K* [1990] 1 All ER 331, DC. D poured acid into an electric drier in his school toilets so that when the next user operated the drier the acid was blown on to his skin. It was held that this would undoubtedly constitute a battery if D had the appropriate *mens rea*. The case was subsequently overruled by the Court of Appeal, but not on this point. (Note that the same reasoning would apply if a harmless liquid such as water were poured in rather than acid.) The Divisional Court in *Haystead* v *Chief Constable of Derbyshire* [2000] 3 All ER 890 held that it was not essential that the force be directly inflicted by a blow with D's fist or weapon held or missile thrown by him. In the case, D deliberately punched X causing her to drop on the floor V, the 12-month child she was holding. He obviously committed a battery against the mother, but did he also commit battery against V, the baby? In a poorly articulated judgment, it was held that D was guilty of battery on V seemingly on the basis that there was a direct application of force in that 'the movement of ... [X] whereby she lost hold of the child was entirely and immediately the result of the appellant's action in punching her.' But surely the force applied to V was when he hit the ground and that was indirect? The conviction can be supported but only on the basis that D's causing of an indirect application of force suffices for battery. Although *Wilson* [1983] 3 All ER 448, HL implies that there must be some cases where causing an indirect application of force is not battery, it is likely to be forgotten in the light of its marginalisation by the House of Lords' decision in *Burstow* (see 4.4.2.1 below).

Battery by omission?

The Divisional Court in *Fagan* v *MPC* [1968] 3 All ER 442 expressed the view that a mere omission to act, even though it results in an application of force to V, could not constitute a battery. Thus, if D fails to move even though he knows that V is about to come round a corner and bump into D, it could not be a battery. In *Fagan* a policeman instructed a motorist not to park in a particular place. Instead the motorist parked his car on the policeman's foot. It was accepted by the court that this was inadvertent and that he did not realise he was parking on the policeman's foot. The policeman apprised him of this in no uncertain terms but D refused to move the car.

This looks very much like an omission to act and, as we have said, the court's view was that a mere omission to act cannot amount to an assault. However, the court managed to find a way to convict D. It held that, although D's act in driving onto the policeman's foot in the first place was unaccompanied by the appropriate *mens rea*, it was an act which *continued* for as long as the vehicle stayed on the policeman's foot, continuing to apply force to it. So long as D had the appropriate *mens rea* at any time during the continuance of this act, he could be convicted. Therefore, as soon as he realised that the car was on the policeman's foot, his refusal to move the car meant that he had the necessary intention to apply force and his continuing act was applying force and therefore he could be convicted. It must be said that this is a rather contrived view and it would surely be better to admit that it is possible in exceptional circumstances to perform a battery by a mere omission. There seems no reason why the standard rules governing liability for omissions should not apply to battery.

? QUESTION 4.5

How would those principles apply in the *Fagan* situation and with what result?

Is *DPP* v *K* (see above) a case of omission? If so, it would surely come within the *Miller* [1983] 1 All ER 978, HL principle—failure to rectify a dangerous situation D has inadvertently created—just as surely as *Fagan* does. Whether it is a case of omission, however, depends on whether or not D had the necessary *mens rea* at the time he did the positive act—putting the acid in the machine. If his realisation that the acid might squirt on someone only came after pouring it into the drier, any liability would have to be based on his omission to avert the danger once the realisation came. That was the line taken by the Divisional Court in *DPP* v *Santana-Bermudez* [2003] EWHC Admin 2908. V, a policewoman, decided to conduct a lawful search of D. He produced some syringes from his pockets and she asked him if he had any other needles or sharps in his pockets. He said not which was a deliberate lie. In the course of going through the pockets, V pricked herself on a syringe needle. D was convicted of assault occasioning actual bodily harm under the *Miller* principle. He had created the dangerous situation by his conduct and words and he was under a duty to V to take reasonable steps to obviate that danger. His omission to inform her of the remaining needle breached that duty caused the application of force when the needle pricked her finger and constituted a battery. It therefore seems clear that a battery can be committed by an omission to act, at least where D's earlier conduct has created a reasonably foreseeable risk of an application of force.

Unlawful force

To constitute the *actus reus* the force applied to the victim must be **unlawful** force (**'unlawfulness' is a requirement applicable to all the offences of violence dealt with in this chapter**). We can identify four main situations where the use of physical force could be lawful: self-defence and prevention of crime; parental chastisement; necessity; and consent.

Self-defence and prevention of crime

Anyone is entitled to use reasonable force in self-defence or in the prevention of crime (s. 3 of the Criminal Law Act 1967). This topic is considered in more detail in **Chapter 8** under general defences. A good example is provided by *Reed* v *Wastie* [1972] Crim LR 221. V, a lorry driver, was standing in the carriageway of a motorway and refused police requests to move. Two policemen forcibly frogmarched him off the carriageway and V struggled violently, knocking their caps off. The policemen managed to subdue him and one of them sat on his chest, whilst the other went to radio for assistance. Thus far they had used only reasonable force in the prevention of V's crime of obstructing the motorway. Such force was lawful and not an assault. However, whilst sitting on V's chest, the policeman gratuitously thumped him in the face breaking his nose. This force was clearly unreasonable and no longer used in self-defence, the prevention of crime or in order to arrest. It was therefore unlawful and the policeman was convicted of the assault.

Parental chastisement

Parents are entitled to take reasonable disciplinary measures against their children, including the use of *moderate* physical punishment. Clearly this does not allow the use of force which is excessive or unreasonable in nature, degree or duration (*Hopley* (1860) 2 F & F 202; *Smith* [1985] Crim LR 42).

In *A* v *UK* [1998] Crim LR 892, the European Court of Human Rights decided that the United Kingdom was in breach of Art. 3 of the European Convention on Human Rights in that the then current law failed to protect children from the 'inhuman or degrading treatment' prohibited by Art. 3. The nine-year-old applicant had suffered 'inhuman and degrading treatment' at the hands of his stepfather who beat him with a cane with considerable force on a number of occasions and yet had been acquitted by the jury on a charge of assault occasioning actual bodily harm having claimed it was reasonable chastisement. The ECHR criticised the vagueness of the 'reasonable chastisement' defence and the fact that the burden of proving that the force used was not reasonable chastisement, was on the prosecutor. However, the Court was at pains to stress that Art. 3 did not require the State to outlaw 'any form of physical rebuke, however mild, by a parent of a child'. This led the Government to propose legislative reform although it 'explicitly' ruled out any move 'to make unlawful all smacking and other forms of physical rebuke' (Dept. of Health: *Protecting Children, Supporting Parents: A Consultation Document on the Physical Punishment of Children* (2000), para. 1.5).

Subsequently, the Court of Appeal in *H* [2002] 1 Cr App R 59 held that the common law rules on what is reasonable correction are evolutionary and can be and have been modified by changing social standards and the impact of the European Convention. Thus, the current standard of reasonableness complies with Art. 3 of the Convention and its interpretative case law so long as the trial judge spells out for the jury the factors identified by the ECHR in *A* v *United Kingdom* as bearing on the issue. The jury must be instructed to consider 'the nature and context of the defendant's behaviour, its duration, its physical and mental consequences in relation to the child, the age and personal characteristics of the child and the reasons given by the defendant for administering punishment.' To be 'degrading' contrary to Art. 3, the punishment must 'attain a particular level of severity' which depends on 'the facts of each case, in particular, the nature and context of the punishment'.

The Government initially responded to this decision by declaring that it made our law consistent with Art. 3, thus rendering legislation unnecessary. However, legislation was subsequently passed in s. 58 of the Children Act 2004 which, whilst not superseding the common law defence, does impose a significant limitation on it. The effect of this rather oddly drafted provision is that any punishment which results in actual bodily harm or worse (whether deliberate or inadvertent) or which amounts to child cruelty under s. 1 of the Children and Young Persons Act 1933, even though no actual bodily harm is caused, cannot constitute reasonable chastisement and must therefore be unlawful. We shall see shortly when we examine s. 47 of the Offences Against the Person Act 1861 that relatively trivial injury including visible bruising can constitute actual bodily harm and it is no excuse that the parent did not intend or even foresee the causing of injury. Therefore, only limited force can **possibly** be permissible and even then it must still pass the reasonableness test in *H*. For example, it would be unlikely to be reasonable to smack a sick child, however moderately, because it will not stop crying. An instance of cruelty without bodily harm might be rubbing a small child's face in its own urine or defecation because it has soiled its bed.

All teachers are prohibited from administering corporal punishment (new s. 548 of the Education Act 1996 as substituted by s. 131 of the School Standards and Framework Act 1998 (as interpreted in *Williamson* v *Secretary of State for Education and Employment* [2003] 1 All ER 385, CA)).

Necessity

Emergency situations can justify a deliberate application of force even if that would otherwise amount to a battery. This is considered more fully in **Chapter 9**, but examples could include medical treatment of an unconscious patient (unless the patient had previously forbidden it) (*F v West Berkshire Health Authority* [1989] 2 All ER 545, HL); pushing V, frozen with fright, down the emergency chute of a blazing aeroplane (after landing!). One school of thought would view such cases as based on implied consent rather than necessity as such.

Consent

Consent may be a 'defence' to a number of crimes, including battery. Sometimes this is explicit in that the crime is expressly defined as requiring an absence of consent. Rape is a clear example because, naturally, the *actus reus* requires that the penile penetration be **without the consent of the victim**. In battery, the need for an absence of consent is implicit rather than express. However, it does appear to be an ingredient of the definition of the offence because force applied with V's consent would not be **unlawful** force (*Kimber* [1983] 1 WLR 1118, CA). By contrast, the majority's obiter view in *Brown* [1993] 2 All ER 75, HL was that the absence of consent was not a 'definitional' element of the crime so that the presence of consent would not negate the *actus reus*. Rather, consent was simply a defence which could be raised once the elements of the offence had been established by the prosecution. Normally this would make no difference to the end result, although it may affect questions as to whether D bears an evidential burden to establish consent. The one area where it seems to be a critical distinction is where D makes a mistake that the victim is consenting. We will be explaining these issues later in this chapter and in **Chapter 8**, so that you need not worry if you find the point difficult to grasp at this stage. Suffice to say that the House of Lords in *B v DPP* [2000] 2 WLR 452 gave a powerful endorsement to *Kimber* which in our (not universally accepted) view currently represents the law (see also *Barnes* [2005] 2 All ER 113, CA at [17]).

What must be consented to?

It is important to realise that what must be consented to depends on the particular offence with which D is charged (For a good illustration of this point, see *Cort* [2004] 4 All ER 137, CA particularly at [19], a case on kidnapping by fraud). In rape we are looking for consent to the act of penile penetration of the vagina, anus or mouth (see 5.3.1.2 below). In battery, it is consent to the application of force or physical touching whereas, as we shall see later in this chapter, in the offence of unlawful infliction of grievous bodily harm under s. 20 of the OAPA 1861, it is consent to the risk of injury. Thus, in *Dica* [2004] EWCA Crim 1231 (see *Cases and Materials* (4.3.3.1)), the Court of Appeal stated that, where a victim became infected with HIV (the virus which often causes AIDS) as a result of agreeing to have unprotected sexual intercourse with D in ignorance of the fact that D was HIV positive, D would not be guilty of rape because V had consented to the sexual intercourse. On the other hand, V would not have consented to run the risk of harm or disease so that D could be guilty of unlawfully inflicting grievous bodily harm.

What constitutes consent?

The most obvious case is where V expressly consents whether in writing (e.g., signing a form consenting to a medical operation) or orally (e.g., asking for a massage). However, there are many instances where V's consent, though not explicit, may be implied. Remembering that the merest touching can constitute an application of force for the purposes of battery, it is not surprising that the courts are often willing to **imply** consent to physical contact in everyday situations. Everyone is deemed to consent to the normal physical contacts in everyday life, such as touching to attract attention, ordinary jostling associated with crowds and so on. It has even been suggested that a patient rendered unconscious in an accident would be deemed to consent to any necessary emergency operation (Goff LJ in *Collins* v *Wilcock* [1984] 3 All ER 374 and, again, as Lord Goff, in *F* v *West Berkshire Health Authority*).

EXERCISE 4.1

Read the extract from *Collins* v *Wilcock* in *Cases and Materials* (4.3.3.1). Goff LJ gives two possible bases for the rule that normal everyday contact does not constitute a battery. Identify them and say which one he prefers.

We shall see in the next chapter that, for the purposes of sexual offences, consent is statutorily defined as 'agreeing by choice' assuming V has 'the freedom and capacity to make that choice' (s. 74 of the Sexual Offences Act 2003). It is likely that this will be influential in assessing consent in non-sexual offences too and you should also read the discussion at 5.3.1.2 below.

Invalid consent

A consent which would otherwise prevent liability will be treated by the law as invalid where V lacks the capacity to consent or where the apparent consent is not freely given, usually due to fear, force or fraud.

Incapacity—age

If the victim is too young to understand the nature of the act he is consenting to, the consent will be of no legal effect. Thus, in *Burrell* v *Harmer* [1967] Crim LR 169, two children of 12 and 13 years of age were held to be incapable of consenting to a tattooing of themselves (such conduct is now in any case prohibited by the Tattooing of Minors Act 1969). In a case raising a number of interesting issues, *Gillick* v *West Norfolk Area Health Authority* [1985] 3 All ER 402, the House of Lords held that a girl under 16 did not, merely by reason of her age, lack legal capacity to consent to contraceptive advice and treatment. If the girl had reached an age where she had a sufficient understanding and intelligence to enable her to understand fully what was proposed, her consent would be valid. It was a question of fact in each case.

Incapacity—mental disorder or learning difficulties

A person may be unable to consent by reason of mental disability, and the test is broadly the same as that for age laid down in *Gillick* (see *Kimber* for an example): has V the ability to understand the nature and effects of the decision he is taking.

Freedom to choose—duress

If the victim's apparent consent has been procured by threats or pressure, the consent could be vitiated and invalid (*Day* (1841) 9 C & P 722). The difficulty is in identifying precisely what gravity of threat or pressure will negate consent, a problem which is particularly acute in a sexual context (e.g., sexual assault and rape). According to the Court of Appeal in

McAllister [1997] Crim LR 233, where D was convicted of indecently assaulting his wife from whom he was separated, the jury must, in each case, 'decide whether an alleged agreement to a sexual act may properly be seen as a real consent or whether it should be regarded as a submission founded on improper pressure which this particular complainant could not reasonably withstand from this particular defendant.' Submission brought about by threats of violence is clearly not consent whereas submission secured by promises of advancement (whether genuine or not *cf. Linekar* below) probably would be regarded as consent (the actor/actress and the casting couch; employer holding out hope of promotion to employee). What if submission is secured by a husband threatening to leave his wife, an employer threatening dismissal, or a teacher threatening to report a pupil's misconduct to their headteacher? The gradations in between are infinite and are left to 'the good sense of the jury' focusing on the particular victim and the particular defendant in the particular circumstances. (For the special provisions governing offences under the Sexual Offences Act 2003 see 5.3.1.2 below.)

Freedom to choose—fraud and mistake

The traditional rule is that, if the apparent consent has been procured by D's fraud (or even V's spontaneous mistake) as to the identity of the accused or as to the nature of the act, the rule is that it will be invalid. However, as long as the victim knows of the nature of the act, it is irrelevant that he is mistaken about a collateral detail of it due to D's economy with the truth. Thus, in the case of *Clarence* (1888) 22 QBD 23 (*Cases and Materials* (4.3.3.1)), there was held to be no assault where a man had sexual intercourse with his wife, knowing that he had venereal disease, which she thereby caught. He did not disclose his condition and the prosecution argued that this 'fraud' vitiated his wife's consent to the intercourse, thus rendering the bodily contact a battery. The court rejected this argument since the wife understood that she was consenting to sexual intercourse, the act that took place. As Smith and Hogan explain, it is like consenting to the injection of a vaccine, not knowing that the needle is contaminated. The consent to the physical touching is valid. On the other hand, if D has replaced the vaccine with something entirely different, e.g., heroin, and injects it into V without disclosing this, V's apparent consent would be vitiated by D's fraud as to the nature of the act. It is true that *Clarence* has been dismissed as outmoded by the Court of Appeal in *Dica* and, as we shall see, V's consent to the intercourse will not prevent conviction for inflicting grievous bodily harm under s. 20 of the OAPA 1861. Nonetheless, we think it is still accurate in regard to battery. If V had not, in fact, contracted any disease or suffered any harm from the intercourse, we doubt that D could be convicted of battery. This was the point we made earlier that it is important to be clear about what exactly needs to be consented to for the particular offence charged. The fact is that V did consent to the touching (albeit in ignorance of D's condition)—the issue in battery—even though she did not consent to run the risk of injury thereby—the issue in s. 20. (For a contrary view see Herring: *Mistaken Sex* [2005] Crim LR 511.)

? QUESTION 4.6

In each of the following situations say whether you think V's consent should be invalid for the purposes of preventing a **battery**.

(a) V consents to undergo a medical examination by V, who has falsely claimed to be a doctor.

(b) V consents to undergo a medical examination by D, a doctor, who falsely pretends that this examination is medically necessary.

(c) V consents to undergo a necessary medical examination by D, a doctor, in the presence of X, whom D falsely represents as a medical trainee, but who is present for sexual gratification.

(d) V consents to sexual intercourse with D, who deliberately fails to tell V that he (D) is HIV positive and has AIDS.

As previously stated, the traditional rule is that if the apparent consent has been procured by fraud as to the identity of the accused or as to the nature of the act, it will be invalid. The question is: has V consented to (a) the act which was done (as opposed to an act fundamentally different) and (b) that act being done by the person who did it and not somebody else (*cf.* para. 5.20 Law Commission Report: *Consent in Sex Offences*)? It follows that in situations (a) and (b) above, the 'consent' would be invalid whereas in (c) and (d) it would be valid. If in (c) X took part in the examination it would be the same as (a). However, in (d), the consent would only extend to the act of sexual intercourse and not to the risk of contracting the disease (*Dica*).

The reasoning of the Court of Appeal in *Tabassum* [2000] Crim LR 686 casts some doubt on the traditional formulation. D's false claims that he was a breast cancer specialist doing a scientific study induced women to allow him to examine their breasts. The prosecution could not establish a sexual motive and there was no evidence to disprove his claim that he was collecting information for a database on the disease, even though his medical experience was confined to a few years as a drugs salesman and the database had not been started. The Court thought there was no true consent to D's acts because, although the women had consented to the nature of the acts, they had mistaken the quality of those acts in that they would not have submitted to them if they had known D was not medically qualified and acting for a bona fide medical purpose. This is a questionable holding and certainly conflicts with general principle and the next case we consider, *Richardson*. In order to negate the validity of the victim's consent, the victim should have to mistake either the identity of D or the nature of the act, not simply an attribute or quality thereof. However, it is surely arguable that the victims here made both types of mistake suggesting the right result for the wrong reasons! The nature of the act here is not merely an examination of breasts but an examination of breasts for bona fide medical/research reasons. Further, the identity of the person here is so bound up with medical qualification and expertise that a mistake about the latter is a mistake of identity. That is for the victim the crucial identifying feature of D.

Interestingly, it was held in *Richardson* [1998] 2 Cr App R 200, CA, that D, a dentist who treated patients after she had been suspended from practising by the General Dental Council, was not guilty of assaulting them. The patients' consent to the treatment was valid notwithstanding their ignorance of D's disqualification. Seemingly a 'qualified' dentist under suspension is not qualitatively different from one not under suspension so that there was no mistake as to the identity of the accused or the nature of the act performed. A dentist is a dentist even though disqualified! This is a rather surprising conclusion and could surely not apply if the dentist had been struck off permanently, say, for gross incompetence. Qualification to practise is **the** crucial identifying feature of D for many, if not most, prospective patients, not the fact that she is Mrs Richardson!

Better applications of the basic principles occurred in two rape cases. In *Linekar (Gareth)* [1995] Crim LR 320, CA, a prostitute consented to sexual intercourse with D who had agreed to pay £25. Following the intercourse, D refused to pay. The Court of Appeal held that the prostitute's consent to the sexual intercourse negatived rape and was not vitiated by D's fraudulent misrepresentation that he was going to pay for it. Payment was only a collateral detail. There was no mistake about the nature of the act. On the other hand in *Elbekkay* [1995] Crim LR 163, CA, D was guilty of rape where he knew the woman's 'consent' was given under the mistaken apprehension that D was her boyfriend (the effect of sleepiness and drink). This issue is further considered in the context of sexual offences where statutory provisions in ss. 75 and 76 of the Sexual Offences Act 2003 may well modify the common law position applicable to non-sexual offences (see 5.3.1.2 below).

When can consent be a defence?

Even where there is an actual consent by a victim of full capacity, the law is far from saying that it is a defence to any offence of violence. The degree of violence to which a person can validly consent is limited.

The degree of harm Euthanasia is illegal and anyone deliberately killing another, even though the victim consents or even begs to be killed (perhaps because they are suffering from a painful, terminal illness) will be guilty of murder. Similarly in manslaughter by gross negligence, the fact that V consents to D's grossly negligent act is irrelevant to liability (*Wacker* and *Willoughby*—see 6.6.3.2 below). The victim's consent cannot affect liability for unlawful homicide.

However, the law's view is much stricter than this, though there is now an element of uncertainty as to how much stricter. Lord Lane CJ in *Attorney-General's Reference (No. 6 of 1980)* [1981] 2 All ER 1057, CA held that the victim's consent will not prevent criminal liability 'if actual bodily harm is intended and/or caused'. This incredibly broad principle was accepted as correct by the House of Lords in *Brown* [1993] 2 All ER 75, a case involving the intentional causing of injury during the course of consensual sado-masochistic activities. Lord Lane CJ's justification for this 'is that it is not in the public interest that people should try to cause or should cause each other actual bodily harm for no good reason.' Actual bodily harm means any injury likely to interfere with the health or comfort of the victim which is more than trifling or transient, and, as such, does not have to be at all serious.

? **QUESTION** 4.7

Can you think of any 'good reasons' for permitting consent to actual bodily harm to be a defence?

Taken literally, this means that, subject to the exceptions noted in the next section, consent can **never** be a defence to the more serious offences against the person (ss. 18, 20 and 47 of the OAPA 1861) all of which involve causing at least actual bodily harm. You might be prepared to accept this if D actually intended harm, but the rule goes further. Consent does not prevent liability if bodily harm is actually **caused, irrespective** of whether D intended it or even realised there was any risk of harm! On the present law, D could be liable even if he did not realise there was any risk of injury, let alone serious injury, in doing the acts consented to by the victim. He takes the risk of them going wrong, whether or not that possibility was foreseen by him or was even reasonably foreseeable. Furthermore, if D did intend to cause harm to the consenting V, he would be liable for battery even if he did not succeed in causing any harm.

The adoption of this principle by the House of Lords in *Brown* (albeit by a 3–2 majority) has not prevented attempts by the lower courts to avoid it, the most significant of which can be found in the case of *Dica* [2004] EWCA Crim 1103, CA. Before that, the Crown Court case of *Slingsby* [1995] Crim LR 570 had refused to adopt so harsh a line. D engaged in a number of consensual sexual acts with V culminating in the insertion of his hand in V's rectum and vagina. Injuries and cuts were caused by the signet ring on D's finger. V realised too late the seriousness of these injuries and died in hospital of septicaemia. D was charged with manslaughter and, as we shall see in **Chapter 6**, conviction in this kind of case depended on proving that D had committed an unlawful act—a battery. The court's view was that because D had consented to the sexual activity and the injuries were an accidental result of that, there was no battery. *Brown* was a case of the deliberate causing of harm, albeit consensual, whereas in this case there was no question of V consenting to injury because neither V nor D anticipated any harm resulting from their actions. The decision does seem to contradict Lord Lane CJ's dictum (approved in *Brown*) that consent will not negate liability if 'actual bodily harm is intended and/**or caused**'. However, it is surely preferable to exclude liability where D is not even aware of any risk of injury. The Court of Appeal in *Boyea* [1992] Crim LR 574 did not go that far but at least required that the resultant harm should have been reasonably foreseeable, even if not foreseen by D.

Dica [2004] EWCA 1231, CA (see *Cases and Materials* (4.3.3.1)) could be seen as attempting to impose a radical limitation on the scope of the *Brown* principle. D formed successive relationships with several women with whom he had unprotected sexual intercourse despite knowing that he was HIV positive. As a result, some of the women contracted the virus. D claimed that the women knew of his condition and therefore consented to the risk, a claim which the women denied. The trial judge, relying on *Brown*, ruled that, because bodily harm was caused to the infected women, their consent or otherwise was legally irrelevant. The Court of Appeal, ordering a re-trial, held that this was a misinterpretation of *Brown*. In their view, *Brown* was confined to cases where D **intended** to cause bodily harm whereas in this case there was no evidence that D's aim was to pass on the infection. It was the purpose of the sado-masochists in *Brown* to inflict the bodily harm which resulted and the willingness of the victims to undergo the harm could not render the acts lawful.

Such a limitation is eminently sensible as a matter of policy and it could be argued that the ratio of *Brown* is limited to intentional infliction of harm. However, it must be said that the judgments of their Lordships were not so limited and expressed the principle in the broad terms set out in *Attorney-General's Reference (No. 6 of 1980)*. Furthermore, *Brown* was applied by the Court of Appeal in *Emmett* (1999) *The Times*, 15 October 1999, a case where D appeared to foresee the harm rather than intend it. *Dica* treated it as an intentional harm case, possibly on the basis that D must have realised it was virtually certain to result (sexual games between a consenting, heterosexual, engaged couple involving asphyxiation on one occasion resulting in eye damage and neck bruising and setting fire to lighter fluid on V's breasts resulting in burns). In a more recent case, *Barnes* [2005] 2 All ER 117 (see *Cases and Materials* (4.3.3.1)), the Court of Appeal reverted to the original rule that 'where at least bodily harm is caused, consent is generally irrelevant'. Curiously the Court also asserted that V's consent is 'always a defence' where 'no bodily harm is caused' (at [7]). This is inconsistent with the principle in *Attorney-General's Reference (No. 6 of 1980)* which applies whenever actual bodily harm is '**intended** and/or caused' (our emphasis). *Dica* was interpreted as deciding that non-violent, consensual sexual contact between adults was a socially acceptable activity and thus within the public policy exceptions to the *Brown* rule in accordance with the principles next explained. *Konzani* [2005] 2 Cr App R 198, CA (see *Cases and Materials* (4.3.3.1)) supports this view of *Dica*.

The social utility of the activity   Whether the general rule is limited to the **intentional** infliction of harm or, as seems still to be the law, also includes simply causing harm, it is itself subject to significant exceptions on public policy grounds. Implicit in the quotation from Lord Lane CJ is that consent to actual bodily harm may prevent liability if it is for a 'good reason'. The courts will look at the purpose and utility of the activity in which the victim is consensually engaging and decide whether this purpose is socially acceptable and/or useful so as to override the general rule. Legitimate purposes in this context would include medical surgery for therapeutic reasons, presumably some surgery for cosmetic reasons (face-lifts, etc.) (since some of the Law Lords in *Brown* included tattooing and ear-piercing), dangerous exhibitions and properly conducted contact sports such as rugby and boxing. More abstruse suggestions by the judges in *Brown* were religious mortification (e.g., 'a father confessor ordering flagellation') and 'bravado (as where a boastful man challenges another to try to hurt him with a blow)'. The Court of Appeal in *Konzani* [2005] 2 Cr App R 14 and *Dica* accepted the public interest in promoting personal autonomy in **non-violent** adult sexual relationships (contrast the attitude in *Brown* (below) to **violent** sex). According to *Wilson (Alan Thomas)* [1996] 3 WLR 125, CA (*Cases and Materials* (4.3.3.1)), a husband who branded his initials on the buttocks of his wife at her request, using a hot knife, was not guilty of assault occasioning actual bodily harm, even though he clearly intended to cause harm. The Court distinguished *Brown* and *Donovan* on the ground that there was here 'no aggressive intent' and viewed it as akin to tattooing and body piercing on the basis that 'the appellant's desire was to assist her in what she regarded as the acquisition of a desirable piece of physical adornment.' This was an acceptable purpose which took it outside the general rule in *Brown* and allowed the wife's consent to operate as a defence.

Unacceptable purposes   Unacceptable purposes would include flagellation for sexual gratification (see *Donovan* [1934] 2 KB 498, CA), other kinds of sexual violence (sado-masochism in *Brown*, asphyxiation in *Emmett*) or an agreed fight to settle the combatant's differences (*Attorney-General's Reference (No. 6 of 1980)*). Clearly, it can be a delicate question of public policy to identify what is and what is not socially acceptable and it may be particularly difficult where ethnic minorities act in accordance with traditional customs. In *Adesanya* [1983] Crim LR 720, D was convicted of assaulting her two sons aged 14 and nine when she had their cheeks incised with their consent in accordance with Nigerian tribal custom. A similar view would presumably have been taken of female circumcision practised by some people of east African origin. But if so, where does that leave non-medical male circumcision practised by adherents of the Jewish religion? In fact, female circumcision is an offence punishable with up to ten years' imprisonment under the Female Genitals Mutilation Act 2003 (replacing the Prohibition of Female Circumcision Act 1985). Nonetheless, Lord Templeman in *Brown* viewed 'ritual circumcision' (presumably male!) as a lawful exercise.

A detailed examination of public mores in this context occurred in *Brown* [1993] 2 All ER 75, HL. A group of sado-masochistic homosexuals met in private over a number of years and willingly participated in acts of violence against each other, including genital torture, for the purposes of sexual gratification. It was held, by a slim 3–2 majority, that the victims' consent was no defence where the acts inflicted more than transient or trifling injuries, i.e., actual bodily harm, notwithstanding that no permanent injury was suffered and no medical treatment received.

Emmett (1999) *The Times*, 15 October 1999, CA applied *Brown* in a case involving consensual, heterosexual activity between an engaged couple—asphyxiation on one occasion resulting in eye damage and neck bruising, and setting fire to lighter fluid on another resulting in a breast burn. The Court of Appeal, refusing to differentiate between homosexual and heterosexual sadomasochism, confirmed D's conviction on two counts of assault occasioning actual bodily harm. *Wilson* was distinguished on the basis that the 'actual or potential damage to which the appellant's partner was exposed in this case, plainly went far beyond that which was established by the evidence in *Wilson*.' Although, in contrast to *Brown* (and *Wilson*), the injury was not intended (though erroneously treated as such in *Dica*), D was aware of the risk of it, unlike Slingsby.

You will probably have gathered from the rather haphazard list of exceptions noted that there is no overriding principle used by the courts to determine when an activity is legitimate and when not. This was admitted by Lord Woolf CJ in *Barnes* who stated, 'The advantage of identifying that the offence is based upon public policy is that it renders it unnecessary to find a separate jurisprudential basis for the application of the defence in the various different factual contexts in which an offence could be committed' (at[11]). Thus decisions are based on the court's perception of the social acceptability and/or utility of the particular activity and made on a case-by-case basis. This allows 'changing public attitudes' to 'affect the activities which are classified as unlawful'. (As recently as 1954 Lord Denning expressed the view that a man's vasectomy would be unlawful if it was 'to enable him to have the pleasure of sexual intercourse without shouldering the responsibilities attaching to it' (*Bravery* v *Bravery* [1954] 3 All ER 59, CA). Clearly, there is no question but that today the patient's consent would render a vasectomy lawful.)

Sports Most sporting activity would be regarded as beneficial to the community and so generally legitimate for this purpose. Of course, sometimes the circumstances may lead to a different finding as in the case of prize fighting not conducted under the auspices of the recognised boxing authorities. As a matter of fact, a participant in a properly conducted sport involving physical contact impliedly consents to the physical contact implicit in such a game, notwithstanding that there is always a risk of suffering injury or even death. We should observe that unlike some of the other situations where D consents to a specific course of conduct designed to inflict the harm, e.g., surgical incisions, in sporting situations (except, perhaps, boxing) D is consenting only to run the **risk** of injury inherent in playing that sport. The Court of Appeal in *Barnes* has cautioned against too ready a use of criminal prosecution given that most organised sports have their own disciplinary system for enforcing rules and standards of conduct.

However, a participant's implied consent will be limited to physical contact that, objectively, can be reasonably anticipated as part and parcel of the sport in question. The rules of the game are important, although certainly not conclusive (*Bradshaw* (1878) 14 Cox CC 83; *Moore* (1898) 14 TLR 229), but if D's conduct does not go beyond the rules and practice of the game, it is almost certain that he will not be liable. At the other extreme, D will not be regarded as consenting to a deliberate punch or kick in an off-the-ball incident in games like football (see, for example, *Johnson* (1986) 8 Cr App R (S) 343—D bit opponent's ear in police rugby match; *Lloyd* [1989] Crim LR 513—D kicked rugby opponent's face as he lay on the ground; *Billinghurst* [1978] Crim LR 553 where an off the ball punch fractured V's jaw. Obviously sports like boxing, wrestling and martial arts would be different). These propositions can be derived from *Barnes* where V sustained a serious leg injury as a result of D's tackle during an amateur football match. Between these clear extremes is a grey area where D's conduct is outside the rules (even to the extent of being sent off) but may be 'an instinctive reaction, error or misjudgment in the heat of the game.' Whether the threshold of criminality has been reached is an objective question independent of the views of the players. All the circumstances must be considered including the 'type of sport, the level at which it is played, the nature of the act, the degree of force used, the extent of the risk of injury' and 'the state of mind of the defendant' (at [12]–[16]).

Finally, consent to participation in rough and undisciplined horseplay has been held to negative liability even where serious injury has resulted, provided there is no **intention** to harm (*Jones* (1986) 83 Cr App R 375, CA—teenagers causing serious injury to 14- and 15-year-old boys by tossing them in the air; *Aitken* [1992] 1 WLR 1006, Courts Martial Appeal Court (a very questionable decision); *Richardson and Irwin* [1999] 1 Cr App R 392, CA—student hijinks!).

 EXERCISE 4.2

Read the extracts from *Brown* in *Cases and Materials* (4.3.3.1) for an illustration (a) of the difficulties in drawing the line in this area; (b) of the divergent views of even Law Lords as to where it should be drawn; and (c) of the competing interests which need to be balanced by the law. Where would you draw the line?

4.3.3.2 *Mens rea* of battery

The prosecution must prove an intention to apply **unlawful** force to another or subjective recklessness as to the application of such force, i.e., realisation by D that unlawful force might be applied as a result of his actions. We would reiterate the point made in relation to psychic assault that *Caldwell*-type objective recklessness does not suffice (see *Spratt* [1991] 2 All ER 210, CA and *Parmenter* [1991] 2 All ER 225, CA and later discussion on s. 47 of the OAPA 1861).

We would emphasise that the *mens rea* is not just an intention or subjective recklessness as to the application of force to the victim, but as to the application of **unlawful** force to the victim. The *actus reus* is not just the application of force but the application of **unlawful** force and D must have *mens rea* (intention or subjective recklessness) in relation to all elements of the *actus reus* including the element of **unlawful** force (*Williams* (1984) 78 Cr App R 276, CA; *Kimber* [1983] 1 WLR 1118, CA—*Cases and Materials* (4.3.3.2)). Therefore if D, however unreasonably, mistakenly believed that the facts were such that the force he was applying was lawful, he could not be guilty. For example, in *Williams* D thought he was preventing V from assaulting a third party whereas in fact V was engaged in effecting a lawful citizen's arrest against that third party. Because of his mistake D lacked the intention to apply **unlawful** force, nor did he realise that he might be applying unlawful force, and so was not guilty.

At this point, we need to caution you to be clear on what precisely this means. Although we might tend to refer in shorthand to an intention to apply unlawful force, the actual position is more complicated than that. More accurately, D must intend or be subjectively reckless as to the application of force in circumstances which the law says make the force unlawful. It is not necessary to prove that D realised that the force was or might be unlawful (whether it is or not in any given circumstances is a question of criminal law), but it is necessary to show that he at least realised that he might be applying force in circumstances which, **objectively according to the law (whether he realised it or not)**, rendered the force **unlawful**. This means that if D makes a mistake about those circumstances, he must be judged on the circumstances as he believed them to be rather than as they actually were. This is true even if his belief is unreasonable although, of course, the more unreasonable his belief, the more likely the jury is to conclude that he did not actually hold the claimed belief. In *Williams* the force D used was reasonable and necessary to prevent the crime he thought was being committed. He therefore intended to apply force which, in the circumstances he believed to exist, was not unlawful.

Similarly, belief that a person is consenting in circumstances rendering that consent valid, means that D intends to apply force which, in the circumstances understood by D, is lawful (*Kimber* [1983] 1 WLR 1118, CA; *Jones* [1987] Crim LR 123, CA). It was held in *Richardson and Irwin* [1999] 1 Cr App R 392, CA that even a **drunken** mistake that P had consented to indulge in horseplay would negate the defendants' *mens rea* (see 8.4.7.1 below for a criticism of the case). However, as explained above, the majority House of Lords' decision in *Brown* [1993] 2 All ER 75 cast doubt on the correctness of the view in *Kimber* that the *actus reus* requires proof of the application of non-consensual (unlawful in this context) force and that therefore the *mens rea* requires an intention to apply non-consensual force or realisation by D (subjective recklessness) that he might be applying non-consensual force. The House's view would presumably be that if D mistakenly thinks the victim is consenting, D would still have performed the *actus reus* with the necessary *mens rea*. His mistake would be as to a matter of defence and, as we shall see in the section on mistake in **Chapter 8**, his mistake would be ignored and no defence **unless** it was a **reasonable** mistake.

However, any doubts about the correctness of *Kimber* and *Williams* seem to have been swept aside by the unanimous views, albeit obiter, of the House of Lords in *B* v *DPP* [2000] 1 All ER 833 and again in *K* [2001] UKHL 41 (see 8.5.2.3 and 13.4.1 below). It follows that, contrary to the majority in *Brown*, the element of unlawfulness should be seen as an element of the *actus reus* rather than as a matter of defence. Therefore *mens rea* is required in respect of this element of unlawfulness.

4.3.4 Reform

The view that absence of consent is not a definitional element of the crime but simply a matter of defence underlies both the Law Commission's Consultation Paper on Consent (Law Com. No. 139) and the Government's draft Offences Against the Person Bill. The former provisionally proposes that a valid consent (which is proposed to be extensively defined) should automatically be a defence to any offence against the person save for the intentional or reckless causing of 'seriously disabling injury' (also defined). The preferred view seems to be that **mistaken** belief in consent would not be a defence where it would be obvious to a reasonable person that V might not be consenting. In effect, there would be a positive onus on D to verify consent, given the invasion of V's bodily integrity.

The Government's draft Bill would amalgamate the currently distinct offences of assault and battery into one offence of assault which can be committed in either of two ways:

(a) where D 'intentionally or recklessly applies force to or causes an impact on the body of another'; or

(b) he 'intentionally or recklessly causes the other to believe that any such force or impact is imminent' (cl. 4).

It is made clear that in all the proposed offences against the person, 'recklessly' requires D to be aware of the risk that the relevant result will occur 'and it is unreasonable to take that risk having regard to the circumstances as he knows or believes them to be' (cl. 14).

Interestingly, the issue of the 'unlawfulness' of the force (as for all the proposed new offences) is left to the current law by providing in cl. 18 that any provisions 'have effect subject to any enactment or rule of law providing (a) a defence or (b) lawful authority, justification or excuse for an act or omission.' Thus it appears that, as the majority in *Brown*, the framers of the Act imply that consent is a matter of defence and, even, it seems, actions in self-defence and the prevention of crime. It remains to be seen whether this will affect the current law governing mistakes about consent, self-defence, etc. (see above and 8.5.3 below).

Otherwise, substantively, this seems more or less to reflect the current law.

4.4 The more serious offences

4.4.1 Assault occasioning actual bodily harm

Section 47 of the OAPA 1861 states:

> Whosoever shall be convicted on indictment of any assault occasioning actual bodily harm shall be liable . . . to be imprisoned for any term not exceeding five years . . .

Notice that the statute does not define what is meant by an assault occasioning actual bodily harm and to discover the meaning of these words we have to look at the case law.

4.4.1.1 *Actus reus*

The *actus reus* of the offence is:

(a) an assault

(b) which causes (occasioning)

(c) actual bodily harm.

Assault

The assault required here is the same as that previously discussed and it is important to realise that it can be either a psychic or a physical assault provided that some physical harm results. Curiously, there is no case which definitively establishes this proposition, but most commentators would accept it as undoubtedly correct. The House of Lords in *Savage; Parmenter* [1991] 4 All ER 698 took the view that a technical assault causing actual bodily harm was covered by s. 47 but omitted to consider the case where there was no psychic assault but simply a battery causing harm. However, it would be ludicrous if such a case were excluded from s. 47 and 'assault' must be used in its loose, general sense to mean either psychic or physical assault. Otherwise to injure a sleeping person or, say, a baby unable to apprehend imminent violence would be outside s. 47. In *Parmenter* itself the victim was a very young child so that the House of Lords can be taken to have implicitly endorsed the view that battery without psychic assault is enough. In *Ireland*, the House accepted, obiter, that this view was correct.

Occasioning

For practical purposes, 'occasioning' can be regarded as synonymous with the term 'causing' and whether the assault can be said to have caused the harm depends on applying the normal principles of causation considered mainly in **Chapter 2** in connection with *actus reus*.

The main problem is likely to arise where the harm is an indirect result of an assault, and is illustrated by the case of *Roberts* (1971) 56 Cr App R 95 (*Cases and Materials* (4.4.1.1)). D, who was driving his car, made improper suggestions and threats to a woman passenger, V, and attempted to remove her coat, as a result of which she leapt from the moving vehicle suffering actual bodily harm. D argued that the chain of causation between his admitted assault and V's injury had been broken by the action of V in deliberately jumping out of the moving vehicle.

The Court of Appeal dismissed D's appeal and held that so long as V's actions were the reasonably foreseeable consequence of D's assault, D's actions had caused the injury. In this case V's jumping out of the car was an understandable reaction to what D had said and done and therefore the injury was a reasonably foreseeable result of his assault. On the other hand, where the victim's reaction is totally unreasonable or, in the words of the Court of Appeal, 'daft', the chain of causation would be broken and D not liable for this offence. (He could, of course, be liable for common assault.)

Actual bodily harm

The classic definition comes from *Miller* [1954] 2 QB 282 and means any hurt or injury likely to interfere with the health or comfort of the victim. Clearly, the injury does not have to be terribly serious (although it does have to be more than 'trifling or transient'

(*Brown* [1993] 2 All ER 75, HL)), and, it is submitted, that any medically diagnosable condition would be covered. According to *Miller*, the victim's hysterical and nervous condition could be actual bodily harm but this was rejected by the Court of Appeal in *Chan-Fook* [1994] 2 All ER 552 (*Cases and Materials* (4.2.1)). Psychiatric injury is capable of amounting to actual bodily harm but it must result in some 'identifiable clinical condition'. Strong emotions such as extreme fear, distress or panic are not actual bodily harm. Neither is any other state of mind unless evidencing an 'identifiable clinical condition'. The House of Lords in *Ireland* warmly endorsed the *Chan-Fook* principles holding that bodily harm includes 'recognisable psychiatric illness' such as anxiety neurosis and depressive disorders. Expert psychiatric evidence is required to establish that P's symptoms not only amounted to psychiatric illness or injury but were also caused by D's assault (*Morris (Clarence)* [1998] 1 Cr App R 386, CA).

Although trivial injuries are within the term, common sense would suggest that there must come a point where the discomfort is so trivial that it cannot justify the description 'actual bodily harm'. In practice the decision whether to charge s. 47 rather than plain battery is likely to be determined by the *Offences against the Person Charging Standard* (Crown Prosecution Service: *Charging Standards*, 2005, Oxford University Press, Ch. 3) issued by the Crown Prosecution Service, even though it has no legal status and is advisory only. This recommends a s. 47 charge in the event of loss or breaking of a tooth, temporary loss of sensory function, extensive or multiple bruising, displaced broken nose, minor fractures, minor, but not merely superficial, cuts probably requiring medical treatment such as stitches or psychiatric injury which is more than fear, distress or panic.

What is surprising is that the Law Commission's proposed definition of injury seems to be in even **wider** terms than the existing definition! There might be a case for narrowing the definition, but surely not widening it (see Law Com. No. 218, p. 30 and *Cases and Materials* (4.3)).

? **QUESTION** 4.8

Why is the width of the definition of actual bodily harm important when considering the defence of consent in battery? (Refer back to 4.3.3.1 on 'Consent' if you cannot answer this question.)

4.4.1.2 *Mens rea*

The *mens rea* for this offence was clarified by the House of Lords following a spate of cases which created difficulties (*Savage*; *Parmenter* [1991] 4 All ER 698, HL) (see *Cases and Materials* (4.4.1.2)). Until the case of *Spratt* [1991] 2 All ER 210, the leading authority of *Roberts* (1971) 56 Cr App R 95, CA held sway and required the prosecution to prove only the *mens rea* for

---

? **QUESTION** 4.9

What is the respective *mens rea* for assault and battery? Refer to 4.3.2.2 and 4.3.3.2 if you do not know.

the assault or battery.

Therefore, no *mens rea* needed to be proved in relation to the causing of harm. So, in *Roberts*, D intended to apply force to his victim when he tried to take off her coat. The fact that he did not intend any harm, or realise that he might cause harm thereby, was irrelevant because no *mens rea* was needed in relation to the causing of harm.

After a division of opinion in the Court of Appeal as to the correctness of *Roberts*, the House of Lords in the consolidated appeals of *Savage; Parmenter* endorsed the view in *Roberts* that s. 47 does *not* require proof of any *mens rea* in relation to the causing of harm. It does not matter that D neither intended nor foresaw any harm. The Court of Appeal's contrary view in *Parmenter* and *Spratt* was therefore overruled. The only *mens rea* needed for s. 47 is **either** intention or subjective recklessness as to the application of force (i.e., the *mens rea* for battery) **or** intention or subjective recklessness as to putting someone in fear of immediate force (i.e., the *mens rea* for psychic assault).

Regrettably, the House of Lords failed to resolve the question of whether the recklessness required for assault and battery extended to include *Caldwell*-type objective recklessness. However, most commentators believed that a minimum of subjective recklessness was required. That formed the ratio of *Spratt* [1991] 2 All ER 210, CA and there are dicta in Lord Ackner's speech supporting it. Any doubt has been dispelled by the House of Lords' decision in *G* [2003] UKHL 50.

It follows from the above that the **only** difference between s. 47 and common assault is the requirement to cause actual bodily harm (*G* [2001] Crim LR 898, CA). If there is no common assault, there is no s. 47 offence either (*Blackburn* v *Bowering* [1994] 3 All ER 380, CA).

4.4.1.3 **Reform**

Clause 3 of the draft Offences Against the Person Bill would replace s. 47 with the offence of intentionally or recklessly causing injury to another. As mentioned in relation to the reform of assault, recklessness is confined to subjective awareness of risk on the part of D (cl. 14). Unlike the present s. 47, D would have at least to foresee a risk of injury, which is entirely proper for an offence carrying up to five years' imprisonment. Clearly liability for the new offence would not depend on the **means** by which the injury is caused and there would be no need for any assault (e.g., persistent telephone calls or letters could be caught whether or not they constituted an assault).

The definition of 'injury' (applicable to all the new offences) endorses the recent case law developments culminating in *Ireland* by including both physical and mental injury (cl. 15). Injury 'does not include anything caused by disease but (subject to that)' physical injury 'includes pain, unconsciousness and any other impairment of a person's physical condition' whilst mental injury 'includes any impairment of a person's mental health'. All the new 'injury' offences are expressed to cover cases where the injury is suffered abroad provided the acts causing it occurred in England or Wales (e.g., letter bomb posted in England to France).

4.4.2 **Section 20 of the Offences Against the Person Act 1861**

Section 20 makes it an offence for anyone to 'unlawfully and maliciously wound or inflict any grievous bodily harm upon any other person, either with or without any weapon or instrument'.

There are two alternative ways of committing this offence—(a) maliciously inflicting grievous bodily harm or (b) maliciously wounding. Both alternatives are regarded in practice as more serious than the offence under s. 47, although, surprisingly, the maximum sentence is five years' imprisonment for both s. 20 and s. 47.

4.4.2.1 *Actus reus*

(a) Inflicting grievous bodily harm

The House of Lords in *DPP* v *Smith* [1961] AC 290 defined grievous bodily harm as 'really serious harm'. However, the Court of Appeal in *Saunders* [1985] Crim LR 230 held that it was not necessarily a misdirection for the trial judge to define it as 'serious harm', omitting the 'really'. It is a matter for the judge in the light of the factual situation in the case, but it is certainly not necessary to use 'really' in the context of a deadly attack with a five-and-a-half inch knife blade (*Janjua* [1999] 1 Cr App R 91, CA). There is no definition of what serious means, but it would certainly include broken limbs, severe internal injuries, or anything which results in significant disablement of the victim, whether permanent or merely temporary. The Court of Appeal in *Bollom* [2004] Cr App R 6 confirmed that there is no need to prove the harm was 'life-threatening, dangerous or permanent' or even required treatment. In this case, bruising and abrasions to a 17-month-old child even though superficial and capable of healing spontaneously without treatment, were sufficiently numerous and extensive over the body to constitute grievous bodily harm. The Court emphasised that the gravity of the injuries had to be assessed by reference to the particular individual so that what might be relatively trivial for a healthy adult could be grievous in the case of a frail, old person or, as here, a very young child. The Crown Prosecution Service's non-statutory Charging Standard recommends a s. 18 or s. 20 charge only for injuries resulting in permanent disability or loss of sensory function, non-minor permanent visible disfigurement, broken or displaced limbs or bones, compound fractures, broken cheekbone, jaw, ribs, etc., injuries which cause substantial loss of blood and injuries resulting in lengthy treatment or incapacity.

You may recall from our discussion of s. 47 that the House of Lords in *Ireland* held unanimously that 'bodily harm' embraces 'recognisable psychiatric illness' including neuroses such as anxiety and depressive disorders. The House also held that such psychiatric illnesses, if sufficiently serious as in *Burstow*, will constitute **grievous** bodily harm under ss. 18 and 20.

What does 'inflict' mean? For s. 20, the GBH must be **inflicted** where, as we shall see shortly, the corresponding part of the more serious s. 18 offence requires that the GBH be **caused**. Until the recent case of *Burstow* [1997] 3 WLR 534, HL, it was universally accepted that 'inflict' bore a narrower meaning than 'cause'. The famous old case of *Clarence* (1888) 22 QBD 23 held, in effect, that 'inflict' meant cause **by means of a direct assault**. Several subsequent cases cast doubt on this requirement (e.g., *Lewis* [1970] Crim LR 647; *Cartledge* v *Allen* [1973] Crim LR 530) and it was finally removed by the House of Lords in *Wilson* [1983] 3 All ER 448 (confirmed again in *Mandair* [1994] 2 All ER 715, HL).

The *ratio decidendi* of *Wilson* is that a person can inflict GBH without an assault or battery being committed. However, the House, obiter, approved the view in the Australian case of *Salisbury* [1976] VR 452 that D inflicted GBH only if he caused it **by means of an application of force to the body**. Without a violent impact on the body, there could be no infliction of GBH under s. 20. For example, if D caused GBH by gassing or poisoning, there would be no violent impact and so no infliction (though D would *cause* GBH—the *actus reus* for s. 18).

EXERCISE 4.3

Read the extract from *Burstow* in *Cases and Materials* (4.2.2.1) and then answer the following questions:

(a) Did the House of Lords define 'inflict' as requiring (i) an assault or battery, or (ii) a direct or indirect application of force?

(b) Did the House hold there to be any difference between 'cause' in s. 18 and 'inflict' in s. 20? If so, what?

In the consolidated appeals of *Ireland* and *Burstow* the House of Lords unanimously held that a person can inflict GBH even though no physical violence is applied directly or indirectly to the body of the victim. Thus, although their Lordships confirmed the ratio of Wilson that infliction did not necessitate any assault or battery, they rejected the *obiter* dictum requiring an application of force. Burstow was yet another stalker who made numerous silent and abusive telephone calls to the victim, persistently waited for her outside her home and workplace and sent her a menacing note. This campaign of harassment caused her to suffer a severe depressive illness, which, as we have seen already, was a serious psychiatric injury held to constitute grievous bodily harm. The House held that a stalker whose campaign of harassment caused serious psychological harm inflicted GBH under s. 20 even though no force was applied to the victim and even if, contrary to the situation in *Ireland*, there was no assault because the victim never feared an **immediate** application of force. 'Inflict' had to be given its 'current meaning' in 'present day conditions' rather than its original meaning when enacted in 1861: 'As a matter of current usage the contextual interpretation of "inflict" can embrace the idea of one person inflicting psychiatric injury on another.' Presumably the same would apply where D gasses or poisons another.

Lord Steyn, who spoke for all their Lordships, built on very slender dicta in holding that 'in the context of the Act of 1861 there is no radical divergence between the meaning of the two words ["cause" in s. 18 and "inflict" in s. 20]'. However, he was 'not saying that the words [were] exactly synonymous'. Regrettably no explanation was forthcoming as to how they differed. Lord Hope, with whom only Lord Goff agreed, after asserting that 'for all practical purposes there is . . . no difference between these two words', then identified a difference: 'The word "inflict" implies that the consequence of the act is something which the victim is likely to find unpleasant or harmful' and to his detriment whereas cause is 'neutral' and 'may embrace pleasure as well as pain'. It is not clear what his Lordship had in mind (probably not the sadomasochists in *Brown*!), but it is suggested that it is an unnecessary and inappropriate distinction which will be quietly ignored in the future.

The conclusion we draw is that, in future, where D has caused GBH under the normal principles of causation, it is almost inevitable that he will be held also to have inflicted GBH. In practice, there does not seem to be any difference between 'inflict' in s. 20 and 'cause' in s. 18. Thus, if D infects V with HIV through unprotected sexual intercourse, then it follows from *Burstow* that D inflicts GBH, even if the intercourse is consented to by V. *Clarence* which decided the opposite has been consigned to the historical dustbin by *Dica* [2004] EWCA Crim 1103. It appears that the courts will no longer feel constrained to accept old anomalies arising from the 1861 statute where they make no sense in modern conditions.

One final point emerges from *Bollom* (discussed above) in cases where there is an accumulation of injuries which may have occurred over a period of time. It must be proved that the injuries arising from 'one continuous course of conduct constituting a single assault' are themselves sufficiently serious to constitute grievous bodily harm. It is not permissible to add up the injuries from 'distinct and separate assaults' to reach the threshold of GBH.

(b) Wounding

For a wound to be suffered, both the inner and outer skin, i.e., the dermis and the epidermis, must be broken. It follows that purely internal injuries cannot amount to a wound, so that in *JJC v Eisenhower* [1983] 3 All ER 230, DC it was held that broken blood vessels in the victim's eye caused by airgun pellets did not constitute a wound. We should point out that an injury may constitute both a wound and GBH but it need not necessarily. Thus, a trivial cut will be a wound but not serious enough for grievous bodily harm. Similarly, a serious injury may not involve any break in the skin and therefore, whilst this would be GBH, it would not be a wound. A wound will necessarily amount to actual bodily harm for the purposes of s. 47. Although, literally, even a small cut or laceration would be a 'wound', the CPS's Charging Standard recommends that prosecutors should charge s. 47 rather than s. 20 unless the wounds 'are considered to be serious (thus equating the offence with the infliction of grievous, or serious, bodily harm under the other part of' s. 20).

There are cases (*Taylor* (1869) 11 Cox CC 261 and *Beasley* (1981) 73 Cr App R 44) which hold that in order to wound, D must cause the wound by means of an assault or battery, i.e., the same rule that *Clarence* had enunciated for inflicting grievous bodily harm. You may remember that *Wilson* overturned the *Clarence* principle in relation to the infliction of GBH and it might be assumed that it would have affected the similar rule for wounding. Surprisingly, the House of Lords in *Wilson* specifically disclaimed any intention of affecting the meaning of wounding and indeed seemed to accept that *Taylor* is still good law. Technically, therefore, the *Beasley* rule must still be considered good law, although it seems unlikely, if the matter arose in the future, that the rule would be retained. Certainly, if the point came before the House of Lords, we would expect the rule to be assimilated to the new position on inflicting GBH, so that an assault or battery would not be an essential requirement. This is especially so in the light of the House of Lords' general stance in *Burstow* though 'wounding' was not there considered.

Both the House of Lords and Court of Appeal obiter in *Savage* envisaged that there could be 'wounding' without a battery, although the facts would have to be 'quite extraordinary'. There was no elaboration of what this meant.

Whatever the position on that point, it should again be emphasised that the prosecution must prove that D's conduct caused the wound and the same causation principles discussed previously come into play.

(c) Unlawfully—more about consent

You will recall our extensive discussion about the force applied in battery having to be 'unlawful' force, particularly in relation to the consent of the victim. Equally this is a facet of the other offences against the person including s. 20 which speaks of 'unlawfully wounds or inflicts' GBH. A number of the cases we looked at were charges under s. 20 and/ or s. 47.

? QUESTION 4.10

What is the consequence for charges under both s. 20 and s. 47 of the wide interpretation of *Brown*? What is the narrow interpretation of *Brown* suggested by *Dica*?

If *Brown* is applied literally, consent could never be a defence to a charge under either section unless one of the public interest exceptions applied such as surgery or approved sporting activities. This is because, by definition in these offences, at least actual bodily harm must have been caused. However, one interpretation of *Dica* might be that the ratio of *Brown* should be confined to cases where D **intended** to cause harm and not applied to cases where harm was an incidental, unintended (even if foreseen) result. Thus, in *Dica*, if D had intended to infect the women, he would still have been guilty even where the women victims had consented to unprotected intercourse **knowing** that D was HIV positive. But where he did not intend to infect, *Brown* did not apply and **knowing** consent negated liability under s. 20. Unfortunately subsequent cases have viewed *Dica* as based on a public interest exception in respect of sexual autonomy in non-violent sexual relations rather than generalizing it into a blanket restriction on the scope of *Brown* (*Konzani* [2005] 2 Cr App R 198, CA; *Barnes*—see 'Consent' at 4.3.3.1 above).

Talk about consent raises the question: consent to what. Unfortunately, the cases are often less than clear on this but, logically, the object of the consent must vary according to what must be proved for the crime charged. For ordinary battery, based as it is on a simple touching, it should be consent to the touching or risk of touching whereas for s. 20, inflicting grievous bodily harm, it should be consent to the risk of grievous bodily harm (seemingly the view in *Konzani* [2005] 2 Cr App R 198, CA). For s. 47, assault occasioning actual bodily harm, it should be consent to the risk of actual bodily harm. However, since the section requires the harm to be caused by means of an assault, should it not require V to know he is risking not just harm but harm **by means of an assault or battery**? If so, V's consent to the touching (even if unaware of the risk of harm) would negate the assault or battery and, logically, any offence under s. 47! This question has not been addressed by the courts but it seems highly unlikely that they would regard V as consenting where he was unaware of the risk of harm.

Let us consider how this might work out in the topical area of sexually transmitted disease. For s. 20, it is not enough for V to consent to the activity engendering the risk. V must consent **realising** the harm that is being risked by such activity. Thus, in *Dica*, there was no consent unless it was proved that the victims were aware there was a risk of sexually transmitted disease.

? **QUESTION** 4.11

But surely in this day and age anyone having unprotected sexual intercourse would know that there was always a risk of contracting a sexually transmitted disease (even if not necessarily HIV)? Does not that mean that V does knowingly consent to run the risk?

The answer of the Court in *Dica* was:

> Given the long-term nature of the relationships, if the appellant concealed the truth about his condition from them, and therefore kept them in ignorance of it, there was no reason for them to think that they were running any risk of infection, and they were not consenting to it.

Thus the Court appeared to stress the fact that D's encounters occurred in the context of steady relationships where V would have come to trust D and feel safe in assuming that D would not put them at risk but would disclose any infections he knew or suspected he had. This suggested that casual, unprotected sex might be different. However, the Court of Appeal in *Konzani*, a case with similar facts, recognised no such limitation. In their view, what was needed was **informed** consent and V's ignorance of D's condition at the time of the sexual intercourse would preclude such a consent. Furthermore, 'there is a critical distinction between taking a risk of the various, potentially adverse and possibly problematic consequences of sexual intercourse, and giving an informed consent to the risk of infection with a fatal disease.' This suggests that D's knowledge and consent must relate to the specific risk of contracting HIV. It would not be sufficient to consent to the risk of other non-fatal sexually transmitted diseases such as chlamydia, herpes or gonorrhoea (one of the victims admitted in cross-examination that she was aware of the risk of sexually transmitted diseases though not HIV). This supports the view that for s. 20 the consent must relate to the risk of **serious** injury, i.e., grievous bodily harm. It is clear, therefore, that a person who, despite knowing (or presumably merely suspecting) he is HIV positive, does not convey this to his partner in unprotected sex (whether they are in a relationship or not) is wildly unlikely to escape conviction under s. 20 by pleading consent.

Suppose, however, that V contracts herpes from sexual intercourse with D who knows of his condition. Herpes would be unlikely to be serious enough to be classed as grievous bodily harm so that s. 20 would be ruled out. (It might certainly be argued that chlamydia, which can cause infertility in infected women, and syphilis, potentially fatal if untreated, would amount to grievous bodily harm.) Since it would certainly be actual bodily harm, a charge under s. 47 is possible. Assuming V is ignorant of the risk of any infection, there would be no consent to run the risk of harm. However, it could be argued that V's consent to the intercourse does preclude any idea of assault or battery (in the same way it precludes rape). If so, how could there be an assault occasioning actual bodily harm? We doubt whether the courts would accept such an argument but, if it is wrong, the implication is that anyone who knows (or probably suspects) he is infected with any sexually transmittable disease is guilty of battery every time he has sexual intercourse with someone who is ignorant of his condition, **whether or not the victim is actually infected**.

The whole area of consent is ripe for legislative reform or at least reconsideration by the House of Lords.

4.4.2.2 *Mens rea*

Whether the *actus reus* is based on a wound or an infliction of GBH, the prosecution must prove that D acted 'maliciously'. This word has a strictly technical legal meaning and should not be considered in the light of its everyday meaning. It means that D must intend or foresee a particular result. As we have seen, foresight of a result by D is the same as saying that D must be subjectively reckless as to that result.

When the House of Lords redefined recklessness in *Caldwell*, there was a possibility that it might have been extended to cover offences against the person so as to render proof of objective recklessness as sufficient *mens rea*. This was always unlikely because *Caldwell* itself indicated that it was concerned with cases where the word reckless actually appeared in the statutory definition of the offence and offences using the old-fashioned word 'maliciously' were expressly excluded from the principles enunciated. This expectation was confirmed by the Court of Appeal in cases such as *W v Dolbey* [1983] Crim LR 681 and *Grimshaw* [1984] Crim LR 108.

Therefore, intention or subjective recklessness is required, but what is the consequence which D must intend or be subjectively reckless about? Although logic would suggest that D must intend or be reckless as to the *actus reus*, i.e., causing a wound or inflicting GBH, this is not the law. It was laid down in *Mowatt* [1967] 3 All ER 47, CA that D need only have intended or foreseen the possibility of *some* physical harm occurring to the victim, albeit neither serious nor a wound. This was endorsed by the Court of Appeal in *Sullivan* [1981] Crim LR 46 which made it clear that an intention merely to frighten did not suffice. In *Sullivan*, D drove his car towards a group of pedestrians standing on the pavement. He lost control of the car, which mounted the pavement causing serious injuries to some of the pedestrians. The Court of Appeal quashed his conviction on the grounds that the jury had not been properly directed that it could only convict if it was sure that D had actually realised that he might cause some harm to another. The Divisional Court in *DPP v A* [2001] Crim LR 140 warned that D was not required to foresee that harm **would** occur (that might constitute intention under the *Woollin* rule), but only that it **might** occur.

The principles above were confirmed by the House of Lords in *Savage; Parmenter* (*Cases and Materials* (4.4.2.2)). Although *Mowatt* talks of having to intend or foresee some **physical** harm, in the light of the holding in *Ireland; Burstow* that actual bodily harm includes psychological illness and injury, it seems inevitable that the *Mowatt* principle will be extended to include intending or foreseeing recognised psychiatric harm. We would submit that D must intend some harm, whether physical or psychiatric and whether serious or non-serious, or, alternatively, foresee that such harm might result from his conduct. Once again there may be difficulty in convicting stalkers, for the prosecution will have to prove beyond reasonable doubt that, at the least, the stalker realised that his attentions might result in 'recognisable psychiatric illness' (as opposed to simple fear and anxiety).

In the sexual disease cases, it is therefore usually obvious that a D, who knows or suspects he is infected, has the necessary foresight. It was accepted in *Konzani* that D must also have *mens rea* in respect of V's lack of **informed** consent so that if he honestly (even if unreasonably) believed that V knew of his condition and the risk of contracting the disease, he could not be convicted. In other words, as we discussed under the *mens rea* of battery, an element of *mens rea* in respect of the 'unlawfulness' of D's conduct is required in the same way for s. 20 so that if D's mistake of fact about V's consent negates that *mens rea*, he is not guilty (see *Kimber* and *Williams* at 4.3.3.2 above).

4.4.2.3 **Reform**

The replacement for s. 20 in the draft Offences Against the Person Bill carrying up to seven years' imprisonment is refreshingly simple—where D 'recklessly causes serious injury to another' (cl. 2). V must suffer 'serious injury' (mere wounding is insufficient), but there is no definition of 'serious' which would have to be interpreted by the courts, presumably in the same way as 'grievous' under the current law (see 4.4.1.3 for the meaning of injury). The other major change would be the requirement that D must recognise the risk of **serious** injury thus overturning the current *Mowatt* principle requiring foresight of only **some harm**, whether serious or not. Again there would be no restriction on the means by which the serious injury should be caused, thus avoiding once and for all any arguments about the meaning of 'inflict' or 'wounding' (*cf. Burstow*).

4.4.3 **Section 18 of the Offences Against the Person Act 1861**

Section 18 provides that it shall be an offence to 'unlawfully and maliciously wound or cause any grievous bodily harm to any person by any means whatsoever with intent to do some grievous bodily harm, or with intent to resist or prevent the lawful apprehension or detainer of any person.'

4.4.3.1 *Actus reus*—wounding or causing grievous bodily harm

The terms 'wound' and 'grievous bodily harm' presumably bear the same meaning as for s. 20. As previously intimated, the meaning of cause was traditionally held to be wider than inflict in s. 20. This is underlined by the use in s. 18 of the words 'by any means whatsoever'. Thus, there is no need to prove any assault, nor is there any need to prove that the injuries were caused by a violent impact on the body. Poisoning, infecting or gassing are all within the compass of 'causing'. As we saw earlier, *Burstow* seems to have expanded the scope of 'inflict' so that there now appears to be little difference from 'cause'. It must be remembered, however, that in the case where the harm results indirectly, the normal causation principles must be applied to see whether the chain of causation between D's conduct and the ultimate injuries has been broken.

4.4.3.2 *Mens rea*

The reason why s. 18, carrying a maximum of life imprisonment, is a much more serious offence than s. 20 is because intention and intention alone suffices for the *mens rea*. As can be seen from the words of the section there are two **alternative** possibilities. The most common in practice is the intent to do grievous bodily harm (GBH). Thus, subjective recklessness as to the causing of harm or even grievous bodily harm is insufficient and D must be proved to have the aim or purpose of causing GBH. This was established by the Court of Appeal in *Belfon* [1976] 1 WLR 741 even before the stricter definition of intention propounded by the House of Lords in the murder cases of *Moloney* [1985] 1 All ER 1025 and *Hancock* [1986] 1 All ER 641. The post-*Moloney* case of *Bryson* [1985] Crim LR 669 confirms the *Belfon* rule in relation to s. 18. Presumably foresight by D that GBH was virtually certain to result would suffice by analogy with *Woollin* (see 3.3.2 above).

> ### **?** QUESTION 4.12
>
> In *Mowatt*, the Court of Appeal said that the word 'maliciously' which is part of the statutory definition of s. 18 was superfluous and added nothing to the *mens rea*. Is this correct?

When the prosecution's charge is based on an intention to do GBH it is clear that the word 'maliciously' adds nothing to the *mens rea* because if D intends GBH, he necessarily acts maliciously. He intends some harm.

In fact, the Court of Appeal overlooked the alternative *mens rea* of an 'intention to resist or prevent the lawful apprehension or detainer of any person'. If the prosecution is using this alternative intention as the basis of its charge, then it is clear that 'maliciously' would add an extra ingredient, requiring proof that D at least foresaw the risk of some harm being caused by his conduct. A person can intend to resist lawful arrest, e.g., by pushing past a policeman, without realising that his conduct might cause some harm. In such a case he would not be acting maliciously and therefore should not be convicted of the s. 18 offence, even if he causes GBH (*cf. Morrison* (1988) 89 Cr App R 17, CA).

4.4.3.3 **Reform**

Under cl. 1 of the draft Offences Against the Person Bill, s. 18 would be replaced by the offence of intentionally causing serious injury to another, also carrying a maximum of life imprisonment. Once again 'wounding' is insufficient and you will notice there is no place for intention to 'resist lawful apprehension', etc. In fact, cl. 6 would create a separate offence committed where D 'causes serious injury to another intending to resist, prevent or terminate the lawful arrest or detention of himself or a third person'. (There is also a lesser offence of assaulting another with the same intention (cl. 7).)

Thus, D would have to intend to cause serious injury to another. Having negotiated the convolutions in **Chapter 3**, you will no doubt join us in raising three cheers when you learn that cl. 14 adopts (albeit only for the newly created offences) the definition of 'intention' in the Law Commission's draft Criminal Law Bill (see 3.3.2 above). This is the only one of the offences in cll. 1 to 4 where D could be guilty if 'he omits to do an act which he has a duty to do at common law'. This inevitably implies that none of the other three offences could be committed by omission (although the *Miller* principle is preserved by cl. 16). For liability under cl. 1, the omission must obviously result in serious injury and D must intend it 'to have that result'. An example would be a car mechanic who deliberately omits to repair faulty brakes intending serious injury to result. One final point: the general definition of injury in cl. 15 would be modified for this offence so as to include 'things caused by disease'. It would therefore cover the transmission of diseases such as AIDS (if intentional) which would be outside the scope of the other offences.

4.5 **Reform**

Whatever else you have gleaned from this chapter, you will have realised that the law in this area is in desperate need of rationalisation. As Henry LJ in *Lynsey* [1995] 3 All ER 654,

CA, put it, 'Most, if not all, practitioners and commentators agree that the law concerning non-fatal offences against the person is in urgent need of comprehensive reform to simplify it, rationalise it and make it trap-free.' As we have seen, the draft Offences Against the Person Bill would sweep away the existing offences and substitute a hierarchy of four core offences: intentional serious injury (cl. 1), reckless serious injury (cl. 2), intentional or reckless injury (cl. 3) and assault (cl. 4). Thus, there would be a rough correspondence with the present hierarchy of ss. 18, 20 and 47 and assault/battery, but the anomalies revealed by our examination of the current law would largely be swept away. In addition to these very general 'causing injury' offences, the draft includes proposals for more specific offences to replace existing offences: assault on a constable (cl. 5), resisting arrest offences (cll. 6 and 7), intending or being reckless as to serious injury by dangerous substances (including explosives) (cl. 8), intending or being reckless as to injury by dangerous substances (cl. 9), threatening to kill or cause serious injury (cl. 10), administering a substance capable of causing injury (cl. 11 replacing ss. 23 and 24, OAPA 1861), torture (cl. 12) and causing danger on railways (cl. 13) (see generally *Cases and Materials* (4.3)). Unfortunately this long-awaited reform has remained festering in the bowels of the Home Office since mid-1998.

■ FURTHER READING

Finch: *Stalking the Perfect Stalking Law* [2002] Crim LR 703.

Gardner: *Rationality and the Rule of Law in Offences Against the Person* [1994] CLJ 502.

Horder: *Rethinking Non-fatal Offences Against the Person* (1994) 14 OJLS 335.

Horder: *Reconsidering Psychic Assault* [1998] Crim LR 392.

Kell: *Social Disutility and Consent* (1994) 14 OJLS 121.

Law Commission: Consultation Paper No. 134 (1994).

Law Commission: Consultation Paper No. 139 (1995).

Spencer: *Liability for Reckless Infection* (2004) 154 New LJ 384 and 448.

Weait: *Knowledge, Autonomy and Consent: R v Konzani* [2005] Crim LR 763.

■ SUMMARY

Technical assault is committed where D intentionally or subjectively recklessly causes P to apprehend immediate unlawful force to their person.

- *Actus reus*—no contact needed. D must actually expect **immediate** force. Threat of future force not enough, but courts take a liberal view of what force is 'immediate', e.g., telephone calls or even letters (*Ireland*; *Constanza*). Words alone can suffice (*Constanza*). Words can neutralise threatening actions. Conditional threats probably enough.

- *Mens rea*—requires intention or subjective recklessness as to *actus reus*—*Caldwell* objective recklessness insufficient.

Battery is committed where D intentionally or subjectively recklessly applies unlawful force to another.

- *Actus reus*—'force' includes mere touching. Unclear if indirectly caused force suffices or if a mere omission can constitute battery. Force must be lawful—it may become lawful if used: (i) reasonably in self-defence or prevention of crime; (ii) by a parent reasonably chastising their child; (iii) certain necessity situations; or (iv) where the victim consents to it.

  Consent express or implied generally negates liability—except where actual bodily harm is 'intended and/or caused' (*Brown*). This exception is itself subject to exceptions in the case of socially acceptable (to the courts!) activities, e.g., medical surgery, tattooing, ear-piercing, lawfully conducted sports in respect of risks normally inherent therein (*Barnes* 2005) and non-violent sexual relations between adults (*Dica*; *Konzani*). Consent must be real—could be vitiated by youth, mental incapacity, duress or fraud as to the nature of the act or the identity of the person.

- *Mens rea*— intention or subjective recklessness as to the application of unlawful force needed—objective recklessness insufficient. If D mistakenly believes the facts are such that the force would be lawful, he lacks the necessary *mens rea* in relation to unlawful force, whether or not his belief is reasonable (*Kimber*; *Williams*). Although *Brown* casts doubt on whether this analysis holds good in respect of mistaken belief in consent, it is endorsed by the House of Lords in *B v DPP*.

Assault occasioning actual bodily harm requires a technical assault or battery which causes actual bodily harm.

- *Actus reus*—actual bodily harm means any injury likely to interfere with the health or comfort of the victim which is more than transient or trifling. It includes psychiatric injury only if an 'identifiable clinical condition'. Extreme distress, fear etc. is not in itself enough. Occasioning means 'causing' and normal causation principles apply. Assault means either technical assault or battery.

- *Mens rea*—only the *mens rea* for the technical assault or battery used as the basis for the s. 47 charge is required. No *mens rea* is needed in relation to the occasioning of harm (*Savage*).

Section 20 of the OAPA 1861 makes it an offence to 'unlawfully and maliciously wound or inflict any grievous bodily harm upon' another.

- *Actus reus*—two alternatives: (i) inflicting GBH or (ii) wounding.

  (i) Inflicting GBH—GBH means 'serious harm'. 'Inflict' does not necessitate any assault or battery or application of force and seems, in practice, indistinguishable from 'cause' in s. 18 (*Burstow*).
  (ii) Wound requires a break in the inner and outer skin but need not be serious. Purely internal injuries are excluded. For the time being it seems the wound must be caused by means of an assault or battery, but likely to be reconsidered in the light of *Burstow*.

- *Mens rea*—D must intend some harm (not necessarily GBH or a wound) or realise that some harm might result from his acts (*Mowatt*; *Ireland*). Objective recklessness does not suffice, nor does an intention **merely to frighten**.

Section 18 of the OAPA 1861 makes it an offence to 'unlawfully and maliciously wound or cause any grievous bodily harm to any person by any means whatsoever with intent to do some grievous bodily harm, or with intent to resist or prevent the lawful apprehension or detainer of any person.'

- *Actus reus*—(i) wound—see s. 20 (ii) cause GBH—no limits on how GBH may be caused apart from the normal principles of causation.

- *Mens rea*—one of the two alternative intentions must be proved. Intent to do GBH is the usual one rendering 'maliciously' redundant. If intent to resist arrest etc. is relied upon, 'maliciously' requires the additional intention to cause some harm **or** subjective recklessness as to some harm.

 CHAPTER 4: ASSESSMENT EXERCISE

4.1 Chelsea, a football hooligan, was painting offensive slogans on a wall outside a football stadium using an aerosol paint spray. She turned to her friend, Lester, and jokingly made as if to turn the spray on him. Lester, fearing he was about to be sprayed, ran off in a panic but tripped and fell. As a result, he banged his head on the pavement causing a gash to his forehead.

Chelsea ran off in a panic but straight into the arms of the uniformed Police Constable Plod who had witnessed the entire incident. Plod tried to arrest Chelsea but she managed to wrench herself free. This caused Plod to overbalance into the road into the path of an oncoming car which hit Plod and caused him severe multiple injuries.

Discuss the criminal liability of Chelsea, if any, for offences under ss. 18, 20 and 47 of the Offences Against the Person Act 1861.

NB. You are required to assume that P.C. Plod was at all times acting lawfully within the execution of his duty.

4.2 Bond hails a taxi, but when it stops Kleb rushes into the taxi ahead of him and slams the door in his face jeering, 'Ladies before gentlemen, Mr Bond'. Bond shouts obscenities at her and Kleb yells, 'You're going to pay for that Mr Bond. I'm going to shoot you.' Bond, fearing he is about to be shot, panics and leaps over a wall into the river running alongside the road. He is swept away by the current and, although he is pulled from the river, his breathing has stopped. His breathing is restarted by mouth-to-mouth resuscitation, but it is discovered that he has suffered permanent brain damage, even though he does not die.

Discuss the criminal liability, if any, of Kleb.

See the **Appendix** (4.1 and 4.2) for specimen answers.

5 Sexual offences

5.1 Objectives

By the end of this chapter you should be able to:

1 Define and analyse the offences of rape, assault by penetration, sexual assault and causing a person to engage in sexual activity without consent

2 Explain how they interrelate to each other

3 Explain the concept of consent and how it applies to these offences

4 Identify the problems concerning the meaning of 'sexual'

5 Identify which, if any of these offences, is committed in a given fact situation

5.2 Introduction

The law on sexual offences underwent a much-needed root-and-branch reform when the Sexual Offences Act was passed in 2003. The scheme of offences was rationalised in an effort to provide clarity and general coherence, to reflect more closely current societal conditions and attitudes, to adopt a gender-neutral approach and to eliminate discrimination on the ground of sexual orientation. Concerns about the extraordinarily low conviction rates, especially for rape, led to a tightening of *mens rea* requirements and a raft of evidential provisions focusing on the issue of the victim's consent. However, many commentators feel that the Act goes too far in pursuit of the laudable aim of the protection of children under 16 and criminalises conduct which would be regarded by many as normal and acceptable behaviour. For example, remarkably, two 15-year-olds who kiss each other on the mouth (i.e., have a snog) with mutual consent both commit the serious offence of sexual activity with a child (s. 13)! This over-criminalisation could well lead to claims of infringement of a person's 'right to respect for his private life' under Art. 8 of the ECHR. It is simply not good enough to assert, as the Government did, that we can rely on prosecutorial discretion to ensure that only the 'right' cases get prosecuted.

The Act creates a very large number of offences covering a wide range of conduct from major crimes such as rape to minor ones such as voyeurism (s. 67) and exposure (s. 66). Many of these offences are defined in unnecessarily minute detail and sadly many anomalies resulting from the differing conditions of liability in different offences have already been identified. There is also considerable overlap between offences and prosecutors could be faced with a bewildering array of possible charges, leading to inconsistency in practice (see www.cps.gov.uk/legal/section7/sexoffencesact2003.html for current guidance for prosecutors). There is also the distinct possibility that this problem could be exacerbated by contrasting judicial interpretations of similar provisions in different offences.

As well as creating the numerous fully fledged criminal offences, the Act also uses a device much favoured by the current Government by introducing an array of so-called 'civil' orders, breach of which provokes criminal penalties. They include Sexual Offence Prevention Orders (SOPOs) and Risk of Sexual Harm Orders (ROSHs) and work in a way similar to the increasingly prevalent Anti-Social Behaviour Orders (ASBOs) (see Shute: *New Civil Preventative Orders* [2004] Crim LR 417).

Space restricts us to a consideration of rape (s. 1), assault by penetration (s. 2) and sexual assault (s. 3). We shall also make some points about the child protection provisions. Before embarking on our analysis of the offences, we need to draw your attention to an issue which is often at the heart of trials for rape and sexual assaults, namely, consent. To be criminal, the conduct must generally be without the consent of the victim. Given that the relevant conduct usually occurs in private between previously acquainted persons, it is not surprising that the prosecution often fails to prove beyond reasonable doubt that the victim did not consent. In an effort to assist the prosecutor, the Act imposes certain presumptions as to the absence of consent in ss. 75 and 76, though it is questionable whether they will assist in discharging the prosecution's burden. We will deal with the provisions on consent in the context of rape but it should be borne in mind that they apply equally to all other offences requiring an absence of consent.

5.3 Rape

Section 1 of the Act reads:

(1) A person (A) commits an offence if—
    (a) he intentionally penetrates the vagina, anus or mouth of another person (B) with his penis,
    (b) B does not consent to the penetration, and
    (c) A does not reasonably believe that B consents.
(2) Whether a belief is reasonable is to be determined having regard to all the circumstances, including any steps A has taken to ascertain whether B consents.

? QUESTION 5.1

What is (a) the *actus reus* and (b) the *mens rea* of rape?

5.3.1 *Actus reus*

There are two elements to this. Firstly, D must actually penetrate the vagina, anus or mouth of another with his penis (nothing but the penis will suffice for rape; penetration by any other means is caught by the offence of assault by penetration under s. 2). Secondly, the penetration must be without the victim's consent.

5.3.1.1 **Penile penetration**

The necessity for **penile** penetration means that, in general, only males can perpetrate rape. However, by virtue of s. 79(3), it appears that rape can be perpetrated by a female-to-male transsexual who has undergone reconstructive penile surgery, even if she is still legally classified as female. The victim may be male or female and it seems to include the penetration of a surgically constructed vagina on a male-to-female transsexual (s. 79(3)). (Women may, of course, be guilty of rape by assisting a man to perpetrate it—see **Chapter 14** on accomplices. The reference to penetration by '**his** [i.e., D's] penis' precludes any idea that rape can be perpetrated through an innocent agent as previously suggested in *Cogan and Leak* [1976] 2 QB 217, CA (see 14.3.1 and 14.4.1.7 below).)

The slightest penetration suffices and, under s. 79(9), the vagina includes the vulva. Penetration is a continuing act from entry until withdrawal (s. 79(2)) so that an act which begins with a consensual entry can become rape if D maintains the penetration despite the victim's withdrawal of consent part way through. The Court of Appeal in *Ismail* [2005] EWCA Crim 397 has ruled that the type of orifice penetrated should not affect the sentence imposed on conviction.

5.3.1.2 **The victim did not consent**

The issue of consent is certainly the most difficult aspect of rape and, as noted previously, applies equally to the crimes of assault by penetration and sexual assault. If the prosecution is unable to prove beyond reasonable doubt that the victim did not consent to the penetration, there is no *actus reus* and no crime. However, ss. 75 and 76 attempt to ease the prosecution's burden by invoking certain presumptions that there is no consent in the circumstances there specified.

(a) Agreement by choice

A general definition of consent is given by s. 74:

> . . . a person consents if he agrees by choice, and has the freedom and capacity to make that choice.

The victim must not agree to the penetration but this does not necessarily require him to demonstrate expressly or even impliedly his objection and opposition to D's act. Thus a sleeping, unconscious or drugged victim may not resist or oppose the penetration but would not generally be agreeing to it (*cf. Malone* [1998] 2 Cr App R 447, CA). Even where the victim is fully conscious, consent cannot be assumed from mere passivity.

(b) Capacity to choose

The Act provides no definition but the most likely cause of incapacity will be mental disorder, extreme youth or some kind of intoxication or unconsciousness. It is unlikely that youth (in the absence of an accompanying mental retardation or disorder) will be a problem issue. This is because ss. 5 to 7 create offences parallel to ss. 1 to 3 where the victim is a child under 13. These offences are committed whether or not the victim consents (the unspoken premise is that children of 12 and under are too young to give any meaningful consent). For 13-, 14- and 15-year-olds, it is likely that the views of the House of Lords in *Gillick* v *West Norfolk and Wisbech Area Health Authority* [1986] AC 112 would be applied. If the child has sufficient maturity to understand what is involved in the conduct agreed to, the consent will be effective to negate the offences in ss. 1 to 3. (It should be noted that there are lesser offences, notably ss. 9 to 12, protecting children under 16, where consent is no defence.) We think it likely in practice that, where it is clear that a child over 12 of normal mental capacity has in actuality consented, the prosecution will tend to charge D under s. 9 rather than seek to argue for rape on the ground that the child lacked effective understanding of the act.

Similar considerations apply in respect of mental disability: does it deprive the victim of the ability to understand the nature and effects of the decision he is taking? This would be likely to include not only the mechanics of sexual intercourse but also some idea of its possible consequences in terms of pregnancy and disease transmission.

(c) Freedom to choose

If the victim is coerced into agreeing to intercourse by threats of or the use of violence, that is not a free choice and cannot be said to be a true consent. Lesser threats may also negate free choice. The victim's employer may threaten dismissal; D may threaten to send embarrassing photographs to a tabloid newspaper; D may threaten to expose an illegal immigrant victim to the police. Whether or not the victim had in reality a free choice has to be decided on the individual circumstances of each case. The key question is what effect the threats had on this particular victim in these particular circumstances. It is the victim's perception that counts. Similar threats can affect different individuals in different ways so that one person's freedom of choice might be negated whilst another's might not. Some writers have suggested that a distinction should be drawn between a threat of detrimental action which induces submission on the one hand and a promise of a benefit on the other. The prostitute who agrees to sexual intercourse only because D agrees to pay her for it makes a free choice. Similarly, an actress who sleeps with a film director on the promise of a job makes a free choice. But others have questioned whether there is any real difference between that situation and a case where an actress already given a part sleeps with the director only because he has threatened to replace her unless she does so. We think the distinction provides a useful working (though by no means foolproof) premise.

(d) The conclusive presumptions under s. 76

The Act specifies two situations where in all cases the victim is deemed not to have consented. No amount of evidence to the contrary can shake this irrebuttable presumption.

(i) Inducement by impersonation

The simplest situation is where D 'intentionally induced the complainant to consent to the relevant act by impersonating a person known personally to the complainant' (s. 76(2)(b)). The most likely scenario is where the victim is intoxicated and/or sleepy and mistakenly takes D for her boyfriend or partner. Note that D has to induce by impersonation. That seems to preclude cases where D simply takes knowing advantage of the victim's own spontaneous mistake (*cf.* the facts in *Collins* at 11.6.2.2 below) but it is entirely possible that the courts will give a broad interpretation and consider that to proceed without disabusing the victim of the known error, constitutes both 'impersonation' and 'inducing'. The requirement of personal acquaintance will preclude the application of the presumption in the case of a look-alike who pretends to be a celebrity.

(ii) Deceit as to the nature and purpose of the act

The second conclusive presumption applies where D 'intentionally deceived the complainant as to the nature or purpose of the relevant act' (s. 76(2)(a)). This provision was probably intended to reflect the position reached in the case law prior to the 2003 Act. The reference to the 'nature' of the act covers the case where D deceives the victim into thinking that the sexual act is not sexual. Thus in *Williams* [1923] 1 KB 340, CCA, the young victim's singing teacher persuaded her to engage in sexual intercourse under the illusion that it was a way of improving her breathing and in *Flattery* (1877) 2 QBD 410, CCR the consent was secured by pretending it was a medical procedure designed to cure the victim's fits. In both cases the victim did not appreciate the nature of the act and therefore their consent was vitiated. By contrast, deceit as to a mere quality or attribute of the act would not invalidate the apparent consent. Thus you may recall that in *Dica* (see 4.3.3.1) the Court of Appeal, obiter, thought that consent to sexual intercourse would not be vitiated by D's failure to disclose that he was HIV positive. Presumably the same view would be taken if D had actively deceived the victim, e.g., lied in response to a direct question. We have already seen when discussing consent in the context of non-sexual offences of violence (see 4.3.3.1 above) that this is a distinction which is often difficult to draw and you are referred particularly to the discussion of *Richardson* and *Tabassum* at 4.3.3.1 above. It all depends on how the courts choose to define the essence, the essential nature of the act in each individual case. At some point an attribute or quality of the act can become so central to it as to become part of its defining nature.

That difficulty of interpretation is compounded by the addition of the alternative deceit as to 'purpose'. It was probably intended to support the view in *Tabassum* (see 4.3.3.1 above). D persuaded several women to allow him to touch their breasts by falsely claiming he was medically qualified. This was done in an apparently professional, non-sexual manner and, for this reason, the court thought that this was the 'nature' of the act consented to. However, because D had no medical qualifications, the act could not have been for medical purposes as claimed to the victims and, therefore, even if D had no sexual motive, the victims' consents had been vitiated. Such conduct would certainly be covered by the presumption now.

However, there is potential for an unacceptably wide interpretation of the provision. In *Linekar (Gareth)* [1995] QB 250, CA, D agreed to pay a prostitute for sexual intercourse when he had no intention of paying her. After the intercourse, he ran off without paying. The Court of Appeal held that there was a valid consent to the intercourse. The deception as to payment did not alter that. In terms of the current presumption, the victim certainly understood the nature of the act of sexual intercourse. But did she understand its purpose? That might depend on whether 'purpose' means only D's purpose or includes also the victim's purpose. His purpose was sexual gratification but her purpose was securing payment. She was certainly deceived as to her purpose but not his. We think that 'purpose' will be limited to D's purpose. The criminality of D's conduct lay in his dishonesty, not his sexual penetration and a conviction for rape could not be justified. Even if the statute's 'purpose' is confined to D's purpose, it is still capable of a ludicrously wide interpretation. If D persuades the victim to have sexual intercourse by falsely telling her that he wants to marry her but, before he can do so, he needs to ensure that they are sexually compatible, that might well be deceiving her as to the purpose of the act. It might be despicable conduct but it surely should not be rape.

Finally, we should point out that a court which decides that such 'mistaken consent' cases fall outside the statutory presumptions would not necessarily be precluded from finding that the apparent consent is vitiated under the general principles enunciated in the case law prior to the Sexual Offences Act (see 4.3.3.2 above). To say that the terms of the presumptions dictate the meaning of consent generally would be to put the cart before the horse. Some interesting decisions lie ahead!

(e) The evidential presumptions under s. 75

Unlike those in s. 76, the presumptions that the victim did not consent in s. 75 can be refuted by the introduction of suitable evidence. In the specified circumstances, absence of consent is presumed without the prosecution having to prove it **unless** there is adduced 'sufficient evidence to raise an issue as to whether he [the victim] consented.' Such evidence may arise from D's testimony and/or cross-examination of the victim and/or the testimony of third parties. If credible evidence that the victim may have consented despite the circumstances, is produced, the prosecution must prove absence of consent beyond reasonable doubt in the normal way. If it is not, the judge must direct the jury that absence of consent is proved. Note that the presumptions will only apply where D is aware that the specified circumstances exist (s. 75(1)(c)).

The specified circumstances set out in s. 75(2) are as follows:

(a) any person was, at the time of the relevant act or immediately before it began, using violence against the complainant or causing the complainant to fear that immediate violence would be used against him;

(b) any person was, at the time of the relevant act or immediately before it began, causing the complainant to fear that violence was being used, or that immediate violence would be used, against another person

Both provisions require actual or threatened violence against a person; situation (a) against the victim and situation (b) against any other person. That does not include violence against property (unless indirectly causing the victim to fear violence against himself or another). The violence may be used or threatened not only by D but also by a third party but it has to occur either at the time of the penetration or 'immediately before it began'. The latter phrase creates uncertainty and will need to be interpreted.

? QUESTION 5.2

Where have you encountered similar uncertainties surrounding how immediate is immediate? Refer to 4.3.2.1 above if you cannot answer.

A possible rebuttal scenario might be where there is credible evidence that D and the victim have previously engaged in consensual sado-masochistic practices and that the violence used before penetration on the relevant occasion was similarly consented to.

  (c) the complainant was, and the defendant was not, unlawfully detained at the time of the relevant act;
  (d) the complainant was asleep or otherwise unconscious at the time of the relevant act

These provisions are largely self-explanatory. Situation (c) covers, *inter alia*, hostage-taking and kidnapping, whether initially for sexual purposes or not. The presumption in situation (d) might be rebutted, say, where the victim was D's partner and evidence was adduced to show that the victim had previously (and, D claimed, on this occasion) consented to take a drug causing loss of consciousness to sate D's penchant for sex with an unconscious person. Similarly, if D's partner had regularly, if retrospectively, approved of D's practice of penetrating her whilst she was asleep.

  (e) because of the complainant's physical disability, the complainant would not have been able at the time of the relevant act to communicate to the defendant whether the complainant consented

Again this is largely self-explanatory. An example would be a conscious patient who is completely paralysed and has lost the power of speech. Notice that it refers only to 'physical' disability and does not apply to mental disability.

  (f) any person had administered to or caused to be taken by the complainant, without the complainant's consent, a substance which, having regard to when it was administered or taken, was capable of causing or enabling the complainant to be stupefied or overpowered at the time of the relevant act

Intended to help combat drug-assisted rape, this provision applies only where it is proved that the victim did not consent to the administration of the drug. The provision includes the surreptitious administration not only of drugs such as Rohypnol but also of alcohol. Clearly, if the victim is actually overpowered or stupefied, the provision is superfluous since D cannot possibly have had the freedom and capacity to consent under the general definition in s. 74. However, it is not essential to prove that the victim was actually overpowered or stupefied. If the victim was little affected despite the bad intentions of D but still went ahead with the intercourse, then D might be able to rebut the presumption of no consent. If the victim was not stupefied but disinhibited to the extent that his consent was forthcoming when it would not have been without the effect of the drugs, it seems likely that the courts would view that as not a true consent and apply the presumption to convict. Finally, if D deceived the victim into thinking that a different type of drug was being administered with different effects, e.g., an amphetamine, we would expect the courts to view that as administered without consent and within the presumption.

5.3.2 *Mens rea*

There are two elements: (1) D must **intentionally** penetrate the vagina, anus or mouth of another person with his penis and (2) must *not* **reasonably believe** that the other person consents to the penetration. On proof of actual penetration, there will be an almost overwhelming inference that it was intentional. It is not the sort of thing that generally happens by mistake or accident, although, given the fact that any penetration, no matter how slight, will do and that the vagina includes the vulva, it is possible to envisage such a case, e.g., where a naked, naturist couple agree to a non-penetrative kiss and cuddle.

5.3.2.1 Absence of reasonable belief in consent

This is likely to be the only contentious *mens rea* issue. The old law was based on subjective recklessness and reviled by many as too favourable to defendants. It meant that any belief that the victim was consenting, no matter how ridiculous, would negate the *mens rea*. The new provision is essentially based on proof of negligence. D only escapes if his belief in consent is a reasonable one in the circumstances, although, subject to the presumptions explained shortly, the burden remains on the prosecution to prove beyond reasonable doubt that he did not have such a reasonable belief. D must still actually hold the belief but that will be to no avail unless that belief is a reasonable one.

The all-important question is how to assess the reasonableness or otherwise of the belief. Section 1(2) provides some help:

> Whether a belief is reasonable is to be determined having regard to all the circumstances, including any steps [D] has taken to ascertain whether [the victim] consents

This suggests that there is an onus on D to verify that the victim is consenting. After all, it is easily done and there is no room for a modern Casanova to assume his irresistibility. Any significant ambiguity in the victim's response would need to be clarified before penetration, though, presumably, it is open to the jury to consider the extent to which the victim's objection was made clear.

The reference to 'all the circumstances' potentially waters down the objective reasonableness test in a way similar to that which we will explore in relation to provocation (see 6.5.2.2 below). The question at issue is the extent to which the individual characteristics of D can be taken into account in assessing how reasonable his belief was. D's perception and interpretation of the victim's response may be abnormal because of factors such as mental illness, youth, sexual inexperience, learning disability, deafness or blindness. In fact it is clear from the Parliamentary debates and amendments made during the passage of the Act that it was intended that 'circumstances' should include characteristics of D so that the test would be whether it was reasonable for D, given the person he is, to believe in consent. However, it remains possible that the courts will shy away from allowing such factors to degrade the objective standard and invite the jury to assess whether an average person would have formed D's belief in consent.

Only circumstances which bear upon the perception and understanding of whether the victim was consenting at the time of penetration should be considered so that it should be irrelevant that the victim was, say, wearing a short skirt and a skimpy top.

Presumptions as to absence of belief in consent

In a further effort to assist the prosecution, ss. 75 and 76 apply the same presumptions we looked at in respect of whether the victim **actually** consented to the question of whether D reasonably **believed** the victim consented. Thus D is **conclusively** (i.e., irrebuttably) presumed not to reasonably believe where (a) he has intentionally deceived V as to the nature or purpose of the relevant act or (b) he has intentionally induced the consent by impersonating someone known personally to V (see 5.3.1.2 (d) above). Secondly there is an **evidential** presumption (i.e., rebuttable) in each of the situations set out in s. 75 (see above 5.3.1.2 (e)) that D did not reasonably believe V was consenting. Thus if, for example, D had used violence prior to penetration, it would be presumed not only that V was not consenting (*actus reus*) but also that D did not reasonably believe V was consenting (*mens rea*). Of course, it would be possible for D to rebut this presumption by introducing evidence that V had, say, enjoyed sado-masochistic sex in the past and that he thought (and thus had reasonable grounds for thinking) V was consenting this time.

5.4 Assault by penetration

Section 2 provides:

> (1) A person (A) commits an offence if—
> > (a) he intentionally penetrates the vagina or anus of another person (B) with a part of his body or anything else,
> > (b) the penetration is sexual,
> > (c) B does not consent to the penetration, and
> > (d) A does not reasonably believe that B consents.
> (2) Whether a belief is reasonable is to be determined having regard to all the circumstances, including any steps A has taken to ascertain whether B consents.

This offence (which carries the same penalty as rape) deliberately overlaps with rape where the instrument of penetration is D's penis, though it does not include penetration of the mouth. This is to cater for cases where there is doubt as to how the penetration was effected. The instrument of penetration can be **any** part of D's body (e.g., finger, tongue or toe) or 'anything else' (e.g., stick, bottle, cigar, thermometer, swab, animal or, presumably, a part of someone else's body, as where he inserts the finger or penis of, say, an unconscious person). Consequently, as long as the fact of penetration by something is proved, it would seem unnecessary to identify the instrument of penetration.

The discussion concerning absence of consent in rape applies equally to this offence including the presumptions in ss. 75 and 76 and the *mens rea* requirements of **intentional** penetration and absence of reasonable belief are the same (s. 1(2) and s. 2(2) are in identical terms). One extra requirement is that the penetration must be **sexual**.

? **QUESTION** 5.3

Why is there a requirement of **sexual** penetration in s. 2 but not s. 1? Can you think of any situations where penetration of the vagina or anus would not be sexual?

Penetration by D's penis is self-evidently sexual so there is no need for it to be expressed in rape. However, many medical and quasi-medical procedures (e.g., colonic irrigation) involve penetration and, whilst V would normally have consented to the procedure, there might be instances where this is not so (e.g., if V is unconscious). Hence the necessity to limit the scope to sexual penetrations. Since the same requirement applies to the next offence of sexual assault, it is convenient to postpone consideration of the meaning of sexual for a moment.

5.5 Sexual assault

Section 3 reads:

(1) A person (A) commits an offence if—
   (a) he intentionally touches another person (B),
   (b) the touching is sexual,
   (c) B does not consent to the touching and,
   (d) A does not reasonably believe that B consents.
(2) Whether a belief is reasonable is to be determined having regard to all the circumstances, including any steps A has taken to ascertain whether B consents.

This broad offence covers any non-consensual touching (including penetration) of a sexual nature. Section 79(8) provides that touching '**includes** touching with any part of the body' or 'with anything else' and 'through anything' (our emphasis). Consequently, the slightest contact with V's body or even clothing worn by V could suffice, whether directly by D's hand or body or by something held or controlled (e.g., an animal) by D. In *H* [2005] 2 All ER 859, the first appeal to be heard under the 2003 Act, the Court of Appeal held that touching clothing worn by V, in this case the pocket of V's tracksuit bottoms, was sufficient and there was no necessity for V to feel D's touching through the clothing. Section 79(8) does not provide a complete definition of 'touching' but simply some examples of it. In particular, the reference to touching 'through anything' cannot be taken to preclude a touching which is not felt by V.

Thus the intentionality requirement acquires some significance since it is very easy to touch (as opposed to penetrate) accidentally, e.g., brush against a woman's breast or bottom in a crowded street.

As before, the previous discussion on absence of consent and reasonable belief in consent applies including the presumptions in ss. 75 and 76 though, of course, the relevant act to which the consent and belief relate differs from rape. Here the act is D's intentional sexual touching of V as opposed to intentional penile penetration in rape. It is clear, therefore, that the key legal issue in the definition is the meaning of 'sexual'.

5.5.1 The touching must be 'sexual'

This is what differentiates an ordinary battery from a sexual assault. Section 78 provides:

...penetration, touching or any other activity is sexual if a reasonable person would consider that—

(a) whatever the circumstances or any person's purpose in relation to it, it is because of its nature sexual, or
(b) because of its nature it may be sexual and because of the circumstances or purpose of any person in relation to it (or both) it is sexual.

The definition envisages three possibilities:

(i) The act is indisputably sexual
By its very nature, a reasonable person would regard the touching (or, in the case of s. 2, the penetration) as inherently sexual irrespective of D's motives and the background

circumstances. Examples would include penile penetration, oral sex, or masturbation of another. It would appear that this represents a change from the old law on indecent assault where the House of Lords in *Court* [1989] AC 28 held that any touching of the vagina, even for a non-sexual reason such as medical research, would be indecent (see also *Tabassum* [2000] 2 Cr App R 328—examination of women's breasts possibly for non-sexual, research purposes). The example given in *Court* was of a doctor who misled a patient into thinking a vaginal sample was necessary for diagnosis (thus vitiating her apparent consent) when he took it for a general research project. Such cases cannot be regarded as inherently sexual.

(ii) The act is potentially sexual

Where the touching is ambiguous, i.e., it may or may not be sexual, the prosecution must prove that the context and circumstances of the touching and the motive and purpose of D (secret or manifest) demonstrate that it **is actually** sexual. Examples are numerous: kissing, touching someone's knee, undressing someone, touching someone's anus or vagina, inserting an instrument in another's anus or vagina. Without knowing something about the circumstances and, in particular, D's purpose and motivation, we cannot decide whether it was or was not sexual. If D is a doctor inserting an endoscope, we would conclude that it is not sexual unless we are convinced that the examination was medically unnecessary **and** the doctor was seeking sexual gratification. Therefore, assuming the patient did not consent and in the absence of any sexual motive (as in the above example from *Court*), the doctor would be guilty of ordinary battery rather than assault by penetration or sexual assault. Although D's motive is the key driver in the issue, that does not mean that D's motive for the act has to be sexual gratification or that his **primary** reason has to be sexual. If D's purpose in inserting an instrument in a woman's vagina is to humiliate and/or injure her and there is no element of sexual gratification, it would still be sexual because his purpose is to use what, in those circumstances, are sexual means to achieve his main purpose. Notice also that an act can be rendered sexual by the 'purpose of **any** person' (e.g., a third person encouraging D's act).

The facts of *Court* provide a final example. D put a fully clothed 12-year-old girl across his knee and spanked her bottom. Whether that was sexual would depend largely on whether or not his purpose (wholly or partly) was sexual gratification. If his purpose was purely chastisement, it would not be sexual.

The Court of Appeal in *H* [2005] 2 All ER 859 has stressed that s. 78(b) creates a two-stage process and that the first stage (that the act because of its nature may be sexual) must first be established without reference to the issues raised by the second stage (namely, the surrounding circumstances and D's purpose). Thus, the jury must first be satisfied that a reasonable person would consider the actual touching to be **capable** of being sexual, looked at in isolation and divorced from 'the circumstances before and after the touching' and from 'any evidence as to the purpose of any person in relation to the touching.' Only if that hurdle is jumped should they go on to consider the second question: would a reasonable person, looking at the touching in the context of the surrounding circumstances and the purpose of D or any other person, regard the touching as **actually** sexual. Thus, in *H*, the touching was D's grabbing of V's tracksuit bottoms by the fabric in the area of the pocket and the attempt to pull her towards him. That, in itself had to be possibly sexual (the Court of Appeal were clear that it was potentially sexual) and no account could be taken of the fact that, when he first approached her, he had said, 'Do you fancy a shag?' and he had subsequently but unsuccessfully attempted to cover her mouth with his hand. Those crucial facts could only be brought in at the second stage.

Although this may strike you as unnecessarily complicated and rather artificial (will jurors really ignore evidence as to D's purpose and the overall circumstances in judging the first issue?), it is, as the Court points out, a consequence of the way s. 78(b) is phrased. Furthermore, the implication of this interpretation is that there must be some touchings which are **incapable** of being sexual no matter what the surrounding circumstances are and no matter how much D is motivated by sexual gratification.

(iii) The act is indisputably *not* sexual

Section 78, as interpreted (correctly we think) in *H*, implies that there is a third category of acts which by their very nature cannot possibly be sexual no matter what the circumstances and motive of the actors.

? QUESTION 5.4

In *George* [1956] Crim LR 52, D, a shoe fetishist, removed a girl's shoe from her foot on several occasions for sexual gratification. The trial judge ruled (correctly in the eyes of the House of Lords in *Court*—see also *Price* [2004] 1 Cr App R 12, CA) that a mere removal of a shoe was incapable of being indecent under the old law despite D's sexual motive. Could such conduct now be sexual assault?

There is a divergence of opinion among writers but one view is that there should be no act which is **incapable** of being sexual so that any act has the potential to be turned into a sexual one by D's purpose being sexual gratification. The counter-argument is that, whilst to base conviction on D's purpose (not necessarily an easy thing to ascertain) where the act looks ambiguous is acceptable, that may not be the case where the act looks unambiguously non-sexual. The Court of Appeal in *H* has impliedly rejected the first view and they thought it questionable whether George's actions could be potentially sexual (though they did incline to the view that the final determination of that would have to be left to the jury). It should be remembered that, even if not sexual, the act would still constitute ordinary battery.

As noted above, D must 'intentionally' touch V and **not** 'reasonably believe' that V was consenting. However, it appears from the way the offence is worded that no further *mens rea* in regard to the touching being 'sexual' is required. Therefore, as long as a reasonable person would regard the act as sexual, it is irrelevant that D does not. Because s. 78 bases the definition of sexual on what a reasonable person would think, the effect is to impose a fault element of negligence. It is enough that D failed to see what a reasonable person would have seen.

5.6 Causing a person to engage in sexual activity without consent

Section 4 reads:

(1) A person (A) commits an offence if —
   (a) he intentionally causes another person (B) to engage in an activity,
   (b) the activity is sexual,
   (c) B does not consent to engaging in the activity, and
   (d) A does not reasonably believe that B consents.
(2) Whether a belief is reasonable is to be determined having regard to all the circumstances, including any steps A has taken to ascertain whether B consents.

This offence certainly overlaps greatly with the offences we have already considered since in most cases a D who rapes, sexually penetrates or sexually assaults V will also be causing V to engage in non-consensual sexual activity. However, its purpose is to catch a number of situations beyond the reach of those offences. Examples include where a woman compels an unwilling man to have sexual intercourse with her (though that would seem to be sexual assault by the woman too), where D causes V to strip or touch herself sexually (not sexual assault because no touching, *cf. Sargeant* [1997] Crim LR 50, CA) or causes V to touch him (D) sexually (arguably not sexual assault if D is completely passive). Equally, if D causes an unwilling V to engage in sexual activity with a third party (T), the offence is committed whether or not T is in league with D, an innocent dupe or a co-victim with V.

The most likely situation caught by s. 4 will be where D uses force or the threat of force to compel V but it could also include surreptitiously drugging V so as to induce the activity or deceit as to the nature and purpose of the act. It will be seen that the issue of whether D causes the activity will usually go hand in hand with the question of whether V consented. It remains to be seen how widely the courts will interpret 'cause' given the recent trend to expand that concept in manslaughter cases involving drug overdoses (see 2.8.2.2 above and 6.5.3.4 below). This could prove especially problematic in cases where the sexual activity is between the non-consenting V and a fully aware third party. Mere encouragement of T would make D liable for aiding and abetting the offence (rape, sexual assault, etc.) which T commits but should not constitute causing under s. 4. On the other hand active assistance (e.g., holding the victim down for T) seems clearly to constitute causing V to engage in the activity, given that D's conduct need only be one of the causes.

As before, the previous discussion on absence of consent and reasonable belief in consent applies including the presumptions in ss. 75 and 76 though, of course, the relevant act to which the consent and belief relate differs from rape and the other offences. Here the act is D's intentional causing of V to engage in sexual activity as opposed to intentional penile penetration in rape.

5.7 Child victims under 13

Sections 5 (rape), 6 (assault by penetration), 7 (sexual assault) and 8 (causing or inciting to engage in sexual activity) contain stricter versions of the offences we have considered where the victim is a child under the age of 13. The definitions parallel the adult versions with two huge differences. Firstly, there is no requirement to prove that V did not consent. Consent is irrelevant to liability. Quite simply Parliament regarded anyone under 13 to be too young to consent and removed the issue from the definition. Of course, that meant D's belief in consent was irrelevant also. Secondly, no *mens rea* requirement was expressed in respect of V being under 13. It is universally accepted that the intention of the legislature was to impose strict liability in respect of the age factor (although in the light of *B v DPP*, it might have been prudent to spell this out—see the discussion at 13.4.1 below). The prosecution simply has to prove that V was in fact under 13 and it is no defence that D believed V was over age (even on reasonable grounds because, say, V looked much older and produced an expertly forged birth certificate stating she was 17!). Note these offences can be committed by anyone over the age of criminal responsibility, i.e., 10 and over and theoretically catch the most innocuous sexual experimentation, e.g., consensual kissing where one or both is under 13.

5.8 Sexual offences protecting children under 16

Sections 9 to 15 aim to protect children under 16 from exploitation largely by adults (although under s. 13, under 18s are subjected to a single offence with a lesser maximum penalty for such conduct). Space prevents us from doing more than summarising what these offences cover:

Sexual activity with a child (s. 9)

Causing or inciting a child to engage in sexual activity (s. 10)

Engaging in sexual activity in the presence of a child (s. 11)

Causing a child to watch a sexual act (s. 12)

Arranging or facilitating the commission of a child sex offence (s. 14)

Meeting a child following sexual grooming (s. 15).

These offences apply to any child victim under 16 (including the under 13s) and so overlap with the 'under 13' offences. If V is under 13, no *mens rea* is needed in respect of V's age. If V is 13 to 15, *mens rea* is required—D must not **reasonably** believe that V is 16 or over.

Sections 17 to 19 create offences extending the protection to victims under 18 where D is in a position of trust in relation to V (e.g., teacher–pupil; inmates in care homes, hospitals, etc.). Sections 25 and 26 protect victims under 18 from sexual abuse within the family unit and ss. 30 to 42 create a range of offences designed to protect mentally disordered victims from sexual abuse. You are referred to the Act itself for a number of miscellaneous offences which we have not been able to mention.

■ FURTHER READING

Finch and Munro: *Intoxicated Consent and the Boundaries of Drug-assisted Rape* [2003] Crim LR 773.

Government White Paper: *Protecting the Public etc.* Cm 5668 2002.

Herring: *Mistaken Sex* [2005] Crim LR 511.

Home Office: *Setting the Boundaries; Reforming the Law on Sex Offences* (July 2000).

Lacey: *Beset by Boundaries* [2001] Crim LR 3.

Power: *Towards a Redefinition of the Mens Rea of Rape* (2003) 23 OJLS 379.

Rumsey: *The Review of Sex Offences and Rape Law Reform: Another False Dawn?* (2001) 64 MLR 890.

Spencer: *The Sexual Offences Act 2003: Child and Family Offences* [2004] Crim LR 347.

Temkin: *Rape and the Legal Process* (2nd ed., 2002, Oxford University Press).

Temkin and Ashworth: *Rape, Sexual Assaults and the Problems of Consent* [2004] Crim LR 328.

■ SUMMARY

The Sexual Offences Act 2003 creates a new code with numerous overlapping offences ranging from rape to voyeurism. Criticised for over-criminalisation and reliance on prosecutors exercising their discretion 'properly'.

Rape (s. 1)

Actus reus: penetration with the penis of the vagina, anus or mouth of another without the other's consent. *Mens Rea*: Intention to penetrate in that manner plus absence of any reasonable belief that the other consents.

Penile penetration: slightest penetration suffices and is a continuing act. It must be by a penis though this can include reconstructive surgery (e.g., sex change operation).

Without consent: applicable equally to assault by penetration and sexual assault. Consent means agreement by choice where V has the freedom and capacity to make that choice (s. 74). Capacity to choose: most likely to be mental disorder, extreme youth or some kind of intoxication or unconsciousness—ask: was V able to understand the nature and effects of his decision. Freedom to choose: coercion by threats negates free choice—depends on the individual V's perceptions but problematic as to what threats and/or inducements would count—violence is clear, loss of job maybe but promise of job or other benefit maybe not.

Conclusive presumptions (s. 76): lack of consent **irrebuttably** presumed in the following cases: (1) Intentional inducement by impersonation of someone known **personally** to V; (2) Deceit as to nature and purpose of the act: (a) Nature, e.g., where D persuades V it is a medical procedure (*Flattery*) or to improve her singing (*Williams*); (b) Purpose: Covers cases like *Tabassum* where breast examination claimed to be for medical purposes but unclear how far it extends.

Evidential presumptions (s. 75): absence of consent presumed in following cases **unless** D adduces credible evidence to contrary: (a) Use of violence or threats of immediate violence against V or (b) against another; (c) V was unlawfully detained but D was not; (d) V was asleep or unconscious; (e) inability of V to communicate consent due to physical disability; (f) non-consensual administration of a drug capable of causing or enabling V to be stupefied or overpowered.

Mens rea: (1) **Intentional** penetration—not likely to cause any problems. (2) Absence of reasonable belief in consent: Based on a minimum fault of ordinary negligence. D must actually believe V consents and that must also be reasonable in the circumstances. Reasonableness has to be assessed 'having regard to all the circumstances, including any steps D has taken to ascertain whether V consents.' Suggests D must verify V's consent and clarify any ambiguity. Not clear if 'circumstances' can include characteristics personal to D, e.g., learning disability, deafness. The presumptions in ss. 75 and 76 also apply to the question of whether D reasonably believed V consented.

Assault by penetration (s. 2)

Covers penetration of another's vagina or anus by a part of the body (e.g., finger, tongue or toe and including the penis, thus deliberately overlapping with rape) or anything else (e.g., a cigar, stick or bottle). Ingredients: (a) intentional penetration of another's vagina or anus by a part of D's body or anything else (b) the penetration is sexual (c) without V's consent and (d) D does not reasonably believe that V consents. Largely same concepts as for rape (e.g., consent—ss. 74–76 apply). The extra requirement is for the penetration to be sexual so as to exclude, e.g., non-consensual medical procedures.

Sexual assault (s. 3)

Ingredients: (1) D intentionally touches V (2) the touching is sexual (3) V does not consent and (4) D does not reasonably believe V consents. Touching includes touching with any part of the body or with anything else or through anything (s. 79(8)). The slightest contact with V's body or clothing worn by V whether felt by V through the clothing or not suffices (*H*). But has to be **intentional** not accidental. Consent and belief in consent is as for rape.

Sexual touching: this is what differentiates s. 3 from ordinary battery. It is sexual if a reasonable person would consider that (a) it **is** because of its nature sexual or (b) because of its nature it **may** be sexual and because of the circumstances or purpose of any person in relation to it (or both) it is sexual. Suggests three possibilities: (i) Inherently sexual (s. 78(a)), e.g., penile penetration, oral sex, irrespective of D's motives and the background circumstances; (ii) Potentially sexual (s. 78(b)), e.g., touching someone's knee, anus or vagina, kissing or spanking someone. The act may or may not be sexual depending on the circumstances and, in particular D's purpose and motivation, e.g., a doctor conducting a medically necessary procedure; *cf.* a doctor conducting an unnecessary procedure for sexual gratification. Under s. 78(b), a jury must first conclude that the touching looked at in isolation divorced from D's motives and the circumstances before and after must be **capable** of being sexual. Only then can they take into account D's purpose and motives etc. to decide if it actually is sexual (*H*); (iii) Indisputably **not** sexual: The implication of *H* is that some acts by their very nature cannot be sexual despite a secret sexual motive of D, e.g., **mere** removal of a girl's shoe by a shoe fetishist (*George; Price*).

No need for D to regard act as sexual if a reasonable person would.

Causing a person to engage in sexual activity without consent (s. 4)

Ingredients: (1) D intentionally causes V to engage in an activity (2) the activity is sexual (3) V does not consent and (4) D does not reasonably believe V consents.

Overlaps greatly with other offences but designed for case where D causes (e.g., by threats, drugging or deceit as to nature or purpose) an unwilling V to do something sexual not amounting to assault, e.g., to masturbate in front of D (*cf. Sargeant*) or to touch D sexually where D is completely passive. Same issues arise on the meaning of consent and absence of reasonable belief.

Protection of children under 13 (ss. 5–8)

Section 5–8 parallel the above 'adult' offences where V is under 13 **except** (i) covers consensual as well as non-consensual activity and (ii) therefore belief in consent is irrelevant too and (iii) no *mens rea* needed in respect of V's age.

Protection of children under 16 (ss. 9–15)

See text at 5.8.

6 Homicide

6.1 Objectives

By the end of this chapter you should be able to:

1 Define the basic ingredients of and distinguish between murder, voluntary manslaughter and involuntary manslaughter

2 Explain the difficulties and uncertainties surrounding the *mens rea* of murder

3 Analyse the requirements for the defences of provocation and diminished responsibility

4 Describe the rules governing gross negligence manslaughter

5 Identify the anomalies and shortcomings of unlawful act manslaughter

6.2 Introduction

To kill another may involve the commission of a number of crimes or none at all. It is perfectly possible for someone to kill another without any fault on their part and without any crime being committed. If you are driving along a motorway at 70 mph in a perfectly competent manner when someone intent on suicide jumps in front of your car from a bridge, it may be said that you cause his death when your car hits and kills him but you would commit no crime. Homicide can only be unlawful if the ingredients of a relevant crime can be proved.

The major unlawful homicides are murder and manslaughter, but others, with which we have no space to deal in this work, include causing death by dangerous driving (new s. 1 of the Road Traffic Act 1988), causing death by careless driving when under influence of drink or drugs (new s. 3A of the Road Traffic Act 1988), genocide (the Genocide Act 1969) and infanticide, which, in effect, reduces murder to manslaughter in the case of the killing by a woman of her child under the age of 12 months whilst the balance of her mind was disturbed due to the effects of the birth or consequent lactation (s. 1 of the Infanticide Act 1938).

In addition to these 'true' homicides, the law also protects foetuses in the mother's womb through the offences of child destruction in respect of foetuses 'capable of being born alive' (prima facie presumed at 28 weeks (s. 1 of the Infant Life (Preservation) Act 1929)) and unlawful abortion in respect of foetuses of any age (ss. 58 and 59 of the Offences Against the Person Act 1861). The latter prohibits almost anything done 'with intent to procure the miscarriage of any woman', but is now subject to wide-ranging defences under the Abortion Act 1967. Although those defences were narrowed somewhat by s. 37 of the Human Fertilisation and Embryology Act 1990, they are still broad in respect of foetuses of 24 weeks or less. Suicide is no longer a crime, although, as we shall see, it is an offence to aid and abet another's suicide.

Our treatment is confined to murder and manslaughter and both crimes share the same *actus reus*. There is no doubt that homicide law is a hotchpotch of confused, anomalous and uncertain rules (like many other areas of criminal law!) and badly in need of reform. After much pressure from the Law Commission (see, e.g., *Report on Partial Defences to Murder*, Law Com. No. 290, 2004, para. 2.8) and others, the Home Office has set up a review of the law of murder, announcing its terms of reference on 21 July 2005 (see www.lawcom. gov.uk/murder.htm).

6.2.1 Overview of the current law of murder and manslaughter

For the moment, you can think of murder as the intentional killing of another. The only penalty available on conviction of murder is life imprisonment. The judge has no discretion and is compelled to impose that sentence no matter what the circumstances, whether a cold-blooded, contract killing or the mercy killing of a pain-wracked, terminally ill loved one. Largely to avoid the rigidity of the fixed sentence and to provide judges with sentencing flexibility, the law now allows intentional killings in certain defined circumstances to reduce what would otherwise be liability for murder to liability for manslaughter only. The two most important situations within this type of manslaughter (known as voluntary manslaughter) are (1) diminished responsibility—where D was suffering from some mental disability sufficient to amount to 'diminished responsibility' as defined in s. 2 of the Homicide Act 1957 and (2) provocation—where D was provoked to lose his self-control. Where the killing was not intentional (i.e., without the *mens rea* for murder) but still sufficiently culpable, the crime would also be manslaughter, though this type is known as 'involuntary' manslaughter. The minimum fault requirement for involuntary manslaughter is very serious negligence known as 'gross' negligence.

6.3 *Actus reus*

The *actus reus* of homicide is the unlawful killing of a human being by a human being under the Queen's peace.

6.3.1 Unlawful killing

A killing may not be unlawful if it falls into one of the following categories:

(a) Killing enemy soldiers in the heat of battle. This seems to be the one example where the victim would not be 'under the Queen's peace'. All other persons would be, including enemy aliens and prisoners of war outside the heat of battle (*cf. Page* [1953] 2 All ER 1355, C-MAC).

(b) Killing in the advancement of justice through a lawful execution of a properly imposed death penalty used to be lawful. However, s. 36 of the Crime and Disorder Act 1998 finally abolished the death sentence for piracy and treason so that there is no longer any power to impose such a penalty.

(c) Justified killing. As we shall see in **Chapter 8**, a person may use reasonable and necessary force in self-defence or the prevention of crime, even, in appropriate circumstances, to the extent of killing. You may recall that we touched on self-defence, including mistaken self-defence, in **Chapter 4**. In addition, the defence of necessity may render a killing justified and so lawful (see **Chapter 9** and *Re A (Children)* [2001] 2 WLR 480).

(d) A killing will not be unlawful if it is without fault in the sense that the prosecution is unable to establish the ingredients of any of the homicide offences.

6.3.2 The victim

Only a human being can be the victim of murder or manslaughter. The ancient definitions talked of 'reasonable creatures in being'. The conjoined twins case *Re A (Children)* [2001] 2 WLR 480, held that the non-viable twin was a human being even though she had 'a useless brain, a useless heart and useless lungs' and was dependent for life on the other twin.

? QUESTION 6.1

What are the two problems the law needs to solve in this regard?

We noted above that foetuses are not protected by the law of homicide but by the analogous offences of child destruction and unlawful abortion. The first question which arises, therefore, is at what point the foetus becomes a 'human being' so as to be within the protection of murder and manslaughter. There are no modern authorities on when a foetus becomes a human being and we have to rely on nineteenth-century cases. It appears that the foetus becomes a child when it has an existence independent of its mother and has been wholly expelled from the mother (*Poulton* (1832) 5 C & P 329 (*Cases and Materials* (6.3.2))) and *Enoch* (1833) 5 C & P 539). Although some cases required that the child should have breathed, this was not regarded as essential in *Brain* (1834) 6 C & P 349 (*Cases and Materials* (6.3.2)). It does not matter that the child is capable of surviving for only a short time after birth, but it would appear necessary that it should be capable of breathing.

If D injures the foetus in the womb, e.g., by stabbing or poisoning the mother, he can be guilty of murder or manslaughter if the child is born alive but dies subsequently from the ante-natal injuries inflicted by him (*Attorney-General's Reference (No. 3 of 1994)* [1997] 3 All ER 936, HL). The last case also decided that the same principle applied where the death of the child was wholly or partly due, not to any pre-natal injury to the foetus itself, but to a pre-natal injury to the mother which resulted in a premature birth contributing to the death of the child. (See also discussion on transferred malice at 3.10.)

The second question is to determine at what point the human being dies since it is not, of course, possible to kill someone who is already dead!

In *Malcherek and Steel* [1981] 2 All ER 422, CA (*Cases and Materials* (6.3.2)) the courts countenanced the possibility that a person whose brain stem had ceased to function would be legally dead, notwithstanding that their heart and lungs were kept working by a ventilator. (The brain stem controls reflex functions like breathing and blood circulation.) If accepted, this would mean a brain-dead person could not be 'killed' by switching off the machine. However, the court found it unnecessary to decide the matter and there is still no legal authority confirming this as the position. It is likely that it would be accepted by the courts, and certainly forms the basis of current medical practice. However, it is not an argument which can be applied to those in persistent vegetative states who are not 'brain-dead' (see *Airedale NHS Trust v Bland* [1993] 1 All ER 821, HL discussed under 2.7.4.2 above).

6.3.3 **Causing death**

We have already discussed the difficult issue of causation (see 2.8). Many of the cases used in that discussion are in fact homicide cases.

Until recently there was an additional requirement for homicide offences that death should occur within a year and a day of the accused's lethal conduct. Following a recommendation by the Law Commission (Law Com. No. 230 (1995)), this throwback to times when medical science was undeveloped and of doubtful precision was abolished by s. 1 of the Law Reform (Year and a Day Rule) Act 1996 where D's lethal conduct occurred on or after 17 June 1996, the day the Act was passed.

This could, of course, mean that a defendant who injures someone may have to endure an indefinite period of uncertainty, wondering if he may face a homicide charge even years after the event and even after he has already been convicted of a lesser offence in respect of the incident. Section 2 of the 1996 Act therefore provides the limited safeguard that the Attorney-General must consent to any homicide prosecution where (a) the injury alleged to have caused death occurred more than three years before the death, or (b) D has already been convicted of an offence (of any kind) 'committed in circumstances alleged to be connected with the death'. Such an offence would most likely be a non-fatal offence against the person such as s. 18, OAPA 1861, but it could also be an offence such as burglary or criminal damage. Presumably the Attorney-General would refuse consent to a prosecution thought to be oppressive.

6.4 **Murder**

Murder is one of the very few occasions where a judge has no discretion on sentencing. Since the abolition of the death penalty for the offence by the Murder (Abolition of Death Penalty) Act 1965, the trial judge is compelled to impose a sentence of life imprisonment on conviction for murder. However, he also lays down a **minimum** period of detention (known as 'the tariff'—it can be for D's natural life, i.e., never) before the accused can become eligible for release on 'licence' (s. 269 of the Criminal Justice Act 2003. Chapter 7 of the 2003 Act lays down the factors to be considered by the court in making that recommendation (see Schedule 21)). Upon the expiry of the minimum term, the Parole Board must review the prisoner's suitability for release and, if continued imprisonment is no longer necessary for the protection of the public, direct his release on licence (s. 269). Despite moves to abolish the mandatory nature of the life sentence supported by senior judges in the House of Lords, including the then Lord Chief Justice, the Government has opposed any such change (see House of Lords Select Committee Report (Nathan Report) 1989—HL Paper 78) and continues to do so. The terms of reference of the Home Office Review of Murder require any recommendations to 'take account of the continuing existence of the mandatory life sentence for murder'.

Having already considered the *actus reus* of murder, we can turn immediately to the factor which distinguishes murder from manslaughter—the *mens rea*.

6.4.1 *Mens rea*

The traditional term used for the *mens rea* of murder is 'malice aforethought'. The term 'malice aforethought' is a term of art with a particular technical legal meaning. There need be neither 'malice' nor 'aforethought'. The 'killer' need not be motivated by 'malice' or ill-will, so that a deliberate 'mercy' killing to alleviate the unbearable suffering of a terminally ill loved one is with 'malice aforethought' and therefore murder. Equally there is no need to prove that the intentional killing was done with any pre-meditation or 'aforethought'. A spur of the moment decision to kill suffices.

The House of Lords in *Moloney* [1985] 1 All ER 1025 described 'malice aforethought' as an 'anachronistic and now wholly inappropriate phrase which still lingers on in the definition of murder to denote the necessary mental element'. What then is 'the necessary mental element' for murder?

The answer is surprisingly simple. It means either:

(a) an intention to kill; or

(b) an intention to cause grievous bodily harm.

You may find it surprising that an intention to cause grievous bodily harm will suffice as an alternative to an intention to kill. The House of Lords in *Cunningham* [1981] 2 All ER 863 (*Cases and Materials* (6.4.1)) removed the uncertainties caused by the disparate reasoning used by the individual Law Lords in the case of *Hyam v DPP* [1974] 2 All ER 41 and confirmed that an intention to cause grievous bodily harm was sufficient *mens rea* for murder. This is accepted in both *Moloney* (above) and *Hancock and Shankland* [1986] 1 All ER 646, HL.

? QUESTION 6.2

- What does grievous bodily harm mean?
- If death unexpectedly results from an intentional causing of grievous bodily harm, should it be murder?

Most commentators regard intention to cause grievous bodily harm as unacceptably wide for the *mens rea* of murder. We saw in the previous chapter that grievous bodily harm means no more than 'really serious' harm according to *DPP v Smith* [1960] 3 All ER 161, HL. Thus, it does not necessitate intending to cause a life-threatening injury. Lords Diplock and Kilbrandon in *Hyam v DPP* wanted to narrow this head to require an intention to cause injury likely to endanger life, but were outvoted by the majority. If D aims to break someone's leg, he intends to cause grievous bodily harm. It seems wrong that he should be convicted of murder if the victim dies due to unforeseen medical complications. But that is the law. Clause 54(1) of the draft Criminal Code proposes a narrowing of the current rule so that D must act 'intending to cause serious personal harm **and being aware that he may cause death**'.

 EXERCISE 6.1

Read the extract from the Criminal Law Revision Committee's Report in *Cases and Materials* (6.2.1.2) for the arguments for and against retaining intention to cause GBH as sufficient *mens rea* for murder.

6.4.1.1 Intention again

Although we examined the concept of intention in some detail at 3.3 above, we can use this section to recapitulate and explore that material.

? **QUESTION** 6.3

What states of mind constitute 'intention'?

In everyday language, intention denotes aim or purpose and it has never been disputed that any such state of mind falls within the legal definition. The difficulty has always been the extent to which 'legal' intention extends beyond this paradigm case. At one time it was enough that D realised that death or GBH was highly probable (*Hyam v DPP* [1974] 2 All ER 41, HL) but it is now clear that the present definition is rather narrower. It seems from *Woollin* that intention in practice includes realisation (foresight) by D that death or GBH is virtually certain (**but nothing less than virtually certain**). However, there is an element of doubt which condemns us to explore further *Moloney*, *Hancock and Shankland*, *Nedrick* and *Woollin*.

Before we do so, it is worth reminding you not to fall into a trap for the unwary which snared the trial judge in *MD* [2004] EWCA Crim 1391. The judge had directed the jury that they could find that D intended to kill only if death or serious injury was virtually certain to result from her actions and she realised this. However, he failed to explain that this was only necessary where D acted without the purpose of killing or causing serious injury. The *Woollin* extension is irrelevant and has **no** application where it is D's aim to kill or cause serious injury.

Moloney

The House of Lords here stressed that in the normal case, 'the golden rule is that the judge should avoid any elaboration or paraphrase of what is meant by intent and leave it to the jury's good sense to decide whether D acted with the necessary intent.' Certainly where there has been a direct attack by D, the judge should not define intent, and presumably the jury will take it as meaning aim or purpose. Elaboration is only necessary where the harm to V may have been an unwanted side-effect of D's actions, the latter being aimed at achieving some other purpose, but nonetheless involving a very high risk of serious injury or death to another, e.g., exploding a bomb to cause economic damage or setting fire to a house to frighten someone.

In such cases, although foresight of probability or even high probability was not 'equivalent or alternative to the necessary intention' to kill or cause GBH, the jury should be told that if they found that D foresaw death or GBH as a 'natural consequence of his act . . . it is a proper inference for them to draw that he intended that consequence'. By natural consequence, the House meant that 'in the ordinary course of events a certain act **will** lead to a certain consequence unless something unexpected supervenes to prevent it' (our emphasis), i.e., that the probability of it must be 'little short of overwhelming'. This seems synonymous with virtual certainty. At one point the House stated that D's foresight of this will '**establish** the necessary intent', implying that foresight of such a high degree as virtual certainty **equals** intention. However, this is contradicted by the insistence that foresight of whatever degree is not 'equivalent' to intention but only material from which the jury may infer intention (then left undefined) if they wish.

Hancock and Shankland

The defendants were striking miners in Wales during the protracted 1984–5 miners' strike. In order to stop a strike-breaking miner getting to work, they pushed a concrete post and block from a bridge onto the road below. The block smashed through the windscreen of a taxi, in which the working miner was being carried, and killed the taxi driver. The defendants claimed they meant only to block the road and not to harm anyone. The House of Lords quashed their murder convictions on the ground that the *Moloney* 'natural consequence' direction used by the trial judge was defective.

One unambiguous holding in *Moloney* was the rejection of the majority view in *Hyam* that foresight that death or GBH was highly probable sufficed for the *mens rea* of murder. In *Hancock,* the House of Lords feared that a jury might misconstrue the term 'natural consequence' as meaning simply that the consequence was caused in the natural course of events rather than being the almost inevitable result of D's act. Pregnancy may be a natural consequence of unprotected sexual intercourse, but it is not even likely. Reference to 'natural' should therefore be omitted. However, rather than requiring foresight of virtual certainty, foresight of **probability only** would suffice to entitle the jury, as a matter of evidence, to draw the inference of intention. Thus, although not a return to *Hyam, Hancock* certainly appeared to backtrack a little on *Moloney*.

Nedrick

The facts of *Nedrick* were similar to those in *Hyam* in that D set fire to a house in the early hours of the morning causing the death of a child. He claimed that he had not meant to harm anyone but only to frighten the mother of the victim.

 EXERCISE 6.2

Read the passage from *Woollin* in *Cases and Materials* (3.3.2) headed 'The context of the decision in *Nedrick*'.

- Is *Nedrick* consistent with *Hancock and Shankland*?
- Is foresight by D that death or GBH is virtually certain, 'intention' according to *Nedrick*?

Nedrick appears initially more or less to follow the position set by *Hancock*. However, the final conclusion is frankly inconsistent with *Hancock* and reverts to the position which, we have argued, was arrived at in *Moloney*. In an extra-judicial pronouncement, Lord Lane CJ has stated that the Court of Appeal in *Nedrick* wanted to cut through the obfuscation by establishing that foresight of virtual certainty **was** intention and by eliminating the confusing concept of inferring intention from foresight. However, it felt constrained by the House of Lords' authority of *Moloney* and *Hancock*.

Woollin

This must now be regarded as the leading case which, you will happily recall, provides welcome clarification and simplification of the law. D, in anger and frustration, threw his crying three-month-old son across the room with considerable force causing him serious brain damage from which he died. The prosecution accepted that D did not aim to kill or cause GBH to his son, but he was convicted of murder after the trial judge directed that it was enough if he appreciated there was a 'substantial risk' of GBH to the baby. The House of Lords unanimously held this to be a misdirection and substituted a conviction for manslaughter.

Bolstered by a highly selective interpretation of the cases we have just considered, the House, free of the inhibitions restricting the Court of Appeal, arguably took the step which the latter dared not take in *Nedrick*.

 EXERCISE 6.3

Read the remainder of the extract from *Woollin* in *Cases and Materials* (3.3.2).

Do you agree that *Nedrick* 'merely stated what state of mind (in the absence of a purpose to kill or to cause serious harm) is sufficient for murder'?

If the jury are satisfied that D foresaw the death as virtually certain, are they *compelled* to find that D intended that death?

It is clear that their Lordships were determined to rid the law of the nonsense and confusion which had disfigured it and to lay down a simple and clear definition of the concept of intention in murder. However, they were only partially successful in this. Whilst we may question the assertion that *Nedrick* (a) is not in conflict with *Hancock*, and (b) 'stated what state of mind ... is sufficient for murder' (as opposed to ruling what degree of foresight could, as a matter of evidence, give rise to an inference of intention), we believe that *Woollin* is in accord with the spirit of *Moloney*. The House adopted, with an important modification, what it terms 'the critical direction' in *Nedrick*. It is initially stated that 'the effect of the critical direction is that a result foreseen as virtually certain is an intended result'. That seems to mean that foresight of virtual certainty **constitutes** intention. It is a form of intention. However, as we shall see below, the final conclusion of the House is at odds with that statement.

The 'critical direction' as modified by the substitution of the word 'find' for the less clear word 'infer' now reads:

> Where the charge is murder and in the rare cases where the simple direction is not enough, the jury should be directed that they are not entitled to **find** the necessary intention, unless they feel sure that death or serious bodily harm was a virtual certainty (barring some unforeseen intervention) as a result of the defendant's actions and that the defendant appreciated that such was the case.

? QUESTION 6.4

Does this direction *define* what is 'non-purpose' intention?

It is unfortunate that the House was so wedded to this 'tried-and-tested formula' which retains a potential for confusion between the substantive definition of intention and the evidence which is needed to prove D had such intention—exactly the confusion which the House was trying to eradicate. To say that the jury are 'entitled to find' intention only if D realised death or GBH was virtually certain implies that they have a discretion whether or not to find it in such a case. Where it is not D's purpose to kill or cause GBH, the jury are prohibited from finding intention unless D foresaw death or GBH as virtually certain. D's foresight of death or GBH as virtually certain seems only to entitle and not to compel the jury to find intention. Furthermore, the direction does not appear to give any indication of the definition of intention. It gives no clue that foresight of virtual certainty **is** intention; it rather implies the reverse.

Despite apparently categoric statements (noted above) in early parts of the judgment that the House's understanding of the direction was that it did define 'non-purpose' intention, it seems that it does no such thing. If they are sure that D appreciated that death or grievous bodily harm was virtually certain to result, the jury are **entitled** to find intention, if they wish, but they are not **bound** to find it. They can please themselves. This unsatisfactory position was endorsed by the Court of Appeal in *Matthews and Alleyne* [2003] EWCA Crim 192 (*Cases and Materials* (3.3)). It may be that the House in *Woollin* deliberately wanted to leave an element of discretion for the jury rather than impose a rigid, hard and fast rule and you should re-read the discussion at 3.3.2 above (around Question 3.7) on this and other points made here. Note that *Re A (Children)*, a civil case, implies that the jury do not have a discretion where D foresaw death or GBH as virtually certain but it is inconsistent with *Matthews*.

Another anomaly in the *Nedrick* direction endorsed by the House in *Woollin* is the unnecessary requirement that death or GBH should **in fact** be virtually certain to result. It is not enough that D (mistakenly) **thinks** it is virtually certain (see 3.3.2 above).

? **QUESTION** 6.5

On the basis of the new test in *Woollin,* would you convict of murder:

(a) The arsonists in *Hyam* and *Nedrick*?
(b) A terrorist bomber who telephones a warning but kills a deaf person who failed to hear the call to evacuate?

There is no doubt that *Woollin* narrows the scope of murder. Of course, it still leaves the jury to designate what is and what is not virtually certain, a line-drawing exercise which is incapable of precision and therefore gives them further discretion in deciding whether D's crime is murder or only manslaughter. This is inevitable once *mens rea* is extended beyond aim or purpose. It means that similar fact situations, e.g., the frightening by arson cases such as *Hyam* and *Nedrick*, may easily be decided differently from jury to jury. Our view would be that most burning-out cases would not satisfy the virtual certainty test because there is almost always a realistic chance of the victim(s) escaping injury. However, we are by no means convinced that a jury would see it that way! The same could be said of the terrorist bomber who gives a warning. He could plausibly argue that he did not think it was virtually certain that someone would be killed or seriously injured, even if he would find it hard to deny that he realised it was likely, say, because of the location and short warning time. But would a jury be prepared to say it was not murder? At what point will the trial judge have to refuse to leave the issue to the jury?

Despite these problems, we would suggest that it is right to draw the line of murder to include cases where D acts knowing that the only realistic outcome will be to cause death or GBH. Such extreme and deliberate disregard for life and limb is scarcely less heinous than aiming to kill or seriously injure and deserves to be condemned as murder. However, the same cannot be said if D thinks there is a realistic chance of avoiding that outcome. His conduct may be heinous, but manslaughter is a very serious crime adequate to deal with it.

The major remaining question for reformers of the law of murder is whether *mens rea* in relation to GBH is acceptable given the fact that GBH covers injury which is in no way life-threatening.

6.4.1.2 **Summary**

Since the House of Lords' decision in *Woollin*, we can state the *mens rea* of murder with reasonable, if not complete, confidence. The law is clear that only an intention to kill or cause grievous bodily harm suffices (*Moloney*). Whether he desires them or not, a person intends death or GBH if it is his aim, objective or purpose to bring them about. In this case, it is irrelevant how likely or unlikely he was to achieve this aim (*MD*).

If it is not his aim or purpose, it is **open** to the jury to find intention if, **but only if**, death or GBH was in fact virtually certain to result from his acts and D appreciated that either was virtually certain to result (*Woollin*; *Matthews*). It is in their discretion.

6.5 Manslaughter

6.5.1 Introduction

Manslaughter is an unusual crime in that there are several disparate ways of committing it, which bear little relationship to each other. There are two main types of manslaughter, known as voluntary and involuntary, respectively. Each of these types has its own subdivisions. In voluntary manslaughter, D has killed with the *mens rea* for murder and satisfies the ingredients of murder. However, he is not guilty of murder because he has killed in certain mitigating circumstances which the law designates as reducing his culpability to manslaughter. On the other hand, if D has killed **without** the *mens rea* for murder, he will be guilty of involuntary manslaughter if he has the lesser fault elements required for that offence. **Figure 6.1** indicates the various forms of manslaughter.

6.5.2 **Voluntary manslaughter**

6.5.2.1 **Introduction**

As our **Figure 6.1** indicates, there are three distinct sets of circumstances which can mitigate what would otherwise be murder to manslaughter. One of the main reasons for doing this is to allow the judge a discretion in sentencing to reflect the reduced culpability of the accused, despite the fact that he intended to kill V or cause him serious harm. You will recall that on a conviction of murder, the trial judge is compelled by law to impose a

Manslaughter					
Voluntary (D has the *mens rea* for murder)			*Involuntary* (D does not have the *mens rea* for murder)		
Provocation (D provoked to lose his self-control)	Diminished responsibility (mental disorder)	Suicide pacts	Gross negligence manslaughter	Subjective recklessness manslaughter	Unlawful act or constructive manslaughter

Figure 6.1 Forms of manslaughter

sentence of life imprisonment. We will see later when considering general defences in **Chapters 8** and **9** that there is pressure from some sources to extend this list of mitigating circumstances. Thus duress is currently no defence to murder, but some argue that it should reduce murder to manslaughter. Similarly, if D kills by using excessive force in self-defence, a number of commentators think that what is now murder should be reduced to manslaughter. Let us concentrate on the existing law, dealing in turn with killing under provocation, diminished responsibility and in pursuance of a suicide pact.

6.5.2.2 Provocation

Introduction

The essence of provocation is that D kills someone **in the heat of the moment, having momentarily lost his self-control.** However, to prevent the defence unduly favouring those who are prone to lose their self-control at the slightest provocation, D's loss of self-control is judged against the yardstick of how an ordinary, average person might have reacted in the same situation. The law regards it as fair to excuse D's lack of self-restraint and lethal reaction **only** if the average person might have done as D did in the same circumstances. As we shall see in (c) below, the precise nature of this objective standard has been a matter of acute controversy which has just taken another rather surprising turn in *Attorney-General for Jersey* v *Holley* [2005] UKPC 23. The defence applies only to a charge of **murder** and is only a **partial defence**, reducing the crime from murder to manslaughter.

? **QUESTION** 6.6

Why do you think provocation is not a defence to any other crime, e.g., s. 18 of the OAPA 1861 or attempted murder?

Provocation is unnecessary in the case of offences other than murder because the presence of provocation can be taken into account by reducing the sentence which would otherwise have been imposed. In the case of murder this is impossible because of the mandatory fixed sentence of life imprisonment. Indeed, historically, the judiciary developed the 'defence' of provocation to avoid the death penalty then mandatory on conviction of murder.

Definition of the defence

Provocation is a common law defence and, as such, the definition has to be gleaned from an examination of the case law. Nonetheless, very significant changes to the common law formulation were wrought, both expressly and, as subsequent case law has confirmed, implicitly, by s. 3 of the Homicide Act 1957. Although not a comprehensive definition, s. 3 is undoubtedly the starting point for any study of the defence:

> Where on a charge of murder there is evidence on which the jury can find that the person charged was provoked (whether by things done or by things said or by both together) to lose his self-control, the question whether the provocation was enough to make a reasonable man do as he did shall be left to be determined by the jury, and in determining that question the jury shall take into account

everything both done and said according to the effect which, in their opinion, it would have on a reasonable man.

EXERCISE 6.4

Read the extract from Devlin J's summing up in *Duffy* in *Cases and Materials* (6.5.2.2). Can you identify the three basic elements which make up provocation?

Elements of the defence

For the purposes of analysis, we can identify three basic requirements: (a) provocative conduct causing (b) actual loss of self-control by D (c) where a reasonable person would have done as D did.

(a) Provocative conduct

According to s. 3 the provocative conduct may be 'things done or things said or both together'. This was enacted to overrule the case of *Holmes v DPP* [1946] 2 All ER 124, HL which appeared to hold that words of abuse were incapable of constituting provocative conduct for the purposes of the defence.

It is now clear from *Doughty* (1986) 83 Cr App R 319, CA (*Cases and Materials* (6.5.2.2)), that almost any conduct will be theoretically capable of founding the defence. In that case the trial judge ruled that the constant crying of a young baby was incapable of constituting provocative conduct and refused to leave the defence to the jury. The Court of Appeal held that this was a misdirection and the defence should have been left with the jury. (It is inconceivable that the defence would have succeeded in such a case, had it been left to the jury, because it would surely have found that the third condition (below) was not satisfied.)

Provocation and third parties   At common law, one could only take into account 'acts done by the dead man to the accused' (see *Duffy* [1949] 1 All ER 932).

?   **QUESTION** 6.7

This imposed two limitations. Can you identify them?

Both limitations have been swept away by s. 3. The first was that any provocative conduct from anyone other than the deceased victim had to be ignored. *Davies* [1975] 1 All ER 890, CA (*Cases and Materials* (6.5.2.2)) confirms that this rule is implicitly abolished by s. 3. Second, *Pearson* [1992] Crim LR 193 holds that the rule that provocative conduct by the deceased victim which was directed at someone other than the accused had to be ignored has also been impliedly overturned by s. 3.

In *Davies*, D killed his wife whilst in the presence of her lover. Since s. 3 simply referred to D being 'provoked to lose his self-control', the Court of Appeal held that it was no longer necessary to show that D was provoked to lose his self-control *by the deceased* and therefore it was incorrect to direct the jury that the only source of provocation which could be taken into account was that offered by the wife, as opposed to any offered by her lover.

In *Pearson*, the court held that provocation meted out by V to D's brother over a period of years during D's absence, could nevertheless be taken into account in D's defence on a charge of murdering V, his violent and tyrannical father.

Self-induced provocation   The situation envisaged here is where D's own behaviour causes the provocative conduct upon which D relies as the basis for his defence of provocation. In *Edwards* v *R* [1973] 1 All ER 152, PC the Privy Council appeared to hold that criminal conduct on the part of D (in this case an attempt to blackmail V) which led to provocative conduct by V (namely threatening D with a knife) causing D to stab (27 times!) V to death, could not form the basis of a plea of provocation, where V's provocative conduct was the predictable result of D's initial criminality, seemingly on the basis that no reasonable man would behave in that manner (i.e., 'do as D did').

This certainly contradicted s. 3 which stipulates that once there is evidence that D had actually lost his self-control, the defence **must** be left to the jury. This was recognised by the Court of Appeal in the subsequent case of *Johnson* [1989] 2 All ER 839 which explained away *Edwards* and held that the fact that the provocation was self-induced could not prevent the issue being left with the jury and was simply one factor for the jury to consider in deciding whether a reasonable man would have done as D did.

Mistake and provocation   If D mistakenly believes that he is being provoked when in fact he is not, should he be judged on the facts as he mistakenly believed them to be or as they actually were? As we shall see in **Chapter 8**, in relation to excusatory defences, which provocation by and large is, the general rule is that only if D's mistake is reasonable will it be taken into account (see 8.5.3). However there are cases in provocation which have held that D is entitled to be judged on the basis of his mistaken view of the situation even where that mistake was an unreasonable one, for example, caused by his own voluntary intoxication (see *Letenock* (1917) 12 Cr App R 221, CCA). It is unlikely that this rule would be upheld today (see *O'Grady* [1987] 3 All ER 420, a case concerning intoxication and self-defence).

Of course, even if D is judged on his drunken view of the situation, in judging how a reasonable man would react to that imagined situation, the rule is that the reasonable man is always sober (see *McCarthy* in (c) below).

(b) The subjective limb: actual loss of self-control by D
It is essential that the provocative conduct caused D to lose his self-control. It is an **entirely subjective** test: did the accused actually lose his self-control? If D did not lose his self-control, the defence fails, even if a reasonable person would have (*cf. Cocker* [1989] Crim LR 740). Whether D did lose his self-control is a question of fact for the jury, which must take into account all the circumstances. This includes all of D's characteristics including any mental or other abnormalities making it more or less likely that he lost his self-control, and traits such as short-temperedness and over-sensitivity.

What is loss of self-control?   The nearest the courts have come to defining this is in *Duffy*, where Devlin J described it as 'a sudden and temporary loss of self-control, rendering the accused so subject to passion as to make him or her for the moment not master of his mind'. This entails more than simple 'loss of temper', although 'the line between loss of temper and loss of self-control is...incapable of precise definition and is in each case a matter for the jury' (*Mohammed (Faqir)* [2005] EWCA Crim 1880). However, it does not require complete loss of self-control so that D does not know what he is doing, but rather that D 'is unable to restrain himself from doing what he did' (*Richens* [1993] 4 All ER 877, CA—*Cases and Materials* (6.5.2.2)).

It appears from *Thornton* [1992] 1 All ER 306, CA that this is unaffected by s. 3, a point re-affirmed in the further appeal in *Thornton (No. 2)* [1996] 2 All ER 1023, CA. This highlights what the Court of Appeal in *Thornton* called 'the essential feature that provocation produces a sudden or impulsive reaction leading to loss of control'. It means that, at the time of the killing, D must have 'snapped', 'seen red' or been so angry that he could not stop himself from doing what he did. Thus, the courts have long stated and continue to state that if D has had time to cool down after the provocative conduct, then the defence is likely to fail on the grounds that he is no longer 'out of control'. Reason has had time to resume its seat (see *Hayward* (1833) 6 C & P 157). Carefully planned revenge after the provocative conduct will not constitute the defence of provocation. However, the Court of Appeal in *Ahluwalia* [1992] 4 All ER 889 (*Cases and Materials* (6.5.2.2)) and *Baille* [1995] Crim LR 739 stressed that cooling time is only an evidential factor and it is always a question of fact as to whether D was 'provoked to lose his self-control' at the time of the killing.

> **? QUESTION** 6.8
>
> Does this mean that no account can be taken of past incidents of provocation as, for example, in the case of battered wives, because 'reason has had time to resume its seat' after those incidents?

It is clear from *Humphreys* [1995] 4 All ER 1008, CA that the courts can take into account previous provocative acts and incidents and regard these as cumulative **provided** the killing is an immediate response to a final act of provocation constituting the 'last straw' (even though this could have been relatively trivial). In *Humphreys*, the Court of Appeal held the trial judge to be at fault for not analysing for the jury the complex history of the tempestuous relationship between D and the deceased, who subjected D to violence and sexual abuse. This culminated in 'final straw' taunts about D's propensity to injure herself to draw attention to herself (she had slashed her wrists on the night in question), which led directly to the fatal stabbing by D. In *Thornton*, a *cause célèbre* for a number of feminist organisations, D had been violently abused by her hard-drinking husband over many months. One evening, she stabbed him to death with a carving knife after a row. The defence of provocation failed because, on her own evidence, after the row, she had gone into the kitchen and calmed down. She had then sharpened the carving knife and gone back into the room where her husband was lying on the sofa and stabbed him to death. At the time of the stabbing, it was found that she was in complete control of her actions. Following a reference by the Home Secretary a fresh appeal—*Thornton (No. 2)* was heard by the Court of Appeal which quashed D's conviction and ordered a retrial of the case, for reasons concerned with the reasonable person test (below). The retrial resulted in a conviction for manslaughter being substituted for the murder conviction.

This view was again endorsed by the Court of Appeal in *Ahluwalia* where D killed her husband after a long history of violence and abuse, by pouring petrol over him and setting fire to it. There was evidence of planning and no 'sudden and temporary' loss of control. The argument that the requirement for a 'sudden' loss of control should not apply in this type of 'slow-burn' case where a woman has been violently abused for a long time was rejected. However, the court managed to find the 'compassionate' way out which it had failed to find in *Thornton* by holding that there was evidence that D might have been suffering from diminished responsibility (due to endogenous depression—**not** battered wife syndrome), a defence which, through no fault of hers, was not raised at the trial. A retrial was therefore ordered and that resulted in a finding of manslaughter on the ground of diminished responsibility. Who says judges are not influenced by political considerations?!

The function of the judge We said above that whether the accused actually lost his self-control is a question of fact for the jury. However, the issue of provocation will only be left to be decided by the jury, if the judge is satisfied that there is, in the words of s. 3, 'evidence on which the jury can find that the person charged was provoked ... to lose his self-control ...'. If, therefore, he is satisfied that, on the evidence given, no reasonable jury could possibly conclude that the accused lost his self-control, he must withdraw the issue from the jury and the defence fails.

The House of Lords in *Acott* [1997] 1 All ER 706 (*Cases and Materials* (6.5.2.2)) held that, in such cases, the trial judge could only leave the issue to the jury where there was some actual evidence as to what had been said or done which allegedly caused D to lose his self-control. This had to be more than just speculation arising from suggestions made by the prosecution but denied by D during his cross-examination, or, say, the savagery involved in the attack. How can a jury determine how a reasonable person might have reacted (i.e., the second limb of the test at (c) below) when they have no evidence as to what was said or done to provoke D?

However, once there is *some* evidence fit for the jury, the judge is duty bound to leave the issue to the jury and has no further powers to decide the question. Even if D's counsel, for tactical reasons, has not pleaded the defence of provocation, the trial judge is bound to explain the possibility to the jury, 'wherever there is material which is capable of amounting to provocation, however tenuous it may be' (*Rossiter* [1994] 2 All ER 752, CA). 'Tenuous' here refers to how provoking the provocative acts and words were and not the strength of the evidence that such provocative acts and words actually occurred (*Cambridge* [1994] 2 All ER 760, CA; *Stewart* [1995] 4 All ER 999, CA). The Court of Appeal went even further in a case involving the namesakes of a more notorious duo, *Burgess and McLean* [1995] Crim LR 425. Because the accused's counsel feared it would prejudice his clients' chances of a complete acquittal for which he was contending, he dissuaded the trial judge from directing the jury on provocation, even though the evidence suggested that it was a possibility. The Court of Appeal held that the judge should have directed the jury on provocation despite counsel's opposition and substituted verdicts of manslaughter for the murder convictions. Counsel and the accused were in this case able to have their cake and eat it! However, the Court of Appeal in *Cox* [1995] Crim LR 741 imposed for the future a duty on both counsel to advise the judge of the need for a provocation direction where there is evidence of D's loss of self-control.

As indicated immediately following Question 6.9 below, if there is some credible evidence that D actually lost his self-control, the judge cannot withdraw the defence from the jury on the ground that he thinks that there is no way the objective condition (see (c) next) could be satisfied. The question of whether a reasonable man might have done as D did is exclusively a question for the jury. However, according to *Van Dongen* [2005] EWCA Crim 1728, the judges of the Court of Appeal may stray into the jury's territory. If the trial judge had incorrectly refused to leave the defence of provocation to the jury, where there was evidence of actual loss of self-control, it would be open to the Court of Appeal to conclude nevertheless that the conviction was safe on the ground that it was inevitable that the jury would have rejected the defence.

(c) The objective limb

The traditional view of this limb required the provocative conduct to be such as might cause a reasonable person to lose their self-control **and** do as the accused did (*Stewart*). How a reasonable person might have reacted provided the standard against which D's actions were judged. As Lord Goff put it: 'The function of the test is only to introduce, as a matter of policy, a standard of self-control which has to be complied with if provocation is to be established in law' (*Morhall* [1995] 3 All ER 659, HL—*Cases and Materials* (6.5.2.2)). As we shall see shortly, the House of Lords in *Smith (Morgan)* [2000] 4 All ER 289 (*Cases and Materials* (6.5.2.2)) watered down this standard replacing the yardstick of the average, normal person with a wider test which simply asked: could D in his situation have reasonably been expected to control his reaction? Although subjected to much criticism, this case was generally thought to have settled the law once and for all, barring legislative intervention. How wrong we were! The Privy Council in *Attorney-General for Jersey* v *Holley* [2005] UKPC 23 (*Cases and Materials* 6.5.2.2) has effectively reversed *Smith (Morgan)* and taken us back to the traditional view in *Camplin* and *Morhall*.

> **? QUESTION** 6.9
>
> Would a 'reasonable' person ever react by *killing* someone *with the mens rea for murder* no matter how grave the provocation?

The jury is the sole arbiter of whether a reasonable person might, in the circumstances, ˒ their self-control and do as D did. Prior to s. 3, the judge had power to withdraw thᵣ from the jury by ruling that there was no evidence fit for the jury that a reasonablᵣ might do as D did. In the course of exercising this function to control the scᵣ defence, the judges developed several hard-and-fast rules about how the reasoᵣ would react (see, e.g., the 'reasonable relationship' rule described below). ˒ cifically abolished the judges' 'filtering' function on this question and thiˑ resulted in the abrogation of the various technical rules developed by ˒ 1957 (see *DPP* v *Camplin* [1978] 2 All ER 168, HL).

The nature of the reasonable person   In many ways the courts' use of the term 'reasonable person' was unfortunate as it seems to be a contradiction in terms to contemplate that a **reasonable person** would ever intentionally kill another person. In reality, the 'reasonable person' means no more than the ordinary, average person who can, of course, occasionally lose his temper and act irrationally (*Morhall*).

Prior to s. 3, the courts insisted that the reasonable person was 'normal' or 'average' in every way and did not possess any special characteristics which D had, even if the provocation was directed at these 'special' characteristics. Thus, in *Bedder* v *DPP* [1954] 2 All ER 801, HL, the reasonable man could not be invested with D's sexual impotence, even though the prostitute he killed had taunted him about his inability to perform sex with her and had kicked him painfully on his failure.

The House of Lords in *DPP* v *Camplin* [1978] 2 All ER 168 (*Cases and Materials* (6.5.2.2)) held that s. 3 impliedly overruled the principle laid down in *Bedder*, so that if similar circumstances arose again, the reasonable man would be invested with D's impotence. According to *Camplin*, the reasonable person was someone 'having the power of self-control to be expected of an ordinary person of the sex and age of the accused but in other respects sharing such of the accused's characteristics as . . . would affect the gravity of the provocation on him . . .'.

? QUESTION 6.10

- Does this mean that the reasonable person should be given all D's characteristics?
- Why is this impossible without undermining the whole basis of the present defence?
- What bottom line characteristic(s) should the reasonable person possess in *every case*?

It is important to realise that this did not mean that the reasonable man had to be invested with every characteristic of the accused. If that were done, the reasonable man would **become** the accused and the objective measure against which the accused's reaction was judged would have been abolished. Therefore, to ensure the maintenance of this objective yardstick, there was always one objective characteristic which the reasonable man should possess in **every** case: that is, he should always possess the **average** degree of self-control so that he can never be invested with the accused's 'exceptional excitability (whether idiosyncratic or by cultural environment or ethnic origin) or pugnacity or ill-temper' (per Lord Simon in *Camplin*). Thus *Lesbini* [1914] 3KB 1116, CCA is still good law. Equally, the reasonable man would never become temporarily excitable or pugnacious through the effect of alcohol. *McCarthy* [1954] 2 All ER 262, CCA is still good law. *Morhall* confirmed that, as a matter of policy, the reasonable person is always sober, even if D's self-control is impaired by alcohol or drugs.

As we shall see below, the instinct of the courts to do justice to the individual defendant by recognising abnormalities which are no fault of his has caused tensions with their duty to ensure that the reasonable man possesses the normal degree of self-control. The Court of Appeal in a number of cases tended to lower the objective standard of self-control required of D where he had an identifiable condition which through no fault of his own rendered him incapable of reaching the normal standard.

This approach was in conflict with the Privy Council's majority decision in *Luc Thiet Thuan v R* [1996] 2 All ER 1033 (*Cases and Materials* (6.5.2.2)). By a three to two majority, the House of Lords in *Smith (Morgan)* [2000] 4 All ER 289 (*Cases and Materials* (6.5.2.2)) chose to adopt the Court of Appeal's approach despite the fact that the Privy Council's view seemed to reflect the line previously taken by the House in the leading case of *Camplin* and again in *Morhall*.

The controversy facing the House of Lords in Smith   The Privy Council's view, seemingly supported by the House of Lords, was that the personal characteristics of D were not relevant to the objective, reasonable man question **unless** they affected the gravity of the provocation on D. In *Smith* and several previous decisions, the Court of Appeal rejected this limitation and allowed the jury to take into account personal characteristics of the accused which simply reduced his general capacity to control himself.

(i) Characteristics affecting the gravity of the provocation
Everyone agrees that personal characteristics of D which enhance the seriousness of the provocation must be taken into account. For example, in *Morhall*, D's addiction to glue-sniffing was relevant because the victim nagged and taunted him about that very trait and his inability to kick his habit. What could be laughed off by a non-addict becomes altogether more provocative and wounding to an addict. Possession of the characteristic alters the **nature** of the provocation and magnifies its effect. Bedder's impotence is another example and illustrates the most obvious way in which a characteristic would 'affect the gravity of the provocation' and so be attributed to the reasonable man, namely where it is directed at that characteristic and provides the sting to the provocation. If the taunts in *Morhall* had been about, say, D's sexual orientation, then his addiction to glue would be irrelevant since it would in no way add point to the provocative remarks.

In *Camplin*, D, a boy of 15, was forcibly buggered by V, a man in his 50s, who, in his moment of sexual triumph, taunted and laughed at D. D lost his self-control and killed V by hitting him over the head with a chapatti pan. The House of Lords held that the trial judge misdirected the jury in instructing them to regard the reasonable man as a normal adult and **not** to invest him with D's youth. The reasonable person should always be given the same age and sex as D.

> **? QUESTION** 6.11
>
> Would D's youth affect the gravity of the provocation or alter its nature and provocativeness in this case?

(ii) Characteristics affecting D's general level of self-control
Can a characteristic be taken into account if it did not increase the provocativeness of the particular conduct of the victim but merely made D more prone to be provoked in general (more provocable) whatever the nature of the provoking conduct? For example, the accused in *Luc* claimed that his sexual prowess had been the subject of derisive comments

by V including unfavourable comparisons with her new lover. It was accepted that he suffered 'organic brain damage' which made him easily provoked and prone to outbursts of violence. In *Smith*, there was evidence that D was suffering from serious clinical depression which would have 'disinhibited' him, thus lowering his powers of self-control. In each case, the nature and gravity of the provocation was unaffected by D's characteristic. There were no taunts about D's brain damage or depression. In each case, D did not have the normal or average powers of self-control and would be much more likely to be provoked, whatever the nature of the provocative conduct. Quite simply, he was more provocable than the average person. The legal question was whether we should judge him by the standard of **normal** powers of self-control or whether we should apply a **lower** standard of self-control consonant with what we can reasonably expect of someone with his condition. The majority in *Smith* took the latter view but, in truth, it appears to undermine the reasonable person test expressly endorsed by the legislature in s. 3. If the reasonable person does not have normal powers of self-control, what is left of the reasonable person? What has happened to the objective yardstick against which we are supposed to be comparing D's loss of control?

The majority claimed that they were following *Camplin* but that does not hold much water. You will recall that *Camplin* held that the reasonable person is someone 'having the power of self-control to be expected of an ordinary person of the sex and age of the accused but in other respects sharing such of the accused's characteristics as ... would affect the gravity of the provocation on him ...' This makes quite clear that, apart from age and sex, the **only** characteristics the reasonable ('ordinary') person can share with D are those which 'affect the gravity of the provocation'. It is true that there is no need to show that the particular provocation had any connection with D's gender or age. Even if D's age relates simply to his general level of self-control as in *Camplin* itself (a15-year-old having a lower general level of control than an adult), the reasonable person must be given his age. This was rightly explained in *Luc* as an exception to the general rule. That exception can be justified on the basis that there is nothing abnormal about age— everyone is young at some stage in their lives and is entitled to be judged against the average person of their current age. The same was said (perhaps without a great deal of consideration) of D's gender. This would seem to presuppose that one sex has a lower threshold of self-control than the other—a questionable hypothesis! Perhaps it was a recognition that some types of abuse, though not related to gender as such, may have a generally more wounding effect on one sex than the other, e.g., unjustified remarks about sexual promiscuity may in general affect women more profoundly than men. The reasoning in *Camplin* and *Morhall* strongly suggests that age and sex are exceptional because they are facets of normality and that the rule cannot be extended to **abnormal** characteristics.

(iii) The decision in *Smith (Morgan)*
There is no doubt that the analysis of the dissenting minority (particularly Lord Hobhouse) is far more convincing than that of the majority but, of course, it is the majority's view which prevails. As indicated, characteristics which have no effect on the gravity of the provocation, but which simply affect D's ability to control himself can be taken into account. Thus the brain damage in *Luc* and the depression in *Smith* would be relevant.

? QUESTION 6.12

Does this mean that if D had a volatile and explosive personality, this would be given to the reasonable person? Is anything left of the objective test?

Lord Hoffmann, giving probably the most important majority judgment, emphasised that it is not **obligatory** for the jury to take factors such as D's depression into account. It is a matter for their discretion to decide whether it is relevant. The ultimate question is whether they thought 'the behaviour of the accused had measured up to the standard of self-control which ought reasonably to have been expected of him'. The remarkable thing about this formulation is that the concept of the reasonable person does not feature in it. That is remarkable because it flies in the face of the express preservation of that concept and test by s. 3!

Undeterred, Lord Hoffmann claimed not to be departing from the legal principle of objectivity embodied in s. 3 when he held that trial judges should no longer be required to direct in terms of the reasonable person. The principle of objectivity should be:

> expounded in clear language... The general principle is that the same standards of behaviour are expected of everyone, regardless of their individual psychological make-up... this is a principle not a rigid rule. It may sometimes have to yield to a more important principle, which is to do justice in the particular case. So the jury may think that there is some characteristic of the accused, whether temporary or permanent, which affected the degree of control which society could reasonably have expected of *him* and which it would be unjust not to take into account. If the jury take this view they are at liberty to give effect to it.

One such characteristic would be post-traumatic stress disorder caused by battered woman syndrome, now a medically recognised condition. It is also clear that temporary conditions like eczema or abscesses can be characteristics for this purpose (*Camplin*; *Morhall*). In addition, a relevant characteristic cannot be ignored just because it is morally repugnant, e.g., paedophilia, drug addiction (*Morhall*).

That is not to say that every characteristic is to be left to the jury to make what they will of it. The trial judge should direct the jury to ignore emotional traits 'such as jealousy and obsession' or a 'tendency to violent rages or childish tantrums'. These are 'defects in character rather than an excuse... In deciding what should count as a sufficient excuse, they [the jury] have to apply what they consider to be appropriate standards of behaviour; on the one hand making allowances for human nature and the power of the emotions but, on the other hand, not allowing someone to rely upon his own violent disposition'. No criteria are suggested for identifying which characteristics cannot be taken into account by the jury.

It may be that we must distinguish between cases where D's lower threshold of control is due to some identifiable condition outside of his control such as clinical depression or brain damage and cases where D's exceptional bad temper, pugnacity or excitability are part of his innate temperament without any obvious cause (or due to voluntary intoxication). But, as Professor Sir John Smith has asked, can we sensibly distinguish between abnormal irascibility itself and the mental condition causing it? It seems that we must!

According to *Weller* [2003] EWCA Crim 815,CA, far from settling the law, the *Smith* ruling led to an increase in the number of appeals concerning the appropriate direction on provocation! D strangled his partner when she ended their relationship because he was unduly possessive and jealous. The trial judge's direction on provocation failed to instruct the jury specifically that they could take into account D's excessive jealousy and possessiveness in assessing whether D should reasonably have controlled himself. However, neither did it rule out such consideration, simply referring in general terms to the necessity for the jury to take into account 'all the circumstances' and 'decide what society expects of a man like this defendant in his position'. That was held to be sufficient especially as a specific mention of the characteristics could well be accompanied by unfavourable comment that 'the jury may think that such characteristics constitute defects of character rather than an excuse for killing'. The crucial concern was that 'the jury must not be directed that they should take no account of them [such characteristics] and it is essential that it is made clear that such matters may form part of their deliberations.' In many cases (unlike this one!), 'the better course' will be 'to identify the particular characteristics relied upon whether or not accompanied by further guidance'. The judge is not entitled to rule out any 'matters relating to the defendant, the kind of man he is and his mental state, as well as the circumstances in which the death occurred ... He may give them some guidance as to the weight to be given to some aspects, provided he makes it clear that the question is one which, as the law provides, they are to answer, and not him'. In other words, anything goes. Nothing is ruled out, not even excessive possessiveness or jealousy or, it seems, excessive pugnacity and excitability! The most the trial judge can do is to invite the jury to **consider** whether such traits provide an acceptable reason for lowering the standard of self-control that society could expect of that defendant!

? QUESTION 6.13

If the effect of the provocative conduct on D is increased because D is drunk or drugged, would that be taken into account?

Intoxication through drink or drugs, even though it makes D more susceptible to the provocation, is always excluded on policy grounds (*Morhall*). The reasonable person always displayed the self-control to be expected of a sober person (*McCarthy*). However *Morhall* demonstrated that the reasonable person would take on D's addiction to alcohol, drugs or chemicals if it increased the gravity of the provocation because D was taunted with it. It seems that under *Smith*, alcoholism or true addiction to other drugs, being illnesses, could be taken into account even if they simply lowered D's general level of self-control. However, presumably the *Morhall* rule that the jury must ignore any intoxication at the time of the incident will prevail. D must therefore be judged by how the provocation might be expected to affect a sober alcoholic!

We have seen how the House of Lords effectively rewrote s. 3 by removing the reasonable person from the equation. We must conclude by noting that the House also chose to ignore the wider statutory context of the Homicide Act 1957 and the provision in s. 2 of the defence of diminished responsibility which expressly caters for people suffering from an abnormality of the mind (see 6.5.2.3 below). In *Smith*, D had failed to establish that his depression was severe enough for diminished responsibility. As the minority asked, why should he have a second bite of the cherry to use his depression as a defence via provocation? As Professor Ashworth had explained long ago, provocation is a defence for those who are 'in a broad sense mentally normal' whereas diminished responsibility is the defence for those who are abnormal (see [1976] CLJ 292). Under *Smith*, the abnormal defendant who cannot satisfy the conditions of s. 2 can pray in aid the same abnormality to have a second try under s. 3.

In conclusion, the decision in *Smith* appeared to have rewritten the statutory scheme and to have come close to implementing the statutory reform proposed by the Law Commission in its draft Criminal Code Bill of 1989 (which differed markedly from its 2004 recommendations, on which see 'Reform' below). Nonetheless, it did appear to be the last judicial word on the subject. However, the cat was well and truly set among the pigeons by the Privy Council in *Attorney-General for Jersey* v *Holley* (*Cases and Materials* 6.5.2.2) which disapproved *Smith* and held that the law was correctly stated in its previous decision in *Luc Thiet Thuan* v R.

(iv) The final resolution?—the reinstatement of s. 3 in *Holley*

The accused in *Holley* was a chronic alcoholic who killed his alcoholic partner with an axe after she taunted him about, among other things, just having had sex with another man. Both were drunk at the time. The issue was whether his disease of chronic alcoholism should be taken into account even though the taunts did not in any way relate to this. It simply lowered his general level of self-control and made him more prone to fly off the handle at any provocation. Under *Smith*, the jury would have been able to take it into consideration but the decision in *Holley* was to the contrary—the alcoholism was irrelevant to the objective condition in provocation:

> ... there is one compelling, overriding reason why this view [the majority's view in *Smith*] cannot be regarded as an accurate statement of English law ... The law of homicide is a highly sensitive and highly controversial area of the criminal law. In 1957 Parliament altered the common law relating to provocation and declared what the law on this subject should thenceforth be. In these circumstances it is not open to judges now to change ('develop') the common law and thereby depart from the law as declared by Parliament. However much the contrary is asserted, the majority view does represent a departure from the law as declared in section 3 of the Homicide Act 1957. *It involves a significant relaxation of the uniform, objective standard adopted by Parliament. Under the statute the sufficiency of the provocation ('whether the provocation was enough to make a reasonable man do as [the defendant] did') is to be judged by one standard, not a standard which varies from defendant to defendant. Whether the provocative act or words and the defendant's response met the 'ordinary person' standard prescribed by the statute is the question the jury must consider, not the altogether looser question of whether, having regard to all the circumstances, the jury consider the loss of self-control was sufficiently excusable. The statute does not leave each jury free to set whatever standard they consider appropriate in the circumstances by which to judge whether the defendant's conduct is 'excusable'* ([22]). (Our emphasis)

Accordingly, in judging whether D 'exercised ordinary self-control', no account could be taken of his intoxication or chronic alcoholism. We therefore must in future differentiate factors affecting the gravity of the provocation which are taken into account to determine the seriousness of the provoking conduct, from factors which do not aggravate the particular provocation but simply make D more liable to be provoked in general terms. The latter are irrelevant to the objective question which involves a two-stage process. In the words of the subsequent Court of Appeal case of *Mohammed (Faqir)* [2005] EWCA Crim 1880 (see *Cases and Materials* (6.5.2.2)), 'the first calls for an assessment of the gravity of the provocation [i.e., how seriously provoking the conduct was] and the second for application of an external standard of self-control; what is to be expected of a person of ordinary self-control.' The first question involves consideration of any factors applicable to D which aggravate the provocativeness of the conduct. For the second, the jury must assess whether a person of ordinary self-control subjected to the same degree of provocativeness might have done as D did. At this stage, no account can be taken of personal factors affecting D. That there is a certain air of artificiality to such distinctions cannot be denied and this weighed heavily with the dissentients in *Holley*. They were much concerned with the ability of juries to grasp such refinements, though the majority thought such difficulties to have been 'exaggerated.' Nonetheless, it seems to be an inevitable consequence of s. 3 and its imposition of a fixed standard of self-control against which to judge D's loss of self-control.

The policy rationale for making this distinction has been put in the following way:

> The provocation excuse should be a concession to extraordinary external circumstances not to the extraordinary internal make-up of the accused. The moral foundation for the extenuation is the necessity for very serious provocation. The more trivial the provocation, the more the defendant's reaction is attributable to his or her own personality and make-up and not to the provocative conduct. The more serious the provocative conduct, the more his or her retaliation is attributable to the provocation rather than his or her own deficiencies. That is why a distinction should be made between assessing the gravity of the provocation and assessing the standard of self-control required. If the reaction is essentially due to the internal character of the accused, his or her excusatory claim, if any, should sound in diminished responsibility. That is the proper defence for the abnormal. 'The defence of provocation is for those who are in a broad sense mentally normal' but who snap under the weight of very grave provocation. (Heaton: *Anything Goes* (2001) 10(2) Nottingham Law Journal 50, 55–56 quoted in the Law Commission's Consultation Paper at 4.144)

You may be thinking that, because *Holley* is a Privy Council decision, it is not binding on English courts but persuasive only. Surely if it conflicts with *Smith*, a House of Lords' decision, it is the latter which should prevail and bind future courts, at least to Court of Appeal level. Technically that is true but we are confident that *Holley* will now be taken to represent the law. As Lord Nicholls delivering the majority judgment stated:

> This appeal, being heard by an enlarged Board of nine members, is concerned to resolve this conflict [between *Smith (Morgan)* and *Luc Thiet Thuan*] and clarify definitively the present state of English law, and hence Jersey law, on this important subject. ([1])

Clearly the fact that nine Law Lords sat instead of the usual five and that they explicitly set themselves the task of clarifying 'definitively' the law puts an almost irresistible pressure on future courts to follow the decision. Although the decision was a six to three majority, the three dissenters accepted that the majority view now definitively states the current law. Technically speaking, it might be argued that *Smith* is inconsistent with s. 3 and, of course, the statute must prevail over judicial decision. Furthermore, the Court of Appeal in

Mohammed (Faqir) [2005] EWCA Crim 1880 proceeded on the basis that *Holley* rather than *Smith* represented the current law.

(v) History and circumstances

It is essential not to lose sight of the fact that other matters apart from D's personal 'characteristics' are often significant. Both *Camplin* and *Morhall* recognised that other matters such as D's 'history or the circumstances in which he is placed at the relevant time' might affect the gravity of the provocation. To appreciate the gravity of provocative con-duct, you must view it in its context. A relatively innocuous remark or action may take on an entirely different colour according to whether it is viewed in isolation or in context. Thus 'last straw' provocations can revive past provocations. Taunts, threats or violence from the victim to an accused who has been continually abused over a period of time must be more provocative for that reason. It is unthinkable that the jury should not take into account the fact that D had been subjected to prior, systematic abuse whether this had led to an identifiable psychiatric condition such as battered woman syndrome or not. The severity of the provocation is often defined by its wider context, e.g., D's past experiences or relationships with the victim or others. An example is provided by *Horrex* [1999] Crim LR 500, CA where the provocation (violence and threats by the victim against G) had to be viewed in the light of D's very close relationship to G whom he regarded as a mother figure. That was central to judging the seriousness of the provocation on him and whether his loss of self-control ought, in fairness, to be excused.

Must the retaliation be reasonably proportionate to the provocation?

? **QUESTION** 6.14

Can anyone, even a reasonable person, who has lost their self-control, keep their retaliation propor-tionate to the gravity of the provocation?

Prior to s. 3, the House of Lords in *Mancini* v *DPP* [1941] 3 All ER 272 appeared to lay down a hard-and-fast rule that a reasonable man would never retaliate in a way which was seriously disproportionate to the provocation offered. As they put it, the reasonable man would answer provocative blows with blows and not with a five-inch stiletto dagger. It is now clear that s. 3, in leaving the reasonable man issue entirely to the jury, has relegated this invariable legal rule to becoming simply one factor which the jury must take into account in deciding if the reasonable man would have done as D did. (See *Brown* [1972] 2 All ER 1328, CA and *DPP* v *Camplin*.) This is hardly a surprising development given that s. 3 expressly states that provocation can be by words alone. If the provocation is simply words of abuse, then any killing in response to those words is, of necessity, seriously dispropor-tionate to the provocation. Nonetheless, a seriously disproportionate retaliation will clearly make it more difficult for the jury to say that a reasonable man would have done as D did. Presumably, the sort of case where they could still do so would be where, by chance, D, in the heat of the moment, just happens to find a weapon to hand, e.g., a carving knife, when he happens to be in the kitchen.

It has been argued by some that it is nonsensical to talk of the reasonable man keeping some proportion in his response when, by definition, he has lost his self-control. The answer given is that there are degrees of loss of self-control, meaning that the reasonable man will generally retain some vestiges of control to enable him to link the severity of his retaliation to the severity of the provocation.

We must emphasise one point, namely, that the concept of reasonably proportionate retaliation in provocation is quite different from the concept of using reasonable force in self-defence (see 8.6.3). In provocation, the response of killing will always be more than is reasonable. After all D has lost his self-control and his reaction is by definition 'over the top'. By contrast, using reasonable force in self-defence means only doing what is necessary to defend yourself.

Logically it would seem that in judging whether a reasonable man would have done as D did, one should only consider the time from the provocative conduct to the act or acts which killed the victim. Anything done subsequently must surely be irrelevant. However, the Court of Appeal in *Clarke* [1990] Crim LR 383 appeared to accept that the jury should consider the whole course of the accused's conduct, including acts done to the victim after the act causing death and, if not too remote, even after the victim had died (e.g., disposal of the body). This seems plainly wrong so that the defence should succeed if the reasonable man would in the circumstances have killed as D did, even though the reasonable man would then have regained his self-control and not done the further acts which D did (e.g., mutilating the corpse).

Reform

It is generally recognised that this area of law is unsatisfactory and all of the judges in *Holley* were agreed that legislative reform was essential, not only in respect of provocation but the whole of the law of murder. In 2003, the Government asked the Law Commission to review the law but limited its terms of reference to provocation, diminished responsibility (the defence we consider next) and one other possible partial defence to murder (excessive self-defence) rather than the whole law of murder. The Commission's Report was accompanied by a plea to the Government to allow it to review murder as a whole (Law Com. No. 290: *Partial Defences to Murder* 2004, para. 1.12). In response, the Government has instituted such a review but, in order to retain control of the process, is conducting it under the auspices of the Home Office, not the Law Commission. The Commission's Report follows on from its Consultation Paper No. 173 (2003) which gives a top class review of provocation including its role in other common law jurisdictions and is well worth reading for a deep understanding. You will find extracts from the Report in the *Cases and Materials* section of the Online Resource Centre at 6.5.2.2.

The main recommendation was that the partial defence of provocation should be retained but in a modified form based on the following principles:

(1) (a) D acted in response to
     (i) gross provocation (meaning words or conduct or a combination thereof which caused D to have a justifiable sense of being seriously wronged); or
     (ii) fear of serious violence towards D or another; or
     (iii) a combination of (i) and (ii); **and**
   (b) a person of D's age and of ordinary temperament (i.e. ordinary tolerance and self-restraint) in the circumstances of D might have reacted in the same or a similar way.

(2) In deciding whether a person of ordinary temperament in D's circumstances might have acted in the same or a similar way, the court should take into account D's age and all D's circumstances other than matters whose only relevance to D's conduct is that they bear simply on D's general capacity for self-control.

Pausing there, we can see that the main change is the absence of any requirement that D should have actually lost self-control. That is replaced by a requirement that D's conduct was a 'response to' (i.e., caused by) either 'gross provocation' **or** 'fear of serious violence'. The latter would be a new departure and is aimed at solving the particular problem of domestic killings by battered women or men. Thus, the 'sudden, impulsive reaction' rule instanced in cases like *Thornton* and *Ahluwalia* would no longer be a feature of the defence. D might be in full control of their actions and not even angry and still succeed in the defence.

In case this might be thought to liberalise the defence too greatly, it should be noted that 'gross provocation' necessitates that not only does D actually have a 'sense of being **seriously** wronged' but also that his view was '**justifiable**'. (This is before we even get to applying the person of 'ordinary temperament' yardstick in (b).) Thus it is necessary but not sufficient that D should feel seriously aggrieved. The jury must also conclude that D had legitimate or sufficient reason to feel the way he did. Clearly that would rule out absurd cases like *Doughty* (the crying of a baby). Nonetheless, the Commission would provide further specific safeguards as follows:

(3) The partial defence should not apply where
   (a) the provocation was incited by D for the purpose of providing an excuse to use violence, or
   (b) D acted in considered desire for revenge.
(4) A person should not be treated as having acted in considered desire for revenge if he or she acted in fear of serious violence merely because he or she was also angry towards the deceased for the conduct which engendered that fear.

The exclusion of 'considered revenge' in many ways implicitly restores the focus on impulsive, angry reactions in all cases apart from the 'fear of serious violence' cases. Where D is not acting impulsively, it will be easy for a jury to view it as motivated by a desire for revenge. But one has to question the logic of basing the 'trigger' for the defence on a justifiable sense of serious grievance ('gross provocation') as opposed to the current 'any conduct causing D to lose self-control', and then excluding the defence where D's response to a justifiable sense of serious grievance is (a) 'revenge' and (b) 'considered'. Since all reactions are likely to be motivated to large extent by a desire for revenge (to get back at the provoker for his sleight), the key question is what is meant by 'considered', a word that was preferred to the previously suggested 'premeditated'. It appears that the Commission eschewed the current 'loss of self-control' trigger largely to accommodate killings by a persistently abused partner who waited until their abuser fell asleep before acting. However, aside from such killings (essentially falling within 1(a)(ii) above), they appear to be attempting to ensure the proposed law is effectively restricted to impulse killings. Provision 4 is largely for the benefit of victims of abusive, domestic violence and recognises that killings provoked by fear of continuing violence are often accompanied by extreme anger towards the violent partner. A jury would presumably have the difficult task of deciding what was the predominant motive in cases of mixed emotions.

It is evident from 1(b) and 2 above that the Commission favours the retention of an external standard against which to judge the excusability of D's reaction. Of course, the Commission reported before the decision in *Holley* when the law was as set out in *Smith (Morgan)*. It will be seen from provision 2 above that the Commission thought that *Smith* went too far and needed to be reined in. Their recommendation is more or less in line with the current law as set out in *Holley*.

One final recommendation is to increase the role and power of the trial judge in controlling the use of the defence. He would 'not be required to leave the defence to the jury unless there is evidence on which a reasonable jury, properly directed, could conclude that it might apply.' You may recall that this was one of the powers taken away by s. 3 of the Homicide Act 1957 prior to which the judge had a general power of withdrawal rather than the very limited one (no evidence that D actually lost his self-control) under the current law. This enhanced power could prove very significant in developing rational and sensible principles defining the scope of the novel and often vague concepts proposed.

6.5.2.3 Diminished responsibility

Introduction

This defence was first created by the Homicide Act 1957 at a time when the death penalty still existed for murder. It was intended to provide a partial excuse for those mentally disordered offenders who fell outside the narrow, legal definition of insanity (see 7.4). In practice, it also became a **replacement** for insanity because murder cases which before 1957 would have been pleaded as not guilty by reason of insanity, were invariably dealt with as manslaughter by diminished responsibility after 1957. Thus, in 1991 there were 60 findings of diminished responsibility (80% of them being pleas accepted by the prosecution), whereas only two of insanity. Insanity has been unpopular since the alternative became available because the judge is **compelled** to order indefinite detention in a secure mental hospital such as Rampton or Broadmoor (see 7.4.1). Curiously the recent trend in diminished responsibility has been steeply down: 38 successful pleas in 1998/99, 23 in 1999/2000, 15 in 2000/01 and only 6 in 2001/02.

Section 2 of the Homicide Act 1957 reads:

> Where a person kills or is a party to a killing of another he shall not be convicted of murder if he was suffering from such abnormality of mind (whether arising from a condition of arrested or retarded development of mind or any inherent causes or induced by disease or injury) as substantially impaired his mental responsibility for his acts and omissions in doing or being a party to the killing.

? QUESTION 6.15

- Identify the three ingredients required for a successful defence.
- Why is it only a defence to murder?

Since the defence applies only to reduce murder to manslaughter, it can only come into play if D kills with the *mens rea* for murder. As with provocation, it is only a mitigating factor. With offences other than murder, the mitigation can be reflected at the sentencing stage and no substantive defence is needed. The fixed penalty for murder prevents that, with the result that a partial defence must be created to allow the judge the flexibility in punishment to reflect the mitigating circumstance. A submission that diminished responsibility operates to reduce attempted murder to attempted manslaughter was rejected by the Court of Appeal in *Campbell* [1997] Crim LR 495 and was incompatible with the wording of s. 2. Furthermore, it is not possible for a defendant who has, by reason of his mental disorder at the time of the trial, been found unfit to plead at his trial for murder, to claim diminished responsibility (*Antoine* [2000] 2 All ER 208, HL).

Elements of the defence

If the defence is to succeed, three 'conditions' must be satisfied. D must (a) have been suffering from an abnormality of mind; (b) due to one of the three causes specified in the brackets in s. 2 of the Homicide Act 1957; and (c) which substantially impaired his mental responsibility for his conduct.

(a) Abnormality of mind

The best 'definition' the courts have come up with is that of Lord Parker CJ in *Byrne* [1960] 3 All ER 1 (*Cases and Materials* (6.5.2.3)):

> Abnormality of the mind . . . means a state of mind so different from that of ordinary human beings that the reasonable man would term it abnormal. It appears to us to be wide enough to cover the mind's activities in all its aspects, not only the perception of physical acts and matters and the ability to form a rational judgment as to whether an act is right or wrong, but also the ability to exercise will-power to control physical acts in accordance with that rational judgment.

Byrne was a sexual psychopath whose violent, perverted, sexual desires caused him to strangle a young woman in a YWCA hostel and commit horrifying mutilations of her corpse. The Court of Criminal Appeal, substituting manslaughter for his initial murder conviction, held that inability to control or, even difficulty in controlling, impulses could constitute 'abnormality of mind'. As we shall see later, 'irresistible impulse' cases fall outside the legal definition of insanity (see 7.4.2).

The concept of 'abnormality of mind' is vague and elastic and courts and juries have taken full advantage of the ability to stretch it to cover situations where D engages the sympathy of the court. Often it seems that no more than abnormal stress suffices to find that D was in a 'dissociated' state constituting the abnormality of mind. Thus, some mercy-killing cases have been brought within the net. In *Price* (1971) *The Times*, 22 December, D placed his severely handicapped son in a river and watched him float downstream to death by drowning. He was allowed the defence of diminished responsibility. In *Reynolds* [1988] Crim LR 679, CA and *Smith* [1982] Crim LR 531, pre-menstrual syndrome was the 'abnormality of mind' which allowed a successful defence. Depression can constitute 'abnormality of mind' (*Seers* (1984) 79 Cr App R 261, CA) even if it is endogenous, i.e., arising from within having no identifiable external cause (*Ahluwalia* [1992] 4 All ER 889, CA). In *Reynolds* [2004] EWCA Crim 1834, the Court accepted that Asperger's syndrome constituted an abnormality of mind.

Of course, anything serious enough to constitute a 'disease of mind' for the purposes of insanity will also amount to an 'abnormality of mind' (including, for example, paranoid psychosis—*Sanderson* (1994) 98 Cr App R 325, CA). This has led the courts in some cases to describe 'abnormality of mind' as 'partial insanity' or 'on the borderline of insanity' (e.g., *Byrne*). However, because 'abnormality' can include many conditions which could not constitute insanity, this was frowned on by the Court of Appeal in *Seers*. Certainly such expressions are more likely to confuse than enlighten.

(b) Specified causes

The abnormality must result from one of the specified causes, i.e., arise 'from a condition of arrested or retarded development of mind or any inherent causes or be induced by disease or injury'.

Suitable medical evidence is needed to establish that the abnormality results from one of these specified causes (*Byrne*). The requirement is intended to limit the scope of diminished responsibility, but it is difficult to state what falls within the 'specified causes'. For example, arrested or retarded development would appear to cover not just congenital defects, but also where development has been arrested by illness or brain injury. 'Inherent causes' is the 'elastic' concept which can be stretched to cover what the expert psychiatrist or the court wants it to, e.g., the depression in *Ahluwalia,* the paranoid psychosis in *Sanderson* and the 'dissociation' in cases like *Price.* The point is that the courts cannot say the condition is due to the external circumstances (violent abuse in *Ahluwalia* or the pressure of having a handicapped child in *Price*), otherwise it would not be due to one of the listed causes! Alternatively if D is suffering from a mental disease brought on by external events, such as battered woman syndrome (now classified by psychiatrists as a disease) from years of abuse as in *Hobson* [1997] Crim LR 759, CA, or the depression in *Ahluwalia*, the abnormality of mind which is the symptom of such disease will be regarded as being 'induced by disease'. The difficulty we have is in distinguishing the symptom (the abnormality of mind) from the cause (the disease) in such cases.

It seems less difficult to show what does not come within 'specified causes'. Hate, jealousy or bad temper causing an abnormality would not, according to *Fenton* (1975) 61 Cr App R 261, CA (though even this is contradicted by some first instance decisions—*Miller* (1972) *The Times*, 16 May and *Asher* (1981) *The Times*, 9 June, *cf. Vinagre* (1979) 69 Cr App R 104, CA (jealousy); and *Coles* (1980) 144 JPN 528 (rage)). Neither would the jury normally be allowed to consider the temporary effects of alcohol or drugs (*O'Connell* [1997] Crim LR 683, CA—Halcion sleeping tablets) because they are not 'induced by disease or injury' or within any of the other specified causes.

Where alcohol is one of the causes of the abnormality, the jury must ignore the effects of that and consider whether the other cause brought about an abnormality which substantially impaired the mental responsibility (*Gittens* [1984] 3 All ER 252—*Cases and Materials* (6.5.2.3)). *Gittens* was approved by the House of Lords in *Dietschmann* [2003] UKHL 10 (*Cases and Materials* (6.5.2.3)). At the time he killed the victim, the accused was heavily intoxicated and suffering from a mental abnormality 'described as an adjustment disorder, which was a depressed grief reaction to the death of his Aunt, Sarah, with whom he had a close emotional and physical relationship' (Lord Hutton). Disapproving a holding to the contrary in *Atkinson* [1985] Crim LR 314, CA and *Egan* [1992] 4 All ER 470, CA (which in turn had relied on formulations by Professor Sir John Smith in his commentary on *Gittens* in [1984] Crim LR 554), the House held that, to succeed in a plea of diminished responsibility, it was not necessary for the defendant to prove that he would have killed just the same even if he had not been intoxicated. Even if he would not have killed, had he been sober, it is still possible that his abnormality of mind was a substantial cause of the killing and substantially impaired his mental responsibility for it. Section 2 does not require the abnormality to be the **sole** cause of the fatal acts. Therefore, the jury has the rather difficult and speculative task of weighing the extent to which the accused's conduct was due to the drink or drugs. Any contribution of the intoxicant (or any other cause not specified in s. 2, for that matter) to his abnormality of mind and impairment of responsibility has to be ignored. The question then is: did the abnormality which remains (i.e., due to one or more of the 'specified causes') substantially impair his mental responsibility for the fatal acts, notwithstanding the drink (or other inadmissible factor)?

It appears from *Dietschmann* that the above rules do not apply where D suffers from alcohol dependence syndrome (chronic alcoholism) because that is recognised as a disease. If it causes permanent injury to the brain, that would certainly be an abnormality of mind due to disease (*Tandy* (1988) 87 Cr App R 45—*Cases and Materials* (6.5.2.3)). Alternatively, if the alcoholic's craving for a first drink is irresistible, he may have a defence, because he would not be 'responsible' for his intoxication which would therefore be 'involuntary' (*Tandy*; *Inseal* [1992] Crim LR 35, CA). The latter issue was not considered in *Dietschmann*.

(c) Substantial impairment of responsibility

The abnormality must have substantially impaired the defendant's mental responsibility for his acts. This phrase is just as vague and elastic as 'abnormality of the mind' allowing the jury a large measure of discretion.

? QUESTION 6.16

Do you think 'mental responsibility' refers to D's *legal* responsibility or his *moral* responsibility? Can psychiatrists usefully testify to *such* things?

It appears that the test fuses the two issues of moral and legal responsibility. It seems to require that (a) the abnormality 'had a substantial effect upon one or more relevant functions or capacities (of perception, understanding, judgment, feeling, control)' and (b) in the light of all the circumstances, this substantially reduces D's moral culpability or responsibility with the result that his legal liability is reduced (see Professor Griew [1988] Crim LR 75). Thus, legal responsibility, unusually in the criminal law, directly follows moral responsibility. Although the courts accept 'expert' testimony from psychiatrists on this question, it is in truth for the most part not a 'clinical' question requiring an 'application of psychiatric concepts', but a straight moral decision for the jury: in all the circumstances, does D deserve to be convicted of murder or only of manslaughter?

The question as to whether there has been a **substantial** impairment is a question of fact. Clearly, a total inability to control one's acts would be a substantial impairment, but whether mere difficulty in controlling them would be a substantial impairment is a matter of degree for the jury to decide (*Byrne*). In *Lloyd* [1967] 1 All ER 107 the court said that for it to be substantial, 'the impairment need not be total but it must be more than trivial or minimal'. In *Simcox* [1964] Crim LR 402, the court said that the difficulty which the defendant had in controlling his conduct must have been substantially greater than would have been experienced by an ordinary person without the mental abnormality of the defendant. In *Egan* [1992] 4 All ER 470, the Court of Appeal said that the jury should be told to approach 'substantial' in 'a broad commonsense way' or in terms of the above formulation in *Lloyd*. However, in *Mitchell* [1995] Crim LR 506, the Court of Appeal denied that it was necessary for the judge to explain the meaning of 'substantial'. It also held that it was not essential to consider the element of 'abnormality' **before** the element of 'substantial impairment'.

? QUESTION 6.17

Sutcliffe, the 'Yorkshire Ripper', deliberately killed many women, claiming he was driven by God to rid the world of prostitutes (although several of his victims were not prostitutes). Medical experts all agreed that he was a paranoid schizophrenic and the prosecution wanted to accept a plea of diminished responsibility. The trial judge, in the glare of intense publicity, refused to accept an agreed plea and 'forced' the prosecution to argue for a murder conviction. The jury, no doubt horrified by the serial killings, convicted of murder. What does this tell you about 'diminished responsibility'?

Subsequent events since Sutcliffe's incarceration have clearly demonstrated his mental disorder, fully vindicating the 'expert' evidence. Such cases illustrate that the defence 'operates less on clear psychiatric grounds than on the gut reaction of those who have the final say—the judge and jury' (Clarkson & Keating, *Criminal Law*, 4th ed., 1998, Sweet & Maxwell, p. 403). Who is more mentally disordered—someone like Sutcliffe or someone like Price who sees, perhaps quite rationally, killing as the kindest way for his mentally handicapped son?

Burden of proof

It is possible for the accused to plead guilty to manslaughter on the ground of diminished responsibility and if his plea is accepted by the prosecution and judge, the jury does not need to sit. Where the issue is contested, s. 2(2) of the Homicide Act 1957 places the burden of proof on the accused to establish the defence on the balance of probabilities (*Dunbar* [1957] 2 All ER 737, CCA). As we shall see in **Chapters 7** to **9**, this is unusual for defences, because D normally bears only the evidential burden of adducing some evidence fit for a jury, the burden then switching to the prosecution to disprove the defence beyond reasonable doubt. The Court of Appeal in the consolidated appeals of *Lambert*; *Ali*; Jordan [2001] 1 All ER 1014 held that placing the burden of proving diminished responsibility on D did not contravene the presumption of innocence in Art. 6(2) of the European Convention on Human Rights. It is not, in either form or substance, an ingredient of the offence of murder but simply allows D to establish a special defence or exception to liability.

Medical evidence is required in support of a plea of diminished responsibility (*Dix* (1981) 74 Cr App R 306), but the decision whether it succeeds is a matter for the jury not the doctors. Only the defence can raise the issue of diminished responsibility. However, where the judge recognises evidence of diminished responsibility, he may alert defence counsel who then has to decide whether to raise it (*Campbell* (1987) 84 Cr App R 255, CA).

Reform

The Law Commission has proposed the retention of diminished responsibility in its draft Criminal Code Bill 1989, cl. 56, in the following revised terms:

(1) A person who but for this section, would be guilty of murder is not guilty of murder if, at the time of his act, he is suffering from such mental abnormality as is a substantial enough reason to reduce his offence to manslaughter.

(2) In this section 'mental abnormality' means mental illness, arrested or incomplete development of mind, psychopathic disorder, and any other disorder or disability of mind, except intoxication.

(3) Where a person suffering from mental abnormality is also intoxicated, this section applies only where it would apply if he were not intoxicated.

There is substantial similarity between this formulation and the current s. 2, but also some differences. The most obvious one is the dropping of the requirement to establish that the abnormality arises from one of the listed causes. The cause of it would be irrelevant. In practical terms, the change would be more apparent than real because of the wide interpretation given to 'inherent causes' in the current s. 2.

'Abnormality of mind' is given a clear definition, but the inclusion of the open-ended, catch-all provision 'any other disorder or disability of mind' would enable the current liberal interpretations to continue.

The new formulation would reveal much more clearly than s. 2 that whether the abnormality is serious enough to warrant reduction of liability is a question entirely for the jury and the courts would find it more difficult than hitherto to hide behind the skirts of expert opinion when it suits them.

Finally, the defence would have only an evidential burden, the burden of proof being, as is normal with defences, on the prosecution to disprove it beyond reasonable doubt when D adduces tenable evidence of it.

The Law Commission's recent Report on Partial Defences to Murder rather ducked the issue of diminished responsibility, recommending that the defence should be retained so long as the mandatory life sentence for murder remained in place and that no changes should be made to it pending a review of the law of murder as a whole. They concluded that the current defence operates satisfactorily in practice. However, they did put forward the following reformulation as a possible 'signpost' for a future reconsideration within the context of a comprehensive review of murder:

A person, who would otherwise be guilty of murder, is not guilty of murder but of manslaughter if, at the time of the act or omission causing death,

(1) that person's capacity to:
   (a) understand events; or
   (b) judge whether his actions were right or wrong; or
   (c) control himself,
   was substantially impaired by an abnormality of mental functioning arising from an underlying condition and

(2) the abnormality was a significant cause of the defendant's conduct in carrying out or taking part in the killing.

'Underlying condition' means a pre-existing mental or physiological condition other than of a transitory kind.

6.5.2.4 Suicide pacts

At one time suicide was looked upon as self-murder, but it ceased to be a crime by s. 1 of the Suicide Act 1961. It remains a crime punishable by up to 14 years' imprisonment to aid, abet, counsel or procure the suicide or attempted suicide of another (s. 2 of the 1961 Act).

What has this got to do with voluntary manslaughter? Section 4 of the Homicide Act 1957 gives a partial excuse to a survivor of a suicide pact who has deliberately killed another or been a party to another's killing in pursuance of the pact.

 EXERCISE 6.5

Read s. 4 in *Cases and Materials* (6.5.2.4). What is the *key* requirement for the defence to apply?

As with diminished responsibility, the burden of proof on the balance of probabilities is placed on the defendant where he raises this defence. It is not essential for D to have tried to kill himself and failed; he may have just changed his mind after killing V, being unable to face his own death. No doubt a jury would be more willing, in the former case, to believe what is absolutely essential—that, at the time of killing V, D had 'the settled intention of dying in pursuance of the pact'.

The draft Criminal Code Bill recognises the anomaly that D would be liable for up to life imprisonment if D kills V in pursuance of a pact, whereas if V kills by his own hand in pursuance of it, D would only be liable for up to 14 years' imprisonment for aiding and abetting suicide. It may be a matter of pure chance who does what, e.g., who turns on the car ignition with a hosepipe leading from the exhaust into the car. Clauses 62 and 63 would introduce a maximum of seven years' imprisonment for each offence, the former clause creating a specific offence separate from manslaughter.

6.5.3 Involuntary manslaughter

6.5.3.1 Introduction

Involuntary manslaughter is confined to unlawful homicides which are committed without malice aforethought.

We have seen that the distinction between murder and involuntary manslaughter is not always easily made because of problems on the meaning of intention. Similarly, the distinction between involuntary manslaughter and accidental death is a difficult line to draw both because it is often a question of degree and because of fluctuating judicial and, indeed, jury opinions. The result is an offence of huge breadth ranging from conduct bordering on murder to conduct bordering on mere carelessness. Following judicial calls to modernise the law (*Scarlett* [1993] 4 All ER 629, CA; *Prentice* [1993] 4 All ER 935, CA), the Law Commission produced a blueprint for reform (Law Com. No. 237—*Cases and Materials* (6.5.2.4)), following an earlier Consultation Paper (Law Com. No. 135). In 2000, the Home Office issued *Reforming the Law of Involuntary Manslaughter: the Government's Proposals*, a paper inviting comments on the proposals set out in it. However, nothing further has materialised on manslaughter generally although a draft Corporate Manslaughter Bill, issued by the Government in 2005 for consultation, would create special provision for the liability of companies and the like for manslaughter (see 15.3.1.3 below).

In *Andrews* v *DPP* [1937] AC 576 the dilemma was described by Lord Atkin (at p. 581):

> ...of all crimes manslaughter appears to afford most difficulties of definition, for it concerns homicide in so many and so varying conditions...the law...recognises murder on the one hand based mainly, though not exclusively, on an intention to kill, and manslaughter on the other hand, based mainly, though not exclusively, on the absence of intent to kill, but with the presence of an element of unlawfulness which is the elusive factor.

There are probably three circumstances where the element of unlawfulness is present:

(a) killing **by gross negligence**;

(b) killing with **subjective recklessness**;

(c) the **unlawful act doctrine** (constructive manslaughter).

6.5.3.2 **Killing by gross negligence**

The background

The law on this subject has always been in a state of uncertainty and this uncertainty was compounded by the House of Lords' decision in *Seymour* [1983] 2 All ER 1058. With the House of Lords' decision in *Adomako* [1994] 3 All ER 79, *Seymour* seems to have been consigned to history and the law returned to the principles, such as they are, established in *Bateman* and *Andrews* (see below and *Cases and Materials* 6.5.3.2).

Initially the law here seemed to require gross negligence on the part of D as to death or (possibly) grievous bodily harm for a conviction, i.e., D had failed to guard against a very obvious risk of death or GBH. This seemed to be the view taken in *Bateman* (1925) 19 Cr App R 8, where V died as a result of a medical operation negligently performed by the surgeon. Lord Hewart's famous statement required that 'the negligence of the accused went beyond a mere matter of compensation between subjects, and showed such a disregard for the life and safety of others as to amount to a crime against the state, and conduct deserving punishment.'

This was subsequently endorsed by the House of Lords in *Andrews* v *DPP* [1937] 2 All ER 552. Therefore, very serious negligence (confusingly often referred to by older judges as recklessness—see, e.g., Lord Atkin in *Andrews*) as to death or GBH constituted the fault element in manslaughter.

Later cases developed an alternative form based on **subjective recklessness**. D would be liable if he actually foresaw the possibility of death or any bodily harm (not necessarily GBH). The widest formulation of this head came from the Court of Appeal in *Stone and Dobinson* [1977] 2 All ER 341 (*Cases and Materials* (6.5.3.2)). D was liable if he realised there was a risk of 'injury to the health and welfare' of the victim.

Seymour, a case of motor manslaughter, seemed to overturn the existing law superseding both the previous heads and replacing them with recklessness as defined in *Caldwell* and *Lawrence* [1981] 1 All ER 974, HL. Thus, if D caused V's death, he was guilty of manslaughter if there was in fact an obvious and serious risk of **harm** which D either recognised or gave no thought to. Although similar in some respects to gross negligence, objective recklessness as applied in *Seymour* probably widened the scope of manslaughter to an unacceptable degree (discussed later in this section).

The present law

 EXERCISE 6.6

- Read the extract from *Adomako* in *Cases and Materials* (6.5.3.2).
- Identify the requirements laid down for gross negligence manslaughter.
- What is the relevance now of *Caldwell/Lawrence* recklessness to manslaughter?

Until the House of Lords decided *Adomako* [1994] 3 All ER 79, it would have been essential to have spent three or four pages analysing *Seymour* in detail. This is no longer necessary because *Adomako,* approving *Bateman* and *Andrews,* has impliedly overruled *Seymour* and reverted more or less to the law as it stood before *Seymour*. Thus, *Caldwell/Lawrence* objective recklessness has no application to manslaughter, gross negligence having resumed its former position as the test.

The basic requirements laid down by *Adomako* for this form of manslaughter are as follows:

(a) D owed V a duty of care in the circumstances;

(b) D breached that duty of care;

(c) the breach caused the death of the victim; and

(d) the breach was sufficiently serious to constitute gross negligence.

This follows substantially the general principles based on *Bateman*, laid down by the Court of Appeal in the case of *Prentice and others* [1993] 4 All ER 935. (Adomako was one of the defendants in *Prentice* which involved consolidated appeals in three different cases. Adomako was the only defendant whose conviction was confirmed and so only he appealed to the House of Lords.)

Let us put the matter in context by giving you some fact situations where manslaughter has been charged. Consider in each case whether you think the defendants ought to be guilty of manslaughter. In *Adomako,* a patient undergoing an operation died from cardiac arrest after an endotracheal tube inserted through the patient's mouth to enable him to breathe by mechanical means whilst under anaesthetic, became disconnected. The connection point was hidden beneath a cover over the patient. D, the anaesthetist, first realised something was wrong four-and-a-half minutes after the disconnection when an alarm on a blood pressure machine sounded. He misdiagnosed the problem as an ocular cardiac reflex. However, he failed to advert to the possibility of disconnection, a possibility which one expert witness stated would have been obvious to any competent anaesthetist within 15 seconds. D had failed to notice that the patient's chest had stopped moving, the dials on the ventilator were not operating, its alarm was switched off and the patient was turning blue, **before** or even after the alarm sounded.

In *Prentice and Sullman* [1993] 4 All ER 935, P, under the supervision of S, injected the wrong drug into the patient's spine by lumbar puncture. This caused the patient's death. Both P and S were inexperienced junior doctors; P had never performed a lumbar puncture before and S had only attempted it once—unsuccessfully! P thought that S was supervising the whole procedure including checking the drug and dosage, whereas S thought he was merely supervising the actual injection. S took the syringe containing the drug from a trolley which carried a box of the correct, safe drug and also a box of the unsafe drug injected. The trolley had been prepared by a nurse who was absent. S gave the syringe to P, who injected it into the patient's spine. Neither P nor S checked the labels on the box of syringes nor on the syringe itself before injecting, both of which would have revealed that it was the drug, vincristine, lethal if spinally injected.

Lethal incompetence is not a quality confined to the medical profession. In *Holloway*, the last of the consolidated appeals in *Prentice*, D, a qualified electrician, installed the electrics on a new central heating system. By mistake he connected one of the programmer terminals to earth causing metal parts such as the radiators to become live in a certain mode of operation. The householder and her family suffered shocks and called back D, who agreed to come at once, observing in exemplary fashion 'You do not take chances with electricity'. Regrettably his commendable attitude was not reflected in the standard of his competence for, having checked the system, he failed to find anything wrong. The shocks continued and he returned. He agreed to replace the programmer but, before he could do this, P was killed by electrocution upon touching the kitchen sink whilst standing in his socks on a damp concrete floor.

Duty of care

? QUESTION 6.18

How does the court decide whether a duty of care is owed by D to V? You should have gleaned this from your reading of *Adomako*.

The House of Lords held that 'the ordinary principles of the law of negligence apply to ascertain whether or not the defendant has been in breach of a duty of care towards the victim who has died'. Thus, the law of torts determines if a duty is owed to the victim. A test based on tortious duty in relation to positive acts, in practice, adds nothing to the basic requirement of gross negligence because, in tort (but not in criminal law), the duty to take care to avoid injury by a positive act to anyone in the vicinity is so wide-ranging. It is acceptable that, in the case of positive acts, liability for the death should generally follow the establishment of gross negligence as to death. In all the cases we have described, the doctors clearly owed a duty of care in tort to their patients and the electrician to users of the house and central heating system. Similarly, in *Singh* [1999] Crim LR 582, CA, a landlord and his son who helped him look after his properties owed a duty of care to tenants in respect of a defective gas fire.

In *Wacker* [2003] Crim LR 108 the Court of Appeal rejected a recent attempt to defend a charge of gross negligence manslaughter by reliance on the maxim *ex turpi causa non oritur actio* to deny that D owed a tortious duty to the deceased victims. He was a Dutch lorry driver who had transported across the Channel on his lorry 60 illegal Chinese immigrants hidden in an airtight container whose ventilator D had closed. On arrival at Dover, it was discovered that 58 of them had died from suffocation. The defence argued that, since the victims were engaged on a joint unlawful enterprise with D, D would have no duty of care towards them in tort because no right of action arises from their own illegality. Further, according to *Adomako*, in gross negligence manslaughter too, 'the ordinary principles of the law of negligence' settle whether D owes the required duty of care and therefore if the *ex turpi causa* doctrine prevents a duty in civil law, it equally rules out gross negligence manslaughter. Fortunately, the Court refused to countenance the importation into the criminal law of such a technicality, recognising the very different policy objectives of the criminal law as compared with the civil law. Its view was that *Adomako* was concerned with 'an "ordinary" case of negligence' and did not intend to regard *ex turpi causa* as 'part of those ordinary principles' of negligence.

Wacker was applied in *Willoughby* [2004] EWCA Crim 3365, CA where D, the owner of a disused public house, recruited V to help him burn it down so that he could claim on his insurance policy. D and V went to the building and V spread petrol provided by D and set it alight. This led to an explosion which caused the building to collapse resulting in V's death. The Court of Appeal held that the fact that D and V were engaged in a joint illegal enterprise did not preclude a duty of care owed by D to V, even though V could be said to have accepted an element of risk inherent in the enterprise. That was capable of arising from the fact that, as well as being the owner of the premises, D had enlisted V and instructed him to spread petrol, all for D's financial benefit.

All of this calls into question whether the duty concept in civil law serves any useful purpose in manslaughter. If D's positive acts create an obvious (to a reasonable person) risk of death, that should be enough, tortious duty or no duty.

A test based on tortious duty creates further difficulties when applied to omissions. There are established rules which govern when there is a duty to act for the purposes of criminal law which may well differ from the corresponding rules governing the tort of negligence (*cf.* Law Com. No. 237, 2.22–2.25 and 3.11–3.16). You will recall that the concept of 'duty' is used to determine whether D is liable for an **omission** to act (see 2.7.4), including cases of homicide by omission. For example, in *Khan and Khan* [1998] Crim LR 830, CA, the accused drug dealers supplied V with heroin to snort in their flat. It may have been her first ever dose and she lapsed into a coma. The Ds just left her and came back to find her dead. They dumped her body on some waste ground. Their conviction for manslaughter was quashed on the ground that the trial judge failed to rule whether the situation was **capable** of giving rise to a duty to summon medical assistance. The Court thought this would have entailed extending the existing categories, a possibility it was prepared to envisage without deciding it. However, in tort, there would arguably be no duty. But, in criminal law, would it be an extension of the law relating to omissions? It seems to fall within the existing *Miller* principle because the Ds were responsible for creating the dangerous situation (supplying the heroin and allowing the use of their flat) and so were under a duty to take reasonable steps to rectify the situation by summoning medical assistance. One could also view *Wacker* in the same light. D created the dangerous situation by shutting the ventilator and was under a duty to rectify it.

Although *Khan and Khan* ruled that it was for the judge to decide whether the situation was capable of giving rise to a duty of care and, if so, for the jury to decide whether there was a duty, the later decision in *Singh* held that whether a duty existed was a question of law for the judge alone to decide. However, it is clear from *Willoughby* that *Khan* and not *Singh* represents the current law on this point ([22]–[24]).

Breach of duty

This simply requires that D's behaviour fell below the standard of conduct to be expected of a reasonable person in the same circumstances. Essentially akin to the standard of care required by the tort of negligence, it is actually encompassed within the deeper requirement of gross negligence discussed below. If D owed a duty and was judged to have been grossly negligent in regard to it, he must of necessity have breached it.

Breach causes death

The causation requirement is straightforward and dealt with in accordance with principles explained at 2.8. Again in our cases, the evidence clearly proved causation.

Grossly negligent breach

The crunch issue is whether D's conduct is bad enough to be designated grossly negligent. This is an objective test since D's conduct is to be judged against an **external** standard. It is not dependent on proving any particular state of mind on the part of D, though D's state of mind (e.g., subjective recklessness or indifference) might well be relevant to the jury's assessment of the grossness and criminality of his conduct (*Attorney-General's Reference (No. 2 of 1999)* [2000] 3 All ER 182, CA; *Misra* [2004] EWCA Crim 2375, CA). An attempt to argue that the statements of general principle in *G and Another* ([2004] 1 AC 1034, HL) meant that negligence, even gross, could no longer constitute a sufficient degree of culpability for a serious offence like manslaughter was roundly rejected by the Court of Appeal in *Misra*. Thus, there is still no need to prove any awareness or particular state of mind on the part of D and *G and Another* has no application to gross negligence manslaughter (see also *Mark*, 5 October 2004 (unreported)).

The standard of care thought proper in the situation is decided by the jury and D must fall **seriously** short of this standard to be grossly negligent. Turning eagerly to *Adomako* for their Lordships' view of the meaning of 'gross negligence', we find remarkably little of substance. Responsibility for defining it is effectively abdicated to the jury in each case. Whether D is grossly negligent:

> will depend on the seriousness of the breach . . . in all the circumstances in which the defendant was placed when it occurred . . . The jury will have to consider whether the extent to which the defendant's conduct departed from the proper standard of care incumbent upon him . . . was such that it should be judged criminal . . . This is necessarily a question of degree and an attempt to specify that degree more closely is . . . likely to achieve only a spurious precision. The essence of the matter, which is supremely a jury question, is whether, having regard to the risk of death involved, the conduct of the defendant was so bad in all the circumstances as to amount in their judgment to a criminal act or omission.

The Lord Chancellor, with whom the other Lords concurred, declined to elaborate any further, regarding it as 'unwise to attempt to categorise or detail specimen directions'.

By any standards, this is a disappointing conclusion from the highest court in the land. At least the Court of Appeal gave some examples of gross negligence (even if they were conceptually awry). Its essence is that D's negligence is criminal (i.e., manslaughter) if it is, in the jury's eyes, criminal! The circularity of the argument has been pointed out by writers ever since the principle was first expressed in 1925 in *Bateman* and, indeed, was expressly recognised by the House in *Adomako*!

The House did endorse the *Bateman* view that where 'a person holds himself out as possessing special skill and knowledge'—in this case that of a qualified doctor—the standard against which he is to be judged is that 'of a reasonably competent doctor' (or electrician in the case of *Holloway*). *Adomako* can be taken as approving *Bateman*'s view that the doctor 'owes a duty to the patient to use due caution in undertaking the treatment. If he... undertakes the treatment, he owes a duty to the patient to use diligence, care, knowledge, skill and caution in administering the treatment.' However, it is essential to remember that gross negligence involves not just **any** breach of this standard of competence but **a very serious** falling below that standard.

Thus, the House does little to clarify what constitutes 'gross negligence'. Nor does it expressly clarify the **consequence** in relation to which D must exhibit gross negligence. Does he have to be grossly negligent as to death or something less—grievous bodily harm or even just some harm? The implication of the judgment is that there needs to be a high risk of death, suggesting the first mentioned alternative, but a clear statement would have been welcome. However, the Court of Appeal in *Misra* (approving *Singh*) had no doubt that the correct interpretation of *Adomako* was that nothing short of a risk of death would suffice. 'In short, the offence requires gross negligence in circumstances where what is at risk is the life of an individual to whom the defendant owes a duty of care' (para. 52). The Law Commission's draft Bill (Law Com. No. 237, Appendix A) endorsed in the government's proposals would require an obvious risk of death **or serious injury**.

If we take our cases, both Holloway and also Prentice and Sullman had their convictions quashed by the Court of Appeal on the ground that their trial judges had (not surprisingly at the time) directed in accordance with *Seymour* and *Caldwell/Lawrence* recklessness. Adomako's conviction was confirmed because his trial judge had 'properly' directed in accordance with *Bateman* and gross negligence. It was clear that Adomako fell way below what might be expected of a competent anaesthetist—according to one expert, the standard of care received by the patient was 'abysmal'.

By contrast, a properly directed jury might well have acquitted Prentice, who ought to have checked the drug he was injecting, but who, in the circumstances of apprehension at his first foray in the technique of spinal injection, left it to his supervisor. It was a bad mistake but, in the circumstances, not gross enough for manslaughter. Sullman is more problematic but he might, in the circumstances, get the benefit of the doubt, because of his misunderstanding about his role and the system failure of allowing the unsafe syringes to be on the same trolley as the safe ones.

Holloway, the electrician, did his incompetent best, but his conduct lacked the excusing features of Prentice. He might well have been convicted on the basis that he had ample opportunity to diagnose the fault and fell seriously below the standards of a competent electrician in failing to do so (*cf.* the electrician who wired up railway signals incorrectly causing the Clapham Junction rail crash). But we are bound to question whether a manslaughter conviction in such cases serves any useful purpose.

Ultimately, the test for gross negligence is an elastic standard which is not capable of exact definition because of the vast range of fact situations with which it has to deal. However, this does not justify the almost complete absence of guidance on the meaning of gross negligence in *Adomako*. As the Law Commission explained: 'A general formula can at least try to make clear the considerations which the jury should have in mind and the type of standard they have to set. This is not, in our view, achieved...by a simple resort to "gross" negligence...' (Law Com. No. 135, para. 5.46). Clause 2 of the Commission's draft Involuntary Homicide Bill (Law Com. No. 237, Appendix A) proposes a new but similar offence of 'killing by gross carelessness' which the government accepted in its Consultation Paper (*Reforming the Law on Involuntary Manslaughter*, May 2000). It would require that:

(a) the risk that D's 'conduct will cause death or serious injury would be obvious to a reasonable person in his position'; and

(b) D was 'capable of appreciating that risk at the material time'; and

(c) 'either...his conduct falls far below what can reasonably be expected of him in the circumstances; or...' (see 6.5.3.4 below).

You will see that (a) borrows from the first limb of *Caldwell* recklessness in requiring the risk of death or serious harm to be 'obvious' (by which the Commission means 'immediately apparent' or 'glaring') to any reasonable person **in D's position**. Thus, the reasonable person is given 'knowledge of any relevant facts' which D has and 'any skill or experience professed by him' (cl. 2(2)). A major defect in the *Caldwell* formulation is avoided by providing in (b) that D must have the **capacity** to appreciate the risk. The key provision in (c) defines the standard for what the current law terms gross negligence. D must fall 'far below what can be reasonably expected of him in the circumstances'. Whilst an improvement on *Adomako*, this test still leaves a vague standard presenting juries with a large measure of discretion. The Commission could 'see no way around this problem, without attempting to define the offence in such rigid and detailed terms that it would be unworkable'. The standard which D must fall **far** below is what could have been expected of **him** in the circumstances. Whilst this expressly comprehends circumstances known to him and of which he could be expected to be aware (cl. 2(3)), it would also require consideration of any pressures and conditions particular to him, e.g., inadequate training, overwork, pressure from an employer to get the job done, the fact that D was only a learner driver.

Although we have criticised the decision in *Adomako* on some important detail, the overall thrust of the decision in jettisoning *Seymour* and *Caldwell/Lawrence* recklessness is to be warmly welcomed. The problem with *Seymour* was that (a) D need only have created an obvious risk of **some** injury (not death or even **serious** injury) and (b) if D gave no thought to it, he was guilty irrespective of possible mitigating circumstances explaining his lack of thought. These defects have been remedied by *Adomako*, which thus narrows the unacceptably wide scope of the law in *Seymour*.

Adomako also confirms that its formulation is of general application to all fact situations including motor manslaughter and corporate manslaughter. The latter raises difficult issues of attribution of liability discussed at 15.3.1.1 and 15.3.1.2 below and has led the

Government to propose in its draft Corporate Manslaughter Bill 2005 the creation of a special corporate manslaughter offence (15.3.1.3 below).

The vagueness of the concept of gross negligence led to a challenge in the case of *Misra* that it contravened the certainty principle enshrined in Art. 7(1) of the European Convention on Human Rights. That requires that citizens should be able to know in advance with reasonable certainty what conduct falls within the offence. The Court of Appeal took the view that 'the ingredients of the offence have been clearly defined, and the principles decided in the House of Lords in *Adomako*.' Thus, there is no 'unacceptable uncertainty about the offence itself' even if there is 'an element of uncertainty about the outcome of the decision-making process' because it is difficult to predict how a particular jury might choose to apply the *Adomako* principles to any given fact situation (paras. 62–66). *Adomako* sets out the legal standard, albeit necessarily in rather generalised form, with sufficient clarity to comply with Art. 7. The jury's decision on whether that standard has been breached in the particular case is treated as a finding of fact, not of law. Although the reasoning is unconvincing, it is difficult to see how we can usefully avoid utilising such generalised standards of fault, e.g., negligence, reasonableness, dishonesty, in assessing liability. The detail required for laws which avoid that is too fantastic to contemplate. However, that is not to say that some improvements could not be made, as we have argued above.

Finally, it is not necessary to show that D's grossly negligent acts would have constituted some other offence if death had not resulted. Manslaughter is the only offence against the person which does not require at least **subjective** recklessness. The end result is that, if D is grossly negligent, he will be liable for manslaughter if death results, but, assuming he foresaw no harm to another, he will probably not be guilty of any offence if only injury, even if serious, results. There is no corresponding offence of causing **injury** by gross negligence.

6.5.3.3 Reckless manslaughter

 QUESTION 6.19

Does *Adomako* mean that there is now no such thing as reckless manslaughter?

We have said that *Seymour* has gone from the law and *Caldwell/Lawrence* recklessness been superseded by gross negligence. However, although it is not discussed in *Adomako*, it is likely that a form of manslaughter based on **subjective** recklessness survives. You may recall that in our introduction to this chapter we noted that *Stone and Dobinson* held that **subjective** recklessness as to ordinary injury (i.e., not death or even serious injury) was sufficient for manslaughter. *Adomako* expressly approved *Stone* in its use and definition of 'reckless' (it included where D was 'indifferent', i.e., could not care less). Nonetheless, it did not advert specifically to recklessness merely as to **some injury** being sufficient, still less to an alternative given in *Stone* of realisation by D that there was a risk of 'injury to health or welfare'. The House did not state whether such a wide formulation as the latter is to be adopted. The answer is probably not.

? **QUESTION** 6.20

Since the decision in *Moloney*, the *mens rea* for murder does not include foresight by D that death or serious harm is likely. Mrs Hyam, who set fire to a house killing two child occupants, might not be guilty of murder (although a finding of intention is possible—see *Woollin*). In that case, she should obviously be guilty of manslaughter.

- On what basis?
- Do you think it would be accurate to regard it as the same as gross negligence manslaughter?

It is obvious that there should be manslaughter by subjective recklessness to catch these 'nearly murder' cases. Most commentators would, however, prefer to limit this to subjective awareness of the risk of **death** or, at most, the risk of **serious** harm. Foresight of non-serious harm should not be enough (D might in such a case also be grossly negligent as to death and so convicted under the other head). The Law Commission's draft Bill proposes a new offence of reckless killing which would carry a heavier maximum penalty (life imprisonment) than the offence of killing by gross carelessness previously examined. The twin fault requirements are that (a) D must be 'aware of a risk that his conduct will cause death or serious injury; and (b) it is unreasonable for him to take that risk having regard to the circumstances as he knows or believes them to be' (cl. 1). This is essentially subjective recklessness—D must consciously take an unjustifiable risk of causing death or serious injury. If he makes a mistake (whether reasonable or unreasonable) as to the circumstances, the question whether it was unreasonable to take the risk has to be judged on the circumstances as he imagined them, not as they actually were. The Government's Consultation Paper endorses the Commission's proposals.

6.5.3.4 Unlawful act manslaughter

According to *DPP* v *Newbury* [1976] 2 All ER 365, HL (*Cases and Materials* (6.5.3.4)), the prosecution must prove:

(a) D intentionally did an act.

(b) Which was **in fact** *unlawful*.

(c) Which was **in fact** *dangerous*.

(d) Which did **in fact and law** *cause* the victim's death.

Note that the situation in our last Question would satisfy the requirements of unlawful act manslaughter.

Intentionally doing an act

It is most important to realise that 'intentionally' refers to the doing of the act, **not** to the harmful consequences which flow from the act. As such, it really adds nothing to the notion of doing an act since the very notion of acting implies that the movements are intended. In *Newbury*, the defendants pushed a concrete block from the parapet of a bridge onto an oncoming train. The block crashed through the cab and killed the guard who was sitting next to the driver. To satisfy this element, all the prosecution had to prove was that the defendants intended to push the block off the bridge. They did not have to prove that they intended any of the possible harmful consequences—damaging property, injuring someone or, still less, killing someone. In practice therefore, this requirement is rarely a problem.

Curiously, intentional **omissions** are excluded from the definition according to *Lowe* [1973] 1 All ER 805, CA. *Lowe* held that a failure to act which is unlawful because D is under a duty to act cannot form the basis of a manslaughter conviction under the unlawful **act** head. It would only be manslaughter if D's failure to act was grossly negligent in accordance with the other head of involuntary manslaughter.

? **QUESTION** 6.21

Is there any rational basis for distinguishing in this way between intentional acts which cause death and intentional omissions which cause death?

The facts of *Lowe* were that D was found guilty of the crime of wilful neglect of a child in failing to summon medical assistance for his grossly emaciated and dehydrated child. Even though death resulted from this dangerous criminal omission, the court refused to hold that a manslaughter conviction automatically followed, i.e., the unlawful **act** doctrine literally applied only to acts.

There does not seem to be any moral distinction between these types of conduct—is it any worse to kill a child by striking it (a positive act) than by starving it (an omission)? Perhaps the answer is to abolish the unlawful act doctrine rather than to introduce an unlawful omission doctrine!

The act is in fact unlawful

It is irrelevant whether or not D **realised** that his intentional act was unlawful. Ignorance of the law is no excuse.

The meaning of unlawful in this context

Originally, even torts were regarded as unlawful acts for this purpose. However, in *Franklin* (1883) 15 Cox CC 163 it was held that only **criminal** acts could form the basis of unlawful act manslaughter.

This was further limited by *Andrews v DPP* [1937] 2 All ER 552, HL which narrowed the definition by excluding negligently committed crimes:

> There is an obvious difference in the law of manslaughter between doing an unlawful act and doing a lawful act with a degree of carelessness which the legislature makes criminal. If it were otherwise a man who killed another while driving without due care and attention would necessarily be guilty of manslaughter.

In other words where the basis of the criminality of D's conduct is that he was negligent, he can only be convicted of manslaughter if he falls within the other head of 'gross negligence' manslaughter. Driving is lawful but if performed negligently it becomes criminal.

The usual offences forming the basis of unlawful act manslaughter will be assault or battery, but this is by no means always the case. For example in *DPP* v *Newbury* it appeared to be criminal damage (throwing a paving stone onto a train) although the court failed to articulate what was the crime relied on as the 'unlawful act', presumably because counsel for the defence had **conceded** that his clients' acts were 'unlawful'. In *Cato* [1976] 1 All ER 260, CA it was administering a noxious thing contrary to s. 23 of the Offences Against the Person Act 1861 (the injection of heroin), in *Goodfellow* (1986) 83 Cr App R 23, CA arson (setting fire to a flat) and in *Andrews* [2003] Crim LR 477 the unlawful injection of the prescription drug, insulin, contrary to s. 67 of the Medicines Act 1968 (this last being a strict liability offence).

The Court of Appeal in *Dias* [2002] 2 Cr App R 96 thought that it could be based on the supply of a controlled drug (an offence under s. 4 of the Misuse of Drugs Act 1971) to another who took it with fatal consequences. (As we shall see shortly, there are severe problems as to whether D's act of supply can be said to cause the death where the victim has made a 'free, deliberate and informed' choice to take them.) However, the act of self-injection or other taking of a drug was not a crime under the Act and so could not be an unlawful act for this purpose (disapproving *Kennedy* on this point). Even while accepting this point, the Court of Appeal in *Rogers* [2003] 2 Cr App R 160 held that if D 'actively participates in the injection process' by, for example, holding a tourniquet on V's arm to raise a vein for V to inject into, D would himself be 'administering a noxious thing' contrary to s. 23 and therefore be guilty of manslaughter if the injection caused the victim's death. In reality, of course, D was helping V to administer rather than administering himself (see further 14.3 below). The saga was taken a step further in *Finlay* [2003] EWCA Crim 3868 where D supplied and prepared heroin, loaded it into a syringe and handed it to V who injected herself with fatal results. Since D had not participated in the actual injection, he did not 'administer a noxious thing'. However, he was held to have committed the s. 23 offence in its alternative form: 'cause to be administered or taken' (a very questionable holding in the light of causation principles, as we discuss later in this chapter—the various issues are explored in Heaton: *Dealing in Death* [2003] Crim LR 497 and Heaton: *Principals? No Principles!* [2004] Crim LR 463). Following a reference by the Criminal Cases Review Commission, *Kennedy* was revisited by the Court of Appeal ([2005] EWCA Crim 685). Their view was that D's making up of the syringe and handing it to V for 'immediate injection' enabled a jury to conclude that, as in *Rogers*, D and V were jointly administering a noxious thing because they were 'acting in concert'. It now seems that the rather vague notion of whether D and V were 'acting in concert' determines whether D commits the s. 23 offence and so manslaughter. It must be said that the reasoning is unconvincing and drives a coach and horses through established principles of both causation and the difference between perpetrators (principals) and accessories.

In order to be an unlawful act, both the *actus reus* and any necessary *mens rea* must be present otherwise the act would not be unlawful. This is well illustrated by *Lamb* [1967] 2 All ER 1282, CA (*Cases and Materials* (6.5.3.4)) where D having checked that there was no bullet in the chamber opposite the firing pin, fired a gun at V and killed him. Both V and D were treating the matter as a joke, having failed to realise that the mechanism revolved one chamber before the firing pin struck. At first sight, this may seem an obvious case of unlawful act manslaughter. However, although D performed the *actus reus* of battery when the bullet struck the victim, it was not the offence of battery because he did not intend to apply force to the victim nor did he realise, because of his stupid mistake, that he might apply force to the victim.

? QUESTION 6.22

- Why was there no psychic assault?
- Could D be convicted of manslaughter under the other head?

The necessity for both the *actus reus* and any necessary *mens rea* of the unlawful act was regarded as axiomatic until the House of Lords in *DPP* v *Newbury* threw doubt on it by appearing to say that all D needed was an intention to do the act, i.e., throw the paving stone, rather than, e.g., an intention to damage property belonging to another. However, although this would be a correct literal interpretation of its statements, it is unlikely that the House of Lords meant to say that D needed only the *actus reus* without the necessary *mens rea*. It would not be a crime without the necessary *mens rea*. *O'Driscoll* (1977) 65 Cr App R 50, CA supports this latter contention and, most recently, *Scarlett* [1993] 4 All ER 629, CA and *Attorney-General's Reference (No. 3 of 1994)*. The problem in *Newbury* was that the House were led astray by Lord Denning MR in *Gray* v *Barr* [1971] 2 All ER 949, CA and confused the issue of whether the act was unlawful (which D's counsel had conceded) with the issue of whether it was dangerous.

The act is in fact dangerous

Only acts which are dangerous in the sense of being likely to cause harm to another person count as unlawful acts for this purpose. This limitation surfaced in *Larkin* [1943] 1 All ER 217, CA and was further refined in *Church* [1965] 2 All ER 72, CA (*Cases and Materials* (6.5.3.4)): 'The unlawful act must be such as **all** sober and reasonable people would **inevitably** recognise must subject the other person to, at least, the risk of some harm resulting therefrom albeit not serious harm' (our emphasis). This formulation was approved in *Newbury* where the House of Lords stressed that it was an entirely objective test and that it did not matter whether **the accused** appreciated that his unlawful act was dangerous. Putting it another way, what seems to be required is that there was an obvious and serious risk of harm to another, which it would be grossly negligent not to recognise and guard against. The House of Lords in *Attorney-General's Reference (No. 3 of 1994)* [1997] 3

All ER 936 (*Cases and Materials* (6.5.3.4)) held that it was unnecessary to show there was an obvious or forseeable risk of injury to the person who died. It was enough to establish a serious risk of injury to **another** person whether the victim or someone completely different. That would make the unlawful act 'dangerous' and it would then simply require proof that it caused the victim's death. Thus D's stabbing of his pregnant girlfriend was clearly an unlawful battery carrying an obvious risk of injury to the woman. The stabbing brought about a grossly premature birth and the baby died 121 days later of a lung condition related to its immaturity at birth. Even though the baby was not a person at the time of the battery, and risk of injury to it **as a person** from D's battery would not be obvious,

D was guilty of manslaughter because injury to **someone** (the mother) was and the battery was a legal cause of the baby's death.

It was held by the Court of Appeal in *Dawson* (1985) 81 Cr App R 150 (*Cases and Materials* (6.5.3.4)) that 'harm' means physical harm. An obvious risk of mere emotional disturbance produced by terror was insufficient, although, of course, if there was an obvious risk of physical harm (e.g., a heart attack) resulting from that emotional disturbance, the act would be dangerous.

Dawson also made it clear that in deciding whether a reasonable man would regard these acts as dangerous, he should be given the same knowledge of the circumstances as D had. In *Dawson*, where the defendants robbed a petrol station cashier using a replica gun and a mask, causing the cashier to have a heart attack, the reasonable man was given no knowledge that the cashier already had a severe heart condition, because the defendants had no idea.

Nonetheless, if the reasonable man observing the accused's actions would have become aware of any special circumstances making these actions dangerous, then he will be given this knowledge notwithstanding that the defendant himself failed to appreciate such circumstances and draw the obvious conclusion. This is clear from *Watson* [1989] 2 All ER 865, CA, where it was held that the burglary of a house, whose occupant was a frail 87-year-old man, became a dangerous act as soon as the occupant's frail condition could be appreciated by a reasonable observer. If therefore the occupant dies of a heart attack caused by the defendants' persisting with the burglary after their continuing unlawful act had become dangerous, they would be guilty of manslaughter. Similarly, in *Ball* [1989] Crim LR 730, CA it was held that if D makes an **unreasonable** mistake about the situation, it will be ignored because no '**reasonable** observer' would make it. D loaded his gun from a mixture of live and blank ammunition in his pocket. He fired at the victim thinking (he claimed) that his gun contained only blanks. The court regarded this mistake that he was taking no risk as irrelevant. No reasonable observer would have concluded that there was no risk of live ammunition being fired unless the cartridges had been thoroughly checked before firing.

The act in fact causes death

Whether the unlawful act caused the death is determined in accordance with normal principles of causation as previously discussed at 2.8. For example, in *Dalby* [1982] 1 All ER 916, CA, D committed an unlawful act in supplying heroin to the deceased but death was caused, not by this unlawful act, but by the deceased's voluntary act in injecting it into himself. If D had injected it into the victim, he would have committed the crime of administering a poison or noxious thing contrary to s. 23 of the OAPA 1861 and this would have caused the death (*Cato* [1976] 1 All ER 260, CA). *Dalby* was distinguished in the rather suspect decision of *Kennedy* [1999] Crim LR 65, CA. D supplied heroin to the deceased and made up the syringe with which the deceased voluntarily injected himself. Surprisingly his conviction for manslaughter was upheld. It is difficult to see any unlawful act committed by D apart from supplying the drug and this could not be said to be a legal cause of death because the chain of causation would surely be broken by the voluntary action of the deceased in injecting. The fact that D made up the syringe and encouraged V to inject was seen by the court as distinguishing the case from *Dalby* but, in truth, the sole legal cause was still the administration of the drug by the deceased himself.

In a very similar fact situation, the Court of Appeal in *Dias* [2002] Cr App R 96 distinguished *Kennedy* on the ground that the question of whether D's act had caused death had there been properly left to the jury, whereas, in this case, it had not. D's conviction for manslaughter was quashed. The Court rejected the *Kennedy* notion that D's unlawful act could be based on his aiding and abetting the victim's self-injection because the latter was not unlawful under the drugs legislation. D did commit the unlawful act of supplying the controlled drug but the Court doubted whether this could be said to cause the death because of the intervention of the victim's own voluntary act. However, it is important to note that the Court did not rule out legal causation in this kind of case, holding that it was a 'question of fact and degree' to be left to the jury to decide. Nonetheless, the Court's view seemed to be that, in the ordinary way, chosen self-injection would break the chain of causation between D's acts and the death. For it not to, it would require 'somewhat different facts' from the present case. Unfortunately, no inkling is given as to what differences are needed but we may surmise that it would include situations where the victim's self-injection was not 'free and informed'. Thus, if he were forced to inject, deceived as to the contents of the syringe or under incapacity due to age or mental condition, his self-injection would **not** break the chain of causation. Absent any such circumstances, the application of normal causation principles would rule out liability in self-injection cases.

However, the latest cases show the courts' determination to find a way of convicting in such circumstances. The preferred solution, adopted in *Rogers* [2003] 2 Cr App R 160, CA and *Kennedy (No. 2)* [2005] EWCA Crim 685 (see *Cases and Materials* (6.5.3.4)), is to circumvent the causation problem by regarding a defendant who 'actively participates in the injection process' (e.g., as in *Rogers* where D held a tourniquet on V's arm whilst V injected himself or as in *Kennedy* where D supplied the heroin and prepared the syringe for immediate injection by V), as himself 'administering' the drug because, according to *Kennedy (No. 2)*, D was 'acting in concert' with V. That concept borrowed from the doctrine of joint unlawful enterprise in the law of complicity (see **Chapter 14**) is vague and uncertain in scope and, given that it is the jury which decides whether it applies in each individual case, creates a serious potential for different treatment of stereotypical situations. The plain fact is that in self-injection cases, it is V not D who administers the drug. It is not made an offence by s. 23 to administer a noxious thing to oneself, therefore V commits no offence and D's assistance cannot amount to aiding and abetting because there is no principal offence committed. D could only be liable under s. 23 if he satisfied the alternative *actus reus* of 'causing to be administered to or taken by' V. This was the line (we think correctly) apparently taken in *Finlay* [2003] EWCA Crim 3868 but regarded as unnecessary in *Kennedy (No. 2)*. D again supplied, prepared and handed a syringe of heroin to V for immediate injection. However, *Finlay* went wrong in holding that V's free and informed decision to inject was not a *novus actus interveniens* which broke the causal link between D's actions and the ingestion of the drug. On standard principles, D did not legally cause the drug to be taken (see 2.8.2.2 above).

To summarise: Anyone preparing the drug for immediate injection or assisting the injection is likely to be regarded as 'acting in concert' with V and thus 'administering' the drug contrary to s. 23. This unlawful act will form the basis for D's manslaughter conviction. It appears that the Court of Appeal is willing to ride roughshod over normal principles of accessorial liability and/or causation and a proper interpretation of s. 23 in order to secure the conviction of those who assist victims of inadvertently fatal drug overdoses in ingesting the dose. There is a desperate need for the House of Lords to clear up the mess and reassert traditional principles (see Heaton: [2004] Crim LR 463).

There appears to be no requirement in recent case law that the death should be due to the element of unlawfulness in D's act as opposed to the act itself. Thus, in *Watson*, the unlawful act was burglary which is committed by one who enters a building as a trespasser with intent to steal. If D entered as a trespasser intending only to find shelter for the night, there would be no burglary. Yet in *Watson* the frail old occupant would have been just as frightened. In other words, the element of unlawfulness was incidental to the causing of death. Nonetheless, it would still have been manslaughter if the intrusion as a whole caused V's death and it was burglarious. To paraphrase Howard's comment in relation to Australian law, the act does not have to be unlawful **because** it is dangerous; it is enough that it is dangerous and incidentally unlawful (*Criminal Law*, 5th ed., 1990, Law Book Co., p. 127).

? QUESTION 6.23

- Suppose D knocks down and kills a pedestrian by careless driving. Would this be unlawful act manslaughter?
- Suppose D is at the time, as he well knows, uninsured or disqualified from driving under the points system. Would this be unlawful act manslaughter?

In the first case, although the act is objectively 'dangerous', causes death and is criminal (driving without due care and attention), it would not be 'unlawful' for the purposes of the doctrine. It would fall within the 'negligence' exception in *Andrews* v *DPP*. Unless the carelessness was so extreme as to amount to gross negligence under the other head of involuntary manslaughter, it would not be manslaughter on that account. In the second situation, D intentionally commits the offence of driving whilst uninsured (or disqualified). The act is dangerous and, if the element of dangerousness does not have to be causally linked with the unlawfulness, D would satisfy the requirements and be convicted, even if his driving was exemplary!

This possibility helps to illustrate the potential for absurdity in the current rules and suggests that some limitation along these lines ought to be articulated. In the next section, we focus on an attempt to establish a differently formulated rule which would produce a similar practical effect.

Must the act be directed at another?

The Court of Appeal in *Dalby* [1982] 1 All ER 916 invented an extra requirement that the unlawful act must be 'directed at another'. Therefore, someone who unlawfully supplied heroin to the victim could not be guilty of unlawful act manslaughter when the victim used the drug and died. It appeared that *Dalby* was in this respect inconsistent with *DPP* v *Newbury* which never mentioned this alleged requirement in a situation where it was far from self-evident that the unlawful act—presumably criminal damage to the train—was directed at any *person*. It was not therefore a surprise when the Court of Appeal in *Good-fellow* (1986) 83 Cr App R 23 rejected the requirement and explained away *Dalby* as meaning no more than that the death should be a direct result of D's unlawful act with 'no fresh intervening cause' (per Lord Lane CJ). D, desperate to be rehoused, set fire to his council house. His wife, girlfriend and son were all killed. The court rejected his argument that, because his act of arson was not directed at any person, he could not be convicted of unlawful act manslaughter. It appears that the last rites on *Dalby* have been pronounced by the House of Lords in *Attorney-General's Reference (No. 3 of 1994)* which held that there is no such requirement.

In practical terms, the requirement would have been a welcome limitation on a doctrine which could lead to outlandish results. For example, without the 'directed at' requirement, someone who throws a banana skin down in a crowded shopping street would seem to satisfy the requirements of unlawful act manslaughter if someone, slipping on the banana skin, crashes their head on the pavement and dies!

Reform

It is not surprising that the Law Commission proposes the abolition of unlawful act manslaughter. It produces capricious and unpredictable results and is confused and uncertain in its scope. It allows conviction where no risk of death or serious injury would be obvious to a reasonable person and/or where D would not be capable of appreciating any such risk. It is, therefore, surprising to find that the Commission proposes to resurrect an admittedly attenuated form of unlawful act manslaughter as an alternative form of the offence of killing by gross carelessness. Where there is an obvious risk of death or serious injury which D is capable of appreciating, D could be convicted not only if his conduct falls far below reasonable expectations, but also if 'he intends by his conduct to cause some injury or is aware of, and unreasonably takes, the risk that it may do so' (cl. 2). This could apply 'only if the conduct causing, or intended to cause, the injury' is itself an offence. The rather suspect justification for this unnecessary complication is that 'the alternative adds little or nothing to the reach of the offence; it serves only to simplify it for the jury, by dispensing with the need to consider a question [the other alternative—did D's conduct fall far below what could be expected?] which will almost inevitably be academic.'

However, despite this criticism, the overall scheme proposed by the Commission in its draft Involuntary Homicide Bill would be a welcome improvement on and clarification of the existing law. The Commission's Report devotes almost half its content to a consideration of the liability of companies for manslaughter. It recommends that a company might commit the offences under cll. 1 and 2, already discussed, under the principles currently applied to general corporate liability (see **Chapter 15**). In addition, there would be a new, separate offence of corporate killing based on the concept of death being caused by 'a management failure' falling 'far below what can be reasonably expected of the corporation in the circumstances'. The proposal was prompted by widespread disquiet about the role of companies in a run of high profile disasters causing multiple loss of life (see **Chapter 15**). The government has announced that it intends to bring forward legislation on corporate killing in the near future.

The provisional proposals contained in the government's recently issued Consultation Paper, *Reforming the Law on Involuntary Manslaughter*, accept all these proposals except one, namely the abolition of unlawful act manslaughter. A more limited version would be enacted which would be committed where D commits a criminal offence causing death with the intention of causing injury or being subjectively reckless thereto. Unlike the Law Commission's cl. 2 provision noted above, there would be no necessity to prove that there was an obvious risk of death or serious injury resulting from D's unlawful act. At least the proposal would appear to require some offence against the person and rule out the more outlandish possibilities under the current law.

■ FURTHER READING

Ashworth: *The Doctrine of Provocation* (1976) 35 CLJ 292.

Ashworth & Mitchell (eds.): *Rethinking English Homicide Law* (2000, Oxford University Press).

Gardner: *Manslaughter by Gross Negligence* (1995) 111 LQR 22.

Goff: *The Mental Element in the Crime of Murder* (1988) 104 LQR 30.

Griew: *The Future of Diminished Responsibility* [1988] Crim LR 75.

Heaton: *Anything Goes* (2001) 10(2) Nottingham Law Journal 50.

Heaton: *Dealing in Death* [2003] Crim LR 497.

Heaton: *Principals? No Principles!* [2004] Crim LR 463.

Home Office: *Reforming the Law on Involuntary Manslaughter: The Government's Proposals* (2000).

Horder: *Provocation and Responsibility* (1991, Clarendon Press).

House of Lords: *Report of the Select Committee on Murder and Life Imprisonment* (Session 1988–89) HL Paper 78-1.

Keating: *The Law Commission Report on Involuntary Manslaughter: The Restoration of a Serious Crime* [1996] Crim LR 535, 580.

Law Commission: *Involuntary Manslaughter*—Report, Law Com. No. 237, 1996.

Law Commission: *Partial Defences to Murder*—Consultation Paper, Law Com. No. 173, 2003 and Report, Law Com. No. 290, 2004.

Mackay: *Mental Condition Defences in Criminal Law* (1995, Oxford University Press).

Mackay & Mitchell: *But is this Provocation? Some Thoughts on the Law Commission's Report on Partial Defences to Murder* [2005] Crim LR 44.

Seneviratne: *Pre-Natal Injury and Transferred Malice: The Invented Other* (1996) 59 MLR 884.

Virgo: *Reconstructing Manslaughter by Defective Foundations* (1995) 54 CLJ 14.

Williams: *The Mens Rea for Murder: Leave it Alone* (1989) 105 LQR 387.

■ SUMMARY

Murder

- *Actus reus*—(i) unlawfully (ii) causing the death (iii) of a human being. *Causing death*—for causing see 2.10. For 'death' see below. *Human being*—excludes foetuses. Foetus becomes a 'child' when wholly expelled from mother and born alive. Death occurs when brain stem ceases all functioning even though heart/lungs kept working by machine *(Malcherek)*.

Unlawfully—excludes killing: enemy soldiers in the heat of battle; where justified; e.g., reasonable force in self-defence or prevention of crime; without fault (purely accidental).

- *Mens rea*—see 6.4.1.2 above.

Manslaughter

Voluntary manslaughter

D has *actus reus* and *mens rea* for murder, but reduced to manslaughter by one of three mitigating circumstances.

- *Provocation*—needs (i) provocative conduct causing (ii) D to lose his self-control (iii) where a reasonable person would have done as D did. *Provocative conduct*—can be things done and/or said whether directed at D or not (*Pearson*; *Doughty*) and whether coming from the deceased victim or not (*Davies*) and whether or not such provoking conduct is blameworthy (*Doughty*). No rule that D cannot rely on provocative conduct for which he is to blame (*Johnson*). There must be **some evidence** of what was said/done not just speculation (*Acott*). *The Subjective Limb*—requires *actual* loss of self-control by D—entirely subjective test for the jury, although the judge may withdraw the defence from it if no credible evidence of actual loss of self-control. Requires a sudden and temporary loss making D so angry he is unable to restrain himself from doing what he did (*Duffy*; *Richens*). A significant time gap between the provocation and D's reaction normally rules out the immediate reaction in the heat of the moment usually regarded as the hallmark of loss of self-control (*Thornton*; *Ahluwalia*). But previous provocation can be revived by a 'last straw' provocation (*Ibrams*). *The Objective Limb*—the test is: would a reasonable (i.e., essentially an ordinary, average) person have lost their self-control and reacted as D did? (s. 3 Homicide Act 1957). (The reformulation of the test in *Smith*—could D have been reasonably expected to control his reaction in all the circumstances?—was disapproved in *Attorney-General for Jersey* v *Holley* 2005, PC, and should now be ignored (*Mohammed* 2005, CA)). In judging the reasonable man's reaction, the jury should take into account (a) personal characteristics of D which affected the gravity of the provocation (*Camplin*; *Morhall*) (b) the age and sex of D (*Camplin*) but **not** (c) other characteristics which merely affect D's general ability to control his reactions to provocation in general (*Holley*; *Mohammed*). Thus once the seriousness of the provocation has been assessed taking into account any characteristics or circumstances personal to D which increase the provocativeness of the provoking conduct, the standard of self-control expected by the law is fixed by reference to how an ordinary person of average temperament might have reacted. At that stage no allowance is made for any personal characteristics of D (even if not his fault) which might lower his threshold of self-control below the norm. *History and circumstances*—provocation must always be viewed in its wider context, e.g., past relationships, history of abuse, to appreciate its severity and effect on D, i.e, in assessing the gravity of the provocation (*Morhall*; *Horrex*). No rule of law that retaliation must be reasonably proportionate to the gravity of the provocation (*Mancini*, overruled by s. 3—*Brown*; *Camplin*).

- *Diminished responsibility*—D must prove (i) abnormality of mind (ii) due to: arrested or retarded development of mind; or inherent causes; or disease or injury (s. 2 Homicide Act 1957) (iii) leading to substantial impairment of responsibility. *Abnormality of mind*—an elastic concept which covers perception of physical matters, ability to judge right and wrong and to resist impulses and control actions (*Byrne*). Also 'dissociated states', depression, pre-menstrual syndrome and anything which constitutes a 'disease of mind'. *Specified causes*—medical evidence needed. *'Inherent causes'*—a vague and elastic concept enabling courts to include most cases they want to. Excludes mere emotions albeit strong such as hate, jealousy, anger (*Fenton*) and the factor of intoxication must be disregarded (*Dietschmann*) unless possibly chronic alcoholism (*Tandy*). *Substantial impairment of responsibility*—vague and elastic giving jury wide discretion. Largely a moral question to be approached 'in a broad, common sense way' (*Egan*).

- *Suicide pacts*—see text.

Involuntary manslaughter

Three forms: (a) gross negligence (b) subjective recklessness (c) unlawful act (constructive) manslaughter.

- *Gross negligence*—law transformed by *Adomako* rejecting *Seymour*. Requires (i) breach of a duty of care owed by D to V which (ii) caused V's death and (iii) was sufficiently serious to constitute gross negligence (*Adomako*). *Duty of care* is owed when owed under the law of torts—rarely likely to be a problem. Much wider than the duty concept used to ground liability for omissions. *Causes death*—see 2.10. *Grossly negligent breach*—the crunch issue. External standard of conduct in effect set by individual juries because of lack of definition by courts. But D must fall **seriously** short of the standard of a reasonable person. If D holds himself out as possessing special skill or expertise, the standard is a reasonably competent 'expert'—doctor, electrician, etc. (*Adomako*). Not clear what risk D has to be grossly negligent in regard to, but probably a risk of death (or at least serious injury) (*Adomako*). *Adomako*'s overturning of *Seymour* probably a welcome narrowing of manslaughter. Formulation in *Adomako* is of general application and includes 'motor manslaughter' (*Adomako*).

- *Subjectively reckless manslaughter*—not discussed in *Adomako* but presumably survives it. Scope uncertain—would cover where D is aware of risk of death and probably of serious injury. The unknown question is whether it extends to awareness of the risk of **non-serious injury** as held in *Stone and Dobinson*.

- *Unlawful act*—requires (i) D intentionally did an act which (ii) was in fact **unlawful** (iii) was in fact **dangerous** and (iv) did in fact cause V's death (*DPP v Newbury*). The *intention* required is to do the act **not** cause the harmful consequence. Intentional **omissions** not covered (*Lowe*). *Unlawful* means at least 'criminal' which probably requires the *actus reus* of the crime to be accompanied by any necessary *mens rea* (*O'Driscoll; Scarlett*) (despite some indications to the contrary). If the act is unlawful only because of D's negligence, it is not 'unlawful' for this purpose (*Andrews v DPP*). *Dangerous* is an entirely objective test (D does not have to realise it is dangerous (*Newbury*)). Act must be 'likely to cause harm' or carry a very obvious risk of harm (*Larkin; Church*). 'Harm' includes non-serious harm (i.e., risk does not have to be of death or serious harm) but must be physical harm as opposed to mere fright or emotional disturbance (*Dawson*). Danger is judged on the basis of any knowledge D had or ought reasonably to have had of the circumstances (*Watson; Ball*). *Causes death*—normal causation principles apply (see 2.10). Seems unnecessary to show death was caused by the element of unlawfulness in D's act as opposed to just the act itself (*Watson*). No requirement that the act should be 'directed at another'. *Dalby* which 'invented' the requirement rejected by *Goodfellow* and *Attorney-General's Reference (No. 3 of 1994)*.

CHAPTER 6: ASSESSMENT EXERCISE

6.1 Melvin, having been violently abused over a period of many years by Alan, his homosexual partner, finally escapes the relationship when Alan throws him out of their house for another man. Melvin feels extremely depressed and vulnerable and goes to live with Rock. Shortly afterwards, Rock comes home drunk one night and starts making advances to Melvin who rebuffs him. Rock becomes angry, severely beats Melvin and tries to rape him. However he is too drunk to do this. Melvin, who is physically weak but has himself an explosive temperament, waits for Rock to fall asleep and then stabs him six times intentionally causing his death. Psychiatric evidence establishes that Melvin was suffering from the male equivalent of battered woman syndrome.

Discuss the criminal liability of Melvin, if any, for the death of Rock.

6.2 Smart, a student, decided to play a practical joke on his lecturer, Dream. When Dream entered the lecture theatre to give a lecture, Smart set off a smoke canister which he had bought from a joke shop, and shouted, 'Fire!'

As a result of these actions, Dream, who already had a weak heart, had a serious heart attack and blacked out. Upon recovering consciousness after initial hospital treatment, Dream instructed the medical staff that they were not to give him any further treatment or medication because he wanted to die, being unable to cope with the pressures of his job. No further treatment was given and he lapsed into a coma and died.

Discuss the criminal liability of Smart, if any, for (a) unlawful act manslaughter and (b) gross negligence manslaughter in respect of Dream's death.

See also **Assessment Exercise 9.1** below.
See the **Appendix** (6.1 and 6.2) for specimen answers.

7 General defences I: Age and insanity

7.1 Objectives

By the end of this chapter you should be able to:

1 State how age affects criminal liability

2 Define the requirements for the defence of insanity with particular reference to the concept of 'disease of mind'

3 Identify the shortcomings of the legal definition of insanity

7.2 Introduction to and overview of general defences

We now turn to consider a number of defences (sometimes termed 'negative fault requirements') which are not specific to any particular crime but apply to crimes generally. Except where the contrary is indicated in our treatment of the individual defence, these defences are available to negative liability whatever crime is charged. The common feature is that even though the positive fault requirements, i.e., the *actus reus* and *mens rea* laid down by the offence definition appear to be present, the accused may avoid conviction by raising one of these general 'defence' issues. They are called 'negative fault requirements' because they are assumed to be inapplicable unless the defence puts them into play by adducing credible evidence of their applicability. For most of them (insanity and diminished responsibility are major exceptions), D's burden is not to prove the defence applies but merely to adduce credible evidence that it may apply. The burden then switches to the prosecution to prove beyond reasonable doubt that it does not apply.

It must be said that these defences form a motley collection that cover vastly different circumstances and operate in quite disparate ways. Attempts to group them into organising themes have been numerous but always flawed in some way or other. In this chapter, we look at two defences where by reason of age or mental condition, D does not have the moral capacity to enable us to regard him as legally responsible for his actions, even though he may have performed the *actus reus* of the crime along with the necessary *mens rea*. (Diminished responsibility dealt with at 6.5.2.3 above falls into the same category.)

In **Chapter 8** we examine a group of 'defences' which operate by negativing an element of the *actus reus* or, more usually, the *mens rea* of the offence charged (automatism, intoxication, mistake and self-defence/prevention of crime).

? **QUESTION** 7.1

Why have we implied, by putting the term 'defences' in quotes, that 'defences' may not be an entirely appropriate description for this group?

Although usually regarded as defences, automatism, intoxication and mistake are not truly defences at all. Rather they amount to a claim by the accused that the prosecution is unable to prove the ingredients (usually the necessary *mens rea*), i.e., the positive fault elements of the crime charged. For example, intoxication can only ever succeed as a defence where it prevents D forming the *mens rea* specified by the crime charged. Thus, if it succeeds, it succeeds **because** the prosecution cannot prove beyond reasonable doubt that D had the relevant *mens rea*. Automatism is usually classed as an incapacity defence similar to insanity. Indeed many instances of it do amount to insanity. Its essential feature is that, although D appears to be acting with purpose and performing the prohibited *actus reus*, his **conscious** mind is not in control of his muscular movements, usually because he is in some kind of trance-like or unconscious state. He lacks the capacity to modify his actions. However, in practice, the defence has striking affinities with intoxication (it can be caused by intoxicating drugs) in that it prevents D forming the *mens rea*. Indeed, most writers argue that it negates the *actus reus* because acts which are not the product of the conscious mind cannot be regarded as acts at all (see 2.7.1 above). For this reason we examine it in **Chapter 8**.

We saw in **Chapter 4** (see 4.3.3.1 and 4.3.3.2 above) that legitimate self-defence or prevention of crime would negate the *actus reus* of battery and other offences of violence and in that respect parallel the 'defences' in the previous paragraph. However, it could just as easily and, perhaps more plausibly, be regarded as an independent matter of defence divorced from the *actus reus* of the crime (*cf.* the attitude of the majority in *Brown* to the 'defence' of consent). It differs markedly from those other defences in that legitimate self-defence is correct and acceptable conduct. The act is permissible. It is the 'right' thing to do in the circumstances. In legal terms, it is 'justifiable'. The other defences simply provide an excuse for the doer. The law excuses him from liability but does not regard the action as acceptable. The conduct is still viewed as wrongful even though it does not incur criminal liability because of the excusing circumstances. As Robinson observes (*Criminal Law Defences: A Systematic Analysis* (1982) 82 Col LR 199), 'Acts are justified; actors are excused...'

Finally in **Chapter 9**, we discuss the defences of duress, necessity and marital coercion where, although the prosecution can prove the elements of the offence—that D has caused the *actus reus* with the appropriate *mens rea*, the law may allow pressure created by the circumstances to negate D's liability. We may view duress as an excuse because D's act is still wrongful even though the law recognises that some threats are so serious that even a law-abiding citizen cannot realistically be expected to resist them, even though ideally they should. We concede that in the circumstances D could not fairly have been expected to act otherwise. True necessity on the other hand may be seen as not just excused but justified—the right thing to do.

7.3 Age and criminal responsibility

The law recognises that children's immaturity may impair their understanding of right and wrong so that it would be unjust to hold them criminally responsible in the same way as an adult. Thus an age is set below which no criminal responsibility can attach. In England and Wales, ten is the minimum age for conviction although most Western European countries have a significantly higher minimum. Curiously, Scotland and Northern Ireland set the age at eight—the age applicable throughout the UK until 1963.

The law **conclusively** presumes that children under ten years of age are incapable of committing a crime and, therefore, whatever they have done, it is impossible to convict them of any crime (s. 50 of the Children and Young Persons Act 1933, as amended). It is, of course, possible for the local authority to apply for a care or supervision order under s. 31 of the Children Act 1989, but these are civil proceedings. However, the commission of what would otherwise be a criminal offence is only one factor for the court to take into account in adjudging whether to make such an order, the welfare of the child being the paramount consideration.

7.3.1 The 10–13s inclusive

Until recently, there was a **rebuttable** presumption that children of ten years and over but under the age of 14 were incapable of committing any crime (*'doli incapax'*). The presumption could be rebutted only by proof that the child had 'mischievous discretion', which meant that he understood that his act was not merely naughty but was seriously wrong in a moral or legal sense. Thus the prosecution had to prove not only that D performed the *actus reus* of the crime charged with any requisite *mens rea* but also that he appreciated that his conduct was seriously wrong—an additional burden which did cause significant practical problems. The Divisional Court in *C v DPP* [1994] 3 All ER 190 tried to abolish this presumption but, on appeal, the House of Lords held that the rule was so well established in law that only Parliament could properly abrogate it ([1995] 2 All ER 43). The legislature soon took the hint and did abolish the presumption by s. 34 of the Crime and Disorder Act 1998.

The intention was probably that children of ten or over should be treated in exactly the same way as adults in terms of criminal **liability**, but it is not entirely clear that this is the effect of s. 34. Professor Walker has argued that s. 34 only abolishes the **presumption** of incapacity, leaving the old substantive law requiring capacity intact (see (1999) 149 NLJ 64). Thus the law would now assume that the 10- to 13-year-olds have adult capacity unless the defence raises the issue with credible evidence to the contrary, in which case the prosecution would have to prove 'mischievous discretion'. On the literal wording of s. 34, the argument is strong but it is thought that the courts will be unlikely to apply it.

7.3.2 **Sexual incapacity**

Previously, boys under the age of 14 were **conclusively** presumed to be incapable of having sexual intercourse. As a result, they could not be convicted as perpetrators of any offence requiring sexual intercourse, such as rape (*Groombridge* (1836) 7 C & P 582), or unlawful sexual intercourse with an under-age girl (*Waite* [1892] 2 QB 600). This anachronistic presumption was abolished by s. 1 of the Sexual Offences Act 1993, in respect of all forms of sexual intercourse, conventional or not. It is now a simple question of fact as to whether the boy did or did not penetrate the relevant orifice with his penis, whether erect or not.

7.4 **Insanity**

7.4.1 **Introduction**

Madness has proved an enduring source of fascination and academic lawyers have not been immune. Indeed it could be argued that its practical importance nowadays does not justify the amount of time spent discussing it. Relatively few cases per year result in a finding of insanity and, prior to 1991, it was very rare for the defendant to plead it as a defence because, although a successful plea will result in a verdict of 'not guilty by reason of insanity', there used to be, until recently, a sting in the tail. On reaching such a verdict, the court **had to** order the accused to be detained indefinitely in a secure mental hospital. Whilst this may have been a useful alternative to hanging when murder carried the death penalty, once this was abolished, there was little point in pleading insanity. Furthermore, the introduction of the defence of diminished responsibility to the crime of murder in 1957 had a dramatic effect in reducing the number of insanity pleas.

Although this used to be the position, important changes were effected by the Criminal Procedure (Insanity and Unfitness to Plead) Act 1991 (as amended by s. 24 of the Domestic Violence, Crime and Victims Act 2004). This gives the trial judge the discretion to dispose of D in ways other than indefinite detention in a secure mental hospital where the verdict is 'not guilty by reason of insanity'. He must choose one of the following alternatives: (a) a hospital order (with or without a restriction order) (effectively a custodial order requiring detention in a mental hospital); (b) a supervision order (a non-custodial order which may prescribe compulsory treatment for the mental condition); or (c) an order for absolute discharge. (new s. 5 of the Criminal Procedure (Insanity) Act 1964 substituted by s. 24 of the 2004 Act). However, it is expressly provided that where the offence involved carries a sentence 'fixed by law' (s. 5(3)), the judge **must** impose a hospital order **with** a restriction order. In practice, this means murder where the only available sentence is life imprisonment. Consequently, in the case of murder, defendants will presumably continue to plead diminished responsibility rather than insanity, preferring a fixed sentence of imprisonment for manslaughter to indefinite detention in a secure mental hospital, which is still the price of an acquittal by reason of insanity.

Research comparing the five years before the 1991 Act with the first five years since shows a doubling of successful insanity pleas, increasing from 20 to 44 and mostly involving offences of serious but non-fatal violence (Mackay & Kearns: *More Fact(s) about the Insanity Defence* [1999] Crim LR 714).

The other major change made by the 1991 Act is to prohibit a finding of insanity unless supported by the written or oral testimony of at least two registered medical practitioners, of whom at least one is approved by the Home Secretary as having special experience in the field of mental disorder (s. 1).

The act makes no changes to the substantive legal definition of what constitutes insanity. We should point out that, if the defendant pleads diminished responsibility, it is open to the prosecution to allege that, in truth, the defendant was legally insane. The same is true where the defendant alleges that he was in a state of automatism when he committed the alleged crime. This defence, which was touched on at 2.7.1, is dealt with in **Chapter 8** but the essence of it is that D's conscious mind was not in control of his muscular movements at the time he did the relevant act. If the defendant's automatic state was caused by a disease of the mind, it would be insane automatism and therefore insanity, whereas if it was due to some other cause, it would be non-insane automatism and D could be completely acquitted of the crime. In several of the leading cases on insanity, D claimed acquittal on the grounds of non-insane automatism but had to change his plea to guilty to the crime charged when the trial judge ruled that his defence was in reality one of insanity because the automatic state was caused by a disease of the mind.

7.4.1.1 The rationale of the insanity defence

Criminal law proceeds on the assumption that individuals are rational and autonomous beings who are responsible for their actions. Serious mental disorder will negate that assumption and fairness dictates that a sufferer cannot be regarded as morally or legally responsible for their actions. The function of the law on insanity is to define the point at which mental disorder dissolves responsibility.

The law of insanity also has another, conflicting agenda which is often uppermost in judges' minds. For Lord Diplock in *Sullivan* [1983] 2 All ER 673, HL, 'The purpose of the legislation relating to the defence of insanity, ever since its origin in 1800, has been to protect society against recurrence of the dangerous conduct.' This is reflected in the coercive powers of disposal given to the judge over a person found not guilty by reason of insanity (see above). As we shall see at 7.4.2.1 below, this public protection ideal has led the courts to sweep into the net of legal insanity people such as diabetics, sleepwalkers and epileptics who seem far from the medical notion of insanity. If they were not legally insane, they might escape criminal liability and sentence altogether on the basis of non-insane automatism, even though there was a danger that the same condition could arise again (see generally **8.3** below). Conversely where D's disorder could not amount to automatism, the tendency is to operate unmodified the very restrictive notion of insanity embodied in the original M'Naghten Rules, arguably on the basis of an instinctive judicial bias in favour of responsibility for one's actions and general suspicion of claimed excuses.

7.4.2 The definition of insanity

Before concerning yourself with the detailed definition of insanity, it is important for you to appreciate that the legal notion of insanity does not correspond at all with the medical notion of insanity. Legal insanity is in some fundamental respects a great deal narrower than medical insanity. It may be said that the legal definition puts all its eggs in the intellectual or cognitive basket. If D understands two simple things—(a) the physical nature of his action and its consequences and (b) that it is against the law, he cannot be found insane, no matter how 'mad' doctors would regard him.

? QUESTION 7.2

Can you suggest some examples of people who would be regarded as medically insane but who are not legally insane because they understand what they are doing physically and that it is wrong? You will encounter several examples in the course of this section.

Doctors would undoubtedly class the 'Yorkshire Ripper' as medically insane but, because he knew that he was killing people and that his acts were against the law, he could not establish that he was legally insane. (He was certainly suffering diminished responsibility in legal terms, although the jury, against the medical evidence, in fact rejected such a plea.)

On the other hand, the legal notion of 'disease of mind' is far wider than psychiatrists would accept. For example, the law regards epileptics and diabetics performing acts during blackouts caused by their disease, as insane (*Sullivan* [1983] 2 All ER 673, HL and *Hennessy* [1989] 2 All ER 9, CA). Similarly, those who commit violence whilst sleepwalking (*Burgess* [1991] 2 All ER 769, CA—*Cases and Materials* (7.4.2)).

Insanity is a common law defence and the basic definition is still that laid down in the M'Naghten Rules. D must prove on the balance of probabilities that he was suffering from a defect of reason arising from a disease of the mind with the result that **either** he did not know the nature and quality of his act, **or** he did not realise that his actions were wrong. There are four elements here and each of them needs further explanation.

7.4.2.1 Disease of the mind

The courts have taken a largely pragmatic view of what constitutes a disease of the mind and their major policy concern has been to ensure that people who have shown themselves to be dangerous to the public should be detained until the authorities are satisfied that the public's safety is not in jeopardy. It is likely therefore that any internal bodily disorder which affects the functioning of the brain and has resulted in violence which might recur will be held to be a disease of the mind (see Lord Denning in *Bratty v Attorney-General for Northern Ireland* [1963] AC 386, HL), although the absence of a danger of recurrence does not preclude a finding of 'disease of mind' (*Burgess*). Indeed the House of Lords in *Sullivan* focused on the **cause** of the mental disorder rather than its possible future consequences.

The concept was explained as follows in the leading case of *Sullivan* (*Cases and Materials* (7.4.2.1)):

> ... 'mind' in the M'Naghten Rules is used in the ordinary sense of the mental faculties of reason, memory and understanding. If the effect of a disease is to impair these faculties so severely as to have either of the consequences referred to in the latter part of the rules, it matters not whether the aetiology of the impairment is organic, as in epilepsy, or functional, or whether the impairment itself is permanent or is transient and intermittent, provided that it subsisted at the time of the commission of the act.

This view adopts the line taken by Devlin J in *Kemp* [1956] 3 All ER 249 (*Cases and Materials* (7.4.2.1)). What matters is that there should be some derangement of the mental faculties affecting the functioning of the mind. It does not matter whether this has an organic cause, i.e., some physical disorder within the body itself, whether this is within the brain cells (e.g., epilepsy—*Sullivan*) or outside of the brain but affecting its functioning (e.g., arteriosclerosis—*Kemp*) or, alternatively, which merely affects the way the brain functions without any identifiable organic cause, e.g., schizophrenia, melancholia or paranoia. Disease of the mind is certainly wider than disease of the brain. Nor does it matter that it is of only temporary or transient effect causing no degeneration of the brain cells, e.g., an epileptic seizure, or the arteriosclerosis in *Kemp* which cut off the blood supply to the brain causing temporary unconsciousness. The fact that the condition is curable or controllable, for example by medication, does not prevent it from being a disease of the mind.

A major limitation on the definition formulated by the Court of Appeal in *Quick* [1973] 3 All ER 347 (*Cases and Materials* (7.4.2.1)) was approved by the House of Lords in *Sullivan*:

> The fundamental concept of a disease of the mind was of a malfunctioning of the mind caused by disease. A malfunctioning of the mind of transitory effect caused by the application to the body of some external factor, such as violence, drugs, including anaesthetics, alcohol and hypnotic influences, could not fairly be said to be due to disease.

In *Quick*, the defendant nurse was convicted of assault occasioning actual bodily harm on a paraplegic patient. He had claimed the defence of non-insane automatism on the basis that, at the time of the alleged assault, he was suffering from hypoglycaemia and was not aware of what he was doing. Hypoglycaemia is a deficiency of blood-sugar caused by the use of insulin prescribed by the defendant's doctor to counteract the diabetes from which he suffered. The defendant had withdrawn his defence and changed his plea to guilty when the trial judge ruled that his defence amounted to insanity. The Court of Appeal quashed the conviction on the ground that the defendant's condition was caused by an **external factor**, i.e., the injection of insulin, which did not constitute a disease of the mind. This condition was only **transitory** in the sense that it would not recur unless the external stimulus was reintroduced.

Ironically, a diabetic may act unconsciously in a similar fashion through **failing** to take insulin. This can lead to a condition known as hyperglycaemia caused by an excess of blood-sugar and in this case the courts would regard the condition as constituting insanity. This was confirmed by the Court of Appeal in *Hennessy* [1989] 2 All ER 9.

> **? QUESTION** 7.3
>
> • What is the factor which led the Court of Appeal in *Hennessy* to distinguish *Quick*?
> • Do you think it makes sense to classify Hennessy as insane and Quick as not?
> • How would you class someone who was violent whilst sleepwalking?

In practical terms, we would see no reason to regard a diabetic who goes into a coma through failing to take insulin as any more dangerous to the public than one whose coma is caused by the injection of insulin. Both are known risks and both can be cured by ingesting a lump of sugar. Yet one is liable to be detained on the ground of insanity and the other is a non-insane automaton and may well be acquitted without strings. This calls into question the validity of making 'disease of the mind' turn on the internal/external distinction. Nonetheless, it is firmly established that if the condition affecting the functioning of the mind results from any internal bodily disorder (e.g., the diabetes **itself** in *Hennessy*), it is a disease of the mind and all the elements of the M'Naghten Rules will be satisfied. If the trigger is an external factor originating outside of the body, e.g., injection of the drug insulin and/or failing to take food to counteract it as in *Quick*, then it is not a disease of the mind and D is not insane.

Despite statements in previous cases to the contrary, the Court of Appeal has now held that sleepwalking, during which D is violent, constitutes a disease of the mind since it is due to an internal bodily disorder (*Burgess—Cases and Materials* (7.4.2.1)).

> **↟ EXERCISE** 7.1
>
> Write down any examples you can think of which would constitute external factors negating a 'disease of the mind'.

You might have suggested a blow on the head causing temporary concussion, anaesthetics, drugs such as LSD, alcohol or hypnotic influences. A more controversial example of an external factor was given in the Crown Court case of *T* [1990] Crim LR 256. The defendant had been raped a few days before she committed a robbery and wounding. A psychiatrist testified that as a consequence, at the time of the alleged offences, she was suffering from post-traumatic stress disorder which had caused her to enter a dissociative state. As a result, she had committed the offences during a psychogenic fugue (an amnesial flight from reality inducing a dream-like trance) without any conscious mind or will. The trial judge ruled that the rape was an external factor and that the resulting post-traumatic stress did not amount to a disease of the mind and so was not insanity.

On the other hand, where the dissociative state is caused by a 'psychological blow' resulting from 'the ordinary stresses and disappointments of life' (as opposed to an extraordinary event like the rape in *T*), it cannot be said to be due to an external factor. The real cause is D's own abnormal 'psychological or emotional make-up' and this is an internal factor constituting 'disease of mind' (see *Burgess* [1991] 2 All ER 769, CA approving the Canadian case of *Rabey* (1978) 79 DLR 435). In *Rabey*, D, on discovering that the girl he was infatuated with, did not care for him, hit her on the head with a rock he had taken from a geology laboratory. He was in a dissociative state which was due to a disease of the mind. The exceptional effect on him of one of life's standard disappointments was due to an internal factor in his make-up. The Court of Appeal made the same distinction in *Hennessy*, holding the diabetic D to be an insane automaton when his failure to take insulin caused a hyperglycaemic coma. D had argued that his failure to take insulin had been due to clinical depression brought on by marital and work problems, which should be regarded as external factors as the rape in *T*. That was rejected because such problems were an everyday feature of life and lacked the necessary 'feature of novelty or accident'. In other words, D's depression was viewed as more the function of his internal make-up leading to an 'abnormal' reaction to standard external events and circumstances.

The Court of Appeal in *Quick* said that the external factor must be of **transitory** effect to avoid a finding of insanity.

? **QUESTION** 7.4

Can you say what is the significance of the requirement that the effect be 'transitory'?

Let us consider a case where D is concussed by a blow on the head. This would be an external factor and if D commits the alleged crime whilst so concussed, this would be non-insane automatism. However, if the blow on the head had caused permanent brain damage so that D might have further attacks spontaneously without the re-introduction of any external stimulus, what started out as an external factor, would have become an internal bodily disorder and would constitute a disease of the mind and therefore insanity.

7.4.2.2 **Defect of reason**

This requires that the disease of the mind has deprived D of or made him incapable of exercising the powers of ordinary reasoning. It does not apply where D retains his reasoning power but, due to momentary confusion or absent-mindedness, fails to use it. This was established by the Court of Appeal in *Clarke* [1972] 1 All ER 219 (*Cases and Materials* (7.4.2.2)). D was accused of theft by shoplifting from a supermarket and claimed that she had no intention to steal in that she had put the items in her own shopping bag in a moment of absent-mindedness whilst suffering from depression. When the judge ruled that this constituted insanity, the defendant rapidly changed her plea from not guilty to guilty. She then appealed to the Court of Appeal who quashed her conviction on the grounds that she was not suffering from insanity because there was no defect of reason. She retained her powers of reasoning even though at the relevant time she did not use those powers properly.

If D is suffering from a defect of reason due to a disease of the mind, he will be insane if **either** he did not know the nature and quality of his act **or**, if he did know this, he did not know it was wrong.

7.4.2.3 **Not knowing the nature and quality of his act**

This refers exclusively to the **physical** nature and the **physical** quality of D's acts. It has nothing to do with whether D appreciates the **moral** nature or **moral** quality of his act. In essence, the court is asking whether D appreciated what he was physically doing and what the physical consequences of that act were. In order not to appreciate the nature and quality of his act, a person would have to be completely divorced from reality. A nineteenth-century judge, Stephen J, gave the colourful example of the man who cut off a sleeping person's head because it would be great fun to see him looking for it when he woke up. Such a person clearly has not the faintest notion of what decapitation means. There is a huge gulf between what D **thinks** he is doing and what he **is** doing. Clearly, people who are acting automatically in an unconscious state would not know what they were doing and so would satisfy this condition.

7.4.2.4 **Not knowing his act was wrong**

You should bear in mind that this is an alternative to the last heading. Lack of knowledge of **either** the nature and quality of his act **or** its wrongness will constitute insanity provided the other conditions are met. 'Wrong' has been interpreted narrowly to mean 'contrary to law' (*Windle* [1952] 2 All ER 1, CCA) (*Cases and Materials* (7.4.2.4)). D gave his wife, who had constantly spoken of committing suicide, a fatal dose of 100 aspirins because he thought it would be beneficial for her to die. There was evidence that the victim was medically insane and that the defendant was also suffering from a form of communicated insanity known as *folie à deux*. However, the defendant made the mistake of telling the police that he supposed he would be hanged for what he had done. He was correct and his insanity plea was rejected by the trial judge on the ground that he clearly knew that what he did was against the law.

> **? QUESTION** 7.5
>
> We stated above that 'wrong' has been interpreted narrowly to mean 'against the law'. Can you suggest an alternative broader meaning for 'wrong' which might be more appropriate for someone suffering from a disease of the mind?

Even if the accused, because of his disease of the mind, is convinced of the moral correctness of his actions, if he knows that what he is doing is against the law (or probably would be condemned by people generally—see *Codère* (1916) 12 Cr App R 21 (*Cases and Materials* (7.4.2.4)), he would not be legally insane. This can work particularly harshly and exclude from the defence people who, on any commonsense view, are mad. An example is provided by the so-called 'divine inspiration' cases where D believes he is acting on the instructions of God and, due to his disease of mind, believes that, not only is he justified in acting, but that it is his duty to act. The uncompromising response of Stephen J in the nineteenth century was that in such a case, he would certainly hang a defendant who killed under orders from God, unless he received an order from God not to. As Fitzgerald has put it, English law rests 'on the quaint assumption that those who are so un-English as to put the edicts of God before the law of the land must be not mad but very wicked!' (*The Guardian,* 25 March 1982).

The current attitude of the courts would not be dissimilar, as is illustrated by the Court of Appeal's decision in *Bell* [1984] 3 All ER 842. The defendant was convicted of reckless driving, having used his van as a battering ram to drive through the entrance gates of a Butlins Holiday Camp. He told the police, 'It was like a secret society in there. I wanted to do my bit against it'. Whether he was hoping to facilitate the escape of some of the campers or had had bad experiences with Redcoats is not clear, but he thought he was driven by God. The Court of Appeal in dismissing his appeal held that the fact that he believed himself to be driven by God did not provide any excuse (i.e., the defence of insanity or automatism), but merely an explanation for what he had done. He knew what he was doing and he knew it was against the law. His perception that he was morally right was irrelevant.

7.4.2.5 **Insanity and *mens rea***

For a verdict of insanity to be possible, the prosecution must establish that D 'did the act or made the omission charged', i.e., performed the *actus reus* of the offence alleged (s. 2(1) of the Trial of Lunatics Act 1883 as amended). Failure to prove the *actus reus* would mean a complete acquittal. However, there is no need to prove the *mens rea* for the offence charged (*Attorney-General's Reference (No. 3 of 1998)* [1999] 3 All ER 40, CA approved by the House of Lords in *Antoine* [2000] 2 All ER 208). It is evident that an insane person may or may not have the *mens rea* for the crime charged. If he does not understand the nature and quality of his act, he is unlikely to have the requisite *mens rea*. On the other hand if he does not understand that his act is wrong in law, this by no means precludes his having the relevant *mens rea*. Once insanity is accepted, the *mens rea* for the offence charged ceases to be relevant. Confusion on this point was at the root of the surely untenable holding in *DPP* v *H* [1997] 1 WLR 1406, DC that insanity could never be a defence to a strict liability offence—in this case drink driving. The view rests on the unwarranted assumption that insanity depends on the disease of mind negating *mens rea* and is contradicted by *Hennessy* [1989] 2 All ER 9, CA which held that insanity could be a defence to the strict liability crime of driving while disqualified. A finding of not guilty by reason of insanity is in no way dependent on proof that D's disease of mind prevented him having the *mens rea* for the offence charged.

7.4.2.6 **Insanity and summary trials**

The legislation on insanity and therefore the judges' powers of disposal apply only to trial by jury and not to summary trials before magistrates. However, the common law defence does apply to summary trials where a finding of insanity would result in a complete, no-strings acquittal (*Horseferry Road Magistrates' Court, ex parte K* [1997] QB 23, DC).

7.4.2.7 **Burden of proof**

Under the M'Naghten Rules, everyone is presumed sane and, therefore, if D claims insanity, he has the burden of proving it on the balance of probabilities (*Sodeman v R* [1936] 2 All ER

1138). You may recall that this is the position where D pleads diminished responsibility (the other 'mental disorder' defence) as a defence to murder (see 6.5.2.3). However, it seems that it is open to the prosecution to allege insanity, especially where D claims some other defence based on his mental condition, e.g., diminished responsibility or non-insane automatism (*Bratty* v *Attorney-General for Northern Ireland* (above); s. 6 of the Criminal Procedure (Insanity) Act 1964 where D pleads diminished responsibility). In such a case, the burden of proving insanity is on the prosecution, although it is not clear whether this is beyond reasonable doubt or only on the balance of probabilities (*Bastian* [1958] 1 WLR 413). Finally, under s. 1 of the Criminal Procedure (Insanity and Unfitness to Plead) Act 1991, a finding of insanity is only possible on the evidence of at least two registered medical practitioners, one of whom must be a specialist approved by the Home Secretary. The draft Criminal Code would place a burden of proof on the balance of probabilities on whoever alleges insanity.

7.4.3 Conclusion

As is evident from the case examples given above, insanity is technically available as a defence to any crime. Even since the wider powers of disposal were conferred on the trial judge by the 1991 Act, the plea is relatively little used and tends to be utilised in serious offences of violence (see [1999] Crim LR 714, 718–19). However, in relation to murder, the mentally disordered defendant is almost certain to plead the defence of diminished responsibility in preference to insanity. A fixed sentence for manslaughter is preferable to indefinite detention in a place like Broadmoor, still the only option available to the judge on a murder charge even after the 1991 Act. The definition of diminished responsibility is, as we have seen, wide enough to encompass any conditions falling within the M'Naghten Rules and, unless the prosecution contends or the trial judge rules that the accused's defence amounts to one of insanity, the verdict will **not** be 'not guilty by reason of insanity'. In practice, the prosecution is likely to accept the plea of diminished responsibility and not to press for an insanity verdict.

We would like to emphasise one final point. We have been dealing with the question of whether D was insane **at the time of the commission of the alleged crime**. However, insanity whilst the accused is in detention for the alleged crime or at the time of the trial, can also affect his liability and result in the trial not being held because D is unfit to stand trial. Important changes governing the rules on fitness to plead and to stand trial were introduced by the Criminal Procedure (Insanity and Fitness to Plead) Act 1991. Since these issues are concerned with procedure rather than the substantive law, they are outside the scope of this work.

7.4.4 Reform

It will be evident that the present definition of insanity is out of touch with modern thinking on mental disorder and has attracted constant criticism. The Butler Committee on Mentally Abnormal Offenders (Cmnd 6244, 1975) proposed radical reform which was never enacted. The basis (but not the entirety) of its recommendations has resurfaced in cll. 35 and 36 of the draft Criminal Code Bill (Law Com. No. 177). The M'Naghten Rules would be abolished and the insanity verdict replaced by one of 'not guilty on evidence of mental disorder'. This would be returned:

(a) where the offence was 'attributable' to D's 'severe mental illness or severe mental handicap' (cl. 35); **or**

(b) where D 'acted in a state of automatism, or without the fault required for the offence, or believing that an exempting circumstance existed . . .' **solely because** of his mental disorder (or a combination of that and intoxication) (cl. 36).

The terms 'severe mental illness' and 'severe mental handicap' in cl. 35 are defined in detail in cl. 34 in the terms proposed by the Butler Committee (we reproduce them, along with cll. 35 and 36 in *Cases and Materials* (7.4.4)). For the purposes of cl. 36, 'mental disorder' includes not only, 'severe mental illness or severe mental handicap' but also 'a state of automatism . . . which is a feature of a disorder . . . that may cause a similar state on another occasion' (cl. 34).

In broad terms, this would widen the scope of 'disease of mind' including, for example, the divine inspiration cases, schizophrenia, paranoia (delusional belief cases), without excluding cases like the diabetic in *Hennessy,* the sleepwalker in *Burgess* or the epileptic in *Sullivan.* Cases like the insulin-taker in *Quick* would still be outside the scope. It is claimed that the new verdict would at least remove the stigma of a finding of insanity, but would a 'mental disorder' verdict come to be seen in the same light as the insanity verdict if it replaced it?

■ FURTHER READING

Dell: *Wanted: An Insanity Defence that Can Be Used* [1984] Crim LR 431.

Mackay: *Mental Condition Defences in Criminal Law* (1995, Oxford University Press).

Mackay & Kearns: *More Fact(s) about the Insanity Defence* [1999] Crim LR 714.

Walker: *The End of an Old Song* (1999) 149 NLJ 64.

Wells: *Whither Insanity?* [1983] Crim LR 787.

Wilson, Ebrahim, Fenwick & Marks: *Violence, Sleepwalking and the Criminal Law; (2) The Legal Aspects* [2005] Crim LR 615.

■ SUMMARY

Age

Under 10s—incapable of committing any crime. 10–13s (inclusive)—now treated as adults for purposes of liability—**rebuttable** presumption of incapacity abolished by s. 34 Crime and Disorder Act 1998. No longer any presumption of sexual incapacity.

Insanity

D must prove on the balance of probabilities he suffered (i) a defect of reason (ii) due to disease of mind so that he did not know **either** (iii) the nature and quality of his act **or** (iv) that it was wrong (M'Naghten Rules).

Defect of reason—D must be deprived of (i.e., incapable of exercising) the powers of ordinary reasoning (*Clarke*). *Disease of mind*—any internal bodily disorder, whether originating inside the brain or not, which seriously affects the mental faculties of reason, memory and understanding (*Sullivan*). It is irrelevant that the disease is curable, controllable or only temporary or not prone to recur (*Kemp*; *Burgess*). Does not include a **temporary** malfunctioning of the mind due to an **external** factor, e.g., drugs (*Quick*). *Nature and quality*— means **physical** nature and quality not moral. Does D realise what he is doing physically and its physical consequences? *Wrong*—means **legally** wrong not morally wrong (*Windle*). It is irrelevant whether or not D has the *mens rea* for the offence charged (*Attorney-General's Reference (No. 3 of 1998)*).
(See **Figure 7.1**.)
See also **Assessment Exercise 8.1** below.

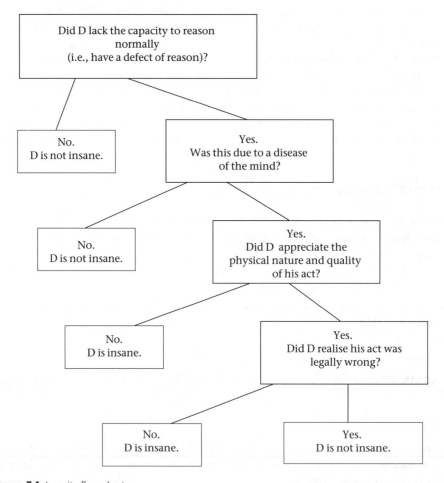

Figure 7.1 Insanity flow chart

8 General defences II: Automatism, intoxication, mistake and self-defence

8.1 Objectives

By the end of this chapter you should be able to:

1 Explain the meaning of automatism and the difference between insane and non-insane automatism

2 Distinguish between offences of specific intent and offences of basic intent

3 Define self-induced automatism and state how it affects criminal liability

4 State the basic rules governing the effect of intoxication in respect of (a) specific intent crimes and (b) basic intent crimes

5 Explain the complications introduced by *Caldwell*

6 Show how the law on intoxication in relation to matters of defence diverges from that in relation to definitional elements of the crime

7 Identify how the treatment of voluntary intoxication by alcohol or dangerous drugs differs from (a) voluntary intoxication by non-dangerous drugs and (b) involuntary intoxication

8 Appreciate the significance of the relationship between mistake and *mens rea*

9 Explain when mistake needs to be reasonable to affect liability

10 Describe the effect of a mistake of law on liability, distinguishing a mistake as to civil law from a mistake as to criminal law

11 State the basic conditions for the applicability of the statutory and common law defences of self-defence and prevention of crime

12 Explain the concept of 'reasonable force'

13 Analyse how mistake affects self-defence

8.2 **Introduction**

We now examine a group of 'defences' which turn out on closer examination not to be 'defences' at all. Rather they are cases where the prosecution is unable to prove all the ingredients of the crimes (usually) because D lacks the *mens rea* because he has made a mistake about the circumstances, is intoxicated or is acting unconsciously (automatism). However, it is common to refer to them as defences since D will normally have to adduce some credible evidence of them to raise the issue. In other words, he bears the evidential burden of producing sufficient material which would enable a reasonable jury to entertain a reasonable doubt as to whether the elements of the offence were present. Once D has produced such evidence, the prosecution has the burden of proving beyond reasonable doubt that the *mens rea* or other ingredient of the crime was not negated by intoxication, a mistake or automatism. This is the normal position with general 'defences', insanity, as we have just seen, being exceptional in this regard.

8.3 **Automatism**

It is an absolutely fundamental requirement of criminal liability that D's acts should be 'voluntary'. It is said that if D's actions are involuntary, it would be a misnomer to describe them as D's acts. The very concept of an act involves muscular movements by D willed or directed by his conscious mind. You may recall that we have already dealt with this issue to some extent when discussing *actus reus* (see 2.7.1).

It is for this reason that most academic writers regard the 'defence' of automatism as, in fact, a claim that D has not committed any *actus reus*. Thus, the plea is more fundamental than a denial of *mens rea* and should provide a 'defence' even to offences not requiring proof of *mens rea* at all. The courts have yet to pronounce definitively on the matter but it is extremely likely that they would hold automatism to be a defence to any offence, whether requiring *mens rea* or not (see *Burns v Bidder* [1966] 3 All ER 29).

8.3.1 **What is automatism?**

The essence of automatism is that the act is done by D's muscles but they are not, at the time, under the control or direction of his conscious mind. The most likely examples involve loss of consciousness, such as concussion (*Bratty v Attorney-General for Northern Ireland* [1963] AC 386, HL—*Cases and Materials* (7.1)), a hypoglycaemic coma (*Quick* [1973] 3 All ER 347, CA) or other blackouts (*Charlson* [1955] 1 All ER 859; *Kemp* [1957] 1 QB 399; *Sullivan* [1983] 2 All ER 673, HL). Equally, actions performed whilst sleepwalking or during nightmares will be regarded as automatic (*Burgess* [1991] 2 All ER 386, CA; *Bratty v Attorney-General for Northern Ireland*; *Lillienfield* (1985)*The Times*, 17 October; *Cogdon*, an unreported Australian case in 1950). In *T* [1990] Crim LR 256 the Crown Court found that actions performed during a psychogenic fugue caused by a post-traumatic stress disorder resulting from a rape on D, so that D was acting as though in a 'dream', could constitute automatism.

This is because D's conscious mind, which evaluates and decides what and what not to do, is dissociated from that part of the mind which controls what the muscles do.

Automatism also includes certain 'acts' whilst D is conscious, such as reflex actions, spasms, convulsions or even sneezing, where they are not **willed** by his conscious mind and are physically out of its control. Similarly, D may be regarded as no longer 'driving' his car where he is incapable of controlling it due to an attack by a swarm of bees (*Hill* v *Baxter* [1958] 1 QB 277) or sudden brake failure (*Burns* v *Bidder* [1966] 3 All ER 29).

However, in *Broome* v *Perkins* [1987] Crim LR 272 the Divisional Court stressed that to succeed with automatism, D had to have lost all control and the plea would fail if he retained what it termed 'partial control'. D was held guilty of careless driving even though he was at the time in a hypoglycaemic state, on the basis that, because he swerved to avoid collision with other vehicles and braked violently, he was apparently exercising **some** conscious control over his vehicle and was therefore 'driving'. This decision has been criticised on the ground that D was incapable of acting in any other fashion because of his hypoglycaemic state. Nevertheless, it was relied on and endorsed by the Court of Appeal in *Attorney-General's Reference (No. 2 of 1992)* [1993] 4 All ER 683 where D drove his lorry into a broken down vehicle on the motorway hard shoulder. He claimed automatism through a condition known as 'driving without awareness'. However, because D retained some, albeit impaired or reduced, control and there had not been total destruction of voluntary control, his plea of automatism was rejected. The case of *Isitt* (1977) 67 Cr App R 44, CA held that D has no defence even though as a result of hysterical amnesia or hysterical fugue he is unaware of 'legal restrictions or moral concern', provided that he knows the facts constituting the offence charged.

 EXERCISE 8.1

- There are other cases where D would be regarded as an automaton even though he is fully conscious. Can you write down an example?
- If D shoots someone, do you think he would be an automaton in either of the following situations?
    — D is acting under an irresistible impulse as a result of a psychopathic disorder.
    — X is holding a loaded gun to D's head threatening to kill D unless D shoots the victim.
- Write down your reasons.

Apart from cases where D is unconscious, automatism includes reflex actions or spasmodic or convulsive acts (*Bratty* v *Attorney-General for Northern Ireland*). The term 'automatism' certainly does not cover cases where D acts under an 'irresistible impulse' (e.g., as a result of a psychopathic disorder) or duress, although these may constitute other defences— diminished responsibility and duress, respectively. In each case, D's muscles perform the relevant acts because they are directed to do so by his conscious mind.

Aside from 'automatic' actions, where D's muscles, albeit without direction of the conscious mind, are causing the actions, D's 'acts' will be classed as involuntary in only very limited circumstances. For example, if D is holding a knife and is held by a more powerful man who forces D to stab the victim, D would be acquitted of any offence.

Another example, according to *Bell* [1984] 3 All ER 842, would be where a motorist is suddenly deprived of control over his vehicle by a sudden blowout or unforeseen brake failure.

It cannot be stressed too strongly that, as will be seen from the foregoing discussion, the legal notion of when conduct is involuntary, and so a complete defence to criminal liability, is extremely narrow and defined purely in **physical** terms. It will not be an easy plea for a defendant to sustain. In the courts' eyes, there is no room here for a wider concept of **moral** involuntariness—that would open the door to all sorts of considerations of the individual's background and motivation, and the social context of his actions, which the law's generally uncompromising emphasis on individual responsibility seeks to avoid. As we shall see later, the law has been forced by general notions of fairness to counter-balance the narrowness of physical involuntariness with a defence of duress to excuse a 'morally' involuntary defendant who commits a 'crime' only due to unbearable pressure brought about by threats of serious harm.

8.3.2 Insane or non-insane automatism?

> **?** **QUESTION** 8.1
>
> Do you remember from our discussion on insanity, when automatism will be classed as insane automatism?

If a defendant raises the defence of automatism, the first question to be decided is whether it is insane or non-insane automatism. If the automatism is caused by a disease of the mind, i.e., an internal bodily disorder, it is classed as insane automatism and the court's verdict will be 'not guilty by reason of insanity'. (See 7.4.2.1 for the meaning of disease of the mind.) If it is caused by an external factor, e.g., the taking of medication, it will be non-insane automatism. This may not be easy to decide where the condition is due to a combination of both internal and external factors. In *Roach* [2001] EWCA Crim 2698, D claimed to be in a state of automatism due to the interaction of prescribed drugs and alcohol on his latent mental illness. The trial judge treated this as a plea of insane automatism and refused to leave the defence of non-insane automatism to the jury. The Court of Appeal disapproved and held that if the external factors affected 'an underlying condition which would not otherwise produce a state of automatism', the defence of non-insane automatism ought to be left to the jury.

Naturally, an insanity verdict, bringing with it the possibility (or certainty if the charge is murder) of indefinite detention in a secure mental hospital, would be disastrous for the accused. Therefore, D will, in almost every case, be contending for non-insane automatism, which, if successful, will result in a complete acquittal without strings. However, where D's state is due to a disease of the mind, the judge is entitled to rule that D's plea is in fact one of insanity.

> **?** **QUESTION** 8.2
>
> Why would automatism caused by a disease of the mind be legal insanity? Refer back to the section on insanity if you cannot answer.

8.3.3 Non-insane automatism

The most frequent cause of non-insane automatism is the taking of drugs, which are often, but not necessarily, medically prescribed. We have already seen that the injection of insulin can give rise to automatism. Equally, it is possible for barbiturates and tranquillisers to result in an automatic state, and drugs taken for 'kicks', such as hallucinogenic drugs like LSD.

Is it the case that non-insane automatism is always a defence resulting in every case in a no-strings acquittal? The answer is that it is **always** a defence to crimes requiring proof of 'specific intent' for a conviction. For all other offences, the defence could well be lost if the automatism was 'self-induced'. As we shall see below, there are detailed rules governing the position where the offence charged is not one requiring specific intent.

8.3.3.1 Crimes of specific intent

If D does not have the *mens rea* for a crime of specific intent due to his non-insane automatism, he must be acquitted, however the **non-insane** automatism arose. (The only exception to this would be where D formed the appropriate *mens rea* before becoming an automaton and deliberately got himself into a state of automatism hoping to commit the offence in that state.) Remember that we are assuming that the automatism here was not due to a disease of the mind, since that would, of course, constitute insane automatism.

The crucial question to be answered, therefore, is what constitutes an offence of **specific intent**. As we shall see, this question is also critical in considering the defence of intoxication and most of the textbooks discuss it under that head. Regrettably, the concept of specific intent is shrouded in mystery and the courts have proved unable or unwilling to give a satisfactory theoretical explanation of the difference between crimes of specific intent and other crimes (usually referred to as crimes of **basic intent**). In truth there is no satisfactory explanation which fits all the case law and the courts' categorisation of offences as specific or basic intent crimes is based largely on public policy. It is no coincidence that specific intent crimes tend to be serious offences of violence, which have a safety net of still serious but lesser offences of violence which have been designated basic intent crimes. The consequence is that, although D may be acquitted of the specific intent crime, he may still be convicted of the basic intent crime.

Lord Simon in *DPP* v *Morgan* [1975] 2 All ER 347 (*Cases and Materials* (8.5.2)) defined a specific intent crime as one where the *mens rea* 'goes beyond the contemplation of the *actus reus*' whereas the *mens rea* of a basic intent crime 'corresponds exactly' to the *actus reus* of the crime.

EXERCISE 8.2

On that basis, tick those of the following crimes which would be specific intent crimes:

- battery;
- s. 18 of the Offences Against the Person Act 1861;
- murder.

For example, the *actus reus* of battery is an application of unlawful force to the victim. *Mens rea* is intention or subjective recklessness as to the application of such force. It is therefore a basic intent crime. On the other hand, s. 18 of the Offences Against the Person Act 1861 is a crime of specific intent because not only must D have *mens rea* in relation to the *actus reus* of the 'wounding', but he also needs a further or ulterior intention to do grievous bodily harm. The *mens rea* goes beyond what is needed for the *actus reus*.

The difficulty with this definition is that it does not accord with the case law. For example, murder has been held time and again to be an offence of specific intent. Yet the *mens rea* needed—an intention to kill—'corresponds exactly' with the *actus reus*—killing. Indeed, far from going beyond the *actus reus*, it can fall short of it in that a mere intention to cause grievous bodily harm short of death suffices for the *mens rea*. A similar argument may be applied to a s. 18 of the OAPA 1861 charge based on 'causing grievous bodily harm with intent to do grievous bodily harm'.

For this reason, Lord Simon modified his stance in *DPP* v *Majewski* [1976] 2 All ER 142, HL (*Cases and Materials* (8.3.3.1)), the leading case on the defence of intoxication. He said that his definition of 'ulterior intent' in *Morgan* was simply one kind of 'specific intent'. 'The *mens rea* in a crime of specific intent requires proof of a purposive element.'

? **QUESTION** 8.3

Can you guess what he means by 'purposive element'?

He appears to mean a direct intent or aim (i.e., purpose) as opposed to subjective recklessness. Therefore, if proof of intention and intention alone is sufficient, and subjective recklessness is not enough, the crime will be one of specific intent. Whilst this would explain murder being a specific intent crime (at least after the redefinition of murder in *Moloney* [1985] 1 All ER 1025, although not at the date of Lord Simon's pronouncement when *Hyam* [1974] 2 All ER 41 held sway), it seems inconsistent with the classification of rape as a crime of basic intent (*Woods* [1982] Crim LR 42). Rape requires a 'purposive element', namely, an intent to have non-consensual sexual intercourse. It is easy to see why the courts have classed rape as a basic intent crime. It would be possible to commit a rape without causing any injuries (e.g., by threats of violence) and, in such a case, acquittal of rape might leave only the relatively trivial offence of indecent assault available. Even where serious injury did result enabling a conviction under s. 20 of the OAPA 1861, for example, this would not be seen as a true reflection of the nature of the offence.

The lack of a satisfactory definition of specific intent means that it is necessary simply to learn a list of those offences which have been regarded as specific intent offences by the courts and those which have been regarded as basic intent offences. Specific intent offences include murder, s. 18 of the OAPA 1861, theft and attempts. Basic intent offences include manslaughter, rape, assault, battery, ss. 47 and 20 of the OAPA 1861 and criminal damage.

? **QUESTION** 8.4

What is the effect of non-insane automatism in respect of specific intent crimes? Go back to 8.3.3 if you cannot answer.

8.3.3.2 Crimes not requiring specific intent

The rules here are more complicated and mean that D may often be convicted even though he was in a state of non-insane automatism. Whether D will be convicted depends largely on whether or not his automatism was **self-induced**.

If the non-insane automatism is not self-induced, then D cannot be guilty of the offence even if it is not a specific intent offence. An example would be where D crashed his car after being knocked unconscious by a stone thrown through the window whilst he was driving. He could not be convicted of careless driving, still less dangerous driving or criminal damage. Another example would be an automatic state caused by the taking of drugs in accordance with medical advice and prescription, unless, perhaps, D was aware that this might lead to automatism. (This is implicit in the Court of Appeal's judgment in *Bailey* [1983] 2 All ER 503, the leading case on self-induced automatism.)

8.3.3.3 Self-induced automatism

The basic notion underlying self-induced automatism is that D is in some way at fault in getting into the automatic state. Thus, if D takes a drug, other than one medically prescribed or in a greater dosage than prescribed (*Lipman* [1969] 3 All ER 410, CA) or fails to eat food after taking insulin for his diabetes or takes alcohol against advice whilst on medication (*Quick* [1973] 3 All ER 247, CA; *Bailey*), his automatism is self-induced.

Similarly, where D falls asleep whilst driving his car, the onset of the automatic state is reasonably foreseeable when D feels tired before he actually falls asleep, and so it would be regarded as self-induced automatism. Alternatively, it could be said that it would be negligent to continue driving when D felt tired. Therefore, D would commit careless driving before he became an automaton.

What is the result of the automatism being self-induced in a crime not requiring specific intent? *Bailey* lays down the following rules:

(a) If the automatism was caused by D's voluntarily intoxicating himself with alcohol or a 'dangerous' drug, the normal rules governing the defence of intoxication set out in *DPP* v *Majewski* [1976] 2 All ER 142, HL apply. This means that, even though D does not have the necessary *mens rea* for the basic intent crime, he is nevertheless always guilty. The self-induced automatism will **never** be a defence. The theory behind this is that it is common knowledge to everyone that alcohol and 'dangerous' drugs can cause states where D is unaware of what he is doing and may become aggressive and violent whilst in such a state.

A 'dangerous' drug is one commonly perceived to be 'liable to cause unpredictability or aggressiveness' such as LSD and crack (*Hardie* [1984] 3 All ER 848, CA). The intoxication rules do not apply to 'non-dangerous' drugs such as sedative-type, tranquillising drugs (in *Hardie*, valium), since it is not common knowledge that such drugs can give rise to automatic states where the accused becomes unpredictable and violent. This situation is governed by rule (b) below. This is true even if a sedative or soporific drug is taken in excessive quantities (*Hardie*). (In fact it is well known to medical experts that valium and other drugs in the benzodiazepine group although given clinically as sedatives and relaxants, can increase aggression as in *Webb*, Archbold News, 29 April 1994 (unreported)—see Law Com. No. 229, para. 5.42.)

(b) If the automatism was due to the taking of a non-dangerous drug or to some other cause such as a diabetic's failure to eat after taking insulin, D will not be convicted of a basic intent crime **unless** the prosecution can prove 'the necessary element of recklessness. In cases of assault, if the accused knows that his actions or inaction are likely to make him aggressive, unpredictable or uncontrolled with the result that he may cause some injury to others and he persists in the action or takes no remedial action when he knows it is required', he will be judged reckless and found guilty (*Bailey*). It would seem to follow from this that what is required is **subjective** recklessness (**before** the onset of the automatism), not only as to the possibility of becoming an automaton but of engaging in aggressive, unpredictable or uncontrolled behaviour whilst an automaton. *Caldwell*-type recklessness will not do.

> **? QUESTION** 8.5
>
> Why does the law require the prosecution to prove that D realised he might become 'aggressive, unpredictable or uncontrolled' in the case of non-dangerous drugs, but not in the case of dangerous drugs?

The rationale of this is that where alcohol and dangerous drugs are involved, it is universally known that dangerous, impulsive behaviour may result and therefore D is **conclusively** presumed to have the necessary recklessness. In the other cases, which we have just examined, such knowledge cannot be presumed and therefore the prosecution is required to prove in every case that D had actually appreciated the possible consequences of what he was doing or failing to do prior to the onset of automatism.

Finally, it should be noted that sometimes an offence may be committed before the onset of automatism. For example, a defendant who falls asleep whilst driving will have committed the offence of careless driving **prior** to falling asleep because he would be negligent in not stopping to drive when he felt tired before he nodded off (*Kay* v *Butterworth* (1947) 173 LT 191; *Moses* v *Winder* [1980] Crim LR 232). The prosecution can prove the *actus reus* and the necessary fault element without recourse to what happened whilst D was in the automatic state.

You will find the flow chart on automatism reproduced in the summary at the end of this chapter an extremely useful guide to the law.

8.3.4 Reform

The draft Criminal Code Bill provides for a defence of automatism which would apply to all offences including strict liability offences (Law Com. No. 177, cl. 33). It would apply where (a) D is conscious but his act is 'a reflex, spasm or convulsion' and (b) D is 'in a condition (whether of sleep, unconsciousness, impaired consciousness or otherwise) depriving him of effective control of the act'. The reference to 'impaired consciousness' would reverse the harsh rule in *Broome* v *Perkins*. There is a sting in the tail of cl. 33 which takes away the defence given by cl. 33(1)(a) if the act or condition is due to (a) voluntary intoxication or (b) something 'done or omitted with the fault required for the offence' (cl. 33(1)(b)). Thus, if in a crime of negligence, D exhibits negligence in getting himself into the automatous state, he will be guilty. This may be seen as an exception to the rule requiring the coincidence of *mens rea*/fault and *actus reus*. Finally, you should realise that if the automatism is attributable to 'mental disorder', the verdict must be 'not guilty on evidence of mental disorder' (cl. 36). This corresponds to the current distinction between non-insane and insane automatism (see *Cases and Materials* (8.3.4 and 7.4.4) for the full text of cll. 33 and 36).

8.4 Intoxication

8.4.1 Introduction

'This area of the law is controversial, as regards the content of the rules, their intellectual foundations, and their capacity to furnish a practical and just solution' (Lord Mustill in *Kingston* [1994] 3 All ER 353, HL).

If the defendant commits the offence whilst intoxicated, will this excuse him from criminal liability? The answer is generally no, but there are significant exceptions to that general rule.

Further, it should be noted that generally the following discussion concerns intoxicants knowingly and voluntarily taken, although we do deal with the special rules governing **involuntary** intoxication. The rules governing intoxication are the same whether the intoxication is due to alcohol or other dangerous drugs such as LSD (*Lipman* [1970] 1 QB 152, CA; *DPP* v *Majewski* [1977] AC 142, HL). The Court of Appeal in *Hardie* [1984] 3 All ER 848 held that different rules apply to voluntarily taken 'non-dangerous' drugs, i.e., sedative and soporific drugs, where there is not common knowledge that they can cause the taker to become aggressive and unpredictable. The precise classification of drugs into 'dangerous' and 'non-dangerous' awaits clarification by the courts. In *Hardie*, valium was regarded as 'non-dangerous'. Cocaine, heroin, amphetamines and hallucinogens like LSD, would all, presumably, be 'dangerous', but it is questionable whether opiates like heroin would make anyone 'aggressive and unpredictable'.

8.4.2 The basic rules

(a) The general rule is that voluntary intoxication, by alcohol or dangerous drugs, is **not** a defence even if it prevents D having the *mens rea* normally required for the crime charged.

(b) However, exceptionally, it will be a defence if:
   (i) it brings on a distinct disease of the mind such as delirium tremens so that D is insane within the M'Naghten Rules (*Attorney-General for Northern Ireland* v *Gallagher* [1963] AC 349, HL); or
   (ii) the crime as charged is a crime of specific intent and the intoxication prevents D from having the necessary specific intent (*DPP* v *Majewski* [1976] 2 All ER 142, HL).

(c) It is **never** a defence to crimes of basic intent or which as charged can be satisfied by proof of recklessness, whether subjective or objective (*Caldwell* [1982] AC 341, HL).

(d) There appear to be special rules governing the effect of intoxication on other defences, such as self-defence, which are out of line with the principle in (b)(ii) above (*O'Grady* [1987] 3 All ER 420, CA; *O'Connor* [1991] Crim LR 135, CA; *Hatton* [2005] EWCA Crim) 2951.

(e) Involuntary intoxication will be a defence to any crime, whether of specific or basic intent, but only if it prevents D having the *mens rea* for the crime charged (*Kingston* [1994] 3 All ER 353, HL).

8.4.3 Insanity

If the drink or drugs trigger a distinct disease of the mind, e.g., permanent damage to the brain cells, and as a result D does not know either the nature and quality of his act or that it is wrong, he will be insane within the M'Naghten Rules.

? QUESTION 8.6

Does this apply where the effect of the drink is only transient and does not cause permanent damage to the brain? If you cannot answer refer back to the discussion of *Quick* at 7.4.2.1.

You may recall that if the drink causes 'an abnormality of mind' it can only be diminished responsibility if it results in permanent injury to the brain (see *Fenton* (1975) 61 Cr App R 261, CA).

8.4.4 **Specific and basic intent**

It is evident from the principles stated above that the key to whether voluntary intoxication can be a defence is whether the offence charged is one of specific intent or basic intent. Only if it is a crime of specific intent is there a **chance** that voluntary intoxication **might** be a defence.

Lord Mustill's cryptic obiter remark in *Kingston* [1994] 3 All ER 353, HL that 'it has not yet been decisively established whether…there is a line to be drawn between offences of "'specific'" and of "basic intent"'' is puzzling in the light of *Majewski*, but can perhaps be explained as a nod in the direction of the blurring of that distinction by the House of Lords in *Caldwell* considered below.

 QUESTION 8.7

Where have you previously encountered the specific intent/basic intent distinction?

 EXERCISE 8.3

Re-read the section on specific intent and basic intent at 8.3.3.1 above to refresh your memory on the distinction between the two. This will also give you the answer to the last Question.

In summary, the hallmark of a specific intent crime is that it 'requires proof of a purposive element' (Lord Simon in *DPP* v *Majewski*). This seems to mean an offence where intention and intention alone suffices for a conviction. The House of Lords in *Caldwell* [1981] 1 All ER 961 (*Cases and Materials* (8.4.4)) was certainly of the view that *Majewski* decided that self-induced intoxication can never be a defence to a crime which, **as charged**, is satisfied by proof of mere recklessness (whether subjective or objective), or less.

This rule in *Caldwell* has curious consequences. Under s. 1(2) of the Criminal Damage Act 1971 it is an offence intentionally or recklessly to damage or destroy property with intent to endanger life or being reckless thereto. Before *Caldwell*, this was universally regarded as a crime of specific intent because *mens rea* was required as to a matter going beyond the *actus reus*—what Lord Simon defined as 'ulterior intent'. It contrasted with ordinary criminal damage under s. 1(1) which required only *mens rea* in relation to the *actus reus*, namely intentionally or recklessly damaging another's property.

 QUESTION 8.8

Since *Caldwell*, can you see that how the prosecution frames its charges is crucial?

According to *Caldwell*, whether voluntary intoxication is available as a defence to a charge under s. 1(2) depends not on whether the offence is one of specific or basic intent but on how the prosecution frames its charge. If it charges D with **intentionally** damaging property **with intent to** endanger life, then the defence of intoxication is potentially available. On the other hand if the charge is framed in terms of the alternative *mens rea*, namely, **recklessly** damaging property **being reckless** as to the endangering of life, then self-induced intoxication **cannot** be a defence. *Caldwell* can be read as marginalising the hitherto central distinction between specific intent and basic intent crimes. What matters is not how the offence charged is classified but whether, on the basis of that charge, the prosecution **must** prove intention and intention alone. If so, intoxication which prevents D having that intent is a defence. However, if the charge requires the prosecution to prove something less than intent, such as recklessness, the self-induced intoxication cannot be a defence. Putting it another way, a voluntarily intoxicated person is to be regarded as having been aware of any risk or circumstance of which he would have been aware had he been sober (*Bennett* [1995] Crim LR 877, CA). Possibly this is what Lord Mustill was referring to in the passage cited at the beginning of 8.4.4. The case of *G* (see 3.4.3 above) which rejected *Caldwell*'s definition of recklessness did not involve any suggestion of intoxication on the part of the defendants and no opinion was expressed on the views advanced in *Caldwell* on the intoxication aspects. Consequently, the position is unaffected by *G*.

8.4.5 The rule for specific intent crimes

As we have seen (subject to the *Caldwell* complications), whenever the intoxication actually prevents D having the *mens rea* necessary for the specific intent crime, D must be acquitted of that crime. You should be aware that the intoxication does not have to render D **incapable** of forming the necessary *mens rea*. The question is simply: has he or has he not formed that *mens rea* (*Pordage* [1975] Crim LR 575; *Sheehan* [1975] 1 WLR 739, CA)? We should emphasise that if D does in fact have the necessary *mens rea*, his intoxication will be irrelevant to liability. The fact that he would not have committed the crime had he been sober, has no effect on liability.

One exception to the first mentioned rule is the so-called 'Dutch courage' situation. Here, if D forms the necessary intention before he gets himself intoxicated, using the intoxicant to give himself Dutch courage, he will be guilty of the offence if he performs the *actus reus,* notwithstanding that at the moment of such performance he did not have the appropriate *mens rea* because of the intoxication (*Attorney-General for Northern Ireland* v *Gallagher* [1963] AC 349, HL).

Offences which the courts have decided are specific intent offences include murder, s. 18 of the OAPA 1861, attempt, theft, robbery and burglary. We noted above that with the offences of violence, there are less serious, basic intent crimes, i.e., manslaughter, s. 20 of the OAPA 1861 or s. 47 of that Act, waiting as a safety net to catch people acquitted of a specific intent charge. However, the same is not true of the property offences where there may be no lesser offence available if D is acquitted of the specific intent offence.

8.4.6 The rule for basic intent crimes

Voluntary intoxication is no defence to a crime of basic intent **even if** it prevents D having the *mens rea* as long as D would have had the requisite *mens rea* (foresight) had he been sober. According to *Majewski*, there is 'a substantive rule of law that in crimes of basic intent the factor of intoxication is irrelevant'. This means that where D claims that he did not have the necessary *mens rea* for the offence due to intoxication, the law says that no such *mens rea* need be proved. Therefore, it is positively detrimental to D to claim the defence of intoxication in a crime of basic intent because it immediately relieves the prosecution of the necessity to prove that D had the *mens rea* normally required. **No *mens rea* need be proved where its absence is due to D's intoxication.**

It is this principle which enables the courts to sidestep s. 8 of the Criminal Justice Act 1967 even though, at first sight, the rules on intoxication appear to contradict that section. You may remember that s. 8 states that wherever it is necessary to prove intention or foresight on the part of D, the court must satisfy itself that D actually had the prescribed intention or foresight by looking at 'all the evidence' which, since it is not excluded by the section, presumably includes evidence of intoxication. It would appear, therefore, that if the offence requires proof of some intention or foresight on the part of D and he has not got it because of intoxication, s. 8 should ensure his acquittal of the offence (irrespective of whether the offence is specific intent or basic intent). However, s. 8 is only a rule of evidence and instructs the court **how** intention or foresight must be proved **if and when** the substantive definition of the offence requires it. If, therefore, the offence does not require proof of any intention or foresight, then s. 8 has no application—it never comes into play. In order to square this circle and to avoid the application of s. 8, the House of Lords in *Majewski* has, in effect, redefined at a stroke **all** basic intent offences so as not to require proof of any intention or foresight where its absence is due to D's intoxication, even though, whenever D is not intoxicated, intention or foresight is required! Judicial sleight of hand!

Whilst these rules defy logical analysis, they can be explained by the courts' understandable desire severely to curtail the possibility of intoxication defences succeeding. As was said in *Majewski*, 'acceptance generally of intoxication as a defence would undermine the criminal law'. The House in *Majewski* justified the rule governing basic intent crimes in the following terms:

> His course of conduct in reducing himself by drink and drugs to that condition in my view supplies the evidence of *mens rea*, of guilty mind. Certainly for crimes of basic intent it is a reckless course of conduct and recklessness is enough to constitute the necessary *mens rea* in assault cases, *Venna* [*per* Lord Elwyn-Jones LC].

You may think that this seems a reasonable enough proposition: D is reckless in getting himself into an intoxicated state and since the crime requires proof only of recklessness, it is correct to convict him. Unfortunately the reasoning has a number of flaws.

First, it does not require proof that D himself realised that he might become intoxicated and unpredictable or uncontrolled in his behaviour; rather it **conclusively presumes** that D realised this (on the basis that the effects of taking alcohol and dangerous drugs are common knowledge—but remember the position in relation to non-dangerous drugs is different (*Hardie*)). Second, even if there is *mens rea*, it does not coincide in time with the *actus reus* which is performed whilst in the state of intoxication. Third, the recklessness in question is recklessness in a **general** sense of realising one might become unpredictable or uncontrolled, whereas the recklessness required normally for a basic intent offence is much more **particular**, e.g., s. 20 of the OAPA 1861 requires foresight of harm to another at the moment of acting. Is it self-evident that a person taking LSD, amphetamines or barbiturates **always** foresees that he might harm someone during his state of intoxication?

8.4.7 Intoxication and defences

The law here is particularly confused and lacking in principle and does not even adhere to the standard specific intent/basic intent dichotomy described above.

The issue of intoxication arises in relation to defences where D, due to his intoxicated state, makes a mistake about the situation, which if true would give him a defence to the crime. We explore in detail the effect of mistake on criminal liability at 8.5 below where, in some cases, the mistake would only be relevant if it were reasonable, whereas in other cases even an unreasonable mistake could be a defence. You may find it easier to read that section before considering the material under the present sub-heading. The point to be made here is that, by definition, a mistake caused by voluntary intoxication will always be unreasonable.

8.4.7.1 Justificatory defences

Actions performed in self-defence or in the prevention of crime are justified as long as only reasonable and necessary force is used (see 8.6 below). If D mistakenly believes he is being attacked or is preventing a crime, it does not matter that his mistake is unreasonable. His mistake prevents him from forming the necessary intention to apply **unlawful** force (*Williams* (1984) 78 Cr App R 276, CA; *Beckford v R* [1988] AC 130, PC).

If that mistake is a drunken mistake, D would still lack the *mens rea* required for the crime and one would expect the normal principles governing voluntary intoxication to apply.

> **? QUESTION** 8.9
>
> What would be the result of applying those 'normal' principles if the charge was (a) s. 18 of the OAPA 1861 and (b) s. 20 of the OAPA 1861?

On normal principles, the intoxication would be a defence to a crime of specific intent but not to a crime of basic intent or one involving recklessness. Thus, if D causes grievous bodily harm to V because, due to D's intoxicated state, he mistakenly believes that V is about to attack and kill him, he should, on principle, not be guilty under s. 18, a specific intent crime, but he should be guilty under s. 20, a basic intent crime. For the purposes of s. 18, D lacks the specific intent to do **unlawful** grievous bodily harm. Equally, for s. 20, he lacks the intent to inflict **unlawful** harm nor, because he believes he is acting in lawful self-defence, does he realise he might be inflicting **unlawful** harm. However, for the basic intent crime of s. 20 absence of *mens rea* due to alcohol is no defence (*Majewski*).

However, the Court of Appeal in *O'Grady* [1987] 3 All ER 411 (*Cases and Materials* (8.4.7.1)) took a different view. It stated quite baldly that a defendant 'is not entitled to rely, so far as self-defence is concerned, upon a mistaken belief that one is under attack which has been induced by voluntary intoxication'. Thus, it would appear that even if the offence charged is a specific intent offence like murder or s. 18, the drunken mistake has no effect on liability. Despite its inconsistency with general principle, *O'Grady* was followed by the Court of Appeal in *O'Connor* [1991] Crim LR 135. However, in both cases these statements appear to have been made obiter and it seemed to be open to a future Court of Appeal to reassert the *Majewski* principle. It appears that Lord Lane CJ in *O'Grady* ignored the decisions in *Kimber* and *Williams* that the term 'unlawful' is a definitional element of the offence. He 'moved from the definitional analysis to the defence analysis' enabling him to disregard the relevance of whether the crime was one of specific or basic intent (see M. Giles [1990] MLR 187, 197 and 8.5.3 and 8.6.5). However, the Court of Appeal in *Hatton* [2005] EWCA Crim 2951 chose to endorse *O'Grady* and *O'Connor* and refused to accept that those decisions were obiter in respect of murder and other specific intent crimes. In their view, the cases were expressed to be founded upon a general principle which applied to all crimes, namely that mistakes of fact brought about by self-induced intoxication were to be ignored and the defendant judged on the facts as they were, not as he drunkenly perceived them to be. That principle was binding on future Courts of Appeal in respect of all crimes since it was not expressed to be confined to manslaughter or basic intent crimes and was clearly intended to be generally applicable.

The case of *Richardson and Irwin* [1999] 1 Cr App R 392, CA appears to go to the opposite extreme to *O'Grady* and is also inconsistent with the *Majewski* principle. The accused dropped the victim over a balcony during a bout of drunken, student horseplay, causing him GBH. On a charge under s. 20 of the OAPA 1861 (a basic intent crime), the accused asserted that, as a result of a drunken mistake, they believed that V had consented to the horseplay in circumstances which would have rendered the force applied not unlawful. The Court thought that this would negate liability seemingly because Ds would not have the *mens rea*—realisation that they might cause harm which, in the circumstances they believed to exist, would be unlawful. Thus the fundamental *Majewski* principle that voluntary intoxication by alcohol can never be a defence to a crime of basic intent even where it negates *mens rea* was overlooked. Neither *O'Grady* and *Hatton* nor *Richardson* can be supported.

8.4.7.2 Excusatory defences

This is largely concerned with the defences of duress in both its forms and provocation. It is clear from the formulation in *Graham* [1982] 1 All ER 801, CA (approved by the House of Lords in *Howe* [1987] 1 AC 417 and *Hasan* [2005] UKHL 22 discussed at 9.3.1.1 below) that if D unreasonably believes that he is being subjected to duress, his plea of duress must fail. It would seem to follow that a drunken mistake as to duress will be no defence. Exactly the same reasoning applies to duress of circumstances (see *Martin* [1989] 1 All ER 652, CA and 9.4 below).

The same should be true of the defence of provocation where, because of his intoxication, D mistakenly believes that he is being provoked when he is not. However, in *Letenock* (1917) 12 Cr App R 221, CCA it was held that, in such a case, D must be judged as if the facts were as he mistakenly believed them to be. However, this is out of line with the current attitude of the courts and the case may well not be followed in the future.

8.4.7.3 Specific statutory defences

For a number of offences, the statute expressly provides that D is not guilty if he holds a certain specified belief. For example, s. 2(1)(a) of the Theft Act 1968 provides that D is not dishonest and can therefore not be convicted of theft if he genuinely believes he has a right to the property he takes. The belief need not be reasonable (*Holden* [1991] Crim LR 480). It seems likely that a drunken mistake leading to D having such a belief will be a defence. Whilst this may be satisfactory and in accordance with principle where the offence concerned is, like theft, one of specific intent (*Ruse* v *Read* [1949] 1 All ER 398, DC), the same is not true where the offence is one of basic intent. Yet the same principle applies (*Jaggard* v *Dickinson* [1980] 3 All ER 716, DC—*Cases and Materials* (8.4.7.3)).

The facts of *Jaggard* v *Dickinson* were simple. D was drunk and there was no doubt that she intentionally broke windows in X's house to gain entry. However, due to her voluntary intoxication, she mistakenly thought the house belonged to her friend, Y, with whom she lived. She believed, correctly as it turned out, that her friend would have consented to her damaging the windows of her house to get into the property. D was charged with criminal damage under s. 1(1) of the Criminal Damage Act 1971.

 EXERCISE 8.4

Read ss. 1(1), 5(2)(a) and 5(3) of the Criminal Damage Act 1971 in *Cases and Materials* (12.10.1 and 12.10.2.1) and then answer the following:

- In the circumstances of *Jaggard* v *Dickinson* was the damage done 'without lawful excuse'? Write down your reason.
- Would it have mattered if Y had given evidence to say that he would not have consented to D's breaking in to the house?
- If D, because of her intoxication, had mistakenly thought that X's house was her own, would she have been guilty of criminal damage?

The Divisional Court quashed D's conviction for the basic intent crime of criminal damage under s. 1(1) of the Criminal Damage Act 1971. Under s. 5(2) of the Criminal Damage Act 1971 a person has a lawful excuse if he honestly believes that the owner would have consented to the damage to his property in those circumstances. Of course, if D had been sober, she would have realised that the property was not her friend's and that the owner would not consent to the damage. However, despite the fact that her mistake was due to intoxication, the court held that she did have a lawful excuse and was not guilty because of her honestly held belief. It was irrelevant whether the mistake stemmed from stupidity, forgetfulness, inattention or intoxication. Equally, if D actually believed that the owner would have consented it would not matter whether the belief was correct or not.

One might have expected the court to have held that a drunken belief in consent was irrelevant where it related to a basic intent crime, thus aligning with the general position on intoxication. Its decision not to so decide leads to anomalous results. If D, because of intoxication, thinks another's property is his own, he will be convicted of criminal damage, despite his lack of *mens rea*, because it is a basic intent crime. On the other hand, according to *Jaggard* v *Dickinson*, if, because of his intoxication, he mistakenly believes the property belongs to Y and that Y would consent to him damaging it, he has a defence!

The Law Commission would apply the general rule to specific statutory defences based on belief by providing that D can only rely on his mistaken belief if he would have held it had he not been intoxicated (Law Com. No. 229, para. 7.18).

8.4.8 Involuntary intoxication

The most obvious example is where D is unknowingly drugged or has his drinks spiked. However, it is also regarded as including some instances of self-administered drugs, namely, where drugs are taken strictly in accordance with medical advice. If the stated dose is exceeded or mixed with other drugs and/or alcohol against medical advice, the intoxication will be regarded as voluntary. According to *Allen* [1988] Crim LR 698, CA the intoxication is not involuntary where D knows he is drinking alcohol but mistakes its strength.

If D is involuntarily intoxicated, he has a defence to **any** crime including those of basic intent, whenever his intoxication negatives the *mens rea* (*Majewski*). However, what if the involuntary intoxication does **not** prevent D having the *mens rea* for the crime charged? Until the Court of Appeal decision in *Kingston* [1993] 4 All ER 373, it would have been regarded as axiomatic that D would have to be found guilty because he had the *mens rea* and the fact that this was due to involuntary intoxication could affect only sentence and not liability.

In *Kingston* there was evidence that D had been given coffee which, unknown to him, had been spiked with sedatives. Following this he intentionally, as the jury found, indecently assaulted a young boy. In a short-lived decision, the Court of Appeal, quashing D's conviction, ruled that if the surreptitiously administered drink or drug caused D 'to lose his self-control and for that reason to form an intent which he would not otherwise have formed...the law should exculpate him because the operative fault was not his. The law permitted a finding that the intent formed was not a criminal intent or, in other words, that the involuntary intoxication negatived the *mens rea*.'

The Court in this case invented an entirely new principle employing novel concepts lacking in clarity. For example, the notion of 'criminal intent' in the sense used here was previously unknown and creates great imprecision because it depends on the jury's speculation as to whether D would have formed the intent and have done what he did without the involuntary intoxication. How could that have been answered in *Kingston* itself? Put another way, the Court seemed to be formulating an entirely new and alarmingly vague defence for a defendant who performs the *actus reus* with the necessary *mens rea*. He would not be guilty if the *mens rea* arose out of circumstances for which he was blameless.

Not surprisingly the House of Lords overruled the Court of Appeal's decision (*Kingston* [1994] 3 All ER 353—*Cases and Materials* (8.4.8)), holding that if D commits the *actus reus* with the *mens rea* prescribed by the offence charged, then he must be guilty of that offence notwithstanding that D exhibits no moral fault in forming that *mens rea*—in the instant case because of involuntary intoxication. The House emphasised that *mens rea* referred to the technical state of mind defined by the crime charged rather than the moral character of D's state of mind, so that the fact that D might be free of any moral blame is irrelevant to criminal **liability**, although relevant when it comes to sentencing for the crime. Therefore, if D forms the intent prescribed by the offence, for whatever reason, he **does** have the necessary criminal intent.

The House also rejected the argument that there was or should be created a new exculpatory defence excusing liability for 'crimes' committed whilst involuntarily intoxicated. If such a defence existed, it would presumably operate (in a way similar to duress) to negative liability even though D had the necessary *actus reus* and *mens rea*. The House's firm view was that there was no distinct defence of involuntary intoxication. In terms of criminal **liability**, involuntary intoxication had to be ignored unless it prevented D forming the required *mens rea*, or brought on a state of insanity or automatism at the time of the prohibited acts. It was certainly insufficient that it merely loosened or destroyed D's inhibitions causing him to commit the offence.

The Law Commission would preserve the current rule that involuntary intoxication would be a defence only if it negatives any necessary fault element in the crime (Law Com. No. 229—cl. 1(4) of its draft Criminal Law (Intoxication) Bill). However, cl. 5 gives a clear definition of what constitutes involuntary intoxication (*Cases and Materials* (8.4.8)).

8.4.9 Self-induced intoxication by non-dangerous drugs

> **? QUESTION** 8.10
>
> Do you recall from the previous section on automatism how self-induced intoxication by a non-dangerous drug affects liability?
> Does the specific intent/basic intent distinction matter in this situation?

Following from hints in *Bailey* regarding the injection of insulin, the Court of Appeal in *Hardie* [1984] 3 All ER 848 adopted different rules where the intoxication, though voluntary in the sense that it is voluntarily taken and self-induced, is due to a 'non-dangerous' drug. 'Non-dangerous' drug implies one that does not normally lead to aggressive and unpredictable behaviour or where it is not common knowledge that it can lead to such behaviour. So far, the only drugs which we can be sure would be classified as 'non-dangerous' would be those like the valium in *Hardie* which are in the benzodiazepine group, although, as we noted at 8.3.3.3, it is well known to medical experts that they can cause aggression. Although barbiturates are sedatives and were commonly prescribed as sleeping tablets at one time, they have an effect similar to alcohol and might be classified as dangerous. The defendant in *Majewski* had taken a mixture of alcohol, amphetamines and barbiturates.

If it is a non-dangerous drug, the rule is that D must be acquitted of any **basic** intent crimes for which, through the intoxication, he has no *mens rea* **unless** the prosecution proves that D actually **knew** he might become aggressive and unpredictable and a risk to persons (in the case of offences of violence), or presumably to property (in the case of criminal damage). This rule applies even if the drug is taken in large quantities and/or is not medically prescribed.

In other words, whereas in the case of alcohol and **dangerous** drugs, there is a **conclusive** presumption that D knows he is liable to become aggressive and unpredictable—it is such common knowledge—in the case of **non-dangerous** drugs, there is no such presumption and the prosecution must establish that D realised what might happen.

Of course, in the case of a specific intent crime, the rule is the same whether the intoxication is through a dangerous drug or a non-dangerous drug—if it negatives the *mens rea* for the crime, D is not guilty.

The Law Commission's intoxication proposals would abolish the 'unsatisfactory' distinction between dangerous and non-dangerous drugs. However, if D took a drug 'solely for medicinal purposes' **and** either (a) on and in accordance with medical advice or (b) he was not aware that it 'might give rise to aggressive or uncontrollable behaviour', he would be regarded as **involuntarily** intoxicated (Law Com. No. 229, paras. 8.21 to 8.30).

8.4.10 **Reform**

The Law Commission's Report on Intoxication and Criminal Liability (Law Com. No. 229 (1995)) represents a remarkable about-turn on the provisional proposals contained in its previous Consultation Paper (Law Com. No. 127) which recommended the radical step of allowing intoxication to be a defence to any offence where it prevented D having the requisite *mens rea*. Thus, the *Majewski* rule and the specific/basic intent dichotomy would have gone. This would have been counterbalanced by the creation of a new offence of 'criminal intoxication'.

It appears that those involved in the 'practical operation' of the law (particularly the judges) have prevailed over academic commentators in persuading the Law Commission to abandon any radical proposals and to keep largely with *Majewski* and the current law, with some minor changes and clarification of the uncertainties.

In order to avoid the uncertainties associated with the specific/basic intent categorisation, the Commission recommends that it be replaced. However, the basic idea of *Majewski* is preserved by allowing intoxication to negative offences of intention but not offences requiring proof of recklessness. Thus, 'a voluntarily intoxicated defendant should be treated as being aware of anything of which he would have been aware but for his intoxication' (para. 1.34). Where a person becomes an automaton through voluntary intoxication, he should be in the same position as any other voluntarily intoxicated person.

The Commission proposes to define both voluntary and involuntary intoxication which would be a big step forward on the current position.

Even accepting the premise that the law should go in the direction proposed, the provisions of the Commission's proposed Criminal Law (Intoxication) Bill seem an unnecessarily complex and convoluted way of achieving it. That was certainly the view of the government when preparing its draft Offences Against the Person Bill (see **Chapter 4**). Although limited in application to the offences created by that Bill, we suspect that cl. 19

(*Cases and Materials* (8.4.10)) would be more likely to form the blueprint for a more general reform than the Commission's proposal. Anyone voluntarily intoxicated would be treated '(a) as having been aware of any risk of which he would have been aware had he not been intoxicated, and (b) as having known or believed in any circumstances which he would have known or believed in had he not been intoxicated'. Voluntary intoxication occurs when D (a) 'takes an intoxicant [i.e., "any alcohol, drug or other thing which, when taken into the body, may impair the awareness or understanding of the person taking it"] otherwise than properly for a medicinal purpose, (b) he is aware that it is or may be an intoxicant, and (c) he takes it in such a quantity as impairs his awareness or understanding' (cl. 19(3)). An intoxicant taken for a medicinal purpose is not taken 'properly' if either it is not taken on medical advice or D fails at any time to comply with any condition forming part of the medical advice to take it and, in both cases, D is aware that, as a result, he may commit the *actus reus* of the offence.

8.5 Mistake

8.5.1 Introduction

Mistake is a topic which has always confused students of the criminal law and this is due, in no small measure, to the fact that the courts have struggled to establish and apply consistent principles.

It is vital to appreciate that although criminal lawyers often refer to the 'defence' of mistake, in fact we are dealing with the other side of the *mens rea* coin in most cases. D is claiming that because of his mistake about the circumstances in which he acted, he did not have the *mens rea* required for the crime charged. This should become clearer later, but first let us summarise the essence of the law on mistake in three intertwined propositions:

(a) Mistake or ignorance of fact about an element of the *actus reus* of the crime charged, whether that mistake is reasonable or unreasonable, will render D not guilty **if** it prevents D having the *mens rea* necessary to constitute the crime charged (*DPP* v *Morgan* [1975] 2 All ER 347, HL; *B* v *DPP* [2000] 1 All ER 833, HL).

(b) Even though the *mens rea* of the offence is not negatived, a **reasonable** mistake as to the facts of the situation will in many cases be a defence **if** D would have been not guilty **had the facts been as D supposed** (*Tolson* (1889) 23 QBD 168).

(c) Ignorance or mistake as to the law is generally no defence, except where the mistake is as to the **civil law** and **it prevents D having the** *mens rea* **necessary for the crime** (*Smith* [1974] 1 All ER 632, CA).

8.5.2 Mistake as to the existence of an element of the *actus reus*

The most important proposition is that D cannot be convicted if he makes a mistake as to an element of the *actus reus* (sometimes called 'a definitional element' of the crime) which prevents D having the *mens rea* of the crime. It does not matter how unreasonable the mistake is. If it is genuine and therefore prevents him having the *mens rea*, he cannot be guilty—because the prosecution cannot prove a fundamental element of the crime. This proposition was firmly established in and is well-illustrated by the case of *DPP* v *Morgan* (*Cases and Materials* (8.5.2)) which provided the popular press of the day with a few column inches and left many members of the public outraged. The result was a redrawing of the offence of rape by means of the Sexual Offences (Amendment) Act 1976, which, incidentally, preserved the principle enunciated by the House of Lords in *Morgan*. (The offence of rape was extended to cover non-consensual intercourse *per anum* with a woman or a man by the Criminal Justice and Public Order Act 1994. Section 1 of the Sexual Offences Act 2003 extends it to cover non-consensual oral penetration by D's penis and redraws the *mens rea* requirement in respect of V's consent in a way considerably less favourable to the accused.)

At the time of *Morgan*, the offence of rape was committed by a man who had vaginal sexual intercourse with a woman without her consent, coupled with an intention to do so. In this case, although the woman did not consent to the sexual intercourse, the defendants claimed that they believed that the woman was consenting. The evidence for this rather incredible claim was that the defendants had been told by the victim's husband, who had invited them home to have sexual intercourse with his wife, that she would pretend to struggle but that they should ignore it because that was how she enhanced her sexual pleasure. The trial judge refused to put this defence to the jury on the basis that, even if such a mistake had been made, it would prevent liability only if it was reasonable, which this mistake clearly was not. By a three to two majority the House of Lords decided that this was a misdirection. The *mens rea* for rape was an intention to have non-consensual sexual intercourse and, if D believes, however unreasonably, that the woman is consenting, he does not have the necessary intention. Although subsequent statutory reform has altered the *mens rea* for rape, it does not affect the general principle laid down in *Morgan*.

In order to illustrate how that principle operates, let us examine some subsequent cases. In *Kimber* [1983] 3 All ER 316, CA, D was charged with indecently assaulting a mentally disordered woman. The issue was whether his admitted indecent interference with her constituted an assault. D claimed to believe that the woman had consented to his action, although she had not.

? QUESTION 8.11

Bearing in mind the *Morgan* principle:

- What do you need to know first before you can assess the effect, if any, of D's mistake, irrespective of whether it is reasonable or unreasonable?
- Battery involves an unlawful touching. What might make a touching lawful? Refer back to 4.3.3.1 if you cannot answer.
- In the light of the facts of *Kimber*, what must the prosecution prove was D's *mens rea* in order to secure his conviction for assault?
- Would it matter if his mistake, assuming it was genuine, was unreasonable?

The court held that the *mens rea* for the assault was an intention to touch V unlawfully and, in these circumstances, that meant without her consent. If D did believe that she was consenting, however unreasonably, he lacked the necessary *mens rea* in respect of the absence of consent and therefore could not be guilty.

 EXERCISE 8.5

Read the case of *Williams* (1984) 78 Cr App R 276 in *Cases and Materials* (8.5.2).

Summarise the Court of Appeal's reasoning on how mistaken self-defence or prevention of crime affects liability. You may find the structure of the last Question helpful in some respects.

Williams was endorsed by the Privy Council in *Beckford* v *R* [1987] 3 All ER 425 so that an honest belief that D was using reasonable and necessary force in the prevention of crime or self-defence means that D lacks the necessary intention to apply **unlawful** force and therefore cannot be guilty of the offence. The prosecution cannot prove the necessary *mens rea*.

This kind of mistake is a mistake relating to a matter forming part of the definition of the crime and it is a mistake which must negative the *mens rea* required by the definition of the crime in respect of the element about which the mistake has been made. Therefore, it should be obvious that the first step in every case where mistake is claimed, must be to decide what must be proved according to that crime in terms of *mens rea* in respect of the part of the *actus reus* about which D is mistaken. Only then can one say whether the mistake will negative liability. The House of Lords in *B* v *DPP* and now *K* (see 8.5.2.3 below) provides a huge endorsement of the *Morgan* principle.

The House of Lords' decision in *Forbes (Giles)* [2001] UKHL 40 provides an example of a mistake which does not negate the *mens rea* and is therefore immaterial. D was convicted of being 'knowingly concerned' in the fraudulent evasion of the prohibition on the importation of prohibited goods contrary to s. 170(2) of the Customs and Excise Management Act 1979. It was held that, as long as D knew or believed he was importing 'prohibited goods', it was irrelevant that he did not appreciate their precise nature, in this case child pornography. The *mens rea* of the offence required only that D should know or believe that the goods being imported were prohibited, not what category of prohibited goods they fell into. Hence a mistake that the videos, though obscene, featured adults rather than children would not negate this *mens rea* because obscene adult pornography is a 'prohibited' good. On the other hand, if D had mistakenly thought that the videos contained adults only and were merely indecent and **not** obscene, his *mens rea* would have been negatived because non-obscene, adult (as opposed to child) videos are not 'prohibited goods' under the legislation.

8.5.2.1 **Crimes of negligence**

Let us suppose that the offence charged requires a fault element only of **negligence** in relation to that part of the *actus reus* about which the mistake has been made.

Would the mistake be a 'defence'? Would it matter whether it was reasonable or unreasonable?

To answer this question we can look at the old case of *Tolson* (1889) 23 QBD 168 (*Cases and Materials* (8.5.2.1)) which involved a prosecution for bigamy. Bigamy is committed by anyone who, whilst already married, 'marries again'. In this case D 'married' again believing incorrectly that her husband had been lost at sea and that she was therefore free to marry. The court held that an honest belief that D was free to marry was insufficient to negative liability. Only if the belief was also based on reasonable grounds would the defendant escape conviction.

At first sight this seems to contradict the principle laid down in *DPP* v *Morgan* and yet it was approved by the House of Lords in that case. The explanation is that, in the eyes of both courts, the prosecution does not need to prove any *mens rea* (in the strict sense) on the part of D in relation to the fact that he is already married at the time of the second ceremony, in order to secure a conviction for bigamy. The only intention required on the part of D for the offence is an intention to go through the second ceremony. A mistake that he is free to marry at this time can have no bearing on that intention. However, by allowing a **reasonable** mistake defence, the courts are in effect incorporating a lesser fault element into the crime of bigamy, namely, negligence as to whether D is already married. Clearly, if D makes an **unreasonable** mistake about this fact, he makes a negligent mistake and, by definition, the prosecution will have established negligence as to the fact that D is already married. (See also *Gould* [1968] 1 All ER 849, CA.) If this mistake is reasonable he cannot by definition be negligent, so that the necessary fault element is missing.

8.5.2.2 **Crimes of strict liability**

Sometimes the courts will hold that an offence requires no fault element at all, not even negligence, in relation to one or more elements of the *actus reus*. Such offences are known as strict liability offences, to which not even a reasonable mistake will be a defence. The classic example is *Prince* [1874–80] All ER Rep 881 involving the offence of abduction later reproduced by s. 20 of the Sexual Offences Act 1956 (but recently repealed in the Sexual Offences Act 2003). D took an unmarried girl under 16 out of the possession of her parents without their consent. He claimed that he believed she was over 16. The court held that the prosecution merely had to prove that she was in fact under 16. D did not have to know she was under 16 or realise she might be under 16 or even be negligent as to the fact that she was under 16. Even if D made the most reasonable mistake in the world about her age, it would not prevent a conviction because no fault needed to be proved in relation to that element of the *actus reus*. It was a strict liability offence.

In other words, the effect of the mistake in question depends on whether it prevents D having a fault element laid down by the definition of the crime charged. Although the House did not formally overrule *Prince* and other sexual offence decisions applying strict liability to the age factor, the correctness of their decision to impose strict liability is thrown into doubt by *B* v *DPP* [2000] 1 All ER 833, HL and also *K* [2002] 1 Cr App R 121,

HL (see below and 13.4.1). Although the Court of Appeal in *K* [2001] Crim LR 134 took a similar view of the crime of indecent assault under s. 14 of the Sexual Offences Act 1956, their view was overturned by the House of Lords which described *Prince* as 'discredited'. Section 14(2) provides that a girl under 16 cannot legally consent so as to negate the assault element. It was held that the offence required full *mens rea* in respect of this age factor so that even an unreasonable mistake that the girl was 16 or over would prevent liability (see further 13.4.1 below). (The Sexual Offences Act 2003 reverses both *B* v *DPP* (s. 10) and *K* (s. 9) in respect of the specific offences in issue but that does not affect the general principle they enunciate.)

8.5.2.3 Conclusion

In summary, the effect of the mistake in question depends on whether it prevents D having a fault element laid down by the definition of the crime charged.

The above principles were strongly re-asserted by the House of Lords in the most important (and perhaps surprising in view of the subject matter) decision of *B* v *DPP*. D, a 15-year-old youth, had persistently asked a 13-year-old girl sitting next to him on a bus for a 'shiner' which 'in the language of today's gilded youth apparently means, not a black eye, but an act of oral sex'. He was charged with inciting a child under 14 to commit an act of gross indecency contrary to s. 1(1) of the Indecency with Children Act 1960. (The particular offence no longer exists, having been replaced by the Sexual Offences Act 2003.) Over-ruling the Divisional Court decision ([1999] 1 Cr App R 163) that the offence was one of strict liability in respect of the age factor, the House held that *mens rea* was required. D had to intend to incite someone **under 14** so that he must either know the girl was under 14 or realise she might be ('reckless indifference'). It followed that a genuine belief by D, whether based on reasonable grounds or not, that the victim was 14 or over would negate such *mens rea* and thus liability.

The House refused to hold that the offence was strict liability in respect of age (see 13.4.1 below) in which case **any** mistake about age would have been irrelevant. Perhaps the best policy solution would have been to adopt the *Tolson* compromise of imposing a fault element but the lesser one of negligence by requiring D's mistake to be **reasonable** (the corresponding offence under s. 10 of the Sexual Offences Act 2003 adopts just such a solution). It seems fair to demand of D that he at least takes reasonable steps to verify that the person he seeks to involve in gross indecency is not under 14. Similarly, this applies for other age-based sexual offences. However, the decision once again illustrates the courts' reluctance to adopt what is often a sensible policy compromise of negligence-based liability.

8.5.3 Mistake as to a matter of defence

These mistakes concern non-definitional elements of the crime charged. The prosecution can prove all the elements of the crime, including the *mens rea*, so that D is prima facie guilty. However, D claims that, if the facts he mistakenly believed to exist were true, they would establish a defence to liability, such as duress or necessity. The general rule here is that in order to be a defence, the mistake must be **reasonable** (*Graham* [1982] 1 All ER 801, CA; *Martin* [1989] 1 All ER 652, CA). For example, if D mistakenly believes he is being subjected to duress, he will only be judged on the facts as he saw them and, therefore, have the defence of duress if his belief was a reasonable one. However, this differentiation between duress and self-defence was challenged by the Court of Appeal in *Martin (David)* [2000] 2 Cr App R 42 which asserted that D should be judged on the circumstances as he saw them, whether his mistake was reasonable or unreasonable. Even if desirable in principle, the decision flatly contradicted previous, binding authority and was overruled by the House of Lords in *Hasan* [2005] UKHL 127, which reasserted the necessity for the mistake to be reasonable in respect of the defence of duress (see 9.3.1.1 below).

The problem with this rule is that it is often very difficult to determine whether something is a definitional element of the crime or merely a matter of defence. Indeed, it is often a matter of pure chance and of form rather than substance. For example, as we saw when considering *Kimber* the victim's consent may prevent liability for an intentional application of force by D. We could say that D satisfies the *actus reus* and *mens rea* of the crime (an intentional application of force) but has the defence of consent. Or we could say that D does not satisfy the *actus reus* and *mens rea* of the crime (intentional application of **unlawful** force) because the victim's consent renders the force applied **lawful**.

? **QUESTION** 8.13

- Which view did the court take in *Kimber*?
- Which view did the majority of the House of Lords take in *Brown* (the case involving sado-masochists)?

Refer back to 4.3.3.2 if you do not know.

In fact, the Court of Appeal in *Kimber* chose the latter analysis so that consent in battery was a definitional element of the crime, although doubt was cast on this by *Brown*. A similar line to *Kimber* was taken where D mistakenly believed he was acting in self-defence or the prevention of crime (*Williams*; *Beckford* v R). Thus, in both consent and self-defence/prevention of crime cases, the mistake does not have to be reasonable (though see *Martin (Anthony)* [2002] Crim LR 137 at 8.6.5 below). You might also consider *O'Grady* (now followed in *Hatton*—see 8.4.7.1 above) where Lord Lane's treatment of self-defence as a 'defence' proper rather than as being part of the definition of the offence (under the guise of 'unlawful') enabled him to ignore the *Majewski* rule that intoxicated mistake which prevents D having the *mens rea* for a specific intent crime is a defence. In Lord Lane's eyes the specific intent in murder is simply an intention to kill not an intention to kill **unlawfully**. This approach is directly contrary to *Williams* and *Beckford* but, as we have seen in *Brown*, the courts are willing to move the goalposts on this issue when it suits them to do so (see also 4.3.3.2). However, the 'defence' approach is contradicted by the House of Lords in *B* v *DPP* which gives a powerful endorsement of *Williams*, *Beckford* and *Kimber*.

However, we could just as easily argue that force inflicted whilst acting under duress is prevented from being **unlawful** by the operation of the defence of duress. This would then relate to a definitional element of the crime rather than 'a matter of defence'. As we have seen, the courts have chosen not to do this. One rationale which has been suggested is that the courts' attitude depends on whether the 'defence' in issue is a justificatory defence or merely excusatory. We should emphasise that this is not a distinction the courts have made but rather a rationalisation by academics. The idea is that where defences like consent and self-defence apply, D's conduct is regarded as justified. He is perfectly entitled to do what he did—it is socially and legally acceptable and D has a right to defend himself from attack.

Other defences such as traditional duress, duress of circumstances and intoxication, may allow the accused to be **excused** from liability but this does not imply that his conduct is acceptable or that he was morally entitled to act in that way. If someone lies in the witness box because he has been terrified by threats of violence, it is not acceptable for him to commit 'perjury', still less for him to be entitled to do so, but it is understandable in the circumstances and therefore he may be excused from legal liability.

In the context of mistake, the law states that the excusatory defences will be permitted only where the accused's belief in the existence of the excusing circumstances was reasonable. In contrast, for justificatory defences the law states that if he honestly believed the circumstances were such that the law would entitle him to do as he did, the accused will not be guilty even if his belief was unreasonable.

Clause 41 of the draft Criminal Code Bill would make no distinction between justificatory and excusatory defences and would allow D any defence he would have had if any circumstance he mistakenly believed to exist had existed. Thus, there is no requirement that his belief be a reasonable one, no matter which defence is in issue (Law Com. No. 177).

8.5.4 Mistake of law

8.5.4.1 Mistake as to civil law

A mistake as to the civil law is treated in exactly the same way as a mistake of fact and so is governed by the rules above. An example is provided by *Smith* [1974] QB 354, CA (*Cases and Materials* (8.5.4.1)), where D was charged with criminal damage to fixtures in a flat of which he was the tenant. D had installed the fixtures to cover the wiring for his stereo equipment. On the termination of the tenancy, D damaged the fixtures in removing the wiring. He believed that as he had installed the fixtures, they were his property and therefore he was damaging only his own property. However, he had made a mistake as to the civil law because under the law of landlord and tenant, fixtures, even if installed by the tenant, become the property of the landlord. Criminal damage can be committed only by someone who intentionally or recklessly damages property **belonging to another**. His conviction was quashed on the ground that his mistake meant that he did not have the necessary *mens rea* in relation to the definitional element of the *actus reus* requiring the property to 'belong to another'.

8.5.4.2 Mistake as to the criminal law

Almost everyone will be aware of the maxim, 'ignorance of the law is no excuse'. Putting it another way, everyone is deemed to know what conduct is prohibited by the criminal law and the fact that D mistakenly believes that what he is doing is not a criminal offence will in no way absolve him from liability. Thus a company director was guilty of the offence of consenting to the acceptance of a money deposit by the company without the authorisation of the Bank of England contrary to the Banking Act 1987 even though he had no idea that such authorisation was required. He knew the deposits were being taken and he knew the company had no licence from the Bank to do it (*Attorney-General's Reference (No. 1 of 1995)* [1996] 1 WLR 970, CA). Even if there was no way D could have known that the conduct in question constituted a criminal offence, he would still be liable. For example, in *Bailey* (1800) Russ & Ry 1, D committed the offence whilst on a voyage on the high seas. When he left England, the conduct in question was not against the law but, unknown to D, it had been made a criminal offence during his voyage. The court found him guilty. Similarly, if a foreigner does an act in England which is lawful in his own country but which, unknown to him, is illegal in England, his ignorance of the criminality of his conduct will be no defence (*Esop* (1836) 7 C & P 456).

We can explain this another way by stating that, in general, the *mens rea* needed for criminal offences does not include a requirement to prove that D realised that his conduct was or might be against the law. For example, the offence of rape is committed by someone who has unlawful sexual intercourse with a woman without her consent either realising that she does not consent or that she might not be consenting. Until relatively recently, it was impossible legally for a husband to rape his wife, unless they were separated. The House of Lords in *R* [1991] 4 All ER 481 abolished the husband's immunity so that the wife has the same protection against unwanted advances from her husband as from any other man. Even though this change in the criminal law was recent, any husband who claimed that he thought it was lawful to have sexual intercourse with his wife whenever he wanted, irrespective of whether she consented, would receive short shrift from the courts. If the prosecution could prove that the intercourse was without his wife's consent and that he knew she was not consenting, it will have established the offence; it would not have to prove that he realised that his actions were against the law so his mistake would be irrelevant. (The decision in *R* was put on a statutory footing by s. 142 of the Criminal Justice and Public Order Act 1994. For rape see now s. 1 of the Sexual Offences Act 2003 discussed in **Chapter 5**.)

The Court of Appeal's decision in *Scarlett* [1993] 4 All ER 629 and its departure from the above principle should be regarded as an aberration (see 8.6.5 below). Another decision, *Secretary of State for Trade and Industry v Hart* [1982] 1 WLR 481, DC, (See *Cases and Materials* (8.5.4.2)) which might appear at first sight to contradict that principle, is in accord with it. D acted as an auditor of two companies whilst disqualified to do so under the Companies Acts by virtue of the fact that he was a director of the two companies. He was charged with the offence of acting 'as auditor of a company at a time when he knows that he is disqualified for appointment to that office'. D did not know he was disqualified from acting as auditor to the companies because he was ignorant of the relevant Companies Act provision disqualifying 'officers of the company' such as directors. He could not therefore be convicted for he lacked the knowledge explicitly required by the offence's *mens rea*. It was not enough that he knew the facts rendering him disqualified. His ignorance of the law saved him but it was ignorance of the **civil law** (the company law governing when people are disqualified) which prevented his having the necessary *mens rea*. If he had known he was disqualified, but had not realised that it was a criminal offence to then act as an auditor, his ignorance would have been as to the criminal law and thus no defence to liability.

8.6 Self-defence, prevention of crime and defence of property

8.6.1 Introduction

The essence of this 'defence' is that in some circumstances D is justified in using violence to meet unjustified aggression against an interest which the law deems worthy of protection. Such interests comprise defending yourself or others, preventing crime, defending your own or another's property and lawfully arresting actual or suspected offenders. It is important for you to realise that the law has to regulate the competing interests of the aggressor and the defender, although naturally the balance is tilted very much in favour of the defender. The aggressor is the source of the problem and is to blame for threatening D's protected interests, but that does not mean that he warrants **no** consideration from the law. It is for this reason that the law allows the defender to use only **reasonable** force. You cannot shoot a vandal who is about to scratch the paintwork on your car!

Although it is common to refer to self-defence and prevention of crime as 'defences', the view currently predominating is that they form part of the 'definitional elements' of crimes of violence. The force must be 'unlawful' and if D uses reasonable force in self-defence, he does not apply 'unlawful' force and therefore the *actus reus* is not established (see 4.3.3.2 and 8.5.3). It follows that it is for the prosecution to disprove self-defence, etc. where D adduces credible evidence of it, because 'unlawfulness' is one of the elements defining the offence (*Beckford* v *R* (below); *Anderson* [1995] Crim LR 430, CA). It is important for you to bear this in mind throughout this section even though, for ease of explanation, we often refer to them as 'defences'.

8.6.2 The basis of the law

There exist two separate defences, one under the common law and the other a statutory defence governed by s. 3 of the Criminal Law Act 1967. In both cases, the essence of the defence is that a person is entitled to use reasonable force in self-defence or the prevention of crime. D must be acting **in order to** prevent physical harm or a crime. If that is not his motive he cannot be acting in self-defence, etc. and his violence will be unlawful. If he acts in retaliation or to teach the aggressor a lesson, he cannot use the defence. He must therefore believe that the force he uses is **necessary** to prevent the harm or crime.

In practical terms, it matters little whether the defendant uses the statutory defence or the common law defence, since the Court of Appeal in *McInnes* [1971] 3 All ER 295 established that the rules to be applied to the common law defence would be the same as for the statutory defence under s. 3. However, s. 3(2) provides that the statutory defence 'shall replace the rules of common law on the question when force used for a purpose mentioned in the subsection is justified by that purpose'.

Section 3(1) reads:

> A person may use such force as is reasonable in the circumstances in the prevention of crime, or in effecting or assisting in the lawful arrest of offenders or suspected offenders or of persons unlawfully at large.

The common law rules permit anyone to use reasonable force (a) to defend himself from an attack, (b) to defend another person from attack, and (c) to defend his property. It will be seen that there is a great deal of overlap between the statutory and common law defences, in that acting in the prevention of crime would embrace most situations covered by (a), (b) and, to a lesser extent, (c) above.

? QUESTION 8.14

Can you think of a situation where the statutory 'prevention of crime' defence in s. 3 would not apply, but the common law defence of self-defence would?

Theoretically, the statutory defence is wider in that the crimes you would be entitled to use reasonable force to prevent are not limited to crimes of violence, as appeared to be the case under the common law defence. Thus, you might be entitled to use reasonable force to prevent someone from indecently exposing himself.

? QUESTION 8.15

Does this mean that you can use force to prevent *any* crime?

No matter how trivial the offence, theoretically you are entitled to use **reasonable** force to prevent it, although it is open to the court to find that, in the circumstances, the offence is so trivial that **no** force would be reasonable to prevent it. In *Jones* [2004] EWCA Crim 1981, it was held that, for the purposes of s. 3, 'crime' meant only a crime according to English domestic law. It did not include conduct which was criminal in accordance with international law or some other country's law **unless** it was also criminal under our law. The defendants claimed that they had damaged property at an RAF air base in order to try to prevent US and UK attacks on Iraq. They contended that such attacks constituted the crime of aggression under international law. The Court of Appeal held that, even if aggression against a foreign country is unlawful under international law, it is not a crime under our law and therefore s. 3 is not engaged.

Sometimes the common law defence may apply where the statute does not. Thus, if D acted in self-defence against an attack by a person who was insane under the M'Naghten Rules, or by a person under the age of criminal responsibility (ten years), technically no crime would be being prevented so that s. 3 would be inapplicable. A most important situation where the statutory defence is not applicable is where no crime is actually being prevented or attack on D being made but D mistakenly thinks there is. As we shall see in 8.6.5 below, the common law may well allow a defence in such cases.

8.6.3 What is reasonable force?

Traditionally 'reasonable force' embraces two distinct ideas—necessity and proportionality. Necessity means that the force used was necessary in the sense that lesser violence would not have been adequate to defend oneself or prevent the crime. Proportionality means that it was reasonable to use that necessary force in the sense that it was not disproportionate to the mischief sought to be avoided.

 What amounts to reasonable force is a question of fact for the jury and not a question of law for the judge. The test is objective and depends on the jury's view of whether a reasonable person would have used such force in the circumstances as perceived by the accused (*Williams* [1987] 3 All ER 411, CA). However, the courts take a robust view of the situation and recognise that the defendant will have no time to consider his reaction. Lord Morris in *Palmer* v *R* [1971] AC 814, PC (*Cases and Materials* (8.6.3)) expressed it thus:

> If there has been an attack so that the defence is reasonably necessary, it will be recognised that a person defending himself cannot weigh to a nicety the exact measure of his necessary defensive action. If a jury thought that in a moment of unexpected anguish a person attacked had only done what he honestly and instinctively thought was necessary that would be most potent evidence that only reasonable defensive action had been taken.

According to the Court of Appeal in *Scarlett*, the jury must be 'satisfied that the degree of force used was plainly more than was called for by the circumstances as he believed them to be' in order to convict.

Thus, the courts lean heavily in favour of the defender in judging the reasonableness of his force. Although the test is objective—the court lays down the external standard of what amounts to reasonable force in the given situation—it is given a subjective twist by ruling that the defender's belief that it was necessary is 'most potent evidence' that it was reasonable. It is almost as if the reasonableness of the force goes to establishing that D acted in genuine self-defence. In fact some authorities seem to slide over into regarding this as the decisive issue—if D was genuinely acting defensively and only doing what he thought was necessary for that purpose, he has the defence (no matter how 'excessive' a jury might view the amount of force), whereas if he was acting offensively he does not (see *Shannon* (1980) 71 Cr App R 192, CA). This was essentially the line taken by the Court of Appeal in *Scarlett*, but, as we shall see at 8.6.5 below, it was rejected in *Owino* [1996] 2 Cr App R 128, CA and cannot be regarded as correct.

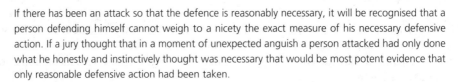

? QUESTION 8.16

Do you think someone who fails to retreat and stands his ground should be disqualified from using the defence? What about someone who makes a pre-emptive strike, fearing an imminent attack?

There used to be a rule at common law that, unless the defendant had retreated as far as he possibly could, until his back was literally against the wall, he was not entitled to use any force. It is now clear that this rule no longer holds, although the courts will normally expect a defendant to indicate his willingness to 'temporise and disengage' (i.e., 'to demonstrate by his actions that he does not want to fight' (*Julien* [1969] 2 All ER 856)). However, in the final analysis, everything depends on whether the defendant acted reasonably in standing his ground (*Bird* [1985] 2 All ER 513, CA—*Cases and Materials* (8.6.3)). 'A failure to retreat is only an element in the considerations on which the reasonableness of the accused's conduct is to be judged' (*McInnes*). This is the position adopted in cl. 28(8) of the draft Criminal Code Bill 1993. Indeed, some cases have accepted that it may be reasonable for D to make a pre-emptive strike to prevent an attack which he apprehends is about to be made (*Attorney-General's Reference (No. 2 of 1983)* [1984] 1 All ER 988, CA; *Beckford* v *R* [1987] 3 All ER 425, PC).

? QUESTION 8.17

Does this mean a battered wife who has reached the end of her tether can choose her moment to despatch her tormentor, knowing that this is the only way to prevent inevitable, further, violent attacks on her?

You will appreciate that the likely physical disparity between a battered wife and her abusing husband would tend to make any attempts to defend herself at the time of an attack both unsuccessful and unwise. If the woman sees no hope of extricating herself from the situation, her only means of defending herself from further violence may be a pre-emptive strike. For the reasons above, this would need to be when her husband is incapable of defending himself because asleep or senselessly drunk, for example. The strike would be aimed to kill because, otherwise, retribution from the abuser would be severe. We have already seen that in this kind of situation, the defence of provocation reducing murder to manslaughter, would be unlikely to succeed although diminished responsibility might. The latter involves regarding the woman as mentally disordered, which may be neither accurate nor appropriate.

Self-defence (although embracing pre-emptive strikes), currently requires apprehension of an **imminent** attack (*Attorney-General's Reference (No. 2 of 1983)* [1984] 1 All ER 988, CA). This would rule out the defence in the case of a sleeping husband or one in a drunken stupor. If there were no restriction of this nature, it could leave the door open too wide for pre-emptive strikes by vigilantes taking their own 'preventive' action far in advance of any threat. However, Professor Williams argues that the focus should be on the immediacy of the necessity for the pre-emptive strike to prevent a future attack rather than the immediacy of the threatened violence (*Textbook of Criminal Law*, 2nd ed., p. 503). The draft Criminal Law Bill has deleted any reference to an 'imminence' requirement preferring to leave it to the jury to decide whether, in all the circumstances, the pre-emptive strike was reasonable (Law Com. No. 218, paras. 39.6 and 39.7). This would give more scope for a jury to exonerate the battered wife in the sort of situation we have posited.

Just as an actual pre-emptive strike can be rendered lawful so also can acts carried out in preparation for defensive action, provided the attack apprehended is imminent and D believes that the means he intends to use are 'no more than reasonably necessary to meet the force...' (*Attorney-General's Reference (No. 2 of 1983)*—shopkeeper's possession of petrol bombs during Toxteth riots).

8.6.3.1 Defence of property

The same basic principles apply where D is defending his own or another's property, whether real (e.g., his home) or personal (e.g., his car).

> **? QUESTION** 8.18
>
> Does this mean that a householder can kill a burglar in defence of his property?

The first point we need to make is that defence of property situations usually become self-defence and prevention of crime situations. For example, the householder attacking a burglar may claim (correctly) that he was making a pre-emptive strike in fear for his own life or safety. However, it seems clear that, in modern times, the **amount** of force which will be permitted as **reasonable** must surely be less where the motive is defence of property as opposed to defence of person. It is difficult to believe that the statement in *Hussey* (1924) 18 Cr App R 160, CCA, that a person is permitted to kill if necessary to prevent a trespasser dispossessing him of his home, would represent the law today. D had fired through the door of his home and wounded some friends of his landlady who were endeavouring to break in to throw him out when they had no right to do so. His conviction for unlawful wounding was quashed because the jury had not been directed on the issue of defence of property.

In a recent **civil** case, *Revill* v *Newbery* [1996] 1 All ER 291, CA, an old-age pensioner was ordered to pay damages for injuries caused to someone breaking into his allotment shed. Fed up with repeated break-ins to his shed and vandalism to his allotment, D had spent the night in the shed armed with a shotgun. When he heard the men outside trying to get in, he fired through a hole in the door seriously injuring V. Despite D arguing that he feared for his safety as well as his property, the High Court and subsequently the Court of Appeal held the force to be out of all proportion to the threat. Public and newspaper outrage followed and D was showered with public donations to a fund set up by the local mayor! In general, however, the courts would be keen to discourage this kind of vigilantism. The notorious conviction of Tony Martin, the Norfolk farmer, for the murder of a teenage burglar (later reduced to manslaughter) provides another example though it must be said the victim was shot in the back whilst trying to get out of the farmhouse.

In *Scarlett* V was killed when he fell down some steps after being ejected forcibly from a pub by D, the landlord, having refused requests to leave. D was acquitted of manslaughter on the basis of defending his property, even though there was no question of the drunken V trying to dispossess him. The Court in *Pownall* (1994) *The Times*, 19 February found it not reasonable for a person to protect their property using dangerous methods such as electrified fences and mantraps.

Finally, we should point out that if D damages another's property (as opposed to a person) in order to protect his own property, the matter is covered by specific provision in s. 5(2)(b) of the Criminal Damage Act 1971 (see 'without lawful excuse' under 12.10.2.1 below). That provision seems to be phrased in entirely **subjective** terms (although, as we shall see, the courts have managed to introduce an objective element which is not really there). Thus, if D is defending his property, his damage to another's property is lawful provided he **believes** that the action is immediately necessary and reasonable in the circumstances.

The curiosity and illogicality is that if D damages V's property (e.g., kills V's attacking dog) in order to defend his **person** (i.e., an interest worthy of greater protection) the test of reasonableness is objective, not what D **believes** is reasonable. The Law Commission's solution to this anomaly would be to amend the Criminal Damage Act 1971 provision by introducing a clearly stated objective element (Law Com. No. 218, paras. 37.3 to 37.6).

8.6.4 **The effects of the defence**

If the defence succeeds, whether common law or statutory, D's conduct is regarded as lawful and he is completely acquitted. It can be a defence to any crime including murder.

However, it should be noted that a defendant who acts in self-defence or the prevention of crime but who uses more force than is reasonable, will be convicted, although the fact that he acted in self-defence will, no doubt, be reflected in a lesser sentence. In the case of the fixed-penalty crime of murder, this is not possible and has led to suggestions that there should be a halfway house defence which acts like provocation and reduces murder to manslaughter. Indeed, such a defence currently exists in the Republic of Ireland and did exist in Australia until it was abolished in 1987. Our courts have firmly set their face against any such partial defence and the use of excessive force completely deprives D of the defence (*McInnes*; *Palmer* v *R*). This view was endorsed by the House of Lords in *Clegg* [1995] 1 All ER 334 (*Cases and Materials* (8.6.4)). Private Clegg, a British soldier, shot dead a 'joyrider' in the rear of a car which failed to stop when ordered to do so by soldiers in Northern Ireland. It was accepted that Clegg feared for the life of a fellow soldier when he fired three shots at the car. However, the judge found as a fact that his fourth and fatal shot was fired into the rear of the car after it had passed all the soldiers, who were therefore no longer in any danger. He could not have fired the final shot in defence of his colleague. (In fact, following submission of new technical evidence by the defence, a further appeal against conviction succeeded on the basis that Clegg might not have fired the fatal shot.)

? **QUESTION** 8.19

- Can you suggest why s. 3 of the Criminal Law Act 1967 *might* still be applicable?
- With reasons, say whether *Clegg* would, in fact, satisfy the terms of s. 3.

The fact that D was not acting in defence of another does not, of course, necessarily rule out s. 3. It could be argued that he was still acting in the prevention of crime—the continuance of the vehicle-taking offence—although this was not raised in the case. In addition, it was possible that he was 'effecting or assisting in the lawful arrest of offenders' and it was accepted by the House that s. 3 therefore came into play. However, the House accepted the Court of Appeal's view that using a high velocity rifle intentionally to shoot a joyrider in order to arrest could not possibly be reasonable force (it might have been different if the occupants of the car had been thought or known to be terrorists). D's force was manifestly excessive and s. 3 was not satisfied.

Following *Palmer* and *McInnes*, the House rejected the existence of any qualified defence reducing murder to manslaughter where D 'has used greater force than was necessary in the circumstances' but otherwise satisfied the requirements of the defence. The rule is the same whether D acts in self-defence, prevention of crime or arresting offenders etc. Soldiers are in the same position as anyone else. The House refused an invitation to create such a new defence, putting the ball firmly in Parliament's court.

8.6.5 Mistake and self-defence

In judging whether the force used by D was reasonable, D must be judged on the facts as he saw them. Thus, if D was mistaken in believing that V was attacking him or committing a crime, then the jury must assume that V was attacking D or committing a crime, and decide whether D used only reasonable force in those imagined circumstances. The same is true of any other mistake about the factual circumstances, e.g., D imagined the attack was more severe than it was (as where D believed V to have a loaded gun, when in fact it was simply an imitation firearm). It is clear from *Williams* [1987] 3 All ER 411, CA and *Beckford* v R that D's mistake need only be an honest one and it does not matter whether it is reasonable or unreasonable. Of course, as a practical matter, the more unreasonable D's claimed mistake is, the less likely the jury is to believe that it was a genuine mistake. The same rules apply where D acts under mistake in the prevention of crime within s. 3 of the Criminal Law Act 1967 or under common law (*Clegg*; *Morrow* v *DPP* [1994] Crim LR 58, DC) and in defence of property at common law (*Scarlett*—below).

Although we therefore judge D on the facts as he saw them, this, according to *Martin (Anthony)* [2002] Crim LR 136, CA, does not extend to his subjective assessment of what those facts mean in terms of the degree of danger created. In *Martin*, D shot and killed someone burgling his isolated Norfolk farmhouse. The jury rejected D's plea of self-defence, presumably on the ground that he used excessive force, and convicted him of murder. On appeal, fresh evidence was introduced that he was suffering from a paranoid personality disorder and depression which exacerbated his paranoia and led to an exaggerated perception of the danger he faced from the burglars. The Court of Appeal held that what mattered was the degree of danger a reasonable person would perceive given the facts as D saw them, not the unreasonable perception of greater danger by the psychiatrically disordered D. Consequently, evidence of his paranoia was inadmissible on the question of whether he used excessive force in self-defence (though it was relevant and admissible on D's alternative plea of diminished responsibility, which succeeded). This is a rather fine distinction since a person's perception of the facts and the judgment he makes of the danger arising from those facts are inextricably bound up together, certainly in terms of assessing D's moral culpability. No doubt the Court was concerned that to allow a paranoiac to be judged by his abnormal perceptions of danger could lead to the complete acquittal of someone whose mental condition made him highly dangerous to the public.

Sir John Smith's solution is to argue that, if D's exaggerated view of the danger he faced was due to a grossly negligent mistake (which presumably it would be in the case of a grossly disturbed defendant), he could be convicted of gross negligence manslaughter. However, it is not clear that the defence of self-defence would be ruled out by the fact that D has made a grossly negligent mistake either about the facts of the situation or the danger arising therefrom. Furthermore, that solution is only available where the victim dies. There is no corresponding offence of causing injury by gross negligence.

However, the Court's stance does contradict a holding by the Privy Council in *Shaw v R* [2002] Crim LR 140 that in judging whether the force used in self-defence is reasonable, the jury must take into account 'the circumstances **and the danger** as the defendant honestly believed them to be' (our emphasis). That authority is, of course, persuasive only and was not specifically addressing the problem at issue.

Therefore, it seems from *Martin* that, if D's perception of the degree of danger would have been greater than that of a reasonable person, assuming the facts were as he saw them, that perception must be ignored and he must be judged on the normal person's assessment of the degree of danger.

There is currently an exception to the rule that D is judged on the facts as he saw them—where the mistake is caused by D's self-induced intoxication. In that case the mistake is ignored and D is judged on the facts as they actually were and not as he drunkenly believed them to be (*O'Grady* [1987] 3 All ER 420, CA; *Hatton* [2005] EWCA Crim 2951). However, we need to remember that *O'Grady* seems to contradict the normal *Majewski* rules on intoxication and is, arguably, obiter on this point (although *Hatton* regarded it as binding—see 8.4.7.1 above). It also contradicts *Williams* and *Beckford* in seeming to regard the self-defence issue as **not** a definitional element of the crime (see 8.5.3 above).

Finally, we should distinguish the above type of mistake about the facts of the situation from a mistake about the amount of force which the law allows D to use in those circumstances. Here there is no mistake about the circumstances of the incident. D simply believes that he is entitled to use more force than the law permits. This is regarded as a mistake as to the criminal law and, as such, should not provide a defence. It is for the law, in the shape of the jury, to prescribe the standard of reasonable force, and if D gets it wrong and acts excessively, he is rightly convicted.

The Court of Appeal in *Scarlett* [1993] 4 All ER 629 ignored this distinction and appeared to hold that if D believed he was entitled to use the amount of force he did, he should be acquitted even though such force was, in the eyes of the jury, excessive in the circumstances believed by D to exist. That view was impliedly rejected by the House of Lords in *Clegg* and expressly rejected in *Owino* [1996] 2 Cr App R 128, CA. There the Court of Appeal explained that the Court in *Scarlett* did not mean what it said and was intending to reiterate the principle expressed in *Williams*.

The *Owino* view of the law was adopted in *Hughes* [1995] Crim LR 956, CA where the judgment was given by Beldam LJ, who had given the controversial judgment in *Scarlett*. We may therefore take it that the statements in *Scarlett* on this point were an aberration and will not be followed.

8.6.6 **Reform**

Clauses 27 to 30 of the Law Commission's draft Criminal Law Bill are partly reproduced in *Cases and Materials* (8.6.6). The suggested provisions are much more detailed than the present s. 3 and extend and clarify the range of purposes for which reasonable force can be used. The *Williams* principle is retained along with an objective test for 'reasonable force' as a single concept. Interestingly, there is no requirement that D should fear an imminent attack and it may be possible for 'battered wives' to argue the defence where they have, e.g., struck while their abusing husband is incapably drunk or asleep, in order to prevent inevitable later injurious attacks.

Following a flurry of failed Private Members' Bills in the wake of public and media concern generated by the Tony Martin case, it appears that the Government has no intention of directly reforming the present law. However, the Crown Prosecution Service has produced 'guidance' to enable prosecutors to judge the appropriateness of prosecution (see www.cps.gov.uk).

You may recall from Chapter 6 that the Law Commission's Report, *Partial Defences to Murder* (Law Com. No. 290), recommended a partial defence reducing murder to manslaughter if D killed 'in response to . . . (b) fear of serious violence . . .' provided that a 'person of ordinary temperament in the circumstances of the defendant might have acted in the same or a similar way.' (See 6.5.2.2 above under 'Reform' for more details.) However, the Commission rejected the introduction of a general partial defence where D, although genuinely acting in self-defence, used more force than was reasonable in the circumstances.

■ FURTHER READING

Gardner J: *The Gist of Excuses* (1998) 1 Buffalo Crim LR 575.

Gardner S: *The Importance of Majewski* (1994) 14 OJLS 279.

Horder: *Drawing the Boundaries of Self-Defence* (1995) 58 MLR 431.

Horder: *Excusing Crime* (2004, Oxford University Press).

Law Commission: *Legislating the Code: Intoxication and Criminal Liability* (Law Com. No. 229, 1995).

Paton: *Reformulating the Intoxication Rules: The Law Commission's Report* [1995] Crim LR 382.

Robinson: *Criminal Law Defences: A Systematic Analysis* (1982) 82 Columbia Law Review 199.

Simester: *Mistakes in Defence* (1992) 12 OJLS 295.

Sullivan: *Making Excuses* in Simester & Smith ATH (eds.): *Harm and Culpability* (1996, Oxford University Press).

■ SUMMARY

Automatism

Automatism is a state where D's conscious mind is not directing his muscular movements (mainly when D is unconscious). D must lose **all** control (*Broome v Perkins*). It is purely **physical** involuntariness not moral involuntariness.

- *Insane automatism*—if due to disease of mind, D is insane.

- *Non-insane automatism*: (i) always a defence to crimes of specific intent (mostly those requiring intention alone as *mens rea*); (ii) Defence to other crimes if **not** self-induced. *Self-induced* (D at fault in becoming an automaton)—always a defence to specific intent crimes. Usually **not** a defence to basic intent crimes: (i) if due to voluntary intoxication by alcohol or dangerous drugs, never a defence; (ii) if due to some other cause, D not guilty **unless** he was reckless in getting into the automatic state and becoming 'aggressive, unpredictable or uncontrolled' (*Bailey*). 'Reckless' means subjectively reckless.

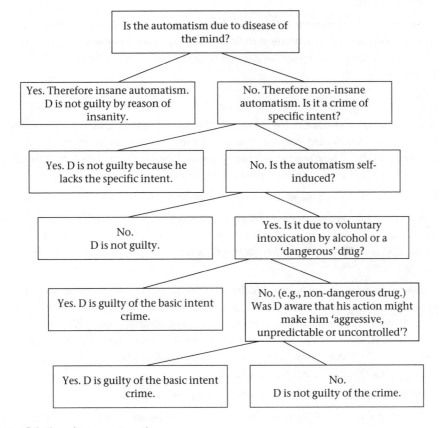

Figure 8.1 Flow chart on automatism

Intoxication

- Refer to 8.4.2.

- *Specific intent crimes*—the framing of the charge is now crucial (*Caldwell*). If offence **as charged** necessitates nothing less than intention, which D lacks, D is not guilty.

- *Basic intent crimes*—no *mens rea* required where absent due to intoxication (*Majewski*). Section 8 of the Criminal Justice Act 1967 irrelevant. D, in getting himself intoxicated, is **conclusively presumed** to be reckless.

- *Defences*—where D would have a defence if the facts were as he intoxicatedly and mistakenly believed them to be. If defence is **justificatory**, e.g., self-defence, it is a definitional element of the crime and **should** be a defence to a specific intent crime where mistake negates the intent but not to a basic intent crime (*Majewski*). But *O'Grady* and *Hatton* say drunken mistake is no defence to **any** crime. With **excusatory** defences such as duress, intoxicated mistake, being unreasonable, should not be a defence. Specific statutory defences based on honest belief are satisfied by a drunken, albeit unreasonable, mistake (*Jaggard* v *Dickinson*).

- *Involuntary intoxication*—defence to **any** crime but **only** if intoxication prevents D having the *mens rea* (*Kingston*).

- *Self-induced intoxication by non-dangerous drugs*—defence to specific intent crimes if *mens rea* negatived. Defence to basic intent crimes if *mens rea* negatived **unless** D reckless as to becoming intoxicated and aggressive, unpredictable and uncontrolled (*Hardie*).

Mistake

- A mistake about an element of the *actus reus*, whether of fact or of **civil** law and whether reasonable or unreasonable, will be a 'defence' **provided** it negatives D's *mens rea* (*DPP* v *Morgan*; B v DPP). Therefore, the first step is to decide what is the fault element in the offence charged in respect of the part of the actus reus about which the mistake has been made.

- If the fault element is negligence then only a **reasonable** mistake can negate it (*Tolson*).

- If the crime is strict liability in respect of the element about which the mistake has been made, not even a reasonable mistake will be a defence, because there is no fault element for the mistake to negate (*Callow* v *Tillstone*; *Prince* though *Prince* doubted in respect of particular offence (now repealed) in *B* v *DPP*).

- *Mistake as to defence*—distinguish (i) 'defences' ('justificatory'?) comprising 'definitional elements' of the crime, e.g., self-defence (*Beckford*; *Williams*), consent (*Kimber* endorsed by *B* v *DPP*) and (ii) other defences (excusatory?), e.g., duress (*Graham*; *Hasan* 2005, HL). Justificatory '*defences*'—falls within (a) above—therefore mistake need not be reasonable. *Other defences*—mistake as to circumstances must be **reasonable** and be such that, if true, would establish the defence, e.g., amount to duress (*Hasan*).

- Mistake as to **civil** law dealt with in exactly same way as mistake of fact (*Smith*).

- Mistake as to criminal law—ignorance/mistake as to **criminal** law is no excuse (*Bailey*).

Self-defence, prevention of crime and defence of property

Parallel common law and statutory defences allowing **reasonable** force in self-defence, prevention of crime, defence of property or in lawfully arresting. Broadly the same but some differences. Where there is overlap, the statutory defence supersedes the common law defence (s. 3 of the Criminal Law Act 1967).

- *Reasonable force*—requires force to be (i) necessary, i.e., no lesser force would be adequate to defend oneself or prevent the crime, etc. and (ii) proportionate to the mischief to be avoided. Amount of force which is reasonable is an external objective standard but, if satisfied D genuinely acting in self-defence, courts lenient in applying standard (*Palmer*). Retreat is only a factor in the general question (*Bird*). Pre-emptive strike possible provided attack imminent (*Attorney-General's Reference (No. 2 of 1983)*). Defence of property—same basic principle but a lesser amount of force would be reasonable than in the case of attack on a person.

- If successful, the defence leads to complete acquittal. If D uses excessive force, plea is destroyed and D guilty (subject to mistake below). No qualified defence reducing murder to manslaughter if force excessive (*Clegg*).

- *Mistake*—D judged on facts as he mistakenly saw them, whether reasonably or unreasonably (*Beckford; Williams*; B v *DPP*) unless due to voluntary intoxication (*Hatton; O'Grady*). Applies even if no actual attack at all or if attack is less severe than believed by D. If D correctly knows the facts but mistakes the amount of force which the law permits in that situation, his mistake as to the criminal law would be no defence (*Owino*).

 CHAPTER 8: ASSESSMENT EXERCISE

8.1 Slater, a college lecturer, had been experiencing nightmares and disturbed sleep and behaving strangely as a result of stress suffered at work brought about by the increase in the number of students on his courses. He was given some tranquilising tablets by a colleague, who told him that they would get rid of his stress. Slater followed his colleague's instructions and took two tablets thinking that they would enable him to get a good night's sleep.

He fell asleep but got up in a trance and walked out into the street in his nightshirt. He picked up a brick and attacked Owl, a passer-by, with the brick causing him grievous bodily harm.

Slater was at all times quite unaware of what he was doing and could remember nothing of the incident. The medical experts were unable to say whether the sleepwalking was due to the tablets or Slater's underlying condition or a combination of the two.

Advise Slater as to his criminal liability, if any, in respect of the injuries to Owl, with particular reference to possible defences.

8.2 Percy is the captain of Radford Rovers football team. He is extremely nervous before a Cup Final and the team manager gives him three amphetamine pills telling him that they will get him buzzing. Percy takes the pills one hour before the match.

The pills make Percy feel hysterical and confused. When the referee comes to shake hands before the game, Percy thinks the referee is attacking him and he punches the referee on the nose causing it to bleed.

Percy then runs to the edge of the pitch, snatches an orange from a spectator and eats it, thinking it is part of the refreshments provided for the players at half-time.

Discuss the criminal liability, if any, of Percy.

See the **Appendix** (8.1 and 8.2) for specimen answers.

General defences III: Duress, necessity and marital coercion

9.1 Objectives

By the end of this chapter you should be able to:

1 Distinguish between traditional duress by threats, necessity and duress of circumstances

2 Describe the conditions required for a successful defence of duress (a) by threats and (b) of circumstances

9.2 Introduction

We have seen, when looking at self-defence and prevention of crime, examples of emergency situations where the necessity to act allows D to inflict force lawfully. In fact we approve his reasonable force to defend himself and would say that he is perfectly justified in using it. However, this is a very particular necessity situation and the question we address in this section is the extent to which the law allows other necessity situations to avoid liability. What if someone threatens to kill you unless you commit the crime? What if a homeless person in danger of freezing to death breaks the lock on an empty house to sleep overnight? Can a surgeon operate on an unconscious patient without the patient's consent? Can someone with a rare blood group have blood extracted forcibly if this is the only way of saving a patient's life?

You may not be surprised to learn in the light of the diversity of these situations that considerable uncertainty surrounds the extent to which necessity is a defence. The courts have been extremely cautious in developing it as a defence, viewing it as something of a Pandora's box. In the words of Lord Denning, 'Necessity would open a door which no man could shut' (*London Borough of Southwark* v *Williams* [1971] 2 All ER 175, CA). The problem for the courts is that necessity opens up considerations which the criminal law prefers to keep out of the criminal liability equation, to be taken into account, if at all, at the sentencing stage. Inevitably, the courts would be drawn into considering the social and political context of D's actions and the motive behind them: the unemployed youth denied social security benefits who steals food from the supermarket to live; the squatter who breaks into an empty house to avoid freezing on the streets; the animal liberationist who releases animals destined for experiments; the Greenpeace activist who blocks with concrete a pipe discharging radioactive or poisonous waste into the sea. Perhaps you can think of others.

Apart from self-defence, there are three defences which might be viewed as necessity situations—duress by threats (traditional duress), duress of circumstances and necessity. The first is the longest established and clearest. The second, although a relatively recent and probably unwitting creation, is now firmly established at Court of Appeal level but has yet to be considered by the House of Lords. It is closely analogous to traditional duress. The third (traditional) necessity, is much more problematic, certainly in terms of the conditions for a successful plea and the extent of its application, though there is a stream of relatively recent House of Lords' authority for its existence (*F* v *West Berkshire Health Authority* [1989] 2 All ER 545; *Airedale NHS Trust* v *Bland* [1993] 1 All ER 821; *R* v *Bournewood Community and Mental Health NHS Trust, ex parte L* [1998] 3 All ER 289), though the prevailing trend in the Court of Appeal is to view it as being limited to cases where doctors act in the best interests of their patient who is incapable of deciding what should happen (see *Quayle* [2005] EWCA Crim 1415, [51]–[53]).

The two duress defences require that the harm to be avoided by committing the alleged crime must be **death or serious injury** (confirmed recently by the House of Lords in *Hasan* [2005] UKHL 22 (*Cases and Materials* (9.2))). D feels compelled to commit the crime by the threat of death or serious harm. His will is overborne by the threats and he feels he has no choice. Duress by threats (traditional duress) is confined to threats of such harm by someone whose **purpose** is to coerce D into committing the crime charged. Do this or else! By contrast, duress of circumstances embraces threats of death or serious harm from any other source whether a human agency or not. The most frequently arising source is in fact from criminal threats by another but where the threatener's objective is to carry out the threats not, as in traditional duress, to use them to force D to commit the crime. For example, D drives dangerously in order to avoid being caught by a vicious gang. The threatening gang does not want D to commit the crime because that will enable him to escape. Aside from this difference, the conditions for a successful plea are much the same in each case and indeed our analysis of traditional duress below sometimes draws on duress of circumstances cases.

The courts often refer to duress of circumstances as necessity but you should be careful not to confuse it with traditional necessity. The latter potentially covers a much wider field than duress because it is not restricted to avoidance of death or serious harm and does not depend on D's will being overborne so as to effectively deprive him of any choice. Traditionally, necessity can apply wherever the commission of the 'crime' is necessary to prevent a greater evil. That 'evil' would frequently be death or physical harm, but it need not necessarily be. The utility of preventing the worse evil than is involved in committing the crime **justifies** what would otherwise be a crime. It is **better** to commit the crime and so it is not a wrongful act. Thus in *F* v *West Berkshire Health Authority*, the House of Lords held that doctors were justified in performing a sterilisation operation on a mentally subnormal woman who was incapable of giving informed consent. This application of force would not be unlawful because, according to the majority, it was necessary to avoid a high risk of pregnancy which would have had a deleterious effect on her health.

Necessity is not such a strong justification as necessary self-defence or prevention of crime because in the latter case the force is used against a person (the attacker) who is necessarily in the wrong and responsible for creating the occasion of the 'crime'. The action is against an 'unjust aggressor'. In necessity and duress, D's 'crime' may affect entirely innocent third parties who had no part in occasioning the circumstances. However, traditional necessity would still be seen as acceptable and morally right conduct because the results of committing the alleged crime are not as bad as the alternative avoided. D commits no wrongful act.

In contrast, duress of circumstances (referred to as 'necessity by circumstances' in *Quayle* [2005] EWCA Crim 1415) along with traditional duress, is based on **excuse** rather than **justification** (*Hasan*, HL). The act of committing the alleged crime is still wrongful—it is not morally acceptable or right to commit it—but, because of the overwhelming pressure, it is understandable and legally **excusable**. D commits the wrongful act but is excused from liability.

It is evident from *Shayler* [2001] Crim LR 986 that the Court of Appeal is reluctant to extend the justificatory idea of necessity beyond the medical sphere, preferring to subsume non-medical cases within the confines of duress of circumstances. Unfortunately, the decision is something of a dog's breakfast, confusing and conflating elements of duress and necessity and clouding the requirements for duress of circumstances. Lord Woolf CJ stated, 'The distinction between duress of circumstances and necessity has, **correctly**, been by and large ignored or blurred by the courts' (our emphasis). On appeal ([2002] UKHL 11) the House of Lords ruled that, on the facts, it was unnecessary to consider these defences and Lord Bingham in the lead judgment expressly stated that he should 'not be taken to accept all that the Court of Appeal said on these difficult topics'. Nonetheless the line taken by the Court of Appeal in *Shayler* was quoted with apparent approval in *Jones* v *Gloucestershire Crown Prosecution Service* [2004] EWCA Crim 1981. More importantly, the Court of Appeal in *Quayle* warmly endorsed Lord Woolf's view that any defence of necessity by circumstances should be treated as governed by tightly prescribed rules governing duress of circumstances. There was no separate defence of necessity proper applicable outside the sphere of medical interventions by doctors acting in the best interests of an incapable patient. Decisions such as *F* v *West Berkshire Health Authority* and *Re A* were confined to their own particular context. However, the door of true necessity is not banged shut since the court did accept that a case-by-case approach should continue to be adopted. It is clear that the Court of Appeal will need some persuading to allow it to be used to avoid the strict requirements of duress of circumstances.

9.3 Duress by threats

Where a person is compelled to commit a crime by threats of violence from another person, he may be able to plead the defence of duress. A successful plea of duress is a complete defence so that D is found not guilty and goes free. You should remember that although D is unconditionally acquitted, the law is not saying that he is **justified** in committing the crime, rather that, in succumbing to the threats, D is **excused** from liability for committing the crime. The rationale of the defence is the law's recognition that, in some circumstances, the threats will be so serious that even ordinary, law-abiding citizens will be unable to resist them and refrain from committing what would otherwise be a crime. We cannot fairly expect D to have resisted the pressure to commit the crime. In other words, it is a concession to human frailty.

In recent years, the popularity of the plea of duress has shown inexorable increase since it is easy to assert (with plausibility in a context of violent crime) and difficult for the prosecution to investigate and discharge its burden of disproving it beyond reasonable doubt, especially when, as is often the case, the defence only raises it (or discloses the details on which the claim is founded) at or just before the trial. Unlike other defences which focus on the factual situation at the time of the alleged crime, the claimed duress will usually have occurred well before the offence. In an effort to put a brake on the advance of duress in the light of such concerns, the House of Lords in *Hasan* [2005] UKHL 22 has, as we shall see in the following sections, narrowed the scope of the defence in a number of ways.

Unlike necessity and duress of circumstances (see 9.4), the coercer's objective is to **make** D commit the crime he does. As it was put in *Cole* [1994] Crim LR 582, CA (*Cases and Materials* (9.3)), 'the defence of duress by threats can only apply when the offence charged (the offence which the accused asserts he was constrained to commit) is the very offence which was nominated by the person making the threat, i.e., when the accused was **required** by the threat to commit the offence charged'. However, the Court of Appeal in *Ali* [1995] Crim LR 303 (*Cases and Materials* (9.3)) assumed that it would be sufficient to make a general demand of D to rob a bank or building society. It would not be necessary for the threatener to require robbery from a specific bank or building society.

9.3.1 What constitutes duress?

9.3.1.1 The standard test for duress

The House of Lords in *Howe* [1987] 1 AC 417 and more recently in *Hasan* approved the test for duress laid down by the Court of Appeal in *Graham* [1982] 1 All ER 801 (*Cases and Materials* (9.3.1.1)), which is analogous to the test used in the defence of provocation, in that there are both subjective and objective elements to satisfy. The essence of the subjective limb is that D was **actually** impelled by the threats to commit the crime. The threats 'directly caused' D to commit the crime charged (*Hasan*). The second objective limb then measures this against the objective yardstick of the average person to see whether an ordinary person might have been similarly influenced to commit the crime by the threats.

What kind of detailed direction to the jury should the judge give when explaining the test to be applied? He should ask:

(a) was D, or may he have been impelled to act as he did because, as a result of what he reasonably believed the threatener had said or done, he (D) had good cause to fear that if he did not so act, the threatener would kill him or cause him serious physical injury; **and**

(b) if so, has the prosecution made the jury sure that a sober person of reasonable firmness, sharing the characteristics of D, would not have responded to whatever he reasonably believed the threatener said or did by taking part in the crime?

? **QUESTION** 9.1

Is the first limb of this test an entirely subjective test? What objective elements does it contain?

The first limb requires that D feels he has no other practical choice than to commit the 'crime'. The pressure of the threats deprives him of the normal freedom to choose his course of action and 'overbears his will' (*cf.* Brooke LJ in *Re A (Children)* at 8.5 below). The pressing need to avoid imminent peril compels his decision to commit the crime.

Although the first limb of this test is termed a subjective test in that it depends on establishing that D committed the crime **because** he **actually** feared death or serious injury, it does contain objective elements. D must additionally have **good cause** to fear that the threatener is serious in making the threats and intends to carry them out. If he mistakes or misunderstands what the threatener has said or done, D will be judged on the facts as he believed them to be only if his belief was **reasonable**. (You should consider the discussion on mistake in this context at 8.5.3.) This means that D may not be judged on what he actually believed was being threatened and/or what he actually feared would be the result of ignoring the threat. This is likely to be so where he is extremely anxious, stupid and/or gullible.

Surprisingly, in view of the approval of *Graham* by the House of Lords in *Howe*, the Court of Appeal in *Martin (David)* [2000] 2 Cr App R 42, held that these objective elements should no longer be applied. Just like mistaken self-defence, D had to be judged on the threats as he perceived them to be, whether his perception was reasonable or unreasonable and whether or not he had good cause to fear they would be carried out. It is now clear that *Martin (David)* cannot stand with *Hasan* and that D's belief will be ignored unless it was based on reasonable grounds. D's belief in the 'efficacy of the threat' must be 'reasonable as well as genuine' (*Hasan*). Notice that, even after *Hasan*, it is not essential that there actually **was** any threat of death or serious injury as long as D **reasonably** perceived such a threat (*Safi* [2003] Crim LR 721, CA).

The second limb is the objective yardstick or control against which D's conduct is to be judged. The test, influenced by *Camplin* in provocation, is whether a person of average firmness or resistance to threats, but having D's age and sex, and sharing any characteristics of D which would affect the gravity of the threat to him, would have reacted by committing the crime perpetrated by D.

> **? QUESTION** 9.2
>
> What two characteristics of D can the reasonable person *never* share?

According to *Horne* [1994] Crim LR 584, CA (*Cases and Materials* (9.3.1.1)) 'a person of reasonable firmness is an average member of the public; not a hero necessarily, not a coward, just an average person'. As in provocation, there may be difficulties over what characteristics of D can and cannot be given to the hypothetical person of 'reasonable firmness'. Whereas in provocation the bottom line, objective characteristic upon which the reasonable person was based was the average degree of self-control, in duress the relevant characteristic is average ability to resist threats of harm. To an extent, *Bowen* [1996] 2 Cr App R 157, CA erodes this requirement (recently reinstated by *Attorney-General for Jersey v Holley* in the parallel case of provocation (see 6.6.2.2 above)). In addition, the reasonable person is always sober and is never under the influence of drink or drugs (*Graham*).

The leading case of *Bowen* holds that the person of average firmness should always be given D's age and sex at least where people of that age or sex might be generally less able to resist threats. Beyond this we encounter similar difficulties to those we faced in provocation (see 6.5.2.2 above) over which characteristics of D are relevant to the objective test. The comparison is not precisely analogous because in duress the necessary threats of death or serious injury are not **about** the relevant characteristic whereas in provocation the provocative conduct often is.

The following propositions can be derived from *Bowen* (*Cases and Materials* (9.3.1.1)):

(a) The reasonable person in duress cannot, without more, be more 'pliable, vulnerable, timid or susceptible to threats than a normal person'. Thus in *Bowen*, D's low IQ of 68 could not be given to the reasonable person even if it did make him less able to resist threats than a person of average intelligence. In *Hegarty* [1994] Crim LR 353, CA, the reasonable person could not be invested with D's 'pre-existing mental condition of being "emotionally unstable" or in a "grossly elevated neurotic state"'. Yet in *Antar* [2004] EWCA Crim 2708, the Court of Appeal ruled that the trial judge had been wrong to exclude the evidence of a psychiatrist that D, who had a very low IQ, functioned cognitively at a significantly impaired level, suffered a moderate (or, at least, mild) learning disability and was more suggestible than the general population. It was for the jury to consider the expert evidence and then decide whether the objective element had been satisfied. The Court saw it as a case of 'recognised mental impairment' (see (b) next).

(b) However, in a distinction foreshadowed in *Horne* [1994] Crim LR 584, CA, it appears that abnormal susceptibility to threats will be given to the reasonable man where it is caused by 'recognised mental illness, mental impairment or psychiatric condition, such as post-traumatic stress disorder leading to learned helplessness'. *A fortiori*, if it is caused by a physical condition such as pregnancy, disability or illness. The latter would clearly be seen as increasing the seriousness of the threats because the pregnant woman would have the added fear for her unborn child and the physically disabled person, e.g., blind or crippled, would be less able to protect himself. The same could be said of a 'recognised mental illness, mental impairment or psychiatric condition' making D exceptionally vulnerable to pressure. But can we really distinguish between a person who, as a matter of personality, lacks normal fortitude for no identifiable reason or for a reason not constituting a recognised psychological condition and one who can point to such a condition to explain it? The former's susceptibility is ignored but the latter's is not. Yet in both cases to give the abnormal susceptibility to a person 'of reasonable firmness' is a logical impossibility. For example, in *Hurst* [1995] 1 Cr App R 82, CA, it was held that D's lack of firmness resulting from being sexually abused as a child did not amount to a psychiatric disorder and could not be given to the reasonable person. Yet *Bowen* gave the example of battered woman syndrome, i.e., 'post-traumatic stress disorder leading to learned helplessness' as a characteristic which could be given.

Of course, duress may, like provocation, be cumulative over a long period of time so that the objective test may be how a person, originally of reasonable firmness, but, e.g., subjected to and cowed by a long period of abuse, would have reacted to the threats. This was the view taken by the Court of Appeal in *Emery* (1993) 14 Cr App R (S) 394 where D pleaded duress to a charge of cruelty to a child, claiming that she had been reduced to a condition of helpless dependency on the coercer after a long period of abuse by him. The court held that the question was whether a woman of reasonable firmness, having been abused as D had, would have succumbed and committed the crime. You may well think that this is a very difficult question to answer and to an extent may be said to undermine the objective test. Nonetheless, *Emery* was accepted in *Hegarty*.

A solution to such convolutions would be to remove the reasonable person from the equation and adopt cl. 25 of the Law Commission's draft Criminal Law Bill: 'the threat is one which in all the circumstances (including any of [D's] characteristics that affect its gravity) he cannot reasonably be expected to resist' (*Cases and Materials* (9.3.1.1)). That would allow the jury to focus on what really matters: in all the circumstances would it be fair to excuse D? It remains to be seen whether a future court might arrive at such a point but the likelihood has receded almost to vanishing point following the rejection of Lord Hoffmann's stance on provocation in *Smith (Morgan)* by the majority in *Attorney-General for Jersey* v *Holley* (see 6.5.2.2 above).

(c) 'Characteristics due to self-induced abuse, such as alcohol, drugs or glue-sniffing cannot be relevant' (*Bowen*). Thus, in *Flatt* [1996] Crim LR 576, CA, D's addiction to crack cocaine could not be given to the person of reasonable firmness in judging how he would react to threats from a drug supplier to whom a large sum of money was owed.

The courts have been keen to emphasise a requirement for proportionality, meaning that the 'act done should be no more than is reasonably necessary to avoid the harm feared and the harm resulting from the act should not be disproportionate to the harm avoided' (Lord Woolf CJ in *Shayler*). Although Professor Sir John Smith has criticised such a requirement given that D's will is overborne, it seems an inevitable result of applying an objective yardstick.

9.3.1.2 Nature of the threats

It is now settled that the only threats capable of constituting duress are threats of death or serious injury (*Hasan*; *Hudson and Taylor* [1971] 2 QB 202; *DPP* v *Lynch* [1975] AC 653). It follows that a threat of non-serious injury and, *a fortiori*, a threat to reveal D's homosexuality (*Valderrama-Vega* [1985] Crim LR 220) or threats to burn down D's home or business premises or to ruin him financially could not found a successful plea of duress, even if the crime committed in response to those threats is relatively trivial, e.g., stealing a magazine from a newsagents. On the other hand, according to *Valderrama-Vega*, if there is a variety of threats **including** threats of death or serious injury, it is permissible to take into account the **cumulative** effect of **all** these threats, not just the threats of death or serious harm, **provided** that D would not have committed the offence but for the threats of death or serious harm.

9.3.1.3 **Against whom must the threat be directed?**

We have established that threats to kill or seriously injure the defendant will suffice, but suppose the threat is against someone other than the defendant.

? **QUESTION** 9.3

Do you think duress should be limited to threats of harm to D himself or extended to threats of harm to *any* third party or perhaps a limited class of third parties?

It seems clear that duress is not limited to threats of violence against D himself and can certainly include threats against D's immediate family or anyone 'for whose safety he would reasonably regard himself as responsible' (*Wright* [2000] Crim LR 510, CA—in that case threats against D's boyfriend would suffice). D may be regarded as responsible for people he does not know or cannot identify provided it is 'possible to describe the individuals by reference to the action which is threatened', e.g., where the threat is to explode a bomb in a building unless D commits the crime (*Shayler* [2001] Crim LR 986, CA). The defence was available in *Conway* [1988] 3 All ER 1025, CA where the threats were to a passenger in D's car, and *Pommell* [1995] 2 Cr App R 607, CA where the threat was to an unidentified group of potential victims. D's answer to a charge of unlawful possession of a loaded gun was to claim that he had taken it from a friend who was threatening to murder various people with it.

The Law Commission's proposal specifically includes threats against **any** other person and, in truth, given the objective yardstick to test the defence of duress laid down in *Graham*, there seems no reason in principle to limit the category of persons in any way. Clearly, the ordinary person is less likely to react to threats against complete strangers than to threats against close friends or relatives or those for whom he feels responsible but that is not to say they might not also be concerned for the safety of others. Nonetheless, the House of Lords in *Hasan*, obiter, would limit it to threats directed at D or a member of his immediate family or 'a person for whose safety the defendant would reasonably regard himself as responsible…**if strictly applied**' (our emphasis). There is no further explanation of what 'strictly applied' means in this context.

9.3.1.4 **Opportunity to escape the threats**

The defence of duress is lost if D fails to take advantage of a reasonable opportunity to escape from the then 'unavoidable dilemma' posed by the threats. D must take 'any evasive action reasonably open to him... in order to avoid committing the crime' (*Hasan*). Seemingly he will be judged on the basis of what an ordinary person of his age and sex with any relevant characteristics (e.g., blindness) would have done (*Baker and Ward* [1999] 2 Cr App R 335, CA). In *Bowen*, the defence belatedly argued on appeal that D's low IQ should have been taken into account as it might 'inhibit his ability to seek the protection of the police'. The Court of Appeal rejected the proposition but seemed to confuse it with the more general issue of 'reasonable firmness' which we explored at 9.3.1.1 above. The House of Lords in *Hasan* regarded the absence of a reasonable opportunity to escape the threats as a 'cardinal feature of the defence', and warned against any general notion that it does not add anything to the basic questions posed in *Graham*.

A safe avenue of escape will kill the defence of duress (*Gill* [1963] 2 All ER 688, CCA; *Hudson and Taylor* [1971] 2 All ER 244, CA—*Cases and Materials* (9.3.1.4)) but it is always a question of fact for the jury as to whether the avenue of escape was 'reasonably open' to D—i.e., was safe (*Hudson and Taylor* which is examined in the next section). However, the House of Lords in *Hasan* emphasised that a jury should be told that, unless D expects 'retribution... to follow immediately or almost immediately on his failure to comply with the threat, there may be little if any room for doubt that he could have taken evasive action, whether by going to the police or in some other way, to avoid committing the crime...' There is a serious element of confusion here in that the question should be whether D can avoid the **retribution threatened without** committing the crime, not whether he can avoid committing the crime as such. D can always avoid committing the crime by simply refusing to do it! But that is not the point. The issue is could he reasonably have nullified the threat by taking some other action, e.g. going to the police, than committing the crime. Whether the retribution would be delayed or immediate seems to be only one factor bearing on that question.

9.3.1.5 Threat must be imminent

As the above quotation from *Hasan* indicates, there is a related principle (propounded in a number of cases) that the threat to D must be 'present and immediate' at the moment he commits the crime (e.g., *Cole* [1994] Crim LR 582, CA; *Hurst* [1995] 1 Cr App R 82, CA). Thus, if it is no longer operative ('present') because D knows it has ceased or become ineffective, duress is not made out (*DPP v Jones* [1990] RTR 33, DC; *DPP v Bell* [1992] Crim LR 176, DC). The 'immediacy' requirement meant that D had to reasonably fear that the threat would be **immediately** carried out unless he committed the offence. This requirement appeared to have been transformed into an **imminence** requirement by a number of Court of Appeal cases (*Hudson and Taylor*; *Baker and Ward*; *Abdul-Hussain et al.* [1999] Crim LR 570, CA). As long as the threat was 'imminent', it mattered not that there was no danger of it being **immediately** carried out. An imminent threat seemed simply to mean that it was hanging over D at the time of the crime with a real chance of being implemented in the foreseeable future (*Hudson and Taylor*; *Baker and Ward*; *Abdul-Hussain et al.* but *cf. Cole* at 9.4.1 below).

Thus, in *Abdul-Hussain*, the accused, Iraqi opponents of Saddam Hussein's regime, were living in Sudan and feared that, at any moment, they might be sent back to Iraq and certain death. They tried unsuccessfully to leave Sudan several times and then hijacked a Sudanese airliner bound for Amman. They forced the crew to fly to England where they surrendered to the authorities. The Court of Appeal held that the trial judge should have left the defence of duress to the jury on the ground that the threat of death, though not immediate, was certainly imminent in the sense of being ever present. It would be unfair to require D to wait until the Sudanese authorities arrived to deport him in order to be able to plead duress! According to *Shayler*, it is enough for D to 'reasonably believe he has to act now to avert harm in the imminent future'.

Hudson and Taylor emphasised that the jury is the ultimate arbiter in this matter. Two teenage girls who lied in giving evidence at the trial of a man for a wounding offence were charged with perjury. The girls had been threatened by associates of the man that they (the girls) would be 'cut up' (literally rather than metaphorically) if they gave evidence against the man. The trial judge ruled that the defence of duress was not available to the defendants in these circumstances since, at the time of committing the crime, the threats of violence were not present and immediate because there was no chance of them being carried out in the courtroom. Furthermore, there was a safe avenue of escape without having to commit the crime.

The Court of Appeal held that this was a misdirection and that the defence should have been left to the jury to determine whether there was in reality a safe avenue of escape, notwithstanding that the threats were not 'immediate'. They were mindful of the youth of the girls, the extremely violent reputation of the threatener, who was present in the public gallery at the wounding trial, and the fact that, although the girls would be safe in the courtroom, the police might be unable to guarantee their safety subsequently in the backstreets of Salford.

It is clear from *Hasan* that the House of Lords was not impressed with the decision in *Hudson*, viewing it as too lax and preferring the stricter line in *Cole*. However, the House appeared to accept that whether there was a reasonably available avenue of escape was a question for the jury to decide but, at least in circumstances such as *Hudson*, there clearly would be, unless D 'reasonably expects' the threat to be carried out 'immediately or almost immediately'. It remains to be seen how strictly this will be construed and what effect it will have in situations such as that in *Abdul-Hussain*. Indeed, it calls into question whether there is any separate 'immediacy' or 'imminence' requirement. *Hasan* seems to view it as simply an important, if not crucial, factor in practice in deciding whether or not D had a reasonably safe avenue to escape the threats. In our view, the stance taken by the Court of Appeal in *Hudson* is preferable to the unforgiving line in *Hasan*.

Under the Law Commission's proposals D would be protected if he knew or believed the threat would be carried out immediately or, if not immediately, before he could obtain 'effective official protection' (Law Com. No. 218). This would presumably cover the *Abdul-Hussain* situation and allow a jury to debate the adequacy of police protection even in a *Hudson* situation. The current law in *Hasan* is also stricter in requiring D's belief to be a reasonable one.

9.3.1.6 Voluntary association with violent criminals

The seemingly inexorable rise and increasing brutality of organised crime is likely to be a major reason for the growth in the plea of duress. The attitude of the House of Lords in *Hasan* (*Cases and Materials* (9.2)) is that if you make your bed by associating with violent criminals, you will have to lie in it and suffer the consequences. The House restated the applicable principle in a much tighter form as follows: 'The defence of duress is excluded when as a result of the accused's voluntary association with others engaged in criminal activity he foresaw or ought reasonably to have foreseen the risk of being subjected to any compulsion by threats of violence' (para. 39). The most obvious case is where D knowingly joins a paramilitary organisation such as the Irish Republican Army or Ulster Volunteer Force and is then forced to commit crimes by his associates (*Fitzpatrick* [1977] NILR 200). The position is the same in respect of 'ordinary' criminal gangs **provided** that D was aware (or, since *Hasan*, ought reasonably to have been aware) of the nature of the organisation **and** its propensity to violence **when** he joined (*Sharp* [1987] 3 All ER 103, CA—no duress where D knew the gang used loaded guns to rob Post Offices, *cf. Shepherd* (1987) 86 Cr App R 47, CA—duress possible where D joined a gang of burglars unaware of any tendency to violence of its members).

Baker and Ward [1999] 2 Cr App R 335, CA demonstrated that it was not even necessary to join an organisation or gang. Simply getting involved in dealing with criminals known to have a propensity for violence could be enough. An example would be drug dealing on a significant scale (*Baker and Ward*; *Ali* [1995] Crim LR 303) or indeed potentially any scale since *Hasan*. *Baker and Ward* made an important qualification: D had to realise that he might be subjected not just to compulsion by violent threats in general (e.g., to pay his debts), but more specifically to compulsion to commit a crime of the type he committed. This limitation was ignored by the Court of Appeal in *Heath* [2000] Crim LR 109 and again in *Harmer* [2002] Crim LR 401. Duress was ruled out in the case of drug addicts who had knowingly and voluntarily exposed themselves to unlawful violence by incurring significant debts to their suppliers. An argument that D had to realise he might be compelled by violent threats to commit crimes similar to the ones committed—drugs supply offences— (rather than just to pay monies owed) was rejected.

The Court of Appeal in *Z* [2003] 2 Cr App R 173 held that *Heath* and *Harmer* were inconsistent with *Baker and Ward* and chose to follow the latter. *Z* was reversed by the House of Lords under the name of *Hasan*. The House preferred *Heath* and *Harmer* to *Baker and Ward*. It is thus no longer necessary for D to foresee the possibility of compulsion being used to make him commit a crime of the type and seriousness that he committed. It is enough that he foresaw **any** compulsion by threats of violence. Furthermore, even though D did not subjectively appreciate the risk of such compulsion, it is sufficient to establish that a reasonable person in the position of D would have foreseen it. It appears that for D to anticipate (or where he ought reasonably to have anticipated) violent compulsion to pay his debts may now be enough to destroy a plea of duress.

> **? QUESTION** 9.4
>
> Identify the two major ways in which the House of Lords in *Hasan* tightened the rules on voluntary association. Re-read 9.3.1.6 above if you cannot answer.

9.3.2 To which crimes is duress a defence?

Although you may expect duress, as a general defence, to be available as a defence to all crimes, this is not so. Most importantly, the House of Lords, after some vacillation, has decided that it can **never** be a defence to the crime of murder (*Howe* [1987] 1 AC 417

(*Cases and Materials* (9.3.2)). No matter how dire the threats against D, the law will not excuse his killing of an innocent person. After all, the threatener may not actually carry out his death threat if D refuses to kill the innocent person, whereas if D succumbs to the threats, then the death of the innocent party is a certainty, assuming D succeeds in his objective.

Initially, the House of Lords in *DPP for Northern Ireland* v *Lynch* [1975] AC 653 held by a slender three to two majority that duress could be a defence to an accessory to murder, i.e., one who merely assisted or encouraged the actual killer to carry out the killing. The court left open the question of whether it could be available for the actual perpetrator of the killing, but the Privy Council in *Abbott* v *R* [1977] AC 755 (*Cases and Materials* (9.3.2)) refused to extend *Lynch* to cover the actual killer. It was felt illogical to distinguish between accessories and perpetrators in this way and that the same rule should apply to each. The House in *Howe* favoured the line taken in *Abbott* and, as we have seen, held as a rule of law that duress was not available to any participant in a murder, whether as perpetrator or mere accessory.

The ruling in *Howe* has been criticised as requiring an unrealistic stoicism or heroism on the part of D. Is it right that an ordinary man who drives a van with explosives to a military checkpoint under compulsion from a terrorist organisation which is holding his wife and family hostage under threat of death, should not have any possibility of pleading duress if the van explodes and kills someone? Perhaps the solution might be to make duress a partial defence to murder, operating just like the defence of provocation to reduce the crime to manslaughter. At least then the court would have a discretion in sentencing and would be able to reflect the fact of the duress in imposing a lighter sentence. However, it would require legislation to effect such a change in the law of duress.

The House of Lords in *Gotts* [1992] 1 All ER 832, by a three to two majority, took *Howe* to a logical conclusion when holding that duress was not available as a defence to **attempted** murder. D, a youth of 16, was threatened with death by his father unless he killed his mother who had escaped to a women's refuge from the violence of the husband. D caused serious injuries by stabbing his mother but she did not die. The House of Lords agreed with the trial judge that duress was not available as a defence to attempted murder.

This leaves one anomaly arising out of the fact that an intention to cause grievous bodily harm is sufficient *mens rea* for murder.

? QUESTION 9.5

Suppose D stabs V intending to cause him grievous bodily harm, as a result of threats to kill D by X unless D 'puts V in hospital'. What would be D's liability if V:

- dies from his wounds; or
- merely suffers grievous bodily harm?

It would appear that if D stabs someone intending to cause them grievous bodily harm, duress could be pleaded as a defence to a charge under s. 18 of the OAPA 1861. However, if the victim dies, D could not plead duress as a defence to murder. Therefore, the chance factor of whether the victim dies or is saved, e.g., by the unusual skill of a particular surgeon, can make the difference between a complete acquittal of any offence and a sentence of life imprisonment for murder!

This was one of the reasons why four of the judges in *Gotts* urged that Parliament should consider whether, as a matter of policy, duress should continue to be a complete defence to crimes generally or simply be regarded as a mitigating factor. Their sympathies seemed to lie with the latter solution (at least in regard to all 'serious crimes').

There is uncertainty as to whether duress is available as a defence to treason. In *Steane* [1947] KB 997, CCA Lord Goddard gave a peculiar definition of intention to avoid convicting the defendant whereas the simpler solution would have been to hold that the defendant acted under duress and so could not be guilty. Unfortunately, Lord Goddard was of the opinion that duress was never a defence to treason, despite a number of old cases and one more recent (*Purdy* (1945) 10 JCL 182 where the facts were very similar to those in *Steane*) where duress was allowed as a defence to treason. It could certainly be argued that *Steane* was decided *per incuriam* because *Purdy* was not cited.

The Court of Appeal in both *Pommell* and *Shayler* was of the view that duress was potentially a defence to all crimes except 'murder, attempted murder and some forms of treason'.

The Law Commission favours the applicability of duress to all crimes including murder. As a fallback position, it would recommend duress as a qualified defence to murder, reducing it to manslaughter (Law Com. No. 177).

You may find the flow chart at the end of this chapter a useful summary of the law.

9.4 Duress of circumstances

Although of recent invention, the defence of duress of circumstances is now firmly established at Court of Appeal level. It has yet to be considered by the House of Lords. As its name implies, it is closely analogous to traditional duress by threats and many of the conditions of its application are similar. Perhaps the imposition of these conditions strictly limiting the scope of the defence enabled the judges to overcome their traditional reluctance to admit a general defence of necessity. Although it is a rather limited version of the defence of necessity, the courts have an unfortunate tendency to call it necessity as well as duress of circumstances. Indeed, the Court of Appeal's view in *Shayler* was that 'apart from some medical cases like *West Berkshire* the law has tended to treat duress of circumstances and necessity as one and the same'. In other words, in non-medical cases, duress of circumstances was the only 'necessity' defence which the law recognised. However this view should be treated with caution in view of the House of Lords' ruling that it was unnecessary to consider duress and necessity in the case and its express refusal to endorse what the Court of Appeal had said on those defences (*Shayler* [2002]

UKHL 11). Nonetheless, it seems from *Quayle* [2005] EWCA Crim 1481 that it represents the prevailing view of the Court of Appeal and will be applied unless and until the House of Lords decides to the contrary.

For the defence to apply, it is essential, as in traditional duress, that D acts to avoid death or serious harm. In *Baker and Wilkins* [1997] Crim LR 497, CA, it was held that the defence was confined to threats of serious **physical** injury and did not extend to threats of serious psychological damage. The same court in *DPP v Rogers* [1998] Crim LR 202 thought, obiter, that this was questionable in the light of *Ireland; Burstow* (see 4.4.2.1 above). In *Quayle* (*Cases and Materials* (9.4)), a series of consolidated appeals where the defendants had claimed to be importing, cultivating or possessing cannabis for medicinal purposes, essentially to alleviate pain from a serious pre-existing medical condition without the side-effects of conventional painkillers, the Court of Appeal held that duress of circumstances was not available where the threat was mere pain, no matter how severe. The commission of the offence had to be necessary to avoid 'imminent risk of serious injury'.

Duress of circumstances covers a much wider range of situations than traditional duress which can only operate where the harm to be avoided by committing the 'crime' arises from the criminal threats of another whose **objective** is to get D to commit the 'crime' charged. By contrast duress of circumstances embraces almost any other situation where a danger of serious harm arises unless the 'crime' is committed. This could be purely fortuitous circumstances, e.g., a fire or shipwreck, or the innocent actions of a third party or the criminal actions of a third party. An example of the latter would be criminal threats of serious injury where the threats are not designed to get you to commit the 'crime' occurring, e.g., taking someone else's car to escape a gang of pursuers. The **source** of the danger is not normally crucial.

However, *Rodger and Rose* [1998] 1 Cr App R 143, CA, held that the circumstances (here suicidal tendencies of the accused following increase by Home Secretary of a minimum sentence of imprisonment to be served) causing the necessity to commit the crime (here breaking out of prison) had to be 'extraneous to the offender himself'. Here it was 'solely the suicidal tendencies, the thought processes and the emotions of the offenders themselves which operated as duress'. The external circumstances, the Home Secretary's decisions, were simply the trigger or background for the 'internal' suicidal tendencies which alone were the legal cause of the necessity to break out of prison. This was approved in *Quayle* where the court stressed the 'need for extraneous circumstances capable of objective scrutiny by judge and jury and as such … more likely to be capable of being checked and, where appropriate, being met by other evidence' ([73]). Here the claimed circumstance was avoidance of pain and the necessity to use cannabis to avoid it was too subjective to be capable of being properly tested objectively. How could a court properly evaluate whether D's internal motivation to avoid pain 'was such as to override the defendant's will or to force him to act as he did'? ([81]).

The defence was the unwitting creation of the Court of Appeal in *Willer* (1986) 83 Cr App R 225 though it was first clearly articulated in *Conway* [1988] 3 All ER 1025, CA. Both cases involved a charge of reckless driving in situations where D claimed he thought it was necessary to drive in that way to escape from pursuers threatening death or serious injury. *Conway* held that 'necessity can only be a defence to reckless driving where the facts establish "duress of circumstances" i.e., where D was constrained by circumstances to drive as he did in order to avoid death or serious bodily harm to himself or some other person...Whether duress of circumstances is called duress or necessity does not matter. What is important is that it is subject to the same limitations as the "do this or else" species of duress.'

? QUESTION 9.6

Both *Willer* and *Conway* involved D committing the crime as a result of criminal threats by another. Why were they not cases for the use of traditional duress? Refer back to the introduction to this chapter if you cannot answer.

Conway held that duress of circumstances was 'subject to the same limitations' as traditional duress and this means that the two-fold subjective and objective test laid down in *Graham* for ordinary duress applies equally to duress of circumstances.

⩓ EXERCISE 9.1

Write down the questions to be answered according to the *Graham* test for traditional duress and consider how it would be adapted to cover duress of circumstances.

The later Court of Appeal cases of *Martin* [1989] 1 All ER 652 and *Cole* [1994] Crim LR 582 (*Cases and Materials* (9.4)), formulated the two questions for the jury as follows:

(i) was the accused or may he have been, impelled to act as he did, because as a result of what he reasonably believed to be the situation, he had good cause to fear that otherwise death or serious bodily harm would result; and

(ii) if so, would a sober person of reasonable firmness, sharing the characteristics of the accused, have responded to that situation by acting as the accused acted? (*Martin*)

If the answer to **both** questions is yes, the jury must acquit because the 'defence of necessity would have been established' (*Cole*). The suggestion in *DPP* v *Rogers* to the effect that the belief referred to in limb (i) (the largely subjective limb) did not have to be a reasonable one cannot stand with the House of Lords' decision in *Hasan*. In any event, the Court (as it had in *Baker and Wilkins*) had confused the current law as enunciated by all the other authorities with the reformulation proposed by the Law Commission in the draft Criminal Law Bill (*Cases and Materials* (9.4)).

The evaluation against the ordinary person of reasonable firmness also means that the commission of the crime must be a reasonable and proportionate response to the danger to be avoided (*Abdul-Hussain*). 'The act done should be no more than is reasonably necessary to avoid the harm feared and the harm resulting from the act should not be disproportionate to the harm avoided' (Lord Woolf CJ in *Shayler*). That is an objective question for the jury and might well not have been satisfied in the case of the extremely dangerous hijacking offence in *Abdul-Hussain*.

In *Martin*, D was charged with driving whilst disqualified. He had pleaded the defence on the ground that his wife, who had already attempted suicide on a previous occasion, had threatened to do so again unless he drove her son to work. The Court of Appeal held that the trial judge had been wrong to refuse to leave the defence of duress of circumstances to the jury and his conviction was quashed.

? QUESTION 9.7

The Court of Appeal in *Cole* questioned whether *Martin* was in fact a case of traditional duress rather than duress of circumstances. Why do you think it took this line?

Presumably it was on the basis that the threatener (D's wife) required D to commit the offence of driving whilst disqualified. Of course, it was an unusual example because D's wife was threatening self-inflicted injuries, not injuries to another, and the threats were non-criminal because suicide is no longer a crime.

In *DPP* v *Bell* [1992] Crim LR 176, DC, D, in terror of serious personal injury from a group of pursuers, jumped into his car and drove off with excess alcohol in his blood. It was held he was entitled to the defence of duress of circumstances because the fear of serious injury caused him to drive. Of course, if he had continued to drive, e.g., 'all the way home', once the threat was no longer operative, he would have been guilty (as was the case in *DPP* v *Jones* [1990] RTR 33, DC). However, in this case, he only drove 'some distance' down the road.

? QUESTION 9.8

Willer, *Conway*, *Martin* and *DPP* v *Bell* all involved threats by another person.

Do you think the same principle would apply in circumstances where the threat arose, say, from natural circumstances, e.g., if in *Martin*, D's wife had taken an overdose and D, on discovering her, had driven whilst disqualified in order to get her to the hospital?

Read the extracts from *Martin* and *Cole* in *Cases and Materials* (9.2) for the Court of Appeal's obiter view.

All of the foregoing 'duress of circumstances' cases involved road traffic offences. In *Pommell* [1995] 2 Cr App R 607 (*Cases and Materials* (9.4)), the Court of Appeal, for the first time applied the principle in a non-traffic case. The defence could be available in the case of charges under the Firearms Act 1968. A similar view, in principle, was taken in *Baker and Wilkins* [1997] Crim LR 497 in respect of a charge of criminal damage and the defence was potentially available to a charge of aircraft hijacking in *Abdul-Hussain* (see 9.3.1.5 above). In fact in *Shayler*, the Court of Appeal endorsed the view in *Pommell* that duress of circumstances applied to all offences except murder, attempted murder and some forms of treason.

The *Abdul-Hussain* case calls into question the requirement in *Cole* for 'a close and immediate' connection between the threat and the crime committed. In *Cole*, D had robbed two building societies following threats of serious violence from a moneylender to whom he owed a large sum. Even though the second robbery was committed at 4.10 p.m. when the moneylender was coming to collect at 6 p.m., this fell 'short of the degree of directness and immediacy required of the link between the suggested peril and the criminal offence charged'. You may recall that in 9.3.1.5 above, we suggested that the immediacy requirement had become an imminence requirement and that it was unnecessary to have to wait for the axe to fall. *Abdul-Hussain* considered *Cole* and rejected the need for immediacy. Surely in *Cole* as in *Abdul-Hussain*, the threat was imminent in that it was hanging over D when he committed the crimes. In the words of Lord Woolf CJ in *Shayler*, D 'must reasonably believe he has to act now to avert harm in the imminent future'. The House of Lords in *Hasan* seemed to view the question of immediacy or imminence not as a distinct requirement but as bearing upon the wider question of whether D could reasonably have avoided committing the crime (see 9.3.1.5 above) (though their view was that normally the harm D seeks to avoid would have to follow 'immediately or almost immediately' upon non-compliance with the threat). In *Quayle*, the defendant's cultivation or import of cannabis could not be said to be to counter an immediate or even imminent threat of pain (even if pain rather than serious injury were sufficient to engage the defence). 'A continuous and deliberate course of otherwise unlawful self-help is unlikely to give rise to the defence' ([80]). The unlawful act of growing cannabis, for example, would occur well in advance of any painful episode necessitating its use.

Another key factor in *Quayle* strongly militating against the defence was the fact that Parliament had provided a very detailed legislative scheme controlling the cultivation, import, possession and use of cannabis even for medicinal purposes. Under that scheme, cannabis may only be used for scientific or medical research. Doctors not engaging in bona fide research are forbidden to prescribe it. It would therefore be anomalous if patients could treat themselves with it or be treated by non-qualified persons by virtue of the defence of necessity. Furthermore the defence of necessity cannot be allowed to undercut the legislative scheme by sanctioning a continuing and regular flouting of the law.

9.4.1 Reform

Clause 26 of the Law Commission's draft Criminal Law Bill formulates the defence of duress of circumstances in more or less the same terms as those for duress by threats. The same comments therefore apply.

9.5 Necessity

Traditional necessity requires a balancing of harms approach. D's action, far from being wrongful, is justified and not unlawful if it is necessary to avoid a greater harm. Unlike the excuse of duress of circumstances, there is no need to prove that, due to the irresistible pressure of another or the factual circumstances, D felt he had no choice but to commit the 'crime' (i.e., that his will was overborne). Nor is it essential that the harm avoided was death or serious harm. Equally, it is not necessary that there should be an 'emergency' where the danger sought to be avoided is imminent. In *Re A (Children)* [2001] 2 WLR 480, CA for example, an operation to separate conjoined twins was held to be justified by the necessity of saving the life of the viable twin despite the inevitable death of the non-viable twin. There was no urgency in the sense that the twins could be expected to live conjoined for some months and the doctors' will was not overborne by the pressure of the circumstances—theirs was a very deliberate and considered choice.

Whereas duress of circumstances is now firmly established with reasonably well defined parameters, the same cannot be said of this more expansive defence, reflecting the courts' reluctance to allow such vague and open-ended possibilities. In the past, the courts have not been willing to formulate a generalised necessity defence, preferring instead to find other reasons to deny conviction in what was in essence a necessity situation. However, there is now compelling House of Lords' authority in the field of medical necessity that such a defence exists though there is little guidance on the limits of its operation and the conditions for its use (*F v West Berkshire Health Authority* [1989] 2 All ER 545; *Airedale NHS Trust v Bland* [1993] 1 All ER 821; *R v Bournewood Community and Mental Health NHS Trust, ex parte L* [1998] 3 All ER 289). All three cases were civil actions seeking a declaration on the lawfulness of actual or proposed conduct by doctors. As we have seen, the Court of Appeal prefers to view these as exceptional cases and to subsume general necessity under the umbrella of duress of circumstances (*Quayle; Shayler; Jones v Gloucestershire Crown Prosecution Service*). Let us consider what principles may be derived from the cases.

9.5.1 **Medical necessity**

The starting point is the fundamental principle of personal bodily autonomy which ensures that any invasive medical treatment or care normally requires the consent of the patient. Thus, the High Court in *Secretary of State for the Home Department v Robb* [1995] 1 All ER 677 (disapproving the earlier suffragette force-feeding case of *Leigh v Gladstone* (1909) 26 TLR 139) held that prison authorities would have to respect a prisoner's decision to fast to death and refrain from unwanted feeding and treatment under the principle of self-determination. This will usually apply even if the patient is pregnant and the foetus is also likely to die unless the treatment—say, a Caesarean section—is given (*St George's Healthcare NHS Trust v S* [1998] 3 All ER 673, CA). Of course, this would only apply to an informed decision by a fully competent person (e.g., refusal might be disregarded in the case of undue influence (*Re T* [1992] 4 All ER 649, CA), non-competence due to the effects of the illness or medication (*Re W* [1992] 4 All ER 177, CA), or in the case of a minor (*Re R* [1991] 4 All ER 177, CA)).

However, the defence of necessity allows such treatment without consent where the patient is incapable of making a decision whether through illness or accident (e.g., he is unconscious) or mental incapacity. In *F v West Berkshire Health Authority* (*Cases and Materials* (9.5.1)), the House of Lords granted a declaration that a sterilisation operation on a sexually active mental patient who, having a mental age of five, was incapable of consenting, was lawful because pregnancy was likely to be disastrous for her psychiatric health. The decision was essentially based on necessity though the judges formulated the conditions for the defence differently. For Lord Brandon, treatment of a patient incapable of consenting would be lawful only if 'carried out in order either to save their lives or to ensure improvement or prevent deterioration in their physical or mental health'. Lord Goff focused more on civil law cases of necessity and concluded, *inter alia*, that the action taken in the necessity situation 'must be such as a reasonable person would in all the circumstances take, acting in the best interests of the assisted person'.

The latter more liberal stance is echoed in *Gillick* v *West Norfolk Area Health Authority* [1985] 3 All ER 402, where a majority of the House of Lords, without expressly referring to necessity, held that a doctor providing contraceptives to a girl under 16 and thereby knowingly encouraging sexual intercourse with a girl under 16 contrary to s. 5 of the Sexual Offences Act 1956, would not be guilty of aiding and abetting the offence if he believed the provision of contraceptives to be necessary for her physical, mental or emotional well-being. Similarly, in the *Bournewood NHS Trust* case, doctors who detained and treated a mental patient incapable of consenting would have the defence of necessity rendering their actions lawful provided they were necessary to avert danger or potential danger to the patient or others (Lord Goff) or to promote the best interests of the patient (Lord Steyn). It therefore appears well established that necessity defends doctors against battery, etc. on their patients provided only that their actions would be seen by reasonable people and doctors as necessary in the best interests of the patient.

However, it appears that the defence will not be extended to medical interventions by non-qualified persons even if these are in the best interests of the patient. You will recall the various consolidated appeals in *Quayle* [2005] EWCA Crim 1415 where, ostensibly in contravention of the Misuse of Drugs Act 1971, cannabis was being imported, cultivated or possessed for use as a pain reliever for people with serious, ongoing medical conditions such as multiple sclerosis and AIDS, on the ground that it was more efficacious and/or had lesser side effects than conventional medication. Some of the defendants were not themselves sufferers but, possibly out of altruism but also in the course of commercially run alternative therapy clinics, supplied cannabis for sufferers. The Court refused to countenance a true necessity defence for non-qualified personnel, which might have allowed the necessity to alleviate pain to be balanced against the harm involved in the illegality. Still less would the defence be available to a self-treating patient. Instead, the only 'necessity' defence potentially available would be duress of circumstances and, on the facts, this was, as we have seen, ruled out for a variety of reasons, not least because there was no avoidance of serious injury or death.

This suggests that true necessity seems to be very much viewed as an exceptional, doctor's defence.

9.5.2 **Necessity and murder**

It could be argued that the famous case of *Dudley and Stephens* (1884) 14 QBD 273 (*Cases and Materials* (9.5.2)) was as clear-cut a case of necessity as is likely to occur and yet the court rejected the defendants' plea of necessity. The accused had spent 20 days in an open boat on the high seas after their ship sank. Only four survivors remained in the boat and, having had no food or water for six days, they all thought they would die shortly unless they got some food. V, the ship's cabin boy was ill and delirious and Dudley and Stephens (although not the fourth survivor) agreed to, and did, kill the cabin boy. All three ate his flesh and drank his blood. By chance, they were rescued four days later, only to be charged with murder when they returned to England. Their defence was necessity. They had killed one person who was near to death anyway as the only way to preserve the lives of three men. Unless one was sacrificed, all four would die.

It was held that the defence failed although the reasoning is far from clear. The decision could be justified on the basis that necessity can never be a defence to murder as is the case with duress (see *Howe*, 9.3.2 above). However, consider the following situation which was reported to have arisen during the sinking of the cross-Channel ferry, *Herald of Free Enterprise*. People desperate to escape from rapidly flooding lower decks were blocked by a passenger who had frozen with fear halfway up a rope ladder. Despite all pleas, he would not move either up or down. Someone forcibly removed him from the ladder and he fell into the water flooding in and is presumed to have drowned. As a result, a number of people were able to escape up the ladder and be saved. Should not a defence of necessity be available in such a case?

An alternative interpretation of Lord Coleridge's judgment in *Dudley and Stephens* is that no necessity situation existed on the facts. The men might have survived without killing the boy or, alternatively, might never have been picked up at all. In either case, the killing of the boy would have been a totally unnecessary act. However, this argument would seem to require clairvoyance on the part of defendants. The fact is that, from their own and any objective standpoint at the time of the killing (without the benefit of hindsight), the only realistic possibility of survival was by killing and feeding on the cabin boy (there might be questions as to why **he** should have to die as opposed to any of the others). It looked like a convincing case of necessity and the refusal to allow the defence threw doubt on whether the defence existed in any circumstances, a doubt reinforced in obiter comments by Lords Mackay and Hailsham in *Howe*.

However, it seems that, at least where D's **purpose** is not to kill the victim, necessity can provide a defence to murder based on 'intention' in the *Woollin* sense of foresight of virtually certain death. For example, in *Moor*, involving the injection of painkilling drugs known by the doctor to be certain to shorten life, the trial judge directed the jury to acquit if they were satisfied that D's purpose was simply to give treatment he believed to be proper for the relief of pain (see 3.3.2 above).

Similarly, the Court of Appeal in *Re A (Children)* [2001] 2 WLR 480 held that necessity was a defence to murder in the very special circumstances arising in that case. Even though the operation to separate the conjoined twins involved the intentional (under the *Woollin* principle) killing of the non-viable twin, Mary, it was justified by the necessity to save Jodie, the viable twin, who would otherwise die with Mary within a few months. Ward LJ based his decision on the utilitarian principle that this involved the lesser of two evils. The doctors owed equal duties to both Mary and Jodie, but the direct conflict between them meant that the court had to choose which took precedence. This had to favour Jodie because the operation would give her a good chance of a relatively normal life whereas, at best, its non-performance would give Mary a few extra months of conjoined life. Brooke LJ distinguished *Dudley and Stephens* on the basis that here there was no need to 'choose a victim' in that Mary was already 'designated for death' by nature. She could not be saved in any meaningful sense whatever happened. Mary's right to life was fundamental but not absolute and it could be overridden by Jodie's right to life. He adopted and found satisfied the three conditions laid down in the nineteenth century by Sir James Stephen:

(a) the act is needed to avoid inevitable and irreparable evil;

(b) no more should be done than is reasonably necessary for the purpose to be achieved;

(c) the evil inflicted must not be disproportionate to the evil avoided.

The decision is to be welcomed and provides a way round *Dudley and Stephens* in non-medical cases like the *Herald of Free Enterprise* example mentioned earlier. Article 2 of the European Convention on Human Rights prescribes a right to life which expresses certain exceptions including one for self-defence situations. However, the right is not expressed to be subject to necessity situations. The unanimous view of the court was that Art. 2 only applied where someone **purposely** deprived the victim of life and therefore had no application here where the doctors would have 'intention' only in the *Woollin* sense of foresight of virtual certainty.

9.5.3 **Non-medical situations**

Outside the medical arena, there is not much authority for the existence of a general defence of necessity going beyond the duress of circumstances defence discussed at 8.4. Indeed, as we have already seen, the Court of Appeal (but not the House of Lords) in *Shayler* and again in *Quayle* endorsed the tendency of the courts to regard duress of circumstances as the only 'necessity' defence 'apart from some medical cases like *West Berkshire* . . .' Thus in *Cichon* v *DPP* [1994] Crim LR 918, DC, the defence was not available to the offence of allowing an unmuzzled pit bull terrier in a public place contrary to s. 1(2)(d) of the Dangerous Dogs Act 1991, even if it was necessary to remove the muzzle to prevent serious harm to the dog. Rather suspectly, the court held that, because the offence was one of strict liability, that precluded any possibility of a necessity defence. As Smith & Hogan point out, that erroneous reasoning would lead to the conclusion that D would not have been entitled to the defence of duress if he had unmuzzled the dog on the instructions of someone with a gun to D's head! Duress of circumstances requires a threat of death or serious injury to a person and could not apply, in any event, because a dog is not a person.

In *Johnson* v *Phillips* [1975] 3 All ER 682, DC, it was held that a police constable has power to direct people to disobey traffic regulations (travelling the wrong way up a one-way street) where it is reasonably necessary for the protection of life or property (in this case to allow access for an ambulance in an emergency). Although not expressly stated by the court, the implication is that a motorist who obeys these lawful instructions would not thereby commit a crime and that could only be on the basis of necessity. Of course, if life was at stake the situation would be covered by duress of circumstances, but not if only property was at risk.

Despite this dearth of authority in favour and the Court of Appeal's hostility, we think that the true necessity defence should not be confined to medical situations. It may be that, in practice, doctors would receive a more lenient application of the test but, as a matter of principle, necessity cannot be their exclusive preserve and should apply generally.

9.5.4 Necessity and statutory provisions

There are many instances where the statutory wording of offences expressly includes necessity-type defences. Section 5(2)(b) of the Criminal Damage Act 1971 gives D 'a lawful excuse' where he damages property believing it to be immediately necessary to protect his own (see 12.10.2.1 below) and under s. 1 of the Infant Life (Preservation) Act 1929, the offence of child destruction (killing a foetus at the time capable of being born alive) is not committed by one who acts 'in good faith for the purpose only of preserving the life of the mother'. Equally, statutory terms like 'without lawful excuse' or 'unlawfully' have some-times been interpreted as impliedly legalising specific instances of necessity. In *Bourne* [1938] 3 All ER 615, CCA, the requirement in the offence of abortion under s. 58 of the Offences Against the Person Act 1861 that D '**unlawfully** uses an instrument' etc. with intent to procure a miscarriage meant that a surgeon committed no offence when, believing it to be necessary to preserve her life or health, he performed an abortion on a 14-year-old girl pregnant by rape.

On occasions, the statutory wording has been interpreted as impliedly **excluding** a necessity defence (*cf. Cichon v DPP*, 9.5.3 above). Thus, the provision of specified necessity excuses in a statute tends to preclude the application of a general necessity defence. For example, in *DPP v Harris* [1995] 1 Cr App R 170, DC statutory regulations prescribed the circumstances in which emergency services could lawfully cross a red light and the court held obiter that there was no room for any general necessity defence where a policeman crossed a red light. It was also stated that necessity could not be a defence to the offence of driving without due care and attention but that view was rejected in *Blackshall* [1999] 1 Cr App R 35 as far as the defence of duress of circumstances was concerned. In contrast to *DPP v Harris*, the House of Lords in the *Bournewood NHS Trust* case held that the existence of a statutory regime governing the circumstances in which mental patients may be compulsorily detained did not preclude the operation of the defence of necessity to justify a detention outside the statutory circumstances. On the other hand, it was held in *Quayle* that the existence of a very detailed and carefully constructed regime covering the importation, cultivation, possession and use of cannabis (including medicinal use) generally precluded the availability of duress of circumstances.

9.5.5 Conclusion

It appears that the existence of a necessity defence distinct from duress of circumstances is firmly established only in the area of medical treatment and care by qualified medical personnel in the best interests of the patient and it remains to be seen whether it will be extended to other areas or whether the courts will confine themselves to duress of circumstances for non-medical situations. The Court of Appeal (but not the House of Lords) in *Shayler* and *Quayle* suggests the latter, but it is unprincipled to give doctors special treatment. We need a general defence of necessity which, unlike duress, is available to murder in appropriate situations (*cf.* the *Herald of Free Enterprise* example at 9.5.2 above).

9.6 Marital coercion

This curious relic of a bygone age has been recommended for abolition by the Law Commission (Law Com. No. 83 (1977), paras 3.1–3.9) and is unsurprisingly omitted from the draft Criminal Code (Law Com. No. 177). But legislation would be needed since s. 47 of the Criminal Justice Act 1925 puts it on a statutory footing. It provides **wives** with a defence to any offence other than murder or treason if they committed it 'in the presence of, and under the coercion of', their husband.

Clearly the defence can only apply if a **wife** (not a mere cohabitee or a child of the man) commits the offence in the **presence** of her husband, but the key question is what constitutes 'coercion' by the husband. It is established that 'coercion' is wider than duress (otherwise it would be redundant and add nothing to the defence of duress!) in that there is no need for threats of death or serious harm or even any physical harm from the husband (*Shortland* [1996] 1 Cr App R 116, CA). The Court of Appeal in *Shortland* approved the formulation by Judge Hutton in *Richman* [1982] Crim LR 507 that D had to prove that her 'will was overborne by the wishes of her husband' but that this could be due to **moral** as well as physical pressure. However, it was more than persuasion 'out of loyalty' and the wife must show she was 'forced unwillingly to participate'. In *Shortland* the wife claimed she had been coerced into signing false passport application forms in the presence of her husband on the basis that 'if I disagree with him he torments me, he keeps on and on at me until I've had enough and I agree with anything he says'. This would, in conjunction with other unspecified evidence, have left it open to the jury to find the defence proved (see *Cases and Materials* (9.6)). *Shortland* was endorsed by *Cairns* [2003] 1 Cr App R 662, where the Court of Appeal accepted that 'moral force or emotional threats' by the husband could suffice. In that case, the wife was charged with a conspiracy to supply heroin lasting over several months. It was held that she had to be in the presence of her husband at the time of the making of the agreement. The fact that she continued with the conspiracy over a long period during which she was often not in the presence of her husband was apparently no bar to a successful plea of marital coercion.

Notice that s. 47 imposes the burden of proving marital coercion on the accused, on the balance of probabilities. Finally, the defence is unavailable to a woman who mistakenly (albeit reasonably) believes she is married to her coercer (e.g., bigamous or polygamous 'marriage') (*Kara* [1988] Crim LR 42, CA). Such a woman is not a 'wife'.

9.7 **Superior orders**

It seems that if D causes the *actus reus* of a crime with the appropriate *mens rea*, he will be guilty of the crime notwithstanding that he was acting on the express orders of his superior. This was recently confirmed by the Privy Council in *Yip Chiu-cheung* v *R* [1994] 2 All ER 924 (*Cases and Materials* (9.7)). N, an undercover US drug enforcement officer, with the approval of the Hong Kong and Australian authorities, participated in a plan which involved his carrying illegal heroin from Hong Kong to Australia. D's conviction for conspiracy depended on establishing that N would have committed a crime had he transported the goods as planned. The court held that N would have committed a crime, even though the authorities would no doubt have declined to prosecute him. The fact that he was acting under the orders or direction of the relevant authorities was no defence. The court adopted as English law the emphatic rejection of a general defence of superior orders which the High Court of Australia had given in *A* v *Hayden (No. 2)* (1984) 156 CLR 532 in the following terms:

> It is fundamental to our legal system that the executive has no power to authorise a breach of the law and that it is no excuse for an offender to say that he acted under the orders of a superior officer.

Although this case concerned the civil authorities, it is thought that the same rule would be applied in military matters notwithstanding the emphasis placed an unquestioning obedience of superior ranks in military training. This was the view of the House of Lords in *Clegg* (noted at 8.6.4 above) in the case of a soldier in Northern Ireland, although the defence was not argued by the accused.

Although superior orders is not **in itself** a defence, it may bring other factors into play and indirectly prevent D from being guilty. For example, it may induce D to make a mistake which prevents D having the *mens rea* for the crime charged. Thus, if D is ordered by his superior to take someone's property and this causes D to believe he has a legal right to take it, he cannot be dishonest (see s. 2(1)(a) of the Theft Act 1968) and so does not commit theft (*cf. James* (1837) 8 C & P 131). Equally, where negligence is the fault element required by the crime, the fact that D was acting under superior orders may lead a jury or magistrate to conclude that D was acting reasonably and therefore not negligently (*Trainer* (1864) 4 F & F 105).

■ **FURTHER READING**

Clarkson: *Necessary Action: A New Defence* [2004] Crim LR 81.

Elliott: *Necessity, Duress and Self-defence* [1989] Crim LR 611.

Gardner: *Necessity's Newest Inventions* (1991) OJLS 125.

Gardner: *Direct Action and the Defence of Necessity* [2005] Crim LR 371.

Horder: *Excusing Crime* (2004, Oxford University Press).

Horder: *Occupying the Moral High Ground: The Law Commission on Duress* [1994] Crim LR 334.

Smith JC: *Justification and Excuse in the Criminal Law* (Hamlyn Lectures, 1989, Sweet & Maxwell).

Smith KJM: *Duress and Steadfastness: In Pursuit of the Unintelligible* [1999] Crim LR 363.

Williams: *The Theory of Excuses* [1982] Crim LR 732.

Wilson: *The Structure of Criminal Defences* [2005] Crim LR 108.

■ SUMMARY

Duress by threats

Requires (i) threats of death or serious injury (ii) aimed at making D commit a particular crime. The threats must (iii) overbear D's will, i.e., impel D to commit the crime because he, with good cause, fears they would otherwise be carried out and (iv) be such that a sober person of reasonable firmness might have committed the crime.

- Threats must be of death or serious harm to either D, his immediate family or another for whose safety D would reasonably regard himself as responsible (*Hasan*), e.g., threats of lesser harm or financial ruin insufficient in themselves (*Valderrama-Vega*; *Conway*).

- The coercer's object must be to secure D's commission of a particular crime (*Cole*) or perhaps a particular type of crime (*Ali*).

- The basic test for duress has a predominantly subjective limb and a predominantly objective limb—(i) was D actually impelled to commit the crime by the threats or what he **reasonably believed** to be threats because he feared **with good reason** that the threatener would otherwise kill or cause serious injury (the words in bold introduce objective elements) and (ii) would a sober person of reasonable firmness, **sharing any of D's characteristics affecting the gravity of the threat to** D, have responded to the threats (actual or reasonably perceived) by committing the crime (the words in bold introduce a subjective element) (*Graham*; *Howe*)? 'Person of reasonable firmness' is 'an average member of the public' and cannot be given D's personal vulnerability to threats (*Horne* and *cf.* provocation). But can be given D's age and sex and any characteristics enhancing the gravity of the threats (*Bowen*).

- *Opportunity to escape*—failure to avail oneself of a reasonably safe avenue of escape destroys duress but always a question of fact for jury as to whether safe avenue existed (*Hudson and Taylor*).

- D must reasonably expect the threat to follow failure to comply 'immediately or almost immediately' (*Hasan*).

- Plea destroyed if D voluntarily associated with criminals whom he foresaw or ought reasonably to have foreseen might subject him to **any** compulsion by threats of violence (*Hasan*).

- Duress never a defence to murder (*Howe*) nor attempted murder (*Gotts*).

See **Figure 9.1** overleaf.

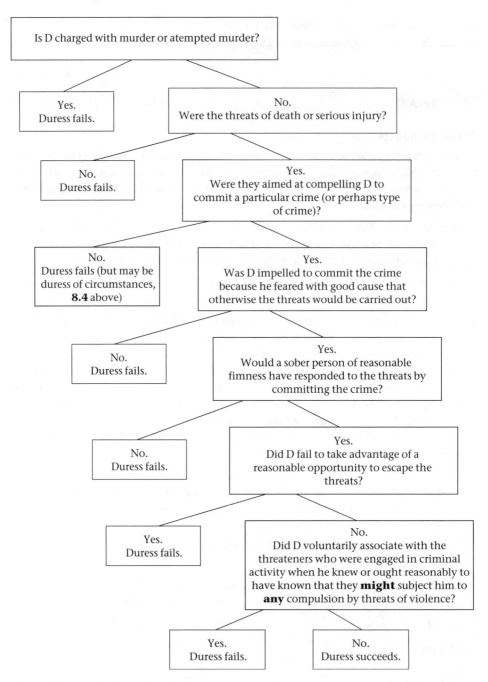

Figure 9.1 Duress by threats flow chart

Duress of circumstances

Now firmly established at Court of Appeal level (*Cole*). Similar to duress by threats but threat can arise from a variety of circumstances. If the harm to be avoided results from criminal threats **designed** to get D to commit the crime, it is duress by threats. If it results from criminal threats without such an object or any other circumstances, it is duress of circumstances (*Martin*; *Cole*). Same two-limbed test as for duress by threats: (i) was D impelled to commit the crime by what he reasonably believed to be the situation because he feared, with good cause, that otherwise death or serious harm would result; and (ii) would a sober person of reasonable firmness, sharing the characteristics of D, have responded to that situation by acting as D did (*Martin*; *Cole*)? This means that D's action must be a reasonable and proportionate response to the threat (*Abdul-Hussain*). The threat must arise from circumstances 'extraneous' to D (*Quayle*) and be 'immediate or imminent' (*Quayle*). Thus, the two defences run closely parallel and both are excusatory rather than justificatory. Note the insistence on threats of death or serious injury (avoidance of serious pain not enough—*Quayle*). Detailed legislative scheme militates against duress of circumstances which could otherwise sanction prolonged, ongoing flouting of the law carefully decided by Parliament (*Quayle*).

Necessity

The traditional view of necessity is that the commission of the 'crime' is **justified** where the harm to be thereby avoided is greater than the harm resulting from the 'offence'. Though there is House of Lords' authority for its existence in the field of medical necessity, its scope and requirements are very uncertain (*F v West Berkshire Health Authority*; *R v Bournewood NHS Trust, ex p. L*). The Court of Appeal view is that, outside of medical necessity, there is no true necessity defence—it is duress of circumstances or nothing (*Shayler*; *Quayle*).

- *Medical necessity*—allows medical treatment by qualified staff believed in good faith to be in the best interests of the patient where they are incapable of consenting, e.g., unconscious or mentally ill (*F v W. Berks. Health Authority*; *R v Bournewood NHS Trust, ex p. L*).

- *Necessity and murder*—arguably *Dudley and Stephens* holds that necessity can never be a defence to murder, but it is open to other interpretations. *Re A (Children)* holds that it can be a defence to murder, though the circumstances would be rare.

- *Non-medical situations*—there is scant authority for the existence of any defence beyond duress of circumstances (*cf. Johnson v Phillips*). The Court of Appeal (but not the House of Lords) in *Shayler* and again in *Quayle* takes the view that any 'necessity' defence must satisfy the requirements of duress of circumstances.

- *Necessity and statutory provisions*—a number of offences **expressly** include necessity-type defences, e.g., s. 5(2)(b) Criminal Damage Act 1971 and more general words have often been construed as importing necessity, e.g., **unlawful** abortion—*Bourne*. The existence of a comprehensive statutory regime does not necessarily preclude a necessity defence in circumstances not expressly provided for (*R v Bournewood NHS Trust, ex p. L*) though it generally militates against it (*Quayle*).

CHAPTER 9: ASSESSMENT EXERCISE

9.1 A fire broke out in an office block trapping the workers on the top floor of a five-storey building. The flames and fumes prevented them from either getting onto the roof or being able to use the stairs. The fire brigade had, however, managed to get a ladder to a window of the top floor and workers were being carried down to safety.

There were still ten more to save when Graham, who had climbed out onto the window ledge became paralysed with fear. He refused either to descend the ladder or to return to the now smoke-filled room, despite the pleas of Helen, who was next in line to escape. The firefighter, Isabel, at the top of the ladder, said to Helen 'If you don't push him off you will all die'. Helen then shoved Graham off the ledge and he fell to his death. She and three more office workers managed to escape down the ladder, but five had become overcome with the fumes and died.

Discuss the criminal liability, if any, of Helen for the **murder** of Graham.

9.2 Coward is of a rather nervous disposition and is in awe of Bully, who lives with him and has ill-treated him over a long period of time. One night Bully comes home from the pub after having had a violent argument with Hard. Bully tells Coward to 'burn out' Hard's house the next night 'because Hard will be away and the house empty'. In fact, Bully well knows that Hard will not be away and hopes that Hard will be seriously hurt.

Coward refuses but Bully threatens to 'spoil your good looks forever' and to reveal to Coward's employer that Coward is homosexual. Faced with these threats, Coward decides to set fire to Hard's house and does so in the dead of the next night, believing the house to be empty. The fire severely damages the house and its contents and Hard suffers serious burns and injuries in jumping through a glass window to escape.

Hard is taken unconscious to hospital where Dr Finlay gives him a life-saving blood transfusion despite protests from Hard's family that Hard is a Jehovah's Witness and would conscientiously object to any blood transfusion. When Hard recovers consciousness he is very angry with Dr Finlay for having given him the transfusion without permission.

Discuss the criminal liability, if any, of:

1. Coward for causing criminal damage by fire (arson) to Hard's property contrary to s. 1(1) and s. 1(3) of the Criminal Damage Act 1971.

2. Bully for causing grievous bodily harm to Hard with intent to do so contrary to s. 18 of the Offences Against the Person Act 1861.

3. Dr Finlay for assault occasioning actual bodily harm to Hard contrary to s. 47 of the Offences Against the Person Act 1861. You are required to assume that the blood transfusion did cause actual bodily harm to Hard.

See the **Appendix** (9.1 and 9.2) for specimen answers.

10 Offences against property I: Theft

10.1 Objectives

At the end of this chapter you should be able to:

1 Define and analyse the basic ingredients of theft

2 Explain how they interrelate with each other

3 Identify whether theft is committed in a given fact situation

10.2 Introduction

A large proportion of cases coming before our criminal courts involve offences against property. Most of the offences we will be examining involve some **dishonest** interference with another's property and are governed by what is left of the Theft Acts 1968 and 1978 and the Fraud Act 2006. Important offences outside of these Acts include forgery under the Forgery and Counterfeiting Act 1981, many kinds of company and commercial fraud dealt with in a number of disparate statutes, e.g., various Companies Acts, Financial Services and Markets Act 2000, Enterprise Act 2002 (none of which are dealt with in this work) and conspiracy to defraud at common law, which we discuss in **Chapter 16**. Finally, the Criminal Damage Act 1971 deals with the damage or destruction of property and does not necessitate proof of any dishonesty on the part of the accused.

Theft is the most significant of the numerous offences created by the Theft Act 1968 (TA 1968) and the Theft Act 1978 (TA 1978). As we will see in **Chapter 11**, many of these offences have been repealed by the Fraud Act 2006 and replaced by a more generalised fraud offence. The TA 1968 was a root and branch reform of the old law, which was of labyrinthine complexity. The Act was largely based on a draft Bill drawn up by the Criminal Law Revision Committee (Cmnd 2977, 1966).

We have no doubt that you will find this a difficult area of law. Such difficulty is inherent in any law which seeks to protect property rights because this will inevitably involve civil law considerations, including property law, contract and restitution. By way of consolation, we can assure you that the Theft Acts have simplified the law, if not as much as was originally hoped. This whole area of the law was reviewed by the Law Commission whose final Report on Fraud (Law Com. No. 276 (2002)) reached radically different conclusions from its initial Consultation Paper: *Fraud and Deception* in 1999 (Law Com. No. 155). This formed the basis of the Fraud Act 2006 which is covered in **Chapter 11**.

Before we turn to the offence of theft, it is convenient to say something about territorial jurisdiction which is applicable to many of the Theft Act offences. As for offences generally, the common law rule, though not beyond doubt (*cf. Smith (Wallace)* [1996] 2 Cr App R 1, CA), required that the last act needed to complete the *actus reus* of the offence must occur in England or Wales (*Manning* [1998] 2 Cr App R 461, CA). Fraud and dishonesty knows no national boundaries and increasing criminal sophistication in our electronic age led to the conclusion that the normal rules concerning when our courts had criminal jurisdiction were inadequate and unduly restrictive. The legislature's response was Part I of the Criminal Justice Act 1993 (*Cases and Materials* (10.2)) which, after an inexplicable delay, was finally brought into force in 1999. It extends our jurisdiction markedly in respect of 'Group A offences', which include theft, blackmail, handling stolen goods and the new fraud offences under the Fraud Act 2006. Offences under ss. 17 and 19 of the TA 1968 are also 'Group A offences', as are offences under the Forgery and Counterfeiting Act 1981 not dealt with in this work. There are other provisions in relation to certain conspiracies, attempts and incitements which we deal with in **Chapter 16**.

By s. 2(3) of the 1993 Act, a person may be guilty of a Group A offence if any 'relevant event' occurs in England and Wales. 'Relevant event' means:

> any act or omission or other event (including any result of one or more acts or omissions) proof of which is required for conviction of the offence.

This means that as long as at least **one** element of the offence (including any result) occurs in England and Wales, the offence is triable here. If Pierre comes from France to Dover and posts a blackmailing letter to Jacques in Paris, his demand (an element of the offence) occurs on posting in England (s. 4(b)(i)). This 'relevant event' in England gives us jurisdiction. It is irrelevant that D was not a British citizen (s. 3(a)).

We have dealt with this question at this point because you will encounter a number of cases with a foreign dimension as we examine the specific offences.

10.3 **Theft**

Before we begin our analysis of theft, let us make some general observations which you will find it useful to bear in mind. Some of these are applicable to other Theft Act offences as well as theft.

First, the system adopted by the legislature is to give a (deceptively simple) basic definition of theft in s. 1(1) of the TA 1968. The five concepts used in this definition are then elaborated upon in the succeeding sections (ss. 2–6). A final overlay of case law interpretations completes the analytical picture. We cannot emphasise too strongly that, whilst some of these succeeding sections give a more or less full definition of the relevant basic concept, others do not, so that some basic concepts (those relating to *mens rea*) remain largely undefined by the statute, allowing the courts a good deal of interpretative freedom. Second, although the courts have on occasion recognised that theft is inextricably bound up with the civil law of property (and contract and restitution), the House of Lords, in particular, has generally striven to exclude civil law complexities by taking an expansive, non-technical view of the elements of the *actus reus* in theft (see, e.g., *Gomez* and *Hinks* at 10.4.1.1 below). As we shall see, this 'simplification' has created acute tension between the criminal law and the civil law (see, e.g., Question 10.5 below) and puts too much weight on the issue of dishonesty, an excess that vague and uncertain concept is ill-equipped to bear. The irony is that the *raison d'être* of theft is to **protect** civil law property rights and its edifice is necessarily built upon the civil law of property!

Finally, although for the purposes of analysis, it is necessary to break down the definition of theft into its constituent elements, you should always bear in mind that in a practical situation they are very much interrelated, and all elements must come together at a particular moment in time to constitute theft.

10.4 **Definition**

Section 1(1) of the TA 1968 reads:

> A person is guilty of theft if he dishonestly appropriates property belonging to another with the intention of permanently depriving the other of it; and 'thief' and 'steal' shall be construed accordingly.

Section 1(3) provides that ss. 2 to 6 shall have effect 'as regards the interpretation and operation of' s. 1. Each of the five concepts used in s. 1(1) has its own interpreting section to be considered. Let us first turn to the *actus reus*—'appropriates property belonging to another'. The three concepts here are elucidated by ss. 3, 4 and 5 respectively.

10.4.1 *Actus reus*

10.4.1.1 **'Appropriates'**

The natural meaning of 'appropriates' conveys the idea of treating something as one's own to the exclusion of the owner. D asserts a right to the property which is inconsistent with the owner's rights. At least for a time, D is exercising dominion over the property and treating himself as the owner. D is in some way laying claim to the property.

However, the legal meaning is undoubtedly wider than this because of the way the courts have interpreted s. 3(1), which states that 'any assumption of the rights of an owner amounts to an appropriation...'

The obvious instance of appropriation is an unauthorised taking or a taking without consent but, as we shall see later, it has also been held to include cases where there is no physical interference with the goods and cases where the taking is with the owner's consent.

How, then, have the courts interpreted the key phrase in s. 3(1), 'any assumption of the rights of an owner'? In *Morris* [1983] 3 All ER 288 the House of Lords held this to mean 'the assumption of **any** of the rights of the owner' of the property in question. This view was endorsed, obiter, by what is now the leading case on appropriation, *Gomez* [1993] 1 All ER 1, HL—although *Morris* was disapproved on the main issue decided by that case (*Cases and Materials* (10.4.1.1)).

Of course, this raises the question of what are the owner's 'rights'. The short answer is that anything that can be done with the property is a right of the owner in this context. It is the owner who has the right to sell property, hire it out, give it away, lend it, mortgage it, damage it, destroy it or throw it away. Equally, it is the owner's right to use it as he sees fit— for example, if it is a book, he can read it, write in the margin, decorate the cover, store it in a drawer, put it on a bookshelf or use it as a doorstop.

The assumption of just one of these myriad rights is enough in the eyes of the House of Lords, even though s. 3(1) talks of 'any' assumption of '**the** rights of an owner'. This would suggest that an assumption of the owner's rights **in general** as a bundle should be required rather than just any **single** right. Nonetheless, the House of Lords has spoken and we must accept that the latter is the position. Thus, a person who switches or interferes with price labels on goods in a supermarket thereby appropriates (even if he does nothing else with the goods) because only the owner has the right to price the goods, a right which the label-switcher has assumed (*Gomez*).

> ### ? QUESTION 10.1
>
> Do you think a shopper who took a packet of smoked salmon from a supermarket shelf and put it into the trolley provided would appropriate the salmon?
>
> Would your answer differ if the shopper had a secret dishonest intention to transfer the salmon to his bag and not to pay for it?

Morris took the view that 'an element of adverse interference with or usurpation of some right of the owner' was essential for there to be an appropriation. For this reason the House of Lords thought that a shopper would not appropriate when he took goods from the supermarket shelf and put them in the wire basket because, since he would be doing precisely what the owner impliedly invited him to do, there would be no 'adverse interference' with the goods. Far from 'usurping' the owner's rights, the shopper would be recognising them by taking the goods to the cash desk in the wire basket.

Gomez held that this aspect of *Morris* was obiter and also inconsistent with the earlier decision in *Lawrence v MPC* [1971] 2 All ER 1253, HL. It therefore disapproved *Morris* and held that adverse interference or usurpation was not necessary and a shopper would assume a right of the owner and therefore appropriate as soon as he took the article from the shelf. This would be as true of an **honest** shopper who intended to pay as of an intending shoplifter. It illustrates the important point that there is nothing inherently wrong with 'appropriating' property. Appropriation is a neutral concept. Only '**dishonest**' appropriations could constitute the offence of theft. Indeed, any self-service shopper will be a compulsive appropriator! The word used is 'appropriates' not 'misappropriates'.

Consent and appropriation

Prior to the Theft Act 1968, the old definition of theft (larceny) required the taking to be 'without the consent of the owner' and therefore a taking with consent could not be theft. However, this express ingredient was omitted from the new definition of theft in the TA 1968. The House of Lords in *Lawrence* confirmed that no such requirement should be implied into the definition of theft. However, 'appropriation' is an ingredient of theft and it could be argued that consent by the owner to the taking may prevent it being an appropriation.

QUESTION 10.2

How might the owner's consent to the taking prevent that taking from being an 'appropriation' according to *Morris*?

This argument found favour with the House of Lords in *Morris* in holding that a shopper does not appropriate when he takes goods from a supermarket shelf. The owner impliedly consents to and authorises this. Its view that appropriation required an 'adverse interference' with or 'usurpation' of the rights of the owner meant that the owner's consent would normally negative appropriation because it would prevent these elements being present.

However, the House of Lords in *Lawrence* (*Cases and Materials* (10.4.1.1)) had stated categorically that consent was irrelevant to the question of appropriation and there could be appropriation even though the owner consents. D, a London taxi-driver, took an Italian student, speaking little English and newly arrived at Victoria Station, for a ride. He demanded the fare at the outset and when the student gave him a £1 note from his wallet, D helped himself to a further £6 from the wallet with the student tacitly consenting to this. The correct regulated fare was just over 50 pence. The House of Lords in the briefest of judgments (which may account for its opacity) found no difficulty in holding that on any view of these facts, D appropriated the student's pound notes. Consent was irrelevant to appropriation, so that even if the student had consented to D's taking, it made no difference.

QUESTION 10.3

Can you suggest another offence which might have been a more appropriate (no pun intended) charge than theft?

Thus, *Lawrence* and *Morris* were essentially inconsistent with each other and there were several Court of Appeal cases following *Morris* and several following the opposite line in *Lawrence*. Little purpose would now be served by rehearsing these cases since the conflict has now been resolved.

The House of Lords in *Gomez* comes down in favour of *Lawrence*. It appears that if D assumes **any** of the rights of the owner whether with or without the consent of the owner, it is an appropriation. Although *Gomez* was a case where V's consent to D's taking of the goods was obtained by fraud, it does not appear to be confined to such cases. Indeed, it is astonishingly wide and means effectively that any deliberate physical touching of the goods constitutes an appropriation.

In *Gomez*, D was employed as assistant manager at an electrical goods shop and was persuaded by B to participate in a fraud whereby B would obtain goods in return for two stolen, and therefore worthless, building society cheques. D asked the manager to authorise the transaction and was told to confirm with the bank that the cheques were acceptable. When D falsely claimed to have done this, the manager authorised the supply to B. B called to collect the goods from the shop, the cheques having been handed over some days before collection, and D helped B load his van. The House held that B's taking of the goods was an appropriation which D assisted even though it was authorised by the manager and even though, in civil law, there was a valid contract under which the ownership in the goods transferred to B. The contract was only voidable for fraudulent misrepresentation unless and until avoided by the victim.

 QUESTION 10.4

Can you suggest another offence (albeit now repealed) which might have been a more appropriate charge than theft?

Let us consider again the basic principles laid down by the House of Lords in *Gomez*:

(a) an assumption of **any** right of the owner is enough; and

(b) it is irrelevant that D has only done what the owner permitted him to do.

These twin holdings have so emasculated the concept of 'appropriation' that to intentionally do **anything** to or with another's property seems now to amount to an appropriation. The reason is that whatever you do physically to or with the property will be **a** right of the owner. *Gomez* has the merit of simplicity, but it is difficult to say anything else favourable.

 EXERCISE 10.1

Read Lord Lowry's powerful dissent for what the framers of the Act intended and what the House should have decided. (There is an extract in *Cases and Materials* (10.4.1.1) but it is worth reading the whole judgment in the Law Reports.)

Does it really matter that 'appropriates' should be given such a wide meaning? After all, only if D's appropriation was dishonest could he be guilty of theft. You will probably have shopped in large chain stores like Marks and Spencer and Littlewoods, perhaps in a large branch with more than one floor. Suppose you wanted to buy several items from different parts of the store, but use only one cheque to pay for the lot. You were descending the stairs, which happen to end close to the exit door, to get the last item from the ground floor when you were arrested by a store detective. Would you be 100% confident that a magistrate would find you innocent if you were charged with theft?

The end result is that the law has put all its 'eggs' in the dishonesty 'basket' and, given that decisions on whether D was dishonest are made by magistrates or juries and may be rather hit and miss, it seems inappropriate that there does not have to be any overt act indicating that D is or may be acting inconsistently with the true owner's rights. 'Appropriation' has ceased to operate as at least a minimal objective control because it no longer requires D to have done anything that looks as though it might be wrong to the observer of D's actions.

Surely what Gomez did was obtain property by deception and that was a perfectly adequate offence. (It would now constitute the offence of fraud by false representation under s. 2 of the Fraud Act 2006, which has replaced obtaining property by deception—see **Chapter 11**). It did not need to be brought within theft. The decision in *Gomez* meant that there were very few cases of obtaining property by deception which were not also theft.

The Court of Appeal's decision in *Gallasso* [1993] Crim LR 459 cannot stand with *Gomez*. D was in charge of patients' finances at a home for the mentally handicapped. She was authorised to draw from a trust account established in the name of V, a patient. On receipt of a cheque for £1,800 payable to V, D, instead of paying it into the V's existing account, opened a new account in V's name and paid it into that account allegedly with a view to dishonestly using the monies for herself. The Court quashed her conviction for theft of the cheque on the basis that paying the cheque into V's account was 'affirming V's rights rather than assuming them for herself' and so not an appropriation. This is clearly untenable. Under *Gomez*, simply handling the cheque, whether honestly or dishonestly, was assuming a right of the owner and the fact that she was doing only what was authorised makes no difference. There was an appropriation.

Acquisition of indefeasible right to the property

In *Gomez*, D acquired the ownership of the property but it was a defeasible ownership because the victim's consent to the transaction had been obtained by deception. In civil law the transaction was **voidable**. Would *Gomez* extend to a transaction where D practised **no** deception on the victim and, in civil law, became the indefeasible (unchallengeable) owner of the property?

? **QUESTION** 10.5

Suppose Shark, a shady second-hand dealer, is engaged to clear out an old lady's attic. He finds a painting he knows to be by Constable worth many thousands of pounds. He offers to buy it for £200 and the old lady delightedly accepts. He knows that the old lady does not know its authorship, or its worth, but he has said and done nothing to deceive her. He simply takes advantage of her known ignorance. Let us assume a jury would regard his actions as dishonest.

- What would be the position under the law of contract?
- Does S dishonestly appropriate the picture?
- Are there any grounds for distinguishing *Gomez*?

On a literal interpretation of *Gomez*, Shark would appropriate when he takes the picture. The fact that the owner consented to and authorised him to take it does not negate appropriation; nor does the fact that the old lady is 'presenting' him with the ownership, because this was what happened in *Gomez*. One of the accused became the owner of the electrical goods by virtue of the contractual transaction. However, there is a difference in our example. The deceit (fraudulent misrepresentation) in *Gomez* meant that the contract was voidable, so that D's ownership could be defeated by rescission of the contract. In our case, the contract, given the absence of any misrepresentation by Shark, is an entirely valid contract which cannot be overturned by the 'victim'. D, in civil law, gets the unchallengeable or indefeasible ownership of the painting. It would seem very odd if he could be convicted of theft for performing a transaction which gives him exclusive ownership of the property which he can defend against all-comers (but *cf.* the court's protective attitude to vulnerable old people in *Silverman* at 11.4.2.1 and the new offence of fraud under the Fraud Act 2006).

The same problem arises where D claims that V made a **valid gift** of the property to D who would thus be presented with the indefeasible ownership of the property which could not be challenged under the civil law. Three recent cases involved defendants who received many thousands of pounds from victims vulnerable due to age and/or limited mental capacity. Of course, if the gift was void or voidable either because the victim lacked the mental capacity to make a gift or because D had exercised undue influence or improper pressure on the victim, the situation would have been similar to *Gomez* in that D would at best have become a **defeasible** owner in civil law. The Court of Appeal in *Mazo* [1997] 2 Cr App R 518 held that if the gift was fully valid, D could not be guilty of theft by receiving it. In truth, it was never completely clear whether this was because D did not 'appropriate' the property or because she could not be dishonest, although the Court did hint that *Gomez* might be confined to cases where V's consent 'was induced by fraud, deception or a false representation', giving credence to the former interpretation. The subsequent decision of *Kendrick and Hopkins* [1997] 2 Cr App R 524, CA doubted this 'apparent gloss on *Gomez*'. However, the fact of mental incapacity was much more clear cut in *Kendrick* in that the victim was an almost blind lady of 99 years and the jury had been told not to convict unless they were sure she lacked the capacity to manage her own affairs. In *Mazo* the evidence was equivocal in that the victim, Lady S, might simply have been eccentric or 'not quite up to it'.

The issue came squarely before the House of Lords in *Hinks* [2000] 4 All ER 833 which is the definitive decision. The victim, a middle-aged man of low IQ, inherited £60,000 on the death of his father. In the space of a few months, virtually all of this money was transferred to D, who described herself as his 'carer'. They paid daily visits to the victim's Building Society where he withdrew the maximum daily cash amounts and gave the money to D, who paid it into her own account. D claimed that the monies were all fully valid gifts or loans to her. The trial judge ruled that an acquisition by way of a fully valid gift could still be an appropriation and, if dishonest, theft. The Court of Appeal agreed and dismissed D's appeal against conviction. By a majority of four to one (on this point), the House of Lords held that the *Gomez* principle was not confined to cases where the transaction was vitiated in some way so that receipt of an indefeasible gift (and presumably receipt of property under a fully valid contract) could be an appropriation even though V has no right to resume or recover any proprietary right or interest in the property. Whether it would be theft, would turn on the jury's view of whether D acted dishonestly (an issue where D's perception of the victim's mental capacity would be of central relevance—see s. 2(1)(b) TA 1968 and 10.4.2.1 below). Virtually any acquisition of property now satisfies the *actus reus* of theft and virtually everything turns on dishonesty. This further extension of *Gomez* is unfortunate and deeply ironic in that the purpose of the law of theft is to protect property rights conferred by the civil law. Yet here the criminal law is allowed to ride roughshod over civil property rights. The civil law says that D is the sole owner of the property and can defeat any legal claim to it, even from the victim, and yet his acquisition of it, if designated dishonest by the court, is theft. Furthermore, so many valid commercial transactions involve dubious or disreputable conduct which, on the *Hinks* view, could be turned into theft at the whim of a jury who chose to categorise the conduct as dishonest, a rather vague and discretionary concept. The answer to the problem of unscrupulous exploiters of vulnerable people surely lies with the development of the civil law concept of undue influence.

Is appropriation instantaneous or continuing?

Another interesting post-*Gomez* case is *Atakpu* [1993] 4 All ER 215, CA (*Cases and Materials* (10.4.1.1)). The defendants hired cars in Belgium and Germany using false passports and driving licences. They then drove them to England intending to sell them to unsuspecting buyers. They were arrested whilst still within the hiring period and charged with conspiracy to steal. The court's jurisdiction for conspiracy at that time depended on the plan involving the commission of a theft in England. (For the current position on jurisdiction for conspiracy see 16.4.3.3.)

 **QUESTION** 10.6

Was there an 'appropriation'? If so, was it abroad when the cars were hired or would it be in England (a) on arrival during the hire period or (b) only when the hiring period expired without the cars being returned?

Applying *Gomez*, the court held that the cars were appropriated as soon as they were hired, it being irrelevant that the owner consented to them being driven off by the accused. The theft therefore occurred abroad. This leads us conveniently to the next question on appropriation.

Could it be said that the appropriation abroad by the defendants in *Atakpu* continued whilst they drove the cars to and within England? If so, they would commit theft in England. The Court of Appeal held that no theft was committed in England but, at the same time, supported the idea that appropriation could be regarded as continuing to a limited extent. As a matter of policy, the Court would prefer to leave it for the common sense of the jury to decide that the appropriation can continue for as long as the thief can sensibly be regarded as in the act of stealing or, in more understandable words, so long as he is 'on the job...' This seems a sensible and pragmatic compromise which views stealing as a process continuing whilst D is still 'on the job', e.g., ransacking a house. On any view, the process of stealing in *Atakpu* had come to an end when the defendants got clear of the hiring premises and long before they reached England.

The 'continuing appropriation' theory does not stop D being guilty of theft immediately he commits the first act of dishonest appropriation. A burglar will steal jewels as soon as he takes them from the drawer and puts them in his pocket. The 'continuing appropriation' theory would simply say that he continues to steal them until the 'job' ends, presumably when he quits the house. As we shall see later, the implications of this are more important for the offences of robbery and aggravated burglary than theft. *Hale* (1978) 68 Cr App R 415, CA and *Gregory* (1982) 77 Cr App R 41, cases involving robbery and burglary respectively, adopted the continuing appropriation theory, whilst *R v Governor of Brixton Prison, ex parte Levin* [1997] 1 Cr App R 335, DC adopted it in a theft case involving D's hacking into a bank's computer in America using his computer in Russia. Appropriation occurred in both places.

This brings us to a related question which would arise whether or not appropriation was regarded as continuing or simply instantaneous. Where D has dishonestly appropriated property and the initial 'job' has come to an end, will subsequent acts done to or with the goods constitute fresh dishonest appropriations and therefore additional thefts of the same property? In *Atakpu*, would the Ds appropriate again when, for example, they resprayed the cars or converted them to right hand-drive or sold them? The prevailing academic view is that generally this is not possible. The opinion of the Court in *Atakpu* was clear:

> In our judgment, if goods have been stolen, even if stolen abroad, they cannot be stolen again by the same thief exercising the same or other right of ownership over the property.

This position is impliedly reinforced by the latter part of s. 3(1).

 EXERCISE 10.2

Read s. 3(1) in *Cases and Materials* (10.4.1.1). Why does this suggest that the last-mentioned proposition in *Atakpu* is correct?

Later assumption of rights

The latter part of s. 3(1) provides expressly for the case where D initially gets the property **'without stealing it'**—which may be entirely 'innocently' or it may involve some tortious or other civil liability without being criminal. 'Any later assumption of a right to it by keeping or dealing with it as owner' amounts to an appropriation.

 EXERCISE 10.3

Write down two examples of a situation where you receive property without stealing it but later steal it by keeping or dealing with it as owner.

Examples you might have chosen include:

(a) where the victim lends you property, e.g., a book and later on you dishonestly decide to keep it or sell it;

(b) where you borrow property without the owner's consent intending to return the property. Although this would be wrongful in civil law terms, it would not be theft initially because you would lack the necessary intention permanently to deprive. A later decision to dishonestly keep it would constitute theft;

(c) if you find property believing the owner cannot be found by taking reasonable steps, you would not be dishonest (s. 2(1)(c) of the TA 1968). However, if you become aware of the owner's identity, it would be theft dishonestly to keep the property.

The forms of appropriation we have considered hitherto all envisage some positive act on the part of D. By contrast it appears that D, without performing any act, can 'keep' property 'as owner' by a mere mental decision not to return it. In other words an omission to return the property is 'keeping it as owner' and therefore 'a later assumption' of the owner's rights. However, the Court of Appeal in *Gresham* [2003] EWCA Crim 2070 thought this might be 'difficult to prove' in relation to the appropriation of a credit balance in a bank account where D, having received a credit due to his bank's mistake, 'does no more than refrain from bringing the mistake to the attention of the bank.' This may be more a problem about proving *mens rea* because if D knows the mistaken credit is there and decides to do nothing about it, he is surely 'keeping it as owner'. *Gresham* itself can be justified on the ground that the bank account in question was in the name of his deceased mother not D himself, the credits being ongoing payments of the mother's teacher's pension after D's failure to notify the payer of her death. Of course, as soon as D deals with the credit balance, e.g., by issuing a cheque or withdrawing cash, that would be a clear case of appropriation by 'dealing with it as owner'.

'Dealing with it as owner' would include selling, mortgaging, hiring, or donating or, presumably, using it in any way as owner. Since this provision expressly applies only to 'later assumptions' where D has initially got the property **without stealing it**, the implication is that 'later assumptions' where D has got the property **by** stealing it do not amount to appropriations, thus supporting the line taken in *Atakpu*.

Innocent acquisition of possession

QUESTION 10.7

D hires a car from V for one week without any dishonest intent. After five days he dishonestly decides to sell it. He drives over to the car auction on day five and, as he is waiting in the queue at the office to enter it into the auction, he is apprehended by the police.
Has he dishonestly appropriated the car?

If D had had the dishonest intent not to return the car at the time he hired it, the case would have been on all fours with *Atakpu* and D would at that point have dishonestly appropriated the car notwithstanding the owner's consent to the hiring. If he was not dishonest then that assumption of a right of the owner, although an appropriation, could not constitute theft.

When he later becomes dishonest, any 'later assumption of a right to it by keeping or dealing with it as owner' would be a dishonest appropriation (s. 3(1)). Has there been a 'later assumption' in our case? Possibly not because all D has done so far is to 'assume' his own proprietary right or interest because he has done nothing he is not entitled to do under the hire contract. The owner has, under the contract, given him the right to possess and use the car for one week. During that week an exercise of either of those rights can only be an assumption of rights which (for that week) belong exclusively to D. Even if he is dishonestly appropriating, it is not of property belonging to V in respect of those rights. The ownership rights have, for that week, been divided up between D and V. Of course, immediately D offers the car for sale or enters it in the auction, he would be assuming a right (to deal with the car) which has been retained by V and therefore still belongs to him. That would be theft (*Pitham and Hehl* (below)).

Innocent purchasers

EXERCISE 10.4

Read s. 3(2) of the TA 1968 in *Cases and Materials* (10.4.1.1). Describe in your own words the situation it is dealing with and say why those protected by it would commit theft without it.

In *Wheeler* (1991) 92 Cr App R 279, D bought some stolen antiques without realising they were stolen. The police informed him they were stolen but subsequently he sold one of the items. The Court of Appeal held that, even though D, having come by the property without stealing it, later assumed the rights of the true owner by dishonestly dealing with the sold item as owner under s. 3(1), he was protected by s. 3(2) and not guilty of stealing the item.

Of course, in cases like *Wheeler*, D would be under civil liability to the original owner. All s. 3(2) does is to prevent criminal liability **for theft**. If, once he becomes aware the goods are stolen, D sells them on to an innocent purchaser without disclosing that they are stolen, he would commit an offence of fraud by false representation under the Fraud Act 2006. He impliedly makes a false representation (that he has a right to sell the goods) with intent to make a gain for himself.

Appropriation without physical interference

We have seen that since *Gomez* any intentional physical interference with property whether with or without the owner's consent is an appropriation. However, can property be appropriated without any physical interference? The case of *Pitham and Hehl* (1976) 65 Cr App R 45, CA (*Cases and Materials* (10.4.1.1)) suggests that it can.

V was sent to prison leaving his house unoccupied. D introduced a prospective buyer to the house and invited him to buy V's furniture. The Court of Appeal held that D appropriated as soon as he invited the buyer to purchase. This is rather suspect because the 'buyer' knew they were not D's goods to sell. In reality, as both knew, they were arranging together to steal the furniture, rather than D at that stage, assuming the owner's rights to it.

? QUESTION 10.8

If D 'sells' the Crown jewels, safely locked up in the Tower of London, to a gullible tourist, has he 'appropriated' them?

We would argue that a purported sale by someone in no position and with no intention to threaten or control the victim's property is not an assumption of a right of the owner to that property but at most a **pretended** assumption of such a right. On this view if D's 'buyer' in *Pitham* had been unaware that D was not the owner, the invitation to buy with the intention of carrying through the transaction would have been an appropriation.

Cheques and bank accounts

A person can steal intangible property with which no physical interference is possible. When you pay money into your bank, the bank becomes the owner of the money but owes you a debt for that sum and for the proceeds of any cheque you pay in. This debt is property and is capable of being stolen. For example, D may dishonestly induce your bank to transfer funds (i.e., the debt or part of it) from your account to another account. It would not matter whether this was done by D's paying in a cheque (forged or otherwise) or sending a letter, fax, telex or computer instruction to the bank. As long as D caused the destruction of the debt (your credit balance) or part of it, he would thereby assume a right of the owner over it and so appropriate it (*Kohn* (1979) 69 Cr App R 395, CA; *Hilton* [1997] 2 Cr App R 445, CA—*Cases and Materials* (10.4.1.1)). This applies even if the bank, which undertakes to accept instructions only from authorised signatories, was not legally entitled to transfer out of (debit) the account because, say, D had forged the cheque or hacked into the bank's computer (*Chan Man-sin v R* [1988] 1 All ER 1, PC; *Hilton*). D would undoubtedly assume the rights of the owner to deal with his credit balance even though the transaction was a legal nullity resulting eventually in the full restoration of the credit balance. The Court of Appeal in *Williams* [2001] Crim LR 253 confirmed that the presentation by D of a valid cheque signed by the account holder causing a reduction in the account holder's credit balance constitutes an appropriation of that credit balance (D, a builder, had frau-dulently overcharged an elderly householder for work and she had paid by cheque).

On the other hand, where D persuades or causes V to make or authorise a transfer directly out of V's account whether by credit transfer, telegraphic transfer or through automatic, electronic payment systems like CHAPS or SWIFT, D does not thereby appropriate the credit balance belonging to V (the debt which V's bank owes to V) (*Naviede* [1997] Crim LR 662, CA). D does nothing which could be described as an assumption of any right of V over the credit balance belonging to V. V is the only one exercising rights over his account. It is V's action, albeit induced by D's deceit, which destroys the relevant part of V's credit balance. (As we shall see later at 11.3.5.1, D does appropriate the new credit balance which is owed by his bank to him when the transfer is received but that debt cannot be stolen by D because from the moment of its creation it never 'belongs to another' but only to D—*Preddy* [1996] 3 All ER 735, HL.)

It was for this reason that the Court of Appeal quashed D's conviction in *Briggs* [2003] EWCA Crim 3662. The elderly victims sold their house to move nearer to their great-niece, the accused. Their house sale was handled by a conveyancing firm whilst the purchase of the new house was handled by the accused. She gave to the conveyancing firm a letter written by her but signed by the victims instructing the firm to transfer £49,950 on com-pletion of the sale directly to the account of the solicitors acting for the vendor of the new house. This was done. Unknown to the victims, the new house was transferred not into their names as they envisaged but into the names of the accused and her father. The defendant's conviction for theft of the £49,950 credit balance was quashed on the ground that the balance was never appropriated by her. The Court's view was that 'where a victim causes a payment to be made in reliance on deceptive conduct by the defendant, there is no "appropriation" by the defendant.'

The first problem with the decision is the failure to identify the property in question. Was it the credit balance in the conveyancing firm's bank account or was it the debt which the conveyancing firm undoubtedly owed to the victims once the proceeds of sale had been received on completion of the sale of the victims' house? If it was the former, then the decision is correct but not, as the Court claimed, because the 'relevant act' was 'committed by the victim'. Rather, the relevant act was committed by the conveyancing firm because, in accordance with the letter signed by the victims, the firm instructed their bank to transfer the £49,950 out of their account to the vendor's solicitors. The immediate cause of the destruction of the credit balance was the account holder's own action. Using the Court's terms, the victims' act in signing the letter of instruction was a too 'remote action triggering the payment which gives rise to the charge' to be regarded as the legal cause of the destruction of the bank account balance. Of course, that conclusion can be and has been questioned ([2004] Crim LR 495; [2005] Crim LR 747, 749) on the basis that the act of the victim does not break the chain of causation because it is not a free and informed act.

However that may be, it is suggested that a conviction for theft could be upheld by analogy with the decision in *Williams (Roy)* if the property in question is the debt owed by the firm to the victims. That debt, which arose when the firm received the sale proceeds, is just as much a chose in action as the credit balance in the bank account. It was extin-guished when the money was transferred in accordance with the letter of instruction. The Court would say that this was caused by the victims themselves but, with respect, the question is not whether the victims' acts caused the extinguishment of the debt but whether the defendant's acts did. In both *Briggs* and *Williams*, it could be said that the transfer was made only because of the instruction of the victims, respectively by the letter and the cheque, but equally it was the actions of the defendants, respectively in presenting the letter and negotiating the cheque, which were the immediate triggers and certainly a significant cause of the transfers. Signing the letter (as signing the cheque) would have no effect on the debt (or bank account balance) without the actions of the defendant in ensuring that those instructions reached the conveyancing firm (or the paying bank). It is submitted that, if the accused in *Williams* was guilty of theft, so the defendant in *Briggs* stole the debt owed by the conveyancing firm to the victims. (For an argument that there was no appropriation in *Williams*, see Heaton: *Cheques and Balances* [2005] Crim LR 747, 750–51.)

Although the Court of Appeal in *Hilton* failed to see the point, you must appreciate that the above only applies where **V himself** activates the transfer process by direct instruction to his bank. If D directly caused V's bank (e.g., by forged instruction or presentation of a cheque) to transfer funds from V's account, D would have assumed V's rights over the relevant portion of the credit balance (*R v Governor of Pentonville Prison, ex parte Osman* [1989] 3 All ER 701, DC; *Williams*).

? QUESTION 10.9

When and where did the appropriation take place in the following situations:

(a) D, in Hong Kong, dishonestly sent a telex to a bank in the USA instructing it to transfer funds in company A's account to company B's account. This was done by the bank in the USA.

(b) D's bank in England mistakenly credited her account with large sums to which she was not entitled. She signed a number of blank cheques and sent them to her sister in Scotland. The sister filled in the amounts and presented them for payment at a bank in Scotland. D's bank in England paid the cheques.

The first situation represents the facts of *Ex parte Osman* and the Divisional Court held that D appropriated company A's credit balance in Hong Kong immediately he sent the telex, thereby assuming a right to draw on the credit balance in the account. It would not matter whether the instruction was acted upon and the account debited or not. D could therefore be extradited to face charges in Hong Kong. In another extradition case, *R v Governor of Brixton Prison, ex parte Levin* [1997] 1 Cr App R 335, D, operating his computer keyboard in Russia, hacked into an American bank's computer located in the USA and successfully instructed the computer to transfer funds from a customer's account to his own account. The Divisional Court held that D would appropriate the credit balance not only in Russia when he sent the instructions but also in the USA when his instructions were received and acted upon the magnetic disks storing the account information.

The second situation in our Question represents more or less the facts of *Ngan* [1998] 1 Cr App R 331 (*Cases and Materials* (10.4.1.1)). The Court of Appeal held that there was no assumption of any right to the mistaken credit balance in D's account until the cheques providing the key to the account were actually presented for payment. That occurred in

Scotland and took the case out of the jurisdiction of the English courts (Part I of the Criminal Justice Act 1993 was not in force at the time but would now give jurisdiction). Simply signing the cheques and even sending them to her sister were merely preparatory to appropriation and did not in any way interfere with V's rights to the excess credit balance. The same is true where D dishonestly draws a cheque in favour of herself, not on her own account as in *Ngan*, but on V's bank account. D appropriates V's credit balance the moment she presents the cheque at a bank for payment whether or not V's account is debited.

In the light of the wide view of appropriation taken in *Gomez*, we are confident that the above ratio of *Ngan* represents the law despite several cases suggesting obiter that appropriation only occurs if and when the account is actually debited (e.g., *Kohn* (1979) 69 Cr App R 395, CA; *Tomsett* [1985] Crim LR 369, CA; *Hilton* [1997] Crim LR 761, CA). The Privy Council in *Chan Man-sin* v *R* [1988] 1 All ER 1 had left the point open, but it may be taken as settled by *Ngan*. Furthermore, it is thought that if D dishonestly writes a cheque drawn on V's account in favour of E, an innocent third party, D will appropriate V's credit balance as soon as he 'issues' the completed cheque, i.e., hands it or sends it to E irrespective of whether E actually presents it for payment. D will have assumed V's rights to deal with the account balance when he puts the completed cheque into circulation and outside of the control of himself or his accomplice.

As we noted above when discussing *Gresham* (see also *Ngan*), the courts seem reluctant to apply the 'keeping as owner' concept where D receives a mistaken credit and simply does nothing about it. He does not draw on it and does nothing to alert the bank to their mistake. He lets it lie fallow. It is true that pure passivity makes it more difficult to establish D's *mens rea*—that he acted dishonestly. But if that can be established, it is difficult to see why a prosecution should fail on the ground that there is no act of appropriation. Surely the whole point of the 'keeping' alternative where D has come by the property without stealing it is to catch any dishonest retention, whether passive or otherwise.

Appropriation of company assets

A significant amount of conflicting case law developed over whether people who represented the sole controlling mind and will of the company (see 15.3.1) would 'appropriate' the company's property if they dishonestly used it for their own purposes. Before *Gomez* it could be argued that the company (through its controlling officers—the alleged thieves!) had consented to the taking and that this would negate 'appropriation'. Since *Gomez* decided that consent is irrelevant to appropriation, this is no longer tenable and there is no difficulty in convicting the officers of stealing from the company. An examination of the case law is, therefore, a luxury we do not need to afford!

10.4.1.2 'Property'

Only 'property' is capable of being stolen. But what constitutes 'property' for this purpose? Section 4(1) (*Cases and Materials* (10.4.1.2)) does not give a comprehensive definition of 'property' but indicates that a wide variety of things can be stolen:

> (1) 'Property' includes money and all other property, real or personal, including things in action and other intangible property.

We cannot regard this as a comprehensive definition because (a) the word sought to be defined—'property'—is repeatedly used in the 'definition' and (b) 'property' is stated to

include rather than to **be** the listed things. Let us examine the types of property specified in the order in which they appear in s. 4(1).

Money

In this context, money means only physically identifiable notes and coins including foreign currency. Therefore there can be no theft of money unless some particular notes and coins are appropriated. In particular, 'money' does not embrace purely paper transactions involving, e.g., cheques and transfers between bank accounts.

Real property

This means land and things attached to land such as buildings and fixtures forming part of buildings, e.g., central heating systems or built-in kitchen units. As we shall see shortly, the remaining subsections in s. 4 cut down dramatically the scope for stealing real property.

Personal property

This covers any item with a physical existence apart from land and includes all the most common items stolen such as videos, cars, cigarettes and works of art. Money itself is also an example of personal property.

 EXERCISE 10.5

Personal property also includes property without any tangible physical existence. Write down two examples of such intangible property.

Things in action

Things in action (also called choses in action—from the French word for 'thing') are personal rights of property which can only be enforced by legal action because they do not have any physical entity which can be physically possessed. The classic example is a debt which is simply a right to sue for money owed. Other common examples include the rights of beneficiaries under a trust, copyright, trademarks, and shares in a company.

If you have a bank account with a credit balance, your bank (the debtor) will owe you (the creditor) a debt for the amount of the balance. If D dishonestly takes one of your cheques and pays it into his own account, he will steal a debt owed by your bank to you for the sum which is transferred from your account to his. However, he will not have stolen the cheque (see 10.4.2.2 below) nor any money—no actual notes and coins were appropriated in this purely paper transaction. On the other hand, if he had gone to your bank and obtained cash for the cheque, then he would have stolen two things—the debt from you and the actual coins and notes handed to him from the bank (*Kohn* (1979) 69 Cr App R 395). The same analysis would hold good if your account were overdrawn and you had a contractual right given by the bank to overdraw. However, it is clear from *Navvabi* [1986] 3 All ER 102, CA (*Cases and Materials* (10.4.1.1)), that where D, knowing that his own account is overdrawn, uses his cheque card so that the bank is obliged to meet cheques drawn by him, he does not steal from the bank. The reason is that, prior to the bank meeting the cheque on presentation by the third party, no debt was owed by the bank to anyone and therefore D has not appropriated any **existing** thing in action. This was a case where D dishonestly drew a cheque on his own account, but the same reasoning would apply if he dishonestly used someone else's cheque to draw on their account in excess of any credit balance and authorised overdraft (*Kohn*).

Other intangible property

All things in action constitute intangible property but not all intangible property constitutes things in action. Section 30 of the Patents Act 1977 declares that a patent or application for a patent is not a thing in action but it is personal property and so covered by 'other intangible property'. In *Attorney-General for Hong Kong* v *Nai Keung* [1987] 1 WLR 1339, PC it was held that export quotas granted to companies which could be sold to other companies were capable of being stolen. It was illegal to export textiles from Hong Kong except in accordance with the quotas granted. Companies which were unable to use their full quotas were allowed to sell them to others. The case held that an unauthorised sale by a dishonest director at a gross undervalue to another company in which he had an interest could be theft.

One general area which has hitherto been held to be outside the scope of this provision is information. Suppose your lecturer carelessly left a copy of your summer examination paper just near a photocopier you happened to be using. Would you steal anything if you photocopied the question paper and replaced it where you found it? You would not steal the question paper itself because you had no intention permanently to deprive the owner of it. In *Oxford* v *Moss* (1978) 68 Cr App R 183 the Divisional Court held that the confidential information contained on a university's exam paper was not property capable of being stolen. Presumably the same would apply to trade secrets obtained by industrial espionage and information held on computer. (Of course, there is an array of special offences created by the Computer Misuse Act 1990 to deal with unauthorised access to and interference with computerised information.)

It was held in *Low* v *Blease* (1975) 119 SJ 695 that electricity is not property for the purposes of theft and this is no doubt why s. 13 of the TA 1968 creates a special offence of dishonestly abstracting electricity (see 12.5 below). Both gas and water constitute personal property and can be stolen.

The human body and its parts

It seems clear that parts of a living person are capable of being stolen. In *Herbert* (1960) 25 Crim LJ 163 it was held that D stole a girl's hair when he cut off a lock without her consent. Similarly, in cases involving drink-drive legislation it has been held that blood and urine samples obtained by the police can be stolen (*Rothery* [1976] RTR 550 (blood); *Welsh* [1974] RTR 478 (urine)).

Corpses or parts thereof **without more** are not regarded as 'property' and cannot be stolen (*Kelly* [1998] 3 All ER 741, CA). However, they are capable of being property 'if they have acquired different attributes by virtue of the application of skill, such as dissection or preservation techniques, for exhibition or teaching purposes.' This was the case in *Kelly*, where D committed theft having taken from the Royal College of Surgeons numerous body parts kept as anatomical specimens for display and the training of surgeons. He was a sculptor who used them to make casts. Furthermore, the Court of Appeal speculated that a future court might hold that it would not be necessary to show that the body parts had acquired 'different attributes...if they have a use or significance beyond their mere existence', e.g., for organ transplantation or as an exhibit in a trial.

Limitations on stealing land

We saw that the general definition of property in s. 4(1) includes real property. This would suggest that land can be stolen just like any other property. A glance at s. 4(2) will reveal that this is very far from being the case. In fact, s. 4(2) provides that land or things forming part of it and severed from it **cannot** be stolen except in the three situations defined in the subsection. Thus, D does not steal his neighbour's land where he dishonestly extends his boundary fence to take in some of the neighbour's garden.

 EXERCISE 10.6

Read s. 4(2)(a) in *Cases and Materials* (10.4.1.2).

- Who can steal land under s. 4(2)(a)?
- How can they steal it?

 EXERCISE 10.7

Read s. 4(2)(b) in *Cases and Materials* (10.4.1.2).
   Who cannot steal land under this provision? Write down two examples of situations falling within this provision.

Section 4(3) creates an exception to the rule in s. 4(2)(b) whereby it cannot be an offence to pick mushrooms or any fungi growing wild on any land unless it is done 'for reward or for sale or for other commercial purpose'. Similarly, it cannot be an offence to pick 'flowers, fruit or foliage from a plant growing wild on any land' unless done 'for reward or for sale or for other commercial purpose'. It would seem that the term 'picking from a plant' would not cover uprooting a plant nor indiscriminate lopping of branches. Those actions would fall within s. 4(2)(b). Other actions caught by s. 4(2)(b) would be stripping lead from a church roof, cutting down a tree, digging up a rose bush or removing a window frame from a building.

  Section 4(2)(c) applies only to those in possession under a tenancy. Because he is in possession of the land, a tenant cannot come within s. 4(2)(b) so that he cannot commit theft by digging up plants or chopping down trees. However, under s. 4(2)(c) he can commit theft if he 'appropriates the whole or part of any fixture or structure let to be used with the land'. Things growing on the land or occurring naturally, such as gypsum or gravel, are neither structures nor fixtures. 'Structure' could include a building, garage, shed or wall whereas 'fixture' could include built-in furniture, plumbing, sanitary fittings and central heating installations.

Wild creatures

Section 4(4) is straightforward and can be found in *Cases and Materials* (10.4.1.2). Untamed wild creatures not ordinarily kept in captivity cannot be stolen unless they have been reduced into another's possession or are in the course of being so reduced. The same rule applies to the carcasses of such creatures. If possession is lost or abandoned, the creature cannot then be stolen.

10.4.1.3 'Belonging to another'

Only property which 'belongs to another' at the moment of dishonest appropriation can be stolen. You may be tempted to think that property belongs exclusively to its owner but this is very far from being the case. The law of theft is designed to protect the rights of the owner of property but it also protects those with a lesser interest in it. Thus, if you pay to hire a car for one week, the property can be stolen from you as well as the car hire firm which owns it.

'Belonging to another' is comprehensively defined by s. 5 of the TA 1968:

> Property shall be regarded as belonging to any person having possession or control of it, or having in it any proprietary right or interest (not being an equitable interest arising only from an agreement to transfer or grant an interest).

It is clear from this basic definition that the legal meaning of 'belonging to another' is far wider than the everyday meaning of the phrase.

Possession or control

Property belongs to anyone having possession or control of it. If you physically have something, you will be in control of it. Someone having possession of property will often be in physical control of it but this is not essential. The precise boundary between the two concepts is not easy to draw, but fortunately it is not important since in either case the property will 'belong to another' for the purposes of theft. When you eat in a restaurant, you will have 'control' of the cutlery you are using to eat your meal but, throughout, it will remain in the 'possession' of the restaurant owner. Similarly, when you are away from your residence, the contents will remain in your possession.

Generally speaking, the owner of private land possesses or at least controls any property on his land, even if it is not owned by him. In *Hibbert* v *McKiernan* [1948] 1 All ER 860, DC it was held that a golf club possessed or controlled golf balls lost and presumably abandoned by their wayward owners. Therefore, even if the balls were ownerless, they belonged to the golf club for the purposes of theft and could be stolen from it. Although this case pre-dates the TA 1968 the current position remains the same. *Hibbert* v *McKiernan* was applied in *Rostron* [2003] EWCA Crim 2206, where a successful prosecution was brought against an accused who donned a frogman's suit to retrieve balls from a golf club's lake.

In the civil case of *Waverley Borough Council* v *Fletcher* [1995] 4 All ER 756, CA, D, using a metal detector, discovered a valuable, medieval brooch buried in the Council's public park. It was held that where, as here, property was found in or attached to the land, the owner or possessor of the land had a better title to it than the finder, who, if dishonest, could therefore steal it from the landowner. Second, if the property were found on the land, unattached to it, the finder would have a better title unless the owner or possessor of the land 'exercised such manifest control over the land as to indicate an intention to control the land and anything that might be found on it'. For example, even if he is unaware of the presence of the property, if he clearly shows an intention to exclude trespassers by, say, fencing, he will be in 'control' of the property (*Woodman* [1974] 2 All ER 955, CA—*Cases and Materials* (10.4.1.3)). It should be noted in passing that if the property fell within the definition of 'treasure' (certain gold or silver articles and antiquities), it would be owned by the Crown by virtue of the Treasure Act 1996.

Ownerless property

It will be seen from *Hibbert* v *McKiernan* that property can become ownerless if **abandoned** by its owner. However, this is unlikely to happen very often. You might have thought that the most obvious case was where D throws his property into the dustbin for collection by the local authority. In *Williams* v *Phillips* (1957) 41 Cr App R 5 it was held that the property in a dustbin is not abandoned by the householder but remains in his ownership until collected, at which point ownership transfers to the local authority. If rubbish is dishonestly taken and sold by dustmen, they would be guilty of theft. It should also be emphasised that losing something is not the same as abandoning it. If you leave your umbrella on a train, you may give up hope of getting it back but that does not mean that you relinquish the ownership of it. Abandonment would seem to involve a deliberate decision to relinquish ownership and one could argue that the owners of lost golf balls do not therefore abandon them. Since putting things in your dustbin does not suffice, it would appear that the owner would have to do something such as dumping the property by the roadside in order to abandon it.

A Crown Court judge reached a rather surprising conclusion in *Sullivan and Ballion* [2002] Crim LR 758. X sold some drugs for £50,000 on behalf of a group of dealers known as 'The Firm'. He went to the home of D1 and D2 where he died of a drugs' overdose. D1 and D2 took the £50,000 cash. The judge ruled that they were not guilty of theft because the cash could not be proved to belong to another. Obviously it no longer belonged to X because he was dead. Neither did it belong to the executors or administrators of his estate because it was not property which he owned at death. He held it on behalf of 'The Firm'. However, because the cash was illegally obtained and the civil law would not permit an action by 'The Firm' to recover it, the judge reasoned that they had no lawful proprietary right or interest in it and therefore it did not belong to them. This is another instance where the policy of the criminal law differs from that of the civil law suggesting that the property should be regarded as belonging to 'The Firm' for the purposes of theft (*cf. Wacker* in respect of manslaughter at 5.6.3.2 above). Even if a pedantic adherence to the civil law were to obtain, the property would presumably pass to the Crown as *bona vacantia* so that, as a last resort, although otherwise ownerless, it would belong to another, the Crown. Surprisingly, prosecuting counsel declined to argue for this when suggested as a possibility by the trial judge!

Proprietary right or interest

Clearly, the owner of property has a proprietary right or interest in it but there are a number of lesser proprietary rights and interests falling short of full ownership. All of these lesser interests are protected by the law of theft. Property may be jointly owned by more than one person, for example, partners, in which case it is possible for one joint owner to steal from the other (*Bonner* [1970] 2 All ER 97, CA). If, as an impecunious student, you deposit your Rolex watch with a pawnbroker as security for a loan, the pawnbroker will acquire a proprietary right or interest in the watch (known technically as a lien) because he has a right to retain possession of the watch until the loan is repaid.

Equitable interests

If you have studied land law, you will probably recall that the legal ownership of property held under a trust vests normally in the trustees of the property, whereas the beneficiaries under the trust have only equitable interests in the property. The latter are, of course, proprietary rights or interests and if the trustees dishonestly appropriated the property, they would steal it from the beneficiaries. If someone else appropriated it, the property would be stolen from both the trustees and the beneficiaries. Trusts are normally expressly created by the original owner of the property (the settlor) who transfers the property to the trustees to hold for the beneficiaries. However, in a number of situations, the law imposes a trust, known as a constructive trust, on the parties, irrespective of their wishes. Such trusts are 'constructed' by the courts on the basis that it is necessary to impose a trust-like framework in order to do justice in the circumstances. For example, an employee who uses his position to make a secret profit (e.g., taking a bribe for awarding a contract) will hold that profit upon trust for his employer. It would seem, therefore, that under s. 5(1), the illicit payment would belong to the employer for the purposes of theft.

Surprisingly, this was denied by the Court of Appeal in *Attorney-General's Reference (No. 1 of 1985)* [1986] 2 All ER 219 (*Cases and Materials* (10.4.1.3)). D was employed to manage a public house and was contractually bound to sell only beer supplied by his employer. He was caught with barrels of beer he had bought from a wholesaler and which he intended to sell in the pub for his own benefit. The court held that it would not have been theft dishonestly to pocket the profit from these sales because D's employer would have no proprietary right or interest in the profit, but merely a right to sue for it in civil law. A similar view was taken by the Divisional Court in *Powell* v *MacRae* [1977] Crim LR 571 where D, a turnstile operator at Wembley Stadium, accepted a £2 bribe to allow someone to enter the ground without a ticket at an all-ticket match. The court quashed D's conviction for theft of the £2, ruling that the bribe money did not belong to D's employer.

On the other hand, in other cases where constructive trusts have arisen, the opposite line has been taken. Where V pays money under a mistake of fact or law (*Kleinwort Benson Limited* v *Lincoln City Council* [1998] 4 All ER 513, HL), the recipient is obliged to repay the money and, according to *Chase Manhattan Bank NA* v *Israel-British Bank (London) Ltd* [1979] 3 All ER 1025, will hold it as a constructive trustee for the payer under the law of restitution (sometimes called unjust enrichment or quasi-contract). The latter proposition was doubted by Lords Browne-Wilkinson and Slynn in *Westdeutsche Landesbank Girozentrale* v *Islington London Borough Council* [1996] 2 All ER 961, HL at 997 but only so long as the recipient was ignorant of the mistake: '...retention of the moneys after the recipient... learned of the mistake may well have given rise to a constructive trust'. In both *R* v

Governor of Brixton Prison, ex parte Levin [1997] 1 Cr App R 335 and *Shadrokh-Cigari* [1988] Crim LR 465, CA (*Cases and Materials* (10.4.1.3)), D knew of V's mistake in crediting the relevant accounts and it was held that V retained an equitable interest therein. In *Shadrokh-Cigari* D was the guardian of his nephew, R, whose bank account was mistakenly credited with $286,000 instead of $286. With the authority of R, D obtained banker's drafts from the bank for most of the money. D was convicted of stealing these drafts, the court holding that they still belonged to another, the bank, which 'retained an equitable proprietary interest in the drafts as a result of the mistake'.

One equitable interest which, by the express terms of s. 5(1), is clearly not protected by the Act is 'an equitable interest arising only from an agreement to transfer or grant an interest'. Transactions involving the sale of shares in a company or land are usually in two stages. When the initial contract to sell is concluded, the vendor becomes, in some respects, a trustee of the buyer, who obtains an equitable right to have the sale completed by the actual transfer of the shares or land to him. The express provision means that the property will not belong to the intending buyer until the sale goes through, so that if, notwithstanding the contract to sell, the vendor were dishonestly to sell the shares to another, he would not steal them from the original intending buyer.

The owner as thief

It is clear from s. 5(1) that it is possible for an owner to steal his own property.

? QUESTION 10.10

Can you think of any situations where this could happen?

In *Turner (No. 2)* [1971] 2 All ER 441, CA (*Cases and Materials* (10.4.1.3)), D took his car to a garage for repair. Following completion of the repair, the garage parked the car in the road and D surreptitiously drove off in the car without telling the garage and dishonestly intending to avoid paying the bill. The court held that because the garage owner was 'in possession or control' of the car, it belonged to him and therefore D stole his own car. A better reason for the decision was that, under civil law, a repairer has a lien (i.e., a right to retain possession) over the repaired goods until the repair bill is paid. This would seem to constitute a proprietary right or interest in the goods. Unfortunately, the Court of Appeal could not use this ground to justify conviction because the trial judge had directed the jury to ignore any question of liens. The problem with basing conviction on the garage owner's 'possession or control' of the car is that, without the lien, D would have, under the civil law, a right to immediate possession of the vehicle from the garage owner, whether he had paid the repair cost or not. It would seem a little odd to be able to convict D of theft for doing something which he has a perfect right to do under the civil law! Other examples you might have given in answer to our Question would be a trustee stealing trust property, an owner stealing a watch he has pawned from the pawnbroker, a joint owner stealing from his co-owner, or the owner of a car stealing it from a person he has hired it to.

Transactions transferring ownership

Since D must 'dishonestly appropriate property belonging to another', it is plain that the time for deciding if property 'belongs to another' is the moment of the dishonest appropriation (*Lawrence*). In most theft cases, this will present no problem because it will be clear that the property belonged to the victim at the outset and continued to belong to the victim throughout, so that at whatever time D dishonestly appropriated it, the property 'belonged to another'. However, in some situations, even though D is acting dishonestly, there may be a transaction involving the property, by virtue of which D ends up becoming the owner of that property under the civil law. We have already come across this situation in *Gomez* and other cases in our discussion of appropriation. If, in the course of the transaction, D becomes the sole owner of the property which has ceased to 'belong to another', it becomes crucial to identify whether the dishonest appropriation occurred before or after the property ceased to 'belong to another'. Unfortunately, this was an issue which the House of Lords in *Gomez* completely ignored even though it was most relevant to a proper disposal of the case.

> **? QUESTION** 10.11
>
> Suppose that D drove into a self-service petrol station, filled up his car with petrol and dishonestly drove off without paying. On these facts, it is not clear whether D is or is not guilty of stealing the petrol. What is the crucial issue upon which his liability for theft would turn?

When D puts the petrol into his tank, there is no doubt that he is appropriating property which belongs to the petrol station owner. The fact that the owner impliedly invites customers to do just that with his petrol is no longer an obstacle to establishing appropriation, because consent is now irrelevant to appropriation (*Gomez*). Clearly, if D intended not to pay when he filled his tank, that appropriation would be a dishonest appropriation constituting theft (*McHugh* (1976) 64 Cr App R 92, CA). However, suppose that D does intend to pay when he fills up and only decides to drive off without paying afterwards when he sees the cashier is otherwise engaged. Accepting that there is a dishonest appropriation of the petrol when he drives off, D would not commit theft because the ownership in the petrol would have transferred to D **before** any **dishonest** appropriation had occurred (*Edwards v Ddin* [1976] 3 All ER 705, DC—*Cases and Materials* (10.4.1.3)). In other words, if D by virtue of the transaction, **innocently** acquires V's **entire** proprietary interest in the property, there is no longer any property 'belonging to another' for him to dishonestly appropriate (unless the special situations described in s. 5(3) and (4) of the TA 1968 apply to artificially deem the property still to belong to the original owner—we consider these below).

You may be wondering how to decide (a) **if** ownership passes to D and (b) if so, **when** it passes to D. This is determined by the rules of civil law, such as those relating to sale of goods, and a full answer is not possible in a criminal law text. The basic rule is that ownership transfers if and when the parties to the transaction intend it to. Unfortunately, the parties often do not make their intentions clear and such intentions must be deduced from the nature of the transaction and its circumstances. In a petrol sale, the implication is that the parties intend the ownership to transfer as it goes into the customer's tank because when it mixes with the petrol already in the tank, it will cease to be identifiable as the original owner's petrol. On the other hand, the courts have decided that in a normal shop or supermarket sale, the implied intention of the shop owner is that ownership should transfer only upon payment for the goods (*Davies v Leighton* (1978) 68 Cr App R 4, DC). Where the parties' intention cannot be determined, expressly or impliedly, s. 18 of the Sale

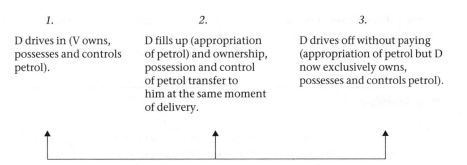

Figure 10.1 The petrol station transaction

of Goods Act 1979 lays down a number of rules for deciding if and when ownership passes in a sale transaction. When money changes hands, the general rule is that ownership in those notes and coins will transfer on physical delivery.

The issues discussed in this section are summarised in **Figure 10.1**.

The crucial issue is whether D's first **dishonest** appropriation came only **after** the ownership transferred to him. The rule is that if D formed his dishonest intention not to pay only after the transfer of ownership, it is not theft. (There is, in fact, a special offence in s. 3 of the TA 1978 which caters for this situation—dishonestly making off without payment (see 11.4.4).) If D dishonestly appropriates **before** any transfer of ownership, there is no problem. However, in our situation, if D never at any time intended to pay, his dishonest appropriation (filling up) seems to occur at the very moment of the transfer of ownership. Where the dishonest appropriation and the passing of ownership are **coincident**, there is a dishonest appropriation of property belonging to another. This is the implication of *Lawrence, Gomez* and *Hinks*. (We consider the whole problem further below.)

There are some special situations defined in s. 5(3) and (4) where, even though D becomes the sole owner of the property in question, it is artificially deemed still to belong to another for the purposes of theft. Let us now examine these situations.

Belonging to another—special cases

It cannot be stressed too strongly that it is only necessary to invoke s. 5(2) to (4) in cases where the property does not 'belong to another' within the general definition in s. 5(1).

As the Court of Appeal recognised in *Arnold* [1997] 4 All ER 1, there is substantial overlap between s. 5(1) and the later subsections and 'the structure of s. 5 is essentially intended to be cumulative in effect'.

Getting property by mistake (s. 5(4))

First it is necessary to consider the wording of s. 5(4):

> Where a person gets property by another's mistake, and is under an obligation to make restoration (in whole or in part) of the property or its proceeds or of the value thereof, then to the extent of that obligation the property or proceeds shall be regarded (as against him) as belonging to the person entitled to restoration, and an intention not to make restoration shall be regarded accordingly as an intention to deprive that person of the property or proceeds.

The two essential features of the section are (a) D must get the property by mistake and (b) he must be under 'an obligation to make restoration'. The provision was prompted by a desire to catch a person who dishonestly kept an overpayment of wages.

? QUESTION 10.12

Suppose D's employer miscalculates the wage due to D and puts too much in his wage packet. He hands the wage packet to D. When D opens the packet at home, he realises for the first time that he has been paid too much. He dishonestly decides to keep the excess and say nothing.

- Explain with reasons when D dishonestly appropriates the excess money.
- At this point does the excess money 'belong to another' under s. 5(1)?

This situation might not constitute theft without the help of s. 5(4) because the civil law rule is that the ownership in money would transfer on delivery, i.e., when the wage packet was handed over. At this moment, the employer would cease to have any proprietary right or interest in (and possession and control of) the money long before there is any question of dishonesty on the part of D. This is when s. 5(4) would come into play. D received the extra money by the employer's mistake and, under the law of restitution, D would be under a legal obligation to repay the extra amount mistakenly overpaid. Thus the extra money would, by virtue of s. 5(4), still be deemed to belong to the employer, notwithstanding that the entire ownership in it and possession and control of it had been transferred to D **before** any dishonesty. Even though D has become the owner of the extra notes and coins, it appears that a dishonest decision to keep it does amount to a dishonest appropriation (see our discussion of appropriation at 10.4.1.1 above).

Of course, the traditional method of paying wages in cash has now been superseded for many employees by a direct transfer from the employer's bank account to that of the employee.

? QUESTION 10.13

Suppose your employer credits your bank account with £100 more than was due. When you discover the error, you dishonestly fail to return the money.

- Have you stolen any money?
- What 'property' has been stolen?

Since the transfer between banks is purely a paper transaction, no money (notes and coins) physically changes hands. We therefore have to look for some other 'property' which is appropriated. The obvious answer is the debt representing the extra amount credited to D's account, which D's bank now owes to D. This was gained by the employer's mistake and D is under an obligation to restore the 'value' of this debt, which therefore, to the extent of the overpayment, is deemed to belong to the employer. These were the facts of *Attorney-General's Reference (No. 1 of 1983)* [1984] 3 All ER 369 (*Cases and Materials* (10.4.1.3)) where the Court of Appeal applied the above reasoning. Exactly the same view was taken in *Ngan* [1998] 1 Cr App R 331, CA, where the bank itself mistakenly credited D's account with the proceeds of cheques meant for X's account. Let us now look at the detailed requirements of the section.

The mistake

You will notice that in the examples given so far, the mistake was made spontaneously by the victim and not in any way induced by D. However, it would seem that mistakes brought about by D's fraud or other conduct would also be covered by the section. In *Gresham* [2003] EWCA Crim 2070, D failed to notify the Department for Education of his mother's death. As a result, they continued to pay for ten more years her teacher's pension into her bank account, which D was able to operate with a Power of Attorney previously signed by her. Of course, the entitlement to the pension and the validity of the Power of Attorney ceased on the mother's death. The Court was in no doubt that s. 5(4) applied equally to 'unforced' mistakes and, as here, mistakes caused by D's own fraudulent conduct. Therefore the credits when the pension was paid into the account each month were deemed to belong to the Department for Education.

We need to remind ourselves at this point that it is necessary to invoke s. 5(4) only in cases where the ownership in the property has passed to D by the time D's dishonest appropriation occurs.

? QUESTION 10.14

Think back to your studies of the law of contract.

- What is the difference between a contract which is void and one which is only voidable?
- What kind of mistakes make a contract void?

Certain fundamental mistakes, e.g., as to the identity of the transferee or of the subject-matter, would render the contract void and ineffective to transfer the ownership as apparently intended. It follows that whenever the dishonest appropriation occurs, the victim will still have 'a proprietary right or interest' in the property under s. 5(1). Quite simply, s. 5(4) is unnecessary and irrelevant.

However, most mistakes will not render the transaction void but at most voidable, so that they will not prevent the ownership passing to D. You may recall *Lewis* v *Averay* [1971] 3 All ER 907, CA where the victim was induced to accept a dud cheque for his car when the rogue in front of him falsely claimed to be Richard Greene, once a well-known film actor. This mistake about the standing of the person buying the car, caused by D's fraudulent misrepresentation, rendered the contract voidable only. D therefore became the owner of the car. This looks like a case for s. 5(4) if it is to be theft. However, you would need to think about the effects of *Gomez* which concerned a similar fact situation. The key point of *Gomez* was to abolish any requirement of adverse interference with the owner's rights for an appropriation. Therefore, even though the owner is willingly presenting D with the ownership (albeit under the mistake, fraudulently induced by D, that the cheque will be met), there will still be an appropriation of the property. Given that D knows the cheque is worthless, his appropriation will be dishonest, but is it of property belonging to another?

In *Gomez*, D1, a shop employee, and D2, his 'customer' friend, duped the shop manager into accepting worthless, stolen building society cheques in payment for electrical goods. The goods were ordered and the cheques handed over some days before the goods were loaded from the shop into D2's van by D1 and D2. By a four to one majority the House of Lords was in no doubt that D1 and D2 were guilty of theft. Regrettably, all the argument centred on the issue of the general meaning of 'appropriation' and no consideration at all was given to the issue of what precise conduct actually constituted the appropriation, nor of whether, at the moment of appropriation, the property belonged to another.

The House's failure in *Gomez* to pinpoint precisely what act(s) of the defendants constituted the appropriation is as surprising as its failure to consider whether at this time the goods 'belonged to another'. The only clue we are given by Lord Keith, who spoke for the majority, is in this passage: '... the owner of the goods was induced by fraud to part with them to the rogue ... the taking by the rogue ... amounted to an appropriation.'

In fact we know from the Court of Appeal's judgment that the prosecution case had been argued on the basis that D2 appropriated the goods with the assistance of D1. Lord Keith's view, therefore, seems to be that D2 appropriated when he collected the goods.

Did the goods 'belong to another' at this moment of appropriation or had the ownership already transferred to D2 by virtue of the voidable contract **before** he physically appropriated the goods by collecting them? You will recall that ownership passes when the parties intend it to and that the courts have held that in a shop sale the parties' intention is that the ownership should transfer only upon payment (*Davies* v *Leighton* (above)). However, in *Gomez* the payment (in the form of the stolen cheques) had been handed over some days before the goods were collected. This would suggest that ownership passed **before** D2's dishonest appropriation, probably when D1 earmarked the particular appliances to the contract (e.g., by putting them on one side or sticking D2's name on them). This would also be the position under s. 18(1) of the Sale of Goods Act 1979 which applies where the parties' intention cannot be expressly or impliedly ascertained. In this case, when D2 physically appropriates, nobody else has any 'proprietary right or interest' in the goods which therefore do not 'belong to another'. Thus, he would not commit theft.

There are two possible answers to this argument, even accepting the premise that ownership did transfer **before** D2's dishonest appropriation:

(a) the goods still belonged to the shopowner at the time of collection because he had 'possession or control' of them. This is an unattractive argument because D2, as the owner by virtue of the voidable contract, has an immediate right to possession. You will recall that *Turner (No. 2)*, nonetheless, supports the argument, although it has attracted considerable criticism;

(b) the implication of Parker LJ's view in the civil case of *Dobson* v *General Accident Insurance Corporation plc* [1989] 3 All ER 927, CA is that the very fact of acquisition of ownership is **itself** an appropriation **irrespective** of any **physical** contact with the property. D had telephoned V after V had advertised a diamond ring for sale in a newspaper, and had agreed to buy the ring. He then went round to V's house and took the ring in return for a stolen cheque which bounced. Parker LJ thought that the parties intended ownership in the ring to pass only on delivery. However, if the ownership had passed when the contract to buy was concluded over the telephone, '. . . the result would be that the making of the contract constituted the appropriation. It was by that act that the rogue assumed the rights of an owner and at that time the property did belong to the plaintiff'. The rogue had never even seen the diamond ring but if he had contracted to buy it and the ownership had thereby transferred to him, he had, on this view, already stolen it! It would not matter that he got cold feet and never turned up at V's house to collect and 'pay'. The House of Lords in *Gomez*, whilst approving the general line taken in *Dobson*, did not consider this particular point. The correctness of Parker LJ's obiter dictum is therefore an open question, but it is probable that the House would have approved it.

The arguments above are based on the premise that ownership did transfer to D2 **before** he collected the goods. We would suggest that the probable explanation which the House would have given had it addressed the question, is that the parties did not intend ownership to pass until delivery. This would mean that the moment of appropriation by D2 (collection) was at the same time as the moment of transfer of ownership (delivery). *Lawrence* and *Hinks* implicitly hold that it is an appropriation of property belonging to another and therefore theft where the moment of appropriation coincides with the moment of transfer of ownership.

? QUESTION 10.15

Returning to the situation in *Lewis* v *Averay*:

- When did D dishonestly appropriate the car?
- When did the ownership pass to D?
- Did D dishonestly appropriate property belonging to another under s. 5(1)?

It seems clear from *Gomez* that wherever D has induced V's mistake by fraud and has thus been dishonest at the outset, there will be no need to invoke s. 5(4). If Parker LJ's dictum is correct, provided D is dishonest all along, it would not matter when ownership transferred because the actual acquisition of ownership, whenever it comes, will be a dishonest appropriation of someone else's property. The rogue in *Lewis* v *Averay* would commit theft. (See also the example we gave at (b) above.)

If Parker LJ's dictum is incorrect, the dishonest appropriation would occur only when D took physical control of the car (or possibly the ignition key). This might well be after the ownership has transferred which would be likely to occur when the contract was concluded or at the latest when the cheque was handed over. If the *Turner (No. 2)* principle is correct (which we doubt), it would enable a conviction for theft because when D dishonestly appropriates by taking possession of the car or key, it is then still possessed by V, to whom it therefore belongs for the purposes of theft. If *Turner (No. 2)* was rejected, it would mean that *Lewis* v *Averay* was distinguishable from *Gomez* in that the dishonest appropriation of the car came only after the transfer of ownership. In order to convict of theft in that case, we would need to utilise s. 5(4). Of course, it is possible that a court would decide that, as we suggested might be the case in *Gomez*, the parties' intention was to transfer ownership only on delivery. In that case, it would be identical to *Gomez* and theft would occur without recourse to s. 5(4).

These are difficult and complex arguments but the important point to grasp is that since *Gomez*, it is unlikely to be necessary to invoke s. 5(4) where V's mistake is caused by D's fraud. However, as we have seen, *Gresham* [2003] EWCA Crim 2070 is clear that s. 5(4) can be applied in situations where V's mistake is induced by D's deception and, indeed, the Court expressly preferred to base its decision on s. 5(4).

What about where the mistake is V's own, uninfluenced by any conduct of D? As we have seen, the most likely instance is where D is mistakenly paid too much money, whether in the form of cash, cheques, drafts or credit transfer to a bank account. D does not usually find out about the overpayment until the ownership has been transferred to him, so that it looks as though the property will have ceased to belong to another by the time he dishonestly appropriates (unless s. 5(4) deems it to belong to another). In fact, even here, there is authority for the view that s. 5(4) is unnecessary and that notwithstanding the transfer of ownership, the property still belongs to another under s. 5(1). The basis of this view is that when someone pays money, whether by cash, cheques, bank drafts or credit transfers to a bank account, under a mistake, they retain by virtue of a constructive trust an equitable interest in the property, which is a 'proprietary right or interest' under s. 5(1). You may remember the case of *Shadrokh-Cigari* [1988] Crim LR 465, CA, where it was held that a bank retained an equitable interest in drafts sent to a dishonest D under a mistake as to the amount held in a bank account. Section 5(4) was held not to be needed. If this case is correct, we would not even need s. 5(4) to cover the very situation it was enacted for— overpayment of wages!

On the other hand in *Ngan* [1998] 1 Cr App R 331 where D's bank account had been credited with someone else's cheques due to bank error, the Court of Appeal, without considering the constructive trust argument, relied on s. 5(4) to deem these wrongful credits to belong to that other person. In line with *Shadrokh-Cigari*, Lords Browne-Wilkinson and Slynn, two of the majority in the civil case of *Westdeutsche Landesbank Girozentrale* v *Islington London Borough Council* [1996] 2 All ER 961, HL, thought that in such cases 'retention of the moneys after the recipient . . . learned of the mistake may well have given rise to a constructive trust'. Thus s. 5(4) would be unnecessary. However, it does appear that the courts prefer to avoid complex analysis of difficult civil law concepts and take the more straightforward route offered by s. 5(4) where possible (*Gresham*).

The obligation to restore

Having established that D got the property by mistake, s. 5(4) can only operate if he is thereby under an obligation to restore in whole or in part the property or its proceeds or its value. Obligation here means a **legal** obligation. In *Gilks* [1972] 3 All ER 280, CA (*Cases and Materials* (10.4.1.3)) ethnic confusion prompted a bookmaker to pay D winnings on a race won by 'Fighting Taffy' when D had actually backed 'Fighting Scot'. D realised the mistake when he was paid but refused to repay. D certainly got the money by mistake but he was not under any legal obligation to repay because it was a gambling debt which the law treats as unenforceable. Section 5(4) was therefore inapplicable. (Rather suspectly the court held that the ownership of the notes and coins did not pass to D on delivery and therefore still belonged to the bookmaker under s. 5(1).)

? QUESTION 10.16

In the light of *Gomez*, would it make any difference to D's conviction in *Gilks* if the correct view that D did become the owner of the notes and coins handed over, prevailed?

When does an obligation to restore arise? In the mistaken overpayment cases, the law of restitution imposes an obligation to restore not the property (i.e., the actual notes and coins handed over) but its 'value' (i.e., the equivalent 'money'). In the voidable contract cases, it can be argued that no obligation arises unless and until the contract is avoided (by its rescission) by V. However, if the contract is successfully rescinded, under civil law the ownership would in any case revert to V who would then have a proprietary right or interest in it under s. 5(1). There would once again be no need for s. 5(4).

In answer to our Question, it would seem that D dishonestly appropriated the money when he took delivery of it because he realised the mistake at that point. The case is the same as the delivery of the money to the dishonest taxi-driver in *Lawrence*. It is irrelevant that V consents to D becoming the owner of the notes and coins. Where the appropriation and transfer of ownership are coincident there is an appropriation of property belonging to another without the need for recourse to s. 5(4).

Obligation to retain and deal in a particular way (s. 5(3))
Section 5(3) states:

> Where a person receives property from or on account of another, and is under an obligation to the other to retain and deal with that property or its proceeds in a particular way, the property or proceeds shall be regarded (as against him) as belonging to the other.

Once again the section is only needed if the property is found not to belong to another under the normal principles in s. 5(1). In effect therefore it can apply only where D becomes the owner of the property he 'receives from or on account of another'. It almost inevitably involves D receiving 'money', whether in cash, cheque or some other form. D becomes the owner of the cash or cheque on delivery by virtue of the civil law rules we examined in the previous section. The crucial requirement is the imposition on D of an obligation to 'retain and deal with the property or its proceeds in a particular way'.

In *Wain* [1995] 2 Cr App R 660, the Court of Appeal, disapproving *Lewis v Lethbridge* [1987] Crim LR 59, DC, held that monies collected on behalf of a charity would fall within s. 5(3). D ran discos in aid of a 'Telethon' charity event organised by Yorkshire Television. He paid the proceeds into a bank account he had opened for the purpose, but subsequently dishonestly transferred them to his personal account for his own use. He received the money (the original notes and coins) 'on account of the charity', the credit balance in the special account represented 'the proceeds' of this money and D was 'under an obligation' to the charity 'to retain and deal with the proceeds in a particular way' (i.e., pay it to the charity). The credit balance in the special account was therefore to 'be regarded as belonging to' the charity by virtue of s. 5(3).

In *Dyke and Munro* [2002] 1 Cr App R 404, CA the defendants were the trustees of a charity and therefore became the legal owners of monies donated to the charity by members of the public in street collections conducted by innocent volunteers. The monies never reached the charity's bank account, having allegedly been misappropriated by the trustee defendants. The prosecution alleged that these monies belonged to the donating members of the public but the Court rejected that view, observing that the monies ceased to belong to them the moment they put them in the charity's tin, at which point the ownership transferred to the defendant trustees. Consequently, the monies did not, as alleged in the charge, belong to the donating members of the public at the time of the trustees' later appropriations, so that their convictions were quashed. However, had the prosecution alleged theft from the beneficiaries of the charity, the charge would have succeeded because the trustees held the monies on trust for those beneficiaries. The latter would therefore have an equitable 'proprietary right or interest' under s. 5(1). (In fact, under s. 5(2), it would also be deemed to belong to the Attorney-General because he has a right to enforce charitable trusts.) Alternatively, s. 5(3) would apply because the trustees received the monies 'on account of' the beneficiaries and were 'under an obligation to retain and deal with that property in a particular way' (i.e., to apply it for the benefit of the beneficiaries). It is not entirely clear why s. 5(3) could not have been used to uphold convictions of at least one of the defendants of theft from the donating members of the public. The evidence showed that Dyke actually collected the money direct from the public and then dishonestly appropriated at least some of the monies donated. It would appear that, in the words of s. 5(3), he received the monies 'from' the public and was 'under an obligation to them to retain and deal with those monies in a particular way'.

? QUESTION 10.17

In modern commerce, it is quite common to require advance payments for goods and services. You pay in advance for your package holiday, flight tickets or mail order goods. You send your inheritance to the company you have selected to invest this fortune for you. If the people you have entrusted your money to, dishonestly use it for their own purposes and fail to provide the goods or services promised, would they steal it by virtue of s. 5(3)?

It is clear from *Gomez* that if D is dishonest from the start and never intends to deliver the holiday tickets or the goods or invest the money, he dishonestly appropriates property belonging to another when he receives it, and no recourse to s. 5(3) is necessary.

However, it may be difficult to establish dishonesty at this stage and the question would be whether D commits theft by dishonestly using the money subsequently. The problem is that D will have become the legal owner of the money when he receives it, fully intending to deliver what he has contractually promised. His subsequent dishonest dealing with the money or its proceeds will therefore be with property which, under s. 5(1), belongs only to him and no longer to another—unless we can use s. 5(3) artificially to deem it to 'belong to another'.

The prosecution must prove that D is under an obligation to the person he received it 'from or on account of' to 'retain and deal with it in a particular way'. (*Meech* [1973] 3 All ER 939, CA is surely wrong in suggesting that it is enough that D believes he is under such an obligation even if he is not.) Obligation here means, as for s. 5(4), a legal obligation (*Mainwaring* (1981) 74 Cr App R 99, CA—*Cases and Materials* (10.4.1.3)). A moral obligation is not enough. Whether D is under such an obligation is a question of civil law, as before, and, once the facts are clear, it is a question of law for the judge. If the facts are disputed, the judge should direct the jury as to what findings of fact would establish a legal obligation (*Dubar* [1995] 1 All ER 781, C-MAC, following *Mainwaring* and disapproving *Hall* [1972] 2 All ER 1009, CA and *Hayes* (1976) 64 Cr App R, CA on this point).

In *Hall* (*Cases and Materials* (10.4.1.3)), D, a travel agent, was paid money in advance by a number of clients for flight tickets which never materialised and no monies were refunded. D was convicted of theft on the basis of his subsequent dishonest use of these monies. The Court of Appeal allowed his appeal on the basis that the monies did not at that time belong to another. When he received the monies, D became the sole owner of them. Section 5(3) did not apply because he was never put under any obligation to retain and deal with the monies in any particular way. The court regarded the payments simply as income for the business to be utilised in the business as D saw fit. In the absence of some 'special arrangement' with his clients that he would earmark the monies only, for example, to pay for their flights, he had no obligation in relation to that property (the monies paid). His only obligation was the contractual promise to come up with the flight tickets at the appropriate time. His failure to meet that obligation was only a breach of contract (*cf. Re Kumar* [2000] Crim LR 504, DC where a travel agent had a contractually imposed obligation to airlines covered by s. 5(3) in respect of monies paid by customers).

It would seem that D must be put under a legal obligation to retain a distinct and separate fund earmarked for a particular purpose and that this will occur only when there is 'a clear understanding' by both parties that this is to happen (*McHugh* (1993) 97 Cr App R 335, CA). An example is provided by the facts of *Hallam and Blackburn* [1995] Crim LR 323, CA (*Cases and Materials* (10.4.1.3)) where the accused were charged with theft of monies (a) received from investors which were not invested as stated and (b) received from insurance companies for policies encashed on behalf of clients where the monies were not passed on to clients. In both cases, the Court found that the accused were under an obligation to deal with the property or its proceeds in a particular way. However, the Court did not think that s. 5(3) was needed on the basis that the clients had an equitable interest in the property or proceeds which would therefore belong to them under s. 5(1).

In *Klineberg and Marsden* [1999] 1 Cr App R 427, CA, it was held that deposits paid by purchasers of timeshare holiday homes (whether by cash, cheque or bank transfer) still 'belonged to' them by virtue of s. 5(3) because they had been assured that they would be held safe by trustees until the homes were ready for occupation. The accused were thus under an obligation to deal with the credit balance in their account ('the proceeds') in that particular way. (See also *Floyd* v *DPP* [2000] Crim LR 411, DC and commentary thereon.)

Similarly, in *Dubar*, D was held to be under such an obligation. V had given him £1,800 to buy a Ford Orion car which D said he had seen advertised. D did not buy the car and soon spent the money for his own purposes. There was an obligation to spend the money only on buying the Ford Orion for V.

> **? QUESTION** 10.18
>
> Suppose D, an employee in charge of placing contracts on behalf of his employer, receives a secret payment from a company in return for giving them a contract. In civil law, he is under a duty to account to his employer for this secret profit made by abusing his position. Does the profit belong to his employer for the purposes of theft?

At first sight, this kind of case looks tailor-made for s. 5(3). D is under a legal obligation to deal with the property (the secret payment) or its proceeds in a particular way (pay it to his employer). However, according to *Attorney-General's Reference (No. 1 of 1985)* [1986] 2 All ER 219, CA (*Cases and Materials* (10.4.1.3)) the money is not received 'on account of' his employer because 'he received the money on his own account as a result of his private venture'. A similar view was taken in *Powell* v *MacRae* [1977] Crim LR 571, DC where a turnstile operator at Wembley Stadium did not steal from his employer the bribe he received for admitting someone without a ticket.

Trust property

>
>
> **⚐ EXERCISE** 10.8
>
> Read s. 5(2) in *Cases and Materials* (10.4.1.3).
>   Why is this provision necessary when any beneficiary of a trust has a 'proprietary right or interest' under s. 5(1)? Would not trust property always 'belong to another' without s. 5(2)?

Some trusts have no identifiable beneficiaries and there are therefore no 'proprietary rights or interests' other than the trustee's legal ownership. It would be possible for a single trustee to use the property in the trust dishonestly for his own purposes without committing theft. This provision ensures that if there is anyone with a right to enforce the trust (whether beneficiary or not), the trust property is deemed to belong to them. For example, rather than leaving money to a particular charitable organisation such as the RSPCA, a benefactor may leave money to be used by the trustee for the welfare of animals. There are no identifiable persons who are beneficiaries, but all trusts for 'charitable purposes' are enforceable by the Attorney-General. Their property therefore is deemed to belong to him and a sole trustee could steal from him (*cf.* commentary on *Dyke and Munro* [2002] Crim LR 153, CA).

10.4.1.4 Cheques, banks and loose talk about money

Before we leave the *actus reus* of theft, it is appropriate to say a little more about a problem we touched upon when we discussed the meaning of 'property' at 10.4.1.2. Strictly speaking 'money' means only physical notes and coins. In many cases V's 'money' is taken in a purely paper transaction through the banking system. This can be done by issuing cheques, using cheque and debit cards or by causing a transfer between accounts in some other way, e.g., electronically through the 'CHAPS' transfer system (see *Preddy* [1996] 3 All ER 735, HL).

> **?** **QUESTION** 10.19
>
> If D dishonestly borrows V's debit card and uses it to pay a £40 bill before returning it to V with the result that V's bank account is debited with £40, what property has D stolen?

You should not have had too much difficulty in deciding that no notes or coins ('money' in the strict sense) were stolen. The card itself was not stolen because there was no intention to permanently deprive V of the card. The property which has been stolen is a thing in action—the debt of £40 owed by V's bank to V. You should always bear in mind that the only person who has money in the bank is the bank. The customer's 'money' does not exist—it is merely a contractual right to be paid by the bank in accordance with the terms and conditions of the account. Nonetheless, even lawyers talk loosely about having money in the bank.

In *Hallam and Blackburn*, the defendants were investment advisers who obtained cheques from investors and paid them in some cases into their own bank accounts and in other cases into their trading company's bank account. The agreed investments were never made. At some point the 'funds' were improperly used by the defendants. Despite *Preddy* (below), it seems clear that the defendants stole things in action. If they were dishonest at the outset, they stole the debt owed by each investor's bank to the investor when they paid the relevant cheque into their own account and caused the investor's account to be debited with the amount of the cheque. By paying in the cheque, D assumed a right of the owner (namely the right to destroy or extinguish V's credit balance) over the debt owed by V's bank to V and thus appropriated property belonging to another (*Williams (Roy)* [2001] Crim LR 253, CA). If they only became dishonest after the cheques had been met, then they could only steal the debt owed by their own bank to them (their bank balance would be 'proceeds' of the original property and, as in *Klineberg*, would belong to the investor by virtue of s. 5(3)).

Would the cheque itself also be stolen if D was dishonest at the outset? According to *Mitchell* [1993] Crim LR 788, CA it would. There are, however, considerable difficulties standing in the way of such a conclusion and *Mitchell* was regarded in this respect as wrongly decided by the House of Lords in *Preddy* [1996] 3 All ER 481. The most significant difficulty is that the cheque as a thing in action (the right to sue for the amount of the cheque) never belongs to anyone but D. It only becomes a thing in action when it is drawn in favour of D and issued to him. From the moment of issue it belongs only to D. He was the only person who ever had the right to sue on it. The thing in action represented by the cheque cannot be stolen by D or obtained by deception in this example because it does not 'belong to another' (*Horsman* [1998] Crim LR 128, CA applying *Preddy*).

On the other hand, the cheque form (the piece of paper) does 'belong to another' and D will dishonestly appropriate it under *Gomez* when he receives it. Unfortunately, other problems arise in relation to whether D intends permanently to deprive V of the cheque form, which we can postpone until later.

A third possibility suggested by Professor Smith and finding some support in *Arnold* [1997] 4 All ER 1, CA and *Kohn* (1979) 69 Cr App R 395, CA, overcomes such problems (see 10.4.2.2 below). This would view the cheque form as a piece of paper which becomes something more when it is completed and issued by the drawer, namely a valuable security because it is effectively the key to the victim's bank account. It is a means of accessing that account. The cheque though a valuable security is not itself a thing in action; it merely **creates** a thing in action, namely, the right to sue on the cheque. The Court of Appeal in *Clark* [2001] Crim LR 572, although finding Professor Smith's analysis 'highly persuasive', felt that it was contrary to *Preddy* and *Graham* [1997] 1 Cr App R 302, CA. It was therefore not open to the Court of Appeal to adopt it.

Because of the difficulties caused by the House of Lords' decision in *Preddy*, the prosecutor's armoury was strengthened by the Theft (Amendment) Act 1996 which created offences of obtaining a money transfer by deception and dishonestly retaining a wrongful credit (see 12.9.2.1 below). However, the former offence has in its turn been repealed by the Fraud Act 2006 which introduces a much broader fraud offence (see **Chapter 11**).

10.4.2 *Mens rea*

At the time he appropriates the property belonging to another, D must (a) be acting dishonestly and (b) have the intention permanently to deprive V of that property. Under s. 1(2) of TA 1968, 'It is immaterial whether the appropriation is made with a view to gain, or is made for the thief's own benefit.' Thus, taking for the benefit of others or with an intention simply to spite the owner by destroying or throwing away his property, may constitute theft.

10.4.2.1 'Dishonestly'

We have seen that in relation to offences against the person, *mens rea* usually comprises some intention, knowledge or recklessness with regard to some consequence of D's act or circumstance(s) surrounding it. 'Dishonestly' is only partly about knowing of the circumstances constituting the *actus reus* of theft, e.g., knowing that the property does or might belong to another. It is fundamentally a moral marker used to judge **standards** of behaviour to see whether criminal blame should be attached to D for his conduct in interfering with another's property rights in disregard of the values inherent in the law's notion of property.

 EXERCISE 10.9

Read s. 2 of the TA 1968 in *Cases and Materials* (10.4.2.1).

- Does this define what is and what is not dishonest?
- If D's state of mind falls outside the provisions in s. 2(1), does that mean that he is dishonest?

Dishonesty is a peculiarly difficult concept to define and Parliament was unable to produce a suitable definition in the TA 1968. You should have realised that s. 2(1) does not tell us positively what **is** dishonest. Rather it gives three instances where, come what may, D is **definitely not** dishonest. The basic definition has to be gleaned from the case law, and is vague and uncertain. It follows that the first port of call for any defence counsel wishing to dispute dishonesty will be s. 2(1), for he knows that if D comes within any of its provisions, an acquittal for lack of dishonesty is **certain**. Only if s. 2(1) is or might be inapplicable would he have to worry about the general rules on dishonesty in the case law. Let us therefore begin with s. 2(1).

Section 2(1)
D is not dishonest if he believes one of the three things set out in s. 2(1)(a), (b) or (c). In each case D's belief need not be based on reasonable grounds. No matter how stupid or ridiculous his mistake, if his belief is genuine he cannot be dishonest (*Holden* [1991] Crim LR 480, CA; *Small* (1988) 86 Cr App R 170, CA).

Belief in legal right to the property
Under s. 2(1)(a), D must believe 'that he has in law the right to deprive the other of' the property 'on behalf of himself or of a third person'. The words 'in law' require D to believe that he is **legally entitled** to take the property. Essentially, D will be making a mistake about the civil law in regard to property rights. A belief in mere **moral** entitlement will not satisfy s. 2(1)(a).

Belief in consent
Under s. 2(1)(b), D must believe 'that he would have the other's consent if the other knew of the appropriation and the circumstances of it'.

> **? QUESTION** 10.20
>
> Suppose your milkman has forgotten to deliver the milk and you are anxious to ensure your consumption of three shredded wheat to sustain you in a long day at university. Your neighbour has left for work and you take one of the bottles on his doorstep believing your neighbour will not mind provided you pay for it as you intend. In fact, your neighbour is furious when he comes home for lunch and finds himself short of milk. Are you dishonest?

Since *Gomez*, the owner's consent to D having the property is no longer a bar to appropriation. However, a genuine belief that V has truly consented knowing all the circumstances, although not strictly speaking covered by s. 2(1)(b) which talks of 'would have' rather than 'has', would negative dishonesty according to *Lawrence* v *MPC* [1971] 2 All ER 1253, HL.

Of course, once the belief is established, the question of whether the owner would or would not have consented is irrelevant, so that in the example in our Question you would not be dishonest.

Belief that owner cannot be found

Under s. 2(1)(c), D must believe that the 'person to whom the property belongs cannot be discovered by taking reasonable steps'.

The most obvious situation is where D finds property which has been lost by the owner. You will recall that such property will usually still belong to the loser, and when D picks it up he will appropriate property belonging to another. Nonetheless, if he has the above belief he does not commit theft.

? QUESTION 10.21

Suppose D finds a ring in the street and, believing that the owner would not be traceable, keeps it. Three days later, as a result of overhearing a chance conversation in a pub, she discovers the identity of its owner but decides to keep it. Would D commit theft?

What are 'reasonable steps' will vary according to the circumstances of the case—the nature and value of the property, the location of the find (remember it may belong to the landowner as well as the loser), any identifying marks (e.g., postcode stamped on a bicycle) and so on. But we must be clear that what ultimately matters is D's **belief** about what are reasonable steps.

Even if D is not dishonest when she initially appropriates because she holds the relevant belief, she will still commit theft if she later discovers the true owner and dishonestly decides to keep the property (see the discussion on s. 3(1) at 10.4.1.1).

Finally, s. 2(1)(c) by its terms does not apply to a person who got the property by virtue of being a trustee or personal representative. If the beneficiaries cannot be found, the trust property will belong to the Crown. The trustee cannot rely on s. 2(1)(c) to negative dishonesty. However, if he believes that he is legally entitled to the property where the beneficiaries cannot be traced, he will be able to rely on s. 2(1)(a).

Willingness to pay

Section 2(2) provides that D **may** be dishonest 'notwithstanding that he is willing to pay for the property'. Whilst an intention to pay may often negative dishonesty (e.g., picking up goods in a supermarket; taking your neighbour's pint of milk), there are clearly situations where it would not. If you own a painting by Van Gogh, you may not wish to sell it at any price. It would be ridiculous if a millionaire could take your painting and avoid any criminal liability simply by paying for it—even a price in excess of the market value. Going back to the doorstep milk example, if you did not know whether the owner would consent, so that s. 2(1)(b) was inapplicable, your intention to pay might still negative dishonesty. On the other hand if you knew that the owner would object, it is unlikely that your intention to pay would absolve you.

Dishonesty outside s. 2(1)

You have seen that s. 2(1) defines three situations where D cannot be dishonest and s. 2(2) defines one situation where D might be. However, there are many other situations not provided for which fall to be determined by the courts. What do the cases have to say?

As we noted above, the function of the concept of dishonesty is to set the standards to reflect the values implicit in society's notion of the sanctity of property. Whose standards are to be used: the accused's, the jury's or the State's (as represented by the judges)? It would be surprising if the courts were to regard D as dishonest only if he regarded himself as dishonest. That would allow each individual defendant to set his own standards of right and wrong. The courts have now rejected such an extreme, subjective view of dishonesty (*Feely* [1973] 1 All ER 341, CA; *Ghosh* [1982] 2 All ER 689, CA). In *Feely* the Court of Appeal, unusually sitting with five judges, held that the issue of dishonesty was in each case a question of fact for the jury rather than a question of law for the judge. In its view the word 'dishonestly' being an ordinary word in common usage was not to be construed as bearing a technical meaning and, hence, applying the general view of statutory interpretation advanced by the House of Lords in *Brutus* v *Cozens* [1972] 2 All ER 1297, its meaning was not a question of law but one of fact.

? QUESTION 10.22

The decision in *Feely*, although still good law, has attracted considerable criticism from leading academics. Can you think why?

Many writers feel that the case mixes two distinct issues. One is the archetypal jury question of what D was actually thinking and believing at the time of the appropriation. Did D, as he claims, intend to repay when he took the money or did he believe that the owner had given him permission to take it? Such questions can clearly have a crucial bearing on whether D is dishonest. However, once D's state of mind has been established, there is the further question of whether D's conduct with that state of mind constituted dishonesty by ordinary standards. Most writers consider that this latter question should be a question of law for the judge. Their reasons centre on the fact that there is an absence of known and shared values in our culturally diverse society so that different juries are quite likely to make inconsistent decisions. If an employee takes home a roll of Sellotape for his personal use, would a jury regard that as dishonest or simply a 'perk' of the job? You can examine these arguments more fully by reading the extracts from Professor Williams in *Cases and Materials* (10.4.2.1)). On the other hand, some feel that the jury is a more appropriate arbiter of these standards because it is more likely to reflect society's changing values. However, in this context, it should not be forgotten that most theft cases are tried summarily by magistrates, jury trials being the exception.

Although the Court of Appeal in *Feely* held that dishonesty was a question of fact for the jury in each particular case, it did lay down guidelines for the jury's decision. The jury 'should apply the current standards of ordinary decent people. A taking to which no moral obloquy could reasonably attach...' is not dishonest. ('Obloquy' means 'moral degradation or shame'.)

In *Feely* the trial judge had, in effect, ruled that to take money from an employer's till against instructions would automatically be dishonest, even though D intended to repay it, left an IOU for the money in the till and believed on reasonable grounds that he could repay it. The Court of Appeal held that such conduct might or might not be dishonest—that was a decision which had to be left to the jury. As it had not, D's conviction was quashed. In fact, D was actually owed more in commission and wages than the amount he had taken from the till.

If there is any significant risk to the owner's money, the taking is likely to be held by the jury to be dishonest. In *McIvor* [1982] 1 All ER 491, CA, D was found to be dishonest when he took £300 from his employer's safe for use as a deposit on a holiday. He claimed that he intended to repay it and had no doubt that he would be able to because his brother had agreed to send him the money from Canada. In fact he did subsequently receive this money and repaid it. Nonetheless, there was no guarantee that the money would arrive from his brother and it was dishonest to impose this risk to the employer's property. The court rejected the idea that because D thought he was not acting dishonestly, he could not be dishonest. This objective test contrasted with other cases where D's own standards, however deplorable, were decisive (*Gilks* [1972] 3 All ER 280, CA; *Boggeln* v *Williams* [1978] 2 All ER 1061).

The matter was resolved by the Court of Appeal in *Ghosh* (*Cases and Materials* (10.4.2.1)) where a middle course was steered in establishing a test which, although fundamentally subjective, did take into account objective matters. The court put forward a two-stage test:

(a) the jury must decide, in the light of the defendant's actions, intentions and beliefs, whether he was dishonest, judged by 'the ordinary standards of reasonable and honest people';

(b) if he was dishonest by those standards, the jury must decide whether D himself realised that his conduct was **by those standards dishonest**. 'It is dishonest for D to act in a way which he knows ordinary people consider to be dishonest, even if he asserts or genuinely believes that he is morally justified in acting as he did.' In other words, D is judged not by his own standards of honesty and morality but by his understanding of the standards of ordinary people.

> ### ? QUESTION 10.23
>
> Would Robin Hood fail the *Ghosh* test?

There have been a number of instances in recent years where animal welfare activists have broken into premises and released animals used or to be used for experimentation. No doubt they would regard taking these animals as morally justified and not in any way dishonest. If a totally subjective test prevailed, they would not be dishonest. On the other hand if a totally objective test prevailed there is little doubt that they would be held to be dishonest because the law's protection of property is paramount. By the same token it is apparent that the first stage of the *Ghosh* test would be satisfied. Dishonesty would then turn on the purely subjective question of whether D realised that his conduct would be regarded as dishonest by people generally. If the passion of his belief in the injustice to animals blinded him to the reality of general opinion, he would be acquitted under *Ghosh*. Robin Hood's case turns on the same considerations.

Despite continuing criticism of the rule in *Ghosh*, there is something to be said for it. It is not a case of D deliberately disregarding the community's values and playing by his own rules. Rather, it is a case where he thinks he is abiding by those values but is mistaken about them. However, it is only in cases where there is evidence that D did not consider his actions dishonest that it is necessary to direct the jury to apply the *Ghosh* test (*Atkinson* [2004] Crim LR 226).

? **QUESTION** 10.24

Refer to Question 10.5 above in which we previously asked you to assume that our shady antiques dealer was dishonest. Can he be dishonest if, in civil law, he acquires unchallengeable ownership of the property by virtue of the contract he has made?

You may recall that the case of *Hinks* appears to establish that a person who acquires indefeasible ownership by virtue of a valid contractual or gift transaction does appropriate property belonging to another. But can such a person, even if his actions are morally dubious, be dishonest in doing what, according to the civil law, he has a perfectly legal right to do? Clearly *Hinks* admits that very possibility and, given that dishonesty is currently regarded as a question of fact for the jury, it is impossible to predict the outcome in individual cases. It is likely that D would plead s. 2(1)(a) (which could also apply even if D did **not** acquire indefeasible ownership). Our shady antiques dealer or the recipient of a valid gift (or one thought by D to be valid) may plausibly claim that once the contract or gift had been made, they believed they then had a legal right to deprive V of it (as indeed they would have in civil law if the transaction were valid!).

In addition, the House of Lords in *Lawrence* v *MPC* by analogy with s. 2(1)(b) held that a defendant who believed that V, with full knowledge of the circumstances, *had* validly consented to D's appropriation, could not be dishonest. For this reason, Lord Hutton in *Hinks,* dissenting on this point, thought it 'contrary to common sense' to regard someone as dishonest for accepting a fully valid gift no matter how 'morally reprehensible' ordinary people would think their behaviour. However, the majority view in *Hinks* is that dishonesty cannot automatically be ruled out where there is a fully valid transaction transferring ownership to D.

It is curious that the general definition of dishonesty has yet to be considered by the House of Lords, and it is conceivable that such a consideration could bring radical changes to the current position. Indeed such changes may be necessary on the ground that the current formulation fails the 'certainty' test prescribed by the European Court of Human Rights (see *Hashman and Harrup* v *UK* [2000] Crim LR 185, ECHR and commentary thereon). The present rules afford too little guidance on what is and what is not theft. (The issue is extensively discussed by the Law Commission in Part V of its Report on Fraud (Law Com. No. 276, 2002). See also the strictures of the Law Commission in Part V of its Consultation Paper: *Fraud and Deception* (Law Com. No. 155, 1999).)

However, the Crown Court in *Pattni and Ors* [2001] Crim LR 570 rejected a claim that the vagueness of the *Ghosh* test for dishonesty contravened Art. 7 of the European Convention. It remains to be seen whether the appeal courts will take the same view.

10.4.2.2 'Intention permanently to deprive'

Time and time again students make the mistake of thinking that in order to establish an intention permanently to deprive, the provisions of s. 6 of the TA 1968 must be satisfied. This is emphatically **not** the case since s. 6 does not define the phrase. It simply **deems** there to be an intention permanently to deprive in certain situations where there would otherwise **not** be an intention permanently to deprive. The phrase should be given its ordinary, everyday meaning and only if you decide that there is no intention permanently to deprive on this basis, do you need to consider the extended meanings in s. 6.

We should also stress that what is needed is an **intention** permanently to deprive at the moment of dishonest appropriation. There is no need to prove any **actual** permanent deprivation. If this were not the case, there would be no theft whenever the property was recovered from the thief and returned to the owner. A pickpocket would commit theft even though he was apprehended as he was withdrawing V's wallet from V's pocket. Explaining it another way, the law is in effect punishing D's **attempt** permanently to deprive the owner, whether the attempt is successful or not.

> **? QUESTION** 10.25
>
> Suppose X hires a car from Y for one week. If D dishonestly takes the car from X, intending to keep it for two weeks, does he commit theft?

You will recall the wide definition of 'belonging to another' which means that people with relatively limited interests in property can be stolen from. In such cases the intention permanently to deprive means simply an intention to deprive V of his entire interest in the property. Therefore, in our example D would intend permanently to deprive X but not Y. He would be guilty of theft from X but not from Y.

Dishonest borrowing

The requirement of an intention permanently to deprive means that in general it is not theft to borrow someone's property, albeit dishonestly. Sections 11 and 12 of the TA 1968 create special offences which catch some situations of dishonest borrowing (see 12.4 below). There is also another exception contained in s. 6 which we shall be examining shortly.

> **? QUESTION** 10.26
>
> - Suppose you borrowed money from your employer's till in order to back a horse which was a 'dead cert'. You intended to repay the money the next day. Did you have an intention permanently to deprive your employer of his property?
> - Suppose you had run out of milk for your shredded wheat. If you borrowed a pint of milk from your neighbour's doorstep intending to replace it with another pint when you had been to the shops, would you have an intention permanently to deprive your neighbour of his property?

In everyday language, we often talk about 'borrowing' money from another, and you might be tempted to conclude that in such a case D would not have an intention permanently to deprive. However, this overlooks the fact that the law regards each individual coin and note as a distinct piece of property.

When we talk of intention permanently to deprive we mean of the actual property taken and, in the case of money, this means the actual notes and coins originally taken. It follows that D will have the necessary intention where he 'borrows' V's money unless he intends to return the exact same notes and coins first taken (*Velumyl* [1989] Crim LR 29, CA). The fact that D intends to return **equivalent** notes and coins is relevant to the issue of whether D is dishonest, but it does not prevent the necessary intention permanently to deprive. Similarly, an intention to return an **equivalent** pint of milk does not negate the intention D had permanently to deprive of the pint of milk originally taken.

Section 6
This section is badly drafted and, in the words of JR Spencer, 'sprouts obscurities at every phrase' ([1977] Crim LR 653).

Section 6 states:

(1) A person appropriating property belonging to another without meaning the other to lose the thing itself is nevertheless to be regarded as having the intention of permanently depriving the other of it if his intention is to treat the thing as his own to dispose of regardless of the other's rights; and a borrowing or lending of it may amount to so treating it if, but only if, the borrowing or lending is for a period and in circumstances making it equivalent to an outright taking or disposal.

(2) Without prejudice to the generality of subsection (1) above, where a person, having possession or control (lawfully or not) of property belonging to another, parts with the property under a condition as to its return which he may not be able to perform, this (if done for purposes of his own and without the other's authority) amounts to treating the property as his own to dispose of regardless of the other's rights.

There are two key points which you must appreciate. First, s. 6 only comes into play if D does not 'mean' (i.e., intend) V 'to lose the thing itself' (i.e., the property appropriated).

Second, s. 6(1) ought to have ended at the semi-colon after 'other's rights'. The remainder of that subsection should then have become s. 6(2)(a) and s. 6(2) should then be s. 6(2)(b), because both are simply giving instances of conduct which could (in the first case) and would (in the second case) amount to treating 'the thing as his own to dispose of regardless of the other's rights'. It is the intention to do this which must be proved in order to trigger the operation of s. 6, which will then **deem** D to have an intention permanently to deprive which he has not **actually** got! This view was endorsed by the Court of Appeal in *Fernandes* [1996] 1 Cr App R 175, CA (*Cases and Materials* (10.4.2.2)).

Treating as one's own to dispose of
The Court of Appeal in *Lloyd* [1985] 2 All ER 661, CA viewed s. 6 as being restricted to situations where D would have been guilty prior to the TA 1968. However, it seems that this cannot stand in the light of subsequent decisions and pronouncements (e.g., *Chan Man-sin* v *R* [1988] 1 All ER 1, PC; *Fernandes*; *Marshall* [1998] 2 Cr App R 282, CA) and s. 6 will be given its ordinary meaning unconstrained by the pre-Theft Act position.

What then does the concept of 'treating as one's own to dispose of regardless of the owner's rights' embrace? The first point is that it is not enough for D to intend to treat the thing as his own simply by using the property regardless of the owner's rights. The section requires an intention to treat it as his own **'to dispose of'**. According to *Cahill* [1993] Crim LR 141, CA the words 'to dispose of' mean more than 'merely to use the thing as one's own'. They suggested that D must intend 'to get rid of; to get done with; to...sell' the property. On the other hand, without referring to *Cahill*, the Divisional Court in *DPP v Lavender* [1994] Crim LR 297 rejected such a construction as too narrow. D had taken two doors from a council house undergoing repair and used them to replace two damaged doors in his girlfriend's council house. The court found him guilty and seemed to regard the words 'to dispose of' as unimportant. The crucial question for them was whether D had intended to treat the doors as his own regardless of the owner's rights.

 It was held in *Marshall* [1998] 2 Cr App R 282, CA (*Cases and Materials* (10.4.2.2)) that to acquire another's unexpired ticket and sell it on to a third person could be theft. D obtained unexpired London Underground tickets and Travelcards from passengers completing their journeys and sold them on to passengers embarking on theirs. D argued that he lacked the intention permanently to deprive London Underground of the tickets since when expired the tickets would be retained by London Underground's machines. However, the Court applied s. 6(1) holding that by acquiring and reselling the tickets, D had an intention to treat them as his own to dispose of regardless of the owner's rights, even if he envisaged that, ultimately, they would find their way back to London Underground. The same might apply if you donate your unexpired parking ticket to a new arrival, but would a jury or even magistrate be prepared to designate such conduct as dishonest where you give the ticket away without any gain for yourself?

Similarly, if D by means of forged cheques causes V's account to be debited and his own to be credited, he will steal the relevant part of V's credit balance (a thing in action), notwithstanding that, because the transaction is a nullity, V will suffer no loss or deprivation (the bank stands the loss). Even if D envisaged that the fraud would be discovered so that V's credit balance would remain intact, he still intended to treat it as his own to dispose of regardless of V's rights. Another example would be where D intends to return the property **only** if V pays for it in some way or satisfies some other condition imposed by D. Some years ago someone took a painting by Goya from the National Gallery and demanded a large payment to charity for its return. According to *Lloyd*, such ransom cases are caught by s. 6(1) and it would be the same if the demand was, say, to free a prisoner rather than payment of money. Equally, if you take V's property intending to sell it back to him, you would intend to treat it as your own to dispose of regardless of the owner's rights.

The remainder of s. 6(1) and the whole of s. 6(2) give specific instances of where D would be 'treating the property as his own to dispose of regardless of the owner's rights'. Let us consider them.

Borrowing or lending equivalent to outright taking

A borrowing or lending of the property may amount to treating it as one's own, etc. but 'only if' it 'is for a period and in circumstances making it equivalent to an outright taking or disposal'.

Suppose D dishonestly takes your railway season ticket which has one month to expiry. Would D commit theft if he intended to return it to you (a) the next day or (b) two days before expiry or (c) the day after expiry?

The leading case on this provision is undoubtedly *Lloyd* (*Cases and Materials* (10.4.2.2)) where D, a cinema projectionist, removed feature films from the cinema for a few hours to enable pirate copies to be made. He then returned the originals to the cinema as he had intended to do all along. It was held that there was no intention to treat the films as his own within s. 6(1). A borrowing or lending would only be 'equivalent to an outright taking or disposal' if D's intention was to return the property 'in such a changed state that it can truly be said that all its goodness or virtue has gone'. When the films were returned they could still be shown as before and therefore retained their 'virtue'. The fact that their exclusivity had been lost to the official distributors through the pirating did not deprive them of **all** their virtue.

On the other hand, an intention to return a season ticket only when it expires would suffice. If the *Lloyd* test were applied literally, an intention to return the season ticket at any time before expiry would not be good enough because some virtue would remain. However, if the virtue remaining is insignificant in relation to the virtue lost, it is possible that the courts might leave it as a question of fact for the jury, enabling it to stretch it and regard it as 'equivalent to an outright taking'. Another possible solution to the problem would be to allege that D had stolen not the ticket but the chose(s) in action represented by it. V has a contractual right to travel with the ticket and this contractual right (chose in action) to travel is intended to be lost to V permanently for the time D intends to retain the ticket.

Parting with property under a condition as to its return (s. 6(2))
D treats the property as his own, etc. if he parts with it 'under a condition as to its return which he **may** not be able to perform'. This provision is intended to catch the case where D without authorisation uses V's property as security for a loan, e.g., from a pawnbroker. D may not be able to pay back the loan when the time comes, even though when he first takes V's property, he does intend to return it. It does not matter that D may be in possession of V's property quite lawfully, e.g., he may have hired it from V, at the time he uses it as security.

If D knows he **may** not be able to redeem the property, it does not seem to matter that he thinks it is very likely that he **will** be able to redeem it. If he is certain that he will be able to redeem it but, objectively, there is a clear risk that he may not be able to do so, the terms of s. 6(2) suggest that he would still be caught—but the matter has yet to be decided.

It is arguable that s. 6(2) is in fact unnecessary since the situations it covers come within the general provision in s. 6(1). If D pawns the property, he is intending to treat it as his own to dispose of regardless of the owner's rights. We can now leave s. 6 to consider one final matter.

Cheques

As always cheques raise difficult problems. The problem in this context is that where D dishonestly gets a cheque payable to him, he intends it to return to the owner's bank (which will hold it on behalf of the owner) because that is the way he will transform it into money.

In order to solve this conundrum, we have first to identify precisely what property we are discussing. The cheque form represents a thing in action because, ostensibly, it gives the payee a right to sue the drawer. It is clear from *Preddy* [1996] 3 All ER 735, HL (*Cases and Materials* (11.3.5.1)) (overruling *Duru* [1973] 3 All ER 715, CA and *Mitchell* [1993] Crim LR 788, CA on this point) that where the payee is D, this thing in action cannot be stolen by D because it is never property 'belonging to another'. It is simply a right to sue V which from the moment of its creation belongs only to D. V cannot have or own a right to sue himself!

The cheque is also a physical entity—a piece of paper distinct from what it represents—which does belong to V at the time of appropriation. The House of Lords in *Preddy* thought D would lack any intention to permanently deprive V of the cheque form which would have to be returned to V's bank (as agent for V) in order to obtain payment. They would presumably reject the view in *Duru* that D intended permanently to deprive V of the **unpaid** cheque since he only intended the **paid** cheque form to return to the owner. Once the cheque was stamped paid, it completely changed its character and became a different piece of property from the cheque form originally taken! This solution is flawed because what has been lost from the cheque by the stamping 'paid' is its character as a thing in action. But, as we pointed out in the previous paragraph, this never ever belonged to V who could not therefore have been deprived of it by the stamping. A more convincing possibility is that D intends to return the cheque to V's bank **only in return for payment**. As previously discussed, by intending V to 'buy back' his cheque form in this way, D, under s. 6(1), will be treating it as his own to dispose of regardless of V's rights. However, the Court of Appeal in *Clark (Brian)* [2001] Crim LR 572, whilst not considering this precise argument, held that Preddy had decided that s. 6 was inapplicable and, in any event, D did not 'treat' the cheque 'as his own to dispose of regardless of the owner's rights' by, as the owner anticipates, paying it into D's own account.

A final suggestion put forward by Professor Smith is that a cheque is a piece of property which is at once more than the physical piece of paper on which it is written and yet distinct from the thing in action created by its issue. It is also a 'valuable security', because it is effectively the key to V's bank account. Viewing the cheque as a 'valuable security', the argument from *Duru* (see previous paragraph) becomes convincing. D's intention is that the cheque form as a piece of paper should return to V's bank, but not as a valuable security. The cheque ceases to be a valuable security when it is stamped paid and so is no longer a key to V's account. It is in that condition only that D intends V to get it back and thus he does intend to permanently deprive V of the 'valuable security'. If this view is correct, it would provide a simple and elegant resolution in cases like *Arnold* (see above) thus avoiding the necessity of becoming embroiled in the vagaries of s. 6. Unfortunately, the Court of Appeal in *Clark (Brian)* [2001] Crim LR 572 although finding Professor Smith's analysis 'highly persuasive' felt it was implicitly rejected by the House of Lords in *Preddy* (though it was probably obiter on this point) and by the Court of Appeal in *Graham* [1997] 1 Cr App R 302. The matter needs a final resolution by the House of Lords.

Conditional intention to deprive

> **? QUESTION** 10.28
>
> Suppose D dishonestly picks up a handbag. On searching through it he discovers nothing he regards as worth taking because it contains only a few tissues and some cosmetics. He replaces the bag intact.
>   Has D stolen anything? If so, what?
>   Has he committed any other offence? If so, what?

The above were roughly the facts of *Easom* [1971] 2 All ER 945, CA which held that D must have formed a definite intention permanently to deprive V of the particular property alleged to be stolen. In this case D never formed any such definite intention to keep the handbag or any of the items actually in it and could not be convicted of theft. However, he could now be convicted of attempting to steal **from** the handbag since he did have a definite intention permanently to deprive the owner of money and any other items worth stealing. The fact that this was impossible because no such items existed is no longer a bar to a conviction for attempt under the Criminal Attempts Act 1981 (see 16.3.4).

■ FURTHER READING

Beatson & Simester: *Stealing One's Own Property* (1999) 115 LQR 372.

Campbell: *The Test of Dishonesty in* R v Ghosh (1984) 43 CLJ 349.

Elliott: *Dishonesty in Theft: A Dispensable Concept* [1982] Crim LR 395.

Gardner S: *Property and Theft* [1998] Crim LR 35.

Griew: *The Theft Acts 1968 and 1978* (7th ed., 1995, Sweet & Maxwell).

Griew: *Dishonesty: The Objections to* Feely *and* Ghosh [1985] Crim LR 341.

Halpin: *The Test for Dishonesty* [1996] Crim LR 283.

Heaton: *Cheques and Balances* [2005] Crim LR 747.

Heaton: *Deceiving Without Thieving* [2001] Crim LR 712.

Shute: *Appropriation and the Law of Theft* [2002] Crim LR 450.

Shute & Horder: *Thieving and Deceiving; What is the Difference?* (1993) 56 MLR 554.

Smith ATH: *Property Offences* (1994, Sweet & Maxwell).

Smith JC: *The Law of Theft* (8th ed., 1997, Butterworths).

Smith JC: *Obtaining Cheques by Deception or Theft* [1997] Crim LR 382.

Smith JC: *Stealing Tickets* [1998] Crim LR 723.

Spencer: *The Metamorphosis of Section 6* [1977] Crim LR 129.

■ SUMMARY

Theft is committed when D (i) appropriates (ii) property (iii) belonging to another (*actus reus*) (iv) dishonestly and (v) with an intention permanently to deprive the other of it (*mens rea*) (s. 1(1) Theft Act 1968).

- *Actus reus*—(i) 'appropriates' means 'any assumption of the rights of an owner' (s. 3(1)). Interpreted in *Morris* and *Gomez* to mean 'the assumption of **any** of the rights of the owner'. No adverse interference required and the owner's consent to the taking does not prevent appropriation which is therefore a **neutral** concept (*Gomez*). This is so even if V consents to D becoming the **owner** of the property, certainly if induced by D's misrepresentation. There is appropriation even where V presents D with the **indefeasible** ownership (*Hinks* disapproving *Mazo*). Thus, intentionally to do anything to or with another's property whether with or without the owner's consent is an appropriation. Appropriation usually involves **physical** interference with the property but need not, e.g., offering for sale (*Pitham & Hehl*) or interfering with a credit balance in V's bank account (e.g., procuring a transfer to another account by paying in V's cheque whether forged or otherwise, sending instructions by fax, letter, computer etc. to V's bank (*Kohn*; *Hilton*)). D appropriates by destroying/diminishing V's credit balance (*Williams* [2001]) so if **V** institutes the transfer to D's account as a result of D's deception, D does not appropriate V's credit balance (*Briggs*). Although appropriation is instantaneous it can probably also be regarded as continuing whilst D is 'on the job' (*Atakpu*; *Hale*). Later assumption of rights by keeping or dealing with the property as owner, D having initially come by it without stealing it, is an appropriation (s. 3(1)). Innocent purchaser for value cannot be guilty of theft by later assumption of rights he believed himself to be acquiring by his purchase (s. 3(2)). (ii) 'Property' includes money and all other property, real or personal, including things in action and other intangible property (s. 4(1)). Money means only physically identifiable coins and notes. Things in action include debts (e.g., balance at bank), shares, rights under a trust. Other intangible property includes patents and export quotas but not electricity, trade secrets or confidential information, e.g., in an exam paper (*Oxford* v *Moss*). Land not stealable **unless** (a) D, a trustee, does it in breach of trust (b) D takes something forming part of the land which has been severed from it (c) D, a tenant, takes fixture or structure let with the land (s. 4(2)). No theft for picking wild mushrooms, flowers etc. unless done for sale or reward (s. 4(3)) or for taking untamed wild creatures unless in someone's possession (s. 4(4)).

  Belonging to another given exceptionally wide meaning by s. 5. Includes anyone (a) having possession or control of the property or (b) having in it any proprietary right or interest (s. 5(1)). A landowner generally possesses or controls things on his land even if not owned by him and presence unknown to him (*Woodman*; *Waverley BC* v *Fletcher*). Abandoned property does not belong to anyone, but quite rare situation (*Williams* v *Phillips*). Proprietary right or interest includes not only full ownership but lesser rights such as liens, hire and equitable interests, e.g., beneficiaries under a trust. Position uncertain where law **imposes** a constructive trust on the property—should be within s. 5(1) (*Shadrokh-Cigari*; *Ex parte Levin*; *Westdeutsche*) but denied in *A-G's Reference (No. 1 of 1985)*. Section 5(1) expressly excludes equitable interests arising on the making of a contract to sell the property. Owner can steal his own property from someone with lesser interest (*Turner (No. 2)*).

Transactions transferring **ownership** to D. The property must 'belong to another' at the moment of D's dishonest appropriation (*Lawrence* v *MPC*). If ownership transfers from V to D after **or** at the moment of dishonest appropriation, the appropriation is of property belonging to another (*Lawrence* v *MPC*). If it transfers **before** the moment of dishonest appropriation, the appropriation will not be of property belonging to another **unless** the special deeming provisions in ss. 5(3) or 5(4) apply: (i) *Getting property by mistake*—if D (a) gets the property by another's mistake (whether induced by D or not) and (b) is **legally** obliged to restore (in whole or in part) the property, its proceeds or its value, the property is deemed for the purposes of theft to belong to another, even though at civil law D is the sole owner. D is normally under such obligation when he is paid money under a mistake of fact, but only on rescission when he gets ownership under a contract voidable for misrepresentation. In the light of *Gomez* and *Dobson* v *General Accident*, it is unlikely that s. 5(4) will be needed to secure conviction where V's mistake is caused by D's fraud. Even if V's mistake not caused by D, it is arguable that V retains an equitable interest in the property or proceeds which thus belongs to V under s. 5(1) without the need for s. 5(4) (*Shadrokh-Cigari*; *Westdeutsche*). (ii) *Obligation to retain and deal* (s. 5(3)). If D (a) receives property from another or an account of another and (b) is under a **legal** obligation to the other to retain and deal with that property or its proceeds in **a particular way**, the property or its proceeds is deemed to belong to that other. There must be a 'clear understanding' or agreement that D is to retain V's money or other property as a distinct and separate fund earmarked for a particular purpose, e.g., payment to a charity, purchase of a particular investment (*Hallam and Blackburn*). Not normally the case with 'advance payment' transactions e.g., to travel agents or for mail order goods. Arguable that, in any s. 5(3) case, D would be a constructive trustee of V's monies and V would therefore retain an equitable interest within s. 5(1) (*Hallam & Blackburn*). Section 5(2) provides that trust property is deemed to belong to anyone having a right to enforce the trust.

- *Mens rea*—(i) dishonestly (ii) with an intention permanently to deprive. (i) Dishonestly is vague and uncertain concept embracing a court's moral judgment of D's conduct. The general notion is defined by case law but s. 2(1) specifies three situations where D is **definitely not** dishonest: where D **honestly** (need not be reasonably) believes (a) he is legally entitled to appropriate the property; (b) he would have V's consent if V knew of the circumstances; or (c) (unless D is a trustee of the property taken) that the owner cannot be discovered by taking reasonable steps. A willingness to pay for the property will not necessarily negate dishonesty (s. 2(2)). Dishonesty outside s. 2(1) is a question of fact for the jury who must apply the current standards of ordinary decent people (*Feely*). In the light of D's actions, intentions and beliefs, was D's conduct dishonest by those standards and, if so, did D himself realise it was **by those standards** dishonest? (*Ghosh*). D can be dishonest where he acquires the indefeasible ownership of the property (*Hinks*). (ii) Intention permanently to deprive—needed at moment of dishonest appropriation. No need for **actual** deprivation. The Theft Act does **not** define the basic concept which bears its everyday meaning. Enough to intend to deprive V permanently of whatever interest (e.g., hire for week) he has in the property. Dishonest borrowing not theft but intention to return 'equivalent' property does not negate intent permanently to deprive, e.g., money where D intends to return **different** notes and coins from those he took. Section 6 **only** applies if D does not intend permanently to deprive: it deems D to so intend if he intends to treat the property as his own to dispose of regardless of the owner's rights (s. 6(1)), e.g., where D intends to return it to V only upon payment (e.g., ransom demand, tricking V into buying it back). Section 6 specifies two examples where D could or would treat the property as his own etc.: (i) a borrowing or lending may amount to so treating **only if** it is for a period and in circumstances making it **equivalent** to an **outright** taking (s. 6(1)). Equivalent to an outright taking only if D's intention is to return the property when it has lost 'all its goodness or virtue' (*Lloyd*) (ii) D treats the property as his own etc. if he parts with it 'under a condition as to its return which he **may** not be able to perform' (s. 6(2)), e.g., using property as security for a loan. D must have made a firm decision to permanently deprive—a conditional intention to deprive will not suffice (*Easom*).

 CHAPTER 10: ASSESSMENT EXERCISE

10.1 Discuss the criminal liability of Flash for **theft**, if any, in each of the following situations—
    Flash, an animal rights activist, broke into a research laboratory and released several dogs which were being forced to smoke cigarettes as part of a medical research project.
    Flash drove into a self-service petrol station, filled up with petrol and drove off without paying.
    Flash rented a car for one week from a car hire company. After four days, he decided to sell the car and pocket the proceeds. He drove it over to the local car auction and was standing in the queue to enter it into the auction, when he was arrested by the police.

10.2 Twitch, a keen bird-watching student, orders a pair of binoculars from Kwikmail plc, a mail order company which guarantees same day despatch of all orders sent with payment. Twitch sends with his order a cheque for the appropriate amount, notwithstanding that he knows there is no money in his bank account.
    Two days later Twitch receives the binoculars from Kwikmail plc. After trying out the binoculars Twitch decides they are not suitable for his purpose and sells them to Crow.
    The next day Twitch receives a letter from Kwikmail plc informing him that his bank has refused to pay the cheque and demanding the return of the binoculars.
    Discuss the criminal liability, if any, of Twitch for theft. Would your answer differ if the letter from Kwikmail plc demanding the return of the binoculars had been received before Crow bought the binoculars?

See the **Appendix** (10.1 and 10.2) for specimen answers.

11 Offences against property II: Fraud*

11.1 Objectives

By the end of this chapter you should be able to:

1 Define the offences of fraud and obtaining services dishonestly

2 Analyse their ingredients

3 Identify which of the offences, if any, apply in any given fact situation

11.2 Introduction

It is estimated that fraud costs the UK economy £14 billion annually, a sum which dwarfs that attributable to burglary, retail theft and vehicle crime combined. The increasing complexity, sophistication and internationalisation of fraud have led to pressure for reform to which the Government has been keen to respond. Much of this has been in relation to evidence and procedure in fraud trials and the tracing and confiscation of the proceeds of crime which are outside the scope of this work. However, dissatisfaction with the substantive law has resulted in major reform.

Largely based on recommendations of the Law Commission (*Report on Fraud*, Law Com. No. 276, 2002), the Fraud Act 2006 has completely revolutionised the law sweeping away most of the offences previously discussed in this chapter. The hotch-potch of individual offences based on deception in the Theft Acts 1968 and 1978 are replaced by a new wide-ranging offence of fraud committable in three different ways. This simplifies the law and overcomes a number of problematic features of the old law. A further offence of dishonestly obtaining services replaces and extends the former offence of obtaining services by deception under s. 1 of the Theft Act 1978. It is convenient to end the chapter with an examination of the only offence created by the Theft Act 1978 which is retained by the Fraud Act—dishonestly making off without payment.

* This chapter has been written on the basis that the Fraud Bill will be enacted in its original form in or shortly after April 2006 and readers are warned to check that there have been no significant changes to the original Bill. As soon as the Bill is enacted, an update will be added to the Online Resource Centre detailing any changes affecting the accuracy of the text or confirming that the text stands as written.

11.3 A brief summary of the old law of deception

The old law comprised a sometimes bewildering array of overlapping offences largely based on the concept of dishonestly obtaining something by deception. The law lacked coherence because it had grown up piecemeal with new offences being enacted to correct problems and plug perceived loopholes in 1978 and 1996. This resulted in some very specific offences defined by reference to the production of a particular type of consequence.

The old offences were:

Obtaining property by deception (s. 15 of the Theft Act 1968)

Obtaining a money transfer by deception (s. 15A of the TA 1968, inserted by Theft (Amendment) Act 1996)

Obtaining a pecuniary advantage by deception (s. 16 of the TA 1968)

Procuring the execution of a valuable security by deception (s. 20(2) of the TA 1968)

Obtaining services by deception (s. 1 of the Theft Act 1978)

Obtaining the evasion of a liability to pay by deception (s. 2 of the TA 1978) (evasion of a liability to pay meant (a) securing the remission of an existing liability to pay (b) inducing a creditor to wait for or forgo payment or (c) obtaining an exemption from or abatement of a liability to pay).

You will notice that all but one of the offences follow a similar pattern. They are based on dishonestly obtaining something by deception, the difference lying in what must be obtained. The key to understanding how these offences worked undoubtedly lies in the concept of 'obtaining by deception'.

The common elements of the offences were as follows:

(a) D must deceive someone;

(b) D must obtain a relevant thing (property, services, etc.);

(c) D's deception must cause the obtaining; and

(d) D must act dishonestly.

11.3.1 Deception

The concept of deception was in many ways at the heart of the difficulties experienced under the old law and it has been replaced by the simpler concept of false representation in the new offence. This shares a number of features with deception and indeed, in our discussion at 11.4.2.1 below, you will see that we have utilised a number of cases under the old law. The essential difference, however, is that representation is a one-sided concept whereas deception was two-sided. The first requirement for deception was that D must in some way have made a false representation. For example, a jeweller may state that a ring is solid gold when it is only gold-plated. Under the new law based purely on the false representation, this is now the only requirement.

The second element required for a deception was that someone was deceived by this untrue representation. The victim must have been taken in or 'conned' by the representation so that he was induced to believe that it was true. It must have operated on his mind. Deception was a two-sided thing—D deceived only if and when someone was fooled by his false representation. Thus, not only would the representation have to be communicated to V but V would have to be taken in and influenced by it. The general view was that this precluded 'deceiving' a machine where the transaction was fully automated without the involvement of any human mind (e.g., internet orders; computerised banking).

11.3.2 D must obtain property, a pecuniary advantage, services or the evasion of a liability

This aspect is discussed below under each individual offence.

11.3.3 Deception must cause the obtaining

D's false statement must have operated on V's mind so as to deceive him and this must have caused V to give up the property, perform the service or whatever was required by the offence in question. This immediately raised questions of causation and turned the offence into a result crime. The 'thing' had to be successfully obtained to constitute the crime. By contrast, the new offence of fraud focuses purely on D's conduct and motivation and is not concerned with the result of his actions. Even if nothing is obtained or, indeed, lost, the new offence can still be made out.

The causation requirement caused problems in a number of situations. For example, in *Coady* [1996] Crim LR 518, the Court of Appeal held that where D filled up at a self-service petrol station, he did not obtain the petrol by deception unless he made a false representation which operated on the mind of the cashier **before** the petrol went into his tank. In this case, the only deception alleged by the prosecution was D's statement to the cashier, **after** he had filled up, that the price should be charged to the account of D's former employer when he was not entitled to do so. The prosecution was unable to prove that this deception was practised before the petrol into the tank. At the other end of the timescale, some cases held that D's deception occurred too early and was too remote a cause of the obtaining to count (*Clucas* [1949] 2 All ER 40, CCA (*Cases and Materials* (11.3.3)) cf. *King and Stockwell* [1987] 1 All ER 547 (*Cases and Materials* (11.3.3))).

The courts found it necessary to skate over the causation requirement in a number of important cases where, in truth, V did not consider whether D's false representation was true or false because it was a matter of no concern to him. Thus, if an employee served his own products to customers instead of his employer's, could we say that the implied representation that they were his employer's operated on the customer's mind and caused him to buy them? (*Cf. Cooke* [1986] 2 All ER 985 HL; *Doukas* [1978] 1 All ER 1061 CA.) The customer would never have given a thought to the origin of the goods and could not truly be said to have been deceived into thinking the goods were the employer's. Similarly, if D proffered to a retailer a cheque, credit or debit card which he knew he was not authorised to use, did he obtain the goods purchased **because of** his deception? It is true that he would make a false, implied representation that he had authority to use the card but would this have operated on the shop assistant's mind so as to cause him to go ahead with the transaction? That is unlikely because the whole point of the card systems is to guarantee the retailer payment without having to worry about the state of the customer's account. Quite simply, the system is designed to obviate the need for the retailer to concern himself with D's authority to use the card and the retailer proceeds with the transaction because he knows he will get paid in any event. Nonetheless, the House of Lords in *Metropolitan Police Commissioner* v *Charles* [1977] AC 177 (*Cases and Materials* (11.3.3)) and *Lambie* [1981] 2 All ER 776 held that it was enough that V remained ignorant of the truth because D did not reveal it and V would not have gone ahead with the transaction if he had known the truth. A similar line is evident from *Cooke*.

11.3.4 D must act dishonestly

Although 'dishonestly' was not defined in the statute (s. 2 of the Theft Act 1968 is expressed to apply only to dishonestly in the offence of theft (s. 1(3)), the same case law tests applicable to theft including *Ghosh* were applied (*Woolven* (1983) 73 Cr App R 231, CA; *Melwani* [1989] Crim LR 565, CA).

11.3.5 The old offences

11.3.5.1 Obtaining property by deception

Section 15(1) read: 'A person who by any deception dishonestly obtains property belonging to another, with the intention of permanently depriving the other of it...' committed the offence.

The *actus reus* involved obtaining property belonging to another by deception. It covered obtaining ownership, possession or control of the property but unless 'property' (as defined for theft—10.4.1.2 above) was actually obtained, no offence was committed. In fact, due to the wide interpretation of 'appropriation' in theft in *Gomez* and *Hinks* (see 10.4.1.1 above), most commentators concluded that, apart from some minor exceptions, all cases of obtaining property by deception would also be theft (see Heaton: *Deceiving without Thieving* [2001] Crim LR 712 for a challenge to the orthodox view). The *mens rea* required dishonesty, an intention permanently to deprive (as in theft—10.4.2.2 above) and deliberation or subjective recklessness in respect of the deception, i.e. essentially knowing that the representation was false or might be and that V would or might be taken in by it.

A major difficulty surfaced in *Preddy* [1996] 3 All ER 735 (*Cases and Materials* (11.3.5.1)) in relation to cheques and bank accounts. D practised a straightforward mortgage fraud, securing the grant of a mortgage advance by giving false details of identity, income etc. on his application form. This deception caused the mortgage lender to instruct its banker to transfer the advance monies electronically direct from the lender's bank account to D's bank account. It was held that D did not contravene s. 15 because he did not obtain any property which **belonged to another**. The credit balance in the lender's account was cancelled or extinguished when its bank transferred the money to D's bank. D did not obtain the lender's credit balance—what he obtained was a new and different (albeit reciprocal) credit balance which, being a debt which D's bank owed to D, from the moment of its creation never ever belonged to anyone but D. The new offence of fraud cuts out this problem because there is no need to prove that D obtained anything by his false statements.

11.3.5.2 Obtaining a money transfer by deception

Banks and building societies were aghast at the apparent loophole for mortgage fraudsters exposed by the House of Lords' decision in *Preddy*. Remedial action was swift and by s. 1 of the Theft (Amendment) Act 1996, a new s. 15A was inserted into the Theft Act 1968. This made it an offence dishonestly to obtain for oneself or another a money transfer by any deception. A money transfer occurred when one account was credited with a sum of money and another debited with a sum of money and either the credit resulted from the debit or the debit resulted from the credit.

11.3.5.3 Obtaining a pecuniary advantage by deception

The original s. 16 prompted one judge to declare, a touch ironically, 'So obscure is s. 16 that it has created a judicial nightmare. It has even puzzled some academic lawyers' (Edmund Davies LJ in *Royle* [1971] 3 All ER 1363). However, the part of s. 16 which gave rise to the difficulty was repealed and replaced (and extended) by the Theft Act 1978. What was left of s.16 was a very restricted rump which gave the concept of 'pecuniary advantage' a narrow, technical meaning totally divorced from its everyday meaning.

Section 16(1) of the TA 1968 provided that the offence was committed by 'A person who by any deception dishonestly obtains for himself or another any pecuniary advantage.' The *actus reus* required that D must (a) obtain for himself or another (b) a pecuniary advantage (c) by a deception. D obtained a pecuniary advantage within the meaning of the section **only** if, by means of his deception, (i) he was allowed to borrow by way of overdraft, or to take out any policy of insurance or annuity contract, or obtained an improvement of the terms on which he was allowed to do so; or (ii) he was given the opportunity to earn remuneration or greater remuneration in an office or employment, or to win money by betting.

As you can see, these provisions were very specific and covered very limited ground.

11.3.5.4 Obtaining services by deception

By s. 1(1) of the Theft Act 1978, 'any person who by any deception dishonestly obtains services from another' committed the offence. Section 1 did for services what s. 15 did for property and remedied a gap in the law prior to 1978. It was designed to cover the case where D got V to expend labour by his deception. The *actus reus* required D to (a) obtain from another (b) services (c) by a deception. Section 1(2) provided an exhaustive definition of what constituted 'services':

> It is an obtaining of services where the other is induced to confer a benefit by doing some act, or causing or permitting some act to be done, on the understanding that the benefit has been or will be paid for.

Examples would include obtaining a taxi ride, a haircut, a massage, a house survey, or a repair of your property when you have no intention of paying; obtaining a university education by falsely claiming to have entrance qualifications; and the obtaining of a loan by deception.

11.3.5.5 Evasion of liability by deception

Section 2 of the Theft Act 1978 covered, in a more coherent fashion, the ground which was covered by the original s. 16(2)(a) of the 1968 Act. It provided a variety of clearly over-lapping ways in which D might evade a debt. Under s. 2(1), the offence was committed by one who 'by any deception':

(a) dishonestly secures the remission of the whole or part of any existing liability to make a payment, whether his own liability or another's; or

(b) with intent to make permanent default in whole or in part on any existing liability to make a payment, or with intent to let another do so, dishonestly induces the creditor or any person claiming payment on behalf of the creditor to wait for payment (whether or not the due date for payment is deferred) or to forgo payment; or

(c) dishonestly obtains any exemption from or abatement of liability to make a payment.

Securing remission of a liability to pay

Here, D had to be under a liability to make a payment and by then practising a deception he got the creditor to agree either to extinguish his liability altogether ('remit in whole') or to reduce it ('remit in part'). So D first incurred the liability to pay, e.g., have a haircut and **then** made the deception, e.g., pretending to be over 60 which fooled the creditor into remitting in part the liability to pay the normal charge, e.g., by applying the concessionary over-60s rate. If the creditor was conned into waiving the whole charge, D would have secured the remission 'in whole'.

Inducing a creditor to wait for or forgo payment

Again the sequence was that D must first have incurred a liability to pay and then used a deception to cause the creditor to postpone payment ('wait for') or forget it altogether ('forgo'). Essentially it covered the stalling debtor who deceived the creditor (e.g., by falsely claiming to be out of work) into either postponing the payment date or writing off the debt altogether. The offence required D to intend **never** to pay ('make permanent default') so that if he only intended to put off the evil day to ease the immediate financial pressure, he could not commit the offence.

Obtaining exemption from or abatement of a liability to pay

The previous two provisions were intended for the case where D used his deception to affect a **pre-existing** liability to pay whereas this provision was intended to catch cases where D used the deception at the outset to affect a **prospective** liability not yet incurred. For example, if D, **before** starting his journey, told a taxi driver a false hard luck story so that he agreed to carry D for nothing, D would obtain an 'exemption from liability' to pay. If D falsely claimed to be an old age pensioner so as to secure half-price admission to a Nottingham Forest football match, he would obtain an 'abatement of liability' to pay. Because of the deception, D ostensibly, in the first case, never incurred the liability for the ride he would otherwise have incurred, and, in the second case, did not incur the normal charge which he would otherwise have incurred. The deception came first and prevented him from incurring the liability he should have incurred.

11.3.5.6 **Procuring the execution of a valuable security by deception**

Section 20(2) was a useful, though often overlooked, offence in the prosecutor's armoury, since it could in some cases avoid difficulties with the more general offences such as theft and obtaining property by deception in the area of banking frauds. The gist of it was dishonestly procuring the execution of a valuable security by deception. 'Valuable security' was defined in broad terms by s. 20(3) and included cheques, banker's drafts, share transfer forms, etc. If, therefore, D dishonestly practised a deception which caused V to 'execute' a cheque (i.e., sign and issue it) or banker's draft, etc., he would commit this offence.

11.3.6 **Defects of the old law**

Part III of the Law Commission's Report detailed a number of undesirable consequences arising from the disorganised 'over-particularisation' of the plethora of 'overlapping but distinct statutory offences'. (See also Annex B of the Home Office's *Fraud Law Reform: Government Response to Consultations*.) Firstly, the lack of generality failed to ensnare new and unforeseen methods of fraud (e.g., in 1968 personal computers were unheard of and the internet did not exist) and encouraged technical arguments about the interpretation of the specific provisions. Thus unsatisfactory loopholes were created as evidenced by the decision in *Preddy*. On a practical level, it was all too easy for a prosecutor to charge the wrong offence or, in adopting a 'belt and braces' approach, to over-complicate the trial by charging too many offences.

As we have seen, the necessity for someone to actually be deceived created a number of difficulties, even where D had clearly made a dishonest, false representation. The absence of any deception where D manipulated computers programmed to dispense services etc. automatically, without human intervention, was a particular problem. The Commission was also concerned that the deception requirement enabled dishonest exploitation to escape the net in certain situations where D abused a position of trust he held in relation to V or, alternatively, failed to disclose information which he ought, in order to dispel the ignorance which he knows V to be labouring under.

11.4 **The new offence of fraud**

11.4.1 **Introduction**

The defects with the old law persuaded the Law Commission and the Government that the existing offences should be replaced by a much simpler, more general offence of fraud 'that targets the nature of fraudulent behaviour, rather than particular instances of such behaviour in a set of defined circumstances. The *Preddy* difficulty also suggests that fraud should cover situations where there is loss to a victim, whether or not the defendant or anyone else obtains (or appropriates) what the victim has lost.' (*Government Response*, [6].) In its initial Consultation Paper (*Fraud and Deception*, Law Com. No. 155, 1999), the Law Commission rejected the idea of a general offence of fraud, still less a general offence of dishonesty, and preferred amendment to the existing offences to cover loopholes which had arisen. However, its Report (*Fraud*, Law Com. No. 276, 2002) revealed a change of mind and a recommendation for a general fraud offence to replace the existing deception offences.

The Government broadly accepted the recommendations but issued its own consultation paper (*Fraud Law Reform: Consultation on proposals for legislation*, Home Office, 2004) and subsequently, its response to the consultation exercise (*Fraud Law Reform: Government Response to Consultations*, Home Office Criminal Policy Unit, 2005). This resulted in some modifications to the detail of the Commission's proposals but left them fundamentally intact to form the basis of the Fraud Act. Thus the Act replaces the deception offences summarised above with a general offence of fraud committable in three different (but probably overlapping) ways and adds a further offence of dishonestly obtaining services. The intention of the Commission, and initially the Government, was to abolish the common law offence of conspiracy to defraud (an extremely wide and vague offence committable only by two or more persons acting together— see 16.4.4.1 below) when the new fraud offence was introduced. However, the Government's consultation produced strong support for its retention, at least until it was seen how the new law operated in practice, and persuaded the Government to retain it for the time being.

11.4.2 Fraud

The concept of fraud is not directly defined by the Act but by implication it is confined to conduct falling within sections 2, 3 and 4 which provide three different ways of committing the offence of fraud (s. 1(1)). These are fraud by false representation (s. 2), fraud by failing to disclose information (s. 3) and fraud by abuse of position (s. 4).

11.4.2.1 Fraud by false representation

Section 2 provides:

(1) A person is in breach of this section if he—
   (a) dishonestly makes a false representation, and
   (b) intends, by making the representation—
      (i) to make a gain for himself or another, or
      (ii) to cause loss to another or to expose another to a risk of loss.

1. *Actus reus*

You will notice that the only physical conduct required is the actual making of a representation. In complete contrast to the old law, nothing needs to result from the making of the representation. D does not need to obtain anything as a consequence of the representation and, indeed, unlike the old concept of deception, there is no need for anyone to be fooled or taken in by the representation or even to be aware of it! No communication of the representation is required. The new offence thus has a much wider reach than the deception offences and conduct which, at most, would have been attempt (or even fall short of attempt) under the old law will now constitute the full offence of fraud. It is in effect what we call an inchoate offence (see **Chapter 16**).

What is a representation?

According to s. 2(3):

> 'representation' means any representation by words or conduct as to fact or law, including a representation as to the state of mind of—
> (a) the person making the representation, or (b) any other person.

This partly echoes the definition of deception laid out in s. 15(4) of the Theft Act 1968 and it is to be anticipated that the old case law will be influential in interpreting the new provision. Notice that the legislature has again failed properly to define a basic concept. Is it helpful to be told that 'representation means any representation...'? The basic notion of what is a representation is thus left to the courts to define, though it is a concept familiar in civil law in the topic of misrepresentation which you may well have studied in the law of contract. Section 2(3) in effect tells us in a general way what kinds of representations may constitute representations for the purposes of the Act.

Words   This is the most obvious way of making a representation, e.g., this ring is solid gold; this car has done 20,000 miles. It can be either in writing or orally.

Conduct   There are many situations where D implies that something is so, simply by his conduct or behaviour. Thus, when you book into a hotel, you impliedly represent that you intend to pay for the room (*Harris* (1975) 62 Cr App R 28); similarly when you order a meal in a restaurant (*DPP* v *Ray* [1973] 3 All ER 131, HL). A wine waiter employed by a hotel or restaurant impliedly represents that the wine he offers customers is his employer's and not his own (*Doukas* [1978] 1 All ER 1061, CA).

When you issue a cheque, you impliedly represent 'that the state of facts existing at the date of delivery of the cheque is such that in the ordinary course the cheque will, on presentation for payment on or after the date specified in the cheque, be met' (*Gilmartin* [1983] 1 All ER 829, CA following dicta of the House of Lords in *Metropolican Police Commissioner* v *Charles* [1976] 3 All ER 112—*Cases and Materials* (11.4.2.1)). The rule applies equally to post-dated cheques. If your cheque is backed by a cheque card, that representation is true because the bank is bound to honour the cheque. Consequently, the House of Lords in *Metropolitan Police Commissioner* v *Charles* held that the user of a cheque card also impliedly represents that he has the authority of the bank to use it. This was followed in *Lambie* [1981] 2 All ER 776 where the House of Lords held the same in relation to the use of credit cards (debit cards such as Switch would also come under this rule). It follows that if the bank or card company has instructed D not to use his card, his continued use of it will involve a false representation.

In our commercial society, it is an accepted goal for businesses to maximise their profits and charge what they can get away with (what the market will bear!). Therefore it might seem surprising that to quote an excessive price has been held to be capable of implying a representation that it is a fair price. In *Silverman* (1986) 86 Cr App R 213, CA (*Cases and Materials* (11.4.2.1)), D charged two elderly sisters a grossly excessive price for repair work on their flat. He had given them the quotation and had put no pressure on them to accept it. They trusted him to charge a fair price because they had had dealings with him over a long period of time. It was held that he impliedly represented that he would make only a reasonable profit.

> **?** **QUESTION** 11.1
>
> Does this mean that companies which charge exorbitant prices might be guilty of fraud?

No doubt in *Silverman* the court's sympathies were with the elderly and vulnerable victims, but the key factor seems to have been the long course of personal dealings which had built up a relationship of mutual trust. This would seem to be lacking in the case of dealings with large companies. Another requirement which would be essential for conviction is dishonesty—this was conceded as being present by Silverman's counsel (see also *Williams (Roy)* [2001] Crim LR 253, CA). *Silverman* was applied in *Jones* (1993) *The Times*, 15 February, CA where a milkman was convicted of obtaining a customer's money by deception through overcharging for milk supplied over a period of many years. Whilst lacking the vulnerability of the elderly sisters in the former case, the customer looked upon the milkman as a friend and there had built up the necessary relationship of mutual trust.

Silence It is usually asserted that it is not a representation to fail to correct a misapprehension which D knows V to be labouring under, provided that nothing in D's conduct has caused or contributed to it. However, this applies only if D's conduct has played no part in bringing about V's mistake. We have already seen how ready the courts are to hold that D's conduct has played a part by finding implied representations. In *Williams* [1980] Crim LR 589, CA, D obtained from a bureau de change sterling currency in exchange for Yugoslavian dinars which he knew to be obsolete and worthless. It was held that, in presenting the notes, he impliedly represented that they were of value.

> **?** **QUESTION** 11.2
>
> Suppose you visit an Indian restaurant and consume your favourite meal, chicken vindaloo. You then realise that you have left your wallet at home and decide to leave without paying. You wait until the waiter goes into the kitchen and then make a run for it.
>   Have you made any false representation?

The above situation is similar to that in *DPP* v *Ray* [1973] 3 All ER 131 (*Cases and Materials* (11.4.2.1)). The House of Lords held that D impliedly represented that he intended to pay for the meal when he ordered it. This was true until he had eaten the meal and then decided not to pay. The House held that the representation was a continuing one which became therefore a false representation the moment D decided not to pay. In other words, D would have a duty to correct V's misapprehension as soon as the representation is falsified by later events. A similar duty would arise where the representation is untrue from the outset but D only realises later that it is false.

It is also the case that D may be under a duty to inform the victim even though no conduct of his has led to the misunderstanding. In *Firth* (1990) 91 Cr App R 217, CA

(*Cases and Materials* (11.4.2.1)) a consultant was held to have deceived a hospital by failing to declare that certain of his patients were private patients, intending to avoid payment of fees due to the hospital. His omission to inform when under a duty to do so apparently sufficed as 'conduct' impliedly representing that they were NHS patients. Similarly in *Rai* [2000] 1 Cr App R 242, CA, Birmingham City Council approved D's application for a grant to install a downstairs bathroom in his home for the benefit of his elderly and infirm mother. Two days after the approval, D's mother died but he failed to inform the Council. Subsequently the bathroom was installed with finance from the Council. D was convicted of obtaining services (the building works) by his deception in failing to notify the Council of the changed circumstances which rendered him ineligible for any grant.

Although some of these cases seem to be stretching the notion of a representation to breaking point, it is conceivable that they will be followed. However, the necessity to do so is much reduced by the provision in s. 3 for fraud by failing to disclose information which would catch at least some of the above cases (see below).

Fact or law or state of mind   Statements of fact are clear enough—'This painting is by Picasso'. However, that must be distinguished from statements of opinion—'I believe this painting is by Picasso' (see below). A misrepresentation of law might be: 'Unless you pay that £1,000 you owe, you will be sent to prison'.

Express or implied statements as to a person's state of mind are rightly included because they are statements of fact. *DPP* v *Ray* gave us an example—when ordering his meal, D impliedly states he intends to pay. Whether D intends to pay is just as much a fact as whether he has the money to pay. If you send money for mail order goods and D takes your money without the slightest intention of supplying the goods, he would obtain your money by a false implied representation that he intended to deliver.

> **? QUESTION** 11.3
>
> Suppose D, an 'investment adviser', promises to V that he will double any monies invested with him in two years. He believes he can do this and fully intends to. Unfortunately, he invests in cocoa futures just as the bottom drops out of the market and loses V's money.
>   Has he made a false representation?

Mere statements of opinion are not covered by the Act because they are not statements of fact. If a company director says to you that you will make a lot of money if you invest £5,000 in his company, this is an expression of opinion rather than fact. However, it also includes an important representation of fact, namely that the director genuinely holds that opinion. If he does not, he will have made a false representation of fact because 'the state of a man's mind is as much a fact as the state of his digestion' (Bowen LJ in *Edgington* v *Fitzmaurice* (1885) 29 Ch.D. 459, CA). Promises, however wild and extravagant, are also outside the Act, being statements as to future intentions. Of course, when D makes a promise for the future he also makes an implied representation as to his present intentions, i.e., at the moment he makes the promise he intends to carry it out. If he has no such intention, then he makes a false representation as to fact (see *Lewin* v *Barratt Homes Ltd*

[2000] Crim LR 323, DC for an example). Our investment adviser in the Question would therefore not make a false representation **as to fact**.

False representation

Of course, the representation must be **false** and, under s. 2(2), 'a representation is false if— (a) it is untrue or misleading, and (b) the person making it knows it is, or might be, untrue or misleading.' This appears to be an exhaustive definition containing an element of *actus reus* and an element of *mens rea*. The representation must actually be untrue or misleading and D must at least realise it might be untrue or misleading. Hence the minimum fault element in respect of the representation's falsity is subjective recklessness. Mere suspicion is enough. Of course, if the representation turns out not to be false, the fact that D thought it was or might be false could not lead to a conviction for fraud (though it could be attempted fraud). There is no definition of 'misleading' but the Government thought it meant 'less than wholly true and capable of an interpretation to the detriment of the victim.' (*Government Response*, [19].) An example might be a statement that a door-to-door collection of unwanted items was to raise funds for a charity when only a tiny fraction of the profits were intended for the charity. It is literally true but gives a wholly misleading impression.

2. Mens rea

The *mens rea* comprises three elements: (a) D must know that his representation is or might be untrue or misleading; (b) his intention in making the representation must be to make a gain for himself or another or to cause loss to another or to expose another to a risk of loss; and (c) D must act dishonestly.

(a) Knowing the representation is or might be false

As we have seen above, this is relatively straightforward. Actual knowledge that the representation **is** false is clearly sufficient as where D claims to have a degree when he has never enrolled for any such course. Knowledge that it **might be** false is in essence subjective recklessness so that it is enough that D is aware of a possibility that it is false.

(b) Intending to make a gain or cause loss or expose to a risk of loss

D's object (or one of his objects) in making the representation must be to make a gain or cause loss to another or to expose another to a risk of loss. Section 5 defines 'gain' and 'loss'. They are limited to a gain or loss in 'money or other property' whether 'temporary or permanent' and 'property' means 'any property whether real or personal (including things in action and other intangible property)' (s. 5(2)). The provision mirrors s. 34(2) of the Theft Act 1968 in relation to the offence of blackmail and it is likely that existing case law interpretations will be followed (see 12.8.2.2 below).

? **QUESTION** 11.4

Suppose D, by falsely pretending to be a film director, induces V, an aspiring actress, to

- lend him her car for the weekend; or
- spend the weekend in the country with him; or
- take part in a pornographic video he is making; or

- pay him the £500 she owes him; or
- withdraw an application she has made for a job.

Say whether D would satisfy the gain or loss provision in each of the foregoing alternative situations.

It is clear from this provision that the offence aims to protect only the victim's economic interests in money or property. It follows that the second situation would not be covered because no gain or loss in terms of money or property is envisaged. At first sight the third situation looks the same. However, if D is intending to make money from the video, e.g., sell it to a Sunday newspaper, then he intends to make a gain. The section makes clear that a temporary economic gain or loss suffices so that the first situation is caught.

According to ss. 5(3) and 5(4), ' "gain" includes a gain by keeping what one has, as well as a gain by getting what one does not have'; and ' "loss" includes a loss by not getting what one might get, as well as a loss by parting with what one has.' If D owes V £1,000 and persuades him to accept £500 in full satisfaction of the debt by falsely representing he is about to go bankrupt, he does it with a view to gain by keeping what he has and with intent to cause loss to V who does not get what he might.

Referring to the last situation in the Question, even if D will not make any economic gain if V does not get the job applied for, he still intends to cause loss. Because V withdraws her application, she does not get what she might get—the job with the money that goes with it.

That leaves us with the fourth situation where D is trying to recover only what he is legally entitled to. It depends on whether 'gain' is taken to mean 'getting a profit' or simply 'acquiring or obtaining' whether at a profit or not. If you are paid what you are owed, you are not making any profit and V is not suffering any loss in the sense that it had to be paid at some time. On the other hand, D certainly acquires the money when it is paid and V certainly loses it in the physical sense. In *Lawrence and Pomroy* (1971) 57 Cr App R 64 (a blackmail case), the Court of Appeal assumed without argument that the defendants had a view to gain even though they claimed to be trying only to recover what was lawfully owed to them, and there is nothing in the Act to suggest that this interpretation is incorrect. It was applied in *Parkes* [1973] Crim LR 358 (another blackmail case) where it was held that 'getting hard cash as opposed to a mere right of action is getting more than one already has'. This is surely correct and thus the fourth situation would be caught. Of course, if D is using the trickery merely to get what is legally owing to him, then it may well be that a jury would refuse to characterise that as dishonest, despite the underhand method used to get it.

The reference to 'exposure to the risk of loss' is potentially very far-reaching and was recommended by the Law Commission to cater for cases like *Allsop* (1976) 64 Cr App R 29, CA and *Wai Yu-tsang* v *R* [1992] 1 AC 269, PC. Because in each case more than one defendant acted together, successful prosecutions for conspiracy to defraud were brought (see 16.4.4.1 below). However, the Commission thought that provision should be made in the new offence of fraud for a defendant who acted alone in similar circumstances. In the former case the defendants agreed to give false information in an application form (inflating the price of the car and amount of deposit paid) to induce a hire purchase company to grant a loan for car purchase. In the latter case the defendants agreed to falsify a bank's accounts to disguise huge losses on some dishonoured cheques, in order to prevent a run on the bank which would have caused its demise. In both cases, the defendants were hoping that things would turn out well, in which case the victims would not suffer any loss and indeed would profit from the deceptions. However, it was enough that the victims' economic interests were 'imperilled' or 'put in jeopardy' or that there was a 'threat of financial prejudice'. In the light of the legislative definition of 'gain' and 'loss' we have explained above, it is questionable whether this extension is needed to cover either case. Allsop may not have intended to cause loss to the hire purchase company but he certainly intended to make a gain for himself (the commission he received from the company) and for another (the loan received by the car purchaser). Less convincingly, Wai Yu-tsang also intended to make a gain for another in that he intended by the false representation to enable the bank to keep what it had (i.e., stop a run on the bank by depositors clamouring for their money). It is true that this 'gain' was not intended to be at the expense of anyone else but that is not required by the definition in s. 2. There need be no loss intended, corresponding to the gain.

We must remind ourselves that the element we are discussing is entirely a *mens rea* element. No actual loss, gain or risk of loss needs to occur. D must simply **intend** the gain or loss or exposure to the risk of loss. If any of those is one of his purposes (it need not be his only purpose), he satisfies the requirement. It is also very likely that it will be enough to prove that he believed that gain, loss or exposure to a risk of loss was the virtually certain result of his false representation, even if he did not aim to secure any of them (by analogy with *Woollin* at 3.3.2 above). Thus, Wai Yu-tsang may not have aimed to expose customers of the bank to a risk of loss but he certainly knew that the inevitable result of mis-representing the financial position by falsifying the accounts was to expose, for example, new depositors to a risk of loss.

Finally, it is not enough to intend to make a gain etc.; the intention must be to make a gain, etc. **by means of** the false representation. This is likely to make little difference in practice but it might come into play where the representation is implied by D's conduct. The Commission quotes as an example the use of a cheque, credit or debit card where D might argue that he believed the retailer would go ahead with the transaction even if he knew D was not authorised to use it. He would then intend to make the gain but not by means of the implied representation as to authority to use. However, in practice, a jury would be unlikely to accept that D believed that the retailer would definitely take the card if he knew of D's lack of authority. Such an assertion would only ever seem plausible where the card had been legitimately issued to D and he had exceeded the credit limit by a relatively small margin which had not yet provoked a demand for the return of the card. In that event, D might well not be regarded as dishonest anyway, especially as the reaction of many credit card companies to an unauthorised exceeding of the credit limit is to raise it!

(c) Dishonestly

D must **dishonestly** make the false representation. No definition of 'dishonestly' is provided and it will almost certainly be construed in accordance with existing case law. It is clear that both the Commission ([7.59]–[7.72]) and the Home Office (Explanatory Notes to Fraud Bill, [9]) envisage that the *Ghosh* test will apply. Of course, this imports the same elements of uncertainty and criticism we noted when discussing theft (see 10.4.2.1 above).

(d) Some observations on fraud by false representation

There is no doubt that the new offence eradicates a number of problematic features of the old law. No longer do we have to worry about whether anyone has been deceived, thus disposing of the unsatisfactory artificiality evident in cases like *Charles* and *Lambie*, and the problematic features of machine manipulation. The *Preddy* obstacle falls away because there is no need to prove that anything was actually obtained or lost or even at risk of loss. In addition, the generalised nature of the offence seems apt to catch new types of fraud which will no doubt be developed in the future as technology thunders on.

The price of this is a very wide-ranging offence of a general nature where a huge amount rests on the issue of dishonesty. The offence effectively criminalises dishonest lying for an economic motive even where this produces no adverse consequences. False (at least in the sense of 'misleading') representations with a view to gain are so rife in our commercial society as to be almost standard practice in sales and marketing. The difference between merely dubious or sharp practice and criminality will come down to whether or not the fact-finders, i.e., the jury or magistrates decide to designate the conduct as dishonest. As we explained when discussing theft (see the discussion of *Hinks* at 10.4.1.1 above and also 10.4.2.1), the vagueness of the concept of dishonesty and the unpredictability of an individual jury's attitude is a recipe for uncertainty and inconsistency.

11.4.2.2 Fraud by failing to disclose information

Section 3 provides:

> A person is in breach of this section if he—
> (a) dishonestly fails to disclose to another person information which he is under a legal duty to disclose, and
> (b) intends, by failing to disclose the information—
>   (i) to make a gain for himself or another, or
>   (ii) to cause loss to another or to expose another to a risk of loss.

Examples given by the Explanatory Notes to the Bill are: the failure of a solicitor to share vital information with a client within the context of their work relationship, in order to perpetrate a fraud on that client; or failure by a person intentionally to disclose information relating to his heart condition when applying for life insurance. It is certainly arguable on the basis of the cases we discussed under the heading 'silence' above that, if there is a legal duty to disclose, then failure to disclose is a representation by omission falling within s. 2 above. However, it is easier and more sensible to locate these cases under a separate head thus obviating the necessity to strain to find a representation.

1. *Actus reus*

This is simply failing to disclose to another, information you are under a legal duty to disclose. The provision is rather narrower than that recommended by the Law Commission ([7.22]–[7.34] esp. [7.31]–[7.34]). It is confined to cases where D has a **legal duty** to disclose the information whereas the Commission would have extended it to situations falling short of **legal** duty where V trusted D to make disclosure of such information and it was reasonable to expect D to disclose it. The Explanatory Notes adopt the Commission's explanation of when a legal duty will arise:

> Such a duty may derive from statute (such as the provisions governing company prospectuses), from the fact that the transaction in question is one of the utmost good faith (such as a contract of insurance), from the express or implied terms of a contract, from the custom of a particular trade or market, or from the existence of a fiduciary relationship between the parties (such as that of agent and principal). ([7.28])

It is clear that this may raise difficult questions of civil law and may well give rise to the sort of conflicts between civil law and criminal law cases we noted in the law of theft in connection with *Hinks* (see 10.4.1.1). In addition, there are bound to be issues about the extent to which non-statutory standards imposed on members of professions, trade organisations and the like will be seen as constituting **legal** duties.

As indicated above, the Commission wanted to embrace some cases of **mere moral** duty to disclose where V trusted D to make disclosure. An example they gave was of an 'antiques dealer who calls on vulnerable people and buys their heirlooms at unrealistically low prices, making no representation as to the value of the items but exploiting the victims' trust.' Another example might be the *Silverman*-type situation (see above). This was a step too far for the Government which probably felt that it opened up too many uncertainties in the area of commercial activity. It would blur even more the line between the mildly dubious and the criminally fraudulent activity.

2. *Mens rea*

For the *mens rea*, you will notice that s. 3 parallels two of the requirements of s. 2: the intention to make a gain, etc. by not disclosing the information and the need for the non-disclosure to be dishonest. The same discussion therefore applies.

There is no requirement for D even to realise he might have a legal duty to disclose the information as long as one in fact exists—ignorance, even of the civil law, is no excuse! The Commission proposed a specific requirement that D must at least be aware of the **circumstances** which gave rise to the duty (even though he might not realise they gave rise to a duty) but that was dropped for the Bill. It is possible that the courts could read in a *mens rea* requirement under the principles in *B* v *DPP* [2000] 2 AC 428 (see 13.4.1 below). However, it is more likely that D will use his ignorance to support a claim that he was not dishonest and the issue will be subsumed under that general question.

11.4.2.3 Fraud by abuse of position

Section 4 provides:

(1) A person is in breach of this section if he—
   (a) occupies a position in which he is expected to safeguard, or not to act against, the financial interests of another person,
   (b) dishonestly abuses that position, and
   (c) intends, by means of the abuse of that position—
      (i) to make a gain for himself or another, or
      (ii) to cause loss to another or to expose another to a risk of loss.
(2) A person may be regarded as having abused his position even though his conduct consisted of an omission rather than an act.

This provision is designed to catch defendants who have been put in a privileged position in relation to V by virtue of which they can prejudice V's financial interests without further reference to V. In the previous two types of fraud we have considered, D intends to induce V to act or refrain from acting by either his false representation or his non-disclosure of information. Here D's position enables him to make the gain, etc. without any involvement of V.

1. *Actus reus*

D must (a) occupy 'a position in which he is expected to safeguard, or not act against, the financial interests of another person' and (b) abuse that position.

The necessary relationship

The question of what relationships will qualify is bound to prove problematic because of the rather loose 'definition' of the type of 'position' envisaged. The Commission gives these examples of such relationships: trustee and beneficiary, director and company, professional person and client, agent and principal, employee and employer and partners [7.38]. Another example would be that between a carer (with, say, authority to administer a bank account) and an elderly or mentally ill person. These situations may be said to import fiduciary duties under the civil law. More controversially, the Commission was adamant that such a fiduciary relationship was not essential and envisaged that the necessary relationship might arise 'within a family, or in the context of voluntary work, or in any context where the parties are not at arm's length.' However, to rein in the possible reach of such a provision in the hands of a jury, they pointed out that it would be for the judge to rule on whether the facts were capable of constituting the necessary relationship [7.38]. In general terms, V has voluntarily put D in a privileged position so that he is able to control or affect V's financial interests for good or ill independently of V. He does not need any further co-operation from V. He has already been given access to or authority over V's assets such as bank accounts, premises, equipment or customers [7.37].

Abuse of position

There is no indication of what conduct constitutes 'abuse of position' and it is left entirely to the fact-finders, i.e., the magistrate or jury in each individual case. The Commission proposed a requirement that the abuse be done 'secretly', i.e., undisclosed to V but this requirement was omitted from the Bill and the Act itself. In truth, there seems no reason why secrecy should be required.

? QUESTION 11.5

Suppose D, a financial adviser, recommends to V, his client, to invest in a fund run by company X rather than by company Y because company X pays a higher commission to D than company Y. He does not disclose this fact to V.

Would D commit fraud?

Generally speaking abuse will be found in actions which are (or may be) against the financial interests of V, e.g., an estate agent who fails to communicate an offer to purchase V's house because he wants it to go to a relative at a lower price; or a waiter who profits from supplying his own wine to customers instead of his employer's. Of course, if the prejudicial action is merely negligent or foolish, D will lack the *mens rea* (certainly of dishonesty) for the offence.

Although the section defines the required **relationship** in terms of safeguarding (or not acting against) V's interests, that is not expressed as a requirement for an **abuse** of that relationship to occur. This opens the possibility that the financial adviser in our question may be said to be abusing his position even if the investments in the two companies are similar and equally suitable for V. *A fortiori*, if the investments are materially different and/ or not equally suitable. Guilt would then turn on whether a jury regarded D's actions as dishonest or perhaps merely a bit underhand. (Another possibility would be non-disclosure under s. 3. Authorised financial intermediaries are under a duty to disclose in writing the amount of commission they will receive (though this would not necessarily include any comparison with rejected investments).)

Section 4(2) makes it crystal clear that a mere omission to act can amount to an abuse of position. The Commission's example is of an employee who passes up the chance of a profitable contract for his employer's business because he wants it to go to an associate instead.

2. *Mens rea*

The twin requirements are (1) dishonestly and (2) intention by means of the abuse to make a gain etc. and these have already been discussed in the context of s. 2. As in s. 3, no further requirement is expressed in respect of knowledge by D that he is in a position of trust, etc. and it is likely that any such issues will be subsumed within the general question of dishonesty.

11.4.2.4 **Miscellaneous offences**

Section 6 makes it an offence for D to have 'in his possession or under his control any article for use in the course of or in connection with any fraud'. This replaces the offence of going equipped to cheat (i.e., obtain property by deception) under s. 25 of the Theft Act (that still remains as going equipped for theft or burglary). That offence only applied to possession of the article away from D's 'place of abode'. The new offence covers possession anywhere including D's home. Examples could include computers, machines for making credit cards, credit cards themselves, false passports or an Old Etonian tie. Section 8 specifically includes 'any program or data held in electronic form'. Thus, D might have on his computer files containing people's credit card details or templates for 'scam' letters or e-mails or to produce blank utility bills. The term 'for use' implies the need for possession for fraudulent purposes though it need not be for a specific, identified fraud. A general intention that it should be used for a fraudulent purpose will suffice.

Section 7 outlaws making, adapting, supplying or offering to supply any such article '(a) knowing that it is designed or adapted for use in the course of or in connection with fraud, **or** (b) intending it to be used to commit, or assist in the commission of, fraud.' This would include supplying machines which can send an electricity meter into reverse when electricity is used, thus defrauding the supplier, or credit card cloning machines.

The offence of fraudulent trading under s. 458 of the Companies Act applies essentially only to companies and corporate bodies who trade with intent to defraud their creditors or for any other fraudulent purpose. Section 9 creates a parallel offence for individuals falling outside the reach of s. 458 (essentially non-corporate traders), who are knowingly parties to the carrying on of a business with intent to defraud their creditors or for any other fraudulent purpose.

Finally, although space does not permit us to analyse them, we can note the continued existence of ss. 17–20 of the Theft Act 1968 (*Cases and Materials* (11.4.2.4)). These sections house practically important offences aimed at company frauds and the world of high (and low) finance. Section 17 covers false accounting, s. 18 deals with the liability of company officers where a company commits an offence under s. 17, and s. 19 prohibits publication of false or misleading information by company officers. The suppression of original court or government department documents, valuable securities and wills is forbidden by s. 20(1).

11.4.2.5 Summary overview and conclusion on fraud

The very general formulation of the new offence of fraud would cover a wide range of conduct including much, but not all, of the conduct currently caught only by the offence of conspiracy to defraud as well as almost the entire range of conduct caught by the existing deception offences. The problems associated with the troublesome concept of 'deception' (explained earlier) are avoided by substituting a requirement for a false representation only. Thus, in the paradigm case based on s. 2, it will be unnecessary to show that anyone was taken in by the false representation. Further, there is no need to show that any loss or gain actually resulted from the false representation, non-disclosure or abuse of position. An intent to make a gain or cause loss **by** making the false representation etc. is what is required. The non-disclosure/abuse of trust provisions certainly extend beyond the former deception offences and would accord protection to the vulnerable from unscrupulous exploitation. The difficulty is that the distinction between mere sharp practice and criminality would be hugely dependent on the jury's (or magistrate's) view of whether D's conduct was dishonest—a notoriously vague and unpredictable concept. Although the offence of fraud may attract criticism on account of its width, unpredictability and unspecific nature, there is no doubt that it will greatly simplify the law and make it easier to understand.

11.4.3 Obtaining services dishonestly

Section 11 provides:

(1) A person is guilty of an offence under this section if he obtains services for himself or another—
   (a) by a dishonest act, and
   (b) in breach of subsection (2).
(2) A person obtains services in breach of this subsection if—
   (a) they are made available on the basis that payment has been, is being or will be made for or in respect of them,
   (b) he obtains them without any payment having been made for or in respect of them or without payment having been made in full, and

(c) when he obtains them, he knows—
  (i) that they are being made available on the basis described in paragraph (a), or
  (ii) that they might be,
but intends that payment will not be made, or will not be made in full.

The main purpose of this offence is to catch automated (generally electronic) transactions where there is no human involvement. The difficulty under the old law was that it was thought impossible to deceive a machine and the previous offence under s. 1 of the Theft Act 1978 required the obtaining of services **by** deception. Unlike the fraud offence, it is essential under s. 11 to prove that D's dishonest act **caused** an obtaining of services though deception is no longer necessary. Examples include dishonestly using a decoder to obtain unauthorised access to cable or satellite television with intent to avoid payment, hacking into internet services to avoid payment and inputting false credit card or personal details to obtain a service, e.g., download a film. On a less technological note, it would include climbing over a wall to get into a football ground to avoid paying the entrance fee.

11.4.3.1 *Actus reus*

Essentially, D must obtain by an act, chargeable services without having paid the charge at all or in full.

Chargeable services

The offence applies only to services for which payment is required and, as the old offence under s. 1, does not embrace gratuitous services. If your silver-tongued mendacity persuades V to offer you his service, e.g., a taxi ride for nothing, you do not obtain 'services' under s. 11 because no payment is envisaged. If you deceive your neighbour into mowing your lawn by falsely pretending you have injured your leg, there are no 'services' because there is no expectation that the neighbour will be paid. Of course, such cases involve a false representation but would constitute fraud by virtue of s. 2 only if you intended a gain or loss in 'money or property'. This would be so in the taxi example but probably not in the lawn example. The obtaining of banking or credit card facilities, or even the ability to operate a bank or credit card account, although apparently 'services' would not suffice unless there was a charge to be levied, e.g., annual credit card fee or monthly bank charge (*cf. Sofroniou* [2003] EWCA Crim 3681 concerning the former offence under s. 1 of the Theft Act 1978). Again it is likely that some false representation will have been used enabling use of the fraud offence, assuming D's ultimate intention is to make a gain or cause loss in terms of money. It is probably immaterial that the liability to pay for the services is not legally enforceable as where D, aged 17, obtains non-necessary services.

Payment probably includes not only payment in money, whether by cash, cheque or credit card, but also payment in kind, e.g., by vouchers, goods or other services in return. If you falsely promise to lay a patio for V in exchange for his painting your house, it should be within s. 11. Of course, it is necessary to show that, at the time of obtaining, the expected, or an acceptable alternative, payment has not been made either at all or in full. Even a relatively minor shortfall would satisfy this requirement (though its triviality or otherwise might be relevant to the issue of dishonesty).

There is no definition of what constitutes 'services' and it seems that the term must therefore be interpreted in the light of its everyday meaning. That would make it rather narrower than the now obsolete definition given in the former offence under s. 1 of the TA

1978 where any act which conferred a chargeable benefit was 'services'. It is therefore suggested that previous case law is at best persuasive only. The Commission certainly intended to include the provision of a service through the medium of a machine whether directly by, for example, an unauthorised switching on of, say, a computer giving access to restricted information or indirectly as where D takes advantage of a program designed to generate automatically, in the future, a service to anyone satisfying certain criteria. Often the latter will involve a misrepresentation (constituting fraud as well) but whether it does or not, it can still be an offence under s. 11. As the Commission puts it, the offence is a 'theft-like offence' which can 'be committed *either* by deception *or* by simply "helping oneself" to a service' ([8.7]–[8.9]).

Obtains by a dishonest act

 QUESTION 11.6

Does this mean that you commit the offence if you listen to music or use a software program which you know has been illegally downloaded in breach of copyright?

The key to answering the question posed is to remember that the offence requires D to 'obtain' services by his dishonest act. The Commission's view is that simply using items 'already obtained' does not constitute the offence. Illegal file-sharers should not take too much comfort from this because the attitude of the courts remains to be seen. It could be said that D's act in opening up the program or music file (and *a fortiori* downloading it from a website or installing it from a CD) does get **him** the services and if it is designated dishonest by the jury, he commits the offence. The necessity for an obtaining by a dishonest **act** precludes liability for getting the services by a mere omission to act.

11.4.3.2 *Mens rea*

There are three elements to the *mens rea*: (1) The act(s) causing the obtaining must be **dishonest**; (2) D, at the time of the obtaining, must **know** that the services **are or might be** being made available on the basis that payment has been, is being or will be made for or in respect of them; and (3) D **intends** that payment will not be made or not be made in full.

(1) Dishonest act
Dishonesty is said by the courts to be a question of fact for the jury and the *Ghosh* test applies as before.

(2) Knowledge that payment might be expected
This requirement is self-explanatory and we need only observe that it suffices that D realises that payment might be required for the services.

(3) Intent to avoid payment in whole or in part
It must be D's object that either no payment will be made or a lesser payment than that due. This was not required for the replaced offence where the deception need not have been related to the prospect of payment (*Naviede* [1997] Crim LR 662, CA).

? **QUESTION** 11.7

Suppose that parents lied about their religious beliefs in order to obtain a place for their child at a private, fee-paying school which admitted only children of a certain religious persuasion. Would they commit an offence (a) under s. 11 and (b) under s. 2?

It follows that if parents lied about their religious beliefs in order to secure their child's admission to a private denominational school, they could not commit this offence if they fully intended to pay the fees, even assuming that their conduct was regarded as dishonest. Their dishonesty was not related to payment of the fees and they did not intend to avoid any payment. Of course, they did make a false representation about their beliefs and you might be thinking that there would be a contravention of s. 2. However, this would seem not to be so because the parents lack the necessary intention to make a 'gain' or cause 'loss'. Remember gains and losses are limited to 'money or other property' and the speculative, intangible benefits of an education at that school would be unlikely to be categorised as 'property', notwithstanding that the ultimate long-term objective of the parents might be to better secure their child's economic future.

It is not totally clear when D must have the intention to avoid payment but it is likely that he must have it at the time he obtains the services. If there is a time interval between performing the dishonest act which triggers the obtaining and the receipt of the services, it is thought that, in practice, he must have the intention both when he performs the act (otherwise he is unlikely to be dishonest) and when he receives (i.e., obtains) the services. If, on or before receipt, he changes his mind and decides he will pay, it will not be the offence.

As in the offence of 'making off without payment' under s. 3 of the Theft Act 1978, which we discuss shortly, it is not made explicit whether there must be an intent to make permanent default so that if D intended ultimately to pay but not at the due time, he would escape liability. However, it is thought that this is the natural meaning of the words used so that an intent to avoid payment **temporarily** would be insufficient. Furthermore, in a penal statute, ambiguity should be resolved in favour of the accused. This accords with the interpretation of s. 3 by the House of Lords in *Allen* (see 11.4.4.2 below).

11.4.3.3 Conclusion

You will have noticed that at various points, we have remarked that obtaining services cases very often involve a false representation creating a clear overlap with the offence of fraud. Even where D manipulates a machine without human intervention, it is arguable that there will usually be a false representation. Instances of obtaining services by inputting false information to a website would surely involve a misrepresentation as to the identity of the inputter or the accuracy of the information. Unlike deception, there does not appear to be any necessity for the representation to involve or be addressed to a human being. It would, on this basis, be relatively easy for the courts to construct an implied representation (e.g., that D is authorised to access the site) in most cases of electronic manipulation of machines. Even our dishonest football spectator, sitting in the stadium, could be said to impliedly represent that he is authorised to be there. There is therefore a question mark as to whether the offence adds anything to the fraud offence or, if it does, whether what is added is worth criminalising by the creation of a special offence with all the extra complications that implies. On the other hand, in practical terms, it is easy to understand and does avoid the need to scratch around for an implied representation.

Notice that the requirement under the repealed offence to obtain 'by deception' is dropped in favour of 'by a dishonest act'. The new offence is narrower in requiring an intent to avoid payment. No definition of 'services' is provided other than to exclude gratuitous services.

11.4.4 Making off without payment

Making off without payment is the only offence in the Theft Act 1978 that survives the Fraud Act. Section 3 provides:

> A person who, knowing that payment on the spot for any goods supplied or service done is required or expected from him, dishonestly makes off without having paid as required or expected and with intent to avoid payment of the amount due shall be guilty of an offence.

The offence is aimed at situations where D tries dishonestly to avoid payment of what is due in circumstances liable to make him difficult to trace. Examples are: running out of a restaurant without paying for a meal; driving off from a self-service petrol station without paying for the petrol; or leaving a hotel without paying for the stay.

It may well be that D also commits other offences but there are times when he does not or, at least, where it is far easier to prove s. 3. For example, we saw the problems and artificiality involved in trying to find a deception by the dishonest diners in *DPP v Ray* (see 11.4.2.1) prior to the creation of this offence. Section 3 does not require any deception or false representation and would now be the obvious charge for such conduct.

? QUESTION 11.8

Would the person who dishonestly drives off from a self-service petrol station without paying for the petrol he has taken commit theft or only the making off offence?

The answer depends on the facts. If D is dishonest at the time he fills up, he dishonestly appropriates the petrol belonging then to the garage and commits theft (*Gomez*; *McHugh*). If he decides not to pay only after he has filled up, his dishonest appropriation would come at a time when the ownership had transferred to him and would not be of petrol 'belonging to another'. There would be no theft of the petrol (*Edwards v Ddin*) only making off contrary to s. 3 of the 1978 Act.

11.4.4.1 *Actus reus*

D must (a) make off from the spot where payment is required or expected (b) without having paid as required or expected (c) for goods supplied or service done.

Makes off

The main question at issue is whether 'makes off' means simply departing from the spot or whether it connotes 'decamping' or 'disappearing: leaving in a way that makes it difficult for the debtor to be traced' (JR Spencer [1983] Crim LR 573—*Cases and Materials* (11.4.4.1)).

There does not appear to be any need for haste or stealth (running out at top speed or sneaking out when the waiter has left the room). It would certainly cover the case where D, who is of gigantic physique, just ambles out telling the waiter what to do with his parsnips. According to *Brooks and Brooks* (1982) 76 Cr App R 66, in a rare biblical reference, making off 'may be an exercise accompanied by the sound of trumpets or a silent stealing away after the folding of tents'.

It was held in a Crown Court case, *Hammond* [1982] Crim LR 611, that if the creditor consents to D's leaving, albeit because of D's dishonest deception, there would be no making off. Thus, if D pays with a dud cheque or gets the creditor's consent to leave by a false statement (e.g., deceives a taxi driver into thinking that he is going into his house to get the money for the fare and then disappears into the night), *Hammond* would say there is no making off. It seems unlikely that this narrow view will be accepted by higher courts.

? QUESTION 11.9

Suppose you are the Marquess of Barchester and you take a taxi ride. At the end of the ride, you announce to the driver that you are the Marquess of Barchester and that you are not paying because the driver refused to open the cab door for you. Would you 'make off' when you walk up the steps to your flat in Belgravia without having paid?

The matter is unresolved but this is where Spencer's argument above might come into play. If making off means disappearing in a way making it difficult to trace, there would be no making off. The same would be true of the case where D pays with a worthless cheque but writes his true name and address on the back. We would guess the courts are more likely to favour the less complicated view implied by *Brooks and Brooks* that 'makes off' simply means 'leaving'. Thus, the question of conviction would largely revolve on whether D was dishonest. It would be difficult to draw the line if Spencer's concept were accepted. Think of the self-service petrol situation: would that be caught where D's car registration number is taken?

The spot

D can only 'make off' when he leaves 'the spot' where 'payment is required or expected'. Section 3(2) specifically, but seemingly unnecessarily, provides that ' "payment on the spot" includes payment at the time of collecting goods on which work has been done [e.g., clock repair] or in respect of which service has been provided' (e.g., clothes dry-cleaned).

The precise identification of the 'spot' in any given case may be crucial in deciding whether D has committed the full offence or merely an attempt. In *McDavitt* [1981] Crim LR 843 the 'spot' was V's restaurant, so that when D made his way to the door intending to leave without paying for his meal but did not actually go through the door, he only attempted to 'make off'. This suggests that the 'spot' will generally be the premises as a whole rather than, say, the cash point for payment.

Of course, there may be no 'premises' involved. In the case of a taxi ride, the 'spot' will normally be at the agreed destination but, if D refuses to pay at that point and the taxi driver sets off for a police station, D commits the offence if he gets out and runs off on route (*Aziz* [1993] Crim LR 708, CA). Presumably, leaving without paying at any time after the agreed destination is reached suffices. In *Moberly* v *Alsop* [1991] TLR 576, DC a London Underground traveller was held to be still 'on the spot' when he passed through the exit barrier at his destination station even though he should have bought a ticket at the beginning of his journey.

This suggests that 'making off' is to some extent a continuing act. If D runs out of a restaurant hotly pursued down the street by a waiter, we would suggest that the 'making off' continues whilst the pursuit continues. This is important because the power of arrest for the offence or an attempt given by s. 3(4) is a 'then and there' power available only whilst the offence or attempt is in the course of being committed. Surely, if the waiter apprehends D, this would be within s. 3(4)? *Drameh* [1983] Crim LR 322 held that the 'making off' had certainly ceased by the time D got home after running off without paying a taxi fare. The police therefore had no power to arrest him in his own home.

Without having paid as required or expected

V must require payment on the spot. If the victim has agreed to postpone payment, even as a result of being duped by D's dishonest deception, he no longer requires or expects payment 'on the spot'. D cannot therefore commit the offence when he leaves without paying (*Vincent* [2001] Crim LR 488, CA). In addition the 'on the spot' payment must in fact be legally due. In *Troughton* v *Metropolitan Police* [1987] Crim LR 138, DC, D, who had had a lot to drink, took a taxi home to Highbury. The driver had difficulty getting the precise address and D accused him of deliberately going a long way round. The driver then drove to a police station. The court held that no payment was due because the driver had broken the contract by not carrying D to the agreed destination. There could therefore be no question of a s. 3 conviction.

The main problem yet to be solved is whether payment by a worthless cheque is 'payment as required'. It would seem that the section envisages that D must pay in a manner known to be expected and acceptable to V. It would therefore cover not only payment in cash but payment with credit cards, cheques, luncheon vouchers, etc. It would presumably not cover payment with forged notes. If D pays with a cheque guaranteed by a cheque card or by a credit card, even if D's authority to use it has been withdrawn or he has stolen it (*cf. Re Charge Card Services Ltd* [1988] 3 All ER 702), it will be payment acceptable to V, provided that the bank or card company is bound to meet the payment.

It seems that payment with a dud cheque is the same as payment with counterfeit money and therefore not payment within s. 3. Although *Hammond* suggests otherwise, this Crown Court decision is unlikely to be followed.

Goods supplied or service done

The offence requires goods actually to be supplied or the service actually to be done. Goods will be supplied only where they come into D's hands with the express or implied consent of the 'supplier'. This will include cases where D helps himself to the goods at the implied invitation of the owner, e.g., self-service supermarkets or petrol stations. Of course, D may well commit the offence of theft in addition to s. 3. On the other hand, if D helps himself to cigarettes at a non-self-service store whilst the assistant is distracted, that will be theft, but not s. 3 because no goods are 'supplied'.

Similarly, 'service done' means a service given at the express or implied invitation of V, e.g., knowing provision of a hotel room for D, giving D a taxi ride. It would probably not include a case where D sneaks into the hotel by the fire escape and sleeps there for the night before leaving the way he had come. By contrast, if D takes advantage of a facility at the implied invitation of the owner, e.g., a car park open to the public, we would suggest that a service is 'done' for him.

Section 3(3) provides that the offence cannot be committed if 'the supply of the goods or the doing of the service is contrary to law, or where the service done is such that payment is not legally enforceable'.

?   **QUESTION** 11.10

If a minor offers to buy 'non-necessary' goods from a market stall-holder but runs off without paying as soon as they are handed over by the stall-holder, would he commit a s. 3 offence as well as theft?

The supply of a prohibited drug, an obscene video or alcohol to someone under 18 might be 'contrary to law', as may services provided in a brothel or unlicensed casino or by a back-street abortionist. As regards legally unenforceable payments, this provision relates only to unenforceable services done and not goods supplied under an unenforceable but not illegal contract. Thus, a person who leaves a prostitute without paying for the service done does not commit the offence, but the youth in our Question would commit the offence not-withstanding that his obligation to pay for the non-necessary goods supplied cannot be enforced under the law on infants' contracts!

11.4.4.2 *Mens rea*

D must (a) act dishonestly (b) know that payment on the spot is required or expected from him and (c) intend to avoid payment of the amount due.

Little needs to be said about 'dishonestly' since the meaning has already been discussed at 11.4.2.1. D must be dishonest **at the time of** 'making off'. If he believed that payment was not due because, for example, the food supplied in the restaurant was inedible, he would not be dishonest.

D must know payment on the spot is required. This is self-explanatory and overlaps with the requirement of dishonesty. If D believes that the goods were offered on credit and that he would be invoiced for them or that someone else has paid or has agreed to pay for them, he would not be guilty.

According to the House of Lords in *Allen* [1985] 2 All ER 641 (*Cases and Materials* (11.4.4.2)) intent to avoid payment means an intent **never** to pay. An intent merely to avoid payment on the spot and gain a temporary respite is not enough. At the time of the making off, D must intend to make **permanent** default. The main reason for this is that a defendant who dishonestly makes off without paying must of necessity intend to avoid paying **at the time** and if that is all that 'intent to avoid payment' meant, it would add nothing to the section and be redundant. That compels the interpretation which gives it some additional point, namely, that D must intend to avoid paying altogether, as opposed to just delay payment.

■ **FURTHER READING**

Binning: *When Dishonesty is not Enough* (2004) 154 New LJ 1042.

Home Office: *Fraud Law Reform: Consultation on Proposals for Legislation* (May 2004).

Home Office: *Government Response to Consultations* (2005).

Law Commission: *Fraud and Deception: A Consultation Paper* (Law Com. No. 155, 1999).

Law Commission: *Report on Fraud* (Law Com. No. 276, 2002).

Sullivan: *Fraud and Efficacy in the Criminal Law: A Proposal for a Wide Residual Offence* [1985] Crim LR 616.

Sullivan: *Fraud: The Latest Law Commission Proposals* (2003) 67 J Crim L 139.

■ **SUMMARY**

The Fraud Act 2006 has replaced the previous deception offences with a new general offence of fraud.

The repealed offences

The old law comprised a disordered list of offences whose common core was '**dishonestly obtaining something by deception**'. The main difference lay in the 'something' that had to be obtained: s. 15 of the TA 1968 covered obtaining property by deception; s. 15A, a money transfer; s. 16 a pecuniary advantage; s. 20(2) the execution of a valuable security; s. 1 of the TA 1978 services and s. 2 the evasion of a liability to pay.

Dishonestly—as for theft except s. 2 did not apply, i.e., *Ghosh* applies. *Deception*—generally required (i) a false representation by D which (ii) 'fooled' V (operated on his mind). It was a two-sided thing. Section 15(4) partially defined what could be a deception—(i) words—written or oral (ii) conduct, e.g., ordering meals, issuing cheques (iii) silence—D under duty to correct misapprehensions he knew to have been brought about by his conduct (iv) fact or law—either would do (v) present intentions—**promises** to do things (e.g., send goods) or statements of **opinion** not covered unless **when given** D did not intend to deliver or did not hold the opinion (vi) deliberate or reckless—**subjective** recklessness. *By deception*—the deception must have **caused** the obtaining and so must have occurred **before** the obtaining (*Coady*). It must not have been too remote (*Clucas*), but courts reluctant to so hold (*King and Stockwell*). D did not have to positively address his mind to the false representation, nor did it have to be a matter of **concern** to D. It was enough if he 'relied' on it in the negative sense that he would not have acted as he did if he had known the truth (*Charles*).

- **Obtaining property (s. 15)**—D must (i) obtain (ii) property (iii) belonging to another (iv) by deception (v) dishonestly (vi) with intent permanently to deprive. *Obtaining*—could be of **ownership**, possession **or** control (s. 15(2)).

- **Money transfer (s. 15A)**—D must dishonestly obtain a money transfer by deception. Involved the reciprocal crediting and debiting of bank accounts.

- **Pecuniary advantage (s. 16)**—D must (i) dishonestly (ii) obtain for himself or another (iii) a pecuniary advantage (iv) by deception. Pecuniary advantage narrowly defined to mean **only** (i) allowed to borrow by way of overdraft or get better terms therefor (ii) allowed to take out insurance or annuity or better terms therefor (iii) given the opportunity to earn remuneration or greater remuneration in employment or win money by betting (s. 16(2)).

- **Procuring the execution of a valuable security by deception (s. 20(2))**—D must dishonestly cause V to execute, i.e., sign and issue a cheque, banker's draft or other valuable security, by deception.

- **Obtaining services (s. 1 of the TA 1978)**—D must for himself or another (*Nathan*) (i) dishonestly (ii) obtain from another (iii) services (iv) by any deception. *Services*—**exhaustively** defined by s. 1(2)—V was (i) induced to confer a benefit by doing, causing or permitting some act (ii) on the understanding the benefit has been or will be paid for. *Paid for*—free services were excluded. Included mortgages and other loans.

- **Evasion of liability (s. 2 of the TA 1978)**—three offences all involving dishonestly 'obtaining' by deception:

  (a) Securing the remission in whole or in part of any existing liability to pay (b) Inducing V to wait for or forgo payment (c) Obtaining an exemption from or abatement of a liability to pay.

The **new offences**

The Fraud Act 2006 replaces the deception offences summarised above with a general offence of fraud and adds a further offence of dishonestly obtaining services.

- **Fraud (s. 1)**: the offence is committable in three different (but probably overlapping) ways:

  (1) **Fraud by false representation** (s. 2): D must (a) dishonestly (b) make a false representation (c) intending by that false representation to make a gain for himself or another or to cause loss to another or to expose another to a risk of loss. *Actus reus*: Simply making a false representation whether or not any gain, loss or risk of loss results from it. In contrast to deception, no need to show anyone was taken in by it or even aware of it. **Representation** means any representation by words or conduct as to fact or law and as to the state of mind of D or any other person (s. 2(3)). (i) Words can be written or oral. (ii) Conduct, e.g., ordering meals, issuing cheques, using payment cards. (iii) Silence—D probably under duty to correct misapprehensions he knows have been brought about by his conduct (though see non-disclosure below). (iv) Fact or law—either will do. (v) State of mind—covers express or implied representations of D's present intentions or beliefs but **promises** to do things (e.g., send goods) or statements of **opinion** not covered unless **when given** D does not intend to deliver or does not hold the opinion. **False** representation: means 'untrue or misleading' (provided D knows it is or might be untrue or misleading) (s. 2(2)). *Mens rea*: comprises three elements: (a) D must know that his representation is or might be untrue or

misleading; (b) his intention in making the representation must be to make a gain for himself or another or to cause loss to another or to expose another to a risk of loss; and (c) D must act dishonestly. Dishonestly interpreted in accordance with *Ghosh* and pre-existing case law. Intent to make a gain, etc.: covers only gain or loss in money or other property (i.e., real or personal including things in action and other intangible property) whether temporary or permanent (s. 5(2)). Non-economic gains or losses outside the offence. Gain includes keeping what one has and loss includes not getting what one might (s. 5(3) and 5(4)). Includes also exposing to a **risk** of loss. Remember it is D's **intention** that counts—no need to show there was any actual gain or loss or risk of loss.

(2) **Fraud by failing to disclose information** (s. 3): D must (a) dishonestly (b) fail to disclose to another information which (c) he is under a legal duty to disclose (d) intending by the non-disclosure to make a gain for himself or another or to cause loss to another or to expose another to a risk of loss. *Actus reus*: failing to disclose information D is under a legal duty to disclose. Only a **legal** duty will do and can arise from statute, contract, trade custom and practice or fiduciary relationship. Involves difficult issues of civil law. *Mens rea*: dishonestly and with the intention to make a gain, etc.—see s. 2 above.

(3) **Fraud by abuse of position** (s. 4): D must (a) occupy a position in which he is expected to safeguard, or not to act against, the financial interests of another person and (b) dishonestly (c) abuse that position (d) intending by that abuse to make a gain for himself or another or to cause loss to another or to expose another to a risk of loss. This provision is designed to catch defendants who have been put in a privileged position in relation to V by virtue of which they can prejudice V's financial interests without further reference to V. *Actus reus*: D must (a) occupy 'a position in which he is expected to safeguard, or not act against, the financial interests of another person' and (b) abuse that position. **The necessary relationship**: examples include trustee and beneficiary, director and company, professional person and client, agent and principal, employee and employer and partners, carer and an elderly or mentally ill person. Likely to prove problematic at the margins. **Abuse of position**: no definition but likely to be found in actions which are (or may be) against the financial interests of V, e.g., an estate agent who fails to communicate an offer to purchase V's house because he wants it to go to a relative at a lower price. A mere omission to act can be an abuse (s. 4(2)). *Men rea*: dishonestly and with the intention to make a gain, etc.—see s. 2 above.

- **Obtaining services dishonestly (s. 11)**: D must (a) by a dishonest act (b) obtain services which (c) are chargeable (d) without payment having been made for or in respect of them either at all or in full (e) knowing that they are or might be chargeable and (f) intending that payment will not be made either at all or in full (s. 11(1) and 11(2)). Mainly intended to catch manipulation of machines which provide services automatically without human involvement. *Actus reus*: essentially D must obtain by an act chargeable services without having paid for them at all or in full. **Services**: no definition therefore has everyday meaning. **Chargeable**: excludes gratutitous services where there is no expectation of payment, e.g., provision of a no fee credit card or bank account. **Obtains by an act**: D must obtain the services so that merely using, e.g., a computer program or CD already obtained may not be covered. Needs a positive act—a mere omission is not enough. **Without having paid in full**: any shortfall is enough. Payment will include any method, e.g., cash, cheque, in kind acceptable to V. *Mens rea*: (i) the act(s) causing the obtaining must be **dishonest**; (ii) D, at the time of the obtaining, must **know** that the services **are or might be** being made available on the basis that payment has been, is being or will be made for or in respect of them; and (iii) D **intends** that payment will not be made or not be made in full. (i) Dishonesty: the *Ghosh* test applies as before. (ii) It is enough that D knows the services **might** be chargeable. (iii) D must aim to avoid the payment in whole or in part. Probably means an intent to make **permanent** default as opposed to merely delay payment though not certain.

- **Making off without payment (s. 3 of the TA 1978)**: this offence was retained by the Fraud Act. D must (i) make off (ii) from the spot where payment is required or expected (iii) without having paid as required or expected (iv) for goods supplied or service done (*actus reus*) (v) knowing payment on the spot is required or expected (vi) with intent to avoid payment of the amount due (vii) dishonestly (*mens rea*). **No** deception is required. *Makes off*—no need for haste or stealth. Does it require 'decamping' or merely 'departing'? Probably the latter (*Brooks and Brooks*). Creditor's 'consent' to leaving is probably irrelevant (although see *Hammond*). To some extent a continuing act. Question of fact where the 'spot' is (*Aziz*). *Without having paid*— payment must be legally due 'on the spot' (*Troughton v Metropolitan Police*). Payment with forged money or bad cheque probably not 'payment' for this purpose (although see *Hammond*). *Goods supplied/service done*—goods must actually be supplied and service actually done. Illegal supply or service excluded and if payment for service (but not for supply of goods) is legally unenforceable (s. 3(3)). *Intent to avoid payment*— requires an intent to make **permanent** default at the time of the making off (*Allen*).

12 Offences against property III

12.1 Objectives

By the end of this chapter you should be able to:

1 Define the offences covered

2 Analyse their ingredients

3 Identify which of the offences, if any, apply in any given fact situation

12.2 Introduction

In this chapter we deal with the remaining offences in the Theft Act 1968 which are within the scope of this work, along with the main offences created by the Criminal Damage Act 1971. Most of these offences are important in practice although there is no particular connecting theme between them other than that they are property offences.

12.3 Robbery

Section 8(1) of the TA 1968 provides:

> A person is guilty of robbery if he steals, and immediately before or at the time of doing so, and in order to do so, he uses force on any person or puts or seeks to put any person in fear of being then and there subjected to force.
>
> By s. 8(2), both robbery and assault with intent to rob are punishable with up to life imprisonment.

12.3.1 Theft plus

Robbery is a form of stealing aggravated by the threat or use of force. The reference to 'steals' in s. 8(1) is shorthand for all the ingredients of theft. (The doubts expressed in *Forrester* [1992] Crim LR 793 are surely untenable.) The simple rule is: no theft, no robbery. It follows that D cannot be convicted of robbery if he believed he was entitled to the property taken notwithstanding that he knew he had no right to use force to obtain the property (*Robinson* [1977] Crim LR 173).

The robbery is complete when the theft is complete. Because of the wide definition of appropriation, robbery can occur even though the robber does not escape with the property. In *Corcoran v Anderton* (1980) 71 Cr App R 10, D dragged a handbag forcibly from V's grasp so that it fell to the ground. That in itself was a complete robbery whether or not he picked it up. The court thought that forcible tugging at the handbag would also have been sufficient, even if V had been able to hang on to it.

12.3.2 Use or threat of force

12.3.2.1 The meaning of force

The term used is 'force' rather than the slightly narrower term, 'violence'. In *Dawson* [1976] Crim LR 692, CA (*Cases and Materials* (12.3.2.1)), D1 nudged against V whilst D2 stole his wallet. Their conviction for robbery was upheld by the Court of Appeal which rejected the argument that such action could not amount to force. Rather surprisingly the court held that whether such a nudge amounts to 'force' was in every case a question of fact for the jury.

12.3.2.2 'Force on any person'

It is not sufficient to use force against property; it must be used on a person. Under the old law, it was not enough to use force on the property to get control of it, so that bag-snatching was not in itself robbery. However, the Court of Appeal in *Clouden* [1987] Crim LR 56 (*Cases and Materials* (12.3.2.2)) held that 'the old distinctions have gone' and the case should be left to the jury to decide if D used 'force on any person' in order to steal. D had wrenched V's shopping bag from her grasp and run off with it. The jury decided that this was robbery and the Court of Appeal upheld the conviction. It seems therefore likely that bag-snatching or ripping off someone's jewellery will constitute robbery.

'On any person' clearly includes where D uses or threatens force on someone other than the owner or possessor of the property. If D is engaged in breaking into V's car in order to steal it when he is challenged by V's neighbour, use of force on the neighbour in order to complete the theft will suffice for robbery; *a fortiori*, if the person is a night-watchman or security patrolman charged with looking after V's property.

12.3.2.3 Threat of force

Actual force is not essential. If D 'puts or seeks to put any person in fear of being then and there subjected to force', he can be guilty of robbery. It is not even necessary to put V in actual fear of force as long as D 'seeks to put' someone in fear. The reference to 'then and there' rules out a threat to apply force at some time in the future (although this may amount to blackmail).

12.3.2.4 Immediately before or at the time of the stealing

If the only force used or threatened comes a long time before the commission of the theft, there can be no robbery (although there may be blackmail). Equally, there is no robbery if the only force used or threatened comes after the theft is completed.

On a literal view, the theft is committed as soon as D touches the jewellery with the dishonest intention permanently to deprive. In other words it was committed upstairs. However, you may recall that when we discussed appropriation in theft, we considered the issue of whether appropriation could be a continuing process (see the discussion under 10.4.1.1 above). According to *Hale* (1978) 68 Cr App R 415, CA (*Cases and Materials* (12.3.2.4)) for the purposes of robbery the appropriation should be regarded as continuing and D would be in the course of the stealing whilst he is removing the goods from the premises. *Lockley* [1995] Crim LR 656, CA, confirms that this principle is unaffected by *Gomez*. At what point the theft will cease must be left to the common sense of the jury, but presumably this will normally occur once D gets to the street. In the words of *Atakpu* [1993] 4 All ER 215, CA the question was whether D was still 'on the job' when he used or threatened the force. In our Question he clearly would be.

12.3.2.5 **And in order to steal**

The force must be used or threatened 'in order to steal'. If D attacks V because he does not like the look of him and during the attack, V's wallet falls to the ground, D would not commit robbery if, after knocking V unconscious, he spies the wallet and makes off with it. The force must be used or threatened for the purpose of effecting the theft (*Shendley* [1970] Crim LR 49, CA; *James* [1997] Crim LR 598; *Harris* (1998) *The Times*, 4 March 1998).

12.4 **Offences of temporary deprivation**

We saw when dealing with theft that apart from the special cases falling within s. 6(1) of the TA 1968, dishonest borrowing is not theft because of the lack of an intention permanently to deprive. Sections 11 and 12 have been enacted to cover two particular situations where this intention does not exist or may be difficult to prove. By far the most important is s. 12 which prohibits 'joy-riding' and other temporary 'borrowings' of vehicles and other means of transport.

12.4.1 **Taking a conveyance without the owner's consent**

The taking of vehicles, particularly by youngsters, has caused growing public concern in recent years, so much so that the Aggravated Vehicle-Taking Act 1992 inserted an additional, more serious form of the s. 12 offence into the TA 1968—s. 12A.

The basic offence in s. 12 makes D guilty 'if, without having the consent of the owner or other lawful authority, he takes any conveyance for his own or another's use or, knowing that the conveyance has been taken without such authority, drives it or allows himself to be carried in or on it'.

By s. 37(1) of the Criminal Justice Act 1988, this offence is now only a summary offence punishable by up to six months' imprisonment. If the court acquits D on a charge of theft of a conveyance, it is open to it as an alternative to convict of a s. 12 offence.

12.4.1.1 Conveyance

By s. 12(7)(a) ' "conveyance" means any conveyance constructed or adapted for the carriage of a person or persons whether by land, water or air, except that it does not include a conveyance constructed or adapted for use only under the control of a person not carried in or on it.' The definition is wide and includes motor vehicles, boats, whether or not powered, aircraft, gliders and hang-gliders. Bicycles would be caught by the definition were it not for the fact that they are expressly excluded by s. 12(5) which creates a separate offence for pedal cycles along similar lines but punishable only by a fine. A horse or other animal is not 'constructed or adapted for the carriage of a person' and so is not within s. 12 (*Neal v Gribble* [1978] RTR 409). It is arguable that the notion of driveability is implicit in s. 12(1) and that would predicate at least some basic controlling mechanism (see *McDonagh* [1974] QB 448). It follows that roller-skates and skis would be excluded.

12.4.1.2 Takes for his own or another's use

According to *Bogacki* [1973] 2 All ER 864, 'takes' occurs when D (a) assumes possession or control of the conveyance and (b) intentionally moves it or causes it to be moved. There is no necessity for D to ride on or drive, sail or fly the conveyance because the basis of the offence is not 'stealing' a ride but temporarily depriving the owner of his conveyance. Thus, in *Pearce* [1973] Crim LR 321, D was convicted when he loaded an inflatable rubber dinghy belonging to a lifeboat station onto a trailer and towed it away.

> **? QUESTION** 12.2
>
> Suppose D, employed as a lorry driver to deliver a load from Nottingham to London, decides to come back via Birmingham so that he can visit his aged mother. Would he be guilty of the offence?

It is possible for those who have lawful custody or possession of the conveyance, such as employees about their employer's business, to 'take' the conveyance. Clearly, it would be unfair to make an employee guilty of the offence immediately he made any unauthorised deviation from the route, however slight. The courts have taken the pragmatic view that it is all a question of degree (*McKnight v Davies* [1974] RTR 4, DC). In general, the courts would be more likely to overlook an unauthorised deviation **during** the working day than one **after** the working day has ended (*Wibberley* [1965] 3 All ER 718). They would probably view our Question as a roundabout way of making the return journey for the employer rather than as a 'taking' for the employee's own purpose. According to *Mc Knight v Davies*

(*Cases and Materials* (12.4.1.2)), the test is whether D appropriates the conveyance to his own use 'in a manner which repudiates the rights of the true owner and shows that D has assumed control of the vehicle for his own purposes'. D damaged the roof of his lorry whilst on his way back to the depot at the end of the day. He was frightened to face his boss and drove to a pub for a drink. He then drove three men home, drove to another pub and finally to his own home. He took the lorry back to the depot early the next morning. It was held that D 'took' the lorry when he left the first public house.

Similarly, if D is not an employee but is loaned a car for a specific purpose, he would 'take' it if he seriously deviated from the permitted route. In *Phipps and McGill* (1970) 54 Cr App R 300, V loaned his car to D to enable D to take his wife to Victoria Station on the strict understanding that he would return the car as soon as he dropped off his wife. Because she missed the train, he drove her to Hastings and returned the car two days later. The Court of Appeal held that there was a fresh 'taking' without the owner's consent when D drove from Victoria Station towards Hastings.

The section requires that D's taking is 'for his own or another's use'. This means that when D takes the conveyance, his intention must be either to use it at that time as a conveyance for himself or another, or to use it as such at some time in the future (*Bow* (1976) 64 Cr App R 54, CA).

? QUESTION 12.3

In *Bow*, D, a suspected poacher, found his car's exit from a private lane blocked by the gamekeeper's Land Rover. The gamekeeper refused to move his vehicle and so D got in, released the hand brake and allowed it to coast down the lane for 200 yards. Was D 'using it as a conveyance'?

Since he was riding in it, even though his object was simply to clear the exit for his own car, D was held to be 'using' it. Had he simply pushed it out of the way without getting in or on it, he would not have been guilty because 'use' means 'use as a conveyance'. In *Stokes* [1983] RTR 59, CA, D did not 'use' V's car when, as a joke, he pushed it around the corner so as to make V think that it had been stolen. Had D done it with a view to driving the car off later, that would have been 'using' it within the section. *Pearce* indicates that an intention to use it in the future as a conveyance is sufficient (towing away a rubber dinghy).

12.4.1.3 Without the consent of the owner or other lawful authority

Other lawful authority covers the case where the police or other authorised personnel remove the vehicle under statutory powers, such as where it is parked illegally in a tow-away zone.

The 'owner's consent' is largely obvious although it will not include consent obtained by force or intimidation (*Hogden* [1962] Crim LR 563). If the owner has not in fact consented, it is irrelevant that he gives evidence that he would have consented if asked (*Ambler* [1979] RTR 217). The major controversy which has arisen has been in relation to cases where the owner's consent is obtained by D's deception.

According to *Whittaker* v *Campbell* [1983] 3 All ER 582, DC and *Peart* [1970] 2 All ER 823, CA, D's fraud will not vitiate V's consent. One would have thought that a fundamental mistake as to the identity of the person should, as is normally the case in law, vitiate the apparent consent. This was denied by the Court of Appeal in *Whittaker* v *Campbell*, although the actual mistake in that case was probably not a mistake as to identity. D used a stolen driving licence to hire a car. It could be said that the employees of the hire company intended to deal with the man in front of them and were merely making a mistake about one of his attributes, namely that he held a valid driving licence.

However, even if the mistake is not a fundamental one as to identity, it is questionable whether the consent should be treated as valid.

? QUESTION 12.4

Suppose D gets your consent to borrow your car in Newcastle by falsely claiming that he has an urgent appointment in Alnwick, about 30 miles north. Would he commit an offence (a) if he drives straight off to Burnley, about 100 miles to the west or (b) if he first drives to Alnwick and then drives off to Burnley?

The facts in situation (a) are those of *Peart* whereas the facts in situation (b) are similar to those of *Phipps and McGill*. The Court of Appeal in *Peart* held that V's consent was not vitiated by D's misrepresentation as to the nature and purpose of his journey. However, because the trial judge's direction did not raise the issue, the court did not consider whether 'there could have been a fresh taking...at some time after the car was originally driven away'. It is not inconceivable therefore that if this aspect had been considered, the court might have applied *Phipps and McGill*. Situation (b) is indistinguishable from *Phipps and McGill* (see 12.4.1.2) and would presumably constitute a 'taking without the owner's consent' when D sets off from Alnwick to Burnley. It cannot make any sense that an immediate, unauthorised use is not a 'taking without the owner's consent' merely because possession of the vehicle has been obtained by deception. If *Peart* is correct, the moral is to deceive V about the **whole** of the use rather than just part of it!

12.4.1.4 *Mens rea*

Section 12(6) of TA 1968 provides that:

a person does not commit an offence under this section by anything done in the belief that he has lawful authority to do it or that he would have the owner's consent if the owner knew of his doing it and the circumstances of it.

Once D has adduced some credible evidence of his belief, the onus is on the prosecution to disprove that belief beyond reasonable doubt (*Briggs* [1987] Crim LR 708, CA).

12.4.1.5 **Driving or allowing oneself to be carried**

This provision creates a secondary offence distinct from the 'taking' offence. It is essential for this offence that the vehicle has already been 'taken' and that D 'knows' this to be the case. There is no decision as yet on whether 'knows' is to be taken literally or whether it also embraces wilful blindness. Of course, if D persists or encourages someone to 'take' the conveyance in the first place, he will be guilty of aiding and abetting the primary offence of 'taking'. This provision extends the scope of liability to include the case where D accepts a ride after the car has been taken or drives it subsequently at the invitation of the taker. If the original 'taker' has abandoned the vehicle, it is no longer a 'taken' vehicle for this purpose. However, it is, of course, then available to be 'taken' again and the new taker would commit the primary offence if he did not have the owner's consent or lawful authority (*DPP* v *Spriggs* [1993] Crim LR 622).

D must either drive the conveyance himself or 'allow himself to be carried, in or on it'. It is therefore essential that the vehicle must move whilst he is in or on it (*Diggin* (1980) 72 Cr App R 204, CA). In *Miller* [1976] Crim LR 147, CA, D was on a motor launch which he knew had been taken without authority, anticipating a journey. Because it did not actually move while he was on it, he was not guilty of the offence. D allows himself to be carried where, although ignorant of the 'taking' offence at the start of the journey, he learns of it during the course of the journey, but then stays in the vehicle to avoid having to walk home (*Boldsizsar* v *Knight* [1980] Crim LR 653).

12.4.1.6 Aggravated vehicle-taking

The Aggravated Vehicle-Taking Act 1992 inserted s. 12A into the TA 1968 (*Cases and Materials* (12.4)). This new offence requires that:

(a) D committed the basic offence under s. 12 (see above) in relation to a **mechanically propelled** vehicle; and in addition

(b) at any time after the unlawful taking of the vehicle (whether by D or another) and before its restoration to the owner or other lawful custody, it was driven or injury or damage was caused, in one or more of the circumstances set out in s. 12A(2).

The listed circumstances are:

(a) the vehicle was driven dangerously on a road or other public place;

(b) an accident involving personal injury occurred as a result of driving it;

(c) an accident involving damage to property (other than the vehicle itself) occurred as a result of driving it;

(d) damage was caused to the vehicle.

This hasty response to the perceived 'epidemic' of teenage car crime departs quite markedly from the normal principles of criminal liability for serious crimes. In none of the circumstances (b)-(d) does any fault have to be proved on the part of D, as long as he has committed the basic offence under s. 12. If someone accidentally crashed into the car through no fault of D, D would commit the aggravated offence. This is confirmed by *Marsh* [1997] 1 Cr App R 67, CA where, through no fault of D, the car he had taken and was driving without the owner's consent was in collision with a pedestrian crossing the road. It was held that s. 12A(2)(b) was satisfied by proof that the accident involving the injury was caused by the driving of the vehicle by D whether or not there was any fault in the way he drove it. Furthermore, the term 'accident' includes the deliberate causing of injury by using the car as a weapon (*B* [2005] Crim LR 486).

It seems that the prosecution does not even have to prove that D himself was a party to the damage to the vehicle or the driving which involves personal injury or damage to other property!

However, s. 12A(3) provides that D has a defence if he proves:

(a) that the relevant driving, accident or damage occurred *before* he committed the basic offence; *or*

(b) that he was not in nor on nor in the immediate vicinity of the vehicle when that driving, accident or damage occurred.

In *Davies* v *DPP* [1994] Crim LR 604, D tried to drive off in a car which was a specially adapted decoy put there by the police. After being driven about 30 yards, the car's engine switched off and the doors locked. D had obviously committed the basic offence under s. 12. However, he damaged the car in trying to escape from it. The Divisional Court held that D was guilty of the aggravated offence under s. 12A. The damage to the vehicle occurred after the unlawful taking and before it was restored to lawful custody, and whilst D was in the vehicle. His detention was lawful and it was unnecessary to decide whether the offence would have been made out if he had been trying to escape from an unlawful detention.

12.4.2 Removal of articles from places open to the public

12.4.2.1 Introduction

It is questionable whether this offence is necessary but it was prompted by the famous incident where Goya's portrait of the Duke of Wellington was taken from the National Gallery and subsequently returned four years later. There had also been an earlier occasion when some Scottish nationalists had taken the Coronation Stone from Westminster Abbey, but again had subsequently returned it some years later.

The taker of the Goya ended up being convicted only of larceny (the old version of theft) of the picture's frame which was never recovered and was presumed destroyed. The difficulty in proving an intention permanently to deprive of the articles in these cases led the Criminal Law Revision Committee to propose the offence which is now s. 11. Of course, in the ransom case there would now be no problem in establishing a deemed intention permanently to deprive under s. 6(1) (see 10.4.2.2). But what of the art student who simply wants to enjoy the Renoir for a couple of years or the activist who wants to gain publicity for his cause?

12.4.2.2 The offence

Let us look at the terms of s. 11:

(1) Subject to subsections (2) and (3) below, where the public has access to a building in order to view the building or part of it, or a collection or part of a collection housed in it, any person who without lawful authority removes from the building or its grounds the whole or part of any article displayed or kept for display to the public in the building or that part of it or in its grounds shall be guilty of an offence.

12.4.2.3 *Actus reus*

D must (a) remove (b) any article (or part) displayed or kept for display (c) without lawful authority (d) from any building (or its grounds) to which the public have access to view the building or a collection housed in it (e) excluding collections exhibited for sales or other commercial dealings.

Removal

'Removal' can be at any time even though the building is closed to the public **provided** that the thing taken is part of a **permanent** exhibition. Otherwise, the removal must take place 'on a day when' the place is open to the public (s. 11(2)).

Any article displayed or kept for display

The section only protects articles being exhibited or 'kept for display', which would include paintings, etc. kept in store. Ordinary articles such as a towel in a museum's toilet are not accorded the special protection of the section, for obvious reasons. In *Barr* [1978] Crim LR 244 it was held that a cross put in a church solely for devotional purposes was not 'displayed'.

From any building (or grounds) to which the public has access in order to view

Removal from the building **or** its grounds is enough and therefore removal from the building to its grounds would suffice. However, if the item is displayed in the building, it would not be enough to remove it to some other part of the building. The same would apply in relation to the grounds.

The building must be open to the general public and not just a particular section of it, e.g., Old Etonians. In respect of items displayed in the building, public access to the grounds only is not enough.

The public must have access 'in order to view the building' or a collection housed in it. If public access is allowed purely for some other purpose, the offence cannot be committed. Presumably, however, if a library or a theatre were to have an exhibition of paintings, the public would have access not only for the usual pursuits of consulting books or seeing plays but also simply for viewing the exhibition.

Exhibitions for the purpose of effecting sales or other commercial dealings

This would exclude art and antique shops, auction rooms and trade exhibitions. However, if the primary purpose is to put on an exhibition rather than to sell the exhibits, the works would appear to be protected notwithstanding that some or all of the exhibits may be available for purchase. Clearly, the mere fact that an admission fee is charged to the public does not exclude the exhibition from the protection of the section.

12.4.2.4 *Mens rea*

D must intend to remove the article from the building or its grounds but no dishonesty is required. Section 11(3) provides:

> A person does not commit an offence under this section if he believes that he had lawful authority for the removal of the thing in question or that he would have it if the person entitled to give it knew of the removal and the circumstances of it.

12.5 Abstracting electricity

Section 13 of the TA 1968 provides:

> A person who dishonestly uses without due authority, or dishonestly causes to be wasted or diverted, any electricity shall on conviction on indictment be liable to imprisonment for a term not exceeding 5 years.

> **?** **QUESTION** 12.5
>
> Why would it not be theft dishonestly to use someone else's electricity?

The usual instance is where D by-passes the electricity meter to escape the electricity company's charges. However, since causing electricity to be wasted or diverted is expressly an offence, there is no need to prove that D intended to gain any economic benefit from his actions. For example, if he has a grudge against his employer and deliberately goes around the workplace switching lights on in order to waste electricity, he could commit the offence. The section does not specify 'mains' electricity and is therefore wide enough to cover using a battery, e.g., another's camera or torch.

Dishonesty is necessary and the case law definition under *Feely* and *Ghosh* applies. The partial definition in s. 2 of the TA 1968 is not expressed to apply to s. 13.

Section 13 is necessary because electricity does not come within the definition of property in s. 4 and therefore cannot be stolen.

12.6 Burglary

12.6.1 Introduction

The old law of burglary was horrendously complex and s. 9 of the TA 1968 greatly simplifies the position. It creates two separate offences of burglary which, nonetheless, have some common elements. It is a serious offence and carries a maximum sentence of 14 years' imprisonment where a dwelling is burgled, or ten years in any other case.

12.6.2 The offences

Section 9 of the TA 1968 provides:

> (1) A person is guilty of burglary if—
>   (a) he enters any building or part of a building as a trespasser and with intent to commit any such offence as is mentioned in subsection (2) below; or

(b) having entered any building or part of a building as a trespasser he steals or attempts to steal anything in the building or that part of it or inflicts or attempts to inflict on any person therein any grievous bodily harm.

(2) The offences referred to in subsection (1)(a) above are offences of stealing anything in the building or part of the building in question, of inflicting on any person therein any grievous bodily harm, and of doing unlawful damage to the building or anything therein.

It should be noted that s. 63 of the Sexual Offences Act 2003 has replaced burglary based on entry with intent to rape (the words 'or raping any person' have been excised from s. 9(2)) with a far wider offence (but still carrying a maximum of ten years' imprisonment) of (knowingly or recklessly) being a trespasser on any premises with intent to commit one or more of the numerous sex offences contained in Part 1 of the Act (*Cases and Materials* (12.6.2)). These range from rape down to genital exposure (s. 66) or voyeurism (s. 67).

? QUESTION 12.6

- Explain what elements burglary under s. 9(1)(a) shares with burglary under s. 9(1)(b).
- Explain how the two forms of burglary differ.

Burglary under s. 9(1)(a) is committed as soon as D enters the building with the necessary intent to commit one of the offences listed in s. 9(2). It is unnecessary to prove that D actually committed an offence in the building. However, it is sometimes difficult to establish that D had the necessary intent, when he entered the building and, indeed, he may not have had any such intent, e.g., where he just intends to find somewhere to sleep for the night. In this case s. 9(1)(b) will be necessary if D is to be convicted of burglary. Here, D must have actually committed or attempted to commit one of the offences specified in subsection (1)(b). (You will notice that the list of offences sufficing for s. 9(1)(b) burglary is a little less extensive than that for s. 9(1)(a) burglary.)

Both forms of burglary require that D should 'enter a building or part of a building as a trespasser' and it is those common elements that we examine first.

12.6.2.1 'Enters'

There is no need to show that D broke into the building but merely that he entered it. 'Enters' is not defined in the Act and the case law has not been particularly illuminating. It may well be that many of the old common law rules will be applied.

According to *Collins* [1972] 2 All ER 1105, CA (*Cases and Materials* (12.6.2.1)) 'an effective and substantial entry' is required. The Court of Appeal in *Brown* [1985] Crim LR 212 agreed that the entry must be 'effective' but thought that the word 'substantial' did not help. In neither case were the terms explained, and, in truth, neither seems helpful in resolving the issue. The simplest rule would be the old common law rule that entry by any part of the body would suffice, although *Collins* especially casts doubt on the current validity of this test. The defendant in *Brown* did enter a shop when, with his feet on the ground, he leaned into the broken shop window to rummage for articles displayed there. Whether there was an 'effective' entry was a question of fact for the jury in each case, but it is clear that it falls short of requiring entry by the whole of D's body. The Court of Appeal in *Ryan* [1996] Crim LR 320 held that it was irrelevant that D was in no position to commit the alleged ulterior offence because he was found at 2.30 a.m. stuck fast in a house window with just one arm and his head in the building and the rest of his body outside! It was open to the jury to conclude that he had entered the building. In the light of this, it is difficult to see what 'effective' entry can mean and the decision seems implicitly to cast doubt on the requirement.

It would appear that D can enter by means of an innocent agent under the normal principles of that doctrine (see 14.3.1). Thus, if Fagin sends in a nine-year-old child to steal from the building, or even a well-trained monkey, there seems no reason why Fagin would not commit burglary even though he himself does not enter the building. The court might have rested a conviction for burglary on the innocent agency principle in *Wheelhouse* [1994] Crim LR 756, but chose another route (see **Chapter 14**). D dishonestly got V to take another's car from the other's garage, V believing it was D's to take and therefore lacking the *mens rea* for theft or burglary.

It is uncertain whether D can enter a building by means of an instrument either held or even thrown by him, where no part of his body enters. The old law distinguished between an instrument used to commit the ulterior offence, e.g., sticking the barrel of a gun through a window in order to shoot someone inside, and an instrument used merely to gain entry, e.g., putting a key in a lock or inserting a jemmy to force a window. The former was an entry, the latter was not. In *Klass* [1998] 1 Cr App R 453, the Court of Appeal held that D did not enter a caravan when he smashed its window with a pole. However, they did not rule out the possibility of entry by means of an instrument, raising the prospect of the old distinction being continued. This would be unfortunate since it extends the notion of 'entering' some way beyond ordinary conceptions and would mean that if D threw a petrol bomb through a shop window to burn it out (or even sent a parcel bomb through the post), he would enter the shop. Entry by some part of D's body should surely be essential. That said, in *Richardson and Brown* [1998] 2 Cr App R (S) 87, D was convicted of burglary where he used a mechanical digger to rip a cash machine from the wall of a bank.

12.6.2.2 As a trespasser

It is clear that when D enters the building, he must be committing the tort of trespass. That will occur where D enters another's building without permission or legal right. However, it is not **sufficient** that D is committing the tort of trespass because that can be committed by mere negligence. *Collins* held that for the purposes of burglary, D must either know he is a trespasser or be reckless as to that fact, i.e., realise that he **might** be a trespasser.

If D enters the building lawfully, he does not become liable for burglary if he then commits theft in that building, unless he **becomes** a trespasser (e.g., by being told to leave) and then enters **another** part of the building, where he commits the theft (see *Laing* [1995] Crim LR 395, CA).

Lawful entry

The most frequent reason why an entry may be lawful is because it is with the express or implied consent of the owner or occupier. In some circumstances, of course, the law permits entry to specified persons even if this is opposed by the owner or occupier, e.g., where the police have a valid search warrant. Express invitations to enter are obvious but implied invitations are very common. Shop owners impliedly invite the public to enter the public parts of their shops during public opening hours. Quite obviously this invitation does not extend to the time when the shop is closed nor to the non-public parts of the shop, such as stockrooms.

The person with authority to give permission to enter is the person in possession of the building or the relevant part of it but he may expressly or impliedly authorise others to grant permission too. According to *Collins*, the authority to consent will extend to any members of the household of a dwelling. The facts of *Collins* were bizarre and Edmund-Davies LJ's recital of them a *tour de force*! D, naked except for his socks, climbed a ladder to the window of a girl's bedroom. He admitted that he intended to have sexual intercourse by force if need be, i.e., he had an intention to rape in the building. (At that time, burglary would be committed by one who entered a building as a trespasser with intent to rape someone therein.) He was in the process of climbing through the window when the girl, who was the worse for drink, noticed him and invited him in for sexual intercourse, mistaking him for her boyfriend.

QUESTION 12.7

Did he enter the bedroom as a trespasser?

The person with authority to grant permission was in fact the girl's mother, who lived in the house and was in possession of it. It may be inferred that she impliedly authorised her daughter to invite people in. By contrast, if she had specifically forbidden the daughter to entertain her boyfriend in the house, it could not be said that her consent would negative trespass. However, D must know he is or might be a trespasser and therefore if he believes that the girl is authorised to permit his entry, he will not have the appropriate *mens rea*. The critical question then would be whether the girl's permission came before or after he had made 'an effective and substantial entry' into the bedroom. If he was entirely outside the bedroom when the girl's invitation became clear, he did not enter as a trespasser. If he was already fully in, the position is the reverse. If only part of his body had entered, we are left with the question of fact for the jury: how much and of what is needed for 'an effective' entry!

Exceeding the terms of the permission

We have already seen that the permission to enter may be expressly or impliedly limited to a particular part of the building, e.g., the public area of a shop. If D is employed to tile V's kitchen, he has no permission to enter V's bedroom and, if he did, he would enter that part of the building as a trespasser. Suppose, however, that D sticks to the permitted parts of the building but enters with a quite different purpose in mind to that envisaged by the owner.

? **QUESTION** 12.8

If D entered a shop intending to shoplift, would he commit burglary?

In the Australian case of *Barker* v *R* (1983) 7 ALJR 426, V asked his neighbour, D, to keep an eye on his house whilst he was on holiday and told him where he had hidden the key in case he needed to enter. D was held guilty of burglary when he entered in order to steal. D's authority to enter was limited to purposes necessary for looking after the house and certainly did not extend to entry for stealing. In *Barker*, the particular purposes of permitted entry were made explicit. Is the position different where there is a general public invitation to enter? Two of the majority in *Barker* thought so, with the result that a person entering a shop intending to shoplift would not be a trespasser, on the basis that the permission to enter is unlimited.

However, it seems likely that English courts would construe even a general invitation as impliedly limited to those who enter for lawful purposes. This was the view taken by the Court of Appeal in *Jones and Smith* [1976] 3 All ER 54 (*Cases and Materials* (12.6.2.2)). D, who lived in his own house, went one night with J to D's father's house and stole two television sets. Was this admitted theft also burglary? It was accepted that D's father had given D a general permission to enter the house at any time and without specifying any purposes for which entry was permitted. The court was clearly of the view that the father's permission, however general, could not extend to entry for the purposes of theft. On this basis the person who enters a shop with a secret intention to steal enters as a trespasser and commits burglary. It would seem that all permissions are liable to be construed as expressly or impliedly limited to certain purposes and if D enters for a purpose other than the ones permitted, he enters as a trespasser. As Scrutton LJ said in *T* v *Calgarth* [1926] P 93, 'When you invite a person into your house to use the staircase you do not invite him to slide down the banisters.'

The same principle will apply with even greater force where D procures V's permission to enter by fraud, e.g., if he poses as an official from the water company in order to gain access to steal. Logically, these rules would suggest that whenever D enters with the intent to commit one of the offences listed in s. 9(2), he will necessarily be entering as a trespasser (unless of course the occupier knows of his intent, e.g., where he wants to get rid of a lodger and invites D in to damage or steal the lodger's possessions).

? **QUESTION** 12.9

In *Collins*, when D got to the window, he intended to enter in order to rape the girl if necessary. The Court of Appeal quashed D's conviction on the basis of doubts over whether he entered the bedroom as a trespasser. Is this consistent with the decision in *Smith and Jones*?

Professor Glanville Williams argues that it is not (*Textbook of Criminal Law*, pp. 812–14). If when D entered, he intended to have sexual intercourse by force if necessary, it seems inconceivable that he could argue that the girl's permission to enter would extend to raping her. He could not be sure that she was inviting him in for sexual intercourse. On the other hand, as Professor Smith points out, the facts were that she realised that D was 'a naked male with an erect penis' before she invited him in. It could be inferred therefore that she invited him in for the purpose of sexual intercourse and that his intention to rape had lapsed.

Alternatively, it could be argued that *Collins* did not squarely address the issue of possible limitations on the permission to enter and is therefore authority only for the issue of *mens rea* in relation to being a trespasser. There is a need to prove that D has *mens rea* in relation to trespassing in these 'permission' cases just as in the ordinary case. As *Smith and Jones* puts it, D must enter 'knowing that he is entering in excess of the permission that has been given to him, or being reckless as to whether he is entering in excess of the permission that has been given to him to enter. Providing the facts are known to the accused which enable him to realise that he is acting in excess of the permission given or that he is acting recklessly as to whether he exceeds that permission, then that is sufficient for the jury to decide that he is in fact a trespasser.'

12.6.2.3 Any building or part of a building

The term 'building' is not defined in the Act and presumably bears its ordinary, everyday meaning. It seems likely that some degree of permanence will be required so that a tent or marquee would not be a building. It certainly covers dwellings, shops, factories and offices and also outbuildings such as sheds, garages, greenhouses and barns. When a house which is under construction becomes a building is undecided. In *B & S v Leathley* [1979] Crim LR 314 a freezer container 25 feet by 7 feet which had been in position for two years and was fitted with electricity was held to be a building. On the other hand in *Norfolk Constabulary* v *Seekings & Gould* [1986] Crim LR 167 two articulated trailers used for temporary storage at the back of a supermarket were not buildings even though electricity was fitted. Section 9(4) (formerly s. 9(3)) extends the meaning of building to include 'an inhabited vehicle or vessel', whether the person inhabiting it is there or not. Thus, caravans and houseboats which are used as someone's home are covered, and presumably a camper van during the period when it is being lived in, e.g., a touring holiday. You should realise that whilst a vehicle or vessel is only protected when inhabited, this is not the case with a building proper.

What is a part of a building?

Where a building is divided into rooms, even by temporary partitions, each room will be a distinct 'part of a building'. Therefore hotel guests may 'burgle' another guest's room since, although he may be in the hotel by permission, that does not include other guests' rooms. He would therefore enter that part of the building as a trespasser. The same rule would apply in relation to a customer who enters a shop's storeroom. The case of *Walkington* [1979] 2 All ER 716, CA (*Cases and Materials* (12.6.2.3)) goes further. In that case there was a moveable, three-sided, rectangular counter in the public part of a shop. D, a customer, noticed that the till on the counter was slightly open and went behind the counter intending to steal from it. In fact the till was empty because it had been cashed up for the day. It was held that the area behind the counter was capable of being a part of the building distinct from the public part of the shop. Since it was clearly out of bounds to customers, D entered it as a trespasser and committed burglary. Thus, if D goes from somewhere in the building he is permitted to be to anywhere in the building he is not permitted to be, then, whether or not there is any physical barrier to overcome, D would enter a different part of the building.

? QUESTION 12.10

Would D commit burglary in either of the following cases:

- at closing time, he hides behind a display of baked beans in the supermarket and when the staff have gone helps himself to goods on the shelves;
- at closing time, he hides in the shop's toilet and when the staff have gone, he emerges into the store and helps himself to some goods?

In the first case, D clearly becomes a trespasser after closing time, but the problem is that he does not appear to have entered any part of the building as a trespasser. He entered the public part of the shop before closing time lawfully and never subsequently went to any other part of the building to steal. Of course, if, when he entered before closing time, he intended to steal, he would be guilty of burglary at that moment. The same point applies to the second case, but even if he had no such intention when he first went into the shop, he would still commit burglary. When he emerges from the toilet after closing time, he enters another part of the building (the public part of the shop) as a trespasser because he knows that he is not allowed there after closing time.

The extent of the building and its constituent parts

It is likely that a block containing a number of flats, offices or shops can be regarded for this purpose as a 'building'. It follows that if D enters any part of that block as a trespasser with intent to steal from any of the constituent flats, offices or shops, he will commit burglary. He does not need to have entered the particular flat, office or shop from which he intends to steal.

Complex problems can arise where D is lawfully in the block as a whole. Let us say that D lives in Flat 1 and unlawfully enters Flat 2 in order to get to Flat 3 where he intends to steal. If he is caught in Flat 2, he has clearly entered a part of the building (Flat 2) as a trespasser, but the problem is that he did not intend to steal '**therein**'. However, Professor Smith suggests that the solution to the problem in cases like this is to divide the building (the block) into only two parts—the part D is permitted to enter and the remainder. Entry as a trespasser in any part of the remainder (all the other flats lumped together) is therefore sufficient irrespective of which flat he intends to steal from (see *Law of Theft*, 8th ed., 11–18–11–21).

12.6.2.4 *Mens rea*

You have already learned that D must intend to enter the building or part knowing of the facts which render his entry a trespass in law or at least realising that such facts may exist (recklessness) (*Collins*). In addition, for s. 9(1)(a) burglary D must intend (a) to steal in the building or part or (b) to inflict grievous bodily harm therein or (c) to do unlawful damage to the building or anything in it. (The list formerly included rape but that was removed by the Sexual Offences Act 2003.)

Stealing means committing theft contrary to s. 1 of the TA 1968. Presumably 'inflicting grievous bodily harm' means the offence under s. 20 of the OAPA 1861 and it is best to regard the Court of Appeal's observations to the contrary in *Jenkins* [1983] 1 All ER 1000 as incorrect. Unlawful damage means damage contrary to s. 1 of the Criminal Damage Act 1971.

A conditional intention is enough (*Attorney-General's References (Nos. 1 and 2 of 1979)* [1979] 3 All ER 143). Thus, D commits burglary if he enters the building as a trespasser intending to steal anything worth stealing or intending to injure seriously anyone who happens to be in the building. It is irrelevant that the building turns out to be deserted or to contain nothing worth stealing.

Under s. 9(1)(b), D must actually commit theft or inflict grievous bodily harm contrary to s. 20 of the OAPA 1861 or attempt either of these offences. Therefore, if there is no theft or attempt or no s. 20 offence or attempt, there is no s. 9(1)(b) burglary. You should be aware that, unlike s. 9(1)(a), this imports a requirement that D must have committed the *actus reus* of one of these offences or the attempt, as well as having the appropriate *mens rea*. For example, if D is attacked by another intruder wielding a knife and inflicts grievous bodily harm in reasonable and necessary self-defence, the force used will not be unlawful and he will not commit any offence against the person.

Finally, since the Criminal Justice Act 1991, if the building is a 'dwelling' burglary carries a heavier sentence than if it is not. 'Dwelling' is not defined, but presumably means any building in which someone is living, even if they are temporarily absent. It is not clear whether D must have any *mens rea* in regard to the fact that the building is a dwelling. The Court of Appeal in *Collins* imported a *mens rea* in relation to being a trespasser and it is likely that it would apply a similar requirement to this ingredient. That would mean that D must either know that someone was living in the building or part or realise that someone might be (recklessness).

12.7 Aggravated burglary

By s. 10 of the TA 1968, 'A person is guilty of aggravated burglary if he commits any burglary and at the time has with him any firearm or imitation firearm, any weapon of offence, or any explosive'. The maximum sentence is life imprisonment.

D must (a) have with him (b) any firearm, imitation firearm, weapon of offence or explosive (c) at the time of committing a burglary.

12.7.1 The aggravating articles

Section 10(1) contains some definitions:

(a) 'firearm' includes an airgun or air pistol and 'imitation firearm' means anything which has the appearance of being a firearm, whether capable of being discharged or not; and

(b) 'weapon of offence' means any article made or adapted for use for causing injury to or incapacitating a person, or intended by the person having it with him for such use; and

(c) 'explosive' means any article manufactured for the purpose of producing a practical effect by explosion, or intended by the person having it with him for that purpose.

EXERCISE 12.1

Write down one example of an article:

- 'made for causing injury';
- 'made for incapacitating';
- 'adapted for causing injury'.

If the 'weapon of offence' falls within the above parameters there is no need to prove that D intended to use the articles—merely that he had them with him. Any article not made or adapted for such use will, nonetheless, be a 'weapon of offence' if it could be used to cause injury or incapacitate and D had it with him **intending** to so use it if the need arose. Examples might be a kitchen knife, an axe, a baseball bat, rope or sticking plaster. Things made for causing injury would include a cosh, a knuckle-duster or a sword. Things made for incapacitating would include handcuffs, manacles or a strait-jacket. A chair leg studded with nails or a razor blade in a potato would be articles 'adapted for causing injury'. In *Bentham* [2005] UKHL 18, the House of Lords refused to accept that the term 'imitation firearm' could include the pointing of D's finger inside his coat pocket so as to resemble a gun. D must have with him 'a thing' which, unlike D's hand or fingers, is 'separate and distinct from oneself' ([8]).

12.7.2 At the time of committing the burglary

 QUESTION 12.11

Why will the relevant time for deciding whether D has with him the firearm, etc. differ according to whether the burglary is charged under s. 9(1)(a) or s. 9(1)(b)?

In the case of s. 9(1)(a), the relevant time is the moment of entry whereas under s. 9(1)(b), it is the time when D commits the ulterior offence. Consequently, if D enters as a trespasser without any intention to commit one of the listed offences, but with a weapon, he would not be guilty of aggravated burglary if he discards the weapon and only **after** that commits theft (*Francis* [1982] Crim LR 363, CA). Equally, if D enters the building as a trespasser unarmed, he will commit aggravated burglary if he arms himself with a weapon in the building and then commits one of the specified offences (*O'Leary* (1986) 82 Cr App R 341—*Cases and Materials* (12.7.2)).

 The issue is one which we have discussed in theft (at 10.4.1.1) and robbery (at 12.3.2.4). Presumably, reasoning by analogy with *Hale* (see robbery above) and gaining some support from *Gregory* (1982) 77 Cr App R 41, the courts might regard burglary as a continuing offence just as they regard theft as a continuing offence, so that if D picks up an article intending to use it to cause injury in order to escape, he would be guilty of aggravated burglary.

> **? QUESTION** 12.12
>
> How long does the burglary last? Suppose that D breaks in and steals jewels from V's bedroom. D has just come downstairs and is on his way out when he is challenged by Jeeves, the butler. D picks up a bronze sculpture and hits Jeeves with it. Would D then commit aggravated burglary?

Although a similar provision relating to weapons of offence in the Prevention of Crime Act 1953 requires the intention to use the article to cause injury to be 'formed before the actual occasion to use violence has arisen' (*Ohlson* v *Hylton* [1975] 2 All ER 490, DC; *C* v *DPP* [2002] Crim LR 322, DC) and not 'ad hoc' (*Humphreys* [1977] Crim LR 225), no such limitation applies to aggravated burglary. The idea behind these decisions is that the 1953 Act aims to prevent the carrying of weapons rather than their use, and the same rationale could be said to apply to aggravated burglary—it aims to prevent people arming themselves with a weapon 'just in case'. The Court of Appeal in *Kelly* (1992) 97 Cr App R 245 refused to adopt this construction for s. 10 and held that D was guilty when he used a screwdriver, which he had brought to gain entry, to prod V in the stomach.

It is clear from *Klass* [1998] 1 Cr App R 453, CA that, if the weapon at no time enters the building, e.g., is carried by an accomplice who remains outside, there can be no aggravated burglary, even if the weapon is used to beat the occupier of the building after he comes outside.

12.7.3 'Has with him'

Normally these words mean 'carrying' (*Kelt* [1977] 1 WLR 1365, CA; *Klass*). According to *Russell* (1985) 81 Cr App R 315, it requires that D **knows** he has the 'firearm', etc. with him and if he has completely forgotten all about its existence, he does not know he has it. *McCalla* (1988) 87 Cr App R 372 and *Wright* [1992] Crim LR 596 go against the latter point. In *McCalla* D was guilty even though he had forgotten he had put a cosh in the glove compartment of his car one month previously. If D1 and D2 burgle a house and D1, unknown to D2, is carrying a firearm, only D1 would commit aggravated burglary. Presumably D would also need to know that the article possesses the characteristics making it a 'weapon of offence', etc. under the Act.

12.8 Blackmail

12.8.1 Introduction

Section 21 of the TA 1968 created a new offence using the appellation 'blackmail' for the first time in our law. It greatly simplified the law replacing 'an ill-assorted collection of legislative bric-a-brac which the draftsman of the 1916 Act put together with scissors and paste' (Professor Hogan [1966] Crim LR 474). The essence of blackmail, often called extortion, particularly in North America, is that D obtains some advantage by the use of improper threats usually involving the revelation of something to discredit the victim.

12.8.2 **The offence**

The first part of s. 21(1) reads:

> A person is guilty of blackmail if, with a view to gain for himself or another or with intent to cause loss to another, he makes any unwarranted demand with menaces...

12.8.2.1 *Actus reus*

This entails (a) a demand (b) with menaces.

Demand

There must be a demand, but under s. 21(2) 'the nature of the act or omission demanded is immaterial'. However, as we shall see the requirement to demand with a view to gain or with intent to cause loss is an implicit limiting factor on the kind of demand caught.

The typical demand will be an express one for payment of money, but it can be implied. If 'the demeanour of the accused and the circumstances of the case were such that an ordinary reasonable man would understand that a demand for money was being made upon him and that the demand was accompanied by menaces—not perhaps direct, but veiled menaces—so that his ordinary balance of mind was upset...', there would be a demand with menaces (*Collister and Warhurst* (1955) 39 Cr App R 100—*Cases and Materials* (12.8.2.1)). In that case two policemen indicated that V would be prosecuted for an offence, but that they would hold back on filing their report until they met V the next day. At that meeting, they asked if V had anything for them saying, 'Remember, sir, I am now making an appeal to your benevolence' and V handed over £5. They were convicted of what would now be blackmail.

? QUESTION 12.13

Suppose D threatens to expose a politician's liaison with a prostitute unless he is paid £25,000. He writes and posts the letter in Germany to the politician's address in England.

Does D make the demand (a) when he writes the letter (b) when he posts the letter (c) when the letter is delivered or (d) when the politician reads it?

The answer to this question might be crucial in a number of situations. Is the offence committed in Germany or England? Will our courts have jurisdiction? What if D never posts it after writing it, or if it gets lost in the post, or if it is never read by V?

A demand in a letter is made when and where the letter is posted (*Treacy v DPP* [1971] 1 All ER 110, HL—*Cases and Materials* (12.8.2.1)) but it continues until it is received and read by the recipient (*Treacy*; *Baxter* [1971] 2 All ER 359, CA). Thus, if, as in our Question, the letter was posted in Germany, a demand would be made there but it would continue and also be made in England on receipt by the addressee. It would not matter that the letter was never read by the addressee. Nor would it matter that the letter was never delivered, provided it reached England (or, according to Lord Diplock in *Treacy* whether or not it reached England). Under Part I of the Criminal Justice Act 1993 jurisdiction depends on proof that 'a relevant event' (i.e., an event, proof of which is an essential ingredient of the crime, such as the making of the demand here) occurred in England. Section 4(b) codifies the position in *Treacy* that a demand would be made (and so a 'relevant event' would occur) in England as soon as the letter reaches England: there is a communication in England and Wales of any information, instruction, request, demand or other matter if it is sent by any means— (i) from a place in England and Wales to a place elsewhere; or (ii) from a place elsewhere to a place in England and Wales.

The same analysis would presumably apply to faxes and telexes, and even oral demands would appear to be made when uttered irrespective of whether they are heard by the victim.

Menaces

Since the Act does not define 'menaces', it must be presumed to mean what it meant under the old law. This gave it a very wide meaning, in no way limited to the natural meaning of threats of violence. According to Lord Wright in *Thorne* v *Motor Trade Association* [1937] 3 All ER 157, HL 'the word "menace" is to be liberally construed and not as limited to threats of violence but as including threats of any action detrimental to or unpleasant to the person addressed. It may also include a warning that in certain events such action is intended.'

This is qualified by *Clear* [1968] 1 All ER 74 where the Court of Appeal held that the threat must be 'of such a nature and extent that the mind of an ordinary person of normal stability and courage might be influenced or made apprehensive so as to accede unwillingly to the demand.' An exception to this is where D is **aware** that V is unusually timorous and would be likely to be influenced by the threats which would have no effect on an ordinary person (*Garwood* [1987] 1 All ER 1032, CA—*Cases and Materials* (12.8.2.1)). If the threats were sufficiently serious to affect an ordinary person, it is irrelevant that they were not taken seriously by or did not affect V (*Clear*; *Garwood*).

> **? QUESTION** 12.14
>
> In *Harry* [1974] Crim LR 32, D sent a letter to local shopkeepers on behalf of a student rag committee offering to sell them 'indemnity posters' rendering them 'immune from all rag week activities whatever they may be'. Evidently one of the shopkeepers was not wild about Harry and complained to the police. Did D 'demand with menaces'?

The answer to the problem depends largely on the precise circumstances. The test to be applied would be how the threat would strike a shopkeeper of ordinary stability and courage unless D knew of any extra susceptibility of any particular shopkeeper addressed. That, in turn, would presumably depend on what sort of activity previous rag weeks had generated and the shopkeeper's knowledge of them. In the event Harry was acquitted. The case also illustrates the provision in s. 21(2) that 'menaces' include threats of action to be taken by others rather than the person making the demand.

Finally, we would refer you back to *Collister and Warhurst* (above) for an illustration that the 'menaces' like the 'demand' can be implicit as well as explicit.

12.8.2.2 *Mens rea*

This comprises three elements:

(a) the demand is unwarranted;

(b) D intended to make a demand with menaces;

(c) with a view to gain for himself or another or with intent to cause loss to another.

Unwarranted demand

It is the crucial word 'unwarranted' which draws the line between justifiable demands with menaces (demand for repayment of money due with a threat to take legal proceedings) and unjustifiable ones (same demand coupled with a threat to 'carve you up'). By the express terms of s. 21(1) whether a demand is unwarranted depends entirely on D's beliefs when he makes it:

> . . . a demand with menaces is unwarranted unless the person making it does so in the belief
>
> (a) that he has reasonable grounds for making the demand; and
> (b) that the use of the menaces is a proper means of reinforcing the demand.

On the face of it, this test is entirely subjective because it is a question of whether D actually **believed** he had reasonable grounds and that the means used were proper, not whether he actually **had** reasonable grounds or that the means used **were** in fact proper.

? QUESTION 12.15

Suppose you are a passionate anti-abortion campaigner and you threaten a surgeon that unless he stops performing abortions and contributes the fees he received for his last three private abortions to your campaign fund, you will send to his wife compromising photos of him in bed with a nurse. You believe that you are justified in doing this. Could your demand be unwarranted?

The beliefs referred to in the test are beliefs not, as is usual in offences, about facts, but about what are correct standards of behaviour. The problem is that D's conception of acceptable behaviour may be quite different from people generally. If the test is entirely subjective—D thinks it is all right to make the demand and use those threats to enforce it, then the law is allowing D to set his own standards of behaviour and is judging him on his own ideas of what he is and is not entitled to do. A drug dealer who is owed money for drugs supplied to one of his pushers might regard it as acceptable to threaten to beat him up unless he pays within the week.

 However, this is not the law (*Harvey* (1980) 72 Cr App R 139, CA—*Cases and Materials* (12.8.2.2)). Since D must believe that the menaces are a 'proper' way of reinforcing his demand, this effectively brings into play society's objective standard as to what is and what is not 'proper'. Therefore, if D thinks the means are proper, but he knows that people generally would regard them as improper, his demand is unwarranted. To escape, D must believe that his actions would be regarded as proper by society generally. You may be struck by the parallels between this test and the *Ghosh* test for dishonesty.

For example in *Harvey*, D paid V £20,000 for a consignment of cannabis which turned out to be 'rubbish'. Incensed by the swindle, D kidnapped V's wife and child and threatened to rape, maim and kill them unless his money was returned. The Court of Appeal held that it should have been left to the jury to assess whether D believed that his demand was reasonable and his menaces proper. However, the Court thought that no sane person could believe that threats of killing, maiming and rape were a 'proper' means of enforcing the demand and therefore applied the proviso to uphold the conviction despite the trial judge's error.

Harvey ruled that 'no act which was not believed to be lawful could be believed to be proper within the meaning of the subsection', but the jury still have to decide that D knew that what he was threatening was or might be a crime. However it would be wrong to surmise that if what D is threatening is not a crime, it is proper. *Harvey* recognised that it was 'a word of wide meaning, certainly wider than (for example) "lawful"'.

The conduct threatened in our Question does not involve any crime, but would be likely to be regarded as improper. In fact threats to expose the sexual peccadilloes of prominent figures to the Sunday newspapers might be regarded as a typical blackmailing situation. Only if D believed that people generally would view it as permissible (socially and morally acceptable), would the demand be 'warranted'. D was convicted in *St Q* [2002] Cr App R (2) 40 where, in order to persuade his wife to agree a divorce settlement, he threatened to distribute videos of them having sex. In a civil case, *Arthur v Anker* [1997] QB 564, it was said that car clampers would commit blackmail unless they believed their clamping was a proper means of enforcing their demand for payment.

With a view to gain or with intent to cause loss

'Gain' and 'loss' are defined by s. 34(2)(a) 'as extending only to gain or loss in money or other property, . . . whether temporary or permanent . . .'

? QUESTION 12.16

Suppose D threatens to inform V's husband of a homosexual affair she is having unless she:

- lends D her car for the weekend; or
- spends the weekend in the country with D; or
- takes part in a pornographic video D is making; or
- pays him the £500 she owes him; or
- withdraws an application she has made for a job.

Say whether D would satisfy the gain or loss provision in each of the foregoing alternative situations.

It is clear from this provision that blackmail protects only the victim's economic interests in money or property. It follows the second situation would not be covered because no gain or loss in terms of money or property is envisaged. At first sight the third situation looks the same. However, if D is intending to make money from the video, then he will make the demand with a view to gain. It is not necessary for D to directly demand money or property as long as that is one of the purposes he has in mind. The section makes clear that a temporary economic gain or loss suffices so that the first situation is caught.

According to s. 34(2)(a) '(i) "gain" includes a gain by keeping what one has, as well as a gain by getting what one has not; and (ii) "loss" includes a loss by not getting what one might get, as well as a loss by parting with what one has.' If D owes V £1,000 and threatens him with violence unless he accepts £500 in full satisfaction of the debt, he does it with a view to gain by keeping what he has and with intent to cause loss to V who does not get what he might.

> **? QUESTION** 12.17
>
> Does this mean that blackmail is committed where a firm, owing V £1,000 and realising that he is in financial difficulties and needs immediate funds, threatens not to pay V unless he agrees to accept £750 in full satisfaction of the debt?

Clearly, the view to gain and intent to cause loss is present and blackmail will turn on whether the demand with menaces was 'unwarranted'. If D was deliberately taking advantage of V's desperate plight, he might find it hard to convince a jury that he believed that he had 'reasonable grounds' for making the demand (*cf.* the contract case of *D & C Builders Ltd* v *Rees* [1955] 3 All ER 837, CA).

Referring back to the last situation in the last but one Question, even if D will not make any economic gain if V does not get the job applied for, he still intends to cause loss. Because V withdraws her application, she does not get what she might get—the job with the money that goes with it.

That leaves us with the fourth situation where D is trying to recover only what he is legally entitled to. It depends on whether 'gain' is taken to mean 'getting a profit' or simply 'acquiring or obtaining' whether at a profit or not. If you are paid what you are owed, you are not making any profit and V is not suffering any loss in the sense that it had to be paid at some time. On the other hand, D certainly acquires the money when it is paid and V certainly loses it in the physical sense. In *Lawrence and Pomroy* (1971) 57 Cr App R 64, the Court of Appeal assumed without argument that the defendants had a view to gain even though they claimed to be trying only to recover what was lawfully owed to them, and there is nothing in the Act to suggest that this interpretation is incorrect. It was applied in *Parkes* [1973] Crim LR 358 where it was held that 'getting hard cash as opposed to a mere right of action is getting more than one already has'. This is surely correct and thus the fourth situation would be caught.

12.9 Handling stolen goods

12.9.1 Introduction

It is probable that most people look upon handling stolen goods as not so serious as theft or burglary. The person who succumbs to the temptation to buy goods 'on the cheap' attracts relatively mild disapproval. Even the backstreet dealer who regularly sells stolen goods, is probably viewed as a shady character in the Arthur Daley mould. However, the law treats this offence as more serious than theft, carrying a maximum of 14 years' imprisonment, and on a par with burglary of a dwelling. The reason is the recognition of the professional handler's supreme importance in providing a market-place for stolen goods, thus providing thieves with the necessary economic incentive. Despite this, it is likely that the public at large will regard the thief or burglar, the primary causer of harm, as more blameworthy and the more serious menace than the handler.

12.9.2 The offence

Section 22 looks deceptively simple:

(1) A person handles stolen goods if (otherwise than in the course of the stealing) knowing or believing them to be stolen goods he dishonestly receives the goods, or dishonestly undertakes or assists in their retention, removal, disposal or realisation by or for the benefit of another person, or if he arranges to do so.

Professor Smith once described this offence as 'a source of endless fascination'. You may have a different description when you have attempted to negotiate its complexities! Section 22 replaces the very simple offence of 'receiving stolen goods' in the old law with a much more wide-ranging offence which includes 'receiving', but is by no means confined to that. There are no fewer than 18 different forms of handling identified by s. 22(1).

12.9.2.1 *Actus reus*

D must (a) handle (b) stolen goods. We will be discoursing below on the concept of 'handling', but first we must examine the meaning of 'stolen goods'.

Stolen goods

Unless the goods are stolen, D cannot possibly be guilty of handling. However, if he thinks they are stolen, when they are not, he can be guilty of an attempt to handle stolen goods (Criminal Attempts Act 1981; *Shivpuri*—see 16.3.4).

  Section 24(4) extends the meaning of 'stolen' by providing that goods are stolen not only where they are obtained contrary to s. 1 (i.e., theft) but also by fraud contrary to s. 1 of the Fraud Act 2006 or contrary to s. 21 (blackmail). By s. 24(1), goods stolen in foreign countries can be 'handled' in England and Wales but only if the act in the foreign country was a crime there and would have been one here, if the act had been done here (see *Ofori and Tackie* (1994) 99 Cr App R 223, CA).

Ceasing to be stolen

Goods which are stolen may not stay 'stolen' forever. By s. 24(3) they cease to be stolen 'after they have been restored to the person from whom they were stolen or to other lawful possession or custody, or after that person and any other person claiming through him have otherwise ceased as regards those goods to have any right to restitution in respect of the theft'.

  The subsection identifies two types of situation.

Restoration to lawful possession or custody

Once the goods are returned to the owner or other person from whom they were stolen, they are no longer stolen and cannot be handled, unless they are first stolen again. Goods also cease to be stolen when they are reduced to possession by the police. According to *Attorney-General's Reference (No. 1 of 1974)* [1974] 2 All ER 899, CA (*Cases and Materials* (12.9.2.1)) whether the goods have been taken into possession by the police depends on the intention of the officers concerned. A policeman, suspecting that goods in a car were stolen, removed the rotor arm from the car's engine to immobilise it. He questioned D when he returned to the car and then arrested him. It was held that the jury should have been told that whether the goods had ceased to be stolen depended on whether the policeman had intended 'to reduce the goods into his possession or to assume the control of them' by immobilising the car, or whether he was merely intending 'to ensure that the driver, when he appeared, could not get away without answering questions'. Of course, as pointed out above, even if the goods have been 'restored to lawful custody', it would still be possible to convict D of attempting to handle stolen goods.

No longer a right to restitution

Whether the owner has lost his right to restitution of the goods originally stolen from him is a question of civil law. For example, in some exceptional circumstances a thief can pass a good title to stolen goods to an innocent purchaser for value. The exception for sales in market overt was abolished by the Sale of Goods (Amendment) Act 1994, but in many cases where D obtains the goods by deception, he obtains a voidable title to the goods and if he sells them to an innocent purchaser before the owner discovers the fraud and rescinds the contract, the innocent purchaser will obtain the ownership of the goods and the original owner's right of restitution will have gone forever.

You may recall the House of Lords' decision in *Hinks* (see 10.4.1.1 above) that dishonest receipt of a fully valid gift can be theft even though D becomes the indefeasible owner of the property. However, if D is the unchallengable owner according to the civil law, it follows that V, the donor, no longer has a right to restitution of the property which, by virtue of s. 24(3), is **not** stolen property. According to *Hinks,* D commits theft but, according to s. 24(3), the property appropriated is not 'stolen'!

Goods and their proceeds

Under s. 34(2)(b) goods 'includes money and every other description of property except land, and includes things severed from the land by stealing'. This closely parallels the definition of 'property' in theft and extends to intangible property such as debts and other things in action. 'Land' is not capable of being handled and it cannot be the subject of a theft (see 10.4.1.2 above). It can, however, be the subject of fraud under the Fraud Act 2006.

Section 24(2) is a complicated provision which extends the notion of 'stolen goods' to include any other goods which (a) have at some time been in the hands of the thief or a handler and (b) which have represented the original stolen goods in the sense of being the proceeds, direct or indirect, of a sale or other realisation of the original goods (see Criminal Law Revision Committee's Report—Cmnd 2977, para. 138).

In other words, you can have a progression of 'stolen' goods. Thus, if D sells a lorry load of stolen whisky for £10,000, that money becomes 'stolen goods'. Anything he buys with it is also tainted so that any other person handling any such items with the requisite knowledge that they were bought with the proceeds of a theft will be a handler. If D uses the proceeds to buy a diamond ring for his wife, the ring will be 'stolen'. If he pays part of the money into his bank account, the debt owed to him by his bank for that sum will become a stolen thing in action. (*Attorney-General's Reference (No. 4 of 1979)* [1981] 1 All ER 1193, CA though see *The Law of Theft*, 8th ed., pp. 13–19 for a consideration of the possibility that s. 24(3) might prevent this thing in action from being stolen.)

In the hands of the thief or a handler

Goods representing the originally stolen goods can only be themselves 'stolen' and so capable of being handled by D if they were 'at some time...in the hands of the thief' or a handler of the original stolen goods. In this regard particular problems arise where stolen monies are paid into bank accounts. If T, the thief, pays stolen monies into his own account, clearly the thing in action created will be 'in the hands of the thief'. But suppose T then transfers monies out of it to D's account, either by direct transfer or by paying a cheque into D's account. Would the thing in action owed by D's bank to D be stolen property so that it would be handled by D if he dishonestly received the credit to his account? It certainly seems to be 'the proceeds direct or indirect' representing the original stolen monies and this is unaffected by anything in *Preddy*. However, this new thing in action (D's bank's debt to D) was never in the hands of the thief (T) or any handler of the originally stolen monies. In *Forsyth* [1997] 2 Cr App R 299, the Court of Appeal held that 'in the hands of' meant 'in the possession of or under the control of the thief'. Therefore credits in accounts in the name of others (e.g., companies) over which T exercises control will be stolen property but not those in accounts which he does not control. If D withdraws cash from an account with a 'stolen' credit, it is thought (despite an assumption to the contrary in *Forsyth*) that the cash itself will not be stolen property because it was never in the hands of the thief.

Dishonestly retaining a wrongful credit

Section 2 of the Theft (Amendment) Act 1996 now ensures that this kind of activity will be caught first by creating a new offence of dishonestly retaining a wrongful credit (new s. 24A of the TA 1968) and second by providing specifically that money dishonestly withdrawn from an account to which a wrongful credit has been made is stolen property to the extent to which the money derives from the wrongful credit (s. 24A(8)). The latter provision thus extends the range of property which can be handled contrary to s. 22. It means that, in the situation described in the final sentence of the previous section, D would be guilty of handling stolen goods notwithstanding that s. 24(2) would not be applicable and, indeed, any additional person who handles that cash with the requisite *mens rea* would also be guilty.

The offence under s. 24A is committed by a person who dishonestly fails to take reasonable steps to secure the cancellation of a credit to his account (or one in which he has 'any right or interest') which is 'wrongful' and which he knows or believes to be wrongful. Under s. 24A(2A), a credit is wrongful 'to the extent that it derives from' theft, blackmail, fraud (contrary to s.1 of the Fraud Act 2006 or stolen goods. It is immaterial that the account is overdrawn at any stage (s. 24A(5)).

On learning of the credit and its wrongfulness, D is required to take reasonable steps 'to secure that the credit is cancelled'. This is a rather odd provision since literally it could be satisfied by a dishonest D who immediately drew out the money (thus securing the cancellation of the credit!) and spent it on the holiday of a lifetime! Presumably the courts will interpret that as not taking 'such steps as are reasonable in the circumstances' even though it does secure cancellation of the credit. Reasonable steps to secure cancellation will embrace some notion of righting the wrong **by** getting the credit cancelled.

Handling

The better view is that s. 22(1) creates a single offence which can be committed in a variety of ways—at least 18! (*Nicklin* [1977] 2 All ER 444, CA.)

Following the decision of the House of Lords in *Bloxham* [1982] 1 All ER 582, we can now identify four basic forms of 'handling':

(a) receiving the goods;

(b) undertaking the retention, removal, disposal or realisation of the goods for the benefit of another person;

(c) assisting in the retention, removal, disposal or realisation of the goods by another person;

(d) arranging to do (a), (b), or (c).

Receiving or arranging to receive

This necessitates that D receives the goods into possession whether alone or shared with others, one of whom could be the thief. In *Wiley* (1850) 2 Den 37 the police burst into D's house and found him haggling over the goods with the thieves. It was held that he had not received them because the goods still remained in the exclusive possession of the thieves. Nor will it be 'arranging to receive' until negotiations have been successful and a definite arrangement concluded. A temporary possession suffices so that if you get possession of the goods to hide them on behalf of the thief until the 'heat is off', you would receive them (*Richardson* (1834) 6 C & P 335). It is irrelevant that the receiver receives no profit or advantage from the possession of the goods.

> **? QUESTION** 12.18
>
> If D, an art collector, agrees to pay X and Y £1 million to steal *Whistler's Mother*, would D be guilty of arranging to receive stolen goods?

An agreement to handle goods to be stolen in the future may constitute conspiracy to handle stolen goods (see below), but it cannot possibly constitute handling stolen goods itself because the goods must be stolen at the time of the handling. Nor does it become handling when the goods are actually stolen (*Park* (1988) 87 Cr App R 164, CA). Of course, once the goods have been stolen, **subsequent** actions by D may constitute handling.

Undertaking or assisting

D must undertake or assist in one or more of four activities—the retention, removal, disposal or realisation of the goods. A person 'undertakes' if he himself does the retaining, removing, etc. He assists if he helps another to do the retaining, removing, etc.

EXERCISE 12.2

Read s. 22(1) in *Cases and Materials* (12.9.2). What limitation applies to the undertaking/assisting forms of handling but does not apply to receiving?

All forms of handling other than 'receiving or arranging to receive' are subject to a very important qualification designed to prevent the original thief automatically becoming also a handler. The activity must be done 'by or for the benefit of another'. The House of Lords in *Bloxham* held this to require that in all cases of 'undertaking' the activity has to be done 'for the benefit of another' and in all cases of 'assisting in' the activity has to be done 'by another'. This qualification applies equally to cases of 'arranging to undertake' and 'arranging to assist in', respectively. It is the retention, removal, disposal or realisation which must be done 'by or for the benefit of another'.

? **QUESTION** 12.19

Suppose D buys a stolen car from a thief, without realising it is stolen. Subsequently he discovers the truth and then sells the car to a shady dealer at a knock-down price. Would D be guilty of handling and, if so, what is the precise form of handling in question?

We have just given you the facts of *Bloxham* (*Cases and Materials* (12.9.2.1)). It is quite clear that when D initially receives the stolen goods he does not commit the offence because he lacks the necessary knowledge or belief that they are stolen. What does he do with the car when he becomes aware that it is stolen? Initially we might say that he undertakes its retention, but this could not be handling because he does not undertake it 'for the benefit of another'. When he sells the car, he undertakes its 'disposal' and its 'realisation' ('exchanging goods for money'). However, the disposal and realisation are not 'for the benefit of another' but for his own benefit. It is irrelevant that the other may incidentally 'benefit' from the transaction. The realisation is **by** D, the seller, and not the purchaser. As Griew puts it, 'the House of Lords effectively treats the notion of an act undertaken "for the benefit of another person" as that of an act done on behalf of another person; it is an act that the other might do himself' (*The Theft Acts 1968 and 1978*, 6th ed., pp. 14–22). Accordingly, the realisation would only be 'for the benefit of another' within the section if D undertook it as agent for the thief or another. Whilst it is difficult to justify such a reading on the strict wording of the provision, it probably achieves the result intended by the legislators.

The four activities which must not be undertaken or assisted in are by and large straightforward, but it may help your appreciation of the wide scope of the section if we look at each one in turn.

Retention

According to *Pitchley* (1972) 57 Cr App R 30, CA to retain means 'keeping possession of, not losing, continuing to have'. It is clear that this is a continuing activity and D may commit the offence where he 'undertakes the retention' when he finds out that the goods are stolen, having been ignorant of this when he originally received them. In *Pitchley*, D paid a stolen cheque into his bank account on behalf of his son, unaware that it was stolen. He then later discovered that it was stolen but did nothing. It was held that he assisted in the retention of the stolen money, by remaining inactive. In fact this looks more like a case of undertaking the retention for the benefit of his son.

In order to assist in the retention, D must do something 'intentionally and dishonestly, **for the purpose** of enabling the goods to be retained' (*Kanwar* (1982) 2 All ER 528, CA— *Cases and Materials* (12.9.2.1)). Thus, where a wife merely used furniture brought home by her husband which she knew to be stolen, she did not thereby assist in its retention. However, when she told lies to the police to convince them that the goods were lawfully hers, she did assist in their retention. Physical assistance is not, therefore, essential. In *Brown* [1969] 3 All ER 198, CA it was held that a mere failure to disclose to the police the presence of stolen goods on his premises, even coupled with advice to, 'Get lost!', is not in itself assisting in their retention, but it can be evidence of the fact that D is permitting the goods to remain on his premises and is thereby assisting in (or, better, undertaking) their retention.

Removal
If D transports the goods in any way to another place, he undertakes their removal. He could assist another in removing them by, for example, lending him a van.

Disposal
This includes giving or throwing away the goods, destroying them or melting them down. Simply for D to sit back and take the benefit of a disposal does not mean that he has assisted in it. In *Coleman* [1986] Crim LR 56, CA, D's wife used stolen money to pay some of the solicitor's fees in respect of the purchase of a flat in joint names. It was not enough to show that D knew that the money was stolen; it had to be shown that he encouraged or agreed to her using it.

In *Forsyth* [1997] 2 Cr App R 299, CA, D was charged with undertaking or assisting in the disposal of a stolen thing in action, a credit balance in a Swiss bank account. She had gone to Switzerland where she instructed the Swiss bank to transfer the monies to an account in England. The Court of Appeal held that, although all D's acts were performed in Switzerland, the disposal she undertook or assisted in continued until the funds reached the account in England, so that our courts had jurisdiction to try the case.

Realisation
'Realisation' means 'exchanging goods for money or other property' (*Bloxham*). D undertakes the realisation of goods if he sells them, although we saw in *Bloxham* that he would only do this 'for the benefit of another' if he was doing it **on behalf of** some other person. He could assist in their realisation by, say, introducing a buyer to the thief.

Otherwise than in the course of the stealing
All forms of handling including 'receiving' and 'arranging to receive' must occur 'otherwise than in the course of the stealing'. This is another provision inserted in an effort to prevent the original thieves from necessarily also being handlers. Whilst the provision may help in that regard, it in no way prevents handlers from being thieves!

- Where D receives stolen goods contrary to s. 22, will he also necessarily steal them?
- If D undertakes the retention, removal, disposal or realisation of the goods contrary to s. 22, will he also necessarily steal them?

The section refers to 'the course of **the** stealing'. This is intended to refer to the original stealing when the goods take on the character of being 'stolen'. Whenever a handler receives the goods, in taking possession of them he will inevitably be 'appropriating' them by virtue of *Gomez*. He would clearly have the *mens rea* of theft—dishonestly and with the intention of permanently depriving the owner of the property. Although this is a stealing, it is not 'the' stealing referred to in the section and so the handler's receipt is 'otherwise than in the course of the stealing'. The 'undertaking' forms of handling would also appear to involve appropriations and to constitute theft, and this would also apply to 'assisting' forms where D physically handles the goods.

Without the provision, two or more people jointly committing theft would be likely to become handlers as well as thieves. When D1 takes the goods from the shop's storeroom and hands them to D2, who loads them into a van, D2 'receives' the stolen goods. Both presumably would either undertake or assist in the removal of the goods.

The phrase 'the course of the stealing' suggests that 'the stealing' is a continuing act which includes the whole process of taking the goods and carrying them off. This would accord with the view of 'appropriation' as a continuing act in *Hale* (see 12.3.2.4) and *Gregory* (1982) 77 Cr App R 41. Precisely how long it would continue in any given case would be a question of fact for the jury. *Pitham and Hehl* (see 10.4.1.1) would appear to contradict this view and to regard 'appropriation' as an instantaneous act. It is best to regard the case as incorrect on this point. You may recall *Atakpu* (see 10.4.1.1) where it was thought that the stealing would continue as long as the accused were 'on the job'. It could be argued that this would not extend to driving off with the goods and would certainly limit the exclusionary efficacy of this provision.

If the thief parts with possession of the stolen goods, e.g., gives them to a friend to hide, he will become a handler when he regains possession of them because 'the course of the stealing' has long since finished. Difficult problems of evidence arise where D is apprehended in possession of stolen goods some time after the theft. It may not be clear whether he is the thief or a handler. If D is charged with handling, the prosecution need not prove that he received the goods 'otherwise than in the course of the stealing', unless there is some evidence indicating that D might be the thief (*Cash* [1985] QB 801, CA; *Ryan* v *DPP* [1994] Crim LR 457; *Wells* [2004] EWCA Crim 79).

Innocent receipt and subsequent dishonesty

You should find this section a useful way of recapitulating on some of the points you have learned so far. D will come by the goods innocently if he does not realise they are stolen or, alternatively, if he intends to return the stolen goods to the true owner. If he then finds out that the goods are stolen or decides not to return them to the true owner, will his dishonest decision to keep them constitute any offence?

? QUESTION 12.21

- If D bought the goods innocently from the thief, will he commit (a) theft or (b) handling or (c) neither, when he dishonestly decides to retain them?
- Would the same apply if D was given the goods by the thief without at first realising they were stolen?

Theft

Although D would dishonestly 'keep or deal with the property as owner' (later assumption of the owner's rights under s. 3(1)), he cannot be guilty of theft because s. 3(2) prevents such later assumption of the rights D believed himself to be acquiring in the sale from being theft. Of course, if it is a *Gomez* theft by deception case, the original thief will have acquired ownership under a voidable contract. If he then sells the goods to D, an **innocent** purchaser, before the original owner has avoided the contract, D will become the indefeasible owner of the property. Therefore, he will not need to rely on s. 3(2). The property will not 'belong to another' and D cannot be dishonest in keeping his own property. The original owner's right to rescind will have been lost.

If D was given the goods, then s. 3(2) would be inapplicable and offer D no protection because there was no transfer 'for value'. Even if D gets the ownership by virtue of the 'gift', the original owner might still have the right to rescind. This would have been lost if, before D was given it, there had been an innocent purchase for value from the rogue who obtained the property by deception. Once the contract is rescinded, the ownership reverts to the original owner and dishonest retention by D is an appropriation of property belonging to another and theft.

Handling

D 'receives' the goods but without the necessary *mens rea*. When he has the *mens rea*, he 'undertakes the retention' of the goods (or 'realisation' if he sells them), but he is not guilty of handling (unless he is acting on someone else's behalf) because he does not retain or realise 'for the benefit of another' (*Bloxham*). If D got the ownership of the goods as a result of his purchase, the goods would cease to be 'stolen' because the original owner would no longer have 'any right to restitution', his right to rescind having been lost.

If D was given the goods, he would, as above, be guilty of handling only if he retained or sold the goods on somebody else's behalf. This is so even if he gets the ownership by the gift, provided, as will be the case if there has been no prior innocent purchaser for value, the original owner still has the 'right to restitution' (i.e., to rescind). The goods will therefore remain 'stolen goods' and it is then a question of whether D undertakes their retention or realisation 'for the benefit of another'.

12.9.2.2 *Mens rea*

D must handle the goods (i) dishonestly (ii) 'knowing or believing them to be stolen goods'.

Dishonestly

This is the same concept as discussed previously, and *Feely* and *Ghosh* would apply (*Roberts* (1987) 84 Cr App R 117, CA). One obvious case where D would not be dishonest is where he intends to return the stolen goods to the rightful owner or to hand them over to the police.

Knowing or believing them to be stolen

D must know or believe the goods to be stolen at the time he 'receives' the goods or handles them in whatever other way(s) is alleged (*Brook* [1993] Crim LR 455; *Williams* [1994] Crim LR 934, CA). The test is entirely subjective. D must actually know or actually believe that the goods are stolen. The fact that it would have been obvious to any reasonable person that the goods were stolen does not establish that D believed them to be so, and the two must not be confused (*Brook*).

We have seen that the courts generally interpret the word 'knowing' as embracing not just actual knowledge but also knowledge of the second degree, i.e., wilful blindness (see 3.6.2 above). However, it is clear that the use of the 'believing' alternative in this section compels the narrow meaning of **actual** knowledge, as where D is 'told by someone with first-hand knowledge (someone such as the thief or burglar)...' (*Hall* (1985) 81 Cr App R 260). Otherwise, 'believing' would be entirely redundant, being encompassed by second degree knowledge. The Court of Appeal has stressed repeatedly that mere suspicion that goods are stolen is not enough. Wilful blindness does not itself suffice, although it may be evidence that D actually believed that the goods were stolen (*Griffiths* (1974) 60 Cr App R 14, CA; *Belleni* [1980] Crim LR 437, CA).

The section requires D to believe that the goods **are** stolen and not that they might be stolen. However, 'belief' can range from absolute conviction (certainty) to lukewarm (possibility). The latter, being mere suspicion is not enough. According to *Reader* (1977) 66 Cr App R 33, CA (*Cases and Materials* (12.9.2.2)), 'To believe that goods are **probably** stolen is not to believe that they are stolen.' Thus, even **strong** suspicion does not suffice. According to the Court of Appeal in *Forsyth* [1997] 2 Cr App R 299 (*Cases and Materials* (12.9.2.2)), 'belief is the mental acceptance of a fact as true or existing'. In *Hall*, the Court of Appeal thought that a person who knew that the only reasonable conclusion in the light of all he had heard and seen was that the goods were stolen would have the necessary 'belief' even though he refused 'to believe what my brain tells me is obvious'. This was frowned on by *Forsyth* as having an inherent 'potential for confusion'. What seems to be the minimum required is that D must believe with virtual certainty that the goods are stolen. D has no significant doubt that they are stolen. This seems to be a surprising and unwarrantedly high standard for the prosecution.

No doubt in recognition of this, the court in *Reader* and *Forsyth* stated that the trial judge should not explain the meaning of believe to the jury because it is an ordinary, everyday word which they will understand! Presumably, in practice juries might well take it to include someone who has strong suspicion and deliberately turns a blind eye, but, as Professor Smith comments, 'No one will ever know'!

It is enough that D knows or believes the goods to be stolen even though he is ignorant of or mistakes their nature. In *McCullum* (1973) 57 Cr App R 645, CA, D was convicted of assisting in the retention of stolen guns contained in a locked suitcase. It was held to be no defence that she did not realise that the suitcase contained guns as long as she knew it contained **some** stolen goods.

12.10 **Criminal damage**

12.10.1 **Introduction**

Criminal damage is a useful offence to study because it reinforces a number of important general principles discussed at other points of this work, e.g., the concept of recklessness, the defence of intoxication, the issue of mistake.

The Criminal Damage Act 1971 resulted from the work of the Law Commission (Law Com. No. 29 (1970)) and provided an entirely new code for offences of damage to property to replace the antiquated Malicious Damage Act 1861. It creates five offences which can be termed basic or simple criminal damage (s. 1(1)), aggravated criminal damage (s. 1(2)), arson (criminal damage by fire—s. 1(3)), threatening to damage (s. 2) and possessing anything with intent to damage (s. 3). Sections 2 and 3 are reproduced in *Cases and Materials* (12.10.1) and are more or less self-explanatory. We shall accordingly concentrate on the offences in s. 1. The aggravating factor in s. 1(2) is that when D commits basic criminal damage, he intends or is reckless as to the endangering of another's life.

12.10.2 **Basic criminal damage**

Section 1(1) reads:

> A person who without lawful excuse destroys or damages any property belonging to another intending to destroy or damage any such property or being reckless as to whether any such property would be destroyed or damaged shall be guilty of an offence.

The maximum penalty is ten years' imprisonment although this is increased to life imprisonment if the damage is by fire and is charged as arson under s. 1(3).

12.10.2.1 *Actus reus*

The *actus reus* comprises four elements: (a) destroys or damages (b) any property (c) belonging to another (d) without lawful excuse.

Destroys or damages

'Destroy' admits of no half-measures and guidance may be gained from the non-Criminal Damage Act case of *Barnet London Borough Council* v *Eastern Electricity Board* [1973] 2 All ER 319, DC. It requires 'at least elements of finality and totality . . . and must . . . go further than merely material change'. Thus, it would include killing an animal, demolishing a building or structure, breaking up a machine, crushing a car or razing crops.

'Damage' is a much more fluid concept and is dependent on the circumstances. It does not matter whether it is temporary or permanent. It involves some physical harm to or impairment of the value or utility of the property. Thus, in *Hardman* v *Chief Constable of Avon* [1986] Crim LR 330, CND supporters painted human silhouettes on the local authority's pavement using water soluble paints and chalks. This constituted damage because, although the pavement could be restored relatively easily to its former condition, it still involved the local authority in the expense of removing the drawings with high pressure water jets. The same was decided in *Roe* v *Kingerlee* [1986] Crim LR 735, DC where it was held that mud graffiti put on the wall of a cell could be 'damage'. (Presumably the same would apply to the daubing of excrement, a form of protest at one time used by imprisoned para-militaries in Northern Ireland.) Similarly where a prisoner deliberately stuffed a clean blanket down his police cell's toilet and repeatedly flushed the toilet causing the blanket to be soaked and the waterproof floor of the cell to be flooded, it was held to be damage to both the blanket and the cell despite the fact that the water was clean and no permanent damage occurred (*Fiak* [2005] EWCA Crim 2381). Even though the damage was remediable, both the blanket and the cell had been rendered unusable for the time being. On the other hand, in *A* v *R* [1978] Crim LR 689, spitting on a policeman's coat did not cause 'damage' because the waterproof coat could be restored simply by wiping off the spittle with a damp cloth. No expense such as dry cleaning was necessary. The court thought that the article had to be rendered imperfect or inoperative in some way.

The latter point illustrates that damage can be caused by simply dismantling a machine or removing parts from it without otherwise physically harming any of the parts (*Tacey* (1821) Russ & Ry 452; *Fisher* (1865) LR 1 CCR 7, DC). However, merely to deprive V of the use of his property is not in itself 'damage'. For example, *Lloyd* [1991] Crim LR 904, DC held that to place a wheel clamp on a car was not to damage it unless, of course, the car was physically damaged in the process. Unlike the machinery cases, the car itself is unchanged and not rendered unfit for use. The same view was taken in *Drake* v *DPP* [1994] Crim LR 855, DC.

Property can be rendered imperfect even though its utility is unaffected. Thus, a scratch on car bodywork is 'damage' not least because it would involve the owner in expense in repairing it. By contrast, in *Morphitis* v *Salmon* [1990] Crim LR 48, DC it was held that a scratch on a scaffolding pole could not be 'damage' because scratching was a normal incident of scaffolding poles. It did not render it any less valuable or imperfect.

An important question in modern times is whether damage to or the destruction of electronically stored data is within the Criminal Damage Act 1971. *Cox* v *Riley* (1986) 83 Cr App R 54 held that wiping the programs from a printed circuit card used to operate a computerised saw was 'damage' and *Whiteley* (1991) 93 Cr App R 25, CA (*Cases and Materials* (12.10.2.1)) held the same where data stored on computer disks had been corrupted by a computer 'hacker' without physically damaging the disks. In fact these cases have, in relation to computers, been superseded by the Computer Misuse Act 1990 which creates special offences. It also limits the definition of 'damage' in the Criminal Damage Act by providing that 'modification of the contents of a computer shall not be regarded as damaging any computer or computer storage medium unless its effect on that computer or computer storage medium impairs its physical condition'. Nonetheless, the principles of the two cases still apply to other electronic/magnetic storage media such as audio and video cassettes. Impairing the value or utility of the tapes by corrupting or wiping the stored data will be 'damage'.

Property

 EXERCISE 12.3

Read s. 10(1) in *Cases and Materials* (12.7). What are the differences between this definition of property and that in s. 4 of the Theft Act 1968 (reproduced in *Cases and Materials* (10.4.1.2))?

There are similarities between the two definitions, but also significant differences. There is no exclusion of land from criminal damage, and damaging buildings (which are real property because attached to and forming part of the land) is the archetypal arson case. Criminal damage does not cover intangible property which is, of course, a common subject-matter of theft. In *Whiteley*, Lord Lane CJ held that tangible property (computer disks) was damaged when the magnetic particles representing the stored data were altered. It is the property damaged which has to be tangible not the damage itself. Finally, wild mushrooms and the flowers, fruit or foliage of any wild plant cannot be the subject of criminal damage whereas they can, albeit in limited circumstances, be stolen.

Belonging to another

 EXERCISE 12.4

Read s. 10(2)–(4) in *Cases and Materials* (12.10.2.1) and say how the definition differs from that contained in s. 5(1) of the TA 1968 (reproduced in *Cases and Materials* (10.4.1.3)).

The offence under s. 1(1) can be committed only against property 'belonging to another'. As we shall see, this limitation does not apply to the aggravated form of criminal damage under s. 1(2). You will have seen that the definition in s. 10(2) broadly follows that in s. 5(1) of the TA 1968 and this means that property may belong to more than one person, leading to the possibility of the owner being guilty for damaging his own property. If D hires out his car for a week to V, V will have 'custody or control', if not a 'proprietary right or interest' for the week. If D disables the car surreptitiously by removing a vital part, he may be convicted of criminal damage.

The differences with the TA 1968 definition are not great and some are more apparent than real. The main one is the use of 'custody or control' rather than 'possession or control'. This would seem to require actual physical custody or control although there is no case law on the point. The inclusion by s. 10(2)(c) of a person having a charge on the property seems superfluous since such a person will, in any event, have 'a proprietary right or interest' in it coming under s. 10(2)(b).

Without lawful excuse

There are many instances where D would have a lawful excuse for damaging V's property. For example, police executing a lawful search warrant may have to smash down a door to gain entry. A public health official may be empowered to destroy infested or infected property. Equally, it might be said that D would have a lawful excuse if he can use any of the normal defences to criminal liability, such as self-defence or duress (although presumably these would have been available anyway even without the express inclusion of the words 'without lawful excuse'). Thus, if D throws V's china ornament at V in reasonable self-defence, the damage would be with lawful excuse (see also s. 5(5)).

In addition to such undefined 'lawful excuses' which are to be gleaned from the general law, s. 5 expressly adds two more which might not otherwise amount to 'lawful excuse'. This extended meaning of 'lawful excuse' does not apply to the aggravated offence under s. 1(2) because that involves the risk of endangerment of life.

EXERCISE 12.5

Read s. 5(1)–(3) in *Cases and Materials* (12.10.2.1).

- Identify what constitutes the 'lawful excuse' in each case.
- Indicate what, if anything, they have in common.
- Does any relevant belief have to be reasonable?

Belief in consent

Section 5(2)(a) parallels s. 2(1)(b) of the TA 1968 in respect of dishonesty in theft. D need only 'believe' that the owner has or would have consented with full knowledge of the circumstances. It is not necessary to show that the owner has in fact or would in fact have consented (although, as a matter of evidence, this will help to give credence to D's claim to have held the belief). Thus, it does not matter whether D was correct in his belief or mistaken. If mistaken, it is immaterial whether the mistake was reasonable or unreasonable because s. 5(3) expressly provides that the belief does not have to be 'justified' as long as it is 'honestly held'.

If D has the relevant belief, he has a 'lawful excuse' even though he is damaging the property for a dishonest purpose. In *Denton* [1982] 1 All ER 65, CA (*Cases and Materials* (12.10.2.1)), D set fire to his employer's mill because his employer had asked him to do so to enable him to make a fraudulent insurance claim. Because he believed (correctly) that the owner had consented to the damage, he had a lawful excuse under s. 5(2)(a) and the prosecution could not therefore prove an essential ingredient of the crime. Both D and the owner could have been convicted of conspiracy to defraud (see 16.4.4.1 below).

An unreasonable mistaken belief even if due to voluntary intoxication still provides a 'lawful excuse'. In *Jaggard* v *Dickinson* [1980] 3 All ER 716 (*Cases and Materials* (8.4.7.3)), D lived in a house belonging to V. D came home drunk one night and went to the wrong house by mistake. Finding it locked, she broke windows to get in. The court held that she had a 'lawful excuse' because she genuinely believed (a) that V was 'entitled to consent' to the damage (because of her mistake that it was V's house) and (b) that V would have consented to her damaging the house to get in, had she known of the circumstances. Section 5(2)(a) did not exclude beliefs due to intoxication from its scope and the court refused to read in a general implied restriction from the general law on intoxication (see 8.4.7.3).

In *Blake* v *DPP* [1993] Crim LR 586, DC, D tried a novel argument in respect of s. 5(2)(a). He was a vicar who, in a protest against the Gulf War, used a marker pen to write a Biblical quotation on a concrete pillar outside the Houses of Parliament. He claimed that he believed he was acting on the instructions of God whom he believed to be the person 'entitled to consent to' the damage to the pillar. He therefore had a 'lawful excuse'. Not surprisingly his argument found no favour with the Divisional Court which confirmed his conviction. In any event, is God a 'person'?

Protection of other property

The feature which s. 5(2)(b) has in common with s. 5(2)(a) is that they are both based on D having a specified belief or beliefs, and the points we made in relation to s. 5(2)(a) beliefs apply equally to s. 5(2)(b).

> **?** **QUESTION** 12.22
>
> What are the three basic ingredients of this type of lawful excuse?

Essentially, s. 5(2)(b) exempts D in a very particular type of necessity situation in which a much more lenient test of necessity is prescribed than applies in the general defence of necessity (or duress of circumstances) or even self-defence. The three requirements are (a) D damages the property 'in order to protect property belonging to himself or another' (b) believing that it is 'in immediate need of protection' and (c) believing that 'the means of protection adopted or proposed to be adopted were or would be reasonable having regard to all the circumstances'. There is no need to show that the damage to his property that D was seeking to prevent would have been unlawful damage (*Jones v Gloucestershire Crown Prosecution Service* [2004] EWCA Crim 1981).

In order to protect property

D must cause the damage 'in order to protect property' whether his own or another's. This means that his purpose must be to protect property. In *Hunt* (1977) 66 Cr App R 105 (*Cases and Materials* (12.10.2.1)) the Court of Appeal made the astonishing assertion that this is an 'objective test'. D assisted his wife who was deputy warden at a block of old people's flats. He had complained to the owner to no avail that the fire alarms did not work. He set fire deliberately to a bed in the guest room in an isolated part of the flats with a view to forcing the owner to repair the alarm. He then 'discovered' the fire, called the fire brigade and evacuated the occupants of the flats. He broke the glass of the alarm which did not work. The Court ruled that because the act of causing the damage did not protect and was not capable of protecting other property, D did not do it 'in order to protect property', whatever his subjective beliefs and aims.

The case of *Hill* (1988) 89 Cr App R 74, CA (*Cases and Materials* (12.10.2.1)) modified this position a little. D, a nuclear protester, was arrested outside a US nuclear submarine base in Wales, with a hacksaw blade. She admitted that she intended to use it to cut the wire surrounding the base. Her purpose was to persuade the Americans to leave in order to reduce the chances of a Russian nuclear strike in the area in order to protect, inter alia, her property nearby. The Court explained that the test was twofold. First, there was the subjective question of deciding what was actually going on in D's mind. Second, there was the objective question of whether, as a matter of law, 'it could be said on those facts as believed by [D], snipping the strand of the wire...could amount to something done to protect either [D's] own home or the homes of her adjacent friends.' The trial judge was right to rule that her proposed act (cutting the wire) 'was far too remote from the eventual aim [protecting her property]...to satisfy the test'. Thus, the court required an immediate causal connection between the damage and the protection. The objective test was applied to similar effect in *Blake v DPP* where the writing on the pillar was held not to be capable of protecting property in Iraq and Kuwait and was accepted as correct in *Jones v Gloucestershire Crown Prosecution Service* [2004] EWCA Crim 1981.

Although the objective test is firmly entrenched, it is difficult to justify since a purpose can only exist in D's mind and D cannot act 'in order to' do something unless it is his purpose. We may be sceptical about D's claim to have the purpose of 'protecting property' where this is so remote from his actions or where they are not reasonably capable of in fact protecting property. Nonetheless, if we accept that that was his purpose, however misguided or ineffectual his actions to achieve it and whatever additional purposes he had, can we deny that he acted 'in order to protect property'?

Belief in immediate need of protection

This would have been a more satisfactory ground for deciding *Hill* since D admitted that she did not believe a nuclear strike was imminent if the wire was not cut at that moment. The same could be argued in relation to *Hunt* in that he did not believe that a fire would break out in the immediate future. On the other hand, it could be argued that the need for the protection a fire alarm would give was 'immediate' because of the ever-present risk of fire. However, in that case, could not *Hill* have pointed to the ever-present risk of a nuclear strike so long as the base remained? Belief that property may need protection at some future time (even if in the reasonably near future) does not suffice (*Johnson* v *DPP* [1994] Crim LR 673, DC). In that case, a squatter, whilst changing the locks of a house he had begun to occupy, damaged the door-frame. Because at that time he had not moved any of his belongings into the house, he could not have believed that they were in immediate need of protection. Thus, the court is entitled to rule on what is 'immediate' for this purpose once it has found what D believed—another element of objectivity worming its way into a subjective test. If D believes that one week's time is sufficiently 'immediate', the court can rule that it is not.

In *Chamberlain* v *Lindon* [1998] 2 All ER 538, D's demolition of a wall obstructing his right of way was excused under s. 5(2)(b). He was acting to protect a 'right or interest in property' in immediate need of protection because it was being obstructed and he thought delay in asserting his access would prejudice his legal rights. The fact that he was also motivated by a desire to avoid the cost and trouble of civil litigation did not matter. By contrast, the courts have rejected similar arguments by car owners damaging wheel clamps to free their cars on the ground that the car is not in immediate need of protection (*Mitchell* [2004] Crim LR 139 CA; *Lloyd* v *DPP* [1992] 1 All ER 982).

Belief that means are reasonable

This is again **apparently** an entirely subjective test dependent purely on D's belief that it is reasonable to damage the property in order to protect the other property. There is no need to show that it was in fact objectively reasonable to take those measures.

> **? QUESTION 12.23**
>
> Does this mean that if D, who is fanatically proud of his Skoda motor car and who believes that its paintwork is being damaged by air pollution caused by a nearby factory, burns down the factory, he will have a 'lawful excuse' because he believes it is immediately necessary to prevent further damage and that it is reasonable for him to do it?

You may remember the *Ghosh* test for dishonesty in theft. It is probably the case that a similar test applies here, so that even if D thinks his actions are reasonable, if he realises that people generally would not so regard them, he does not believe the means are reasonable. Once again, a hidden element of objectivity emerges in the sense that the standard of reasonableness is set by D's view of ordinary people's attitudes rather than by his own attitudes (see also 8.6.3.1).

12.10.2.2 *Mens rea*

D must either intend to destroy or damage property belonging to another or be reckless thereto. Intention bears its usual meaning (see **Chapter 3**) and applies to the 'belonging to another' requirement as well as the causing of the damage. In other words, D must aim to damage the property knowing or believing that the property belonged to another. Thus, in *Smith* [1974] 1 All ER 632 the Court of Appeal held that D's mistaken belief that boarding and wiring which he had himself installed as a tenant of V's premises in connection with his stereo system, meant that he did not have the *mens rea* for s. 1(1). He had made a mistake as to the civil law of property because the boarding damaged became the landlord's property once it was affixed to the property (see 8.5.4.1).

There is no need to prove intention where the alternative *mens rea* of recklessness is charged, as will almost invariably be the case.

> **? QUESTION** 12.24
>
> What does 'reckless' mean? Refer to 3.4 if you cannot answer.

As the House of Lords' decision in *G* [2003] UKHL 50 demonstrates, the framers of the Act intended to include only subjective recklessness as the alternative *mens rea* so that D would need to realise that he might cause damage to property belonging to another (as was held in *Smith*). However, that orthodox view was overturned by the House of Lords in *Caldwell* which held that either subjective or objective recklessness would suffice. The House in *G* finally recognised its error and decided that *Caldwell* should no longer be followed. Henceforth, 'reckless' in the Criminal Damage Act requires nothing less than subjective recklessness so that D must be proved to have actually realised that his conduct might cause damage to another's property. Subsequent to *G*, the Court of Appeal in *Cooper* [2004] EWCA Crim 1382 asserted that D had to foresee the risk as being an 'obvious and significant' one. That seems to hark back to one of the requirements in *Caldwell* and it is an unwarranted gloss on the test laid down in *G*. If D foresees the risk as a mere possibility (whether he regards it as 'obvious and significant' or not) and it is unreasonable to take that risk, D will be reckless (*cf. Chief Constable of Avon* v *Shimmen* (1986) 84 Cr App R 7, DC at 3.4.2 above. See 3.4 generally for a more detailed analysis of *G* and recklessness. You should bear in mind when reading cases between 1981 and 2003 that they would have proceeded on the (now declared incorrect) basis that objective recklessness would suffice).

Section 30 of the Crime and Disorder Act 1998 (as amended) creates a more serious offence where criminal damage committed under s1(1) is 'racially or religiously aggravated'.

12.10.3 **Aggravated criminal damage**

Section 1(2) of the Criminal Damage Act 1971 provides:

> A person who without lawful excuse destroys or damages any property, whether belonging to himself or another—
>
> (a) intending to destroy or damage any property or being reckless as to whether any property would be destroyed or damaged; and
> (b) intending by the destruction or damage to endanger the life of another or being reckless as to whether the life of another would be thereby endangered;
>
> shall be guilty of an offence.

The offence is punishable by up to life imprisonment (s. 4).

? QUESTION 12.25

What are the two main differences between this offence and basic criminal damage under s. 1(1)?

The present offence is essentially s. 1(1) criminal damage plus. The additional ingredient is the extra *mens rea* requirement that D intends or is reckless as to the endangering of life and this is what makes the offence so much more serious. The one ingredient of simple criminal damage which is missing from s. 1(2) is the need for the property to belong to another. The s. 1(2) offence can be committed equally by the destruction or damaging of D's own property because of the risk to life aspect.

? QUESTION 12.26

Does s. 1(2) require proof that someone's life was in fact endangered by D's acts of damage or destruction?

One further difference, which is not apparent from s. 1(2) itself, flows from the risk to life element. By the terms of s. 5(1), the extended meaning given to 'lawful excuse' by s. 5(2) does not apply to a charge under s. 1(2). Thus, although 'without lawful excuse' is still an ingredient of s. 1(2), it is left entirely undefined and must be gleaned from the general law. It would include cases where D uses reasonable force in self-defence or the prevention of a violent crime, e.g., by smashing a beer glass over someone's head. It might also include some duress of circumstances situations (e.g., where D, in escaping from pursuers, crashes his car into another vehicle—see 9.4). However, because of the assumed danger to life, the courts are likely to be tougher in deciding what is reasonable in the circumstances than they would be in the case of basic criminal damage under s. 1(1).

12.10.3.1 *Mens rea*

The major distinction between the two offences lies in the enhanced *mens rea* requirement for s. 1(2). Not only must the *mens rea* for basic criminal damage be proved—intention or recklessness as to damaging the property—but also the further intention or recklessness in respect of endangering life by the damage. It is no part of the *actus reus* that life should actually be endangered by the damage. It is purely a *mens rea* requirement. If D intended it or was reckless as to it, it is irrelevant that, as it turned out, the actual damage did not endanger life (*Sangha* [1988] 2 All ER 385, CA discussed at 3.4.3.2; *Parker* [1993] Crim LR 856, CA). This is fairly obvious because otherwise D might escape liability where he sets fire to a house thinking that it is occupied when it is not.

The offence definition gives intention and recklessness as alternatives both in respect of the *actus reus*—the damaging of property—and the endangerment of life, which is not part of the *actus reus*. It is open to the prosecution to frame the charge using any combination of these states, but prudence would dictate that all of them are charged in the alternative, i.e., D intended or was reckless as to damaging the property and intended or was reckless as to thereby endangering another's life.

> **? QUESTION** 12.27
>
> Why, according to *Caldwell*, is the wording of the charge crucial in the case where D pleads no *mens rea* because of voluntary intoxication? Refer to 8.4.4 if you are unable to answer.

The meaning of intention and recklessness is the same as discussed for s. 1(1), i.e., a minimum of **subjective** recklessness is required since *G* overturned *Caldwell*. The wording of the section does, however, impose a very important limitation on what situations are caught leading to the necessity to make what 'may seem to many a dismal distinction' (Lord Taylor CJ in *Webster; Warwick* [1995] 2 All ER 168, CA).

> **? QUESTION** 12.28
>
> Suppose D, being reckless as to endangering V's life, fires a shot through a bedroom window behind which V and his wife are standing. Is he guilty under s. 1(2)?

These were the facts of *Steer* [1987] 2 All ER 833, HL (*Cases and Materials* (12.10.3.1)) which came to the apparently surprising conclusion that D did not commit aggravated criminal damage under s. 1(2) but only simple criminal damage under s. 1(1). However, their Lordships' conclusion is compelled by the section's insistence that D should intend to endanger life 'by the destruction or damage' or be reckless as to whether the life of another would be 'thereby' (i.e., by the destruction or damage) endangered. Any danger to life would arise not from the damage (breaking the window) but from the firing of the shot.

The damage was merely incidental. D was reckless as to endangering life **by the act** (shooting) which caused the damage, but not as to endangering life **'by the damage'** as is required by the statute.

The matter was reviewed again by the Court of Appeal in two consolidated appeals, *Webster* and *Warwick*, which involved regrettably common fact situations. In *Webster*, D pushed a coping stone weighing about 100 kilos over the parapet of a bridge onto the roof of a passenger train below. Although it penetrated the roof and showered passengers with insulating material, it was fortuitously stopped from falling through by the carriage's rear bulkhead. Fortunately nobody was injured, although passengers were shocked by the incident. The court had to follow *Steer* and hold that D could only be guilty if he was intentional or reckless as to endangering life by damage to the train, e.g., by causing wood or metal pieces from the carriage to fall on the passengers. It would not be sufficient to show that he was intentional or reckless as to endangering life by the stone itself crashing through the carriage and falling on a passenger. This was 'the dismal distinction' to which Lord Taylor CJ referred.

🚶 EXERCISE 12.6

In *Warwick*, D was driving a stolen car which deliberately rammed pursuing police cars and from which large stones were thrown at the cars causing damage (including broken windows) and direct injury. The defence argued, following *Steer*, that it was not by the causing of damage that D intended or was reckless as to endangering life. Showering the police with glass from throwing the stones or damaging the cars by ramming them bumper to bumper were not capable of endangering life. Read the extract from the case in *Cases and Materials* (12.10.3.1) for the court's answer to these arguments.

You should be clear that the damage by which D must intend or be reckless as to endangering life is the damage he intended or was reckless as to causing, not the damage he actually caused. It is irrelevant that he neither intended nor was reckless as to the endangering of life by the **damage actually caused** (*Dudley* [1989] Crim LR 57, CA; *Webster* [1995] 2 All ER 168, CA). In *Dudley*, D, intending to endanger life, threw a petrol bomb into a house causing a small fire which was quickly put out. There was no need to prove that D intended to endanger life (or was reckless thereto) by the actual (trivial) damage caused. What mattered was whether he intended to endanger life (or was reckless thereto) by that (much more extensive) damage which he intended to cause (or was reckless as to causing). Equally, *Dudley* confirms a point we have already made that it is immaterial that no danger to life is in fact caused by D's acts.

If you are wondering why such difficult nuances of meaning are necessitated by what should be a fairly straightforward offence, you need to remind yourself that the core of the offence is criminal damage. Any liability for the aggravated offence is parasitic upon liability for that. The prosecutor has an array of offences against the person to deploy against the accused in many of the situations we have considered, including attempted murder and attempts to commit other offences. It is right that the mere fortuitous occurrence of incidental damage to property should not be a foundation for the serious 'property damage' crime under s. 1(2).

12.10.4 **Arson**

Section 1(3) provides:

> An offence committed under this section by destroying or damaging property by fire shall be charged as arson.

It follows that any offence under s. 1(1) or s. 1(2) where the damage is caused by fire constitutes arson and *must* be charged expressly as arson (*Booth* [1999] Crim LR 144, CA). Arson carries a maximum sentence of life imprisonment even if D commits only basic criminal damage without any intention or recklessness as to the endangering of life (s. 4). Apart from the extra 'by fire' requirement, the ingredients are exactly the same as for the relevant offence under s. 1(1) or (2). Indeed, several of the cases we have already discussed are arson cases. It would appear that the *mens rea* is slightly more precise in that D would have to intend to damage by fire or be reckless thereto.

? QUESTION 12.29

- If D falls asleep whilst smoking in bed and accidentally sets fire to his mattress and upon discovering the smouldering mattress, does nothing and goes out, does he commit arson?
- If D knew there were other occupants in the house, would he also commit an offence under s. 1(2)?

You may recognise the above as the facts of *Miller* [1983] 1 All ER 978, HL and you can find the answer to the first question by referring back to our section on omissions at 2.7.3. The same principle would apply to convict D under s. 1(2) provided, as seems to be the case, that he was reckless as to the endangering of another's life by the fire damage when he did nothing and walked out.

Where attempted arson is charged based on s. 1(2), D must be shown to have intended to damage the property by fire (intention to perform the *actus reus* is a basic requirement for any offence of attempt). However, it is sufficient to prove that he was reckless as to thereby endangering life (*Attorney-General's Reference (No. 3 of 1992)* [1994] 2 All ER 121, CA). This point is considered more fully at 16.3.3.1.

■ **FURTHER READING**

Alldridge: *Attempted Murder of the Soul: Blackmail, Privacy and Secrets* (1993) OJLS 368.
Ashworth: *Robbery Reassessed* [2002] Crim LR 851.
Elliott: *Criminal Damage* [1988] Crim LR 403.
Elliott: *Endangering Life by Destroying or Damaging Property* [1997] Crim LR 382.
Griew: *The Theft Acts 1968 and 1978* (7th ed., 1995, Sweet & Maxwell).
Hogan: *Blackmail* [1966] Crim LR 474.
MacKenna: *Blackmail* [1966] Crim LR 467.
Pace: *Burglarious Trespass* [1985] Crim LR 716.

Smith ATH: *Property Offences* (1994, Sweet & Maxwell).

Smith ATH: *Theft and/or Handling* [1977] Crim LR 517.

Smith JC: *Burglary under the Theft Bill* [1968] Crim LR 367.

Smith JC: *The Law of Theft* (8th ed., 1997, Butterworths).

Spencer: *The Aggravated Vehicle-Taking Act 1992* [1992] Crim LR 69.

Spencer: *The Mishandling of Handling* [1981] Crim LR 682.

■ SUMMARY

Robbery

Robbery is theft plus (s. 8). No theft, no robbery. In addition to committing theft, D must (i) use or threaten immediate force on a person (ii) immediately before or at the time of the theft **and** (iii) in order to steal. Force against property not enough but left to jury to decide whether there is (i) force and (ii) used/ threatened against a person (*Dawson*; *Clouden*). Actual fear of force not needed if D seeks to cause it. Force used only after completion of the theft or well before it not enough—but theft may be a **continuing** offence (*Hale*). Force used for a purpose other than effecting or completing the theft insufficient (*Shendley*).

Offences **of temporary deprivation**

- Primary offence (s. 12)—D must (i) take for his own or another's use (ii) a conveyance (iii) without the owner's consent or other lawful authority.

- *Taking*—means possessing/controlling and moving the vehicle but D must intend it to be used **as a conveyance** either then or in the future (*Stokes*; *Bow*). A **serious** deviation from a permitted purpose can be a 'taking' *(Phipps and McGill; Wibberley)*. *Conveyance*—includes cars, boats, aircraft but not bicycles (special offence) or horses. *Consent* obtained by D's deception has generally been treated as consent (*Whittaker* v *Campbell*; *Peart*), although consider *Phipps and McGill*.

- *Mens rea*—D not guilty if he believes he has lawful authority or that the owner, with full knowledge of the circumstances, would have consented (s. 12(6)).

- Secondary offence—D drives or allows himself to be carried on or in a conveyance already taken contrary to s. 12 at any time when he knows this to be the case.

- Aggravated vehicle taking (s. 12A)—see text.

Burglary

- Burglary has two main forms (s. 9). Both involve D (i) entering (ii) as a trespasser (iii) a building or part of a building. *Enters*—'effective' entry required but does not require whole body (*Brown*). Probably any part of the body suffices despite *Collins (Ryan)*, but perhaps not by an instrument held by D. Uncertain. *As a trespasser*—D must be a trespasser at the moment of **entry** into the building or relevant part. Express or implied consent of the owner or anyone authorised by him to grant consent negatives trespass (*Collins*). D may exceed such permission and become a trespasser by entering an 'out of bounds' part of the building (*Walkington*) or by entering the permitted part(s) with an unauthorised secret purpose, e.g., to steal (*Smith and Jones*); *a fortiori*, if D gets the permission by fraud. D must either know the facts rendering him a trespasser or be reckless (probably subjectively reckless) as to those facts (*Collins*; *Smith and Jones*). *Building*—includes any fixed structure with a degree of permanence—dwellings, shops, factories, sheds, greenhouses, etc. It also includes **inhabited** vehicles or vessels (s. 9(4)). **Part** of a building includes rooms, etc. with obvious divisions but also any spaces with less obvious physical divisions which are out of bounds, e.g., space behind a counter (*Walkington*). Note problems caused by blocks of flats, shops or offices.

- Those requirements are common to both forms of burglary. Section 9(1)(a) requires in addition, **at the moment of entry of the building or relevant part as a trespasser**, an intent to steal, inflict GBH or do unlawful damage in the building **or relevant part**. It is irrelevant whether D does anything to carry out his intention once he has entered as a trespasser.

- Section 9(1)(b) requires **the actual commission** of a **specified** offence in the building or the part entered as a trespasser. The specified offences are theft, attempted theft, inflicting GBH or attempting to inflict GBH.

- Burglary of a **dwelling** carries a heavier sentence. Probably D must know the building is a dwelling or realise it might be (s. 9(3)).

- Aggravated burglary (s. 10). Burglary plus. D **must** commit burglary and (i) have with him (ii) any firearm, imitation firearm, weapon of offence or explosive (iii) at the time of committing a burglary. Section 10(2) defines the 'aggravating articles'—'weapons of offence' means any article made or adapted for causing injury or incapacitating or, if not, **intended** for such purpose by D. It is uncertain if D must know he has the article with him (e.g., if he has forgotten he has it) (*Russell* says yes; *McCalla* and *Wright* say no). D must have it with him at the moment he commits the burglary. In s. 9(1)(b) burglary, it is when he commits the offence in the building. However, theft and therefore s. 9(1)(b) burglary may be a continuing offence (*Gregory*; *Hale*) and D may commit the offence by arming himself on the spur of the moment in the course of the burglary (*O'Leary*; *Kelly*). No premeditated intention to use as a weapon of offence is needed (*Kelly*).

Blackmail

D must (i) make a demand (ii) with menaces. The demand must be (iii) unwarranted and (iv) with a view to gain for himself or another or with intent to cause loss to another (s. 21). *Demand*—can be express or implied by conduct (*Collister and Warhurst*). There is no formal restriction on what D demands of V (s. 21(2)). A demand need not be heard or read by the addressee. It is made when spoken or, if in writing, when issued, e.g., posting of letter, transmitting telex or fax (*Treacy v DPP*), although it may **continue to be made** until received by the victim. Jurisdictional problems involving foreign countries have been overcome by the Criminal Justice Act 1993. *Menaces*—wide meaning including anything 'detrimental to or unpleasant to' V and not limited to threats of violence (*Thorne v Motor Trade Association*). However, threats must be serious enough to influence an ordinary person (*Clear*) unless D aware that V is unusually timorous (*Garwood*). *Unwarranted*—draws the distinction between justifiable and unjustifiable demands. The test is subjective—if **D believes** (i) he has reasonable grounds for making the demand; and (ii) the use of menaces is a proper means of reinforcing the demand. The beliefs relate not to facts but to correct standards of behaviour and the courts have used the word 'proper' to import an element of objectivity—D must believe that **people generally** would think his menaces a 'proper' means of reinforcing his demand (*Harvey*). This could not include an act known to be unlawful (*Harvey*). *With a view to gain, etc.*—'gain/loss' mean in 'money or other property' **only** (s. 34(2)(a)). Blackmail protects both directly and indirectly only V's economic interests in money or property. 'Gain' includes keeping what you have and 'loss' includes not getting what you might. 'Gain' includes 'obtaining' even if it is only what you are owed (*Parkes; Lawrence and Pomroy*).

Handling stolen goods

D must (i) handle (ii) stolen goods (iii) otherwise than in the course of the stealing (iv) dishonestly and (v) knowing or believing them to be stolen. *Stolen goods*—no stolen goods, no handling—at most attempting to handle stolen goods. Goods stolen if obtained by theft, by fraud contrary to the Fraud Act 2006 or by blackmail (s. 24(4)). Stolen goods cease to be stolen if (i) they are restored to the owner or other lawful possession or custody such as the police (s. 24(3) and see *Attorney-General's Reference (No. 1 of 1974)* or (ii) the owner has in civil law lost his right to restitution (s. 24(3)). 'Goods' includes money and all property (tangible or intangible) except land (s. 34(2)(b)). Anything representing the original stolen goods as the direct or indirect proceeds passing through the hands of the thief or a handler are also 'stolen goods' and can be handled (s. 24(2)). This includes credits in bank accounts which the thief or original handler can control (*Forsyth*) but probably not others. But D would in most cases be caught by the Theft (Amendment) Act 1996 (dishonestly retaining a wrongful credit) which provides that withdrawals of wrongful credits are themselves 'stolen' proceeds which can be handled. *Handles*—four basic forms: (i) receiving (ii) undertaking the retention, removal, disposal or realisation for the benefit of another (iii) assisting in the retention, removal, disposal or realisation by another or (iv) arranging to do (i), (ii) or (iii) (*Bloxham*). Receiving necessitates that D gets possession but this need only be temporary (*Wiley; Richardson*). If D himself does the retention, he undertakes; if he helps another to do it, he assists. Unlike receiving, undertaking/assisting forms (and arranging to undertake/assist) must be done 'by or for the benefit of another'. 'For the benefit' has been interpreted to mean that D must be undertaking the retention, etc. 'on behalf of' another as opposed to for himself. It is irrelevant that another incidentally benefits (*Bloxham*). In order to assist in, for example, the retention by another, D must do something 'for the purpose of enabling the goods to be retained' (*Kanwar*). 'Realisation' means 'exchanging goods for money or other property' (*Bloxham*). *Otherwise than in the course of the stealing*—applies to all forms of handling and is designed to prevent the original thieves from also automatically becoming handlers. Of course, if they part with possession of the goods they have stolen and then receive them back, they would 'handle' them 'otherwise than in the course of the' original stealing. Note evidential problems—is D the thief or just a handler (*Cash; Ryan v DPP*)? *Dishonestly*—same meaning as *Ghosh* in theft (*Roberts*). *Knowing or believing the goods to be stolen*—the test is entirely subjective (*Brook*). 'Know' means actual knowledge that the goods **are** stolen. 'Believe' means 'the mental acceptance of a fact as true or existing' (*Forsyth*). Mere suspicion, even strong suspicion (or wilful blindness) that the goods are stolen is not enough (*Griffiths; Belleni*). D must believe that the goods **are** stolen not that they might be stolen or even that they are **probably** stolen (*Reader*). If D knows/believes that the goods are stolen, he does not need to know what they are (*McCullum*).

Criminal damage

- *Simple criminal damage* (s. 1(1)). *Actus reus*—D (i) destroys or damages (ii) property (iii) belonging to another (iv) without lawful excuse. *Mens rea*—(i) intent to destroy or damage property belonging to another or (ii) recklessness as to that. *'Damage'* includes physical harm or impairment of usefulness or impairment of value or rendering imperfect (especially where expense required to restore). Need not be perceptible, e.g., corruption of magnetic data. Temporary damage suffices. *Property*—similar to theft but includes land, excludes intangible property. *Belonging to another*—includes 'proprietary right or interest' and 'custody or control'— similar to theft. *Without lawful excuse*—covers self-defence, prevention of crime, etc. under general law—s. 5 adds (i) D's **honest** belief that the owner has consented or, knowing of the circumstances, would have consented (ii) D damages in order to protect other property **honestly** believing that it is in **immediate** need of protection and the damage is a reasonable way of protecting it. *Mens rea*—applies to all elements of *actus reus* including 'belonging to another' (*Smith*). Either intention to damage property belonging to another or recklessness thereto suffices. *G* holds that recklessness now means only subjective recklessness. Objective recklessness no longer suffices and *Caldwell* should not be followed.

- *Aggravated criminal damage* (s. 1(2)). Essentially simple criminal damage plus. Needs all the ingredients of simple criminal damage except (i) property damaged need not belong to another and (ii) the s. 5 extension to 'lawful excuse' does not apply. The additional 'aggravating' ingredient is either intent to endanger life by the damage or recklessness thereto. No need to prove life was **in fact** endangered or that the actual damage was capable of endangering life (*Webster*). D must intend or be reckless as to the endangering of life **by the damage he intends or is reckless about** (*Steer*; *Dudley*).

- Arson is where either of the other offences is committed by fire damage.

 CHAPTER 12: ASSESSMENT EXERCISE

12.1 Cain, who is short of money, decides on a plan to take his father's video recorder and sell it. Having supposedly gone to the cinema one evening, Cain secretly returns home knowing that his parents would by then have gone out to play bingo.

He enters the house, takes the video recorder and drives with it to a public house where he persuades the barmaid, Phoebe, to buy it for £50.

Subsequently Phoebe overhears a policeman, investigating the recorder's disappearance, questioning the landlord of the public house about whether anyone had been trying to sell a recorder in his pub.

Phoebe, then suspecting for the first time that the recorder she had bought might be the one to which the policeman was referring, sells it for £50 to Aesop.

Discuss the criminal liability, if any, of Cain and Phoebe.

See the **Appendix** (12.1) for a specimen answer.

13 Strict liability

13.1 Objectives

By the end of this chapter you should be able to:

1 Explain the nature of strict liability

2 Identify those factors likely to influence the courts in deciding whether to impose strict liability

3 State the basic policy arguments for and against the imposition of strict liability

13.2 Introduction

An offence of strict liability means an offence which requires no blameworthiness on the part of D (i.e., no *mens rea* or even negligence) in respect of at least one element of the *actus reus*. Strict liability offences are not necessarily devoid of any *mens rea* or negligence requirement. However, none is needed in respect of at least **one** element of the *actus reus*.

Strict liability offences are not uncommon and must be contrasted with offences of **absolute** liability, which are almost as rare as the dodo and which many writers believe should follow that unfortunate bird into extinction. An absolute offence is an offence which, not only does not require proof of any *mens rea* or negligence, but does not admit of any defence. It does not even require proof that D's conduct was voluntary in the narrow, legal sense that D's conscious mind was controlling his muscular movements. The established **absolute** offences are offences where the *actus reus* involves proof of a 'state of affairs'. Before considering the two most famous examples, we ought to warn you that, confusingly, the courts regularly use the term 'absolute offence' to mean simply 'strict liability offence'. The narrow usage of 'absolute' which we have adopted tends to be used by academics rather than judges!

The most celebrated case is *Larsonneur* (1933) 24 Cr App R 74 where D, a French national, was prohibited by the Home Secretary from remaining in the UK. In compliance with the banning order, she sailed to Eire. She was immediately taken into custody by the Irish police. The Irish Government ordered her deportation and she was escorted by Irish police back to Holyhead where she was handed over to the British police. She was convicted of the offence of 'being found' in the UK whilst a prohibited person. The Court of Criminal

Appeal refused to imply any requirement of culpability or voluntariness and presumably would have arrived at the same decision even if D had been kidnapped in Eire and brought to the UK by her kidnappers!

A similar decision was reached by the Divisional Court in *Winzar* v *Chief Constable of Kent* (1983) *The Times*, 28 March. D had been brought into hospital on a stretcher, although it is not clear from where. The medical staff concluded that he was merely drunk and he was told to leave. Subsequently, he was found slumped on a seat in the hospital corridor and the police were called. They took him from the hospital onto the public highway and then to the police station. He was charged with being found drunk on the highway contrary to s. 12 of the Licensing Act 1872. The Divisional Court convicted him regarding it as irrelevant how D came to be on the public highway. Even if D had originally been drunk in his own home, from where he had been transported to hospital, he would still have been guilty once he was carried to the public highway. No culpability or voluntariness needed to be proved, apparently. Extraordinary state of affairs!

In contrast, strict liability offences, like all other offences, always need this element of voluntariness and may be negated by pleading any of the general defences discussed in **Chapters 7 to 9**. (It is best to regard the statement in *DPP* v *H* that insanity is never a defence to strict liability crimes as wrong—see 7.4.2.5.) However, strict liability crimes will not require any **other** culpability in respect of one or more components of the *actus reus*. You may recall the case of *Prince* [1874–80] All ER Rep 881 (now highly suspect in the light of *B* v *DPP*—see 13.4.1 below) where D was convicted of taking an unmarried girl under 16 out of the possession of her parent or guardian against his will under what became s. 20 of the Sexual Offences Act 1956. D believed on reasonable grounds that the girl was 18. It was held that no *mens rea* or negligence needed to be proved in respect of the element of the *actus reus* requiring the girl to be under 16. Therefore, even though D did not suspect and had no reason to suspect that the girl was under 16, he was guilty. On the other hand, this is not true of other elements of that particular offence. In *Hibbert* (1869) LR 1 CCR 184, D met a girl of 14 in the street and took her away. The court decided that *mens rea* was needed in respect of the part of the *actus reus* requiring the girl to be in the custody of her parents or guardian. Since the prosecution was unable to prove that D knew or suspected the girl to be in the custody of her parents, he was found not guilty. This illustrates the point that most strict liability offences are not completely devoid of *mens rea*— they do not need it in respect of one or more parts of the *actus reus*. (It should be noted that the Sexual Offences Act 2003 has repealed but only partially replaced the s. 20 offence. The new offences only deal with abduction where there is a sexual motive. However, non-sexual abductions would generally be caught by s. 2 of the Child Abduction Act 1984.)

One final example will suffice at this stage. In *Callow* v *Tillstone* (1900) 83 LT 411, D was convicted of the offence of exposing unsound meat for sale. D was a butcher who had asked a vet to examine a carcass to check that it was fit for human consumption. The vet negligently certified that it was so fit and D offered it for sale. In fact, unknown to D, it was unfit for human consumption. Despite being totally blameless and having done all he reasonably could to satisfy himself that the meat was sound, D was convicted of the offence because it was one of strict liability in respect of that part of the *actus reus* requiring the meat to be 'unsound'. We shall be considering this case again in respect of the vet's liability in **Chapter 13**.

13.3 **The development of strict liability**

The idea of strict liability took hold in the nineteenth century with the development of social legislation regulating certain activities affecting the public's health, safety or welfare, such as food and drugs, liquor and health and safety in factories and other places of work. It is largely confined to statutory offences and is possible where the statutory definition of an offence fails to include any express *mens rea* or negligence requirement. Assuming there are no previous case law interpretations on that particular offence, this leaves the court to decide whether to imply a *mens rea* or negligence requirement or whether to hold the offence to be one of strict liability. The main purpose of this chapter is to examine the factors which influence the courts in deciding strict liability or not.

Strict liability is almost exclusively confined to statutory offences. The common law offences of public nuisance and criminal libel are often said to be crimes of strict liability but the matter has yet to be definitively established. However, the House of Lords in *Lemon* [1979] 1 All ER 898 (*Cases and Materials* (13.3)) appears to make the common law offence of blasphemous libel a strict liability crime. The dissenting minority in the House of Lords certainly thought so although, strangely, the majority denied it. It is difficult to place much credence on this denial when the majority held that D, the editor of *Gay News*, who published a poem involving a person who fantasised about Jesus being sodomised after His death on the cross, only needed to intend to publish the material which was in fact blasphemous. He did not need to know it was blasphemous or foresee that it might be. Blasphemy involves the use of indecent or offensive language likely to shock or outrage the general community of Christian believers. The law on blasphemy protects only the Christian religion in this country, a fact confirmed in the attempted private prosecution over comments on the Muslim religion in Salman Rushdie's *Satanic Verses* (*Chief Metropolitan Stipendiary Magistrate, ex parte Choudhury* [1991] 1 All ER 306, DC). Similarly, the common law offence of outraging public decency has been held not to require any intention or recklessness by D that his act might outrage public decency (see *Gibson* [1991] 1 All ER 439, CA where earrings made out of freeze-dried human foetuses were exhibited in a commercial art gallery).

The whole concept of strict liability has been attacked on the basis that it contravenes the presumption of innocence required by Art. 6(2) of the European Convention on Human Rights because once it is proved that D physically performed the prohibited conduct, his guilt is presumed. Thus, in *Barnfather* v *Islington London Borough Council* [2003] 1 WLR 2318, DC, because D's child failed to attend school regularly, D was guilty of a strict liability offence under s. 444 of the Education Act 1996. Even if D had done everything they reasonably could to ensure the child's attendance or was ignorant of the child's failure to attend, she would be guilty. No proof of fault was required. It was held that the Article is designed to ensure a fair trial **procedure** and does not extend to requiring a fair **substantive** law. As the European Court of Human Rights put it in *Salabiaku* v *France* (1988) 13 EHRR 379, 'In principle the Contracting States may, under certain conditions, penalise a simple or objective fact as such, irrespective of whether it results from criminal intent or negligence.' Thus it does not impose any minimum requirements of fairness as to what the ingredients of an offence should be but rather limits the creation of offences where D is required to disprove one or more elements. Essentially Art. 6 is to secure 'fair trials' not 'fair laws'.

13.4 How do the courts decide on strict liability?

It must be said at the outset that the courts have not been consistent in their decisions and this makes predicting what they will decide in respect of an offence which has not been the subject of a court decision a hazardous exercise. There are few hard-and-fast principles and the most we can do is elucidate certain guidelines which will influence, although not necessarily determine, the court's decision. Indeed, some of these 'guidelines' are diametrically opposed to each other!

It must always be borne in mind that, since we are almost exclusively concerned with statutory offences, the exercise is one of statutory interpretation. Theoretically, the court is simply endeavouring to ascertain the will of Parliament as expressed in the wording of the offence. If that wording **expresses** the *mens rea* for the offence clearly, e.g., by using words like 'intentionally', 'recklessly' or 'negligently', there is no problem. Many offences do this. Equally, if the wording expressly provides that the offence is to be strict liability in one or more respects, there is again no problem. It is rare for Parliament to do so (for an example, see s. 1 of the Contempt of Court Act 1981).

The problem comes when, as happens surprisingly often, Parliament does not provide expressly one way or the other. At first sight, one might expect that if Parliament has made no reference to *mens rea,* this must mean that it intended the offence to be strict liability. However, this is emphatically not the case and the courts often imply *mens rea* even though none has been expressed in the statutory wording.

13.4.1 Presumption of *mens rea*

In *Sweet* v *Parsley* [1969] 1 All ER 347 (*Cases and Materials* (13.4.1)), a case famous in its day, the House of Lords reiterated that, where the statute is silent as to *mens rea*:

> there has for centuries been a presumption that Parliament did not intend to make criminals of persons who were in no way blameworthy in what they did. That means that whenever a section is silent as to *mens rea* there is a presumption that, in order to give effect to the will of Parliament, we must read in words appropriate to require *mens rea*.

Having been convicted of being concerned in the management of premises used for the purpose of smoking a prohibited drug, cannabis, contrary to now replaced drugs legislation, Sweet had to take her case to the House of Lords before securing an acquittal. She had let rooms in a farmhouse to students, who, unknown to her, used it for smoking cannabis. She did not reside at the premises and only visited them occasionally. The House of Lords implied a requirement of *mens rea* into the statutory offence, which expressed no such requirement, so that a person could only be guilty if they knew that the premises were being used for the prohibited purpose. Now, s. 8 of the Misuse of Drugs Act 1971 expressly adopts the knowledge requirement.

The strength of the presumption was stressed by the House of Lords in the most important (and perhaps surprising in view of the subject matter) decision of *B* v *DPP* [2000] 2 WLR 452. D, a 15-year-old youth, had persistently asked a 13-year-old girl sitting next to him on a bus for a 'shiner' which 'in the language of today's gilded youth apparently means, not a black eye, but an act of oral sex'. He was charged with inciting a child under 14 to commit an act of gross indecency contrary to s. 1(1) of the Indecency with Children Act 1960 (now replaced by s. 10 of the Sexual Offences Act 2003). It was accepted that he honestly believed she was over 14. Overruling the Divisional Court decision ([1999] 1 Cr App R 163) that the offence was one of strict liability in respect of the age factor, the House held that *mens rea* (knowledge or recklessness) was required so that a genuine belief by D, whether based on reasonable grounds or not, that the victim was 14 or over would negate such *mens rea* and thus liability. 'Unless Parliament has indicated a contrary intention either expressly or by necessary implication . . . the appropriate mental element is an unexpressed ingredient of every statutory offence' (Lord Nicholls). Even though it might be a **reasonable** implication that strict liability was intended by Parliament, that is insufficient to displace the presumption of *mens rea* (Lord Hutton). It had to be a **necessary** implication which 'connotes an implication which is compellingly clear. Such an implication may be found in the language used, the nature of the offence, the mischief sought to be prevented . . . ' (Lord Nicholls). In this case, even the fact that the offence was for the protection of vulnerable children, was not enough. Although the House did not formally overrule *Prince* and other sexual offence decisions applying strict liability to the age factor, they must now be regarded as suspect and liable to be overturned. *B v DPP* was applied by the House in *K* [2001] UKHL 41 to hold that the offence of indecent assault was not strict liability in regard to the age factor in consent. *Prince* was described as 'now discredited'. Similarly, the Court of Appeal in *Kumar* [2004] EWCA Crim 3207; [2005] Crim LR 470 implied a *mens rea* requirement in respect of age in the now repealed offence of buggery contrary to s. 12 of the Sexual Offences Act 1956, even though its provisions had been amended by Parliament as recently as 2000. The offence consisted of having anal intercourse with a person under 16 and it was held that D's honest belief that V was 16 or over would negate liability.

Although the Sexual Offences Act 2003 has replaced the current ragbag of sexual offences, including those in issue in *B v DPP* and *K*, with a comprehensive new code (often prescribing different fault requirements to the current, corresponding offences), it is important to realise that the general principles so strongly endorsed by these two leading authorities are not specific to sexual offences and will endure as the starting point for all strict liability enquiries.

The Privy Council in *Gammon (Hong Kong) Ltd v Attorney-General of Hong Kong* [1984] 2 All ER 503 (*Cases and Materials* (13.4.1)) strongly reiterated the importance of the presumption, stamping on a suggestion by the Court of Appeal in *Champ* [1982] Crim LR 108 that the presumption may not always apply in the case of regulatory offences.

The Privy Council in *Gammon* gave its view of the presumption and when it may be rebutted in the following propositions:

(a) there is a presumption of law that *mens rea* is required before a person can be held guilty of a criminal offence;

(b) the presumption is particularly strong where the offence is 'truly criminal' in character;

(c) the presumption applies to statutory offences, and can be displaced only if this is clearly or by necessary implication the effect of the statute;

(d) the only situation in which the presumption can be displaced is where the statute is concerned with an issue of social concern; public safety is such an issue;

(e) even where a statute is concerned with such an issue, the presumption of *mens rea* stands unless it can also be shown that the creation of strict liability will be effective to promote the object of the statute by encouraging greater vigilance to prevent the commission of the prohibited act.

A good example of the application of these guidelines is found in *Harrow London Borough Council* v *Shah* [1999] 3 All ER 302, DC, where the offence of selling a National Lottery ticket to a person under 16 was held to be strict liability in respect of the age factor.

13.4.2 The social context: truly criminal or merely regulatory?

The quotation from *Sweet* v *Parsley* gives the impression that the courts are extremely reluctant to impose strict liability. In practice, this is not so. Even after *Sweet* v *Parsley*, the House of Lords itself, in a number of cases, found offences to be strict liability. You may be forgiven for thinking that, after the stress on the presumption of *mens rea* in both *B* v *DPP* and *K*, the chances of the courts finding strict liability in the future would be extremely small. However, this has already proved to be far from the case and the Court of Appeal has happily found strict liability in two subsequent cases—*Muhamad* [2003] 2 WLR 1050 and *Matudi* [2003] EWCA Crim 697. The key to understanding this apparent contradiction is to realise that where the court regards the offence as **regulatory** (sometimes also referred to as quasi-criminal), the presumption of *mens rea* is much weaker and, indeed, one suspects that the courts are merely paying lip-service to it. It follows that the starting-point for assessing whether an offence is strict liability or not is to classify the offence as either **truly criminal** on the one hand, or **regulatory** on the other. It should be said that this is hardly a scientific classification and the distinction could be criticised as perpetu-ating the view that what is sometimes called 'white-collar' crime is somehow less heinous than 'ordinary' crime.

The courts' surprising view is that there are crimes and crimes. **Regulatory** offences 'are not criminal in any real sense, but are acts which in the public interest are prohibited under a penalty' (*Sherras* v *De Rutzen* [1895] 1 QB 918 (*Cases and Materials* (13.4.2)), approved by the House of Lords in *Alphacell Ltd* v *Woodward* [1972] 2 All ER 475).

?   **QUESTION** 13.1

Can you suggest some examples of the sort of offences which might be termed 'regulatory'?

Such offences tend to be those regulating a particular activity, often carried on by busi-nesses for profit, which involve potential dangers to the public health, safety or welfare and in which citizens or companies have a choice whether or not they participate. Examples include legislation policing the manufacture and sale of food, health and safety at work and air and river pollution. In adopting strict liability, the courts are telling businesses that if they choose to engage in a particular activity, they must ensure **at all costs** that they carry it on in the manner prescribed by the legislation. (As we shall see later, regulatory statutes often include a generalised no-negligence defence to all the strict liability offences created by the statute.) For example, the offence in *Matudi* was importing animal products without giving the requisite notice to customs. D had ordered a consignment of frozen cassava leaves (i.e., wholly vegetable products) from his supplier in the Cameroons. Unknown to him, she had included a few frozen monkey and pangolin carcasses. It was held to be strict liability, the offence being seen as a regulatory offence concerned with an important issue of food safety to prevent the import of infected meat. Although most regulatory statutes are aimed at the control of businesses, it is not invariably so. Motoring is a closely regulated activity, whose participants are drawn from a wide section of the general public. Many of the offences are strict liability, including both technical requirements governing brakes, lights and construction of vehicles, etc., and offences concerned with the manner of driving, such as failing to conform to a traffic signal and speeding. Although this is a very general activity and not necessarily commercial, it still has the characteristic of being an activity which a person can choose whether to engage in and involves significant dangers to the public.

Truly criminal offences are the sorts of offences which everyone would think of when 'crime' is mentioned and which are generally recognised as morally reprehensible. Examples are offences of violence and property offences involving dishonesty, like theft. As we have noted above, the dividing line is very unclear, particularly as views of what is morally reprehensible can undergo radical changes over time. Consider, for example, the recent change in attitudes to certain motoring offences, such as drink-driving.

Rather suspectly, the Court of Appeal in *Blake* [1997] 1 All ER 963 ignored the suggested distinction in holding that an offence of using apparatus for wireless telegraphy (i.e., broadcasting) without a licence contrary to s. 1(1) of the Wireless Telegraphy Act 1949 was a 'truly criminal' offence. The reason was that 'throughout its history...an offender has been potentially subject to a term of imprisonment' (currently two years but only three months until 1990). If liability to imprisonment is to be the criterion, the distinction will cease to be of any significance since most offences regulating business activity carry a possibility of imprisonment. The offence in question was surely a typical regulatory offence to control use of the airwaves for broadcasting (*cf. Harrow LBC v Shah* [1999] 3 All ER 302, DC where selling a lottery ticket to an under 16 was classed a regulatory offence even though the penalty was up to two years' imprisonment). Ironically, after classifying it as 'truly criminal' and finding the presumption of *men rea* 'particularly strong', the court went on to hold it to be strict liability on the ground that it was prompted by a serious 'social concern in the interests of public safety' because of the possible interference with emergency services and air traffic communications caused by pirate broadcasting. Thus, although D needed to know that he was using apparatus, he did not need to know that 'wireless telegraphy' (i.e., broadcasting) was or might be actually occurring (D, a disc jockey, claimed to believe he was making a demonstration tape).

If the offence is truly criminal, the courts are likely to rule out strict liability, a point strongly underlined by the recent unanimous House of Lords' decision in *B v DPP*. Prior to that, in the area of sexual offences dependent on establishing that the victim was under a particular age, there was a tendency to uphold strict liability in respect of the age factor (see *Prince* (at 13.2 above); *Maughan* (1934) 24 CR App R 130, CCA (indecent assault); the Divisional Court in *B v DPP* [1998] 4 All ER 265; *Land* [1998] 1 All ER 403, CA (possessing indecent photographs of children under 16 contrary to s. 1 of the Protection of Children

Act 1978)). All of these must now be regarded as suspect since *B* v *DPP* and henceforth it will be wholly exceptional to impose strict liability in the case of truly criminal offences. *K* [2001] UKHL 41 specifically overruled *Maughan* and interpreted s. 14 of the Sexual Offences Act 1956 as requiring *mens rea* in respect of age for the crime of indecent assault. As we explain in the next section, the Court found that it was not a 'necessary implication' of the statutory wording and its context that Parliament intended strict liability. Similarly doubt has been cast on *Land* by *Smith*; *Grayson* [2002] Crim LR 659, CA. It is an offence under s. 1(1)(a) of the Protection of Children Act 1978 'to make an indecent photograph or pseudo-photograph of a child' (essentially a person under 16 (raised to 18 by s. 45 of the Sexual Offences Act 2003)). That was held to require a deliberate and intentional act (e.g., downloading images from the internet) with knowledge that the image was, or was likely to be, an indecent photograph or pseudo-photograph of a child. That seems to embrace knowledge of (or of the likelihood of) both indecency **and** the fact that the image is of a child, i.e., is under 16. *Land* held that once D appreciated the image was indecent, it was no defence that he failed to appreciate it was of a child. That looked unlikely to survive after *B* v *DPP* and the implicit effect of *Smith*; *Grayson* is to cast doubt on it. However, an express ruling would have been welcome.

One offence where there was a 'necessary implication' that strict liability was intended was s. 6 of the Sexual Offences Act 1956—having 'unlawful sexual intercourse with a girl under sixteen'. (Now replaced by s. 9 of the Sexual Offences Act 2003.) The recent case of *Kirk*; *Russell* [2002] Crim LR 756, CA confirmed that no *mens rea* was needed in respect of the age of the girl. This was recognised in both *K* and *B* v *DPP*. This interpretation was the inevitable result of the inclusion of the so-called 'young man's defence' by s. 6(3). This provided a defence for a man under 24, not previously convicted of such an offence, who believed on reasonable grounds that the girl was 16 or over. Obviously, this qualified defence would be totally unnecessary if the basic offence required proof of *mens rea* in respect of age in the first place.

The Sexual Offences Act 2003 indicates that Parliament has taken in the lesson of *B* v *DPP* and *K* that it is necessary to pay much closer attention to defining the fault requirements for the offences it creates. Most of the offences created spell out in detail fault requirements leading to a 'necessary implication' that where these are not delineated, the omission is deliberate and strict liability is intended. Thus a number of special offences relate to sexual activity with a child under 13 (e.g., ss. 5, 6, 7 and 8) whilst others concern sexual activity with a child under 16 (e.g., ss. 9 and 10). The latter specifically provide that, in order to be guilty, D must not 'reasonably believe' that the victim is 16 or over. In other words, the requirement in *K* to prove an absence of belief would be modified to proof by the pro-secution of an absence of **reasonable** belief that the victim was 16 or over. When it comes to the under 13 offences (ss. 5–8), no such requirement is expressed and the necessary implication is that no fault element was intended in relation to the victim being under 13. This is reinforced by the configuration of ss. 9 and 10 which apply to all children under 16 including under 13s. These sections provide that D would incur liability if **either** the victim is under 16 and D does not 'reasonably believe' him to be 16 or over **or** the victim 'is under 13'. Even though the intention to impose strict liability seems 'compellingly clear', it might have been prudent to expressly state that no fault was required!

On the other hand, if the offence is classed as quasi-criminal (regulatory), there is a greatly enhanced possibility that the courts will classify it as strict liability and we doubt that *B* v *DPP* will make the courts significantly more reluctant to impose it (*Muhamad*; *Matudi*). It simply makes the classification of the offence even more critical. For example, in *Doring* [2002] Crim LR 817, CA, the Court endorsed, obiter, the view in the pre-*B* v *DPP* case of *Brockley* (1994) 99 Cr App R 385, CA that the offence of taking part in the management of a company whilst an undischarged bankrupt contrary to s. 11(1) of the Company Directors Disqualification Act 1986 required no fault element in respect of being an undischarged bankrupt. Furthermore they thought that a similar offence under s. 216 of the Insolvency Act 1986 was strict liability. It is difficult to see anything in the wording of the relevant statutes which could give rise to this being a 'necessary implication' as required by *B* v *DPP* and *K*!

The criminal/regulatory distinction was thought by the Court of Appeal in *Muhamad* [2003] 2 WLR 1050 to have been replaced by a 'seriousness' test: 'the more serious the offence, the greater weight to be attached to the presumption'. However, given that regulatory offences tend by and large to be 'less serious' offences compared with 'truly criminal' offences, the different approach may not matter unduly in practice. The case concerned s. 362(1) of the Insolvency Act 1986 under which a bankrupt is guilty of an offence if he 'materially contributed to ... his insolvency by gambling ...' within the two years before the bankruptcy petition. The issue was whether the court should imply that D needed to know that his gambling might materially contribute to his (future!) bankruptcy. It was held not. Although the offence was 'significant' (carrying a maximum of two years' imprisonment!), it was 'not one of the utmost seriousness'. Although 'some weight must undoubtedly be given to the presumption, ... it can be readily displaced.' It was not 'a particularly serious offence' and no 'great stigma' was attached to it. Having looked at the various factors explained in the next section, the court concluded that the presumption was displaced and that the offence was one of strict liability. This decision bears out the sceptic's view that the apparently strong statements in *B* v *DPP* and *K* will not in practice prevent the courts from continuing to impose strict liability in the sphere of regulatory offences. The Court also rejected the idea that the imposition of strict liability contravened Art. 7 of the European Convention on Human Rights (as also did *Kearns* [2003] 1 Cr App R 7, CA).

Let us now consider what other factors come into play in determining strict liability.

13.4.3 The statutory context

In the final analysis, the courts are engaged in an exercise of statutory interpretation. It is their job to give effect to the intention of Parliament as expressed in the words used to define the offence. Inevitably, therefore, any decision of the courts must involve a close analysis of the statutory wording, and also the particular and general contexts in which it appears.

13.4.3.1 Section/subsection wording

In *Alphacell Ltd* v *Woodward* (*Cases and Materials* (13.4.3.1)), the company was convicted of causing polluting matter to enter a stream. Polluted water from its factory processes had overflowed into the stream, probably due to a blocked filter. The House of Lords held that this was a strict liability crime and it was unnecessary to prove that the company was in any way at fault over the occurrence. One factor supporting the decision was that the section made it an offence to 'cause or knowingly permit' the pollutants to enter the stream. The

House felt that had Parliament intended *mens rea* to be required for the 'cause' alternative, the word 'knowingly' would have been placed before 'cause'. In its actual position, it was intended only to govern the 'permit' alternative.

? QUESTION 13.2

Suppose the statute had omitted the word 'knowingly' before 'permit', do you think it would have made any difference? Could someone be guilty of 'permitting' the pollution *without* knowing it was happening?

13.4.3.2 **Wording of surrounding sections/subsections**

Light may also be thrown on Parliament's intention by comparing the wording of the offence charged with the wording used for other offences in the surrounding sections or subsections of the same act. Thus, in *Pharmaceutical Society of Great Britain* v *Storkwain Ltd* [1986] 2 All ER 635 (*Cases and Materials* (13.4.3.2)), the House of Lords decided that s. 58(2)(a) of the Medicines Act 1968 which provides that 'no person shall sell by retail...[certain medicinal products]...except in accordance with a prescription given by an appropriate practitioner...', was a strict liability offence. The defendant company was convicted after supplying a medicine to a person who produced an apparently genuine prescription, which unknown to the company's employee, was a forgery. In holding strict liability, the House was much influenced by the fact that Parliament had made detailed *mens rea* requirements for a number of the other offences created by the statute but none for this particular offence. This same factor was influential in both *Muhamad* and *Matudi*. Similarly, where a no-negligence defence was expressly incorporated in the wording of some offences in the National Lottery etc Act 1993, its omission from the offence in question showed it was intended to be strict liability (*Harrow LBC* v *Shah*).

You will recall that *B* v *DPP* decided that *mens rea* must be implied unless 'the language used, the nature of the offence, the mischief sought to be avoided and any other relevant circumstances' creates a 'necessary [i.e., "compellingly clear"] implication' that the legislature intended strict liability. Almost immediately in *K* [2001] Crim LR 134, the Court of Appeal found that there was such a necessary implication as regards the age factor in indecent assault under s. 14 of the Sexual Offences Act 1956 (now replaced by s. 3 of the Sexual Offences Act 2003). The issue arose because, although the victim's consent to D's indecent acts would normally negate any 'assault', s. 14(2) expressly provides that the consent of a girl under 16 cannot in law prevent the acts being an assault. In this case D thought the consenting girl was 16. If the offence required *mens rea* in respect of the girl being under 16, D's mistake would negate it and be a defence; if no such *mens rea* was required, D's mistake would be irrelevant leaving him guilty.

Clearly the 'nature of the offence' was 'truly criminal' where the presumption of *mens rea* could be expected to be at its strongest. The 'mischief sought to be avoided' was, in this context, sexual exploitation of the under 16s but, as is evident from *B* v *DPP*, the protection of children of itself cannot justify the imposition of strict liability. The crucial element which led the Court to find the 'necessary implication' of strict liability was 'the language used' for the offence. This was based mainly on s. 14(4) which provides that, just like that of a girl under 16, a mentally defective woman's consent cannot negate assault. However, unlike s. 14(2), s. 14(4) goes on to provide that, in such a case, D can only be guilty if he knew or had reason to suspect her to be defective. Of course, such a provision is only comprehensible on the basis that, without it, the offence is strict liability in respect of the victim's mental subnormality and, by analogy, the victim's age. The Court felt compelled to hold that the absence of any such provision in s. 14(2) showed that Parliament intended to apply a strict liability rule to the victim's age. However, the House of Lords overturned the decision on the ground that the statutory wording did not give a 'compellingly clear' implication that strict liability was intended. It was not inevitable that s. 14(2) should be read as analogous to s. 14(4). Section 14 would not be reduced to absurdity if *mens rea* was required for age.

A much clearer example is provided by the common drafting configuration used in s. 3 of the Sexual Offences (Amendment) Act 2000 (now replaced by s. 16 of the Sexual Offences Act 2003). It is an offence for someone aged 18 or over to have sexual intercourse or other sexual activity with someone who is under 18 where he is in a position of trust in relation to that person (this includes, for example, the teacher—pupil relationship). Section 3(2) gives a 'compellingly clear' indication that the presumption of *mens rea* in respect of the victim's age and the fact that D is in a position of trust towards him is displaced. This provides that 'it shall be a defence for [D] to prove that ... he did not know, and could not reasonably have been expected to know' that the victim was (a) under 18 or (b) in a position of trust towards the victim. Clearly the 'necessary implication'—indeed, the only sensible interpretation—is that the prosecution is not required to prove any *mens rea* or fault element in respect of the age or the position of trust—otherwise the defence could never come into play. (Of course, this argument would be weakened if the courts were to interpret 'proves' as meaning 'adduces evidence' by analogy with *Lambert*—see 1.5 above.)

13.4.3.3 Historical wording of precursor statues

Where legislation has a previous history and is from time to time updated by Parliament, the court may derive some assistance by examining the wording under the previous enactment and comparing it with the wording for the same offence in the current statute. The same wording would confirm Parliament's intention not to alter the position, whereas changed wording may lead the court to reassess its previous classification (*cf. Smedleys Ltd* v *Breed* [1974] 2 All ER 21, HL). The line taken in *Alphacell* v *Woodward* has been adopted in respect of other, more recent pollution statutes (*National Rivers Authority* v *Yorkshire Water Services* [1995] 1 All ER 225, HL; *Empress Car Co. (Abertillery) Ltd* v *National Rivers Authority* [1998] 1 All ER 481, HL—*Cases and Materials* (2.8.2.2)).

In *B* v *DPP* the House of Lords, in interpreting s. 1(1) of the Indecency with Children Act 1960, paid close attention to the Sexual Offences Act 1956 since the 1960 Act was designed to cover a loophole left by the 1956 Act. However, the ultimate conclusion was that it was of little help since it consisted of a ragbag of various offences without any coherent thread or rationale.

13.4.3.4 Analogous contemporary statutes

The court may also reason by analogy from similarly worded offences in statutes covering different activities. For example, offences involving 'selling' or 'using' appear in many different contexts. We might also point to 'causes', which is generally interpreted as not importing *mens rea* (unless qualified in the statute by an express *mens rea* word).

Similarly, a large number of offences are phrased in terms of 'permitting' or 'allowing' something to occur. The tendency hitherto has been to regard both as implying a *mens rea* of knowledge (including wilful blindness) on the basis that one cannot permit something without being aware that it is or at least may be happening. Thus in *James & Son Ltd v Smee* [1954] 3 All ER 273, DC, D could not be convicted of 'permitting' a lorry to be used with defective brakes when he was unaware of the defect. On the other hand, the offence of 'permitting' a vehicle to be used whilst uninsured has been held not to require any knowledge or even negligence that the vehicle was in fact uninsured (*Chief Constable of Norfolk v Fisher* [1992] RTR 6, DC).

The House of Lords had a chance to impose some consistency in *Vehicle Inspectorate v Nuttall* [1999] 3 All ER 833 but, in a rather unsatisfactory decision, provided little assistance. It held that the meaning of permit varied with the context, ranging from 'authorising' or 'agreeing to' in its narrowest sense to simply 'failing to take reasonable steps to prevent' in its widest. Here the company was convicted of 'permitting' its coach drivers to contravene rules on driving hours and rest periods imposed by European Union regulations contrary to s. 96(11) of the Transport Act 1968 (as amended). It was not aware of the driver's breaches because it failed to check their tachograph record of each journey. The House was unanimous that 'permit' had to be construed to mean 'failing to take reasonable steps to prevent' the drivers' breaches.

For two judges, no further fault element was required whereas for another two D had to be reckless, i.e., knowing there was a possibility of breaches occurring or not caring whether they were occurring. The final judge, without explanation, contrived to agree with both these opposing views! However, it seems that on any view, it is not an offence of strict liability, requiring as a minimum a fault element of negligence. In terms of 'permitting' offences generally, it is as difficult as ever to predict when a requirement of knowledge will be implied and what it is about the context which determines when they will be narrowly construed and when not.

13.4.3.5 Enactment of general no-negligence defence

Finally, in relation to the statutory context, the enactment of a general no-negligence defence in the statute creating the offence charged is an excellent indicator that Parliament must have intended at least some of the offences created by that statute to be construed as strict liability.

? QUESTION 13.3

Can you see why?

If none of the offences was strict liability, there would be no point in having a general defence of that nature since, if the prosecution had to prove fault on the part of D in the first place, before conviction, the defence would never come into play. D would have to be proved to have been at least negligent and then, of course, by definition, D cannot prove that he was not negligent. The defence would be superfluous and totally useless. Hence, because Parliament is assumed not to have put in the defence for nothing, it is a sure sign that one or more of the offences created is strict liability. Such statutory defences are extremely common (see, for example, s. 24 of the Trade Descriptions Act 1968 and s. 21 of the Food Safety Act 1990—*Cases and Materials* (13.4.3.5) and also *Kirkland v Robinson* [1987] Crim LR 643).

A similar line is evident in the Health and Safety at Work etc. Act 1974 where there is no general no-negligence defence but a no-negligence provision is incorporated into some of the individual offence provisions. Thus s. 2(1) requires 'every employer to ensure, so far as is reasonably practicable, the health, safety and welfare at work of all his employees' whilst s. 3(1) requires every employer 'to conduct his undertaking in such a way as to ensure, so far as is reasonably practicable' that non-employees 'are not thereby exposed to risks to their health and safety'. It has been held, in the case of s. 3(1) by *Associated Octel Co. Ltd* [1996] 4 All ER 846, HL, and in the case of s. 2(1) by *Gateway Foodmarkets Ltd* [1997] 2 Cr App R 40, CA, that the presence of the 'reasonably practicable' qualification shows that the offences are prima facie strict liability. If safety, etc. is not ensured, the employer will be liable unless he can show he did all that was reasonably practicable to ensure it.

13.4.4 Gravity of punishment

As a general rule, the more serious the criminal offence in terms of the maximum punishment available, the less likely the courts are to view it as an offence of strict liability. However, this is only one factor and offences imposing severe maximum penalties have been held to be strict liability because of the courts' perception of the danger to the public involved in the regulated activity. Indeed, somewhat antipathetically, the courts often stress that 'the greater the degree of social danger the more ready the courts will be to infer that Parliament's intention was to create a strict liability offence' (*Matudi*). For example, a maximum penalty of two years' imprisonment did not dissuade the House of Lords from holding strict liability in the *Storkwain* case or the Court of Appeal in *Muhamad* and *Matudi*. Similarly in *Howells* [1977] 2 All ER 417, CA the offence of possessing a firearm without a certificate under the Firearms Act 1968 was held to be strict liability despite carrying a maximum penalty of five years' imprisonment. Exactly the same line was taken in respect of the offence of 'having with him' a firearm in a public place, also carrying a maximum penalty of five years' imprisonment (*Vann and Davis* [1996] Crim LR 52, CA). A penalty of up to ten years' imprisonment coupled with the breadth of the conduct (ranging from fairly trivial to very serious) embraced by gross indecency and particularly incitement to gross indecency was a key factor in the denial of strict liability in *B v DPP*. Indecent assault attracts a similar penalty but this did not prevent the Court of Appeal in *K* from imposing strict liability, though the House of Lords reversed the decision.

In some instances, the courts have stressed the public danger element as evidenced by the heavy penalty provided by Parliament as a **reason** for imposing strict liability contrary to the usual stance where a severe penalty is a reason for **not** imposing strict liability and requiring proof of fault. (See *Blake* at 13.4.2 above for evidence of the use of **both** types of reasoning in the same case!) The law relating to firearms is one example and, before its statutory reform, the law relating to drugs was another (see, e.g., *Warner v MPC* [1968] 2 All ER 356, HL).

13.4.5 **Will strict liability serve any purpose?**

Before imposing strict liability, the courts will need to be satisfied that this will be of practical assistance in ensuring observance of the regulatory statute (see, e.g., *Muhamad* [2002] EWCA Crim 1856 at [10] and *Matudi*). As Lord Diplock put it in *Sweet* v *Parsley*, the court would have to be satisfied that 'there is something that the person on whom the obligation is imposed can do directly or indirectly by supervision or inspection, by improvement of his business methods or by exhorting those whom he may be expecting to influence or control, which will promote the observance of the regulation'. This echoes the very similar view expressed by the Privy Council in *Lim Chin Aik* v *R* [1963] 1 All ER 223, PC (*Cases and Materials* (13.4.3.5)).

13.4.6 **Conclusion**

A study of the case law reveals extraordinary inconsistency of approach. Factors seen as crucial in one case are scarcely considered in another. The impression given is that the courts decide as a matter of policy what they desire as the end result and then emphasise those factors which support such a result whilst downgrading or ignoring those which do not. The courts pick and choose those factors which they want to be influential.

13.5 **Is the imposition of strict liability justified?**

The concept of strict liability has often been criticised as being incompatible with our notions of fairness and justice. How can it be right to convict somebody of a criminal offence where he has not been shown to be at fault in any way? In practice, however, the existence of strict liability probably does make the task of law enforcement agencies, for example the environmental health inspector overseeing food retailers or the health and safety inspector overseeing factories and other workplaces, much easier. Studies have shown that such agencies tend to use prosecution in the courts very much as a last resort and only after the defendant has shown a history of contraventions and failures to comply with the inspector's requirements. The point is that in individual incidents it might be difficult for an inspector to produce the evidence if he had to prove fault. In many instances, what D did or did not do to ensure compliance with the regulations is peculiarly difficult to establish and something which is within D's exclusive knowledge. Strict liability essentially says to a person participating in the activity: if you choose to engage in this activity, it is not enough just to take reasonable steps to ensure compliance with the regulations governing that activity; you must, in effect, take all possible steps and, indeed, guarantee compliance with those regulations. This is certainly harsh on a blameless defendant who is convicted, but it does put maximum pressure on business and others to make every effort to comply with the regulations.

Nonetheless, most academic writers feel that justice and fairness dictate that, at the very least, even if the offence is prima facie strict liability, the defendant should always be given a defence if he can prove that he exercised all due diligence to comply with the regulations. In fact, in Canada and Australia, the courts have developed at common law just such a general defence. However, our courts have not done so and there is no such defence unless the particular statute in issue expressly includes one. Fortunately, it is now very common for statutes to do so.

■ **FURTHER READING**

Glazebrook: *How Old Did You Think She Was*? [2001] CLJ 25.

Horder: *Strict Liability, Statutory Construction and the Spirit of Liberty* (2002) 118 LQR 459.

Jackson: *Storkwain: A Case Study in Strict Liability and Self-Regulation* [1991] Crim LR 892.

Leigh: *Strict and Vicarious Liability* (1982, Sweet & Maxwell).

Richardson: *Strict Liability for Regulating Crime: The Empirical Research* [1987] Crim LR 295.

Simons: *When is Strict Criminal Liability Just*? (1997) 87 Journal of Criminal Law and Criminology 1075 (USA).

■ **SUMMARY**

- An offence of strict liability is one that does not require any *mens rea* or fault element in respect of at least one element of the *actus reus* (e.g., *Prince*; *Callow* v *Tillstone*). However, D's conduct must be voluntary (*cf.* absolute 'state of affairs' offences—*Larsonneur*). Mostly confined to statutory offences (but *cf.* public nuisance, outraging public decency (*Gibson*) and blasphemous libel (*Lemon*)).

- Deciding on strict liability if statute silent as to *mens rea*/fault—**always** a presumption that Parliament intended the courts to imply *mens rea* (*Sweet* v *Parsley*; *Gammon* v *A-G for Hong Kong*). Presumption very strong for 'truly criminal' offences (*B* v *DPP*) though can still be rebutted; fairly weak for quasi-criminal or regulatory offences (e.g., *Alphacell* v *Woodward*). Presumption applies unless the language used, the nature of the offence and/or the mischief sought to be prevented creates a 'necessary [i.e., "compellingly clear"] implication' that Parliament intended strict liability (*B* v *DPP*). Because it is a question of statutory interpretation, the statutory context is always important and requires close analysis of wording compared with (i) other offences in the same subsection or section (ii) other offences in surrounding sections (iii) similar offences in analogous statutes (iv) similar offences in past but replaced statutes. Certain words are usually held to imply *mens rea*, e.g., permitting (*James* v *Smee cf. Vehicle Inspectorate* v *Nuttall*). Presence in statute of general 'no-negligence' defence indicative of strict liability. Courts generally (although not invariably (*Howells*)) reluctant to impose strict liability where offence carries heavy penalty and where they do not believe that it will serve any useful purpose (*Sweet* v *Parsley*). The inconsistency of the cases leads to suspicion that courts to an extent decide what they want to be the outcome and then pick and choose those factors which they need to technically justify the decision.

See also the **Chapter 15 Assessment Exercise** below.

14 Secondary participation in crime

14.1 Objectives

By the end of this chapter you should be able to:

1 Identify the perpetrator(s) of a crime and any secondary participants in it

2 Define what conduct amounts to secondary participation in crime

3 Analyse the *mens rea* required of an accessory and distinguish this from the *mens rea* required of the perpetrator

4 Describe the rules applicable to joint enterprise

14.2 Introduction

A person who performs the *actus reus* of a crime is known as the **perpetrator** or the **principal** of that crime. If the *actus reus* is performed by more than one person jointly, then they will be **joint principals** (e.g., if D1 and D2 break into a house together in order to steal, they will both be perpetrators of the burglary).

Perpetrators of crimes often have accomplices who assist or encourage them in the commission of the crime and who are known as accessories to the crime or secondary parties to it. Such accomplices are 'liable to be tried…and punished as a principal offender' for the offence assisted or encouraged (s. 8 of the Accessories and Abettors Act 1861, as amended by the Criminal Law Act 1977; and s. 44 of the Magistrates' Courts Act 1980 in relation to summary offences). The term 'accomplice' includes all the parties to the crime—both the principal (perpetrator) and anyone who encourages or assists (although the Law Commission regards it as synonymous with 'accessory' (Law Com. No. 131, para. 2.3)). The law in this area is often called the law of complicity but is also referred to as the law of participation in crime. There is no doubt that the law is complicated. Fortunately the House of Lords' decision in the consolidated appeals of *Powell and Daniels* and *English* [1997] 4 All ER 545 is most helpful but certainly does not solve all problems.

In this chapter, we use A to denote an alleged accessory and D to denote the alleged perpetrator.

14.3 Perpetrators

It is usually obvious who is the perpetrator of a crime and who is a mere accessory. However, sometimes, in practice, it proves extremely difficult, often due to uncertainties in the evidence as to who did what. There are also instances where the courts have stretched to and beyond breaking point the notion of perpetration because accessorial liability would not have been possible in the circumstances. An excellent illustration is provided by the recent case of *Rogers* [2003] 2 Cr App R 160, CA. V died from an overdose of heroin which he had bought and injected into himself. He was assisted in this process by D, a drinking companion, who held a belt round V's arm to act as a tourniquet in order to raise a vein to facilitate the injection. Although this seemed a typical instance of assisting V to administer a noxious thing to himself, the court astonishingly held that D 'administered' as perpetrator the noxious thing contrary to s. 23 of the Offences Against the Person Act 1861 because D 'was playing a part in the mechanics of the injection which caused death . . . a person who actively participates in the injection process commits the *actus reus* and can have no answer to an offence under s. 23.' The real reason for this rather perverse holding was that it was not an offence for V to administer a noxious thing to himself so that D could not have been liable as a mere accessory. There was no offence for him to assist. Only if he 'administered' it himself (albeit jointly in conjunction with V) could he be liable.

This was stretched even further in *Kennedy (No. 2)* [2005] EWCA Crim 685 (see *Cases and Materials* (6.5.3.4)) where D simply supplied and prepared heroin and handed the syringe to V for immediate injection. D did not directly assist in the injection process itself as had Rogers. Nonetheless, the Court of Appeal held that he perpetrated a s. 23 offence because he was 'acting in concert' with V. They jointly administered the heroin. The Court relied on a misunderstood (wilfully or otherwise) obiter dictum by Lord Steyn in *Latif* [1996] 2 Cr App R 92, 104 to apparently hold that if D acts in concert with another, D perpetrates whatever actions the other person takes! Little assistance is given as to what amounts to 'acting in concert' for this purpose and it is to be hoped that the principle is not applied generally. It should be seen as a limited device to avoid difficult causation problems in an area (drug overdosing) where the judges are determined to secure convictions for those who help where V is not actually committing any crime. Otherwise it risks undermining the basic distinction between perpetrators and accessories (see Heaton: *Principals? No Principles!* [2004] Crim LR 463). The truth is that the Court's reasoning is mightily confused and does not stand up to analysis. The term 'acting in concert' has hitherto been used as a euphemism for participation in a joint unlawful enterprise (see 14.4.3 below), i.e., where two or more people share a common purpose to commit a crime. It does not mean that all participants become perpetrators of whatever acts the others commit in carrying out the enterprise. The getaway driver for armed bank robbers does not perpetrate the robbery; he is simply an accessory to it even though he is clearly acting in concert with the perpetrators who enter the bank. He assists the robbery and is liable for it for that reason but he does not perpetrate it (*Powell*; *English* [1997] 4 All ER 545).

Since an accessory is 'liable to be tried and punished as a principal offender', is there any need to distinguish whether a person is a principal offender or a mere accessory? There are several reasons why it may be necessary, some of which could be crucial to whether a person is criminally liable at all:

(a) As we have already seen in *Rogers* and *Kennedy (No. 2)*, sometimes no offence will be perpetrated unless D is classed as a perpetrator.

(b) The *mens rea* requirement may differ according to whether D is a perpetrator or an accessory. Curiously, it is often (though not always) more exacting in the case of an accessory, particularly, as we shall see, in relation to strict liability offences.

(c) Vicarious liability (dealt with in **Chapter 15**) may be imposed only in respect of the acts of a perpetrator and not those of an accessory.

(d) Some offences may be committed **as perpetrator** only by a specified category of person (e.g., 'a licensee'—see under vicarious liability; or men in the case of rape), whereas persons precluded from being principals can be convicted as accessories.

(e) Where the court is not sure whether D is the perpetrator or merely an accessory, D can be convicted of the crime provided that the court is satisfied that D must have been one or the other and provided that the prosecution has framed the charge in the alternative alleging that D is a principal or an accessory (*Gaughan* [1990] Crim LR 880, CA; *Giannetto* [1997] 1 Cr App R 1, CA). The same is true where two or more people are charged with an offence, but it is not clear which of them was the perpetrator. As long as the court is satisfied that both or all must be either the perpetrator or an accessory, they can all be convicted of the offence (*Mohan* v *R* [1967] 2 AC 187, PC). However, this will mean that for both parties the court must be sure that the more stringent *mens rea* requirements for accessories are satisfied, even if the offence is one of strict liability (*Smith* v *Mellors and Soar* [1987] RTR 210—see 13.4.2).

For the principle to apply, it must be clear that both parties participated in the crime in one way or the other. It is not sufficient to prove that a crime was committed and that it was perpetrated by A or B, if it cannot be established that whoever did not perpetrate the crime was at least an accessory. *Lane* (1986) 82 Cr App R 5 (*Cases and Materials* (14.3)) illustrates the point. The child of D1 and D2 had been killed between noon and 8.30 p.m. Each parent had been present for some of the time and absent for some of it, although the child had always been in the presence of at least one parent. Each was acquitted of manslaughter since the prosecution was unable to prove who had caused the child's death or that each had been involved either as principal or accessory. It may have been the work of one parent alone without any assistance or encouragement from the other.

Disquiet caused by such acquittals led to strong pressure for change from organisations such as the NSPCC and resulted in Law Commission Reports (Law Com. No. 279, 2003 and Law Com. No. 282, 2004 *cf.* Glazebrook's comment on the 2003 Report at [2003] Crim LR 541). The Government's response now embodied in ss. 5 and 6 of the Domestic Violence, Crime and Victims Act 2004 departed from the Commission's preferred solutions. It creates a new offence of 'causing or allowing the death of a child or vulnerable adult'. The offence can be committed only by someone who was a member of the same household as the victim and had frequent contact with him, in circumstances where there was 'a significant risk of serious physical harm being caused to V by the unlawful act' of such a member of the household. The offence can be committed in either of two ways and it is unnecessary to prove which of the alternatives applies to D as long as it is clear that one of them does (s. 5(2)). D must either have 'caused V's death' (obviously if that might be proved, the prosecution would be likely to charge murder or manslaughter alongside this fallback offence) **or** have 'failed to take such steps as he could reasonably have been expected to take to protect V from the risk' of serious physical harm from a member of V's household. The fault requirement for this serious offence (up to 14 years' imprisonment) is remarkably low—simple negligence. It is enough that D either foresaw or ought to have foreseen (i) the aforesaid risk of serious harm and (ii) the 'kind of circumstances' in which the fatal act 'occurred'.

14.3.1 Innocent agent

We have indicated that the perpetrator is the person who physically performs the *actus reus* and is its most immediate causer. However, exceptionally, D may be regarded as the perpetrator even though the *actus reus* was performed by another. This arises where D uses an 'innocent agent' to perform the *actus reus* for him.

> **?** **QUESTION** 14.1
>
> Can you think of a situation where the *actus reus* of an offence is performed by an innocent agent?

The person performing the *actus reus* will be an innocent agent if he is devoid of responsibility because he lacks the capacity to commit the offence (e.g., he is under ten or insane) or he does not possess the requisite *mens rea* for the offence. For example, if a doctor, with intent to kill a patient, instructs a nurse to administer to the patient a drug, which, unknown to the nurse, is lethal, the doctor would be regarded as the perpetrator of the murder when the patient dies from the drug. It can truly be said that the doctor has killed the patient. Conversely, if the nurse knew that the drug was lethal, he would be the perpetrator whereas the doctor would only be an accessory.

Although many offences can, in such exceptional circumstances, be committed through an innocent agent, the nature of some offences would seem to preclude it. A prime example is surely rape which can only be committed by a man. If A persuades X that V consents to the sexual intercourse X has with V, when A knows this not to be the case, X might not perpetrate rape because he might lack the necessary *mens rea* (if he reasonably believes V is consenting). Although X would be A's innocent agent, it is not credible to describe A as raping V, especially if A is a woman! As we shall see (at 14.4.1.7 below), it does not follow that a woman cannot be an accessory to rape. The foregoing is in accord with *DPP* v *K and B* [1997] 1 Cr App R 36, DC though contrary to obiter dicta in *Cogan and Leak* (see 14.4.1.7 below).

14.4 **Accessories**

Section 8 of the Accessories and Abettors Act 1861, as amended by the Criminal Law Act 1977, provides:

> Whosoever shall aid, abet, counsel or procure the commission of any indictable offence . . . shall be liable to be tried, indicted and punished as a principal offender.

Section 44 of the Magistrates' Courts Act 1980 (*Cases and Materials* (14.4)) contains a similar provision in relation to summary offences.

It is important to realise that the prosecution must always prove that the accessory performed the *actus reus* (in essence, assisting or encouraging D to commit the crime) with the necessary *mens rea* (in essence, an intention to assist or encourage). One further essential is that the crime which the accessory is charged with aiding etc. must have actually been committed by the perpetrator, since the accessory can hardly be convicted of a crime which is not committed. (Curiously, this is not entirely true and we will consider some exceptions later in this chapter.) It follows that an accessory's liability is essentially derivative—derived from that of the perpetrator.

It is possible to be guilty of aiding and abetting an **attempt** to commit a crime.

14.4.1 *Actus reus*

The *actus reus* requirement can be minimal since the most marginal assistance can constitute 'aiding' and simply clapping or cheering can amount to 'encouragement'. The *actus reus* is defined by the words 'aids, abets, counsels or procures'. Although each of these words may have a distinct meaning, it is the common practice to charge any accessory with 'aiding, abetting, counselling or procuring' the relevant offence. Usually, no attempt is made to select the one most suitable for the actual conduct of the accessory and Glanville Williams has described this as using the statutory language as a blunderbuss! However, prosecutors have not been helped in producing a more refined approach by the courts' failure to define clearly the differences between the four verbs. The best effort so far comes from Lord Widgery CJ in *Attorney-General's Reference (No. 1 of 1975)* [1975] 2 All ER 684, CA (*Cases and Materials* (14.4.1)). Professor Smith argues that, for historical reasons, it is a mistake to regard the words as having separate individual meanings corresponding with their ordinary usage (see Glazebrook (ed.), *Reshaping the Criminal Law*, pp. 120–37) and, indeed, prior to Lord Widgery's statement, this was the 'received view' (see Law Com. No. 131, para. 2.10).

14.4.1.1 **Aids**

This entails helping or giving assistance to the perpetrator in the commission of the offence, whether before or at the time of the offence and whether or not the aider is present at its commission.

EXERCISE 14.1

Using a separate sheet of paper, write down three examples of how you could aid the commission of a crime including at least one where you are not present at the scene of the crime and one where you help beforehand.

You will find a number of examples as you read further in this chapter.

14.4.1.2 **Abets**

This means encouraging, instigating or inciting the commission of the crime. The view has been expressed that abetting (and, indeed, aiding) means that the encouragement, etc. (or assistance) by A occurred while A was **present** at the actual commission of the crime. However, there have been a number of cases where the court has regarded A as an aider and abettor even though he was not present at the commission of the crime but gave assistance **before** the crime (e.g., *NCB* v *Gamble* [1958] 3 All ER 203, DC where A was regarded as aiding and abetting by supplying, **before** the crime, a weighbridge ticket (an article essential for the crime), which enabled an overloaded lorry to leave the private colliery complex and drive on the public highway; see also the 'generous host' example given by Lord Widgery CJ in *Attorney-General's Reference (No. 1 of 1975)* [1975] 2 All ER 684, CA). However, whilst it seems that a person can 'aid' by giving help either before or at the time of the crime, it may be that 'abet' is limited to encouragement at the time of the crime in order to allow some scope for the counselling alternative we now consider.

14.4.1.3 **Counsels**

'Counsel' means more or less the same as abets except that the encouragement etc. occurs **before** the commission of the crime. In *Calhaem* [1985] 2 All ER 266, the Court of Appeal held that the word 'counsel' should be given 'its ordinary meaning, which is ... "advise", "solicit", or something of that sort.'

14.4.1.4 **Procures**

Procures is different from the other alternatives. It means causing the commission of the offence or bringing about its commission (*Beck* [1985] 1 All ER 571, CA). As it was put in *Attorney-General's Reference (No. 1 of 1975)* [1975] 2 All ER 684, CA 'to procure meant to produce by endeavour. One procured a thing by setting out to see that it happened and taking the appropriate steps to produce it.' There must be 'a causal link' between the procurer's actions and the commission of the offence. In that case, A secretly laced his friend's drink with double spirits knowing his friend would shortly be driving his car home. The friend was stopped and found to be driving with excess alcohol in his blood and A was subsequently charged with 'procuring' this offence. The Court of Appeal held that he would be guilty if he knew (a) that his friend was going to drive and (b) that the ordinary and natural result of the additional alcohol would be to bring him above the statutory limit.

Some further differences between aiding, abetting, counselling and procuring?
The court thought that procuring was different from the other three alternatives in two respects:

(1) Meeting of minds between A and D?
According to Lord Widgery CJ, 'aiding and abetting almost inevitably involved the parties at some stage being in contact so each knew what was passing through the mind of the other. The same applied to counselling, but not procuring.' This seems to involve a shared intention by the accessory and the principal that the offence should be committed but it does not necessarily involve any prior planning or discussion between them. Thus, if A sees D throw V to the ground and shouts to D, 'Go on, put the boot in' and D does, A will have abetted D's crime in kicking V. This is true even if D would have done it anyway without A's encouragement (see (2) below). On the other hand, A may 'procure' even though the perpetrator has no idea what is happening, as in *Attorney-General's Reference* above where the perpetrator was unaware that A had spiked his drink.

Lord Widgery's statement may be an accurate description of when a joint enterprise exists (see 14.4.3) but it seems unduly restrictive at least in relation to 'aiding', because it would seem to be perfectly possible for A to assist in the commission of the crime without the perpetrator realising it. For example, if, unknown to the perpetrator of a crime, A prevents Y from intervening to stop the crime, A would seem clearly to aid its commission. However, it seems applicable to counselling and abetting because it is difficult to envisage how the accessory could 'encourage' the perpetrator without the perpetrator being aware of it! Thus, for procuring and aiding, no meeting of minds between A and D is required but, for counselling and abetting, this would appear to be essential at least in the sense that D was aware of A's encouragement. Whether it is also necessary to show that D was actually influenced by A's encouragement is a contentious question dependent on the role of causation in accessorial liability, to which we now turn.

(2) Causal connection?
Lord Widgery also thought that aiding, abetting or counselling, in contrast to procuring, did **not** require proof of any causal connection between the offence and the actions of the aider, abettor or counsellor. On this view, it does not matter that A's 'encouragement' has, in fact, no effect or influence on the perpetrator of the crime, who would have committed it just the same without such encouragement. Similarly, if A supplies, say, a screwdriver to D for use in a burglary, it would be irrelevant that D could easily obtain one elsewhere and so would have perpetrated the burglary just the same without A's help. Nor would it matter that A's 'assistance' was of no value to the perpetrator or even a hindrance to him in committing the crime, as where A inadvertently gives D the wrong address of a proposed murder victim. On the other hand, procuring does, according to the *Attorney-General's Reference* case, necessitate proof of causation so that if, for example, the friend in that case was already well over the limit when A laced the drink, A would not be liable for procuring because his actions would not have caused the offence. It would have been committed without A's actions.

> **? QUESTION** 14.2
>
> Can you see why requiring proof of a causal connection could make things very difficult for the prosecution especially in cases of encouragement?

The better view, therefore, seems to be that, apart from cases of 'procuring', it is unnecessary to prove that A's acts of 'assistance' in any way caused D to commit the crime and similarly that A's encouragement did in fact influence D in any way. That said, some academic commentators favour the necessity for some (much watered down) causal link and there is support for this in an important Court of Appeal decision on complicity, *Bryce* [2004] EWCA Crim 1231 (see *Cases and Materials* (14.4.1.4)). The Court accepted that a causal connection was an essential element of all forms of accessorial liability. However, 'it seems clear that the requirement for a causal connection is given a wide interpretation where a secondary party prior to a crime has counselled or assisted the perpetrator in actions taken by him which are directed towards the commission of the crime eventually committed' ([26]). It turns out that this 'causal connection' falls far short of any requirement to cause the commission of the crime.

D was instructed by a drug dealer, B, to murder, M, an associate dealer. A, knowing of this, transported D with a concealed shotgun to a caravan located near to where M lived, having arranged for D to stay there. Early the next morning, B visited D at the caravan to stiffen D's resolve and to saw off part of the barrel of the shotgun. Then, some 13 hours after A's acts of assistance, D went to M's house and deliberately shot M dead. The Court endorsed the trial judge's direction that it was necessary to show a causal link between A's acts of assistance and the murder, i.e., that A 'did an act which *in fact* assisted' D (Court's emphasis). (Technically this holding was obiter because, in view of the trial judge's direction, causal connection was assumed on all sides to be necessary.) A had claimed that his acts had actually hindered the murder because, until he suggested the caravan as a 'safe house', D had been going to carry out the murder more or less immediately. However, it was clear that, under the revised plan, his acts were of material assistance to D in the furtherance of the murder and it mattered not that there was a 13-hour time interval before the murder. A's assistance was still 'operative', there being a 'continuing causal connection (by way of facilitation)', and there was no 'overwhelming supervening event' breaking the causal connection between the assistance and the killing.

Clearly there has to be some connection between the accessory's acts and the crime committed otherwise there would be no reason to regard A as participating in D's crime and so convict him. But what it boils down to is that A must have provided assistance and the assistance can still be said to be operating. For example, if D had abandoned his plan to murder and left the caravan but then subsequently murdered M a few days later, it could be said that A's assistance was spent and no longer operative. Although the Court seems to require that D was actually assisted by A's acts, we doubt whether this is strictly necessary. Thus, if A mistakenly gives erroneous information or supplies safe-blowing equipment which is not used or does not work so that his assistance is ineffectual or even a positive hindrance, he would surely still 'aid' D's crime (assuming that D still manages to commit it!).

In terms of encouraging (abetting and counselling), the relevant 'connection' is provided by the fact of communication of the encouragement to D. If D is aware of A's encouragement, it matters not that he is not influenced one jot by it (*Clarkson* [1971] 1 WLR 1402, CA; *Calhaem* [1985] 2 All ER 266, CA) and that he would have committed the crime anyway (*Attorney-General* v *Able* [1984] QB 795, 812). To require proof that D was actually influenced by A, dependent as that would commonly be on the testimony of D, who might well have strong reasons to exonerate A, would make life extremely difficult for the prosecution. Therefore, if D has received A's encouragement (abetting or counselling) and D commits the offence counselled in a way which is within the scope of his authority, A will be guilty (*Bryce* at [26–27] approving *Attorney-General's Reference (No. 1 of 1975)*).

To these differences expressed in *Attorney-General's Reference*, we could add two more. Third, it is clear that one can 'procure' the perpetrator to commit a crime even though the perpetrator made no **decision** to commit a crime (see *Attorney-General's Reference*). However, the other forms, aiding, abetting and counselling which mean assisting or encouraging the perpetrator, seem to imply that it was the perpetrator's objective to perform the conduct constituting the crime. Fourth, it is likely that the *mens rea* requirement for a procurer is more stringent than for an aider, abettor or counsellor (*Blakely, Sutton* v *DPP* [1991] Crim LR 763, DC—see 14.4.2.1).

The probable effect of some of these considerations is neatly summarised by Smith and Hogan as follows (*Criminal Law*, 10th ed., p. 147):

(a) 'procuring' implies causation but not consensus;

(b) 'abetting' and 'counselling' imply consensus but not causation;

(c) 'aiding' requires actual assistance but neither consensus nor causation.

14.4.1.5 Assisting after the commission of the crime

To be guilty as an accessory, the assistance or encouragement must be given **before, or at the time of**, the commission of the principal offence. Someone who assists the perpetrator **only after** the commission of the principal offence is not liable as a party to it, although assisting the perpetrator to escape detection or arrest may constitute the statutory offence of assisting arrestable offenders under s. 4(1) of the Criminal Law Act 1967. This is a convenient point to explain some outdated terminology which you will inevitably come across in both case law and text books, even though it was abolished by the Criminal Law Act 1967. The principal or perpetrator used to be called the 'principal in the first degree'. Anyone assisting or encouraging **at the time of** the offence used to be called a 'principal in the second degree', whereas anyone assisting or encouraging **before** the commission of the crime was 'an accessory before the fact'. Some writers argue that the distinctions made in the old law still continue into the modern law so that the equivalent to a principal in the second degree would now be an aider or abettor, whereas the accessory before the fact would now be a counsellor or procurer. However, as we have seen above, at least aiding would appear to be possible both prior to the crime and at its actual commission. The old law had a further category, 'accessory **after** the fact', which covered assistance rendered *after* the crime had been committed. This category no longer exists in the modern law, having been abolished by the 1967 Act, and such a person would no longer be an accomplice to the offence.

14.4.1.6 **What constitutes 'assistance or encouragement'?**

We have seen above that, apart from the special case of 'procuring', A must have given assistance or encouragement in order to be convicted as accessory to a crime. Assistance or encouragement may occur in any number of ways, from an early stage in the preparation of an offence, through to the moment of commission. Examples would include driving the perpetrator to the scene of the crime (*DPP for Northern Ireland* v *Lynch* [1975] 1 All ER 913), holding a woman down whilst she is raped (*Clarkson* [1971] 3 All ER 344, C-MAC), cheering and clapping an unlawful concert (*Wilcox* v *Jeffrey* [1951] 1 All ER 464, DC), opening a bank account to enable the perpetrator to pay in forged cheques (*Thambiah* v *R* [1965] 3 All ER 661, PC) and supplying equipment or information for use in the commission of a crime (*NCB* v *Gamble* [1958] 3 All ER 203, DC).

> **? QUESTION** 14.3
>
> Suppose D, having been disqualified from driving, lends his car to A for the period of disqualification. D calls on A saying that he needs the car urgently to drive to Scotland and demands its return. If A does return it, knowing D is going to drive whilst disqualified, would he be an accessory to D's offence?

In cases where A supplies items for use in committing the crime, it does not matter whether the item is given, lent or sold to the perpetrator, even in the normal course of business. In all of these cases, it is assistance and whether the supplier will be liable as an accomplice depends on his *mens rea* (see 14.4.2). *Lomas* (1913) 110 LT 239, CCA, as explained in *Bullock* [1955] 1 All ER 15, CCA, provides an exception where the perpetrator is the owner of the item supplied (e.g., a jemmy or knife which the perpetrator had previously loaned to him) and is therefore in civil law entitled to the return of the item. However, many academics have expressed doubt as to the validity of this exception on the basis that a person who returns a borrowed gun to the perpetrator knowing that he intends to kill someone with it should surely be guilty as an accessory to the murder when it takes place.

Presence

A question which has exercised the courts several times is whether mere presence at the commission of the offence **without more** constitutes assistance or encouragement.

> **? QUESTION** 14.4
>
> In the film *The Accused*, starring Jodie Foster, a woman was held down and raped in a café full of people. A number of people watched these events, some clapping and cheering. Anyone holding a woman down would aid and abet the rape, but would the spectators?

The first point to make is that **generally** a person cannot become an accomplice merely because he fails to act to prevent an offence he witnesses. There are two exceptions to this rule: (a) where the accomplice has a right of control over the actions of the perpetrator which he deliberately fails to exercise and (b) in those exceptional cases where the criminal law imposes a duty on someone to act and they deliberately fail to do so. An example of (a) is *Tuck* v *Robson* [1970] 1 All ER 1171, DC where a publican who stood by and watched his customers drinking after hours was guilty of aiding and abetting them in doing so. Similarly, the owner of a car who, sitting in the passenger seat, does nothing to prevent his car from being driven recklessly (or, as it would now be, dangerously) by D is guilty of aiding and abetting D's reckless (or dangerous) driving (*Du Cros* v *Lambourne* [1907] 1 KB 40). *J. F. Alford Transport Ltd* [1997] 2 Cr App R 326, CA, provides an interesting application of the principle. Drivers employed by D were illegally falsifying their tachograph records to 'reduce' the number of hours driven to 'comply' with permitted limits. It was held that, since the company and its managing director had the power to control the actions of the drivers, a deliberate decision to refrain from doing so would be positive encouragement for the drivers to continue falsifying the records. Although in the other two cases cited, A had been present at the commission of the offence, in this case A was not present when the records were falsified. It was held that A's presence was not essential as a matter of law (though it might help, as a matter of evidence, to prove the necessary 'encouragement' by A) (see 14.4.2.1 below on the question of *mens rea*).

An example of (b) would be where a parent stands by and watches another person ill-treat the parent's child when he could reasonably prevent the offence. The parent would be an accomplice to the offence whereas a stranger, who has no duty to protect the child, would not (*Gibson and Gibson* (1984) 80 Cr App R 24, CA; *Russell and Russell* [1987] Crim LR 494, CA; *Forman and Ford* [1988] Crim LR 677).

Because of the general rule stated above, it is clear that a mere accidental spectator of the commission of an offence will not without more be an accomplice. If he does an act of positive assistance or encouragement (such as the clapping and cheering of the spectators of a rape portrayed in the film *The Accused*), then the spectator can be convicted as an accessory, even though his initial presence was entirely accidental. If the accused was present pursuant to a prior agreement that the offence be committed, there is no doubt that his mere presence would constitute encouragement without the necessity for the prosecution to prove that he did anything further (*Smith* v *Reynolds* [1986] Crim LR 559, DC).

In the halfway house situation where A's presence was not accidental but yet equally not in pursuance of a prior agreement with the perpetrator, it is not entirely clear as to whether that voluntary presence itself would constitute encouragement, even though no other act of assistance or encouragement could be proved. The case law seems to show that it is a question for the jury in each case as to whether the accused's presence did in fact encourage the perpetrator (*Clarkson* [1971] 3 All ER 344, Courts-Martial Appeal Court; *Coney* (1882) 8 QBD 534). In many cases passive spectating will not amount to actual encouragement whereas in some it will. Examples of the former include *Clarkson* and *Allan* [1963] 2 All ER 897, CCA (*Cases and Materials* (14.4.1.6)). In *Clarkson*, the accused were attracted to a room by sounds indicating that a woman was being raped. They passively watched whilst a German girl was raped by three British soldiers. As the judge put it, 'To say that they behaved like animals would be unjust to animals.' In *Allan* the accused passively watched a violent fight which constituted an affray. In both cases the accused were acquitted because there was no evidence that the spectators' presence actually encouraged the rape or the fight. On the other hand, in *Wilcox* v *Jeffrey* [1951] 1 All ER 464, A attended the performance of a celebrated alien saxophonist, Coleman Hawkins, who he knew had been refused a work permit, making the performance illegal. In fact he had previously met him on arrival at the airport and subsequently wrote a rave review for the jazz magazine he edited. It was held that his buying a ticket and attending the performance was an encouragement to Hawkins. A similar view would be taken of attendance at, say, an illegal dog fight or an illegal prize fight (see *Coney* above).

 QUESTION 14.5

Is actual encouragement all that the prosecution needs to prove to win its case?

Even if the presence is construed as being an actual encouragement, this will only establish the *actus reus*. In addition, *mens rea* is required. In this context, that means that the prosecution must prove that A **intended** to encourage the perpetrator to commit the crime. This was stressed in *Clarkson* where it was noted that even if presence did in fact encourage the perpetrator, the accused might not realise he was giving encouragement, nor intend to do so. The reason why the conviction of the spectator at the illegal prize fight was quashed in *Coney* was that the Appeal Court thought that the trial judge's direction could have been understood to mean that his voluntary and deliberate presence was **conclusive** evidence of such intention. It could have been somebody who was totally opposed to prize fighting. *Allan* shows that a totally passive spectator at an affray who does not, **by this presence**, intend to encourage the participants, cannot be convicted simply because he secretly intended to join in the fight if the side he favoured needed help.

14.4.1.7 The principal offence

Subject to the exceptions to be noted shortly, since the accessory's liability is derivative flowing from the liability of the perpetrator, it is essential to prove that the principal offence that A is charged with aiding, abetting, etc. was actually committed. How can A aid and abet a non-existent offence? This was why the Court of Appeal in *Rogers* strained to find that D, who in reality merely assisted V to administer the drug injected by V into himself, actually administered it to V and thus acted as a perpetrator of the s. 23 offence (see 14.3 above). In *Thornton* v *Mitchell* [1940] 1 All ER 339, DC (*Cases and Materials* (14.4.1.7)) a bus conductor who negligently directed the bus driver to reverse his bus with the result that two pedestrians were knocked down, could not be guilty of aiding and abetting the driver to drive without due care and attention because it was found that the driver was not negligent in relying on the conductor's signals. The court found that there was no *actus reus* because nobody drove carelessly. The conductor was careless but did not drive, the driver drove but was not careless! (See also *Loukes* and *Roberts and George* below.)

Paradoxically, it seems that an accomplice can be convicted of aiding and abetting an offence for which the perpetrator is acquitted. In *Humphreys and Turner* [1965] 3 All ER 689, A was convicted of aiding and abetting D to obtain money by false pretences. Yet D was found not guilty of perpetrating this offence. In fact, it was not as illogical as it sounds because D's earlier confession of guilt was inadmissible under the rules of evidence in the case against him but was admissible in the case against A. Even if the evidence against the principal and the accomplice is exactly the same, it is perfectly feasible that, if they have separate trials, different juries could reach inconsistent verdicts (see *Hui Chi-ming* [1991] 3 All ER 897, dealt with below, for an example). Thus, there is no need for 'the principal offence to be evidenced by the prior or contemporaneous **conviction** of the perpetrator' (Law Com. No. 131, para. 2.36).

What are the exceptions to the rule requiring proof of the actual commission of the offence alleged to have been aided and abetted?

Where the perpetrator and the accomplice are liable but for different crimes

This situation can arise where different offences share the same *actus reus*, e.g., murder and manslaughter or ss. 18 and 20 of the Offences Against the Person Act 1861. According to some authorities, it is possible for the perpetrator to be convicted of murder and the accessory of aiding and abetting only manslaughter and vice versa, depending on whether they have an intention to kill the victim. Lord Mackay in *Howe* [1987] 1 AC 417, HL gave the following example: A gives D a gun informing him that it is loaded with blanks and telling him to go and scare X by firing it. The ammunition is in fact live, as A well knows, and X is killed. Even if D is convicted as perpetrator only of manslaughter because he lacks any intention to kill or cause grievous bodily harm, four Law Lords agreed with the Court of Appeal that A would nonetheless be guilty of aiding and abetting murder. Conversely, the perpetrator of the offence could be guilty of murder and the accessory of manslaughter if it was the accessory who thought that the ammunition was blank and the perpetrator who knew that it was live (*Reid* (1975) 62 Cr App R 109, CA—there is a question mark over the correctness of *Reid* and the principle itself, which we explore further at 14.4.3.1).

In the case of murder and manslaughter, it is possible that even though both the perpetrator and accessory have the *mens rea* for murder, one of them may have the defence of provocation or diminished responsibility reducing their crime to manslaughter. It would appear that the other party, whether perpetrator or accessory, would nonetheless be guilty of murder. This is expressly provided for in the case of diminished responsibility by s. 2(4) of the Homicide Act 1957 and the implication of *Howe* is that the position would be the same in respect of provocation.

Perpetrator exempt from prosecution

This very unusual situation is not really an exception to the rule since the perpetrator does actually commit the crime, but a special statutory provision exempts him from prosecution for the commission of that offence. Nonetheless, a person can be liable for aiding and abetting the perpetrator who cannot be prosecuted (*Austin* [1981] 1 All ER 374, CA). In *Austin*, the defendants were convicted of aiding and abetting the offence of child-stealing contrary to s. 56 of the Offences Against the Person Act 1861 (since repealed). The child victim was snatched by its father (with the help of the accused) from the lawful custody of his estranged wife. Under the terms of the statute, a father was 'not liable to be prosecuted' for the offence and therefore immune. The Court of Appeal held that this did not prevent the father from committing the offence but merely from being prosecuted for such commission and therefore there was no problem in finding that the accomplices aided and abetted the offence.

Perpetrator not liable because he has a defence

In this situation, the perpetrator causes the *actus reus* of the offence and has the *mens rea* but is not guilty because of the existence of some defence. Can the accomplice be guilty of aiding and abetting the offence, even though the perpetrator does not, because of the defence, commit it?

 EXERCISE 14.2

Read the extract from *Bourne* in *Cases and Materials* (14.4.1.7).

Do you agree with the Lord Chief Justice that Mrs Bourne 'committed the crime' but is 'excused punishment' by virtue of duress?

Do you agree with him that she had no *mens rea* for the crime?

In *Bourne* (1952) 36 Cr App R 125, CCA when A forced his wife to have intercourse with an Alsatian dog, she was not guilty of the offence of buggery because she was acting under duress, though clearly she had caused the *actus reus* of the crime with the appropriate *mens rea*. (In fact the court seemed to be saying, quite wrongly, that the wife did commit an offence but 'duress excused her punishment'. However, it is quite clear that where it operates, the defence of duress negatives liability and therefore the wife committed no offence.) The husband was, nonetheless, convicted of aiding and abetting his wife to commit buggery.

DPP v *K and B* [1997] 1 Cr App R 36, DC, provides another example. V, a 14-year-old girl, was threatened, falsely imprisoned and robbed by A1 and A2, also girls of 14 and 11 respectively. They forced V by threats of violence to have non-consensual sexual intercourse with D, a boy who was certainly over ten but may have been under 14. The boy could not be traced and it was not possible to rebut the presumption of incapacity (*doli incapax*) then applicable, by showing that he knew his acts were seriously wrong. It could not be proved that he committed the crime of rape. Nonetheless, A1 and A2 were guilty of procuring rape. The Court thought that it would be 'quite different' if the boy were under ten but, in truth, there seems no reason why the same principle should not apply. If in both cases D has intercourse knowing the girl does not consent, does it matter that the boy under ten is not guilty because of the irrebuttable presumption of *doli incapax* whereas the 10- to 14-year-old is not guilty because of a rebuttable (but unrebutted) presumption thereof?

Perpetrator not liable because he lacks the mens rea

Here the perpetrator performs the *actus reus* of the crime but does not possess the appropriate *mens rea* so that he commits no offence. In *DPP* v *K and B*, it was not proved that D knew or was reckless as to V's lack of consent. Nonetheless, it was held that such a lack of *mens rea* on the part of the perpetrator did not preclude conviction of A1 and A2 for procuring rape where the *actus reus* was procured and they 'desired' it. This followed the case of *Cogan and Leak* [1975] 2 All ER 1059, CA where the facts were similar though A and D were adults. A was guilty notwithstanding D's acquittal for lack of *mens rea* because he procured D's *actus reus* (non-consensual sexual intercourse) with the intention that D should have intercourse with the victim (A's wife) without her consent. The Court thought that A should have been indicted as a **principal** rather than a mere accessory since, in its eyes, A perpetrated rape on his wife through the innocent agency of D. There are serious problems with this view that someone can have sexual intercourse through the agency of another. Suppose A had been female! Section 1 of the Sexual Offences Act 2003 requires penile penetration and so, by implication, provides that only a man can commit rape as principal (though obviously a woman can be an accessory as held in *DPP* v *K and B*, e.g., if she holds the victim down). The better view is that innocent agency has no application in rape.

Offences where innocent agency could be applied in cases where A uses someone lacking *mens rea* to achieve his purpose are theft and burglary. Paradoxically, when the point arose in *Wheelhouse* [1994] Crim LR 756, the Court of Appeal convicted A of procuring burglary. A told D, to whom he owed money, that he could have his car. He gave D the keys to it and to a garage where the car was located and D took the car from the garage. In fact A had previously sold the car to the owner of the garage. D was acquitted of theft and burglary for lack of dishonesty but A was found dishonest and convicted of procuring D's burglary. He had deliberately procured the *actus reus* of the crime and that was enough.

Wheelhouse followed the Court of Appeal's decision in *Millward* [1994] Crim LR 527 (*Cases and Materials* (14.4.1.7)). Under instructions from A, his employer, D drove on to the highway a tractor towing a trailer. Owing to a badly maintained towing hitch, of which A but not D was aware, the trailer broke away from the tractor and hit a car, killing one of its occupants. D was acquitted of the (now obsolete) offence of causing death by reckless driving because he lacked the *mens rea* necessary for reckless driving. Could A nonetheless be guilty of procuring it?

The Court, rather suspectly, decided that the *actus reus* of reckless driving was committed as soon as D drove on to the highway with the seriously defective tow. It was enough to convict A that he procured D to commit this *actus reus* even though D's lack of fault prevented his having the *mens rea* necessary to convict him (D) of the offence. It is not clear whether this principle is limited to cases of procuring or whether it extends to aiding, abetting and counselling. If the differences in the second and third respects noted at 14.4.1.4 above are applicable, then A cannot aid, abet or counsel where the perpetrator performs the *actus reus* without the necessary *mens rea* because there is no 'consensus' (i.e., meeting of minds) between A and the perpetrator and the perpetrator's objective is not to do what constitutes the crime. We would suggest that it is unnecessary and dangerous to extend the principle beyond 'procuring' (*cf.* Law Com. No. 131, para. 4.207).

It is clear that the *Millward* principle can only operate where D has committed the *actus reus*. If no *actus reus* is perpetrated, then *Thornton* v *Mitchell* will apply, making conviction of the 'accessory' impossible. Thus, in both *Loukes* [1996] 1 Cr App R 444, CA, and *Roberts and George* [1997] Crim LR 209, CA, road users had been killed in accidents caused by defects in badly maintained lorries. The drivers of the lorries were charged with causing death by dangerous driving (which has now superseded 'reckless' driving) and their employers as accessories thereto. It was held that neither driver performed the *actus reus* of the offence because unless 'it would be obvious to a competent and careful driver that driving the vehicle in its current state would be dangerous', there was no 'dangerous' driving. Since it was not proved that either defect would be obvious to the reasonable driver, the death was caused by driving but not **dangerous** driving. An essential ingredient of the *actus reus* was missing. It followed that neither employer (even if aware of the defect!) could be guilty of procuring the offence.

> **?** **QUESTION** 14.6
>
> Could an employer who was aware of the dangerous state of the vehicle (as was the case in *Millward*) be guilty as *principal* on the basis of innocent agency?

No consideration was given to the possibility of the use of the innocent agency principle in either *Loukes* or *Roberts and George* since there was no evidence that either employer knew of the defect. Where the employer is aware of the dangerous state of the vehicle and the employee ordered to drive is not, the latter might be viewed as the innocent agent of the employer. However, it is thought that the principle is inappropriate for 'driving' offences. Like rape, driving is not something that can be done through the agency of another. Only the driver drives.

14.4.2 *Mens rea*

There is still a considerable element of uncertainty in the case law as to the precise *mens rea* needed for accessorial liability. This is because that *mens rea* is uniquely complex in having a dual focus. Not only is there the usual requirement to establish fault in respect of the accessory's own acts including the circumstances surrounding them but also his awareness of the intentions of the perpetrator. Where the assistance occurs beforehand, there is always an element of unpredictability as to what the perpetrator is going to do.

Isolating these two elements, we can summarise the essential requirements: A must (a) intentionally do the acts of assistance or encouragement done, realising they are capable of assisting or encouraging the perpetrator to do what constitutes the crime; and (b) know or believe that the perpetrator is committing the crime (if assisting/encouraging at the time of the crime) or will or **might well** commit the crime. Controversially, the Court of Appeal in *Bryce* [2004] EWCA Crim 1231 insists that there is a further requirement in respect of (a) in the form of 'an intention to assist (and not to hinder or obstruct) the perpetrator in acts which the accessory knows are steps taken by the perpetrator towards the commission of the offence' ([24]).

If A is charged with procuring, then it is submitted that he must also intend, by his acts, to bring about the commission of the crime.

14.4.2.1 **Intentional assistance/encouragement**

It is clear that, aside from 'procuring', the accessory does not need to have an intention that the crime be committed with his assistance or encouragement. That is, it need not be shown that it is A's **purpose** to get the crime committed. He need only intend to do acts he knows to be capable of assisting or encouraging the perpetrator to commit the crime (*National Coal Board* v *Gamble* [1958] 3 All ER 203—*Cases and Materials* (14.4.2.1)—and *J. F. Alford Transport Ltd* [1997] 2 Cr App R 326, CA). Although, as noted above, *Bryce* insists there is a further requirement of intention to assist D, it is not entirely clear what is meant by this and whether it actually adds anything in practice. The Court explains as follows:

> Where a defendant, D, is charged as the secondary party to an offence committed by P in reliance on acts which have assisted steps taken by P in the preliminary stages of a crime later committed by P in the absence of D, it is necessary for the Crown to prove intentional assistance by D in the sense of an intention to assist (and not to hinder or obstruct) P in acts which D knows are steps taken by P towards the commission of the offence. ([24])

Notice that what the accessory must intend to assist is not the commission of the offence itself but acts which A knows are steps taken by D towards its commission. So in *Bryce*, A intentionally arranged for D to stay at and intentionally transported him (and his shotgun) to, a caravan knowing that this was to be used as a safe house from which D was going to murder the victim in his nearby home. Even if A did not intend D to go through with the offence, he was aiming to help him in taking these preliminary steps which he believed were steps D was taking towards the crime. With respect, that does not seem much different to saying A must deliberately do his acts of assistance knowing that they are capable of assisting the perpetrator to commit the crime. However, the Court did imply that if D was motivated to provide his acts of 'assistance' by an intention to 'hinder or obstruct' the execution of the crime, he would lack the necessary intent to assist. In this case, A had claimed that he had come up with the caravan idea in order to delay the attack on the victim and possibly lead to a change of mind by D. Although rejecting this claim on the evidence, the Court seems to have been of the view that this would have precluded the necessary intention to aid. One might say that the provision of 'knowing' assistance will automatically lead to a finding of intention to assist **unless** it is shown that A was aiming to hinder or obstruct the commission of the crime.

Aside from the unusual case where A, by his ostensible assistance, is aiming to hinder D's commission of the crime, our contention would still be that 'knowing' in addition to 'intentional' assistance would suffice. Provided that A does know the full circumstances constituting the offence (see 14.4.2.2), if he voluntarily assists the principal in bringing about its commission he is guilty even though he may be quite indifferent about whether it is committed or even positively hope that it is not committed (*NCB v Gamble*; *DPP v Lynch* [1975] 1 All ER 913, HL). (It is best to regard *Fretwell* (1862) Le & Ca 161 which goes against this principle as incorrect.) In *Lynch*, A drove D to the place where he knew that D intended to murder a policeman and did. It was held that A's intentional driving of the car was aiding and abetting, 'even though he regretted the plan or indeed was horrified by it'. (Of course, since *Howe* [1987] 1 All ER 771, HL duress, which in *Lynch* was held to be a possible defence for A, is no longer available to an accessory to murder.) Thus, it is not necessary that A should have as his **purpose** that the crime he intentionally assists/encourages should be committed. There is no need to show that A provided his assistance/encouragement **in order** that D might commit the crime.

The interesting civil case of *Gillick v West Norfolk Area Health Authority* [1985] 3 All ER 402 (*Cases and Materials* (14.4.2.1)) is difficult to reconcile with the above principle. The House of Lords held that in some circumstances where a doctor knew that the provision of contraceptive advice or treatment to a girl under 16 would encourage or facilitate unlawful sexual intercourse by the girl with a man, such advice and treatment would be lawful. Clearly, the man, but not the girl, would commit an offence if he had sexual intercourse with the girl (s. 6 of the Sexual Offences Act 1956—now superseded by a wider offence in s. 9 of the Sexual Offences Act 2003). Has not the doctor knowingly assisted the man (in making the girl more ready to have intercourse) and encouraged the man (assuming the man knows of the contraception)? Although their Lordships' reasoning is not clear, the decision that the doctor's action can be lawful clearly implies that he does not aid and abet the crime. It seems that the majority of the House thought that the doctor would lack the necessary intention, presumably on the basis that his purpose was not to facilitate or encourage unlawful intercourse but rather to protect the girl if she did indulge in it. However, such an interpretation is contrary to the principles stated above and seems to confuse intention and motive. The better explanation is to regard *Gillick* as based on necessity (see 9.5.1).

It may be that the above analysis suggesting that it is enough to show that the accomplice contemplated (i.e., realised) that his act would or might well bring about the commission of the offence does not apply to a mere 'procurer' of the offence. In *Blakely and Sutton* v *DPP* [1991] Crim LR 763, DC (*Cases and Materials* (14.4.2.1)) the defendants, A1 and A2, put vodka in D's tonic water (unknown to D) in order to put him over the drink-drive limit. Their intention was to tell him later what they had done, believing that he would then decide not to drive home to his wife but to stay the night with A1. In fact he left and drove home before A1 had told him of the vodkas. He was convicted of a drink-driving offence. The issue was whether A1 and A2 were guilty of procuring the commission of this offence. The Divisional Court tentatively suggested obiter that it might not be sufficient for A1 and A2 to realise the offence might be committed. They would have to be proved to have **intended** (i.e., aimed for) the commission of the offence and, of course, here, they intended D **not** to drive—exactly the opposite to what was required!

> **?** **QUESTION** 14.7
>
> If a procurer's intention (i.e., purpose) has to be that the offence should be committed, was the accused in *Millward* rightly convicted of procuring his employee to cause death by reckless driving?

You may also recall that the Court of Appeal in *Attorney-General's Reference (No. 1 of 1975)* [1975] 2 All ER 684 defined 'procure' as 'produce by endeavour' implying that it had to be the procurer's purpose to secure the commission of the offence. If that is correct, it throws doubt on the procurer's conviction in *Millward* [1994] Crim LR 527, CA. A was convicted of procuring the offence of causing death by reckless driving in that he knowingly caused his employee to drive on the road towing a trailer with a defective towing hitch. The employee was acquitted for lack of *mens rea*. What was A's purpose? Certainly not to cause anyone's death—otherwise this would be murder. He was not out to 'produce' a death by reckless driving 'by endeavour'. He was aiming that his employee should drive recklessly because he knew that was the inevitable consequence of driving with the defective tow. A conviction for procuring reckless driving is therefore compatible with the 'purpose' view of procure but not a conviction for causing death by reckless driving.

14.4.2.2 **Knowledge of the principal offence**

The second of the two main elements of the *mens rea* requires that the accessory should know (at the time he assists or encourages) that D is doing or will do or may well do acts (with any necessary state of mind or fault element) constituting the crime. For example, the weighbridge attendant employed by the National Coal Board in *NCB* v *Gamble* knew that, following the issue of the weight ticket, the driver **would** commit the offence by driving his overloaded lorry on the highway. But what if the accessory is not sure that the offence is going to be committed but knows that it **might** be? Although the authorities are not definitive, it does now appear that this would suffice. Indeed if the assistance/encouragement is given beforehand, how can anyone know for sure that the offence **will** be committed? Liability can only be premised on belief that the crime will be committed or realisation that it may be (or is likely to be) committed unless, as in some cases, e.g., *Bainbridge*, the rule is based on A's knowledge of D's **intentions** to commit the crime rather than the commission of the crime itself. As we shall see at 14.4.3 below, the House of Lords in *Powell* [1997] 4 All ER 545 makes it clear that where the accessory is participating in a joint enterprise, there is no doubt that liability is based on A's foresight that the crime **may** be committed. It appears increasingly likely that this applies equally to non-joint enterprise situations (*Bryce*; *Gilmour* [2000] 2 Cr App R 407; *Carter* v *Richardson*; *J. F. Alford Transport Ltd*; *Reardon* [1999] Crim LR 392, CA) though there are some authorities against (e.g., *Bainbridge*; *DPP* v *Maxwell* is ambiguous). All these cases are dealt with below. Let us look at some of these issues in more detail.

To be an accessory A must 'know the essential matters which constitute that offence. He need not actually know that an offence has been committed, because he may not know that the facts constitute an offence and ignorance of the law is not a defence' (Lord Goddard CJ in *Johnson* v *Youden* [1950] 1 All ER 300, DC). The 'essential matters' referred to mean all the circumstances **required** by the *actus reus* of the offence. It should also include any consequences necessary for the *actus reus* **and** any *mens rea* or fault element required by the perpetrator to commit the offence but, curiously, there does not appear any formal requirement for A to foresee the prohibited consequences of D's act. This is because the law seems to be based on whether A is responsible for D's acts. If he is, it seems automatically to follow that he is also responsible for the consequences which ensue from the harm causing acts (see 14.4.3 below).

The requirement for knowledge of the circumstances holds good even if the offence is a strict liability offence requiring no *mens rea* on the part of the principal in relation to one or more elements of the *actus reus*. The accessory can be convicted only if he knows of the existence of those essential circumstances. *Callow* v *Tillstone* (1900) 83 LT 411 (*Cases and Materials* (14.4.2.2)) illustrates the point. Shortly before it would have died naturally from the poison, a farmer slaughtered a cow which had eaten poisonous yew leaves. He asked A, a vet, to examine the corpse and A certified that the meat was untainted. In reliance on A's certificate, D, a butcher, had offered the meat for sale. In fact, A's examination had been negligent and the meat was unsound. The butcher was convicted of the strict liability offence of exposing unsound meat for sale.

? **QUESTION** 14.8

Was the vet guilty of aiding and abetting this offence? Give your reasons.

As argued above, we think that 'knowledge' in this context includes not only actual knowledge but also wilful blindness or subjective recklessness, but certainly **not** *Caldwell*-type objective recklessness (*Carter* v *Richardson* [1974] RTR 314, DC; *Blakeley Sutton* v *DPP* [1991] Crim LR 763, DC; *cf. Roberts and George* [1997] Crim LR 209, CA). It seems reasonably clear that where A knows that D is going to perform his intended actions, it will suffice to establish that A knew that the 'essential matters' constituting the offence **might** or at least were likely to, be present. In *Carter* v *Richardson,* A, the supervisor of D, a learner-driver driving with excess alcohol, was guilty of aiding and abetting D's offence because he knew that it was 'probable' that D was 'over the limit'. A was only subjectively reckless as to the 'essential matter' of the *actus reus*, the presence of excess alcohol. Does the same apply where A does not know for sure that D is going to perform the anticipated actions, e.g., drive at all? *J. F. Alford Transport Ltd* [1997] 2 Cr App R 326, CA suggests it does. The lorry driver employees of A had committed the offence of falsifying their tachograph records. It was held that it would be sufficient for aiding and abetting the offences to show that A knew that such false records were 'likely to be produced' by the drivers. Turning a blind eye to the drivers' falsification would be enough.

To summarise, the accessory must know that there is a significant **risk** that (a) D is going to do the acts constituting the crime and (b) all the ingredients ('the essential matters') of the crime will be present. That is why the vet in *Callow* v *Tillstone* was not an accessory to the butcher's offence. Because of his negligent mistake, the vet believed that the meat was sound. He did not know an 'essential matter' for the offence—he did not appreciate there was a risk that the meat might be unsound.

? **QUESTION** 14.9

Suppose A supplied a gun to D knowing that it would be used in an armed robbery. If D shoots someone dead in the course of the robbery, what would the prosecution need to prove in order to make (a) D guilty of murder and (b) A guilty as an accessory to murder?

If subjective recklessness suffices to fix liability on the accessory, it creates the unusual situation that his *mens rea* may be **less** exacting than that required for the perpetrator. Our Question provides an example. The accessory would be guilty of murder if (a) the perpetrator shot the victim with the intention of killing or causing grievous bodily harm **and** (b) the accessory realised when supplying the gun that there was a significant risk that the perpetrator might use it to **deliberately** (i.e., with the *mens rea* for murder) kill someone in the course of the robbery. Of course, the actual perpetrator can only be convicted of murder if he **intended** to kill or cause grievous bodily harm. It would not be enough that he realised there was a significant risk of killing, e.g., from a ricochet of a bullet fired to frighten.

Support for this can be found in *Reardon* [1999] Crim LR 392, CA. A was drinking in a pub with D and others when D shot two people in the head. They were carried outside and D came back exclaiming to A, 'That cunt's still alive . . . lend us your knife.' A handed his knife to D who went out and stabbed both victims a number of times. Both died partly from the gunshot wounds and partly from the knife wounds. A was held to be an accomplice to both murders even though his assistance was given for the purpose of killing only an unspecified one of the two. This was not a case where it was established that A and D were engaged in a joint enterprise having the common purpose to kill. However, the Court of Appeal applied the *Powell*; *English* principle (see 14.4.3.1 below) holding A liable because he contemplated (a) that the knife would be used to kill one of the victims and (b) that there was at least a strong possibility that it would be used similarly on the other victim if he were found to be still alive. The current principle appears to be that, whether he is participating in a joint enterprise or not, A need only realise that there is a real or significant risk of the crime being committed.

Similarly, in *Bryce*, the Court of Appeal held that it was enough that A, 'at the time of doing the act contemplated the commission of the offence by' D, i.e., he foresaw it as a 'real or substantial risk' or 'real possibility'. As in *Reardon*, the prosecution had not established that it was A's purpose to secure the victim's murder so that it was treated as not a joint enterprise case.

14.4.2.3 Knowledge of the type of crime

In understanding this requirement, it is essential to appreciate that when an accomplice is convicted, he is convicted of the offence the perpetrator has actually committed. There is no special offence of aiding and abetting criminality in general terms. A can be convicted only of aiding and abetting a specific crime which is actually committed with his assistance or encouragement. You might conclude from this that in order to be convicted as a participant in any crime, A would have to know the precise crime he was assisting or encouraging the perpetrator to commit. However, the law is not so strict. Of course, if A is assisting or encouraging at the scene of the crime or procuring, he is likely to know exactly what crime he is helping. The problem we are dealing with is likely to arise where he gives help beforehand (for example, by supplying equipment) without knowing precisely what is planned.

The law does not require a knowledge of the **precise details** of the particular crime to be committed. On the other hand, it would be unfair to convict someone of aiding and abetting whatever crime the perpetrator happens to commit just because he gave assistance to the perpetrator knowing that he was 'up to no good' and had some criminal purpose in mind without knowing what. If A supplies the perpetrator with a jemmy, asking no questions but realising that it is likely to be used for some criminal purpose, it would not be fair to convict A of aiding and abetting murder if the perpetrator used the jemmy to attack and deliberately kill someone. It could not be said that A **intentionally** aided D to commit **that** crime.

EXERCISE 14.3

Read the extract from *Bainbridge* in *Cases and Materials* (14.4.2.3).

- What was the principle formulated by the court?
- Do you see any problems with it?

Read the extract from *DPP for Northern Ireland* v *Maxwell* in *Cases and Materials* (14.4.2.3).

- Did the House of Lords approve the *Bainbridge* principle?
- Did the House depart from it in any way?
- How would you formulate the principles applicable after *DPP* v *Maxwell*?

The actual legal rules applicable sit somewhere in between the two extremes we adverted to earlier. According to *Bainbridge* [1959] 3 All ER 200, CCA it is sufficient to prove that A knew the 'type of crime' to be committed. A supplied oxy-acetylene equipment knowing, as the jury found, that it was to be used for a breaking and entering type of crime. The Court of Criminal Appeal held that it was immaterial that he did not know that it was to burgle the Midland Bank, Stoke Newington, six weeks later. A would have to know (not merely suspect, *cf. Alford Transport Ltd* above) that D intended to commit a crime of the type actually committed and that meant a crime of breaking and entering and stealing. On the other hand, using the equipment to cut up stolen goods would be a crime of a different type. Presumably if D had committed a multiplicity of breaking and entering crimes with the equipment, A would have been guilty of all of them! Another difficulty is that the notion of 'type of crime' is rather vague and could give rise to endless debates. Are all burglaries the same type of crime? If the perpetrator uses a jemmy supplied by A to break into a house, will A be guilty of aiding and abetting the burglary if the perpetrator intended to inflict GBH on someone in the house when A believed that he intended to steal from the house to be broken into?

The principle was adopted and, indeed, extended by the House of Lords in *DPP for Northern Ireland* v *Maxwell* [1978] 3 All ER 1140. It held that an accessory would be guilty of the crime committed by the principal if either it was of the type contemplated by the accessory or (and this is the extension of the principle in *Bainbridge*) it was within the range of a limited number of crimes which the accessory contemplated would be committed (even if the list of possible crimes contemplated contained crimes of different types). In *Maxwell*, A drove his car to a public house knowing that he was guiding another vehicle containing terrorist members of the Ulster Volunteer Force to the pub. A realised that some kind of attack was to be made, but he did not know what form it would take. In the event the men in the following car threw a pipe bomb into the pub which, fortunately, did not explode in the pub. A was held guilty for being an accessory to the crimes of doing an act with intent to cause an explosion and possession of explosives. These were offences within the range of possibilities which he contemplated would be committed. It would not have mattered if the men had carried out the attack with guns or if the pub had simply been a rendezvous point, the attack being carried out at some other venue. A defendant who voluntarily gives assistance to someone being aware that they are going to commit one of a number of possible crimes, makes himself liable for whatever crime the perpetrator chooses to commit, provided, of course, that it is within the range of the offences con-templated.

It will be evident that problems under this head tend to arise when the defendant's assistance or encouragement occurs prior to the commission of the offence since, if it is given at the time the offence is being committed, A will be well aware of the precise offence being committed. However, a similar problem can arise where the parties embark on a joint unlawful enterprise and one of the parties departs from the joint enterprise agreed and perpetrates a further crime. The question then is whether A would be liable as an accessory for that further crime.

14.4.3 Joint unlawful enterprise

Most accessories will in practice be participants in a joint enterprise because they will share with the perpetrator(s) a common purpose to get the crime committed. There is some debate about whether this doctrine is a distinct form of liability but the better view seems to be that it is a (perhaps illegitimate) extension of the standard law on aiding, abetting, counselling and procuring—in the words of Professor Smith 'a bastard appendage' to it ((1994) 144 NLJ 679, 682). The House of Lords in *Powell* seemed to view participants in joint enterprise as accessories but did not discuss the issue specifically. It has traditionally been thought that joint enterprise does import special rules which relax the normal requirements for accessorial liability. However, the precise extent to which they differ, if at all, has never been properly analysed by the courts and continues to be shrouded in uncertainty. The only situation where joint enterprise might differ from normal accessorial rules in our law seems to be where, during the course of carrying out an agreed crime, one or more of the participants deliberately commits a different crime which was not part of the agreed enterprise. The question which is then raised, of course, is whether the other participants are responsible for the unagreed crime as well as the agreed crime.

In many cases, two or more people will embark on a joint enterprise to commit a crime which they have planned and agreed beforehand. That is the clearest case, but it is possible for the agreement to be purely tacit and made immediately before or even during the course of the commission of the offence. The essential ingredient of joint enterprise is a **shared** common purpose—'a **shared** common intention... each has the same intention as the other and each **knows** that the other intends the same thing'—*Petters and Parfitt* [1995] Crim LR 501, CA (our emphasis) (*Cases and Materials* (14.4.3)). The rule is that each party is liable for whatever crimes the others commit which come within the scope of the **common purpose or design**. Thus, if D1 and D2 execute a smash-and-grab raid at a jewellers, A remaining in a car as a get-away driver, all will be liable for criminal damage, theft and burglary. It does not matter who actually broke the window or reached in and took the jewellery. All of these acts were expressly or impliedly agreed upon by all parties as part and parcel of the common design. Does the converse rule apply so that an accomplice is **not** liable for crimes which are **outside** the scope of the common purpose or design? The answer is, not necessarily.

14.4.3.1 **Deliberate departure**

Common purpose

If the perpetrator **deliberately** departs from the joint enterprise without the participation or agreement of A, e.g., vandalises V's property or shoots someone dead during a joint burglary, A will not normally be liable as an accomplice to criminal damage and murder respectively because both are outside the scope of the joint enterprise.

? **QUESTION** 14.10

Imagine that you agree to break into a warehouse with Bonnie and Clyde. When leaving the warehouse, you are challenged by a security guard. Bonnie pulls out a gun and deliberately shoots the guard dead. Should you be guilty of murder if you:

(a) had no idea B and C were carrying weapons;

(b) knew B and C were carrying weapons;

(c) knew B and C were carrying weapons but they had agreed they would be used only to frighten;

(d) knew B and C were violent people who had used guns to murder people before but you did not know whether they were carrying guns on this occasion?

You will find the answers to this Question at the end of our further explanation.

An example is provided by *Davies* v *DPP* [1954] 1 All ER 507, HL. A was a willing participant in a pre-arranged gang fight on Clapham Common which ended with one of the rival gang being stabbed to death. It was held that A was not an accomplice to manslaughter because he did not know that the perpetrator was carrying a knife and the scope of the joint enterprise was limited to assaulting with fists. However, suppose that A had known that the perpetrator was carrying a knife. Clearly, if A had tacitly agreed to the use of the knife if necessary, then its use would be part of the common purpose and A would be liable to the same extent as the perpetrator. Such tacit agreement would normally be inferred from proof that A knew that the knife was being carried. Use of the knife would not be a departure from the common purpose.

Foresight of possible departure

Furthermore, it appears from the House of Lords' decision in *Powell; English* [1997] 4 All ER 545 that, even if A does **not** agree, tacitly or otherwise, to the use of the knife, where 'one party foresees that in the course of the enterprise the other party may carry out, with the requisite *mens rea*, an act constituting another crime, the former is liable for that crime if committed by the latter in the course of the enterprise.' This confirms the position applied by the Privy Council in *Chan Wing-siu* v *R* [1984] 3 All ER 877 and *Hui Chi-ming* v *R* [1991] 3 All ER 897 and by the Court of Appeal in several cases. It would seem clear that the use of the knife is outside the 'common purpose' of the enterprise but it is now clear that it will still be regarded by the courts as 'within the scope of the enterprise' if it was contemplated by A as a possible incident of the agreed enterprise (see, e.g., the Australian case of *McAuliffe* v *R* (1995) 130 ALR 26 approved in *Powell* and *D* [2005] EWCA Crim 1981 at

[20]). Therefore, if A goes along with the joint enterprise realising that D may intentionally kill in the course of the enterprise, A will be liable for murder if D does so kill (or attempted murder if D tries but fails to kill—*O'Brien* [1995] 2 Cr App R 649, CA). A 'has in those circumstances lent himself to the enterprise and by so doing he has given assistance and encouragement to the perpetrator in carrying out an enterprise which [A] realises may involve murder' (*Hyde* [1990] 3 All ER 892, CA).

According to *Powell*, A need only foresee the crime as a '**possible** incident of the joint venture, unless the risk was so remote that the jury take the view that the secondary party genuinely dismissed it as altogether negligible.' This is generally put as 'a real or substantial risk' (*Bryce*; *Chan Wing-siu* v R). As we saw at 14.4.2.2 above, this principle also seems to apply to non-joint enterprise accessories (*Reardon*; *Bryce*).

It follows that, on the current law, the situations in our last Question would be resolved as follows:

(a) Not guilty. The shooting was outside the common purpose and not contemplated.

(b) Guilty. The court would infer your tacit agreement to the use of weapons unless there is evidence to the contrary. Therefore the shooting to kill or cause GBH was within the common purpose. Even if there is evidence to the contrary, you would be liable if you realised B or C might deliberately shoot to kill or cause GBH.

(c) Guilty, **provided** you realised that there was a real risk that B or C might deliberately shoot to kill or cause GBH, notwithstanding that the shooting was outside the common purpose.

(d) Guilty, **provided** you realised that there was a significant risk that B or C would murder with a deadly weapon, if challenged in the course of the break-in.

Foresight and murder

> **? QUESTION** 14.11
>
> But if A is guilty of murder because he realises D might, if necessary, intentionally kill during the course of a break-in, does that not contradict the assertion in *Moloney* and *Hancock* that intention to kill or cause GBH alone suffices for murder? Can it be right that a lesser *mens rea* is required for the accessory than for the perpetrator?

Powell rightly holds that there is no contradiction because *Moloney* and *Hancock* were concerned only with a perpetrator's liability. It should also be pointed out that to be liable, A must not only foresee the possibility that D might do the act causing death but also that D might do so with the requisite *mens rea* for murder, i.e., an intention to kill or cause GBH. Although it is anomalous to require a lesser *mens rea* for the accessory than for the perpetrator (the reverse is usually the case), Lord Steyn explains the policy imperative which underpins the courts' extension of liability in joint enterprise cases:

> It would in practice almost invariably be impossible for a jury to say that the secondary party wanted death to be caused . . . In the real world proof of an intention sufficient for murder would be well

nigh impossible in the vast majority of joint enterprise cases…Experience has shown that joint criminal enterprises only too readily escalate into the commission of greater offences. In order to deal with this problem the accessory principle is needed and cannot be abolished or relaxed.

Lord Steyn gives the game away. The courts want to convict participants whose enterprise escalates beyond the original purpose because in most cases those participants would back D's greater crime. However, because A would always deny it, his agreement (even tacit) might be difficult to prove. To overcome this evidential difficulty, the solution is to soften the substantive law.

Some academic writers argue that it is inherently unfair to convict the merely reckless accessory of murder especially as the mandatory penalty for murder precludes the imposition of a lesser penalty than for the perpetrator. A possible solution might be to make the accessory responsible for the act causing death but only to the extent of his own *mens rea* so that he would be convicted of manslaughter only. However, it is clear that the current law makes the accessory liable for murder. The Court of Appeal in *Concannon* [2002] Crim LR 213 firmly rejected a misguided attempt to challenge the fairness of this rule of substantive law by praying in aid Art. 6 of the European Convention on Human Rights. That article is essentially concerned with the right to a fair trial in procedural terms and acceptance that an otherwise fair trial becomes unfair in contravention of it if the substantive law is unfair would open the floodgates and cause huge uncertainty. Not surprisingly the Court dismissed the point as 'unarguable'.

Assisting or encouraging beforehand

In essence therefore, the accessory is made liable because he is taking a deliberate risk of assisting or encouraging the further crime in the course of committing the agreed crime. This principle applies whether A is present at the time of the crime or merely gives assistance or encouragement beforehand (*Rook* [1993] 2 All ER 955, CA). This was endorsed by the Court of Appeal in *Wan and Chan* [1995] Crim LR 296 (*Cases and Materials* (14.4.3.1)) and again in *Bryce* so that it applies equally to one who counsels or procures the crime beforehand. Regrettably, the Court of Appeal in *Stewart and Schofield* [1995] Crim LR 420, without citing *Rook* (!), seemed to regard joint enterprise as inapplicable to counsellors and procurers, i.e., those not participating at the time of the commission of the offence. Participation beforehand apparently does not count as joint enterprise. This goes too far and would introduce an unwelcome distinction between those present and/or active at the crime and those not. Mr Big, the organiser and instigator of the whole unlawful enterprise, may often not be present or active at the time of the offence. The same rules should surely apply to his 'counselling and procuring'. If the court really meant to exclude counsellors and procurers from the joint enterprise doctrine, *Rook* and *Wan and Chan* are to be preferred. Unfortunately, the House of Lords did not consider this issue in *Powell*.

If *Stewart and Schofield* was simply seeking to say that some people who assist or encourage beforehand are not parties to the joint enterprise, this would be acceptable. Peripheral figures who, for example, merely supply equipment for use by a gang but who are not involved in the 'plan' should not be regarded as participants in the joint **enterprise**. In terms of *Petters and Parfitt* [1995] Crim LR 501, CA the peripheral figures might well lack any 'shared common intention' to commit the crime planned, of which they could easily be ignorant as to the details.

Unforeseen 'fundamentally different' acts

Powell; *English* decides that an accessory is not liable for any acts of the perpetrator which are 'fundamentally different' from any acts the accessory contemplated the perpetrator might perform during the enterprise.

? QUESTION 14.12

In *English*, a consolidated appeal heard by the House of Lords with *Powell*, A and D took part in an agreed joint attack to injure a policeman hitting him violently with wooden posts. During the attack D took out a knife and stabbed the policeman to death. It was assumed that A did not know D had a knife so that he did not foresee that D might stab the policeman. Should A be liable for murder because he realised that the policeman might be intentionally killed or intentionally seriously injured by the beating with the posts?

If the policeman had been killed by a blow with D's post, D would have been guilty of murder assuming he had had an intention to kill or cause GBH. A would have been guilty as an accessory to murder if either intentional infliction of GBH by the posts had been the common purpose or he had realised D might use the post in this way with an intention to at least cause GBH (*Powell*). (There would be no need to foresee the possibility that the blows might **kill** the victim. A will be responsible for D's **act** even if he does not foresee it as potentially lethal and the fact that he realises it will be done with the *mens rea* for murder—intention to do GBH—will make him a party to murder if death does result, whether the death is foreseen or not. If A is responsible for the act, he is also responsible for any of its consequences even if unforeseen and unintended by D, *cf*. 14.4.3.2 below.)

The policeman actually died from D's stabbing with intent to kill or cause GBH. This act was not contemplated as a possibility by A who did not know of the knife. The House of Lords held that A needed to have at least foreseen an act of the **type** which caused the death and 'in the present case the use of a knife was fundamentally different to the use of a post'. Similarly if, as in *Gamble* [1989] NI 268, A participates in an agreed enterprise to 'kneecap' with a gun, he would not be liable for murder where, in an action unforeseen by A, D kills V by cutting his throat with a knife. The House, rather surprisingly, thought it 'more debatable' whether the same would apply if D deliberately fired the gun into V's head as opposed to the anticipated knee! The two cases seem indistinguishable. In either case the lethal act is fundamentally different from the kneecapping because death is very likely and intended whereas death is neither intended nor likely from the contemplated shooting in the knee. In *Attorney-General's Reference (No. 3 of 2004)* [2005] EWCA Crim 1882 A sent D1 and D2 to terrorise V but they deliberately shot him in the head and killed him. They committed murder. It was accepted that A knew they would be armed with a gun and that they might discharge it near to V to maximise his terror. However, it was also accepted that A had not intended, or foreseen the possibility of, any physical injury or death. That precluded a conviction for murder or manslaughter because the deliberate shooting in the head was fundamentally different from any act (shooting to frighten) which A had contemplated might occur. It was therefore outside the scope of the agreed enterprise.

If in *English*, the plan had been to **kill** the victim with the posts as opposed to just causing GBH, should it make any difference that death is caused in a way unforeseen by A? Is a stabbing with intent to kill 'fundamentally different' from a beating with a post with intent to kill? A further qualification (which may partly resolve the questions just posed) was that it should not affect A's liability that he contemplated an attack with one weapon where the actual attack was with a weapon 'different to, but as dangerous as', the contemplated weapon, e.g., a knife instead of the contemplated gun or vice versa. A post is clearly not as dangerous as a knife!

At the end of the day, the House recognised that 'there will be cases giving rise to a fine distinction as to whether or not the unforeseen use of a particular weapon or the manner in which a particular weapon is used will take a killing outside the scope of the joint venture, but this issue will be one of fact for the common sense of the jury to decide.' In *Uddin* [1998] 2 All ER 744 (*Cases and Materials* (14.4.3.1)), the Court of Appeal did not rule that unforeseen use of a knife in a combined attack was 'fundamentally different' from the use of clubs and kicks but only that the issue should have been left to the jury for decision. *Greatrex* [1999] 1 Cr App R 126, CA took a similar line on the question of whether the use of a bar or spanner during a concerted attack was 'fundamentally different' to the use of kicks with shod feet.

The last two cases make it clear that the *Powell*; *English* principle applies not only to pre-planned crimes but also to a spontaneous attack by an irrational group of individuals all intent on doing serious harm to (or even killing) the victim. If death is actually caused by an act fundamentally different to any contemplated by the alleged accessories, they cannot be liable for murder even though they themselves were intent, by a 'fundamentally different' method, on causing GBH (or even killing).

Liability for lesser offence?

This leaves us with one final question to discuss where D's crime deliberately departs from the common purpose. It is a question which is not directly addressed in *English*. If the above principles exclude A's conviction for murder, could he be guilty of the lesser offence of manslaughter? The answer is found in *Uddin* above. Logically, if D's act is fundamentally different from any act foreseen by A, it is outside the scope of the joint enterprise and A cannot be in any way responsible for the act or its consequences. The House clearly endorsed this principle in holding that English was not guilty of either murder or **manslaughter** and it was applied subsequently by the Court of Appeal in *Uddin*.

That is the position where the act causing death is quite different from any act envisaged by A whether because, say, a surprise weapon is used or a known weapon is used in an entirely different way (e.g., the kneecapping example). But there is another situation unresolved by *English*.

? QUESTION 14.13

Suppose that A, a bookmaker, employs D to rough up V to encourage V to pay A a gambling debt. He stresses that D must not hurt him badly since this is more in the way of a warning. Contrary to instructions, D savagely attacks V and intentionally causes him serious injury. D is convicted of causing GBH with intent to cause GBH contrary to s. 18 of the OAPA 1861.

- Would A be guilty of the s. 18 offence?
- If not, would he be guilty of maliciously inflicting GBH contrary to s. 20 of the OAPA 1861?

This factual situation is similar in principle to that in *Wan and Chan* [1995] Crim LR 296, CA. Clearly, D's attack is a deliberate departure from the joint enterprise and not part of the common design. Nonetheless, if A contemplated that there was a real risk that D might **intentionally** cause GBH, he would be liable for the s. 18 offence under *Powell*. If he was not aware of this then, in strict theory, he should not be liable for any lesser offence even if he contemplated that such lesser offence might be committed by the perpetrator (*Wan and Chan*; *Dunbar* [1988] Crim LR 693, CA). The reason is that the nature of the attack (beating **with intent to cause GBH**) was unauthorised and unforeseen and, as it was a **deliberate** departure from the plan, A is totally absolved from responsibility for such acts and their consequences. A is not, on this view, an accessory to any offence because no criminal acts contemplated by A were performed by the perpetrator. He could be convicted of conspiracy to commit an assault occasioning actual bodily harm (which was what was agreed to be done) and inciting such an offence (see **Chapter 16**).

The Court of Appeal in *Stewart and Schofield* [1995] 3 All ER 159 disputes this analysis because, in its view, it is possible for an act done with an intention to cause death or serious injury on the part of one participant to still be within the scope of a joint enterprise with other participants who contemplate no more than non-serious injury. Whether it is within the scope of the joint enterprise is a question of fact for the jury in each case. We can perhaps accept that a distinction can be drawn where the perpetrator begins his beating without an intention to cause GBH and, in the course of the beating, the victim annoys him by fighting back, so that he then forms the intention to injure seriously. In our example situation, D will initially cause the contemplated injury (actual bodily harm) while acting within the agreed scope of the joint enterprise. A therefore immediately becomes liable for the s. 47 offence. It is irrelevant and cannot undo this liability that D **subsequently** departs from the common design. However, where D sets out from the beginning to depart from the agreed design, it is difficult to see how he could ever remain within the scope of the joint enterprise.

In *Stewart and Schofield*, the joint enterprise was to rob V at his shop. D went armed with a scaffolding pole and A1 with a knife. A2 kept watch outside the shop. V was beaten to death with the pole. D pleaded guilty to robbery and murder. A1 and A2 were acquitted of murder but convicted of manslaughter. A1 and A2 appealed contending that D's beating with murderous intent was neither part of the agreed common design nor contemplated by A1 and A2 as a possible departure from it. The court dismissed the appeal holding that, even though the jury's verdict that A1 and A2 were not guilty of murder meant that the jury accepted that A1 and A2 did not contemplate killing by D with the *mens rea* for murder, this did not compel the court to find that D had acted outside 'the course of' the joint enterprise (by which the court presumably means outside 'the scope of' the joint enterprise). It was apparently up to the jury to decide this as a question of fact. Once it decided that D's acts were still within the 'course' (scope?) of the enterprise, A1 and A2 would be responsible for those acts and their consequences. However, since they lacked any intent to kill or cause GBH and did not contemplate that D would have any such intent, they could only be convicted of manslaughter.

The case is in conflict with *Wan and Chan, Dunbar* and a number of other cases. However, there is another line of cases, including *Reid* (1975) 62 Cr App R 109, CA, which supports it.

Does *Powell; English* help to resolve the conflict? Surprisingly, neither *Wan* nor *Stewart* was referred to in *Powell*. It appears from *Powell* that to take an act outside the scope of the enterprise and thus absolve A from **any** responsibility for it, it has to be both uncontemplated itself by A and fundamentally different from any other act that A has contemplated. If, in *Stewart*, as the defendants claimed, they had not foreseen any violence with the iron bar but only that it would be used to threaten, then its actual use to inflict harm would surely be 'fundamentally different' and outside the scope of the joint venture. The defendants would not be responsible for it and would be acquitted of any liability for the death. The more difficult case left open by *Powell* is where the accused contemplated some actual violence with the iron bar but falling short of GBH or to be done without the *mens rea* for murder, i.e., an intention to kill or cause GBH. This would be similar to *Wan* and the facts of our last Question. The key question is whether the beating done by D with the intent to kill or cause GBH is thereby taken outside the scope of the joint enterprise. If the beating is carried out in the basic manner contemplated, does the uncontemplated increase in severity and the unanticipated murderous intent of D make the acts 'fundamentally different' from any foreseen by A? In one sense the acts are done as contemplated (beating with an iron bar), but in another sense (beating to cause GBH or death), they are most definitely not. The general tenor of the remarks in *Powell* and *Uddin* implies that the House might well have viewed the acts as still within the scope of the enterprise, although it should be remembered that it is ultimately an issue 'of fact for the common sense of the jury'.

If the acts were held to be within the scope of the joint enterprise, A would be responsible for D's acts but could not be guilty of murder (or if death did not result as in *Wan*, s. 18 of the OAPA 1861) because, by definition, he lacks the necessary *mens rea*. He does not contemplate that D will act with an intention to kill or cause GBH. However, as D's acts are within the scope of the joint venture, he will be convicted of manslaughter on the basis that he is responsible for the unlawful and dangerous act which has caused death. In the analogous situation in *Wan* where V suffers GBH but does not die, the courts might say that A is responsible for D's acts which inflicted GBH and since A contemplated D would do those acts intending to harm (sufficient *mens rea* for s. 20 of the OAPA 1861), A should be convicted under s. 20 while D is convicted of causing GBH with intent to do so contrary to s. 18.

The Court of Appeal of Northern Ireland supports this thesis in *Gilmour* [2000] 2 Cr App R 407 (*Cases and Materials* (14.4.3.1)). A acted as getaway driver for the Ds who murdered the victims by throwing a petrol bomb into a house where they were sleeping. Although A knew they were going to throw the petrol bomb into the house, he did not realise they were going to do so with intent to kill or cause grievous bodily harm, i.e., with the *mens rea* for murder. It followed that A could not be an accessory to the murder committed by the Ds. However because he contemplated 'the very deed' performed by the Ds, i.e., throwing the petrol bomb into the house, he was responsible for that unlawful and dangerous act which, since it caused death, enabled A to be convicted of manslaughter. He did contemplate the commission of that offence in that way. This was the explanation of *Stewart and Schofield* where A1 and A2 contemplated the possibility that D might injure V with the scaffolding bar but not intentionally kill or seriously injure him. Thus they were not guilty of murder but were rightly convicted of manslaughter.

Essentially, if the act committed by D is that envisaged by A, A will be guilty as accessory 'of the degree of offence appropriate to the intent with which he [A] so acted'. Without giving any examples, the Court thought it 'conceivable... that in some cases the nature of the principal's *mens rea* may change the nature of the act committed by him and take it outside the type of act contemplated by the accessory.' In that case A would not be responsible for the act at all and so could not be guilty of a lesser offence. Presumably, it will be left to the jury in each individual case to decide whether it is or is not an act of the nature contemplated.

The Court of Appeal in *Day* [2001] Crim LR 984, though unaware of the decision in *Gilmour*, adopted a similar view. A participated with D and others in a joint enterprise to harm V. Whilst A was fighting with V's friend, D was kicking V about the head intending to cause him GBH. V died from the kicks and D was convicted of murder. The jury acquitted A of murder (thus implying that A did not foresee that D might intentionally kill or cause GBH) but convicted him of manslaughter. A had admitted that he foresaw that D might kick V about the head in the course of any fight. The Court of Appeal held that such foresight of the physical acts which led to death made A responsible for D's acts and the fatal consequences. However, because he contemplated only some harm might be caused and not GBH, he could only be convicted of manslaughter and not murder. The Court's view was that D's secret, uncontemplated 'larger intentions' (to do more serious harm than agreed) did not take his contemplated kicks outside the course of the joint enterprise. To put it in terms of *Powell; English*, kicking someone's head with intent to do GBH was not 'fundamentally different' from kicking someone's head without the intent to do GBH!

In two further cases, *Attorney-General's Reference (No. 3 of 2004)* [2005] EWCA Crim 1882 ([52]) and *D* [2005] EWCA Crim 1981 ([38]) (see *Cases and Materials* (14.4.3.1)), the Court of Appeal has emphasised that in all cases it is the *Powell* principle which decides the outcome. If D's acts were fundamentally different from any contemplated by A, then they are outside the scope of the joint enterprise and A cannot be liable for them at all, not even a lesser offence than D. However, in *D*, the Court concluded in line with *Day* that because A contemplated 'precisely the actions which caused death, namely punching, kicking and stamping', she was responsible for those actions of D1 and D2 and their consequences, even though she did not contemplate they would be done with the *mens rea* for murder or result in death. Kicking, punching and stamping without an intention to kill or cause grievous bodily harm were not fundamentally different from the same actions with an intent to kill or cause GBH. That is perhaps an easy conclusion where A, as in *D*, is present during the attack but, where A is not present, it is always open to a jury to decide that an uncontemplated savagery of blows is qualitatively and fundamentally different from the blows envisaged, thus negating A's liability altogether.

14.4.3.2 Accidental departure

It is possible for parties who are endeavouring to carry out the common purpose, to go beyond it **accidentally**. The rule is that if D's acts are within the scope of the enterprise so that A is responsible for them, A is also responsible for any unforeseen consequences of those acts to the same extent as D (*Baldessare* (1930) 22 Cr App R 70, CCA). As Lord Parker CJ put it in *Anderson and Morris* [1966] 2 All ER 644, CA:

> Where two persons embark on a joint enterprise, each is liable for the acts done in pursuance of that joint enterprise... [including] liability for unusual consequences if they arise from the execution of the agreed joint enterprise.

Thus, the common purpose may be to beat someone up. If, in the course of the beating up, D pushes V against a wall so that he cracks his head and dies from brain injury, both D and his accomplice, A, will be liable for the unintended death. The offence would be murder if D was intending to do grievous bodily harm and A would be guilty of murder if the common purpose was to inflict grievous bodily harm in the beating up. Alternatively, where the common purpose was to inflict only actual bodily harm and **not** grievous bodily harm, this would be a **deliberate** departure by D governed by the principle explained previously. If D lacked the intention to kill or cause grievous bodily harm, both he and A would be guilty only of unlawful act manslaughter.

It will be seen that this accidental departure principle forms an exception to the general rule in *Bainbridge* that, to be convicted, the accessory must know the type of crime to be committed. It is thought that the rule applies equally to make non-joint enterprise accessories responsible for accidental, unforeseen consequences (*Harris* [1964] Crim LR 54, CCA; *Millward* [1994] Crim LR 527 CA).

14.4.3.3 Is there any difference between the rules for joint enterprise accessories and those for ordinary accessories?

We have seen that the Court of Appeal in *Bryce* held that the basic principle in *Powell*; *English* that A is responsible for those acts of D which A has foreseen or which are not fundamentally different from others that A has foreseen applies to all accessories whether joint enterprise participants or not. Indeed some commentators have viewed it as 'merely a descriptive term of no legal effects' (Ashworth: *Principles of Criminal Law* (4th ed., 2003), 429). However, we would identify the following as possible differences.

The main difference concerns the accessory's *actus reus*. A normal accessory must be proved to have assisted or encouraged the particular crime charged. On the other hand a joint enterprise accessory's assistance or encouragement of the **enterprise** itself suffices. There is no need to show he did any acts of assistance or encouragement for the crime committed in the course of the enterprise which departs from its common purpose. Alternatively, it might be said that participation in the joint enterprise is deemed by the courts to be intentional assistance and encouragement to any crimes foreseen as possible incidents of it. Essentially, given the appropriate foresight, his assistance or encouragement of the crime within the common purpose counts as assistance or encouragement of the crime outside it. The utility of this for the prosecution is evident in instances of gang violence where the scene is often chaotic with conflicting witness evidence so that it is very difficult to be sure who did what. It is easier to prove a more general participation in the enterprise than a specific assistance or encouragement to the (more serious) offence into which it escalates. On the other hand, one might argue that participation in the enterprise whilst aware of the possible extra crime must inevitably assist and/or encourage D in the extra crime as well as the agreed crime. What is lacking is only A's **intention** to encourage/assist the unagreed crime and, as *Powell*; *English* holds, that is not necessary in joint enterprise cases where foresight that it may be committed suffices.

You may recall that *Bryce* identified such an intent to assist/encourage as essential for non-joint enterprise accessories but not applicable to participants in a joint enterprise (discussed at 14.4.2.1 above). Although the nature of such intent is far from clear, it does represent an additional element dispensed with in the case of joint enterprise accessories.

Finally we should mention that Lord Hobhouse has expressed the view in *Stewart and Schofield* and a civil case, *Crédit Lyonnais Nederland NV* v *Export Credits Guarantee Department* [1998] 1 Lloyd's Rep 19, 42–44 and extra judicially that participants in a joint enterprise are **not** accessories but joint **principals** (though, in his view, joint enterprise is limited to participation at the time of the crime, not just beforehand). A similar view is taken in Australia (see *Osland* v *R* (1998) 73 ALJR 173) and South Africa (see Burchell, *Joint Enterprise and Common Purpose* (1997) SACJ 125). This legal fiction seems inconsistent with the approach of the House of Lords in *Powell*; *English* and does not represent the current law. However, there are disturbing echoes of it in *Kennedy (No. 2)* (see 14.3 above).

14.4.4 **Victims as accessories**

Cases suggest that the 'victims' of crimes cannot be guilty as secondary parties where the creation of the offence was for their protection (*Tyrrell* [1894] 1 QB 710; *Whitehouse* [1977] 3 All ER 737, CA). In *Tyrrell* it was held that a girl under 16 could not aid and abet a man to have unlawful sexual intercourse with her, even if she were a willing party or even the prime mover. In *Whitehouse*, a girl under 16 could not aid and abet the commission of incest against her by her father and therefore he could not be guilty of inciting her to commit such an offence. In both cases the offences were created, at least in part, to protect young girls. On the other hand, a woman can be an accomplice to an unlawful abortion performed on her because the offence was not created for her protection (*Sockett* (1908) 1 Cr App R 101, CCA).

14.4.5 **Withdrawal from participation**

An accomplice can avoid liability for an offence which he has assisted or encouraged by making an effective withdrawal from participation before the offence is committed. The rationale for this is not clear but it may be because A is deemed to be less culpable (he will remain liable for an offence, if any, committed before the point of repentance, e.g., incitement) and/or because the law wants to encourage accessories to pull out (that presupposes some idea of what the law is!).

? **QUESTION** 14.14

- What do you think an accessory would have to do in order effectively to withdraw from the offence?
- Should it be possible to withdraw, if the accessory has already given whatever assistance he planned?
- To what extent should an accessory have to take active steps to prevent the crime which he has assisted in order to withdraw from it?

14.4.5.1 **Where the crime is planned in advance**

It seems that withdrawal at the preparatory stage is more easily effected than when the crime is in the course of commission (*Grundy* [1977] Crim LR 543, CA and *Whitefield* (1983)

79 Cr App R 36, CA; *cf. Becerra* (1975) 62 Cr App R 212, CA). At the preparatory stage, it would seem that it is enough for the accessory to communicate unequivocally to the perpetrator (all perpetrators, if more than one) that if he continues with the offence, he will be 'on his own'. This seems to be true even if the accessory has already provided material assistance, e.g., information enabling the perpetrator to commit the crime (*Grundy*; *Whitefield*). In *Whitefield*, A told D that the occupant of the next flat was away and he agreed to break in with D by way of his own balcony. Subsequently, he told D that he was not going to participate but on the night in question he heard D breaking into the adjoining flat and took no steps to prevent him. The Court of Appeal held that there was 'evidence...that he had served unequivocal notice on D that if he proceeded with the burglary he would do so without the aid or assistance of A.' A's conviction was quashed because the trial judge had ruled that such notice was insufficient and that, in order to effect withdrawal, A would need to have contacted the police or taken some other steps to prevent the burglary. Notice that there was no insistence on the necessity to nullify the assistance previously given though if A does act to negate his previous assistance, that would be strong evidence of an effective withdrawal.

Clearly, a decision to back out will be ineffective as a withdrawal unless and until the accomplice effectively communicates it either to the perpetrator or the police or other relevant person. In *Rook* [1993] 2 All ER 955, CA it was held that it was not sufficient for A merely to absent himself on the day appointed for an agreed murder to take place. The court reserved its position on whether, even if A had told the others expressly that he was withdrawing, this would have been sufficient, or whether he would need to have taken some additional steps to neutralise the assistance he had already given.

Where the parties are in the course of commission of the joint criminal enterprise, it will be more difficult to convince the court that an effective and timely withdrawal from the enterprise has occurred. Indeed, in *Becerra* (*Cases and Materials* (14.4.5.1)), the Court of Appeal expressed the view that at some stage a point in time will be reached where only physical prevention of the crime, or at least the taking of all reasonable steps to prevent it, will exculpate the accessory. A and D broke into a house in order to steal and A gave a knife to D to use if necessary on anyone interrupting them. They were disturbed by the tenant of the upstairs flat and A said, 'There's a bloke coming. Let's go.' With that, he jumped out of the window and ran away. D remained and stabbed the tenant to death with the knife. The Court of Appeal held that A was an accessory to the murder, his actions being insufficient to constitute an effective withdrawal from the joint enterprise involving the use of the knife if necessary.

The Court of Appeal, obiter, in *Perman* [1996] 1 Cr App R 24 wondered 'whether once the criminal exercise contemplated in a joint enterprise has commenced, it is possible for a party to the joint enterprise to withdraw.' Of course, even if the withdrawal is effective to avoid liability as an accessory to the offence committed, it will not prevent D remaining liable for conspiracy (offence completed as soon as overt agreement to commit the crime is reached) or possibly incitement.

14.4.5.2 Spur of the moment crimes

The above cases concerned crimes which were planned in advance by all the participants. The Court of Appeal in *Mitchell and King* [1999] Crim LR 496 held that the requirement for timely communication of withdrawal was inappropriate in cases of spontaneous violence, such communication being only 'a necessary condition for disassociation from pre-planned violence'. Presumably the assumption is that if the parties assist and encourage each other in a spontaneously arising fight, the cessation of the accomplice's participation in and so withdrawal from the fight will be obvious, thus dispensing with the normal need to communicate withdrawal. We need only observe that this is not necessarily the case particularly in gang violence involving numerous participants.

In *O'Flaherty* [2004] EWCA Crim 526 (approved and applied in *D* [2005] EWCA Crim 1981), A1, A2 and A3, armed with a cricket bat, bottle and claw hammer respectively, had joined with others in a spontaneous attack on V, part of a rival group. V had managed to run off and was pursued by others but not A2 and A3 to a nearby street, where he was beaten and stabbed to death. A1 did follow with his cricket bat but, although present at the fatal attack, did not join in. The Court held that A2 and A3 had withdrawn from the enterprise even though they did not communicate with anyone but simply failed to follow the pursuers. On the other hand, A1 had clearly not withdrawn because he was still 'encouraging' the killers by his presence and had in no way indicated that he was desisting. An alternative way of looking at it would be to say that the original enterprise that A2 and A3 signed up to had ceased and therefore the fatal blows were outside the scope of that enterprise ([63]). Mantell LJ stated the requirements for withdrawal thus:

> To disengage from an incident a person must do enough to demonstrate that he or she is with-drawing from the joint enterprise. This is ultimately a question of fact and degree for the jury. Account will be taken of *inter alia* the nature of the assistance and encouragement already given and how imminent the infliction or the fatal injury or injuries is, as well as the nature of the action said to constitute withdrawal.

That implies that the test of withdrawal is fluid depending on the extent and importance of A's contribution to the crime as well as the timing and manner of his withdrawal. The greater A's contribution, the more will be required of him to effect withdrawal. It harks back to the earlier point we made about whether A's actions must nullify his previous assistance or encouragement.

14.4.6 Entrapment

This is where someone (usually an undercover police officer or police informer) co-operates and/or participates in a criminal enterprise in order to entrap the other participants by tempting or luring them into committing a crime. Such a person is often called an *agent provocateur*. Two main problems arise:

(a) Does the agent's instigation of the crime affect the liability of the other participants who have been encouraged to commit the crime?

(b) Is the agent himself guilty as an accessory to the crime committed?

In regard to (a), the House of Lords in *Loosely* [2001] UKHL 53 has confirmed:

(i) There is no substantive defence of entrapment which could excuse the other participants from liability.

(ii) However, a court has the power to stay proceedings as an abuse of process if 'it offends the court's sense of justice and propriety to be asked to try the accused in the circumstances of a particular case' (*R v Horseferry Road Magistrates' Court, ex parte Bennett* [1993] WLR 90, HL). This can apply to entrapment cases (*Latif and Shahzad* [1996] 2 Cr App R 92, HL; *Loosely*).

(iii) Section 78 of the Police and Criminal Evidence Act 1984, which allows a court to exclude any evidence having an adverse effect on the fairness of the trial, can apply to entrapment evidence.

(iv) English law is not affected by, because it complies with, Art. 6 of the ECHR (as interpreted by the European Court of Human Rights in *Teixeira de Castro v Portugal* (1998) 28 EHRR 101) which guarantees the accused's right to a fair trial.

The unanimous view of the House was that the proper response to a finding of entrapment would be a stay of proceedings 'to protect the integrity of the criminal justice system' where 'the court's participation in such proceedings would bring the administration of justice into disrepute'. It is necessary to prevent D being tried at all as a way of curbing 'abuse of executive power' (Lord Hoffmann). Unacceptable conduct by the police in causing D to commit the crime means that proceedings should not be brought. Even if the court refuses a stay, it is still open to D to argue for exclusion of the *agent provocateur's* evidence under s. 78 on the ground that it would adversely affect the fairness of the proceedings.

A variety of circumstances will be taken into account in assessing whether police conduct went beyond what was acceptable. A particularly important distinction is whether the police did no more than afford D the opportunity to offend, of which he freely took advantage, where he would have behaved in a similar way if offered the opportunity by someone else, or whether they had caused him, by means of shameful or unworthy conduct, to commit an offence that he would not otherwise have committed? Offering to buy drugs at market price from a willing trader was likely to be acceptable, but dangling large sums of money in front of someone known to be in financial need would not. Similarly, in *Nottingham City Council v Amin* [2000] 2 All ER 946, DC, incognito council enforcers who flagged down a taxi in an area where it was not licensed to pick up merely provided the opportunity for the taxi driver to commit the relevant offence. They did not exert any unfair pressure or offer any special inducements; they behaved in an unexceptional manner, as any prospective customer might. Therefore, as Lord Nicholls put it in *Loosely*, it would be perfectly acceptable to do 'no more than present the defendant with an **unexceptional** opportunity to commit a crime' ([23], our emphasis).

On the other hand, in mainstream criminal offences (as opposed to regulatory offences such as in *Amin*—see **Chapter 13**) it would not normally be acceptable to provide at random opportunities for people to commit crimes, e.g., leaving a bag on a park bench. There must be some reason to suspect that D is about to engage or is engaged in such crime or that there is a known problem of such crime in a particular location. In addition, the action would normally have to be part of a properly authorised and supervised, official investigation complying with Part II of the Regulation of Investigatory Powers Act 2000 and the Undercover Operations Code of Practice issued by the police and customs and excise authorities (*cf. Moon* [2004] All ER (D) 167).

Loosely is a welcome clarification of the principles applicable and seems to provide a reasonable balance between securing justice for the accused and facilitating the prevention, detection and successful prosecution of crime.

Dealing with (b), it seems clear that to instigate an offence which might not otherwise be committed renders the instigator guilty of the offence instigated (*Smith* [1960] 1 All ER 256, CCA). Even if the instigator is a police officer or an agent acting on police instructions, it is not permissible to induce or encourage another to commit an offence (or indeed a more serious offence) which the perpetrator would not otherwise commit (*Birtles* (1969) 53 Cr App R 469; obiter, *Sang* [1979] 2 All ER 1222, HL; *Latif* above). Again it seems that a more lenient view will be taken in respect of regulatory offences where the practice is very common and, arguably, practically necessary (*Nottingham City Council* v *Amin* above).

However, even with 'truly criminal' offences, it seems that if the offence is already 'laid on', the police may to a limited extent participate in it without incurring liability, e.g., where it is necessary to pretend to go along with the proposed crime to avoid their cover being blown and to assist in the apprehension of the offenders (*Birtles*; *Clarke* (1984) 80 Cr App R 344—*Cases and Materials* (14.4.6)). Unfortunately, the extent to which such conduct is permissible is shrouded in uncertainty and awaits clarification by case law. This aspect was not considered in *Loosely*.

14.4.7 Reform

We have seen that under the existing law, the liability of the accessory is essentially parasitic on that of the perpetrator. It derives from the crime he commits and requires the actual commission of the crime.

It is, however, possible to make accessories liable in their own right independently of any offence of a perpetrator. The Law Commission's Consultation Paper No. 131 makes such a proposal for a radical transformation of the present law. It would abolish the existing law making the accessory liable for the offence committed by the perpetrator, and create two specific offences of assisting crime and encouraging crime. The latter would cover the case of incitement which would no longer be needed as a separate crime. These would be themselves inchoate offences not dependent on the commission of the crime assisted or encouraged. It would not matter whether or not that crime was perpetrated and the offence would be committed immediately the accessory gave the assistance or encouragement. We have reproduced the detailed legislative suggestion in *Cases and Materials* (14.4.7). Such is the intractability of the problem of accessorial liability that the Commission has still not produced its follow-up Report. Its web site promised its appearance early in 2005 but there is no sign of it yet.

The rationale of decoupling the accessory's liability from that of the perpetrator is that whether or not the perpetrator ultimately commits the crime, the accessory's conduct in facilitating it manifests a willingness to help bring about criminal harms worthy of punishment and itself endangers society by increasing the risk of crime.

However, Professor Smith has expressed serious reservations about the wisdom of abolishing secondary participation and has pointed out that it is almost universal in foreign jurisdictions. His preferred solution was to enact, in addition to the existing law, a new offence of facilitating crime, but to retain the present law of secondary participation after endeavouring to simplify it and remove anomalies (see (1994) 144 NLJ 679).

■ **FURTHER READING**

Clarkson: *Complicity*, Powell *and Manslaughter* [1998] Crim LR 556.

Kadish: *Complicity, Cause and Blame* (1985) 73 California Law Review 323 (USA).

Kadish: *Reckless Complicity* (1997) 87 Journal of Criminal Law and Criminology 369 (USA).

Lanham: *Primary and Derivative Criminal Liability: An Australian Perspective* [2000] Crim LR 707.

Law Commission: *Assisting and Encouraging Crime: A Consultation Paper* (Law Com. No. 131, 1993).

Smith JC: *Aid, Abet, Counsel or Procure* in Glazbrook (ed.): *Reshaping the Criminal Law* (1978, Stevens).

Smith JC: *Criminal Liability of Accessories* (1997) 113 LQR 453.

Smith JC: *Joint Enterprise and Secondary Liability* (1999) 50 NILQ 153.

Smith K: *A Modern Treatise on the Law of Criminal Complicity* (1991, Oxford University Press).

Smith K: *Withdrawal in Complicity* [2001] Crim LR 769.

Spencer: *Trying to Help Another Person Commit a Crime* in Smith (ed.): *Criminal Law: Essays in Honour of JC Smith* (1987, Butterworths).

Sullivan: *Intent, Purpose and Complicity* [1988] Crim LR 641.

Sullivan: *The Law Commission Consultation Paper on Complicity: (2) Fault Elements and Joint Enterprise* [1994] Crim LR 252.

■ **SUMMARY**

- The perpetrator or principal is the one who physically performs the *actus reus* and is its most immediate causer. Exceptionally, a person can be the perpetrator who does not physically commit the crime where he uses an innocent agent, e.g., child under ten, someone lacking *mens rea*.

- Accessories can be convicted of offences which they aid, abet, counsel or procure (s. 8 of the Accessories and Abettors Act 1861; s. 44 of the Magistrates' Courts Act 1980). Accessory's liability is parasitic on the **actual** commission of an offence by another.

- *Actus reus*—**aiding** means helping either before or at the time of the commission of the offence whether or not the aider is present at its commission. **Abetting** means encouraging, instigating or inciting the crime. **Counselling** means the same but is used for encouraging, etc. **before** the commission of the crime. *Bryce* holds that there must be some causal connection between the help/encouragement and the commission of the crime but it is uncertain what this entails and it is certainly a much weaker connection than for normal causation. Abetting/counseling necessitates that the perpetrator is at least aware of A's encouragement (*A-G's Reference (No. 1 of 1975)*). This is not necessary for aiding. All three probably imply that it must be the perpetrator's **purpose** to do what constitutes the crime. **Procuring** means bringing about or 'producing by endeavour' the commission of the offence. The accessory's conduct must **cause** the commission of the offence. No need for perpetrator to realise that he is performing the conduct constituting the crime (procuring may be limited to cases where he does not (*A-G's Reference*; *Millward*)). If D's conduct occurs only **after** the crime is completed, he cannot be an accessory to it. Mere presence at the crime without intervening is not of itself assistance or encouragement unless, exceptionally, law imposes duty to act (*Gibson and Gibson*; *Clarkson*). Deliberate presence at the crime will be encouragement if in pursuance of prior agreement with perpetrator and maybe if not (*Clarkson*; *Wilcox* v *Jeffrey*; *Coney*). *The principal offence*—because accessory's liability is derivative, it is essential to prove principal offence was **actually** committed (*Thornton* v *Mitchell*), although no need to prove that the perpetrator has been **convicted**. There are exceptions: (i) where different offences share same *actus reus*, perpetrator may be convicted of, say, murder and accessory of manslaughter or vice versa (*Howe*); (ii) where perpetrator commits offence but is immune from prosecution (*Austin*); (iii) where perpetrator has a defence, e.g., duress (*Bourne*; *DPP* v *K and B*); (iv) where perpetrator performs *actus reus*, but lacks *mens rea* for the offence, at least in the case of **procuring** (*Millward*; *Wheelhouse*; *DPP* v *K and B*).

- *Mens rea*—requires (i) intention to assist or encourage (ii) with knowledge of the principal offence (*Bryce*). *Intention to assist/encourage* the crime does not require that A's purpose is to secure the commission of the crime. It means that he intends to do acts which he knows are capable of assisting or encouraging the perpetrator to commit the crime (*NCB* v *Gamble*; *Lynch* v *DPP*). He deliberately gives assistance/encouragement **realising** that the offence might well be committed (*J.F. Alford Transport Ltd*). If he intends by his acts of 'assistance' to 'hinder or obstruct' the crime, he will not intend to aid (*Bryce*). Procuring is probably narrower requiring it to be procurer's **purpose** to secure commission of the crime by the perpetrator (*Blakely, Sutton* v *DPP*). *Knowledge of the principal offence*—A must know that the perpetrator is going to perform the full *actus reus* of the crime with the appropriate fault element (if any). In a strict liability offence, even though no *mens rea* is required for the principal, the above *mens rea* is required for the accessory (*Callow* v *Tillstone*). It is enough if the accessory (unless a procurer) realises that there is a significant possibility of the offence being committed (*J.F. Alford Transport Ltd*; *Reardon*; *Bryce*). A may not know the precise details of the offence, but it is enough if he knows the type of crime to be committed (*Bainbridge*). Similarly, if it is one of a limited number of crimes which he contemplates may be committed at the time of assisting (*DPP* v *Maxwell*).

- *Joint unlawful enterprise*—where two or more have 'a shared common intention . . . each has the same intention . . . and each knows the other intends the same thing' (*Petters and Parfitt*). It now appears that most of the rules are the same as the standard law on accessories and it is uncertain whether there are any special rules extending the law. All participants are liable for all crimes committed **as part of the common design or purpose** irrespective of who does what. Additionally, all participants are liable for all offences committed **outside** the common design **if** they are an **unforeseen and accidental** departure from the common design. If the offences **outside** the common design are a **deliberate** departure from it by one or more participants, the accessory will not be liable for them **unless** he realised there was a real risk that the perpetrator might depart from the joint enterprise and commit the offence (*Powell*). A takes a deliberate risk of assisting or encouraging the further crime in the course of committing the agreed enterprise. Probably applies equally to accessories merely assisting/encouraging the crime **beforehand** and not present at its commission (*Rook*; *Wan and Chan*, although *Stewart and Schofield* (probably wrong!) doubted this). A is not liable where D's act is fundamentally different in type from any foreseen by A, e.g., sudden use of unknown weapon (*Powell*; *Uddin*). Difficult questions still remain as to when D's acts are outside the scope of the joint venture (*Wan and Chan, cf. Stewart and Schofield*) but A remains responsible for any act which he contemplated D might commit albeit with a lesser *mens rea* than he actually had. Even though D commits the greater offence (e.g., murder), A would be liable for the lesser offence only (e.g., manslaughter) because he did not contemplate the possibility of the greater offence (*Gilmour; Day; Attorney-General's Reference (No. 3 of 2004); D*).

- Victims cannot be accessories to a crime created for their protection (*Whitehouse*).

- Withdrawal by accessory—must be effective, i.e., communicated unequivocally to perpetrator or police (*Rook; Whitefield*). Easier if done before the crime is embarked on. Once the crime is in progress, effective withdrawal may require accessory to take reasonable steps to prevent it (*Becerra*) except for participation in a crime of spontaneous violence (*Mitchell and King; O'Flaherty*).

- Entrapment—(1) *Loosely* HL holds: (i) no defence of entrapment excusing other participants from liability (ii) the court has power to stay proceedings for abuse of process in entrapment cases (iii) the judge has a discretion to exclude evidence obtained by entrapment under the powers conferred by s. 78 of the Police and Criminal Evidence Act 1984. (2) The *agent provocateur* is an accessory to the offence even if an undercover police officer or agent (*Sang; Birtles*) unless the participation is limited and in an offence already 'laid on' (*Birtles; Clarke; Latif*).

 CHAPTER 14: ASSESSMENT EXERCISE

14.1 Stan and Ollie decide to steal antiques from Lord Wooster's country mansion. Stan buys a gun from Winchester, who knows Stan to be a violent criminal. Before the raid, Ollie discovers that Stan intends to take a gun and he tells Stan that he is not going ahead. Stan threatens to inform Ollie's wife of the affair Ollie is having with another woman unless Ollie participates. Ollie goes ahead because of these threats but obtains from Stan a promise that, should they encounter anyone, he will not use the gun except to frighten.

The two break into the mansion. As they are leaving the house, they are challenged by Jeeves, Lord Wooster's butler. Stan pulls out his gun and deliberately shoots Jeeves dead. Ollie shouts, 'That's another fine mess you've got me into, Stan' and they rush to escape.

Discuss the criminal liability, if any, of Stan, Ollie and Winchester for the death of Jeeves.

See the **Appendix** (14.1) for a specimen answer.

See also **Assessment Exercises 9.2** and **15.1**.

15 Vicarious and corporate liability

15.1 Objectives

By the end of this chapter, you should be able to:

1 Distinguish between strict liability, vicarious liability and corporate liability

2 State when vicarious liability arises

3 Explain the basis of corporate liability

15.2 Vicarious liability

The essence of vicarious liability in criminal law is that a person may be held liable as **the principal offender**, i.e., the perpetrator of a crime whose *actus reus* is **physically** committed by someone else. We have already considered a similar type of situation earlier in **Chapter 12**, namely the doctrine of innocent agency. However, in the case of vicarious liability proper, the person physically performing the *actus reus* is not 'innocent' and may indeed also be liable for the offence. The law focuses upon the **relationship** between the defendant and the performer of the physical acts and, sometimes, by virtue of that relationship, it attributes (imputes) the acts of the latter (and, occasionally, his *mens rea*) to the former. This is almost always the relationship of employer and employee though it can be something akin to the civil law concept of principal and agent.

It should be emphasised at the outset that this form of liability in criminal law is very much the exception rather than the rule. The general principle is that criminal liability is based on D's personal acts rather than those of another. This attitude contrasts markedly with the courts' attitude in civil law under the law of torts where vicarious liability (mainly of an employer for the negligence or breach of duty of his employees) is extremely common.

15.2.1 **When does vicarious liability arise?**

The general rule is that a person is **not** vicariously liable for acts performed by another. Nonetheless, **by way of exception**, there are certain situations where vicarious liability will be imposed. In all but one instance, these exceptions have been created by the judiciary in case law but, usually, to remedy what they perceive to be defects in the drafting of legislation creating statutory offences. The exceptions are as follows:

15.2.2 **Common law offences**

The only common law offences where vicarious liability is a possibility are public nuisance and criminal libel, for both of which an employer can be held vicariously liable for the acts of his employees.

15.2.3 **Express creation of vicarious liability by statute**

Parliament sometimes specifically imposes vicarious liability in the statutory definition of the offence. For example, until repealed by the Licensing Act 2003 (which adopts a different configuration), s. 59(1) of the Licensing Act 1964 prohibited a person from selling intoxicating liquor on licensed premises outside permitted hours 'himself or by his servant or agent'.

15.2.4 **Implied imposition by statutory wording—the extensive construction principle**

Not infrequently the courts interpret statutory offences as imposing vicarious liability by giving an extended meaning or construction to certain verbs used to define the offence in the statute. They are most likely to do this in the case of employees acting in the course of their employment. The employee physically performs the *actus reus*, but his act is regarded in law as the act of the employer. However, the principle is not confined to employer/employee situations (see, e.g., *Cobb* v *Williams* [1973] Crim LR 243; *Clode* v *Barnes* [1974] 1 All ER 1166—liability for acts of co-partner).

It is important to realise that the extensive construction principle can be utilised only where the statutory offence charged is one of strict liability so that, although the *actus reus* performed by the employee or agent may be imputed or attributed to the employer, the employee's *mens rea* cannot be so imputed (in the absence of delegation—see 15.2.5). Therefore, if the offence requires *mens rea* a person cannot be vicariously liable under this principle (*Vane* v *Yiannopoullos* [1964] 2 All ER 820, HL).

What do we mean by extensive construction? An example will give the general idea. In *Coppen* v *Moore (No. 2)* [1898] 2 QB 306 (*Cases and Materials* (15.2.4)) an assistant in a chain of shops owned by D sold an American ham as a 'Scotch ham'. This was strictly contrary to instructions but D was nonetheless convicted of 'selling' goods to which a false trade description had been applied (now an offence under the Trade Descriptions Act 1968). Although 'selling' in this kind of provision is normally interpreted as the 'physical handling and handing over of the goods by way of sale' rather than the legal transfer of ownership (see *Goodfellow* v *Johnson* [1965] 1 All ER 941), the courts have been willing to 'stretch' it or 'extensively construe' it so as to regard the owner of the shop as 'selling' the goods as well as the shop assistant, since, after all, the ownership in the goods transfers from the shop owner to the customer by virtue of the transaction.

The reasoning was applied in *Harrow London Borough Council* v *Shah* [1999] 3 All ER 302, DC, to convict the owner of a shop of the strict liability offence of 'selling' a national lottery ticket to someone under 16. The owner was in a back room when his employee conducted the offending sales transaction. The owner was a 'seller' even though he was not the sales person.

Furthermore, in relation to the sale of goods such as intoxicating liquors which require a licence, the licensee is regarded as selling them even though he does not own them but is, say, the employee of the brewery which does own them (*Allied Domecq Leisure Ltd* v *Cooper* [1999] Crim LR 230, DC). More questionably it was assumed that this would mean that the owner of the goods (the brewery) did not 'sell' them when their barmaid employee served a customer. This was corrected in *Nottingham City Council* v *Wolverhampton and Dudley Breweries* [2004] 2 WLR 820 which held that the brewery which owned the products could 'sell' intoxicating liquors in their pubs through the agency of a barmaid irrespective of the position of the licensee.

Similarly, a number of offences employ the word 'use', particularly in relation to motor vehicles. For example, in *Griffiths* v *Studebakers Ltd* [1924] 1 KB 102 the defendants were convicted of 'using' a vehicle contrary to certain Licensing Regulations because they were carrying more than the permitted number of passengers. The defendants were the owners of the vehicle which, unknown to them, was being driven with the excess passengers by their employee despite an express instruction to the contrary. Although the employee was physically 'using' the vehicle, it is not too great an extension to regard the employer as also 'using' the vehicle where the employee is about the employer's business.

Similar interpretations have been made in respect of offences requiring D to be 'in possession' of goods etc. (*Melias Ltd* v *Preston* [1957] 2 QB 380) and 'keeping' a van without the requisite licence (*Strutt* v *Clift* [1911] 1 KB 1 though *cf. Attorney-General's Reference (No. 2 of 2003)* [2004] EWCA Crim 785). *Tesco Supermarkets Ltd* v *Nattrass* [1970] 3 All ER 357, HL proceeded on the assumption that when a branch employee displays a poster in the window advertising a special offer price, Tesco thereby 'gives an indication' as to the price at which such goods are offered for sale.

National Rivers Authority v *Alfred McAlpine Homes East Ltd* [1994] 4 All ER 286, DC (*Cases and Materials* (15.2.4)) held that the offence of causing polluted matter to enter controlled waters contrary to s. 85 of the Water Resources Act 1991 could be 'extensively construed' to impose vicarious liability on the company. Wet cement (the polluted matter) was washed into a controlled stream during the construction of a water feature on the company's building site. An application of the identification principle to impose corporate liability directly was not possible because none of the polluting acts was attributable to a person senior enough to be the 'directing mind and will' of the company (see 15.3.1). Therefore, the company could only be liable if it was held vicariously liable for the acts of its employees acting in the course of their employments (the site manager and the construction workers). Not surprisingly the court in effect adopted the extensive construction principle as the only means of bringing the company to book. If its employees caused the pollution in the course of their employment, the company caused it.

The decision is understandable and, we would argue, the only practical one in the circumstances. However, the court relied heavily on *Alphacell Ltd* v *Woodward* [1972] 2 All ER 475, HL interpreting that as also a case of vicarious liability.

 EXERCISE 15.1

Read the extracts from *Alphacell Ltd* v *Woodward* in *Cases and Materials* (13.4.3.1).
   Was this a case where the company was vicariously liable for the acts of its employees or others in causing the pollution?

The company had designed and built its plant to direct the polluted water used in its processes to a settling tank by the river. Pumps were designed to prevent the water reaching a critical level. Can there be any doubt, however, that the constructing of the overflow into the river meant that, if the pumps failed, the polluted water was **designed** to overflow into the river? There is no evidence from the House of Lords' judgments that they regarded this as a case of vicarious liability. Professor Smith views it as a case of direct corporate liability presumably on the basis that the construction of the system and the decision to operate it must have been instituted by a controlling officer or officers of the company ([1994] Crim LR 761). In his view, vicarious liability would only have arisen had it been established that the overflow had occurred through some negligent or wrongful act of an employee, e.g., a failure to inspect the filters or clear away debris revealed. Presumably his reasoning is that only a negligent or wrongful act would break the chain of causation between the company's operating the system as designed and the resultant pollution. It would then be necessary to find vicarious liability for that wrongful or negligent act before the company could be held to have caused it.

The implication of Professor Smith's commentary is that he would not favour the application of vicarious liability in the *McAlpine* case, thus allowing the **company** to escape liability. Whether or not his technical analysis is correct, it would seem essential that the company should be convictable in situations like this and that the vicarious liability principle should apply as held by the court. By analogy with the 'use' cases, if employees 'cause' it in the course of their employment, they are about the company's business and, therefore, the company 'causes' it. (See further 15.3 below.)

It should be emphasised that the person who physically performs the *actus reus* may also be convicted of the offence as the **perpetrator** rather than just as an accomplice (*Green* v *Burnett* [1954] 3 All ER 273, DC). The result is that in a *Coppen* v *Moore* situation both employer and employee could be charged and convicted as **joint principals**. This could be important in practice due to the more stringent *mens rea* requirements needed to convict an accomplice to a strict liability offence (see *Callow* v *Tillstone* at 12.2).

Although vicarious liability most frequently arises under this principle where employers and employees are involved, the courts have on occasion used it (although with conspicuous lack of consistency) to impose liability on one partner for the acts of a fellow partner (*Clode* v *Barnes* [1974] 1 All ER 1166, DC); a licensee of licensed premises for illegal sales by bar staff who were not his employees but like him employed by the owner of the premises (*Goodfellow* v *Johnson* [1965] 1 All ER 941, DC); and in one or two other instances (see, e.g., *Quality Dairies Ltd* v *Pedley* [1952] 1 All ER 380, DC—liability for subcontractor).

15.2.5 **The delegation principle**

In some situations the courts have developed the idea that a person cannot escape the responsibility for observing duties imposed on him under a criminal statute by delegating them to someone else. It seems that the law will apply this delegation principle only where the statutory wording provides that the offence can be committed only by a specified category of person. For example, prior to recent reform by the Licensing Act 2003, many offences created by the Licensing Acts controlling the sale of intoxicating liquors could be committed only by 'the licensee' (see *Vane* v *Yiannopoullos* (*Cases and Materials* (15.2.5)), for an example). Thus, nobody but the licensee was *capable* of committing the offence. This opened up the possibility of public house owners circumventing the legislative controls by having a nominee as 'licensee' who never went near the establishment. To plug this gap, the courts invented the delegation principle whereby, if the licensee left it to others to run the public house, he would be regarded as being responsible for his delegates and therefore having committed any acts committed by them which contravened the statute.

The delegation principle allows both the *actus reus* and the *mens rea* of the delegate to be imputed to the defendant upon whom the legislation placed the duty.

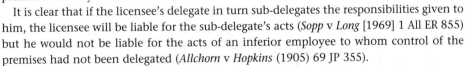

? **QUESTION** 15.1

Is this true of the extensive construction principle? Re-read 15.2.4 if you cannot answer.

This means that under the delegation principle, D can be liable for offences which require proof of *mens rea* as well as strict liability offences, even though he has no knowledge whatsoever that any offence has been committed. Thus, in *Allen* v *Whitehead* [1930] 1 KB 211 (*Cases and Materials* (15.2.5)) the manager of D's cafe knowingly allowed prostitutes to frequent the cafe contrary to the strict instructions of D. This was an offence under the Metropolitan Police Act 1839 which provided that it could only be committed by a person 'who shall have or keep' the cafe. In law the 'keeper' of the cafe was D and not the manager to whom he had delegated the running of the premises. The court found D guilty even though the statutory wording of the offence expressly required D to 'knowingly permit' the prostitutes to frequent the cafe. The manager 'knew' and his knowledge, as well as his act in permitting, could be imputed to D and regarded as D's act **and state of mind**. Similarly, in *Linnet* v *Metropolitan Police Commissioner* [1946] 1 All ER 380, one of two co-licensees was liable for the act of the other in knowingly permitting disorderly conduct in the licensed premises contrary to the same Act.

It is clear that if the licensee's delegate in turn sub-delegates the responsibilities given to him, the licensee will be liable for the sub-delegate's acts (*Sopp* v *Long* [1969] 1 All ER 855) but he would not be liable for the acts of an inferior employee to whom control of the premises had not been delegated (*Allchorn* v *Hopkins* (1905) 69 JP 355).

15.2.5.1 What constitutes delegation?

In modern times the courts have shown themselves to be less than keen on the delegation principle and have sought to limit the scope of its operation. The courts have therefore insisted that there should have been a complete delegation of the licensee's managerial functions and responsibilities (*Vane* v *Yiannopoullos* [1965] AC 486, HL—*Cases and Materials* (15.5.2)). Thus, it seems to require that the licensee be completely off duty, if not absent from the premises altogether, before he will be regarded as having delegated to the person temporarily in charge. In *Vane* a restaurant owner was held not to have delegated to his waitress by going down to the basement. Therefore, he was not vicariously liable for her actions in knowingly serving alcohol to persons not ordering a meal contrary to the conditions of the restaurant's liquor licence (and in contravention of the restaurant owner's instructions).

It is probably best to regard *Howker* v *Robinson* [1972] 2 All ER 786, DC as inconsistent with *Vane*. The licensee who was serving in the public bar was held liable for an illegal sale made by his barman who was in the lounge. This is hardly complete delegation within the *Vane* principle but the court seems to have regarded the issue of delegation as purely a question of fact.

If the delegate is outside the category of persons capable of committing the offence, e.g., not the licensee, then he cannot, of course, be guilty of the crime as perpetrator himself. However, he will be regarded as an accessory to the crime for which D is vicariously the principal offender (*Griffiths* v *Studebakers Ltd* [1924] 1 KB 102; *Ross* v *Moss* [1965] 3 All ER 145).

A person cannot be held vicariously liable for aiding and abetting another to commit an offence (*Ferguson* v *Weaving* [1951] 1 All ER 412, DC) nor for attempting to commit an offence (*Gardner* v *Akeroyd* [1952] 2 All ER 306, DC).

15.2.6 Reform

Clause 29 of the draft Criminal Code Bill would abolish the delegation principle prospectively but would retain vicarious liability via the extensive construction principle (Law Com. No. 177; see *Cases and Materials* (15.2.5.1)).

15.3 Corporate liability

The liability of corporations in the criminal law is a relatively new development necessitated by the proliferation of corporate bodies since the advent of the limited liability company. For this purpose, corporations include public limited companies (e.g., Lucas

Industries plc), private limited companies (e.g., Savage (Enterprises) Ltd), local authorities and other public sector bodies such as nationalised industries like the Post Office.

The general rule is that corporations can be criminally liable to the same extent as individual persons because, legally, the corporation is regarded as a distinct person separate from the individual members and employees making up its organisation. However, there are two exceptions to this rule:

(a) the nature of some offences precludes their commission by corporations, e.g., rape; and

(b) the courts will refuse to convict corporations of offences for which the only punishment is imprisonment, e.g., murder and treason.

This general liability of corporations for offences generally was firmly established only as recently as 1944 (*DPP* v *Kent and Sussex Contractors Ltd* [1944] 1 All ER 119, DC; *ICR Haulage Ltd* [1944] 1 All ER 691, CCA; *Moore* v *I Bresler Ltd* [1944] 2 All ER 515, DC). However, long before this, the courts had been willing to hold corporations vicariously liable for the acts of their employees and others on exactly the same principle as applicable to individuals (*Mousell Bros Ltd* v *London and North Western Railway Company* [1917] 2 KB 836). Therefore, whether the accused employer is a company or a private individual has no bearing on whether it or he/she/it is vicariously liable.

In addition, where a statutory duty was imposed on a particular category of person, e.g., an 'occupier', and the 'occupier' was a corporation, the courts had no hesitation in holding the corporation liable for a breach of that statutory duty. For example, in *Evans and Co. Ltd* v *LCC* [1914] 3KB 315 the Divisional Court held the defendant company guilty of failing to close a shop which it occupied on the afternoon of an early closing day in breach of the statutory duty to do so imposed on occupiers of shops by the Shops Act 1912. A modern example is provided by *British Steel plc* [1995] Crim LR 654, CA (*Cases and Materials* (15.3)) where the company was convicted for failing to conduct its undertaking so as to 'ensure so far as is reasonably practicable' that sub-contractors were not exposed to risks to health and safety contrary to s. 3(1) of the Health and Safety at Work etc. Act 1974. The statutory duty is confined to 'employers'. In this case the company employer had not 'ensured' the sub-contractors' safety (two were killed when dismantling a steel platform) and it did not matter who within the company was responsible for the failure.

This view of s. 3 was endorsed and applied by the House of Lords in *Associated Octel Co. Ltd* [1996] 1 WLR 1543. The duty is imposed on all employers, whether individuals or corporations, because they are in a position to exercise complete control over their undertakings. The same approach was taken by the Court of Appeal in *Gateway Foodmarkets Ltd* [1997] 2 Cr App R 40 to s. 2 which requires 'every employer to ensure, so far as is reasonably practicable, the health, safety and welfare at work of all his employees.' The duties are personal to the employer and if safety etc. is not ensured, the employer will be liable unless it can be proved that all reasonably practicable precautions have been taken by it or on its behalf.

The practical outcome of these cases is that the employer is, in effect, made vicariously liable for all the acts of all its employees performed in the course of their employment. If safety is not ensured by the company and all its employees, the company is responsible. Recent cases like the above signal an important shift by the courts towards a willingness to impose responsibility on companies for the actions and failures of all their employees, without which it would be all too easy for them to divert blame on to lowly employees.

The limited scope of these two principles led to the development of a much more general principle of 'identification', whereby a corporation could be made liable for almost any offence whether requiring *mens rea* or not, and whether as a perpetrator or as an accomplice.

15.3.1 The identification principle

The idea that corporations can be criminally liable in just the same way as a human individual seems strange, since a corporation cannot perform any acts except through the agency of human individuals or have a state of mind independently of one or more individuals within the organisation. The truth is that the courts have invented the fiction that the acts and state of mind of certain senior managers or officials **are** the acts and state of mind of the corporation. What the senior executive does and thinks in the performance of his duties is identified with, and becomes the acts and thoughts of, the company itself. Thus, the frauds perpetrated by Robert Maxwell in the name of various companies could become the frauds of the companies by virtue of this identification principle. Lord Denning's metaphor in the civil case of *H. L. Bolton (Engineering) Co. Ltd* v *P. J. Graham & Sons Ltd* [1956] 3 All ER 624 explains the notion:

> A company may in many ways be likened to a human body. It has a brain and nerve centre which controls what it does. It also has hands which hold the tools and act in accordance with directions from the centre. Some of the people in the company are mere servants and agents who are nothing more than hands to do the work and cannot be said to represent the mind or will. Others are directors and managers who represent the directing mind and will of the company, and control what it does. The state of mind of these managers is the state of mind of the company and is treated by law as such.

This dictum was approved in what is now the leading case, *Tesco Supermarkets Ltd* v *Nattrass* [1971] 2 All ER 127, HL (*Cases and Materials* (15.3.1)) where Lord Reid was concerned to distinguish the personal liability of a corporation under this identification principle from its vicarious liability as an employer:

> A living person has a mind which can have knowledge or intention or be negligent and he has hands to carry out his intentions. A corporation has none of these: it must act through living persons, though not always one and the same person. Then the person who acts is not speaking or acting for the company. He is acting as the company and his mind which directs his acts is the mind of the company. There is no question of the company being vicariously liable. He is not acting as a servant, representative, agent or delegate. He is an embodiment of the company, or, one could say, he hears and speaks through the *persona* of the company, within his appropriate sphere, and his mind is the mind of the company. If it is a guilty mind then that guilt is the guilt of the company.

Although the courts often refer to this form of liability as direct (or personal) liability as a means of distinguishing it from the vicarious liability we examined at 15.2 above, it is in truth a variant of vicarious liability. The reason is that the law is attributing (imputing) to the corporation an *actus reus* performed by and, where the offence requires it, a *mens rea* or fault element displayed by a senior manager **identified** with the company. It differs from the other forms of vicarious liability in that it is **special** to companies and has no application to human individuals. It is more general than those other forms in that it applies to offences generally—not just strict liability offences (as the extensive construction principle) or offences committable only by a particular category of person (as the delegation principle and 'employer' offences). However, it is in practice extremely narrow because of the very limited range of people who will be regarded in law as 'identified' with the company. It is to that last issue that we now turn.

> **? QUESTION** 15.3
>
> Is this anthropomorphic model of the corporation as an alternative individual a realistic representation of a large modern company?

15.3.1.1 Who is to be regarded as the company?

Tesco holds that whether a person is to be identified with the company in this way is a question of law and only those exercising very senior management functions—those constituting the 'directing mind and will' of the corporation—can be identified with the corporation in this way. Whilst this would usually include directors (at least executive directors), it is not confined to directors. However, to qualify, a person would need to have been given a significant area of discretion at a senior management level, although not necessarily over the whole of the corporation's affairs. In the *Tesco* case, the manager of one of 800 branches was clearly far too junior to be identified with the corporation, and the same applied in relation to the operator of a weigh-bridge belonging to the company (*John Henshall Quarries Ltd* v *Harvey* [1965] 1 All ER 725, DC), a car hire company's depot engineer (*Magna Plant Ltd* v *Mitchell* [1966] Crim LR 394, DC) and even the European Sales Manager only four steps down the reporting ladder from Dunlop's chief executive (*R* v *Redfern and Dunlop Ltd (Aircraft Division)* [1993] Crim LR 43, CA). On the other hand, a manager was identified with the company where the directors had delegated him full power in the running of its affairs (*Lennard's Carrying Co. Ltd* v *Azeatic Petroleum Co. Ltd* [1915] AC 705, HL) or part of its affairs (*Worthy* v *Gordon Plant (Services) Ltd* [1985] CLY 624, DC).

Limiting the identification with the corporation to a small core of top management in this way severely restricts the scope for personal corporate liability. In recognition of this, the Privy Council in *Meridian Global Funds Management Asia Limited* v *Securities Commission* [1995] 3 All ER 918 (*Cases and Materials* (15.3.1.1)) held that the acts of employees who were not 'the directing mind and will' of the company could be attributed to the company in some cases. It all depended on the 'interpretation or construction of the relevant substantive rule'. If insistence on the normal, primary rules of attribution would defeat the purpose of the statutory offence, 'the court must fashion a special rule of attribution for the particular substantive rule...tailored as it always must be to the terms and policies of the substantive rule.' In *Meridian*, the defendant company (D) was convicted of an offence of failing to disclose a substantial shareholding in another company. Unknown to anyone who was the 'directing mind and will' of D, the shareholding had been acquired by the actions of D's chief investment officer, K, as part of a corrupt scheme to acquire surreptitiously control of the target company for personal benefit. It was held that the policy of the relevant New Zealand statute to enable immediate identification of substantial shareholdings would be defeated unless corporate holders were identified with the employee (here K) who, acting within his authority, had acquired the holding. K's knowledge of the holding was attributed to D which was therefore guilty.

There is no doubt that the case, if followed in the future, will increase uncertainty in this difficult area since we could never be sure what rules of attribution would be adopted unless and until there had been a definitive interpretation of the offence charged. However, as a matter of policy, there is much to be said for the flexibility it offers to reflect the practical realities of the commercial world.

One important issue is whether a company's 'fault' can be found by aggregating the conduct and blameworthiness of more than one individual controlling officer, where, in isolation, no one officer exhibits the necessary degree of fault. If aggregation is possible, should it be limited to 'controlling officers' or should it include more junior managers? The sinking of the cross-Channel ferry, the *Herald of Free Enterprise*, occurred when it set sail with its bow doors still open. The company owning the ferry was eventually prosecuted for manslaughter, but the case was stopped by the trial judge on the basis that no **one** person sufficiently senior to be identified with the company displayed the necessary fault for manslaughter (*P & O European Ferries (Dover) Ltd* (1991) 93 Cr App R 72—*Cases and Materials* (15.3.1.1)). This contrasts with the view of the report of the inquiry into the disaster that 'From top to bottom the body corporate was infected with the disease of sloppiness . . .' (the *Sheen Report*, para. 14.1). Most other observers and the public (including the jury at the victims' inquest in defiance of the coroner's directions) viewed the company as to blame for the disaster. However, the company's fault was an agglomeration of failures of a number of separate individuals from directors down to the man employed to operate the door-closing mechanism. One employee might appreciate the possibility of the ship's setting off before the doors are properly closed but not realise how dangerous this might be. Another might know of the instability of car ferry design but not realise the possibility of sailing with open doors. Another might not appreciate there were no warning lights on the bridge to apprise the captain when the doors were closed. There might be no director or senior executive with responsibility for reviewing safety (as was the case here). Should this be a reason for escaping liability or imposing it?!

Although there is much to be said for the principle, it is the view of both the Divisional Court and the Court of Appeal that aggregation is not possible even among individuals who are sufficiently senior to be identified with the company (*R v HM Coroner for East Kent, ex parte Spooner* (1989) 88 Cr App R 10 (*Cases and Materials* (15.3.1.1); *Attorney-General's Reference (No. 2 of 1999)* [2000] 2 Cr App R 207, CA). Thus, corporate liability can arise only if an individual identifiable with the company commits the offence. If no individual commits an offence, then there is no possibility of direct corporate liability under the identification principle, even on a charge of manslaughter by gross negligence (*Attorney-General's Reference (No. 2 of 1999)*).

Another problem with the identification principle is the necessity to establish that a particular 'controlling officer' has performed the *actus reus* with the necessary *mens rea*. It may be evident that something within the organisation's systems has gone seriously wrong without it being possible to lay the blame at the door of a particular executive. The company itself will, of course, be keen to devolve the blame to an employee not sufficiently senior to be identified with the company. It remains to be seen how influential the *Meridian* case will be in lowering this threshold of corporate liability. The Court of Appeal held that it had no application to common law offences such as manslaughter where the traditional identification rules applied (*Attorney-General's Reference (No. 2 of 1999)*).

15.3.1.2 Offences to which the principle of identification cannot apply

We now return to the exceptions to corporate liability briefly mentioned earlier. These exceptions were established in *ICR Haulage Ltd* [1944] 1 All ER 691, CCA. The less important exception denies liability where the only punishment available for the offence is imprisonment and it is now limited to murder and treason.

? QUESTION 15.4

Can a company commit (a) perjury (b) bigamy (c) rape or (d) any offence of violence against the person?

The more important exception holds that there are certain offences which, from their very nature, cannot be committed by a corporation. It is said that a corporation cannot commit sexual offences like rape, nor the offences of bigamy and perjury. However, it is doubtful whether perjury is a good example since there seems no reason why the perjury of, say, a director could not, in appropriate circumstances, be identified with the company. The other examples are more apposite, at least in respect of the company being the perpetrator. However, it is possible to envisage the company being an accomplice to bigamy, where, e.g., the company operates a marriage bureau. It is more difficult to envisage liability as an accomplice to a sexual offence like rape, but not impossible. For example, the company might be in the business of making pornographic videos which, to the knowledge of the directors, involved filming an actual rape undertaken for the purpose.

At one time it was thought that a corporation could not be convicted of any crime of violence (*Cory Bros Ltd* [1927] 1 KB 810). However, in *Robert Millar (Contractors) Ltd* [1970] 1 All ER 577, CA the company was convicted as an accomplice to causing death by dangerous driving and, more importantly, in *DPP* v *P & O European Ferries (Dover) Ltd* (1991) 93 Cr App R 72 the case arising out of the sinking of the car ferry, *Herald of Free Enterprise*, the trial judge, after very careful argument by distinguished counsel, ruled that a company could be convicted of manslaughter.

The Court of Appeal accepted that a company could be convicted of manslaughter in *Attorney-General's Reference (No. 2 of 1999)* [2000] 2 Cr App R 207 (a prosecution of a train operating company for manslaughter arising out of a rail crash at Southall). Nonetheless, because of the difficulties in applying the identification principle and the rejection of the aggregation principle even in gross negligence manslaughter cases where it seems especially appropriate (see discussion in the previous section), prosecutors are extremely reluctant to institute manslaughter proceedings against companies. This has attracted considerable public disquiet following a series of high-profile tragedies, e.g., the sinking of the

Marchioness pleasure boat on the Thames; the fire at King's Cross tube station, and a succession of serious rail crashes.

You may recall the ill-fated canoe expedition across Lyme Bay when several sixth-form students died after their canoes capsized after the weather took a turn for the worse. The managing director of the company which ran the adventure centre which organised the trip and the company itself were both convicted of the manslaughter of the victims (*OLL Ltd and Kite* (1994) 144 NLJ 1735). The smallness of the company and its dominance by one individual, the simplicity of the precautions not taken and the fact that former instructors at the centre had written to warn the managing director in the clearest, tragically prophetic terms ('otherwise you might find yourself trying to explain why someone's son or daughter will not be coming home') made it simple to ascribe the blame to the company. The contrast between this case and large company cases such as the *Herald of Free Enterprise* points up the irony that the identification principle works best where it is not really needed. The conviction of a one-man company like *OLL Ltd* adds nothing to the conviction of the one man behind it—the owner and managing director. Conversely, conviction of unknown (to the general public) junior employees does not properly reflect the corporate blame often attaching to large companies where it is currently all too easy for the tiny proportion of top executives who can be identified with the company to insulate themselves from responsibility.

OLL Ltd represented the first conviction for an unlawful homicide recorded against a company in this country. According to the Government's White Paper on Corporate Manslaughter (see next section), since 1992, there have been 34 prosecutions for 'work-related' corporate manslaughter and only six convictions, all of 'small organisations'. The dismissal of manslaughter charges against the contractor responsible for the maintenance failure which caused the Hatfield rail crash has added fuel to already considerable public disquiet and demand for reform.

15.3.1.3 Reform of corporate manslaughter

The Law Commission's proposed Involuntary Homicide Bill (Law Com. No. 237, Appendix A) would retain the liability of corporations for the offences it recommends to replace manslaughter on the same basis as just discussed. However, it would also create a brand new offence of corporate killing which, in essence, adapts the elements of killing by gross carelessness under cl. 2 to the corporate context and seeks to attack fatal safety failures at a management or organisational level. The target is the management's failure to provide a safe **system** of conducting the company's activities and not the casual negligence of the company's employees at a purely day-to-day operational level. The offence would be committed 'if (a) a management failure by the corporation' is a cause of someone's death and '(b) that failure constitutes conduct falling far below what can be reasonably expected of the corporation in the circumstances' (cl. 4(1)). There is a 'management failure' if the way in which the corporation's 'activities are managed or organised fails to ensure the health and safety of persons employed in or affected by those activities' (cl. 4(2)(a)). A management failure can be a cause of the death 'notwithstanding that the immediate cause is the act or omission of an individual' (cl. 2(4)(b)). Thus, although the immediate cause of the death will often be the 'casual' negligence of an employee, this will not preclude a finding that it occurred as a result of a management failure, say, of supervision or training, which would then be also 'a cause' of the death.

The Government initially responded with its own provisional proposals in the form of a Consultation Paper (*Reforming the Law on Involuntary Manslaughter*, May 2000). It accepted the Commission's proposals as outlined above but would have extended them to **any** employer, whether a corporation or not. That massive extension looked too wide and overlooked the rationale of creating the special offence in the first place—to overcome the difficulties caused by the current rules of attribution for corporate liability. There is a strong case for extending the new offence to certain unincorporated associations such as health trusts, police authorities and the like but not to one-man employers and small partnerships. The proposals compounded this error by floating the idea that employees of companies might commit this special corporate offence (or one ancillary to it) and envisaging the imposition of sanctions on individuals. It was not explained why current offences were not adequate to deal with individuals (see Professor Sullivan at [2001] Crim LR 31 at pp. 38-9).

Things have moved on and the Government has issued revised proposals for consultation in the form of a draft Corporate Manslaughter Bill (*Corporate Manslaughter*, Cm 6497, 2005 and see *Cases and Materials* (15.3.1.3)). This accepts those two major criticisms and limits liability under the new offence to bodies corporate (which includes all companies incorporated under the Companies Acts and public bodies such as NHS Trusts, local authorities, universities and colleges which are incorporated under statute or Royal Charter) and, subject to some limitations, Government Departments (cl. 1(2)). Furthermore, there is to be no accessorial liability for the new corporate offence so that an individual cannot be convicted of aiding, abetting, counselling or procuring the new offence (cl. 1(5)). Of course, individuals may still be prosecuted for the existing offence of manslaughter. By the same token, liability of corporations for the existing offence of 'manslaughter by gross negligence' is abolished (cl. 13) (but not apparently 'unlawful act' manslaughter!).

An organisation commits

> corporate manslaughter if the way in which any of the organisation's activities are managed or organised by its senior managers—
>
> (a) causes a person's death, and
> (b) amounts to a gross breach of a relevant duty of care owed by the organisation to the deceased.
> (cl. 1(1))

The penalty is an unlimited fine (cl. 1(4)) (nobody can be imprisoned for this offence) and the court can order the organisation to take remedial steps (cl. 6).

You will notice that this offence shares a number of the ingredients in the existing manslaughter offence. There must be a duty of care which must be breached in a 'gross' way so as to 'cause' someone's death. However, the key difference is that the death must stem from the way in which 'senior managers' have 'managed or organised' any of its 'activities'. The focus is therefore on 'management failures at a senior level within the organization . . . the arrangements and practices for carrying out the organisation's work, rather than any immediate negligent act by an employee (or potentially someone else) causing death.' It looks at senior management's performance and attitude to the management of risk and the design, implementation and supervision of safety systems. Liability is limited to the actions and failures of 'senior managers' though, unlike the present law, it covers both individual and collective failure. There is no longer any need to identify one particular senior manager exhibiting gross negligence. A person is a 'senior manager' if 'he plays a significant role in (a) the making of decisions about how the whole or a substantial part of its activities are to be managed or organised, or (b) the actual managing or organising of the whole or a substantial part of those activities' (cl. 2). This rather vague definition could be interpreted narrowly as roughly equivalent to the existing concept of 'directing mind and will' or quite broadly but it would seem destined to provide much initial dispute in the courts. Arguably, the reference to 'senior managers' (which did not appear in the Law Commission's original proposals) is an unnecessary distraction, the real issue being 'whether the activities and organizational practices of the company were seriously deficient' (Clarkson [2005] Crim LR 677, 689).

Turning to those ingredients which parallel the existing law, we find that an attempt has been made to define the key concepts. The offence requires a 'gross breach of a **relevant duty of care**'. That means a duty owed by the organisation in negligence (a) to its employees, (b) in its capacity as occupier of land and (c) in connection with its supply of goods or services (whether for consideration or not) or its carrying on of any other activity on a commercial basis (cl. 4). Interestingly, cl. 4(3) departs from the existing law (see *Willoughby* at 6.5.3.2 above) in treating the question of whether the organisation owed a duty of care to the deceased as one of law purely for the judge. The judge must rule whether there was or was not a duty owed after making 'any findings of fact necessary to decide that question'. It is debatable whether the duty concept serves any useful purpose here: if a serious management failure has caused a death, why should that not be enough? It just adds an unnecessary layer of complexity and gives a further opportunity for unmeritorious argument (*cf. Wacker* and *Willoughby* at 6.6.3.2 above).

Unlike the existing law of manslaughter where the concept of gross negligence is left undefined and completely open for the jury, cl. 3 provides important guidance on what constitutes a gross breach of duty. The management failure must amount to 'conduct falling far below what can reasonably be expected of the organisation in the circumstances.' That may strike you as just as vague as the existing law but cl. 3(2) does provide some more helpful detail on how that question should be decided. The 'jury must consider whether the evidence shows that the organisation failed to comply with any relevant health and safety legislation or guidance.' That means 'any enactment dealing with health and safety matters' (and any subordinate legislation made under such an enactment) and 'any code, guidance, manual or similar publication that is concerned with health and safety matters' issued by an official enforcement agency. The implication seems to be that if non-compliance cannot be shown, the organisation is likely to be absolved. It does appear from cl. 3(4) that this is not automatic but so wide ranging is the definition of relevant 'legislation or guidance' that it is difficult to envisage a situation where liability could ensue without there being a breach of it. Clarkson has argued that the reference to 'guidance' makes the test too stringent since guidance notes often identify 'best practice' rather than just minimum standards applicable in legislative codes. However, breach of guidance is only a factor for consideration and does not result in an automatic finding of gross breach. It is right to take it into account.

If there is a breach of such legislation or guidance, the jury must further consider

(a) how serious was the failure to comply;
(b) whether or not senior managers

(i) knew, or ought to have known, that the organisation was failing to comply with that legislation or guidance;

(ii) were aware, or ought to have been aware, of the risk of death or serious harm posed by the failure to comply;

(iii) sought to cause the organisation to profit from that failure.

Although it is compulsory for the jury to consider the above matters, that 'does not prevent the jury from having regard to any other matters they consider relevant to the question' (cl. 3(4)). Although culpability is based on negligence and does not require proof of any subjective state of mind, it seems reasonably clear that proof of actual awareness of legislative non-compliance and/or the consequent risk of serious harm will be regarded as an aggravating factor in judging whether the negligence is 'gross'. Provision (b)(iii) invites the jury to view more severely organisations which deliberately cut safety corners for cost saving reasons. Presumably such **calculated** breaches of duty are more reprehensible and therefore more likely than inadvertent breaches to be gross. Again we would surmise that the absence of any of the factors in (b) would in practice preclude a finding of gross breach, though in terms it is not absolutely ruled out.

One final point of interest is that cl. 13, which is misleadingly headed 'Abolition of liability of corporations for manslaughter at common law', only refers to 'manslaughter by gross negligence'. It would therefore still be possible to convict a corporation of common law manslaughter under the unlawful act doctrine using the existing identification principle in relation to the underlying unlawful act. This is presumably deliberate rather than an oversight.

The proposed offence would make it more feasible to prosecute successfully large companies and to allay present public fears that they are currently not fully accountable for their failures. However, the vagueness and elasticity of some of the provisions is sure to provoke keenly contested trials where large corporations will fight tooth and nail to avoid tarnishing their image with a manslaughter conviction. It should be noted that, as for common law manslaughter, there is no corresponding offence of causing injury (or even serious injury) by a gross breach of duty.

15.3.2 Personal liability of directors and executives

Clearly, if a company is liable under the identification principle, then the person identified with it for this purpose will also be liable as perpetrator and, indeed, other officials might also be liable either as perpetrators or accessories. There is no question of the individuals who perform and/or authorise the acts in the name of the corporation being able to shelter behind its criminal liability. In order to be liable, the defendants must have the appropriate *mens rea* for the crime and, as we saw in **Chapter 14** on accomplices, *mens rea* is always required for accessories whatever the requirements of the principal offence. It can therefore be quite difficult to establish liability as an accessory. The Law Commission proposes that it should not be possible for an individual to be an accessory to its proposed new offence of corporate killing (cl. 4(4)). The Government has now accepted that but would allow individuals to be disqualified from acting in a management role.

However, it is now common for regulatory statutes, such as the Trade Descriptions Act 1968 and the Food Safety Act 1990, to provide that where an offence under the Act is committed by a corporation, any director, manager, secretary or other similar officer will also be guilty if the act was done with his 'consent or connivance' or if 'attributable to any neglect' on his part. Consent involves knowledge of what is happening and agreement to it. Connivance implies wilful blindness as to the commission of the offence. In either case a failure to prevent the offence by persons over which D had a right of control can suffice, even though this would not amount to aiding, abetting, counselling or procuring.

The third possibility—'attributable to neglect'—is the real extension here because mere negligence is never sufficient *mens rea* for a person to be an accessory. However, in *Lewin* v *Bland* [1985] RTR 171, DC it was held that, to be attributable to his neglect, it must be the superior officer's duty to check on the conduct of the person which resulted in the offence.

15.3.3 Conclusion

The problem for the criminal law is that its concepts were developed for individual acts or omissions committed by human individuals. Although they might be appropriately transferred to govern small one-person companies, they are unsuited to deal with organisations of any size or complexity. Large companies are not simply the sum of the individuals employed; they are organisations which have their own systems and structures for formulating policies and operating them, and often their own ethos or corporate culture. These tend to operate independently of the particular personnel involved. Because of the vast organisational edifice of larger companies, it may be impossible for an outsider to identify any 'controlling officer' whose actions or inactions and whose blameworthiness have led to the commission of the 'offence'.

Instead, corporate 'fault' may well comprise an aggregation of failures by a number of facets of the organisation and an agglomeration of different individuals whose identities may or may not be known. An 'offence' may be due to the company: (a) having no policy or an inadequately conceived policy to avoid its commission; or (b) failing properly to supervise the operating of an adequately conceived policy; or (c) failing to operate competently the adequately conceived policy.

More likely it will be down to a combination of two or more of these factors. Can the problem be resolved by allowing the court to aggregate the fault of different individuals? This could be a way forward but if the individuals whose fault could be aggregated were limited by the 'identification' principle, i.e., to the most senior management, it would still be restrictive since fault at the operational level ((c) above) and even the supervisor level ((b) above) would almost always be with individuals too junior to be identified with the company. You may recall that, in the limited circumstances where it operates, vicarious liability holds a company liable for the acts of all of its employees no matter how junior. Although, as we have seen, the courts have in the past been reluctant to impose vicarious liability, there are signs that they have been affected by public concern that blameworthy companies can often evade criminal responsibility. A number of important recent cases have adopted a vicarious or quasi-vicarious model of liability (*British Steel plc*; *Associated Octel Co. Ltd* (at 15.3 above); *Director-General of Fair Trading* v *Pioneer Concrete (UK) Ltd* [1994] 3 WLR 1249, HL; *Tesco Stores Ltd* v *Brent London Borough Council* [1993] 2 All ER 718, DC). Coupled with the signs in the *Meridian* case of a broader and more realistic view of the identification principle, this has been heralded by Professor Wells as a 'quiet revolution' in corporate liability ((1995) 145 New LJ 1326). However, it might be thought unfair to impose a general criminal liability on companies for **all** the acts of **all** their employees acting within the scope of their employment, which would be the result of imposing vicarious liability. Objections to this might be met by the imposition of such liability subject to the enactment of an across-the-board defence for companies which can show that they exercised all due diligence in terms of systems, supervision and operation to avoid commission of the offence.

Alternatively, if this is thought to place too heavy an onus on companies, a halfway house might be to require proof of management fault (taking a wide view of management to include relatively junior line managers) but to allow aggregation of fault among managers. As we saw earlier, the Court of Appeal has rejected such a principle (*Attorney-General's Reference (No. 2 of 1999)*).

As we have seen (at 15.3.1.3 above), the Law Commission's and the Government's proposed new offence of corporate killing seeks to by-pass the current constraints of the identification principle and vicarious liability, by focusing on the company's systems of management and organisation and its general attitude to and concern for safety. There is no doubt that the idea of 'management failure' in organising its systems of operation could be applied to corporate liability more generally and we believe it would be a welcome development to help control corporate behaviour. That is not to say that it could not be improved (see [1996] Crim LR 545; [2005] Crim LR 677).

On the other hand, the general proposals on corporate liability in cl. 30 of the draft Criminal Code Bill largely reflect the current law, except that a company would not be liable where the relevant controlling officer acted with intent to harm, or to conceal harm done, to the company itself.

■ **FURTHER READING**

Bergman: *The Case for Corporate Responsibility* (2000, Disaster Action).

Braithwaite & Fisse: *The Allocation of Responsibility for Corporate Crime* (1988) 11 Sydney Law Review 468.

Clarkson: *Corporate Manslaughter: Yet More Government Proposals* [2005] Crim LR 677.

Clarkson: *Kicking Corporate Bodies and Damning their Souls* (1996) 59 MLR 557.

Glazebrook: *A Better Way of Convicting Businesses of Avoidable Deaths and Injuries* [2002] CLJ 405.

Glazebrook: *Situational Liability* in Glazebrook (ed.): *Reshaping the Law* (1978, Sweet & Maxwell).

Gobert & Punch: *Rethinking Corporate Crime* (2003, LexisNexis).

Leigh: *Strict and Vicarious Liability* (1982, Sweet & Maxwell).

Pace: *Delegation—a Doctrine in Search of a Definition* [1982] Crim LR 627.

Sullivan: *The Attribution of Culpability to Limited Companies* [1996] CLJ 515.

Sullivan: *Corporate Killing—Some Government Proposals* [2001] Crim LR 31.

Wells: *Corporations and Criminal Responsibility* (2001, Oxford University Press).

■ **SUMMARY**

Vicarious liability

Courts normally reluctant to make D liable for acts physically performed by another. Two main exceptions: (i) extensive construction (ii) delegation. *Extensive construction*—extended meaning given to statutory verb, e.g., 'selling', 'using' usually to impose liability on employer where employee physically performs *actus reus*. Only possible if offence is strict liability (i.e., only the *actus reus*, **not** *mens rea* of employee can be imputed to the employer). *Delegation*—disliked by courts but firmly established in certain areas, e.g., licensing where, for some offences, only the licensee is capable of committing the offence (*Vane v Yiannopoullos*). Unlikely to be extended. If statute places responsibility on D he will be liable for any offences committed by his delegate (both *actus reus* **and** *mens rea* of delegate can be imputed to D). Complete delegation required.

Corporate liability

Companies are a distinct legal entity and theoretically can be criminally liable to same extent and on same basis as an individual, e.g., they can be vicariously liable in the same way as a human being. Can also be 'personally' liable under the identification principle—the acts and state of mind of senior managers are 'identified with' and treated as the acts and state of mind of the company (*Tesco Supermarkets Ltd v Nattrass*). Only very senior people with large measure of managerial discretion will constitute the 'directing mind and will' of company for this purpose. No facility to 'aggregate' the fault of more than one 'controlling officer' (*P & O European Ferries Ltd*; *Attorney-General's Reference (No. 2 of 1999)*). No corporate liability for offences (i) which carry mandatory imprisonment, i.e., murder, treason or (ii) such as rape, bigamy. Manslaughter possible (*OLL Ltd*). 'Controlling officers' could also be personally liable.

 CHAPTER 15: ASSESSMENT EXERCISE

15.1 Assume that Parliament has recently made it an offence 'to use or permit to be used any land for the conduct of any car boot sale without a licence'.

Crooks Limited, a company which specialises in car boot sales, instructs Sharp, its area manager, to organise a sale on Lord Fauntleroy's land. Sharp reaches agreement with Lord Fauntleroy and applies to the local authority for a licence.

As the date approaches, Sharp telephones the local authority and is told by Duff, a clerk in the relevant department, that the licence for the sale has been granted but that owing to staff shortages it may not be possible to get a letter of confirmation to him in time. Duff assures him that he need not worry because the sale is licensed. In fact Duff has made a mistake and the local authority has refused a licence for the sale.

The sale goes ahead with Sharp thinking that a licence has been granted.

Discuss the criminal liability, if any, of Crooks Limited and Sharp for 'using the land for a car boot sale without a licence', Lord Fauntleroy for 'permitting it to be so used' and of Duff for aiding and abetting Sharp.

See the **Appendix** (15.1) for a specimen answer.

16 Inchoate offences

16.1 Objectives

By the end of this chapter you should be able to:

1 Identify where the law draws the line between attempt and mere preparation

2 Define the *mens rea* of attempt in relation to both consequences and circumstances

3 Explain the issue of impossibility in attempt and how it has been resolved

4 Analyse the requirements of statutory conspiracy

5 Identify what remains of common law conspiracy

6 Explain how statutory conspiracy and common law conspiracy interact

16.2 Introduction

Inchoate ('ch' pronounced 'k') means 'only begun' or 'unfinished'. The so-called 'inchoate offences' presently comprise attempt, conspiracy and incitement. However, a person cannot be guilty of attempt, etc. in the abstract. The offence is attempting to commit a particular crime, e.g., theft or murder, or conspiring to commit it or inciting it. It is the crime D is attempting, conspiring or inciting to commit which is incomplete—not the attempt, conspiracy or incitement. In essence, D is aiming to commit the offence which is not completed and the attempt, conspiracy or incitement is a step towards that objective.

? QUESTION 16.1

- Why do you think the law has developed inchoate offences?
- We saw in **Chapter 14** that someone who assists, encourages or instigates a crime before its commission is guilty of that crime. When would someone who incites another to commit a crime not be guilty of aiding, abetting, counselling or procuring it?

Before an inchoate offence can be committed, the law requires more than the existence of a mental resolve to commit the crime. As with crimes generally, the guilty mind needs to be accompanied by an *actus reus*. D must not only have decided on the crime, he must have done something towards ensuring its commission. With conspiracy, this need not amount to anything more concrete than making a definite agreement with another to commit the crime. Conspiracy is committed immediately two or more people **agree** to commit a crime, whether or not they carry out any practical steps towards its commission. Similarly, incitement consists simply of trying to persuade someone to commit a crime, whether or not any further steps are taken towards its commission. Both incitement and conspiracy necessarily involve one or more others than the accused. By contrast, attempt can be committed without anyone other than the accused being involved. Attempt does require that the defendant has performed acts which fall only a little way short of the completed crime before the *actus reus* of attempt is held to be present.

You may recall that, where D gives assistance or encouragement to a perpetrator before the commission of the crime, in general D can be an accessory to and therefore convicted of that crime only if and when the perpetrator assisted or encouraged actually completes the crime. Liability is parasitic upon the full offence. The big difference with the inchoate offences is that they are not dependent on the full offence being committed as envisaged and can be committed whether or not the planned offence comes to fruition. For example, D will be guilty of incitement to commit an offence immediately he tries to persuade someone to commit it, whereas he could not be convicted as an accessory to the offence incited (encouraged) unless and until the perpetrator actually commits it.

? QUESTION 16.2

In fact the Law Commission Consultation Paper No. 131 (1993) on assisting and encouraging crime proposed radical changes to accessorial liability which involved the creation of two new inchoate offences and the abolition of one existing inchoate offence.

Can you remember the gist of these proposals? Refer back to 14.4.7 if you are unable to answer.

Before moving on to examine the law of attempt, we need to address one final issue raised in the last but one Question. Why have inchoate offences? The rationale is to enable the law and its enforcement agencies to intervene before the planned crime comes to fruition and causes the harm, without sacrificing the chance of a criminal conviction. Clearly, it would be ludicrous if, knowing of a plan to murder X by shooting, the police could only secure a successful prosecution of D for any offence if they allowed him to perpetrate the shooting. If D has shown himself by his actions to be sufficiently serious about committing the offence, he is dangerous enough for the law to intervene. Of course, the key question which we examine in the following sections is where the line of intervention should be drawn.

16.3 **Attempt**

16.3.1 **Introduction**

The old common law offence was repealed and replaced by a new statutory offence of attempt by the Criminal Attempts Act 1981 (*Cases and Materials* (16.3.1)). Under s. 1(1) statutory attempt is committed by someone who, with intent to commit an offence triable on indictment (i.e., an indictable offence or one triable either way), does an act which is more than merely preparatory to the commission of that offence.

Generally it is **not** an offence to attempt to commit a summary offence (i.e., one triable **only** summarily) (s. 1(4)). In addition s. 1(4) provides further limitations, making it no offence to attempt to conspire to commit an offence or to attempt to be an accessory to the commission of an offence. Furthermore, attempt would not lie unless the offence alleged to have been attempted would be triable as an indictable offence in England and Wales if it were completed. Generally speaking, this would exclude attempts to commit an offence abroad since the offence would be outside our courts' jurisdiction. It appears from *Liangsiriprasert* v *US Government* (1991) 92 Cr App R 77, PC that any attempt abroad to commit an offence in England or Wales is triable here even though none of D's acts occurs within the jurisdiction (e.g., parcel bomb sent to England from France).

Sections 3 and 5 of the Criminal Justice Act 1993 greatly extend our courts' jurisdiction over some attempts with a foreign element. Section 3 applies only to attempts to commit what the statute terms 'Group A' offences, which in general terms cover offences under the Theft Acts (but by no means all of them), the Fraud Act 2006 and the Forgery and Counterfeiting Act 1981. D can be convicted here of any attempt to commit a 'Group A offence' **triable here** whether or not—(a) the attempt was made in England and Wales; (b) it had an effect in England and Wales. A 'Group A offence' is triable here if 'a relevant event', i.e., 'any act or omission or other event (including any result of one or more acts or omissions) proof of which is required for conviction of the offence' occurred in England and Wales. It follows that if any element of the 'Group A offence' was intended to be performed here, the attempt would be triable here even though D actually did nothing and planned to do nothing in England and was not even a British subject!

? QUESTION 16.3

Suppose D, an Irish national, takes out a large life insurance policy in favour of his wife, with an insurance company in England. Unknown to his wife, he plans to disappear to Australia to set up home with his lover. On a business trip to the USA he fakes his death by drowning by leaving his clothes on Miami beach and disappears to Australia under an assumed identity.

- If his wife unwittingly obtains the life insurance money from the insurance company in England, what offence is committed by D? (It would be a 'Group A offence'.)
- If D was discovered in Australia before his wife claimed under the insurance, D would be guilty of attempting to commit 'a Group A offence'. Explain why our courts would have jurisdiction.

The facts above are similar to the case of *DPP* v *Stonehouse* [1977] 2 All ER 909, HL (*Cases and Materials* (16.3.1)) involving the former Government Minister, John Stonehouse, which we will examine further shortly. The offence he attempted was obtaining for another (his wife) property (the insurance money) by deception contrary to s. 15 of the Theft Act 1968 (now repeated and replaced by the Fraud Act 2006). Section 15 is a 'Group A offence' by virtue of s. 1 of the 1993 Act. The House of Lords held that, where D's intent was to cause the commission of the offence in England, the attempt would be triable here certainly where D's acts had an 'effect' in England (Lord Keith thought such an 'effect' essential; Lord Diplock thought it unnecessary). Communication of the false report of death to any relevant party in England, e.g., the insurance company or even the English media, could be the necessary 'effect' in England so that, on either view, our courts would be likely to have jurisdiction in our Question situation. What is the situation under Part I of the Criminal Justice Act 1993? The 'obtaining' is 'an act proof of which is required for conviction' of that offence and since this would have occurred in England, the completed s. 15 offence would have been triable here. So therefore is the attempt, by virtue of s. 3. Would the position be the same if D's wife had remained in Ireland and intended to claim and obtain the money there by postal communication? Section 4(a) caters for just such a situation: 'there is an obtaining of property in England and Wales if the property is either despatched from or received at a place in England and Wales.'

If the 'Group A offence' attempted is **not** triable here because no 'relevant event' would occur in England and Wales, s. 5 nonetheless provides that if an act is done in England and Wales which would constitute an attempt here but for the fact that all the elements of the completed offence would occur abroad and therefore not constitute an offence triable here, it shall be treated as an attempt here. There is a proviso that the conduct intended abroad would also involve the commission of an offence in that country. Fortunately, most topics in attempt are much less complicated than the 1993 Act on jurisdiction!

It is important to understand that, like other offences, attempt requires proof of both an *actus reus* and also a *mens rea*. However, unlike most substantive offences, where the emphasis is placed on the actual physical conduct proscribed by the crime (i.e., the *actus reus*), with the mental element acting as a control, with attempts, the focus is on the *mens rea* (the intention to perform the harmful conduct) with the *actus reus* (the physical steps taken towards performing the crime) acting as the control. The law's dilemma is that it does not wish to punish people for guilty thoughts alone but, on the other hand, it needs to be able to intervene at some point before those guilty thoughts have manifested themselves in the actual commission of the substantive crime. The existence of the inchoate offences (attempts, conspiracy and incitement) enables the courts and, more importantly, the law enforcement agencies, to intervene before the crime is completed.

16.3.2 The *actus reus* of attempt

The law is reluctant to intervene until a person's guilty intentions have actually manifested themselves in action—the taking of concrete steps towards the commission of the crime. The perennial problem is to determine how far along the line towards the commission of the substantive offence D must go before he is regarded by the law as having performed the *actus reus* of attempt. This was a major problem before the Criminal Attempts Act 1981 and it remains a major problem after the Act.

The main test, used before the Act, was called the 'proximity' test, whereby D's acts had to be 'proximate' to the crime in order to be an attempt, such acts being contrasted with 'remote' or preparatory acts. The courts' interpretation of this was remarkably restrictive and resulted in situations where D had gone quite a long way towards the commission of the crime, being excluded from the scope of attempt. For example, in *Comer* v *Bloomfield* (1970) 55 Cr App R 305, D, having crashed his van, pushed it into a nearby wood and reported to the police that it had been stolen. He wrote to his insurers stating that the van had been stolen and inquiring whether he could claim for it. Nonetheless, he was acquitted of attempting to obtain money from his insurers by deception on the basis that his actions were insufficiently proximate to the actual obtaining of the money. (See also the famous case of *Robinson* [1915] 2 KB 342, CCA.)

Shortly **before** the Criminal Attempts Act 1981, the House of Lords considered the issue in *DPP* v *Stonehouse* [1977] 2 All ER 909. The former Cabinet Minister John Stonehouse faked his own death by drowning off Miami beach and was discovered some time later in Australia living under an assumed identity. He had effected large insurance policies on his life and was charged with attempting to commit an offence under s. 15 of the Theft Act 1968, i.e., to enable another (his wife) to obtain monies from the companies insuring his life by his deception (pretending to be dead). His wife (who was innocent) had not in fact made any claim under the policies when D was discovered to be alive.

? QUESTION 16.4

Do you think D had done an act sufficiently proximate to amount to attempt?
  Can you see any distinction with *Comer* v *Bloomfield*?

The House of Lords laid down one definite rule for attempt which probably survives the 1981 Act. D would certainly commit the *actus reus* of attempt if he performed the last act **dependent on him**. Lord Diplock, metaphorically mixing it, expressed it thus: '... the offender must have crossed the Rubicon and burnt his boats.' We would emphasise that, contrary to the impression given by Lord Diplock's dictum, the converse proposition is not true. It is **not** essential for D to have done the last act dependent on him to be convicted of attempt (*Gullefer* [1990] 3 All ER 882, CA).

In *Stonehouse* the House of Lords distinguished *Robinson* and *Comer* v *Bloomfield* and held that there was an attempt because, in this case, D had done the last act **depending on him** to enable his wife to obtain the money. There was nothing further he could do, whereas in both *Robinson* and *Comer*, **the accused** had to make a claim before the money could be obtained from the insurance company.

However, the courts were unable to come up with any definitive test and Lord Reid in *Haughton* v *Smith* [1973] 2 All ER 896, HL—*Cases and Materials* (16.3.2)), reflected the practical position thus:

> But no words, unless so general as to be virtually useless, can be devised which will fit the immense variety of possible cases. Any attempted definition would, I am sure, do more harm than good.

It must be left to common sense to determine in each case whether D has gone beyond mere preparation.

At one stage the Law Commission had the idea of providing that if D had taken 'a substantial step' towards the commission of the crime, that would be enough for attempt. Its final view, however, was that this might give too wide a scope to the law of attempt and its 1980 Report recommended the formulation which was ultimately enacted in the 1981 Act.

16.3.2.1 The present law

 EXERCISE 16.1

Read s. 1(1) of the Criminal Attempts Act 1981 in *Cases and Materials* (16.3.1) and answer the following questions.

* Is it an offence to attempt to commit a summary offence? Refer back to the introduction to this chapter if you are not sure.
* Does the Act's definition of attempt cover attempt by *omitting* to act, e.g., if a parent tries to kill their child by deliberately withholding food or medical treatment?
* Where does the Act draw the line that has to be crossed to establish the *actus reus* of attempt? Is it of any practical assistance?

Section 1(1) defines the *actus reus* of attempt as the doing of 'an act which is more than merely preparatory to the commission of the offence'. Regrettably, there is no guidance whatsoever on when an act is to be regarded as more than 'merely preparatory' and the end result is that the courts are given a large measure of discretion in deciding which side of the line any particular case falls. Whether what D has done is 'more than merely preparatory' is a question of fact for the jury, although the judge can rule that the acts in question are not reasonably capable in law of amounting to an attempt (s. 4(3)).

The first point we can make is that the reference to acts in s. 1(1) means that it is presumably not possible to be guilty of attempting to commit a crime of omission. However, the issue has not as yet been raised by any case.

The second point is that the case law so far indicates that the courts seem to be continuing the restrictive interpretation of the pre-1981 case law even though there is no doubt that they are not in any way bound by the pre-1981 Act decisions. We can be reasonably confident that the present courts would follow those pre-1981 decisions where D was held guilty of attempt. For example, there is little doubt that D will always be guilty of attempt if he has performed the last act dependent upon him (see *Stonehouse* above). However, Lord Lane CJ in *Gullefer* [1990] 3 All ER 882, CA (*Cases and Materials* (16.3.2)) stressed that acts could be 'more than merely preparatory' notwithstanding that they fell short of the last act necessary for the defendant to complete the crime, although the test he formulated seemed to be as restrictive as the previous case law. According to him, an attempt 'begins when the merely preparatory acts come to an end and the defendant embarks upon the crime proper [or] the actual commission of the offence.' This echoes a phrase used previously by Rowlett J in *Osborn* (1919) 84 JP 63 that to commit an attempt D must be 'on the job'. The restrictive nature of the test is revealed in *Gullefer*. Gullefer's travels consisted of a trip to the local greyhound track where he placed a bet on a dog which failed to justify his confidence. Because the dog was clearly losing, Gullefer leapt out on to the track at the final bend in an effort to have the race declared void by the stewards so that he could recover his stake money from the bookmaker. The rules required bookmakers to return all stake money if the race was declared void. Unfortunately, Gullefer's second gamble was as unsuccessful as his first because the stewards did not declare the race void. He was charged with attempted theft of his stake money.

? QUESTION 16.5

Do you think that he should have been convicted? Had he done the last act dependent on him?

The Court of Appeal quashed Gullefer's conviction holding that he had engaged in merely preparatory acts even though the only act dependent on him left to perform was to go and collect the stake monies from the bookmaker.

Whilst Lord Lane was keen to stress that the court must look 'at the plain natural meaning' of s. 1(1), it is clear from *Jones* [1990] 1 WLR 1057, CA (*Cases and Materials* (16.3.2)) that it is permissible for the court to obtain guidance by referring to pre-1981 case law. However, in *Jones* again, the Court of Appeal construed as capable of being 'more than merely preparatory', **only** behaviour very close to D's last possible act. The facts of *Jones* illustrate the point. D, with intent to murder V, his rival in love, bought a shotgun and sawed off the barrel. He disguised himself and lay in wait for V with the loaded gun outside V's daughter's school. V arrived in his car and when his daughter had got out, D jumped into the rear seat pointing the shotgun at V, saying, 'You are not going to like this.' V grabbed the gun and managed to escape. It was later established that D had previously obtained some Spanish currency and was intending to flee to Spain after the event. He was convicted of attempted murder, the Court of Appeal dismissing D's argument that he had not gone far enough to commit attempt in that it was not proved that the safety catch was in the off position or that he had his finger on the trigger. It is instructive to read the Court's view of the point at which an attempt had been committed:

> Clearly his actions in obtaining the gun, in shortening it, in loading it, in putting on his disguise, and in going to the school could only be regarded as preparatory acts. But, in our judgment, once he had got into the car, taken out the loaded gun and pointed it at the victim with the intention of killing him, there was sufficient evidence for the consideration of the jury . . . it was a matter for them to decide whether they were sure those acts were more than merely preparatory.

It is therefore clear that D had to have gone very close to the last act before there would even be 'sufficient evidence' fit for a jury to be able to conclude that his acts were 'more than merely preparatory'. Of similar import is the decision in *Campbell* [1991] Crim LR 268, CA. D was observed by police hovering near a sub-post office for half an hour. He was eventually arrested in front of the premises and found to be in possession of an imitation firearm and a threatening note—a clear indication of his intention to rob the post office. The Court of Appeal, holding that D had not gone beyond mere preparation, said, 'If a person in such circumstances has not even gained the place where he could be in a position to carry out the offence, it is extremely unlikely that it could ever be...an attempt.'

Geddes (1996) 160 JP 697, CA further illustrates the unsatisfactorily narrow reach of attempt. D was caught in a school lavatory block with a rucksack containing a large kitchen knife, some lengths of rope and a roll of masking tape. The Court of Appeal held that, even though D's intention was to kidnap a schoolboy who happened along, he was not guilty of attempted false imprisonment. He had not 'moved from the realm of intention preparation and planning into the area of execution or implementation' because he had never confronted nor had any contact with any pupil. There was insufficient evidence to show that 'he had begun to carry out the commission of the offence'. The Court thought it to be 'an accurate paraphrase of the statutory test and not an illegitimate gloss upon it to ask whether the available evidence...could show that a defendant has done an act which shows that he has actually tried to commit the offence..., or whether he has only got ready or put himself in a position or equipped himself to do so.' It appears that lying in wait for the victim intending to pounce when he comes along is incapable of amounting to an attempt!

Tosti [1997] Crim LR 746, CA purported to apply *Geddes* but seems to have reached a rather contradictory decision on the facts. D1 and D2 were convicted of attempted burglary. They had parked their cars in a lay-by near a farm and hidden oxy-acetylene cutting equipment in a hedge near a barn. They were bending down examining a padlock on the barn door when they were disturbed by the owners of the farm. They ran off but were subsequently arrested. The Court held that it was open to a jury to conclude from this evidence that the accused had 'actually tried to commit the offence' as opposed to 'only got ready...to do so'. But were they any nearer to the offence than the accused in *Campbell* or *Geddes*?

It could be said that all acts prior to the last act necessary to complete the crime (and even the last act!) are preparatory to its commission and it is implicit in the statutory wording that the key distinction is not between acts of preparation and acts of commission (the latter will include some of the former), but between acts of **mere** preparation and acts of commission, i.e., acts going beyond **mere** preparation. According to *Tosti*, the latter includes 'acts which were preparatory but not merely so' and which were 'essentially the first steps in the commission of the offence':

> Essentially the question is one of degree: how close to, and necessary for, the commission of the offences were the acts which it was proved they had done.

 The Court of Appeal in *Attorney-General's Reference (No. 1 of 1992)* [1993] 2 All ER 190 (*Cases and Materials* (14.3.2)) held that the trial judge was wrong to rule that there could be no attempted rape **unless** D had made an actual physical attempt to penetrate V's vagina with his penis. If, with intent to do that, he dragged her into the bushes, lowered his trousers and interfered with her private parts, it was open to the jury to conclude he had done something 'more than merely preparatory' to the offence of rape, even if he had not tried to enter her with his penis.

Toothill [1998] Crim LR 876, CA makes the rather obvious point that on a charge of attempting to commit a burglary under s. 9(1)(a), the *actus reus* of attempt relates solely to the entry into the building and not to the ulterior offence which D intended to commit within the building. Thus, in this case, it was enough to show that D attempted to enter the building with the requisite intent to rape; there was no need to show that he had taken any steps towards the actual rape.

16.3.3 *Mens rea*

Under s. 1(1), D must **intend** to commit the offence alleged to have been attempted. There appears to be no change here from the pre-1981 law and, according to *Pearman* (1984) 80 Cr App R 259, CA, *Mohan* [1976] QB 1, CA (*Cases and Materials* (16.3.3)) still applies, requiring 'proof of specific intent, a decision to bring about, insofar as it lies within D's power, the commission of the offence which it is alleged the accused attempted to commit, no matter whether the accused desired that consequence of his act or not'.

Although the general thrust of this definition seems to require a direct intent, i.e., it is D's purpose to bring about the offence, the final words of the quotation, according to *Pearman*, embrace a slightly extended notion of intention similar to the view put forward by the Court of Appeal in *Nedrick* [1986] 3 All ER 1 and now the House of Lords in *Woollin* (see 3.3.2), i.e., in effect, foresight by D that the offence is virtually certain to result. It must be said, however, that this extended notion of intention seems to contradict the inherent nature of an attempt. It is difficult to see that you can be attempting to commit an offence unless you are **trying** to commit it, i.e., that it is your **purpose** to commit it.

In considering the intention requirement in more detail, it is helpful to distinguish **acts and consequences** forming part of the *actus reus* of the crime in question from **circumstances** forming part of that *actus reus*.

16.3.3.1 **Acts and consequences**

In general terms, as we have just seen, D must intend whatever act is required by the crime (e.g., penile penetration of the victim in the case of rape) and, in addition, any consequence defined as necessary by the *actus reus* of the crime (e.g., to cause the death of another in the case of murder). The result of this is that for many crimes, the prosecution's burden in proving *mens rea* is greater in relation to attempt than in relation to the actual completed offence.

> **? QUESTION** 16.6
>
> This is true of murder. Can you explain why?
>   It is also true of maliciously inflicting grievous bodily harm under s. 20 of the OAPA 1861. Why?
>   To answer, you need to know the *mens rea* required for murder and s. 20.

For murder, an intention to cause grievous bodily harm will suffice as well as an intention to kill. However, for attempt, **only** an intention to kill will suffice because D cannot be said to be attempting murder unless he is attempting actually to kill (*Whybrow* (1951) 35 Cr App R 141, CCA). So, if D intends grievous bodily harm **only**, where death actually results he is guilty of murder, but where death does not result he cannot be guilty of attempted murder.

Many offences requiring production of a particular consequence require proof only of recklessness in relation to that consequence (e.g., offences against the person such as s. 20 of the OAPA 1861 and criminal damage where D need only be subjectively reckless as to the harmful consequence). Even though recklessness suffices for the full offence, it will **not** be enough for attempt because D cannot be said to be attempting to harm someone or damage someone's property unless it is his purpose to do so. Mere awareness that your actions might injure someone or damage someone's property is not the same as intending to injure a person or damage their property. For example, in *O'Toole* [1987] Crim LR 759, D was alleged to have tried to set fire to a public house, inside which was a barmaid. The Court of Appeal held that D was not guilty of attempted arson (i.e., attempting to cause criminal damage by fire) because it was not shown that he intended to damage the pub by fire, his recklessness as to causing such damage being held to be insufficient.

? QUESTION 16.7

If such intention had been shown, would D have been rightly convicted of the aggravated offence of criminal damage under s. 1(2) of the Criminal Damage Act 1971 (see 12.10.3 on criminal damage above or *Cases and Materials* (12.10.1)), if he did not intend the barmaid's life to be endangered, but was reckless as to that happening?

That question was answered by the Court of Appeal in *Attorney-General's Reference (No. 3 of 1992)* [1994] 2 All ER 121 (*Cases and Materials* (16.3.3.1)). Provided D **intended** to damage the property, he would be guilty of attempting to commit the offence under s. 1(2) even if he was only reckless as to the endangering of life by such damage. For attempt, the **intention** necessary was an intention to 'supply the missing physical element of the completed offence' (i.e., the *actus reus*—in this case just damage to property); the endangering of life is not an element in the *actus reus* of s. 1(2) because it is not necessary to prove that anyone's life was **in fact** endangered. Therefore, it is not a 'missing physical element of the completed offence'. If D has this intent to supply the missing physical element, the *mens rea* he requires beyond that is exactly the same as for the completed offence. Hence, for attempting s. 1(2), he needs only to be reckless in relation to the endangering of life.

16.3.3.2 Circumstances

In many crimes, the *actus reus* is so defined as to require proof of the existence of certain prescribed circumstances when the accused does the prohibited act. As we have seen when looking at *mens rea* generally, the mental element in regard to such circumstances can vary from none at all (i.e., strict liability in relation to the relevant circumstance) to a requirement of actual knowledge of the presence of that circumstance. Keeping in mind the common sense notion of attempt as **trying** to commit the relevant offence, we would expect to find that the law requires that D should **actually know** of (or at least **believe** in) the existence of any circumstance required by that offence, as well as having the intention to do the act or produce the consequence prohibited by it. This should be true whether the culpability required in relation to that circumstance by the **full offence** is actual knowledge, recklessness, negligence or even none at all.

? QUESTION 16.8

Suppose a law is passed making it an offence to destroy documents more than 100 years old. If D deliberately tries but fails to destroy some 101-year-old documents, would you regard him as having attempted to destroy a document over 100 years old if:

- he never thought about how old they were; or
- he thought they might be over 100 years old but did not bother to check; or
- he knew they were over 100 years old?

D can hardly be said to be attempting to commit that offence unless he is aiming to destroy the documents **knowing** (or at the very least believing) they are over 100 years old. This principle should hold even if the *mens rea* required by the full offence is less than knowledge (or belief) that the documents are over 100 years old (e.g., recklessness (whether subjective or objective) as to their age or even strict liability as to it). However, the Court of Appeal recently departed from this principle that intention/knowledge is required in relation to **every** element of the offence in the case of *Khan* [1990] 2 All ER 783 (*Cases and Materials* (16.3.3.2)) where D was convicted of attempted rape.

? QUESTION 16.9

- What was the *actus reus* of rape prior to the Sexual Offences Act 2003?
- What was the *mens rea* of rape?
- What should be the *mens rea* of attempted rape?

The *actus reus* of the most common type of rape was performed when a man had sexual intercourse with a woman without the woman's consent. The *mens rea* involved an intention to have sexual intercourse with a woman knowing or being reckless as to the fact that the woman did not consent. The Court of Appeal held that for attempted rape, the *mens rea* was precisely the same. The only difference was in the *actus reus*—in the full offence of rape sexual intercourse takes place, whereas in attempted rape it does not. Therefore, in both rape and attempted rape, the only intent required is to have sexual intercourse. The offence is committed 'because of the circumstances in which he manifests that intent i.e., when the woman is not consenting and he either knows it or could not care less [i.e., recklessness] about the absence of consent'.

    In fact, it appears that the principle stated by the Court of Appeal in *Attorney-General's Reference (No. 3 of 1992)* [1994] 2 All ER 121, perhaps unwittingly, extends *Khan* to offences requiring only objective recklessness or negligence or even no fault (i.e., strict liability) in relation to the vital circumstance. According to the court, D 'must be in one of the states of mind required for the commission of the full offence and did [sic] his best . . . to supply what was missing from the completion of the offence.'

Literally, this means that if the complete offence requires no fault element in relation to a particular circumstance forming part of the *actus reus*, then neither does an attempt to commit it. Similarly, if the complete offence is satisfied by proof of negligence in respect of a circumstance of the *actus reus* then proof of such negligence will suffice for attempting that offence. This is because these represent 'the states of mind required for the commission of the full offence' in relation to those circumstances.

Let us take the abduction of a girl under 16 contrary to s. 20 of the Sexual Offences Act 1956 as an example (a good illustration even though the offence was recently repealed by the Sexual Offences Act 2003). Suppose D tries but fails to abduct a girl under 16 mistakenly thinking she is over 16. If we require only the state of mind of the complete offence in relation to the girl being under 16, then D will be guilty of attempt without proof of any *mens rea* (or even negligence) in respect of her being under 16 (see *Prince* (1875) but remember this is suspect since *B v DPP*). All he would require is an intention to supply the 'missing physical element' from the complete offence (i.e., the intention to take the girl).

It is to be hoped that the courts will reconsider this widening of the law of attempt at the first opportunity and require in all cases that D was at least **aware** of the possibility of the relevant circumstance existing before he can be convicted of attempt, no matter what the *mens rea* for the completed offence. This is the position proposed in the latest draft Criminal Code (see *Cases and Materials* (16.3.3.2)).

Even if the courts were later to overturn the decisions in *Khan* and *Attorney-General's Reference (No. 3 of 1992)* and to revert to the view originally favoured by the Law Commission that intention/knowledge would be required in relation to all elements of the offence, it seems implicit in s. 1(3) of the Act (which relates to impossibility of an attempt—dealt with at the end of this chapter) that 'belief' that the relevant circumstance exists would suffice as an alternative to actual knowledge. In this context, belief probably means that D had no substantial doubt that the circumstance existed.

Finally, we would emphasise that in no case does the requirement of an intent to commit an offence mean that the accused must know or believe that what he intends to do is a crime. The Act does not affect the general principle that ignorance of the law is no defence.

16.3.3.3 **Conditional intent**

D has a **conditional** intent where he intends to commit an offence, but only if a particular condition is satisfied. For example, D is caught going through coat pockets in a sports changing room. His intention is to steal, but only if he comes across items he regards as worth stealing. The rule is that he can be guilty of attempt provided he has a **definite** intention to steal if the condition is satisfied. However, care must be taken in the formulation of the charge. If he is charged with attempting to steal **specified** (but worthless and/or rejected) items actually in the pockets (e.g., a handkerchief or comb), the charge will fail because the prosecution will be unable to prove that he had formed a definite intention to steal **those items**. The way round the difficulty is to charge him with attempting to steal **from** the coat pockets without specifying any particular items. There can be no doubt that he had formed a definite intention to steal from those pockets subject to finding something worth stealing (e.g., money) (see *Attorney-General's References (Nos. 1 and 2 of 1979)* [1979] 3 All ER 143, CA and *Toothill* [1998] Crim LR 876, CA).

16.3.4 **Impossibility**

The situation contemplated here is where, unknown to D, the prevailing circumstances make it impossible for him to complete the offence that he is trying to commit. Prior to the 1981 Act, the courts made unconvincing distinctions and excluded from the law of attempts cases which most people thought ought to be included.

 EXERCISE 16.2

Using a separate sheet of paper, write down three examples of situations where, unknown to D, the offence is impossible to commit.

When you have read the next paragraph about *Haughton* v *Smith*, decide which of the three categories each of your examples fits into.

The House of Lords in *Haughton* v *Smith* [1973] 3 All ER 1109 distinguished three situations which will help us in our consideration of the changes brought in by the 1981 Act.

(a) **Insufficiency of means**—the means used by D make it impossible for him to do what he sets out to do and complete the crime, e.g., D's attempt at a burglary fails because the jemmy he uses is not strong enough to force the door of the building.

(b) **Factual (or physical) impossibility**—unknown to D, the facts are such that, whatever means are adopted, it is impossible to commit the crime, usually due to the fact that the subject-matter of the crime does not exist, e.g., trying to pick a pocket which is in fact completely empty (there is simply nothing to be stolen); or trying to kill a 'sleeping' person who is in fact, unknown to D, already dead.

(c) **Legal impossibility**—where D, even if he did all he planned, would not in fact commit a crime because, due to a mistake on his part, this does not constitute the crime owing to the absence of a vital element of the *actus reus*, e.g., D handles goods he mistakenly believes to be stolen but which in fact are not stolen (he has done exactly what he set out to do, but, contrary to his belief, he has not handled stolen goods); D takes an umbrella intending to steal it but, unknown to him, it is his own.

After *Haughton* v *Smith*, only the first of these situations constituted criminal attempt. The exclusion of the second and third situations seemed to contradict the rationale of attempt, which is to catch those who have shown a willingness to put their evil intentions into practice by going beyond mere preparation. It was therefore no surprise that the Criminal Attempts Act 1981 sought to reverse *Haughton* v *Smith* and sweep situations (b) and (c) into the net.

Section 1(2) provides that a person can be guilty of attempt 'even though the facts are such that the commission of the offence is impossible'. This provision clearly catches situation (b) and, arguably, also situation (c). However, to make doubly sure that situation (c) was covered, the legislature went on to provide for the situation where D makes a mistake as to the facts. Section 1(3) expressly provides that, if D would have had the requisite intent, had the facts of the case been as D mistakenly believed them to be, then he is to be regarded as having the necessary intent to commit the offence, even though it is actually impossible to commit it. So, for example, if D has sexual intercourse with a girl he mistakenly believes to be 15 but who is in fact 16, it is conceivable that he would **not**, without s. 1(3), be regarded as having an intention to have sexual intercourse with a girl under 16. Section 1(3) makes it clear that D would have the necessary intent and this, admittedly unconvincing, argument could not possibly succeed. Similarly, if D intends to handle a video recorder which he believes to be stolen but which in fact is not, s. 1(3) makes it clear that he is to be regarded as having an intention to handle a **stolen** video, precluding the argument that, because he intended to handle that ('unstolen') video, he therefore intended to handle an 'unstolen' video.

For a brief period the House of Lords in *Anderton* v *Ryan* [1985] 2 All ER 355 completely disregarded the clear intentions of the legislation and held that s. 1(2) did not make situation (c) an attempt. The facts were similar to the video example given above and this was held not to constitute an attempt on the basis that D had done all he set out to do and his actions were 'objectively innocent' and not an offence. Thankfully, the House of Lords realised its mistake very soon after and overruled *Anderton* v *Ryan* in *Shivpuri* [1986] 2 All ER 334 (*Cases and Materials* (16.3.4)). D was detained while in possession of a suitcase and admitted that he believed it contained either heroin or cannabis. In fact, unknown to him, the suitcase did not contain any illegal drug but only snuff! Nonetheless, D was convicted of attempting to commit the statutory offence of knowingly being concerned in dealing with a drug whose importation was prohibited. According to the House, the question to ask where D is mistaken about the facts of the situation is whether his acts would have been more than merely preparatory if the facts had been as D believed them to be.

We may therefore summarise the law on impossibility as follows. As long as D intended to commit the offence in question and had done an act which was more than merely preparatory to the offence **he intended** to commit, even though, unknown to him, it could not be committed, he would be guilty of attempt no matter **why** it was impossible to commit.

Before leaving impossibility, it must be stressed that s. 1(3) does not apply where what D sets out to do is not, on the facts as seen by him, an offence known to the law. Therefore, if he makes a mistake as to the criminal law and believes that certain conduct is criminal when the law says that it is not, he cannot be convicted of attempt. For example, if a man has sexual intercourse with a girl of 17, mistakenly believing that it is a criminal offence to have intercourse with a girl under 18, he cannot be convicted of attempt because he does not intend to commit an offence known to the law.

16.4 **Conspiracy**

16.4.1 **Introduction**

Regrettably, the law of conspiracy is considerably more complex and uncertain than it need be because the statutory reform of the area largely contained in Part I of the Criminal Law Act 1977 was only partial. As a result, there are now two types of conspiracy— statutory conspiracies governed by the 1977 Act, and an important but limited range of common law conspiracies, which were expressly retained by ss. 5(2) and 5(3) of the Act, still governed by the old common law rules. By far the most significant of the latter group is conspiracy to defraud, the others being conspiracy to corrupt public morals and conspiracy to outrage public decency (although, as we shall see later, there is a doubt about whether there is, in practice, any scope for the latter two). All other common law conspiracies were abolished by s. 5(1) of the Act. A statutory conspiracy is essentially any agreement to commit a crime.

The intention of the reformers was that this hybrid system should only be temporary pending review and reform of the law relating to fraud, and obscenity and indecency. Unfortunately, although the law has now been reformed by the Fraud Act 2006, the Government has decided to wait and see how the new law operates in practice before taking any step to abolish or change common law conspiracy to defraud so that exclusive reliance on statutory conspiracy has still not been achieved.

Major problems were experienced in the early years after the Act over how the preserved common law conspiracy to defraud dovetailed with the new statutory conspiracy to commit a crime. Frequently, an agreement to defraud will necessarily involve an agreement to commit a substantive offence entailing dishonesty such as theft or the new offence of fraud under the Fraud Act 2006. Suppose, for example, A and B agree a scheme to dupe people into investing money in a non-existent company intending to disappear with the money subscribed. To do this would certainly be to agree to defraud the investors, but it would also be an agreement to commit the crime of fraud by false representation under s. 1 of the Fraud Act 2006. Must it be prosecuted as (a) only common law conspiracy to defraud or (b) only statutory conspiracy to commit the fraud offence or (c) whichever one the prosecution chooses?

EXERCISE 16.3

- Read s. 5(3) of the Criminal Law Act 1977 in *Cases and Materials* (16.4.1).
  Is there any overlap between statutory conspiracy to commit a crime and common law conspiracy to corrupt public morals/outrage public decency? When is an agreement to corrupt public morals or outrage public decency *not* a common law conspiracy?
- Read s. 5(2) Criminal Law Act 1977 including the original concluding words now repealed by s. 12 Criminal Justice Act 1987 in *Cases and Materials* (16.2.1).
  Was there any overlap between statutory conspiracy to commit a crime and common law conspiracy to defraud?
    When was an agreement to commit a crime *not* a statutory conspiracy?

- Read s. 12 of the Criminal Justice Act 1987 in *Cases and Materials* (16.2.1).
  Is there any overlap between statutory conspiracy to commit a crime and common law conspiracy to defraud?
  Can an agreement to commit a crime be charged as a common law conspiracy? If so, when?

It is clear from s. 5(3) that there is no overlap between statutory conspiracy and common law conspiracy to corrupt public morals or outrage public decency. They are mutually exclusive. Common law conspiracy is confined to cases where the conduct corrupting or outraging 'would not amount to or involve the commission of an offence...'

The position in relation to conspiracy to defraud under the original wording of s. 5(2) seemed clear enough but was to the opposite effect. Again there was no overlap but this time statutory conspiracy 'shall not apply in any case where the agreement in question amounts to a conspiracy to defraud at common law'. In other words any agreement to defraud, no matter what substantive crimes would be involved in carrying it out, had to be charged as a common law conspiracy. This was a very serious curtailment of the scope of statutory conspiracy since most offences involving dishonesty under the Theft Acts would entail 'defrauding' and would not be within the provisions of the 1977 Act. After much confusion, the House of Lords in *Ayres* [1984] 1 All ER 619 refused to accept this interpretation but itself created such difficulties for prosecutors that two years later in *Cooke* [1986] 2 All ER 985 it gave yet another interpretation. Fortunately, the confusion was finally cleared up by s. 12 of the Criminal Justice Act 1987. This now gives the prosecutor the option to charge common law conspiracy to defraud **or** statutory conspiracy to commit a crime in any case where the agreement to defraud would involve the commission of a crime. Mutual exclusivity has gone and there is now a considerable overlap between the two.

16.4.2 Common features between statutory and common law conspiracies

Although there are important differences between common law and statutory conspiracies necessitating separate treatment, some elements are shared and it is convenient to deal with some of these at the outset.

16.4.2.1 Agreement

The essence of conspiracy is the agreement by two or more people to effect the unlawful purpose. There must be a definite concluded agreement but nothing more is needed. It is unnecessary for any steps to be taken to carry out the agreement. Nor does it matter that important details of the plan have still to be settled—even, for example, the date and place of an agreed burglary.

The offence is committed immediately the agreement is concluded but it then continues for as long as the agreement subsists, i.e., until the plan is carried out, abandoned or prevented by circumstances (*DPP* v *Doot* [1973] 1 All ER 940, HL—*Cases and Materials* (16.4.2.1)).

A number of principles can be derived from the 'continuing' offence analysis. The fact that the agreement was made abroad outside our jurisdiction will not prevent conviction here where the parties did acts in concert in England in pursuance of the agreement (*DPP* v *Doot*). Similarly, it means that others joining in after the initial agreement has been concluded can be guilty of conspiring with the original parties. This means that it is not necessary for all the parties to be in contact with each other or even to know each other's identities (*Ardalan* [1972] 2 All ER 257, CA). However, it is essential that D has communicated expressly or implicitly his agreement to the prohibited purpose to at least one other party to the agreement. It is not enough to have a secret uncommunicated intention to join in (*Scott* (1979) 68 Cr App R 164, CA—*Cases and Materials* (16.4.2.1)).

16.4.2.2 **Agreement with whom?**

Two or more people must agree but it is not essential to be able to identify D's coconspirator(s). Companies can be guilty of conspiring with another company or a human individual (*ICR Haulage* [1944] 1 All ER 691). However, according to *McDonnell* [1966] 1 All ER 193, if a director, who is the sole responsible person running the company, commits an offence in the company's name, neither he nor the company commits conspiracy. Presumably the same rule would apply where a 'controlling officer', without communicating with any other 'controlling officer', uses the company for an offence, even although he is not the 'sole responsible person' running the company's affairs. In both cases the 'agreement' is effectively with himself not another. (See 15.3 for corporate liability.)

A further restriction prevents conspiracy where the **only** parties to the agreement are married to each other (*Mawji* v *R* [1957] 1 All ER 385, PC (common law conspiracy); s. 2(2) Criminal Law Act 1977 (statutory conspiracy)). Of course, a wife and husband can be guilty of conspiracy if they know that another person (e.g., a close relative) is a party to the agreement (*Chrastny* [1992] 1 All ER 189, CA). Under s. 2(2) no statutory conspiracy can be committed where the only other party is under the age of criminal responsibility (currently under ten) or alternatively 'an intended victim' of the offence(s) planned.

There is no authority governing common law conspiracy, but it is likely that a similar rule will apply in respect of the under 10s. It is difficult to envisage how there could be a common law conspiracy to defraud where the 'intended victim' agrees to commit the fraud! No definition of 'intended victim' is provided by the statute, but Smith and Hogan suggest that it should be limited to cases where the offence exists to protect the alleged victim so that he would not be liable as an accessory to D's offence although he cooperates in it with full knowledge. However, a literal interpretation would reach much further. In regard to our Question, examples falling within the narrow interpretation would include a 15-year-old girl who agrees with D (a) to have sexual intercourse with D or (b) to let D take her out of the possession of her parents without their consent. Similarly, a mental defective who agrees with D to have sexual intercourse with him.

? QUESTION 16.12

If a sadist agreed to meet a masochist for the purpose of inflicting on the masochist genital torture involving actual bodily harm, would they be guilty of conspiring to commit an assault occasioning actual bodily harm?

The answer depends on whether the courts adopt the wider literal interpretation of 'intended victim'. The masochist, according to *Brown*, would aid and abet the s. 47 offence if actual bodily harm was inflicted by the sadist and therefore would not come within the narrow interpretation advocated by Smith and Hogan, so that both would commit conspiracy on conclusion of the agreement.

If D agrees to commit the offence with only one other who is exempt from prosecution for that offence (e.g., a mother for abducting her own child), he can be convicted of conspiracy (*Duguid* (1906) 21 Cox CC 200). But what of the person who is exempt from liability? Will they be guilty of conspiracy also? It would appear so. Thus, rape is a crime which can only be perpetrated by a man. However, we saw in **Chapter 14** that a woman could be an accessory to rape. Equally, she can conspire to rape. Similarly, a bachelor or spinster can conspire to commit the offence of bigamy and/or be an accessory thereto. This principle was adopted in *Whitchurch* (1890) 24 QBD 420.

Suppose, however, that D was exempt from liability for the offence planned, both as perpetrator **and** accessory. According to *Burns* (1984) 79 Cr App R 173, CA he could nonetheless be guilty of conspiracy to commit it (see *Cases and Materials* (16.4.2.2)).

16.4.2.3 **Acquittal of all other alleged conspirators**

In the chapter on complicity at 14.4.1.7, we saw that in some circumstances it was possible for X to be guilty of aiding and abetting Y to commit a crime even though Y was acquitted of that crime. Similarly, where D is charged with conspiring with others to commit a crime, it is not necessarily a bar to his conviction that all the other persons with whom he is charged with conspiring are acquitted. This is true even if all the others were tried at the same time as D.

Section 5(8) of the Criminal Law Act 1977 now provides for **all** conspiracies that the acquittal of all the other alleged conspirators 'shall not be a ground for quashing his conviction unless under all the circumstances of the case his conviction is inconsistent' with the other acquittals. (See *Cases and Materials* (16.4.2.3).)

16.4.3 **Statutory conspiracy**

As you would expect, the offence is defined by s. 1 of the Criminal Law Act 1977 and you will find the full text of s. 1(1) and (2) as amended set out in *Cases and Materials* (16.4.3). In essence the offence is committed where two or more people agree 'that a course of conduct will be pursued which, if...' then '...carried out in accordance with their intentions, ...will necessarily amount to or involve the commission of an offence by one or more parties to the agreement.'

Although the offence could be analysed using the conventional division into *actus reus* and *mens rea*, we feel that this is artificial given that the essence of the *actus reus* is the 'agreement'. Agreement is fundamentally a mental operation although, of course, it must be evidenced by some words or conduct of the conspirators. Conspiracy is, therefore, overwhelmingly a crime of the mind. Let us now turn to the ingredients of statutory conspiracy.

16.4.3.1 **Purpose of the agreement**

The parties must agree that:

(a) a course of conduct be pursued;

(b) which if carried out in accordance with their intentions;

(c) will necessarily amount to or involve a crime.

Course of conduct be pursued

It is possible to interpret 'course of conduct' narrowly or broadly. Although there is no definitive case law in favour, most writers conclude that the broad interpretation is correct, not least because the alternative would be absurdly restrictive. The controversy is whether 'course of conduct' is confined to the physical acts planned to be performed or whether it includes in addition (a) the consequences the accused intend to follow from those actions and/or (b) any material circumstances which they know or believe or intend to exist. Suppose that A and B agree that they will set fire to X's house in the dead of night with the intention of killing X.

? QUESTION 16.13

- How would you describe the course of conduct to which A and B have agreed?
- Will this course of conduct 'necessarily involve the commission of the offence of murder'?

If the 'course of conduct' is simply setting fire to the house, then it will not necessarily involve a murder because X may not be in the house or he may escape from it. On the other hand, if 'course of conduct' includes the intended consequence—X's death, then it will necessarily involve the crime of murder. Most writers go for the inclusion of all intended consequences. We should emphasise that it is only **intended** consequences which can be part of the 'course of conduct' in this way (*Siracusa* (1990) 90 Cr App R 340, CA). This would be so even though the conspirators **realise** that the consequence they do not intend may ensue. Thus, if in the factual example above, A and B intended only to frighten X or to cause him only serious injury, they could not be guilty of conspiracy to murder even if they thought that death was a likely consequence. Death was not part of the agreed plan.

You will be aware that many offences require as part of their *actus reus* the presence of defined surrounding circumstances. Since such crimes would only **necessarily** be committed if the relevant circumstance(s) existed, it is crucial to know if 'course of conduct' includes those circumstances which the conspirators envisage or plan will exist. The implication of s. 1(2) of the 1977 Act is that 'course of conduct' does include those circumstances which the conspirators **'intend or know**...will exist at the time when the conduct constituting the offence is to take place'.

? **QUESTION** 16.14

Suppose A and B agree to marry each other in one month's time knowing that B is still married to C. Will this constitute conspiracy to commit bigamy?

If 'course of conduct' was limited to their planned physical acts—going through a ceremony of marriage—it would not 'necessarily' result in bigamy. B might cease to be married to C before the ceremony through divorce or C's death. On the other hand, if 'course of conduct' includes the circumstances which A and B envisage will exist at the time of the second ceremony, bigamy will necessarily result. However, s. 1(2) requires the conspirators to 'intend' or 'know' that B will still be married at the time. We cannot say that, **at the time of the agreement**, B knows that she will still be married because C might die at any time. It is also odd to talk about intending that B should still be married where the matter is outside B's control. No doubt B would be delighted if C were to die leaving her free to marry. The view of most writers is that 'know' must be extended to embrace 'believe'. Thus, 'course of conduct' will include intended consequences and any circumstances which the conspirators intend, know or believe will exist. Conspiracies to handle stolen goods throw up the same problem.

If carried out in accordance with their intentions

Until the House of Lords made a mess of the law in *Anderson* [1985] 2 All ER 961, it was understood that D could not be convicted of conspiracy unless it was proved that he and at least one other party to the agreement intended that the agreement should be carried out. This was certainly the position at common law (*Thomson* (1965) 50 Cr App R 1) and the intention of the architects of the statutory reform, the Law Commission. It is true that Parliament deleted from the draft Bill the provision which made this crystal clear, but this seemed to be in order to avoid what was perceived as unnecessary complexity rather than an attempt to change the law. If A and B agree to murder X but one or both secretly do not intend X to be killed, it cannot be said that the carrying out of **their** combined intentions will necessarily result in the offence of murder.

EXERCISE 16.4

Read the extract from *Anderson* in *Cases and Materials* (16.4.3.1).

- What was the main argument advanced by the defence which Lord Bridge rejected?
- According to Lord Bridge, what intention must be proved to convict a person of conspiracy?
- Lord Bridge was concerned to exclude from the scope of conspiracy, law enforcers who pretend to go along with the criminal plan. Which rule would be more likely to exclude such law enforcers, Lord Bridge's rule or the one he rejected?

The House of Lords in *Anderson* was of the unanimous view that it was unnecessary to prove 'an intention on the part of each conspirator that the criminal offence ... should in fact be committed.' It was only necessary to prove that he intended to play some part in the agreed course of conduct intended by the other conspirators to result in the offence. On this basis, D was guilty of conspiracy to effect another's prison escape even though he did not intend the escape to be effected. He agreed to supply a diamond saw to E and F even though he regarded their plan as having no chance of success. Apart from D, there were three other parties to the conspiracy who clearly did intend the escape to be effected. The agreed course of conduct, if carried out in accordance with their intentions, would necessarily result in the escape offence. However, this could not be the case if none or only one of the parties to the agreement intended that the offence should be committed. The House did not indicate whether its new principle would extend to such cases but there was no indication that it would not cover them. However, we would anticipate that a future court would make a distinction along these lines and confine *Anderson* to cases where there are at least two parties to the agreement intent on carrying it out.

? **QUESTION** 16.15

Lord Bridge thought his rule was necessary to enable the conviction of minor helpers in the plan who might well not care whether the offence planned was committed. He instanced the owner of a car hire firm who hires a car to a gang knowing that it is to be used for a robbery. Would you regard the owner as having agreed to rob or merely to have helped others to carry out their agreement to rob?

The answer to Lord Bridge's worry is that those who assist conspirators without themselves intending the offence to be committed should be regarded as aiding and abetting the conspiracy rather than as being principals in it. Although, for the time being, *Anderson* represents the law, its future applicability seems uncertain in the light of the Privy Council's decision in *Yip Chiu-Cheung v R* [1994] 2 All ER 924 (*Cases and Materials* (16.4.3.1)). Lord Griffiths, pronouncing the unanimous opinion of their Lordships, enunciated a principle apparently in direct conflict with *Anderson* (though he seemed not to recognise any conflict!). Lord Griffiths stated,

> The crime of conspiracy requires an agreement between two or more persons to commit an unlawful act with the intention of carrying it out. It is the intention to carry out the crime that constitutes the necessary *mens rea* for the offence.

This cannot stand with the House of Lords' assertion in *Anderson* that there was no need to prove an intention by each conspirator that the offence should be committed. It is true that *Anderson* was a prosecution for statutory conspiracy whereas *Yip Chiu-Cheung* was for common law conspiracy, but the latter's view is preferable and may well prompt an early reconsideration of *Anderson* by the House of Lords. The Court of Appeal has already overlooked or ignored *Anderson* on several occasions, most recently in *Harvey* [1999] Crim LR 70.

The House in *Anderson* made another surprising change of principle when laying down what **was** required for the offence. The accused must have 'intended to play some part in the agreed course of conduct in furtherance of the criminal purpose'. This would seem to absolve Mr Big who originates and orchestrates the whole plan but who never participates in any actions necessary to carry it out. The requirement was intended to protect the undercover law enforcer who pretends to go along with the agreement but it is unlikely to do so since the law enforcer will usually need to participate, at least in a small way, to maintain his cover.

It is not surprising that the Court of Appeal in *Siracusa* (1990) 90 Cr App R 340 (*Cases and Materials* (16.4.3.1)) should attempt to outflank this aspect of *Anderson*. In its view, 'playing some part in' can include continuing to concur in, or failing to stop the criminal activity of another. On this basis, 'participation in a conspiracy...can be active **or passive**' (our emphasis).

Intention and knowledge as to facts or circumstances necessary for the commission of the crime

Substantive offences often require proof of a particular fact or circumstance in order to establish their *actus reus*. Sometimes the offence definition incorporates a fault element in respect of such facts or circumstances—it could be knowledge of it or recklessness or just negligence as to it. As we saw in **Chapter 13**, offences of strict liability do not require proof of any fault in respect of one or more circumstances forming part of the *actus reus*. However, regardless of the fault requirements of the substantive offence, it appears from s. 1 (2) that D must 'intend or know' that 'any particular fact or circumstance necessary for the commission of' that offence 'shall or will exist at the time when the conduct constituting the offence is to take place' in order to be convicted of conspiracy to commit that offence. As mentioned previously, it is likely that 'intend or know' will be interpreted to embrace cases where D believes the circumstance will exist.

Let us illustrate this with the case of *Harmer (Roy)* [2005] EWCA Crim 01, CA. D was charged with conspiring to commit an offence under money laundering legislation (since replaced by the Proceeds of Crime Act 2002). The underlying substantive offence required proof that the money laundered was in fact the proceeds of criminal conduct or drug trafficking (*Montila* [2004] UKHL 50) but the fault element was simple negligence: it was enough that there were reasonable grounds for suspecting that it was 'hot' money. Nonetheless, for conspiracy, s.1(2) required that D must 'intend or know' that the provenance of the money was criminal conduct or drug trafficking and, since this had not been proved, D was not guilty.

This is surely a correct application of s. 1(2) but, unfortunately, there are apparently conflicting authorities. The most recent is *Sakavickas* [2004] ECWA Crim 2686, another case of money laundering based on a different (but also now replaced) substantive offence. The substantive offence comprised entering into an arrangement whereby the retention of another's proceeds of criminal conduct was facilitated, knowing or suspecting that the other is or has been engaged in or has benefited from criminal conduct. (The charge of conspiracy to commit an offence which **itself** consists of agreeing to launder criminal proceeds is rather strange—it is effectively charging D with agreeing to agree!). The Court of Appeal's decision that s. 1(2) did not require proof that D **knew** the other had been in engaged in criminal conduct but merely that D suspected this has been criticised by academics as contrary to s. 1(2). However, we think that the reasoning is not necessarily inconsistent with the view we have expressed as to the proper interpretation of the subsection. The key point to understand is that, in the Court's view the 'fact or circumstance necessary for the commission of the offence' was not that the other person **was** engaged in criminal conduct but only that D suspected that. The fact that D had to 'know' was that he **suspected** that the other was engaged in criminal conduct and, inevitably, he must know what he himself suspects! The Court purports to apply s. 1(2).

However, what the Court overlooked was that the *actus reus* of the substantive offence does require the monies, whose retention is facilitated, to actually be 'the proceeds of the other person's criminal conduct.' (Any doubts on this are scotched by the subsequent House of Lords' decision in *Montila* [2004] UKHL 50.) Therefore, under s. 1(2), it is necessary to show that D intended or knew (and not merely suspected) the arrangement involved the proceeds of criminal conduct by the other person. Contrary to what the Court implicitly thought, that is a 'fact or circumstance necessary for the commission' of the substantive offence. Accordingly, we are of the view that *Sakavickas* should not be taken to cast doubt on the received interpretation of s. 1(2) as expressed in *Harmer*. The interpretation of s. 1(2) in *Harmer* has now been approved in *Ali* [2005] EWCA Crim 87 so that suspicion that the money being laundered is drugs money is not enough. It must be proved that it was drugs money and that D **knew** it was drugs money.

Conditional intentions

Intentions to commit crimes are almost always subject to 'ifs and buts', usually implicit but sometimes explicit. D intends to burgle X's house but not if, when he gets there, it is ringed by Group 4 security guards. In general such a conditional intention will suffice for conspiracy certainly where the whole point of the agreement was to commit the offence. Clearly, if the object is to burgle X's house, it does not matter that the conspirators agree to burgle X's house only if X is out. If the agreement is carried out in accordance with their intentions, it will necessarily involve the offence of burglary (*Jackson* [1985] Crim LR 442, CA in *Cases and Materials* (16.4.3.1)).

The case of *O'Hadhmaill* [1996] Crim LR 509, CA, follows a similar line. D, a sociology lecturer at the University of Central Lancashire and member of the IRA, agreed with others to make bombs for use in a bombing campaign in England if, but only if, the IRA decided to resume its campaign of violence, then temporarily suspended. It was held that D had conspired to cause explosions even though, if the peace process worked out for the IRA, their bombing campaign would never be resumed and the bombs would not be used.

On the other hand the commission of the offence may not be the purpose of the agreement although the parties contemplate its commission as a possible incident of carrying out the lawful objective of the agreement. Consider the example given in *Reed* [1982] Crim LR 819, CA (*Cases and Materials* (16.4.3.1)). A and B agree to drive to Edinburgh in a time which could be achieved without exceeding any speed limits but only if traffic is exceptionally light.

? QUESTION 16.16

(a) Does the agreed course of conduct necessarily involve the commission of a speeding offence if carried out in accordance with their intentions?

(b) What if A and B agreed that A would have sexual intercourse with X whether or not she (X) consented?

(c) What if A and B agree to burgle a country house and, if necessary in order to escape, to shoot to kill?

The view in *Reed* was that there would be no conspiracy in case (a). A and B were, however, held guilty of conspiring to aid and abet suicide where they agreed that A would visit people considering suicide and then either attempt to dissuade them from ending or assist them to end their life depending on his view of the most appropriate action. This would be analogous to *O'Hadhmaill* and to case (b) above, which would therefore be a conspiracy to rape. The Court failed to explain the distinction between case (a) and the fact situation in *Reed* itself but Smith and Hogan (*Criminal Law*, 10th ed., 2002, Butterworths, p. 307) suggest that it lies in determining the 'object of the exercise' or the main purpose of the agreement. In the driving example, whatever the circumstances, speeding is never the point of the agreement but merely incidental to it. The object is always to get to Edinburgh by the allotted time. With the suicide and rape examples, in certain circumstances (A deciding that suicide is suitable in the circumstances; X does not consent to intercourse) the agreement is that the offences, aiding and abetting suicide or rape, become the 'object of the exercise' or the whole purpose of the agreement. The analysis is not altogether convincing but nobody has come up with a better explanation. If adopted, A and B in example (c) would be guilty only of conspiracy to burgle and not conspiracy to murder because murder would only be incidental to the main purpose and never the 'object of the exercise'. Allen (*Textbook on Criminal Law*, 7th ed., 2003, OUP, pp. 260–61) has suggested that a conviction for conspiracy to murder could be obtained by severing the contingent agreement to kill from the main agreement to burgle. There are thus two distinct agreements and murdering would be the whole point of the second agreement, **if** killing proved necessary. This would be no different to an agreement to burgle subject to X being out. However, could we not equally say that there is a distinct subsidiary agreement to speed, subject to its being necessary, in the driving to Edinburgh example? As you will have gathered, the position is uncertain and unresolved.

Will necessarily amount to or involve the commission of a crime

What matters is that the plan if carried out as intended will certainly amount to or involve the crime. 'Necessarily' does not mean that the offence will inevitably be carried out come what may (*Jackson* [1985] Crim LR 442, CA); it refers to what must happen **if** what is intended according to the agreement is done.

? QUESTION 16.17

What was the basic position adopted by the House of Lords in *Haughton* v *Smith* [1975] AC 476?

- Summarise the changes made to it by the Criminal Attempts Act 1981.
- If you cannot answer these questions, refer back to 16.3.4.

16.4.3.2 **Impossibility**

In the section on attempt, we spent some time discussing the situation where, unknown to D, the crime alleged to have been attempted was in the circumstances impossible to commit.

A similar problem arises in conspiracy where for some reason the crime agreed by the conspirators is in fact impossible to carry out. For example, what if A and B agree to 'marry' thinking that B is and, at the time of the ceremony, will be, married to X, when in fact, unknown to them, X died before the agreement was made? Or suppose that A and B agree to handle goods which they believe to be stolen but which, at the time of the agreement, have ceased to be stolen. In fact, this should not make any difference because if the agreed course of conduct were carried out **in accordance with their intentions**, it will necessarily result in the crimes of bigamy and handling stolen goods respectively. However, the irrelevance of impossibility was implicit rather than explicit in the original definition of statutory conspiracy. The legislature therefore decided to put the matter beyond doubt by modifying the definition of statutory conspiracy to include express reference to impossibility (s. 5(1) of the Criminal Attempts Act 1981). The restrictive common law rules in relation to attempt and impossibility established by *Haughton* v *Smith* [1973] 3 All ER 1109, HL had been applied equally to common law conspiracy and impossibility by the House of Lords in *DPP* v *Nock* [1978] AC 979. Whilst overturning *Haughton* v *Smith*, in relation to attempt, the legislature used the Criminal Attempts Act to insert s. 1(1)(b) into the 1977 Act to avoid any risk of the courts deciding to apply *DPP* v *Nock* to statutory conspiracy. Thus, statutory conspiracy is committed if the agreed course of conduct **would** necessarily amount to or involve the commission of an offence 'but for the existence of facts which render the commission of the offence...impossible'. Curiously, the 1981 Act did not affect the common law position and therefore *Nock* must still govern those common law conspiracies which were not abolished by the 1977 Act. Of course, the same problem does not arise in relation to attempt because the common law crime of attempt was totally abolished by the 1981 Act.

16.4.3.3 **Territorial jurisdiction**

With the growing ease of travel and communication, it is not surprising to find an increasing number of conspiracies with an international dimension. Two fundamental questions which arise are: (a) is an agreement in this country to commit an offence abroad an offence under English law?; and (b) is an agreement made abroad to commit an offence in England the offence of conspiracy under English law? The first question is addressed by s. 1(4) of the 1977 Act which stipulates that the offence agreed must be 'an offence triable in England and Wales'. By and large, the English courts do not have jurisdiction over offences committed entirely abroad. Therefore, subject to a few exceptions, e.g., an agreement to commit bigamy abroad by a British subject, it would not be conspiracy under English law to agree to commit an offence abroad. Section 1(4) creates a blanket exception to that rule for an agreement in England or Wales to commit a murder abroad, irrespective of whether the murder was to be committed by a British subject and therefore triable in this country.

A **major** exception is created by s. 5 of the Criminal Justice Act 1993. This provides that conspiracies (or attempts or incitements) to commit a 'Group A' offence not triable here (because it is intended to be committed entirely abroad), **are** triable here if **any** party to the agreement, either personally or through his agent (a) did anything here (England and Wales) in relation to it before its formation (e.g., writing a letter suggesting it) or (b) joined it here or (c) did or omitted anything in pursuance of it here. If any one party falls within the provision **all** conspirators, wherever they are, are triable here. 'Group A' offences are defined in the 1993 Act and include theft and other crimes under the Theft Act 1968 and the new offence of fraud under the Fraud Act 2006 (see 10.2 above). A similar provision applies to conspiracies to defraud (s. 5(3)). Introduced to combat so-called 'sex tourism' activities, the Sexual Offences (Conspiracy and Incitement) Act 1996 extends jurisdiction in similar fashion for conspiracy and incitement to commit certain specified sexual offences abroad against victims who are under 16, including rape, assault by penetration and sexual assault.

The answer to the second question must be gleaned from case law since the 1977 Act makes no blanket provision for agreements made abroad to commit an offence here. The House of Lords in *DPP* v *Doot* [1973] 1 All ER 940 established that an agreement abroad to commit a crime in England is an offence here at least if an overt act is done here in pursuance of the agreement. The Privy Council in *Samchai Liangsiriprasert* v *United States Government* (1990) 92 Cr App R 77 went further and held that, in relation to a common law conspiracy to defraud, it is unnecessary to prove that any overt act was done in England. As long as the agreement was intended to result in the commission of a criminal offence in England or Wales, it would be a conspiracy under our law. The Court of Appeal in *Sansom* (1991) 92 Cr App R 115 (*Cases and Materials* (16.4.3.3)) decided, arguably obiter, that this principle applied to statutory conspiracies.

Section 3 of the Criminal Justice Act 1993 gives this rule statutory backing in relation to conspiracies (or attempts or incitements) to commit 'Group A' offences triable here. By s. 2 a 'Group A' offence would be triable here if 'any act or omission or other event (including any result of one or more acts or omissions) proof of which is required for conviction of the offence' occurred in England and Wales. It follows that an agreement which would involve the commission here of any element of the 'Group A' offence planned would be a conspiracy triable here even if none of the conspirators had any connection with Britain, joined the conspiracy here or, in the event, actually did anything here! As we have seen, the same principles apply to attempts to commit such an offence (s. 3(2) and (3)).

16.4.4 **Common law conspiracies**

> **?** **QUESTION** 16.18
>
> What are the only three types of common law conspiracy that can exist since the 1977 Act?

16.4.4.1 **Conspiracy to defraud**

Most frauds involved the commission of crimes like theft or the now repealed offence of obtaining property by deception (or now, of course, the new offences created by the Fraud Act 2006), but some involved no offence at all. It was for this reason that conspiracy to defraud was preserved by s. 5(2) of the 1977 Act. This was intended to be a temporary measure pending a comprehensive reform of the law of fraud but, that reform being long postponed, the temporary measure acquired some permanence! After some years waiting, the Law Commission issued its final report (Law Com. No. 276: Fraud) which recommended the abolition of conspiracy to defraud and the enactment of a new offence of fraud (see **Chapter 11** above). An agreement to commit the new offence would be a **statutory** conspiracy in the normal way. However, the Government, whilst legislating for the new fraud offences, was unwilling to abolish common law conspiracy to defraud and the new Fraud Act 2006 leaves it unaffected.

Resolving several years of confusion, s. 12 of the Criminal Justice Act 1987 provided that where a conspiracy to defraud does involve the commission of criminal offences the prosecutor may charge **either** common law conspiracy to defraud **or** statutory conspiracy.

The meaning of defraud

Most typical frauds involve causing economic injury to the victim usually by practising a deceit on him. Investors are persuaded to hand over money to buy shares in non-existent companies or newspaper readers are persuaded by bogus advertisements to send money for goods which never materialise. However, neither deceit nor economic loss is a necessary ingredient of conspiracy to defraud. In *Scott v Metropolitan Police Commissioner* [1974] 3 All ER 1032, HL (*Cases and Materials* (16.4.4.1)), D agreed with cinema projectionists temporarily to remove films without the consent of the cinema owners so that pirate copies could be made and distributed commercially.

> **?** **QUESTION** 16.19
>
> • Would this constitute theft of the films?
> • Was any deception practised on the cinema owners?

The House of Lords held that D was guilty of conspiracy to defraud whether or not the agreement involved committing a substantive criminal offence. No theft was committed because the intention to return the films intact meant that there was no intention permanently to deprive. Equally, wide though the concept of 'property' is under the Theft Acts, it does not embrace the loss of exclusivity in the films. Since no representation of any kind was made to the cinema owners, who were completely unaware of the unauthorised borrowing of the films, it is clear that they were not deceived. This was no bar to conviction. According to *Scott*, conspiracy to defraud includes an agreement by dishonesty (a) to deprive a person of something which is his or to which he is or would be or might be entitled or (b) to injure some proprietary right of his. In this case, the film owners might be deprived of revenue from sales if pirated copies were distributed. They would also be deprived of the profits made by the pirates which, in law, would belong to the film's copyright owners.

This duty to account was at the heart of the recent Privy Council decision in *Adams* v *R* [1995] 1 WLR 52 (*Cases and Materials* (16.4.4.1)). D, a director of a holding company, agreed with members of the company's investment team which he headed to conduct a complex web of share transactions through subsidiary and offshore companies in order to make a secret profit for themselves which they agreed to conceal from the holding company. D's conviction for conspiracy to defraud was upheld on the basis of the agreement to take positive steps dishonestly to conceal the making of the profit. It was not the making of the profit itself which was the defrauding but the impeding of the company's right to recover the profit for which the defendants had a duty to account. As Lord Jauncey put it, a victim 'can only suffer prejudice in relation to some right or interest which he possesses'. Here, the only right possessed by the company was the right to recover the amount of the profit conferred by D's legal duty to account for it. The exercise of that right was prejudiced by the elaborate steps taken in pursuance of the conspirators' agreement dishonestly to conceal the profit. It seems rather surprising that dishonestly making and retaining a secret profit is not 'defrauding' whereas the taking of active steps to conceal it is! (*Cf. Fussell* [1997] Crim LR 812, CA.)

It is not essential that the victim should suffer or be intended to suffer actual economic loss through the carrying out of the agreement. *Allsop* (1976) 64 Cr App R 29, CA and *Wai Yu-tsang* v *R* [1992] 1 AC 269, PC (*Cases and Materials* (16.4.4.1)) held that it is enough that the victim's economic interests are put at risk. In the former case the defendants agreed to give false information in an application form to induce a hire purchase company to grant a loan for car purchase. In the latter case the defendants agreed to falsify a bank's accounts to disguise huge losses on some dishonoured cheques, in order to prevent a run on the bank which would have caused its demise. In both cases, the defendants were hoping that things would turn out well, in which case the victims would not suffer any loss and indeed would profit from the deceptions. However, it was enough that the victims' economic interests were 'imperilled' or 'put in jeopardy' or that there was a 'threat of financial prejudice'.

So far we have indicated that defrauding involves economic loss or at least economic risk to the victim. In fact even this is unnecessary, because a victim can be defrauded even though there is no loss or risk to his financial interests. It is well established that an agreement dishonestly to bring about a situation which would or might deceive a public official to act contrary to his public duty constitutes a conspiracy to defraud even though no financial or economic interests are at stake (*Board of Trade* v *Owen* [1957] AC 602; *Welham* v *DPP* [1961] AC 103, HL).

You might have said an agreement to induce a public official **by deception** to grant an export licence (*Board of Trade* v *Owen*) but the most obvious one would be an agreement to deceive an official into disclosing information to an unauthorised recipient (*DPP* v *Withers* [1974] 3 All ER 984, HL). It is very common for private detective agencies to try to obtain information about people from government agencies such as social security offices, tax offices and the Vehicle Licensing Authority. If the agreement is to use deception to extract this information, it will be conspiracy to defraud. In *DPP* v *Withers* the House of Lords held that the rule did not extend to deceiving non-public officials such as bank employees into breaking their employment duties. However, some doubt is thrown on this restriction by the Privy Council's statement in *Wai Yu-tsang* v *R* [1991] 4 All ER 664 that the public official cases should not be regarded as 'a special category . . . but rather as exemplifying the general principle that conspiracies to defraud are not restricted to cases of intention to cause the victim economic loss.' They seemed to favour the extremely wide propositions enunciated by Lords Denning and Radcliffe in *Welham* v *DPP* [1961] AC 103, HL to the effect that it would be enough if there was a risk that anyone might 'be prejudiced in any way by the fraud'. This would certainly seem to catch private detectives who agree to obtain information about an individual's bank account from a bank employee by, for example, pretending to be employed at other branches of the bank. However, we would regard the adoption of such a broad principle as casting the net of conspiracy to defraud unacceptably wide.

One final point of note is that it is not essential that the actual defrauding be perpetrated by one or more parties to the agreement. Thus, people who agree to make and sell to retailers goods that are counterfeited to resemble well-known brands (*Attorney-General's Reference (No. 1 of 1982)* [1983] 2 All ER 721, CA) or who agree to make and sell electronic devices to by-pass electricity company meters (*Hollinshead* [1985] 2 All ER 769, HL) will not themselves perpetrate any fraud or deceit on anyone. Rather the fraud on the purchasers of the counterfeit goods will be effected by the retailer, and the fraud on the electricity company will be perpetrated by the user of the device. Nonetheless, the original suppliers can be convicted of conspiracy to defraud.

Mens rea of conspiracy to defraud

There are two elements to this. Let us first dispose of the easier one. The defendants must agree to act **dishonestly** in bringing about the situation causing loss or risk to the victims' financial interests or causing risk that a public official might act contrary to his public duty. It was established in *Ghosh* [1982] 2 All ER 689, CA that the test for dishonesty was exactly the same as for theft.

?   **QUESTION** 16.22

Can you remember that two-stage test? If not, refer to 10.4.2.1 above.

The second element is much more difficult. It is said that the defendants must intend to defraud. Unfortunately, the cases reveal considerable divergences of approach to the definition of intention here. It is likely that *Wai Yu-tsang* v *R* [1991] 4 All ER 664, although a Privy Council decision, will prove to be the most influential. The Privy Council thought that dicta that it was necessary to prove that the conspirators' **purpose** was to cause loss or risk to the victims' financial interests were too restrictive and wrong. In *Cooke* [1986] 2 All ER 985, HL the defendants, employed as catering stewards on British Rail trains, agreed to sell their own sandwiches on the trains, passing them off as British Rail's, intending to pocket the profits for themselves.

?   **QUESTION** 16.23

How would you describe their purpose?

It would seem that their object was to make money for themselves rather than to cause any loss to British Rail. Nonetheless, they knew that achieving their objective inevitably meant causing loss to British Rail. It could therefore be said that they intended to cause loss and they were, in fact, convicted of conspiracy to defraud. Similarly, in *Allsop* (1976) 64 Cr App R 29, CA the defendants, in submitting the untrue applications for car loans to the hire purchase company, may not have wanted to cause any loss to the company and, indeed, may have thought that no loss would be caused to the company, but they surely knew that the inevitable result of carrying through their plan would be to cause **risk** to the company's economic interests. Therefore, it could be said that they intended to put those economic interests in jeopardy.

EXERCISE 16.5

Read the extract from *Wai Yu-tsang* v *R* in *Cases and Materials* (16.4.4.1).
   The Privy Council would certainly accept the foregoing as correct, but appears to extend the principle even further. Can you identify how?

The crucial statement of principle in *Wai Yu-tsang* is as follows: 'It is enough for example that as in *Allsop* and in the present case, the conspirators have dishonestly agreed to bring about a state of affairs which they realise will **or may** deceive the victim into so acting, or failing to act, that he will suffer economic loss or his economic interests will be put at risk' (our emphasis). It is one thing to say that D intends to defraud if he realises that the victims' economic interests **will for certain** be prejudiced. It is quite another to say that D intends to defraud where he realises only that the victims' economic interests **may be** prejudiced. Yet, if you refer to the emphasised words in the quotation that is exactly what the Privy Council seems to be saying. If correct, it means that intention to defraud is not required but rather subjective recklessness as to loss or risk to the victims' financial interests. If the conspirators know that their agreed actions **might** cause economic loss or risk to the victim, they would, on this view, have the *mens rea* for conspiracy to defraud. It probably goes too far and was certainly unnecessary for the decision because the defendants knew that the inevitable result of falsifying the accounts would be to prejudice the victims' economic interests.

An agreement in England to carry out the fraud entirely abroad was formerly not a conspiracy to defraud under English law (*Attorney-General's Reference (No. 1 of 1982)* [1983] 2 All ER 721, CA). Under the new s. 1A(3), inserted into the Criminal Law Act 1977 by s. 5(3) of the Criminal Justice Act 1993, such an agreement would be conspiracy here provided (a) the conduct planned to take place abroad would be an offence there and (b) if it had been planned for here, it would have been conspiracy to defraud here.

Conclusion on conspiracy to defraud
It is a pity that the Government suffered a failure of nerve and omitted to repeal the offence of conspiracy to defraud in the Fraud Act 2006. The Law Commission's recommendation for a wide and general fraud offence was partly premised on the abolition of conspiracy to defraud. The new offence is surely broad enough without the need to multiply the vagueness and uncertainty by the preservation of conspiracy to defraud. There is little justification for criminalising conduct which is not a crime when committed by one person acting alone, merely because it happens to involve two or more persons acting in agreement. The Government has not ruled out its ultimate abolition but, bolstered by responses to its consultation exercise prior to the Act, prefers to monitor the workings of the new offences before taking that step.

16.4.4.2 Conspiracy to corrupt public morals or outrage public decency

EXERCISE 16.6

Read s. 5(1) and (3) Criminal Law Act 1977 in *Cases and Materials* (16.4.1).

- Where the defendants agree to corrupt public morals or outrage public decency, they can only be convicted of common law conspiracy to do that if . . . ?
- Does s. 5(3) indicate whether it is an offence for a single person acting alone to corrupt public morals or outrage public decency?

The Law Commission wanted the 1977 Act to abolish common law conspiracies under this head but the government was not prepared to do this pending a review of the whole area of obscenity and indecency. Section 5(3) was intended as a temporary holding operation but has now acquired a degree of permanence. The Committee on Obscenity and Film Censorship reported in 1979, but no action has been taken or seems likely to be taken on its proposals.

Common law conspiracy in this area is only preserved where the agreed conduct 'would not amount to or involve the commission of' a substantive offence. There is strong authority that outraging public decency is a substantive offence and therefore can be committed by one person acting alone (*Knuller* v *DPP* [1972] 2 All ER 898, HL; *Gibson* [1991] 1 All ER 439, CA; *Rowley* [1991] 4 All ER 649, CA). The position is markedly less clear in the case of corrupting public morals. The Court of Criminal Appeal in *Shaw* v *DPP* [1961] 2 All ER 446 held that there was such a substantive offence but, unfortunately, the House of Lords in holding that there was an offence of **conspiracy** to corrupt public morals, did not decide whether one person acting alone would commit an offence. *Gibson* provides some support for the existence of the substantive offence, but the point cannot be said to be settled. Section 5(3) throws no light on the matter.

?   **QUESTION** 16.24

Why is the existence or otherwise of a substantive offence important for conspiracy?

Given that it is now settled that to outrage public decency is an offence, regardless of any conspiracy, it follows that any agreement to outrage public decency must be charged as a statutory conspiracy because it is an agreement to commit a criminal offence. It would seem that there is only room for a common law conspiracy to outrage public decency if the concept of outraging public decency were to be defined more narrowly for the substantive offence than for the conspiracy offence. This seems to be extremely unlikely. Whether the same is true in relation to corrupting public morals remains to be seen. It should be emphasised that whether or not corrupting public morals is itself a substantive offence, if the agreement to do that would involve the commission of some other offence, e.g., under the Obscene Publications Act 1959, s. 5(3) means that the agreement cannot be a common law conspiracy and must be charged as statutory conspiracy.

Corrupting public morals

In *Shaw* v *DPP* [1961] 2 All ER 446, HL it was held that an agreement to publish a 'Ladies' Directory' giving the names, addresses and specialities of prostitutes constituted a conspiracy to corrupt public morals. In *Knuller* v *DPP* [1972] 2 All ER 898, HL (*Cases and Materials* (16.4.4.2)) an agreement to publish advertisements soliciting homosexual acts between consenting adults in private was likewise a conspiracy to corrupt public morals even though such acts were lawful. The House of Lords emphasised that 'corrupt' meant more than 'lead morally astray'. Lord Reid thought it meant 'deprave' whereas Lord Simon required 'conduct which a jury might find to be destructive of the very fabric of society'. The jury should apply the current standards of ordinary decent people—a vague and unpredictable test.

Outraging public decency

The House of Lords in *Knuller* emphasised that outrage is a very strong word which 'goes considerably beyond offending the susceptibilities of, or even shocking, reasonable people. Moreover, the offence is, in my view, concerned with recognised minimum standards of decency, which are likely to vary from time to time.' According to *Choi* [1999] All ER (D), it is 'disgusting' conduct which 'fills the onlooker with loathing or extreme distaste or causes them extreme annoyance', such as D's conduct in videoing a lady using a public toilet.

The conduct must be likely to disgust and annoy ordinary members of the public and be able to be seen by at least two people, although not necessarily at the same time (*Mayling* [1963] 1 All ER 687, CCA). According to *Knuller*, the conduct must be committed in public and *Walker* [1996] 1 Cr App R 111 holds that this entails commission in a place where there was a real possibility that members of the general public might witness what happens. For example, 'the public touting for an outrageously indecent exhibition in private would not escape'. Equally clearly, a magazine, book or video could be caught notwithstanding that it has a wrapper preventing browsers from opening it or that it is available only to those who ask for it. In *Gibson* [1991] 1 All ER 439, CA the defendants were convicted of outraging public decency by displaying earrings made out of freeze-dried human foetuses as an exhibit at a commercial art gallery. However, an act of indecency in D's own home would clearly not satisfy the requirement unless the public would be able to see what takes place (*Walker*).

As with corrupting public morals, the scope of outraging public decency is vague and unpredictable in the extreme. Do we really need either?

16.4.5 The rationale of conspiracy

Is there any need for an offence of conspiracy and should it be committed by a mere **agreement** to effect the unlawful purpose without anything further being done?

In regard to the first question, Fletcher argues: '[T]he phenomenon of people forming criminal bands might be regarded as sufficiently unnerving to be prohibited for its own sake' (*Rethinking Criminal Law* (1978, Little, Brown), p. 133). The underlying assumption is that people working together are likely to be more dangerous than people working alone.

They will generally be able to achieve more complicated and harmful criminal enterprises and peer pressure makes it more likely that the actors will carry out their criminal intentions. The latter argument cuts both ways since it could be said that peer pressure might equally operate to dissuade the actors!

Conspiracy can enable the real nature of a complex criminal enterprise to be revealed where this might not be evident from (specimen) prosecutions for actual substantive offences. This may be so where the conspiracy leads to a continuing course of conduct involving the commission of a large number of offences, which may or may not be in themselves relatively trivial (e.g., a large-scale operation to make, distribute and sell counterfeit goods). It would also make it easier to strike at the organisers of the enterprise who get others to perform the substantive crimes. Of course, it could be argued that they would be accessories to the substantive crimes and that is what they should be prosecuted for. However, there is no doubt that a conspiracy charge might be evidentially easier to prove. (In fact, a quirk of our law of evidence relaxes normal evidential rules on conspiracy charges and in particular evidence of one co-defendant is admissible against another co-defendant.)

The third main justification for conspiracy is that it enables the authorities to act at an early stage to intervene to nip the planned crime in the bud without jeopardising the chances of criminal conviction. Quite apart from the fact that some conspiracies to defraud do not involve an agreement to commit any **crime**, it is questionable whether the law needs to intervene at the agreement stage. Surely, what creates any imperative for the law to intervene is the fact that the conspirators have shown that the agreement is serious by doing something significant to put it into practice.

Therefore, if we are to have conspiracy, we would suggest that a limitation be borrowed from the Model Penal Code of the American Law Institute, art. 5.03 of which requires proof of 'an overt act in pursuance of' the agreement by at least one of the conspirators. However, if this were adopted it would call into question whether the law of attempt could be used to take over this 'preventative' role, thus obviating the need for conspiracy. The present law on the *actus reus* of attempt ('the proximity test'—see 16.3.2) is too narrow to plug the gap. It would require the broadening of attempt to embrace the Law Commission's originally proposed 'substantial step' theory or something similar before it could be seriously argued as, in conjunction with the law of complicity, an adequate substitute for conspiracy. Even then it is questionable.

What is difficult to justify is extending conspiracy beyond agreements to commit criminal offences. If the conduct planned would not constitute a crime if performed by one person acting alone, it is difficult to see that it should become a serious crime merely because more than one has agreed to do it. One of the major reasons used to justify the retention of conspiracy to defraud is its utility in covering 'gaps' in the Theft Acts, e.g., dishonest borrowing, 'stalling debtors' who do not intend to make permanent default (Law Com. No. 228). If Parliament and/or the courts have decided that particular conduct is not caught by the Theft Acts (or now the Fraud Act), it seems improper to use the involvement of two or more people as an excuse for criminalising conduct pronounced not criminal!

16.5 Incitement

16.5.1 Introduction

Incitement is simpler than either attempt or conspiracy. Unlike attempt, which is now wholly statutory, and conspiracy, which is now mostly statutory, incitement is a common law offence. As with attempt and conspiracy, D must incite another to commit a specific offence. Incitement to commit a summary offence must be tried summarily and incitement to commit an offence triable either way *may* be tried summarily. In both cases, the maximum penalty available for the summary conviction for incitement is the same as that prescribed for summary conviction of the completed offence (ss. 17, 32 and 45 of the Magistrates' Courts Act 1980). Curiously, the penalty for incitement tried on indictment is in the complete discretion of the court and in no way geared to the penalty available for the completed offence. This is because incitement is a common law offence and, in the absence of any statutory prescription, the complete range of penalties from absolute discharge to life imprisonment is available to the judge.

This common law offence of incitement to commit another offence is a general offence but it is not uncommon for the legislature to enact specific individual offences with their own prescribed penalties based essentially on the notion of inciting. A notable example is s. 4 of the Offences Against the Person Act 1861 which prohibits soliciting another to commit murder. The Sexual Offences Act 2003 contains numerous offences of 'inciting', e.g., 'inciting a child to engage in sexual activity' (ss. 8, 10, 17 and 26).

16.5.2 What is incitement?

The Court of Appeal in *Goldman* [2001] Crim LR 894 and the Divisional Court in *DPP* v *Armstrong* [2000] Crim LR 379 and *R (On the application of O)* v *Coventry Magistrates' Court* [2004] Crim LR 948; [2004] EWHC 905 (Admin) all approved as an accurate statement of the current law the definition set out in cl. 47 of the Law Commission's draft Criminal Code (Law Com. No. 177, I, 63):

> (1) A person is guilty of incitement to commit an offence or offences if—
>   (a) he incites another to do or cause to be done an act or acts which, if done, will involve the commission of the offence or offences by the other; and
>   (b) he intends or believes that the other, if he acts as incited,
>   (c) shall, or will do so with the fault required for the offence or offences.

16.5.2.1 *Actus reus*

The essence of incitement is trying to persuade or influence another to commit a crime. It can be by words, whether written or oral, or acts, and it can be express or implied. The courts have often used the terms 'soliciting' or 'encouraging' to explain incitement, but it is clear from *Race Relations Board* v *Applin* [1973] 1 QB 815, CA a civil case followed in the criminal case of *Invicta Plastics Ltd* v *Clare* [1976] RTR 251, DC (*Cases and Materials* (16.5.2.1)), that it also includes the use of pressure and threats designed to 'persuade' another to commit the offence. Indeed, it is thought that it is the element of persuasion which is the essence of incitement and mere 'encouragement' without that element of persuasion such as words of approval where D knows that X has already decided to commit the crime, should not suffice, contrary to what is suggested in *Marlow* [1997] Crim LR 897, CA.

According to *Goldman* [2001] Crim LR 822, CA, it matters not that the incitee is only too pleased to be incited. A Dutch company advertised pornographic videos for sale. In response, D requested a video containing child pornography. It was held that D's offer, being an inducement to the company, would incite the company to commit the offence of distributing indecent photographs of children under 16, notwithstanding that the incitee (the company) was the instigator of events.

> **? QUESTION** 16.25
>
> Is a separate offence of incitement necessary? If inciting means persuading and/or encouraging an offence, would not an incitor always be liable anyway for counselling or procuring the offence?

The incitement need not be addressed to a particular person. In *Most* (1881) 7 QBD 244 the publisher of a newspaper article which, following the assassination of the Tsar of Russia, urged readers to murder Heads of State from Constantinople to Washington, was guilty of incitement to murder. Similarly, in *El-Faisal* [2004] EWCA Crim 456, D in speeches and audio tape recordings of the speeches urged his generally Islamic audience to kill non-believers, especially Americans, Hindus and Jews. He was convicted of soliciting murder, the Court of Appeal rejecting on the facts a claim that his urgings were confined to **lawful** killings on the 'battlefield' in self-defence.

Again in *Marlow*, D was convicted of inciting offences under s. 4(2) of the Misuse of Drugs Act 1971 (production of a controlled drug) by authoring a book explaining how to cultivate and produce cannabis. The Court of Appeal frowned on the trial judge's direction that it was enough to show that the book 'may encourage or persuade' or 'is capable of encouraging and persuading'. However, the direction seems correct because when the persuading words or conduct occur, it cannot be known whether they **will** encourage and persuade. Since the offence of incitement can be committed whether or not the incited crime is perpetrated, it ought to be sufficient that D's conduct **might** persuade the incitee. Whereas liability for counselling and procuring an offence requires the commission of the offence because it derives from that principal offence, incitement is a stand alone offence not in any way dependent on successful persuasion. There is no need to prove that D's persuasion had any effect on the mind of the incitee. Guilt could still follow a point blank refusal by the incitee. Of course, if the offence incited is actually committed, then D could be guilty of **that** offence as a counsellor and procurer **in addition to** the offence of incitement.

It is a requirement that the acts or words of persuasion must be communicated to the person sought to be incited so that if the incitee does not hear the incitor's words or does not read them because, for example, a letter of persuasion is lost in the post, the *actus reus* of incitement is not present. However, in such circumstances, D can be convicted of attempting to incite the commission of the offence (*Ransford* (1874) 13 Cox CC 9).

The difficulties created by the notion that incitement necessitates communication with another person were rather brushed aside by the Court of Appeal in *R (On the application of O)* v *Coventry Magistartes' Court* [2004] Crim LR 948; [2004] EWHC 905 (Admin). As in *Goldman*, D had subscribed to a web site offering indecent images of children. The problem was that the procedure for accessing the images was fully automated with no intervention of any other person in the process. Nonetheless, the Court was of the view that, in subscribing, D was inciting the persons running the company to commit the crime of offering the indecent images of children.

There is no offence unless the act incited would, when done, amount to a crime by the person incited. In *Whitehouse* [1977] 3 All ER 737, CA (*Cases and Materials* (16.5.2.1)), D incited his 15-year-old daughter to have sexual intercourse with him. He was not guilty of incitement to incest because by the terms of the Sexual Offences Act 1956, the daughter would commit no offence by participating in the act of incest. This particular gap in the law was quickly filled by the creation of a statutory offence of inciting a girl under 16 to have incestuous sexual intercourse (s. 54 of the Criminal Law Act 1977 now replaced by s. 26 of the Sexual Offences Act 2003 which creates an expanded offence of inciting a child under 18 to engage in sexual activity with specified members of the child's family), but the general principle still holds. Similarly if a person cannot in law be an accessory to an offence because he belongs to the class of people that offence is designed to protect (*Tyrrell* [1894] 1 QB 710), he is similarly incapable of inciting the commission of the offence.

It is uncertain what the position is where the person incited would cause the *actus reus* of the crime with the appropriate *mens rea* but would not be liable for it because he would have a defence. For example, the person incited may be under ten years of age or be acting under duress. But, as noted above, the Court of Appeal in *El-Faisal* accepted that the specific offence of soliciting murder under s.4 of the Offences Against the Person Act 1861 would not be committed if the killing D incited would be a lawful killing in reasonable self-defence. That seems correct but it may well be that the courts would apply that rule only for justificatory defences. It would certainly be odd to excuse D from incitement **because** he has threatened serious violence (duress) to the incitee or alternatively taken advantage of his infancy.

> **? QUESTION** 16.26
>
> If the 'crime' incited in each of the first two examples in the previous paragraph—let us say it was theft—was actually carried out by the persons incited, would D be guilty of theft?
>   Give your reasons. If you are unsure, refer back to 14.4.1.

16.5.2.2 *Mens rea*

D must intend that the person incited will perform the conduct constituting the relevant offence, including any consequences required by its *actus reus*. D cannot incite X's murder unless he intends the person incited to cause X's death.

Equally, D must know or believe (or possibly suspect) that any circumstances required by the *actus reus* of the crime will be present (e.g., to kill in circumstances not constituting reasonable force in self-defence—*El-Faisal* above). Finally, D must know or believe (or possibly suspect) that when the person incited causes the *actus reus*, he will possess any necessary *mens rea* for the offence incited. Thus, if a doctor, wishing to kill a patient, instructs a nurse to inject the patient with a substance which, unknown to the nurse, is lethal, D will commit murder through the innocent agency of the nurse if the patient dies from the injection. However, if the nurse omits to give the injection, the doctor could not

be convicted of incitement to murder. Unfortunately, the Court of Appeal in *Curr* [1967] 1 All ER 478 (*Cases and Materials* (16.5.2.2)) distorted this principle by holding that the person incited must actually have the *mens rea* for the offence incited. In this case, that was knowledge on the part of women agents incited by D to cash family allowance vouchers belonging to others that they were not entitled to cash the vouchers. Of course, the decision cannot be correct because, as we have already seen, the offence of incitement is not dependent on the person incited going ahead with the offence. What matters is that D **believes** the person incited will commit the offence with any requisite *mens rea*, **if** the incitee goes ahead. This is made crystal clear by the definition of incitement proposed

by cl. 47 of the draft Criminal Code (see *Cases and Materials* (16.5.2.2)).

Nonetheless, the Court of Appeal made exactly the same kind of error in *Shaw* [1994] Crim LR 365 (*Cases and Materials* (16.5.2.2)), confusing the *mens rea* required for incitement with the *mens rea* required for the offence incited! The correct line was taken by the Divisional Court in *DPP v Armstrong* [2000] Crim LR 379 where D asked J, an undercover police officer, to supply him with child pornography. It was held that the necessary *mens rea* for incitement, which D had, was an intention that **if** the person incited does what is asked he will commit an offence. It was therefore irrelevant that the police officer had no intention of supplying the pornographic material. *Curr* and *Shaw* must surely be wrong.

16.5.2.3 Impossibility

The problem is similar to the one we met in relation to attempt and conspiracy. Unfortunately, the statutory clarification of the law in respect of those two offences did not extend to incitement so that this is still governed by the common law. In *McDonough* (1962) 47 Cr App R 37 it was held that D could be convicted of an incitement to commit an impossible offence. D incited X to handle what he thought were stolen lamb carcases in a cold store when in fact there were no stolen carcases in that store. This decision appeared to be approved obiter by the House of Lords in *DPP v Nock* [1978] 2 All ER 654. Nonetheless, the Court of Appeal in *Fitzmaurice* [1983] 1 All ER 189 regarded the position in incitement as governed by the decision in *Haughton v Smith* [1973] 3 All ER 1109, HL.

? QUESTION 16.27

What were the three impossibility situations distinguished by that case? Refer back to 16.3.4 if you do not know.

It would appear, therefore, that if *Fitzmaurice* is upheld, it is not a crime to incite an offence which cannot, in the circumstances, be committed, whatever means are adopted. The irony is that it was deemed unnecessary to provide for inciting the impossible in the Criminal Attempts Act 1981 because it was thought the *McDonough* case, having been approved by the House of Lords in *Nock* had already established that it was an offence to incite the impossible in these cases!

■ FURTHER READING

Ashworth: *Defining Criminal Offences Without Harm* in P Smith (ed.): *Criminal Law: Essays in Honour of JC Smith* (1987, Butterworths).

Buxton: *Circumstances, Consequences and Attempted Rape* [1984] Crim LR 25.

Dennis: *The Elements of Attempt* [1980] Crim LR 758.

Dennis: *The Rationale of Conspiracy* (1977) 93 LQR 39.

Duff: *Criminal Attempts* (1997, Oxford University Press).

Smith JC: *Conspiracy to Defraud* [1995] Crim LR 209.

Smith K: *Proximity at Attempt: Lord Lane's Midway Course* [1991] Crim LR 576.

Virgo: *Conspiracy to Defraud—Intent and Prejudice* (1992) 52 CLJ 208.

Williams: *The Problems of Reckless Attempts* [1983] Crim LR 365.

■ SUMMARY

Attempt

D must (i) do an act more than merely preparatory to the commission of an offence (*actus reus*) (ii) with intent to commit that offence (*mens rea*) (s. 1(1) of the Criminal Attempts Act 1981). Territorial jurisdiction over attempts with foreign element (i) if attempt abroad to commit offence here (*Liangsiriprasert* v *US Government*) or (ii) in respect of any attempt (wherever it occurs) to commit a **'Group A' offence triable here** (s. 3 of the Criminal Justice Act 1993) (iii) if attempt here to commit a **Group A offence** entirely abroad (s. 5 of the Criminal Justice Act 1993).

- *Actus reus*—requires act(s) (probably **not** omissions) going beyond mere preparation (s. 1(1)). No definition of where mere preparation ends and attempt begins. It is sufficient but not essential to prove that D did last act dependent on him (*DPP* v *Stonehouse*; *Gullefer*). Question of degree for jury but it is clear from the case law that D must be 'on the job' and have got close to the point of commission or final act (*Jones*; *Campbell*). Has he 'begun to carry out the commission of the offence' (*Geddes*)?

- *Mens rea*—D must have **intended** to commit the offence alleged to have been attempted. In essence, it was his aim or purpose (but may include foresight of virtual certainty—*Pearman*) to do the act or produce the consequence constituting the crime. This is true even where the complete offence requires only recklessness or less in respect of the act or consequence (*O'Toole*).

D needs an intention 'to supply the missing **physical element** of the completed offence' (*Attorney-General's Reference (No. 3 of 1992)*). In relation to **circumstances** forming part of the offence 'attempted' it will be enough if D knows the circumstance exists or, if the full offence only requires it, awareness that it **might** exist (i.e., subjective recklessness) (*Khan*). It may go even further in simply requiring whatever fault element (if any) the full offence requires in respect of the circumstance (*Attorney-General's Reference (No. 3 of 1992)*).

- **Impossibility**—impossibility in completing the full offence for whatever reason is no longer any bar to a conviction for attempting it (ss. 1(2) and 1(3); *Shivpuri*).

Conspiracy

- **Statutory** conspiracy is essentially any agreement by two or more to commit a crime (s. 1 of the Criminal Law Act 1977) and supersedes all common law conspiracies **except** (i) conspiracy to defraud and possibly (ii) conspiracies to corrupt public morals and to outrage public decency (s. 5(2) and (3)). Considerable overlap between statutory conspiracy and conspiracy to defraud— in such cases prosecution can choose to charge whichever it wants (s. 12 of the Criminal Justice Act 1987). Otherwise the other common law conspiracies can only be charged if they do not involve the commission of a substantive offence.

- Common features of **all** conspiracies—(i) agreement—must be definite but nothing needs to be done in pursuance of it. The offence is committed as soon as the agreement is made but **continues** as long as it subsists (*DPP* v *Doot*) thus catching people joining later. (ii) Agreement with whom?—can be with company unless D is controlling officer and acts alone. No conspiracy where the **only** conspirators are married to each other, the only other party is under ten, or an 'intended victim' of the offence, i.e., offence exists to protect such people. Can be conspiracy with someone exempt from liability for agreed offence (*Whitchurch*; *Burns*).

- Statutory conspiracy—the parties must agree that (i) a course of conduct be pursued (ii) which if carried out in accordance with their intentions (iii) will necessarily amount to or involve a crime. *Course of conduct*—probably includes not only the physical acts planned but also their **intended** consequences (*Siracusa*) and any circumstances which the Ds intend, know or believe will exist when the agreed offence occurs. *'In accordance with their intentions'*—seems to imply that D could only commit conspiracy if **he** intended the offence to be carried out and at least one other did. The House of Lords has rejected this holding that D will be guilty even if he does not intend the 'agreed' offence to be in fact carried out (*Anderson* but conflicts with the Privy Council in *Yip Chiu-Cheung* v *R*). Uncertain if this extends to cases where only one or even none of 'conspirators' has intent to carry it out. *Anderson* curiously requires an intent to play some part in the agreed conduct in furtherance of the criminal purpose but *Siracusa* evades this novel limitation by interpreting 'passive' participation as 'playing some part in'. Under s.1(2), D must intend or know (or probably believe) that any facts or circumstances forming part of the *actus reus* of the underlying substantive offence will be present when the intentions are carried out. This is true even if the substantive offence itself requires a lesser (or even no) fault element in respect of the circumstance (*Harmer* 2005 though *cf. Sakavickas* 2005). Conditional intention to commit the offence in general suffices at least if, in certain circumstances, it becomes an object of the exercise (*Reed*). *'Necessarily' involving a crime*—the offence must **certainly** be a result **if** the agreement is carried out as intended. Impossibility of committing the offence agreed is no bar to statutory conspiracy (s. 1(1)(b)). Jurisdiction here over conspiracies with foreign element if (i) agreement here to commit murder abroad (s. 1(4) of the Criminal Law Act 1977) (ii) agreement here to commit offence abroad **if** offence abroad would be **triable here** (iii) agreement to commit 'Group A' offence (not triable here) abroad **if** anyone joined the conspiracy here or did here any act in connection with it (s. 5 of the Criminal Justice Act 1993) (iv) agreement abroad to commit crime here (*Liangsiriprasert* v *US Government; Sansom* and in respect of 'Group A' offences, s. 3 of the Criminal Justice Act 1993).

- Common law conspiracies—(i) conspiracy to defraud and possibly (ii) conspiracy to corrupt public morals (iii) conspiracy to outrage public decency. *Defraud*—normally involves deceiving the victim so that he suffers financial loss but neither is essential. It includes dishonestly with or without deceit (i) injuring someone's proprietary right or (ii) depriving him of something to which he is or would or might be entitled (*Scott* v *Metropolitan Police Commissioner*). It suffices that V's financial interests would be put at risk (even if no actual loss may occur) (*Allsop*) or that a public official (or possibly even non-public employees, e.g., bank employees—*Wai Yu-tsang* v *R*) would be deceived into acting outside their duty (*DPP* v *Withers*). *Mens rea*—(i) dishonesty (as in *Ghosh*) (ii) intent to defraud—not necessary to show the Ds' **purpose** was to cause loss or risk to V's financial interests. It is enough if they knew the loss or risk was the certain result of achieving their objective (*Cooke; Allsop*). *Wai Yu-tsang* v *R* extends this to the Ds knowing the loss or risk **might be** a result thereof.

- Corrupting public morals/outraging public decency—these common law conspiracies preserved only where agreed conduct would not involve commission of a substantive offence. Outraging public decency is a substantive offence (*Knuller* v *DPP*) so conspiracy to outrage public decency is a statutory conspiracy, not a common law conspiracy. Position less certain for corrupting public morals. Corrupting public morals means depraving or doing things 'destructive of the very fabric of society' (*Shaw* v *DPP*). May not be a substantive offence (but see *Gibson*). Outraging public decency—conduct likely to disgust ordinary members of public (*Knuller* v *DPP*). Both concepts vague and unpredictable.

Incitement

- *Actus reus*—trying to persuade, encourage, instigate or influence another to commit a crime. Can be addressed generally (*Most; Marlow*). Irrelevant whether the addressee is in fact persuaded.

- *Mens rea*—D must intend the incitee to perform the conduct constituting the offence including any **consequences** required by it. He must also know or believe (or possibly suspect) that any **circumstances** and any *mens rea* on the part of the incitee will be present. *Curr* goes further and requires **D** to have the *mens rea* for the **offence incited** but that was rightly rejected in *DPP* v *Armstrong*. *Impossibility*—still governed by common law rules which are uncertain. *McDonough* approved obiter in *DPP* v *Nock* holds that impossibility is never a bar to incitement. *Fitzmaurice* holds that incitement is governed by the principles in *Haughton* v *Smith* which means that in some cases of impossibility, incitement cannot be committed.

CHAPTER 16: ASSESSMENT EXERCISE

16.1 Esme married Osama in 1997. In 2003, Osama left Esme and travelled to Iraq to fight on behalf of a militant organisation which was opposing an American-led coalition. The organisation's forces suffered many casualties under sustained aerial bombardment.

Ayub, who had also fought for the organisation in Iraq but who hated Osama, found his way back to England. He told Esme and his friend, Rashid, who he knew had always loved Esme, that he had witnessed Osama's death during a bombing raid, although he knew that Osama had been captured alive by American forces. Rashid, believing Osama was dead, comforted Esme and eventually both he and Ayub persuaded her to 'marry' him. Esme and Rashid arrived at the Registry Office and the Registrar had just begun the ceremony of 'marriage' when Osama's brother arrived with the news that Osama was alive and in American captivity. The ceremony was abandoned.

Discuss the criminal liability, if any, of (a) Esme for attempted bigamy and (b) Ayub, Rashid and Esme for conspiracy to commit bigamy.

Section 57 of the Offences Against the Person Act 1861 defines bigamy and provides: Whosoever, being married, shall marry any other person during the life of the former husband or wife...shall be guilty of felony...Provided, that nothing in this section contained shall extend...to any person marrying a second time whose husband or wife shall have been continually absent from such person for the space of seven years then last past, and shall not have been known by such person to be living within that time...

See the **Appendix** (16.1) for a specimen answer.

APPENDIX:
ASSESSMENT QUESTIONS AND ANSWERS

General hints on answering problem questions in criminal law

The technique and approach which is likely to work best for most people is as follows—

(a) identify the likely offence(s) starting with the most serious (realistic) possibility. If the question specifies the offences to be discussed, make sure that you stick to those offences;

(b) give the basic definition of the offence (usually a statutory provision);

(c) having thus identified the ingredients of the crime, break the definition down into manageable components for discussion (division into *actus reus* and *mens rea* is often—though not always—a good start but it may well be necessary to further sub-divide);

(d) taking each component in turn, analyse the case law in order to explain in more detail and precision the requirements for that ingredient, dealing in particular with any uncertainties, inconsistencies and conflicts within the case law remembering to note the precedential weight of the authorities considered (a good essay would also consider the law critically and suggest how it might be clarified/improved) (It is unwise to get too involved in the problem facts during stage (d) of the discussion but obviously it is necessary to slant the discussion so as to emphasise those issues likely to prove crucial in solving the problem. Do not labour the obvious, i.e., those issues which are clear and uncontroversial on the facts given);

(e) having reached a conclusion on what requires to be proved legally to satisfy that ingredient, it is then necessary to apply that legal principle to the facts by discussing whether it can be established on the given facts (this process is often skated over by students who must remember that they are in the position of both judge and jury in that they should come to some conclusion on both the law and the facts—if, as is often the

case in criminal law problems, the facts are uncertain in crucial respects, this should be pointed out but any ancillary facts pointing one way or the other should be highlighted);

(f) adopt the same process for all the other ingredients in turn and then come to an overall conclusion for the offence as a whole;

(g) if the facts seem to indicate a relevant defence, go through the same process as above substituting 'defence' for the word 'offence';

(h) go through the same process for any other possible offences in turn.

Obviously if you are subject to time constraints in an examination or a word limit in a coursework, you may not be able to afford the luxury of setting out in full that kind of systematic treatment for every offence and defence in issue. You may well have to streamline these steps when you come to write the answer but, even so, it is well worth adhering to them as a preliminary operation to ensure that you have seen all the relevant issues. Above all, remember that part of the exercise is to see how well you are able to judge not only what are the relevant legal issues but also their relative importance. That judgement becomes even more critical where there is a tight word or time limit. **Make sure you use your words wisely**.

Question 4.1

Chelsea, a football hooligan, was painting offensive slogans on a wall outside a football stadium using an aerosol paint spray. She turned to her friend, Lester, and jokingly made as if to turn the spray on him. Lester, fearing he was about to be sprayed, ran off in a panic but tripped and fell. As a result, he banged his head on the pavement causing a gash to his forehead.

Chelsea ran off in a panic but straight into the arms of the uniformed Police Constable Plod who had witnessed the entire incident. Plod tried to arrest Chelsea but she managed to wrench herself free. This caused Plod to overbalance into the road into the path of an oncoming car which hit Plod and caused him severe multiple injuries.

Discuss the criminal liability of Chelsea, if any, for offences under ss. 18, 20 and 47 of the Offences Against the Person Act 1861.

NB. You are required to assume that P.C. Plod was at all times acting lawfully within the execution of his duty.

Indicative Answer to 4.1

Introduction

1. This question involves two distinct incidents and it is probably easier though not essential to consider them separately.

The injury to Lester

Section 18

2. Give the basic definition of the offence. You should then (stepping back from the problem facts to an extent but with one eye on them) seek to elaborate on and elucidate this basic definition by discussing and analysing the surrounding case law. To do this you will need to divide up the basic definition into manageable components. A convenient initial division would be into *actus reus* and *mens rea*.

3. It is obvious that the most likely form of *actus reus* here is 'wound'. You would therefore define 'wound' by reference to the case law and easily conclude that there is a breaking of the inner and outer skin (*JJC* v *Eisenhower*). A 'gash' in itself is unlikely to be serious enough to constitute grievous bodily harm ('really serious harm') though it cannot be entirely ruled out. Either way, it has to be proved that D caused the injury (wound or GBH). In problem questions of this type, you should resist the temptation to write all you know about causation and stick to the particular point(s) about causation raised by the facts.

4. In indirect causation cases, the issue boils down to whether the actions of the victim immediately leading to the injury break the chain of causation between D's actions and the ultimate injury. The test is whether the victim's action is a reasonably foreseeable result of D's conduct, i.e., was it the sort of response you might expect or was it an outlandish or 'daft' action which a reasonable person would not have anticipated (*Roberts*; *Williams*). Any injury flowing directly from the victim's reasonably foreseeable reaction to D's conduct will have been legally caused by D. It seems clear that Lester's attempt to escape was reasonably foreseeable and as a direct result he suffered the gash. Chelsea clearly caused that injury.

5. One anomaly left by the case law is the apparent requirement that the wound must result from an assault or battery committed by D (*Taylor*; *Beasley*). In the light of the case law widening the meaning of 'inflict' (*Wilson*, HL and particularly *Burstow*, HL), the rule relating to 'wound' seems ripe for reconsideration.

6. However, even if assault or battery is required it looks to be present here. Judging by Lester's reaction, he feared that he was about to be sprayed by Chelsea. Spraying would constitute an application of force, no particular violence being necessary. The fact that, unknown to Lester, Chelsea had no intention of spraying does not matter as long as Lester feared it (*DPP* v *Logdon*). The *actus reus* is therefore present. Although Chelsea was joking, it seems probable that she intended Lester to think he was about to be sprayed (or at the very least realised that he might so think) and so exhibited the necessary *mens rea* for assault—intending to put in fear of immediate violence or being subjectively reckless thereto (*Venna*).

7. Although the *actus reus* of s. 18 can be established, there is no evidence that Chelsea had an intention to do grievous bodily harm (or any intention to resist lawful apprehension, etc.) and it is inconsistent with the fact that it was intended as a joke. Therefore s. 18 can be ruled out.

Section 20

8. Give the basic definition. The *actus reus* is the same as discussed in connection with s. 18 and it appears to be present.

9. The *mens rea* is encompassed by the word 'maliciously'. You need to examine *Cunningham* and *Mowatt* establishing that D must either intend **harm** (not necessarily wounding nor GBH but any harm) or be **subjectively** reckless as to **harm**, i.e., foresee the possibility of harm resulting. *Mens rea* as to frightening will not do (*Sullivan*). All of this was confirmed by the House of Lords in *Savage*; *Parmenter*. Applying this to the question,

we cannot really say whether Chelsea realised harm might result from her actions. If she did, she would be guilty. If she did not, she would be acquitted and you would need to consider the next offence in the scale—s. 47 OAPA.

Section 47

10. Assault occasioning actual bodily harm involves a number of issues previously discussed. 'Actual bodily harm' means 'any hurt or injury likely to interfere with the health and comfort of the victim' which is more than 'transient or trifling' (*Miller, Brown* 1993). Clearly a 'gash' will qualify. 'Occasioning' is just another word for 'causing' and it has already been established that Chelsea caused the harm. Equally that she caused it by means of an assault.

11. After a period of confusion, the *mens rea* of s. 47 was clarified by the House of Lords in *Savage*; *Parmenter*. It is unnecessary to prove any *mens rea* in relation to causing the actual bodily harm. The only *mens rea* required is that for the assault or battery. It has already been concluded that Chelsea intended Lester to fear immediate force or, at least, realised that he might. It follows that, at the least, Chelsea could be convicted under s. 47.

The injury to Plod

Section 18

12. Here we can simply refer back to previous discussion and establish that Chelsea caused Plod GBH. It is evident that severe multiple injuries must constitute GBH and it is clear that Chelsea's actions deposited Plod into the road and were a significant cause of the injuries. The fact that the driver is also a legal cause of the injuries does not preclude this and, since it was accidental, the running over would not be regarded as a 'free, deliberate and informed' third party act. Thus it would not break the chain of causation between the injuries and Chelsea's acts.

13. In regard to *mens rea*, there is no evidence that Chelsea intended to do GBH but it seems clear that she had the alternative intention 'to resist or prevent the lawful apprehension or detainer of any person' (herself). However, did she act 'maliciously'? According to *Mowatt*, 'maliciously' is superfluous in s. 18 but this is only true when the prosecution relies on the 'intent to do

GBH' alternative. For the 'intent to resist' alternative, 'maliciously' does add an extra ingredient (*Morrison*). It seems that, as in s. 20, this requires an intention to harm or subjective recklessness (actual foresight or realisation) as to harm. *Morrison* confirmed that at least **subjective** recklessness is required but failed to clarify that this was in relation to simple **harm** (as opposed to GBH). It appears Chelsea is guilty under s. 18 **only** if she at least realised she might harm Plod and it is impossible to say from the facts given whether she did realise this or not.

Section 20

14. If she is not guilty under s. 18, then, for the same reason, she cannot be guilty under s. 20 OAPA. If she did not realise harm might result, she did not act 'maliciously'.

Section 47

15. In regard to s. 47 OAPA she clearly 'occasioned actual bodily harm' but was it by an 'assault'? 'Assault' here is used in a general sense to embrace both technical assault and battery. If Chelsea had pushed Plod into the road, that would have been an intentional application of force (battery) causing the harm. However, she 'wrenched herself free' and according to *Sheriff* [1969] Crim LR 260, CA simply to pull away from someone does not constitute a battery. It may be that this would preclude a conviction under s. 47. In that case, there could not be a conviction for simple assault or battery. You may have come across in Public Law the offence under s. 89(2) of the Police Act 1996. Chelsea could undoubtedly be convicted of 'resisting a constable in the execution of his duty' but this is a relatively trivial summary offence. By the terms of the question, you were not required to deal with it!

Question 4.2

Bond hails a taxi, but when it stops Kleb rushes into the taxi ahead of him and slams the door in his face jeering, 'Ladies before gentlemen, Mr Bond.' Bond shouts obscenities at her and Kleb yells, 'You're going to pay for that Mr Bond. I'm going to shoot you.' Bond, fearing he is about to be shot, panics and leaps over a wall into the river running alongside the road. He is swept away by the current and, although he is pulled from the river, his breathing has stopped. His breathing is restarted by mouth-to-mouth resuscitation, but it is discovered that he has suffered permanent brain damage, even though he does not die.

Discuss the criminal liability, if any, of Kleb.

Indicative Answer to 4.2

Introduction

1. When dealing with any question involving offences of violence, the first task is to decide which offences you ought to discuss. This is easily done by considering the extent of the injury suffered by the victim. If the victim dies, you obviously consider murder and/or manslaughter. If he suffers grievous bodily harm (GBH) or wounding, you need to consider OAPA 1861, ss. 18 and 20; if actual bodily harm, s. 47 and so on. Logically, it is usually best to consider the most serious possible offence first and then work your way down the scale of seriousness until you are sure there is an offence of which D is guilty or you run out of offences.

Section 18

2. In this question, Bond has clearly suffered GBH and that should immediately point you to OAPA 1861, ss. 18 and 20. Section 18 is committed by anyone who unlawfully and maliciously by any means whatsoever wounds or causes grievous bodily harm to another with intent to do grievous bodily harm or with intent to resist or prevent the lawful apprehension or detainer of any person.

3. The *actus reus* is wounding or causing GBH by any means whatsoever. Wounding involves causing a break in both the inner and outer skin and there is no evidence of any such injury here (*JJC* v *Eisenhower*). According to *DPP* v *Smith*, 'grievous bodily harm' means 'really serious harm' although *Saunders* regarded 'serious harm' as GBH. Either way Bond's 'permanent brain damage' satisfies the definition and amounts to GBH. Does Kleb 'cause' this GBH? It is clear that Kleb's actions caused **in fact** the GBH in that the GBH would not have occurred **but for** Kleb's actions sparking off the incident. In terms of **legal** causation, the main issue is whether Bond's reaction in jumping into the river is a *novus actus interveniens* which breaks the chain of causation between Kleb's threats and the ultimate GBH suffered by Bond. If Bond's reaction was a

reasonably foreseeable one in the circumstances and not 'daft' or unexpected, it will not break the chain of causation and Kleb will have caused the GBH (*Roberts*). In other words, his reaction has to be understandable or 'within the range of responses which might be expected from a victim placed in the situation in which he was', otherwise it will break the chain of causation and Kleb will not be responsible causally for any consequences occurring after it (*Williams*). The last case stressed that a jury should bear in mind that the victim 'in the agony of the moment may act without thought and deliberation'. However, its assertion that the jury should also take into account 'any particular characteristic of the victim' is questionable. The issue of reasonable foreseeability must surely be judged on the basis that the victim is a normal person without unusual characteristics, e.g., excessive paranoia or extreme nervousness, **unless** these were known or ought to have been known to D.

4. The causation question could go either way and would require more detailed facts to resolve, e.g., did Kleb appear to have a gun? What was their past relationship? Given that Bond did fear he was about to be shot, his spur of the moment reaction may be thought to be understandable so that Kleb would be held to have caused the GBH he ultimately suffered.

Did she have the *mens rea* for s. 18? It is clear that she did not have any intention to resist arrest, etc. so that the prosecution would have to prove that she intended to do GBH. Essentially this requires that it was Kleb's aim or purpose to cause GBH (*Belfon*; *Bryson*). This cannot be ruled out but it would seem to be a possibility only if Kleb actually had with her a loaded gun which she planned to fire at Bond. There is little evidence of such an intention and Kleb would probably not be guilty under s. 18. As was pointed out in *Mowatt* (1967, CA), the requirement that the acts be performed 'maliciously' is superfluous in a case where D intends to do GBH because such a person would necessarily be acting 'maliciously'.

Section 20

5. Section 20 requires that D 'unlawfully and maliciously wound or inflict grievous bodily harm' upon another, whether with or without a weapon or instrument. The *actus reus* comprises wounding or inflicting GBH. Wounding has

already been ruled out above. It has been established that Bond suffered GBH and the sole issue is whether Kleb inflicted it. It appeared from *Wilson* that the GBH would only be 'inflicted' if it was caused by means of a direct or indirect application of force to the body. Such a rule could exclude a situation like the present where GBH results from drowning not attributable to any 'impact' injuries. However, the House of Lords in *Burstow* has rejected any such limitation in holding that to cause severe psychological injury by means of telephone calls and/or 'stalking' is to inflict it. In truth, there does not now seem to be any practical difference between 'cause' in s. 18 and 'inflict' in s. 20. It is evident that, assuming the chain of causation is not broken, as previously discussed, Kleb has inflicted GBH on Bond.

6. The *mens rea* of s. 20 is prescribed by the word 'maliciously'. The House of Lords in *Savage*; *Parmenter* confirmed that this entails either an intention to cause harm or subjective recklessness as to some harm. There is no need to prove that D intended or foresaw any risk of **grievous** bodily harm or wounding even though one or the other is needed for the *actus reus* (*Mowatt* confirmed by *Savage*; *Parmenter*). An intention to frighten is insufficient and, at the very least, D must realise that some harm might result from his actions (*Sullivan*). It is not possible to say if Kleb had the necessary *mens rea* but it would be enough to prove that she realised that Bond might be slightly injured, say, in a panic to escape. Conviction for a s. 20 offence would turn on whether the *mens rea* can be established.

Section 47

7. Section 47 of the OAPA 1861 requires an 'assault occasioning actual bodily harm'. 'Actual bodily harm' means any hurt or injury which interferes with the health or comfort of the victim and clearly includes brain damage (*Chan Fook*; *Brown*). 'Occasioning' is synonymous with 'causing' and it was concluded above that the injuries were probably caused by Kleb. But was there an assault? It appears that the term 'assault' is used in the general sense in s. 47 to include either a technical or psychic assault or a physical assault (battery) (*Constanza*). Since there was no physical contact with the victim, at first sight there does not appear to be any battery whose *actus reus* requires an actual application of force (*Ireland*). However, there is an indirect application of force when Bond hits the water. *Wilson* implies that cases of indirect force such as this do not constitute battery because it clearly envisages a situation where D causes an application of force which does not constitute a battery. However, both *DPP* v *K* and *Haystead* v *Chief Constable of Derbyshire* have held that it matters not that the impact on the victim is caused indirectly and it could well be that *Wilson* will be quietly forgotten. Even if Kleb is held to have performed the *actus reus* of battery, her *mens rea* is in doubt. She must have either intended force to be applied to Bond or at least foreseen that it might be applied as a result of her actions. It looks unlikely on the facts given that she would have intended or anticipated that Bond might leap into the river though, again that might depend on their previous relationship. It is easier to establish a psychic assault.

8. Was there a technical assault? Did Kleb intentionally or recklessly put Bond in fear of an immediate application of unlawful force to his person (*Venna*)? The question states that Bond feared he was about to be shot and this establishes the *actus reus*. It is possible that Kleb's threatening words may not be accompanied by any threatening actions (the question is not clear). Even so, it is now plain that assault can be by words alone (*Constanza* where D assaulted by letter; *Ireland* where D assaulted by telephone calls).

9. The *mens rea* for s. 47 is clear after the House of Lords' decision in *Savage*; *Parmenter*. It is not necessary to prove D intended or foresaw harm. No *mens rea* in respect of 'occasioning ABH' is needed. All the prosecution has to prove is the *mens rea* for assault or battery. In this case it is assault which requires that Kleb intended to put Bond in fear of immediate violence or (subjective recklessness) realised that Bond might be put in fear of immediate violence. It seems clear that Kleb intends this or at the very least would foresee that Bond might be put in such fear. What is the point of her actions otherwise?

10. Therefore there is a probability that she would be convicted under s. 47 but acquitted of offences under ss. 18 and 20.

Question 6.1

Melvin, having been violently abused over a period of many years by Alan, his homosexual partner, finally escapes the relationship when

Alan throws him out of their house for another man. Melvin feels extremely depressed and vulnerable and goes to live with Rock. Shortly afterwards, Rock comes home drunk one night and starts making advances to Melvin who rebuffs him. Rock becomes angry, severely beats Melvin and tries to rape him. However, he is too drunk to do this. Melvin, who is physically weak but has himself an explosive temperament, waits for Rock to fall asleep and then stabs him six times intentionally causing his death. Psychiatric evidence establishes that Melvin was suffering from the male equivalent of battered woman syndrome.

Discuss the criminal liability of Melvin, if any, for the death of Rock.

Indicative Answer to 6.1

Introduction

1. The question states as fact that Melvin intentionally killed Rock. That should alert you to the fact that the offence involved is prima facie murder but that the questioner is not looking for an extended discussion of murder. The likelihood is that the core of the question revolves around one or more defences. The severity of M's response suggests provocation but always remember that provocation situations are quite often pleaded as self-defence in an effort to obtain a complete acquittal. Another possibility (see, e.g., *Ahluwhalia*) is diminished responsibility.

Murder

2. Although, as appears above, the bulk of the discussion will be on provocation, it is obviously necessary to establish the offence for which the defence is needed, in this case murder. It is quite unnecessary to go into any detail on either the *mens rea* or the *actus reus* since both are obvious and, indeed, given. You should simply give the definition of murder and establish in one sentence that M has caused the death. No need to drivel on about causation unless the question raises a difficulty. Similarly you need a simple statement that the mens rea is an intention to kill or cause GBH (*Moloney*; *Hancock*; *Cunningham*). The question tells you as a fact that M intended to cause death and you are required to assume that all facts given in problems are provable. It follows that M had the *mens rea* and that all discussion of the extended meaning of intention

(foresight of virtual certainty) in *Woollin* is irrelevant (*MD*).

3. So in two or three sentences you can satisfactorily establish that M is prima facie guilty of murder. Since it would result in a complete acquittal, defence counsel might choose to run self-defence as M's defence, even if it looks unlikely. He knows that the judge is legally bound to direct the jury on provocation, even where the defence has not raised it in order to avoid undermining any shred of credibility in the self-defence plea. (*Mancini v DPP*, HL; *Rossiter*; *Burgess and McLean*).

Self-defence

4. You should therefore look **briefly** at self-defence first. State that M is allowed to use such force as is necessary and reasonable to defend himself against attack (*McInnes*; *Palmer v R*). M would argue that his action was necessary to defend himself from further serious violence. Even if it were accepted that his action was 'necessary' as being the only realistic way to prevent further violence against himself (which is doubtful), the plea would almost certainly fail the 'imminence' test. Although a pre-emptive strike is contemplated in some cases (*A-G's Ref. (No. 2 of 1983)*; *Beckford v R*), the courts are always keen to stress that the attack must be imminent for a pre-emptive strike to be justified (*A-G for Northern Ireland's Reference* 1977; *Chisam*). Given that Rock was asleep, it is unlikely that the courts would accept any claim of imminence. Furthermore, the severity of the force used suggests that M was acting in revenge rather than self-defence. Even if D was 'defending himself', the force (several blows with a knife) might be thought excessive and unreasonable thus destroying the self-defence plea. Excessive self-defence has no effect on liability in English law (*Clegg*, HL).

Provocation

5. The first task is to state what has to be proved:

(a) D must be provoked by things done and/or things said to lose his self-control and

(b) in those circumstances a reasonable person would also have been provoked to lose his self-control and do as D did (s. 3 of the Homicide Act 1957).

You now have to use the case law to analyse the principles explaining these two limbs and apply them to the problem facts.

The subjective limb

6. Define loss of self-control drawing on *Duffy* and the more recent CA cases of *Thornton, Thornton (No. 2)* and *Ahluwalia* which all confirm the necessity for 'a sudden or impulsive reaction leading to a loss of self-control' which renders D 'so subject to passion as to make him or her for the moment not master of his mind'. You could also refer to *Richens* to the effect that this does not require 'complete loss of control' so that D does not know what he is doing but rather such loss of control as 'resulted in the defendant's being unable to restrain himself from doing what he did'. *Ahluwalia* demonstrates that the longer the time lapse between the last provocation and retaliation the more difficult it is to show loss of self-control at the time of the killing. Reason will have had time to resume its seat, though remember cooling time is only one factor in the overall question: did D actually kill while out of control due to the provocation. (However, it is also a relevant factor in the objective limb: would a reasonable man have done as D did.) What is also clear from the case law is that past provocations can be revived by later incidents and this can include the abuse from a previous partner even though they were no fault of the victim (*Humphreys*; *Thornton*).

7. Applying these principles to the question facts, although M's reaction was some time after the provocative conduct and is suggestive of considered revenge, *Ahluwalia* demonstrates that the courts are prepared to recognise the possibility of slow burn anger/resentment which erupts some time after the last, triggering provocation, especially in persistent violent abuse cases like this. In addition, the severity and apparently frenzied nature of the reaction suggests a man out of control. There is certainly credible evidence of loss of self-control sufficient to require the trial judge to leave the defence to the jury and it is conceivable that a jury would find that the subjective limb is satisfied.

The objective limb

8. According to s. 3, the provocative conduct must be such as would, in the opinion of the jury, cause a reasonable man to lose his self-control and do as D did. According to *Morhall*, HL, the reasonable man means the ordinary, average person rather than a '100% rational' person and, as laid down in *DPP* v *Camplin*, is always given the actual age and sex of D. Since he provides the objective yardstick against which to judge whether D's loss of self-control should be excused, he should logically have the powers of self-control of the ordinary person, though *Camplin* requires that the reasonable person be given such of D's characteristics as affects the gravity of the provocation.

9. This conventional view was turned upside down by the House of Lords in *Smith (Morgan)*. This case held that the jury had the discretion to take into account **any** characteristics of the accused even those which merely affected D's general capacity for self-control and did not increase the provocativeness of the actual provocation. It is true that the Lords indicated that this did not include a tendency to childish tantrums or unexplained violent outbursts but their desire to exclude innately pugnacious temperaments is actually inconsistent with their insistence that it is all a matter for the jury. The House went even further and recommended trial judges not to use the concept of the reasonable man which they felt tended to confuse rather than illuminate the essential question. In their eyes, that was: could **this** defendant in **these** circumstances have fairly been expected to have restrained himself from acting in this way. No factor is ruled out in considering this. Whilst this may be a more sensible question, it does appear inconsistent with s. 3 and outside the powers of judges to impose.

10. That stance appeared to be inconsistent with s. 3, the decision of the Privy Council in *Luc Thiet Thuan* v *R* and the previous House of Lords' decisions in *Camplin* and *Morhall*. It was heavily criticised by academics as undermining the objective standard. This led to a reappraisal recently by the Privy Council in *Attorney-General for Jersey* v *Holley*. Nine judges heard the appeal in a deliberate attempt to settle once and for all the controversy and by a 6–3 majority held that *Smith* was inconsistent with s. 3 and the previous House of Lords' decisions. The law was as stated in *Luc* and required the jury to take into account the age and sex of D and any characteristics and circumstances which increased the gravity of the provocation. Characteristics which merely affected D's general level of self-control should not be given to the reasonable man who therefore always retained normal or average powers of

self-control. The Court of Appeal in *Muhammed (Faqir)* has confirmed that *Holley* will be taken to represent the law.

11. Looking at the facts, a number of M's characteristics can be identified which might either enhance the provocativeness of the provoking conduct and circumstances. His physical weakness and BWS may aggravate the provocative effect of the further violently abusive conduct—the feeling that his weakness and vulnerability is being exploited might enhance the gravity of the provocation, making it worse than it otherwise would be. Depression might also make M more prone to lose self-control generally (though medical evidence would be needed to that effect) but, since *Holley*, the jury would not be allowed to take this into account in applying the reasonable man test. A major factor in M's loss of self-control may well have been his 'explosive temperament'. It is now clear from *Holley* that the jury cannot make allowance for this since it is only relevant to M's general power of self-control.

12. In judging how a reasonable man might react, many of the factors relevant to the subjective limb will apply equally here; for example, the issues of cooling time (*Thornton*), past provocation, who did the provoking and who was retaliated against are all relevant factors in deciding how the reasonable man might react. It is clear from *Brown* and *Camplin* that the fact that D's reaction looks to be seriously disproportionate to the gravity of the provocation is no longer automatically fatal to the plea, as appeared to be held in *Mancini* prior to s. 3. Nonetheless, it is always an important factor tending against a successful defence. In this case, M would be helped if the weapon were an everyday object (e.g., kitchen knife) that just happened to be to hand, and not a lethal weapon habitually carried around 'just in case'.

13. It would seem that the emotional response of the jury to M might well determine the success of a plea of provocation. The overall conclusion would be that, bearing in mind that the burden of disproving the elements of provocation is on the prosecution, M has a chance of creating a reasonable doubt in the minds of the jury that a reasonable man might have done as he did but not a very good one. The tightening of the law by *Holley* requiring the exclusion of his depression and explosive temperament coupled with the

time lapse between the retaliation and the last act of provocation all militate against a successful plea.

Diminished responsibility

14. You should explain the three requirements laid down by s. 2 of the Homicide Act 1957. There is some evidence in the question suggesting M suffered an 'abnormality of mind', a notoriously and perhaps necessarily vague and elastic concept. Although *Fenton* holds that strong emotions such as hate, jealously and anger are not in themselves abnormalities, it is clear that clinical depression and battered woman syndrome are (*Ahluwalia* and *Hobson* respectively). Presumably the 'male equivalent' of BWS would also be so classified. Thus it is likely that M would be able to establish the first requirement.

15. It is likely that the courts would find that the abnormalities were 'induced by disease' (*Ahluwalia*; *Hobson*) on the basis that depression and BWS are classified as psychiatric diseases. However, this view is problematic in that depression and BWS seem to embrace both the symptom (the abnormality of mind) and its cause (the disease).

16. The crunch issue will be whether there was 'substantial impairment' of his mental responsibility for the act. Again, this is essentially in the discretion of the jury and, in practice, would be heavily dependent on whether M engages the sympathy of the jury. They must decide whether the abnormality was serious enough to warrant excusing D from murder. On balance, it is thought that there is sufficient impairment of responsibility here to enable a plea of diminished responsibility to succeed.

Question 6.2

Smart, a student, decided to play a practical joke on his lecturer, Dream. When Dream entered the lecture theatre to give a lecture, Smart set off a smoke canister which he had bought from a joke shop, and shouted, 'Fire!'

As a result of these actions, Dream, who already had a weak heart, had a serious heart attack and blacked out. Upon recovering consciousness after initial hospital treatment, Dream instructed the medical staff that they were not to give him any further treatment or medication because he wanted to die, being unable to cope with the pressures of his job. No further treatment was given and he lapsed into a coma and died.

Discuss the criminal liability of Smart, if any, for (a) unlawful act manslaughter and (b) gross negligence manslaughter in respect of Dream's death.

Indicative Answer to 6.2

Introduction

1. The question prescribes the offences to be discussed and therefore no credit will be gained for discussing any offence other than involuntary manslaughter, except insofar as it is relevant to unlawful act manslaughter. In particular you should not consider murder or voluntary manslaughter.

Unlawful act manslaughter

2. Set out the basic requirements as laid down in *DPP* v *Newbury*. The 'act' in question here is clearly setting off the smoke canister and shouting, 'Fire!' It is evident that Smart (S) 'intentionally' did these acts because they formed part of his purpose. The intentionality requirement relates only to doing the acts and not to any **consequences** of the acts such as death, injury or even frightening. In reality, this 'intention' adds nothing to the basic idea of doing an act.

3. A crucial requirement is that these acts must have been 'unlawful' and this is the issue liable to cause most difficulty here. 'Unlawful' in this context has, ever since *Franklin*, been held to mean criminal, as opposed to merely tortious. In addition, a criminal act whose criminality arises merely from the fact that the act is performed in a negligent way will not be accepted as an 'unlawful' act for the purposes of this doctrine (*Andrews* v *DPP*). It would seem therefore that the prosecution would have to show that S has committed the *actus reus* of a crime (other than a crime of negligence) with any necessary fault or *mens rea* elements (*Lamb*; *Scarlett*). The apparent denial of the necessity for such *mens rea* in *DPP* v *Newbury* is a case of the House of Lords having got confused the distinct concepts of 'unlawful' and 'dangerous'. They cannot have meant what they appeared to say because an act cannot be a crime unless **all** its ingredients (including *mens rea*) are present.

4. Were S's acts criminal in this case? There is no evidence that the joke shop smoke canister caused any damage to property so that criminal damage seems unlikely. It is equally unlikely that setting off a canister available from a joke shop would contravene any legislation concerning explosives, etc. The most likely possibility is an offence against the person. Since there is no actual violence to Dream's person, we can rule out battery (*Ireland*). For technical assault, it is necessary to prove that S intentionally or recklessly caused Dream (D) to apprehend an immediate application of physical force (*Ireland*). It is clear that D was frightened as a result of S's actions but that is insufficient. He has to have been frightened of a very specific thing, namely, that force is about to be then and there applied to his person. It is questionable whether his generalised terror at the prospect of a fire would embrace that specific fear. However, it should be emphasised that *Ireland* holds that the victim need only fear the **possibility** of immediate force as opposed to the more or less definite application of such force. Arguably D might have feared he would be knocked into or trampled in a rush for the exits. (Could the licking of flames on his body be an 'application of force for this purpose'?) In regard to the *mens rea*, whilst it is reasonably clear that S must have intended to fool D into thinking there might be a fire, it seems rather fanciful to think that he wanted D to fear that force was about to be applied to his person. Subjective recklessness as to such fear also suffices (*Savage*; *Parmenter*) and he may have realised that there was a risk that D might apprehend immediate force, e.g., if he thought there might be a panic for the exits. However, even that seems unlikely.

5. A further possibility which would avoid the problem of fearing an immediate application of force is s. 20 of the OAPA 1861. Did S maliciously inflict GBH? Obviously D suffered serious harm before he died from the heart attack and, in the light of *Burstow*, it is evident that S's conduct, having according to the question facts caused this injury, also thereby inflicted it. There is no longer any necessity for the GBH to have resulted from a violent impact on the body. The *mens rea* of 'maliciously' requires S to have either intended some harm or realised that some harm might result (*Savage*; *Parmenter*). There is no evidence of intention but subjective recklessness is possible depending on the precise circumstances.

Obviously if S knew of D's condition, then he would find it difficult to deny that he realised some harm was a possibility. If he did not know, it may be that he might contemplate the possibility of someone being injured in the event of a panic evacuation—this could depend on the extent to which the remaining audience was a part to the 'joke'.

6. Thus although a crime is possibly committed, it is by no means certain. It goes without saying that there is no need to prove that S realised his conduct was a crime since ignorance of the law is no excuse (*DPP* v *Newbury*).

7. Assuming S's conduct constituted an assault or a s. 20 offence, was it 'dangerous'? Introduced in *Larkin* as meaning 'likely to cause harm', this limitation is now more usually defined by the more convoluted formulation in *Church*: would all sober and reasonable people have inevitably recognised the conduct carried a risk of harm, albeit not serious harm? The requirement for **inevitable** recognition suggests that the risk of harm must be foreseeable as more than just possible but as a pretty obvious risk. The test is objective and there is no need to establish that S appreciated the risk or even that he was capable of appreciating it (*DPP* v *Newbury*). Although *Watson* makes it clear that harm means physical harm and does not include mere emotional disturbance such as extreme terror, it confirms that physical harm brought about by a heart attack resulting from such emotional disturbance is certainly harm for this purpose. Presumably since the decision in *Ireland* to expand the notion of harm to include 'recognised psychiatric illness' for the purposes of non-fatal offences against the person, the notion of harm in this context would be similarly expanded if the matter arose.

8. In applying the test, the notional reasonable person must be given any special knowledge which the accused possesses and any knowledge which S ought to have gleaned from the unfolding situation. Clearly if S knew of D's heart condition, then the risk of harm from such a prank would be obvious to any reasonable person. If he did not, there is still the possibility that it would be obvious from D's appearance that he was less than robust (*Watson*). It should also be remembered that it is sufficient if there is an obvious risk of harm to someone whether the actual victim, D, or any other member of the audience (*Attorney-General's Reference (No. 3 of 1994)*) so that if the rest of the audience was not party to the joke, there could be an obvious risk of injury through a rush to the exits. Thus there is a reasonable possibility of establishing that the conduct was 'dangerous'.

9. The final element requires that the unlawful and dangerous act should cause the death. The question states that D's heart attack resulted from S's conduct. Even though D had a pre-existing heart condition which made the effect of the conduct unforeseeably severe, S is not absolved from causal responsibility in any way because of the well-entrenched principle that the defendant must take his victim as he finds him (*Hayward; Blaue*). The only question is whether D's refusal of medical treatment constitutes an intervening act which breaks the chain of causation between the initial heart attack and the ultimate death. A straightforward application of the rule in *Smith* indicates that it does not. It is clear that the heart attack triggered by S's conduct is a 'substantial and operating cause' hastening on death at the moment of death. The effects of the heart attack are allowed to take their natural course by the withdrawal of treatment. Refusal of treatment for whatever reason will not absolve S (*Holland; Blaue*). It is better to base it on the *Smith* principle rather than the rather dubious extension of the take your victim as you find him rule primarily relied on in *Blaue*.

10. Since the House of Lords' decision in *Attorney-General's Reference (No. 3 of 1994)*, it is no longer necessary to be concerned about whether the unlawful act was directed at the victim (though the test would in any case appear fulfilled on these facts).

Gross negligence manslaughter

11. Following a period of uncertainty when the House of Lords' decision in *Seymour* appeared to have transformed 'gross negligence' manslaughter into 'objective recklessness' manslaughter, the law is now relatively clear again. The House, in the leading case of *Adomako*, has returned the law essentially to the traditional position articulated many years ago in *Bateman*. The requirements are: (1) the accused has broken a duty of care owed to the victim; (2) that the breach has caused the victim's death; and (3) the accused's conduct constituted gross negligence.

12. Whether a duty of care is owed is determined by the law of tort and, particularly by the

tort of negligence (*Adomako*) though this is not to be applied in too technical a way (*Wacker*; *Willoughby*). Obviously, in a criminal law essay, it is imprudent to go to great lengths discussing the duty concept in torts. It is a question of law for the judge to determine whether a duty of care is capable of arising in the circumstances but then a question of fact for the jury to decide if it actually does arise (*Willoughby*). In general, there will always be a duty to take reasonable care to avoid physical injury to anyone who might reasonably foreseeably be injured by one's conduct. That would include everyone in the lecture theatre in this case. Equally a court would have no difficulty in concluding that S's conduct caused the death in accordance with the principles discussed in 9 above.

13. It is plain that a reasonable, prudent student (if one were to exist) would not have acted in this alarmist way so that the standard of conduct fell below that required and constituted ordinary negligence sufficient for liability in tort. However, criminal liability depends on establishing a serious and extreme failure to comply with the standard of the reasonable person. Only then would the negligence be 'gross'. The House in *Adomako* was content to leave it to the jury to decide whether the accused had crossed the boundary between ordinary and gross negligence in any particular case, regarding it as impossible for the law to give any further meaningful guidance on what was essentially a matter of degree. Nonetheless, one important issue implicitly determined by the House was that the risk in relation to which the accused had to be grossly negligent was the risk of **death**. If adhered to, this would represent a tightening of the traditional law in cases like *Bateman* which referred to risks to the 'life and safety' of others and was interpreted (whether correctly or otherwise!) as a risk of death or GBH. However, it is surely correct to require that the accused has fallen seriously short in failing to guard against the risk of death (rather than just injury or even serious injury) for the offence of manslaughter.

14. Has S fallen seriously below the standard of conduct expected of a prudent person in regard to the risk of death? One might say that there is a high risk of injury which a prudent person would have avoided by not doing what S did but could it be said that there was a high risk of death? That would depend on the knowledge of the circumstances which the reasonable person is notionally given. If D's heart condition is taken into account, then it might well be possible to say that there was an obvious and serious risk of death. Otherwise not. As in respect of the issue of 'dangerousness' in unlawful act manslaughter, the reasonable person would be given such knowledge as S had or ought to have gleaned from the unfolding situation. It would therefore appear unlikely that S could be convicted of gross negligence manslaughter unless he was aware of D's heart condition.

Question 8.1

Slater, a college lecturer, had been experiencing nightmares and disturbed sleep and behaving strangely as a result of stress suffered at work brought about by the increase in the number of students on his courses. He was given some tranquilising tablets by a colleague, who told him that they would get rid of his stress. Slater followed his colleague's instructions and took two tablets thinking that they would enable him to get a good night's sleep.

He fell asleep but got up in a trance and walked out into the street in his nightshirt. He picked up a brick and attacked Owl, a passer-by, with the brick causing him grievous bodily harm.

Slater was at all times quite unaware of what he was doing and could remember nothing of the incident. The medical experts were unable to say whether the sleepwalking was due to the tablets or Slater's underlying condition or a combination of the two.

Advise Slater as to his criminal liability, if any, in respect of the injuries to Owl, with particular reference to possible defences.

Indicative Answer to 8.1

Introduction

1. The crucial issues for discussion centre round the intertwining defences of insanity, automatism and intoxication. All can be accessed in a logical sequence through the medium of automatism and you could do worse than use the flow chart in **Chapter 8** as your template. However, logically, before defences can come into play, we need a potential offence(s) but the obviousness of

the 'offence' issues warrants only an economical and succinct treatment.

Potential offences

2. The question states that S caused O grievous bodily harm and that obviously suggests ss. 18 and 20 of the OAPA 1861. Prima facie the *actus reus* of both sections has been committed by S since 'inflicts' in s. 20 is more or less synonymous with 'cause' in s. 20 following *Burstow*. (No need to go into the meaning of GBH, still less wound, because the question states S caused GBH.)

3. It appears that S has the *mens rea* for neither offence because the question states that he was 'at all times unaware of what he was doing', etc. He, therefore, could not have intended GBH as required by s. 18 nor, at the time he attacked O, could he have even foreseen the possibility of harm resulting, the minimum required for s. 20. However, the reason for the absence of *mens rea* was that he was in a state of automatism because, quite clearly, his conscious mind was not directing or willing his muscular movements (*Bratty* v *A-G for Northern Ireland*). The question you need to address is what effect, if any, this has upon liability.

Defences

4. As soon as you see phrases like 'at all times unaware' and 'remembers nothing', you should immediately think about automatism. The effect of automatism depends first on identifying whether it is insane or non-insane automatism since the former will result in a 'qualified' acquittal—not guilty by reason of insanity—whilst the latter has the potential for a complete 'no-strings' acquittal.

Insane automatism

5. If the autonomic state results from a disease of the mind, the finding must be insanity because it means that the definition of insanity—all the elements of the M'Naghten Rules—must be satisfied. Obviously if S is at all material times unaware of what he is doing, he cannot know the 'nature and quality of his acts' or, for that matter, that they were 'wrong'. Equally he suffers from a defect of reason because he is incapable of exercising the ordinary powers of reasoning (*Clarke*). These requirements will be met in **every** case of automatism, the only variable being 'disease of

the mind'. If the last is present, it completes the definition and constitutes insane automatism.

6. Any malfunctioning of the mind caused by an internal bodily disorder seems to constitute a disease of the mind whereas if the malfunctioning is due to an external factor of transitory effect, there is no disease of mind and the case is one of non-insane automatism (*Sullivan*; *Quick*). The problem in this case is that there is no clear indication of whether the cause of S's violent sleepwalking was the taking of the tablets or the work-induced stress. If it was due to the stress rather than the tablets, it would seem from *Burgess* that it would be classed as an internal bodily disorder and so insane automatism. An argument based on *T* that the trigger for the stress, S's job, was an 'external factor' would be doomed to failure. Unlike the rape in *T*, job demands are part of the trials and tribulations of everyday life which everyone has to cope with. An unusual reaction like violent sleepwalking would be attributed to internal abnormality in S's make-up and so be a disease of mind (*Rabey*; *Burgess*).

7. S would be unlikely to plead insanity because of the risk of an indefinite hospital order. He would claim non-insane automatism on the ground that his state resulted from the taking of the tablets. The facts demonstrate that S would easily be able to satisfy the minimal burden on him to produce credible evidence of automatism caused by the tablets. It would then be up to the prosecution to prove beyond reasonable doubt that it was not due to this external factor but to the underlying condition. They would be unable to do this in the absence of very clear medical evidence that the tablets played no significant part in the events. Consequently the finding would almost certainly be non-insane automatism. This is supported by *Roach* where D claimed to be in a state of automatism due to the interaction of prescribed drugs and alcohol on his latent mental illness. The trial judge treated this as a plea of insane automatism and refused to leave the defence of non-insane automatism to the jury. The Court of Appeal disapproved and held that if the external factors affected 'an underlying condition which would not otherwise produce a state of automatism', the defence of non-insane automatism ought to be left to the jury.

Non-insane automatism

8. Whatever the cause of the non-insane automatism, it will **always** be a defence to a crime of specific intent (*Bailey*; *DPP v Majewski*). Section 18 has been held to be a crime of specific intent (*Pordage* 1975; *Davies* 1991). In some configurations (e.g., wounding with intent to do GBH) it requires proof of an ulterior intent (Lord Simon in *DPP v Morgan*) and in all configurations it requires proof of 'a purposive element' for conviction—usually the intent to do GBH (Lord Simon in *DPP v Majewski*). Since S was unconscious at the time of the attack, he cannot possess the requisite specific intent and so must be acquitted of the s. 18 charge.

9. Section 20 is a crime of 'basic intent' (*DPP v Majewski*; *Bratty v A-G for NI*) in that there is no requirement to prove either 'a purposive element' (intention) or any ulterior *mens rea* for a conviction since subjective recklessness as to harm suffices. The effect of the automatism on liability depends on a number of issues. If the automatism is not self-induced, it will effectively be regarded as involuntary and will be a defence to a basic intent crime such as s. 20. 'Self-induced' means that D was in some way to blame for getting into the autonomic state, i.e., it was a reasonably foreseeable result of his actions. In this case, S has voluntarily taken what he knows to be drugs from a non-medical source. Plainly he is at fault and the automatism self-induced.

10. Where self-induced automatism is caused by the voluntary taking of alcohol or dangerous drugs, it is regarded as no different from any other case of intoxication not resulting in automatism and the normal rules laid down in *Majewski* will apply. These state quite categorically that self-induced intoxication by alcohol or a **dangerous** drug is **never** a defence to a crime of basic intent even where D lacks the *mens rea* for the offence. (The juristic basis for this rule is not totally clear but the most likely view from *Majewski* is that D, whether he actually is or not, is automatically **deemed** to be 'reckless', i.e., to know what 'everyone' knows—that alcohol and dangerous drugs may cause D to become 'aggressive, unpredictable or uncontrolled'. This 'recklessness' at one remove from D's *actus reus*, then replaces the normal requirement to prove D had the *mens rea* for the crime at the time of committing it. An alternative view (see, e.g., *Woods* [1982] Crim

LR 42) is that, as a matter of policy, evidence of such intoxication has to be ignored—is 'legally irrelevant'—and guilt depends on establishing that D would have been reckless, i.e., have realised the risk of harm had he done the acts while sober!). Consequently if the courts were to class the drug S took as dangerous, he would definitely be guilty of a s. 20 offence.

11. Since the tablets were to get rid of stress, there is a good chance that they were 'non-dangerous soporific or sedative-type' drugs not commonly known to make takers 'aggressive, unpredictable or uncontrolled' (*Bailey*; *Hardie*). In that case, the normal *Majewski* rules on intoxication do not apply and are superseded by the rules set out in *Bailey*. These would hold that S could only be convicted of the basic intent crime if the prosecution proved that he was 'reckless' as to getting into the automatic state and becoming 'aggressive, unpredictable or uncontrolled with the result that he may cause some injury to others'. *Bailey*, even before *Caldwell* was overturned by *G*, made it clear that, for offences against the person, 'reckless' was confined to **subjective** recklessness so that the prosecution must prove **actual realisation** by S that the tablets might have the relevant effects. Given that S was anticipating 'a good night's sleep', it would be difficult to prove that he was aware of the potential for dangerous or unpredictable conduct and an acquittal of any offence of violence would be likely if the drugs were 'non-dangerous'.

Question 8.2

Percy is the captain of Radford Rovers football team. He is extremely nervous before a Cup Final and the team manager gives him three amphetamine pills telling him that they will get him buzzing. Percy takes the pills one hour before the match.

The pills make Percy feel hysterical and confused. When the referee comes to shake hands before the game, Percy thinks the referee is attacking him and he punches the referee on the nose causing it to bleed.

Percy then runs to the edge of the pitch, snatches an orange from a spectator and eats it, thinking it is part of the refreshments provided for the players at half-time.

Discuss the criminal liability, if any, of Percy.

Indicative Answer to 8.2

Introduction

1. The fact that Percy has taken pills and is 'hysterical and confused' should suggest to you that a major part of the discussion will be on defences—the likely candidates being intoxication and automatism. However, as always it is necessary first to identify the possible offences and since there are two clearly separate incidents involving quite different offences, it makes sense to deal with each situation in turn rather than together.

The injury

Possible offences

2. In relation to the attack on the referee, it would seem that a bloody nose must constitute at least actual bodily harm thus indicating that s. 47 OAPA is possible but it may also (and probably would) constitute a wound, thus raising the issue of ss. 18 and 20 OAPA. There has to be a rupture of both layers of the **external** skin (*JJC v Eisenhower* 1983, DC). However, since this has been held to include a cut on the urethra and the inside of the cheek (*Waltham* 1849), it is likely to include rupturing the blood vessels on the inside of the nostrils. Therefore it would seem that **prima facie** Percy has committed the actus reus for both ss. 18 and 20 in that he has wounded the referee by means of a direct application of force, i.e., a battery. (See *Beasley* 1981, CA.)

3. Does he have the *mens rea* required for these offences? Section 18 requires in this situation proof of an intention to cause grievous bodily harm. It is possible that Percy did intend serious injury but there is nothing in the question to suggest it. Since it cannot be ruled out, it is necessary to consider the situation where he has that intention.

Mens rea and mistaken self-defence

4. Percy's first line of defence would perhaps be to argue that he did not intend to apply **unlawful** force relying on *Williams* 1984, CA and *Beckford* 1988, PC. Obviously, the force was **in fact** unlawful because the referee was not attacking him and therefore he was not using reasonable force in self-defence (or the prevention of crime under s. 3 Criminal Law Act 1967). But he mistakenly, if stupidly, thought he was. *Williams* holds that where D mistakenly believes he is being attacked, he must be judged on the facts as he mistakenly believes them to be, no matter how ridiculous and unreasonable his belief. The question then would be whether the force he actually used was, in the eyes of the court, no more than was reasonable and necessary to defend himself against the **imagined** attack. The force here looks to be reasonable on the premise of an attack by the referee and so Percy would lack the intention to apply force which was unlawful.

5. If the force was judged objectively to be an unreasonable response in the imagined circumstances, that should, on general principle, destroy the defence even if Percy thinks it is only reasonable force. He would be making a mistake as to the amount of force the law allows in any given situation—a mistake as to the criminal law. However, *Scarlett* 1993, CA appeared to hold that Percy would not have the necessary *mens rea* in such a case. Fortunately the later cases of *Owino* 1995, CA and *Hughes* 1995, CA have indicated that *Scarlett* is an aberration and that the principle stated in the first sentence of this paragraph is the correct one.

Intoxication and self-defence

6. Unfortunately a complication arises because the cause of his mistake appears to be voluntary intoxication due to the taking of a **dangerous** drug (amphetamines). The Court of Appeal in two cases, *O'Grady* 1987, CA and *O'Connor* 1991, CA, held, apparently obiter, that where D's mistaken belief that he is defending himself is due to self-induced intoxication, it is to be ignored and D must be judged on the facts as they actually were, namely that he was not being attacked at all. This would mean that Percy would be guilty of the s. 18 offence **if he intended GBH**.

7. Both cases are arguably obiter on the point and go against the general principles governing the defence of intoxication laid down by the House of Lords in *Majewski* 1976, HL. These principles allow intoxication as a possible defence to crimes of specific intent and s. 18 is such a crime since it requires proof of a purposive element. If intoxication prevents D having an intention to do GBH, he cannot be convicted under s. 18. Logic and common sense would

surely likewise dictate that if D does not intend to do **unlawful** GBH, he cannot be guilty because he lacks the *mens rea* (see *Williams* endorsed by the House of Lords in *B* v *DPP* 2000) for a specific intent crime. This inconsistency with the principle in *Majewski* would have enabled a future court to refuse to follow the dicta in *O'Grady* and *O'Connor*. In both of those cases, D was convicted of manslaughter—a basic intent crime—for other reasons and therefore any comments on the effect of drunken mistake in crimes of specific intent were arguably unnecessary for the decision and therefore obiter. However the Court Appeal did not take that opportunity in the recent case of *Hatton*. They preferred to follow *O'Grady* claiming that it was binding on them in relation to all crimes, whether specific intent or basic intent, including murder. Their view was that *O'Grady* and *O'Connor* were enunciating and applying a general principle to the effect that a mistake caused by self-induced intoxication had to be ignored whatever the crime charged. That was the stated principle and it was in no way limited to manslaughter or other basic intent crimes. The mere fact that the crime under consideration happened to be manslaughter did not render the principle obiter in regard to other crimes. It follows that, unless and until the House of Lords decides otherwise, the accused must be judged on the facts as they actually were so that he is deemed not to be acting in self-defence. Therefore if Percy intended to cause GBH he would be guilty under s. 18.

Automatism

8. The fact that the pills made Percy 'hysterical and confused' might suggest automatism. After all in *T* 1990, a Crown Court held that a woman traumatised by rape who committed an offence whilst experiencing a psychogenic fugue (a fugue is an amnesial flight from reality) had no conscious control over her movements. On the other hand this is only a Crown Court decision and *Broome* v *Perkins* 1987, DC, *Isitt* 1978, CA and most recently *Attorney-General's Reference (No. 2 of 1992)* 1993, CA suggest that Percy has probably not lost sufficient conscious control to be classed as an automaton so as to prevent him having the necessary conscious intention to do GBH. Clearly if he had, it would negative a s. 18 offence (specific intent) even though it was self-induced due to the voluntary taking of

dangerous drugs (*Bailey* 1983, CA). Obviously if Percy did not intend any GBH, he could not be convicted under s. 18 even if it was the intoxication which prevented him having the *mens rea* (*Majewski*).

Basic intent offences—ss. 20 and 47

9. Percy appears to have 'wounded' the referee and has certainly caused him 'actual bodily harm'. Clearly there has been an application of unlawful force which caused the injury. It follows that the *actus reus* of both offences is present. The question of *mens rea* might be thought to be crucial but, according to *Majewski*, in a crime of basic intent, where D claims that he lacked the *mens rea* due to his intoxicated state, the normal requirement to prove *mens rea* is simply dispensed with. (In any event in this case, he does seem to have the intention to harm (s. 20) and to apply force (s. 47).) Presumably *O'Grady* and *O'Connor* even without the endorsement of *Hatton* were clearly correct in respect of **basic intent** crimes so that it is likewise unnecessary to prove an intention to apply **unlawful** force (or even foresight as to the application of **unlawful** force) where D thinks it is lawful only because of self-induced intoxication. Nevertheless, the case of *Richardson and Irwin* 1999, CA appeared to deny this, perhaps unwittingly, in a holding which is inconsistent with the *Majewski* principle. The accused believed, as a result of a drunken mistake, that V had consented to student horseplay which, if true, would have rendered the force applied to V lawful. It was held that the defendants could not be guilty under s. 20 OAPA (a basic intent crime) seemingly because they would not have the *mens rea*—an intention to (or realisation that they might) cause harm which, in the circumstances they believed to exist, would be unlawful. It is submitted that this cannot be supported and the *Majewski* principle will apply to deem Percy to have the *mens rea* for ss. 20 and 47.

10. With regard to automatism, even if Percy is acting as an automaton, it is clearly self-induced by the voluntary taking of a dangerous drug (*Majewski* had taken amphetamines). *Bailey* holds that such a situation is caught by the rules in *Majewski* and is treated as voluntary intoxication so that it is no defence to a basic intent crime. D's action in taking the dangerous drug is conclusively presumed to be reckless since 'everyone' knows it

is likely to make one 'aggressive, unpredictable or uncontrolled with the result that he may cause some injury to others'.

11. It follows that Percy is probably guilty under s. 20 (assuming there is a 'wound') and certainly guilty under s. 47.

The orange

Theft

12. Percy clearly appropriates property belonging to another with the intention of permanently depriving him of it. 'Dishonestly' is the problem. The question indicates that he honestly if stupidly (and intoxicatedly!) believed that the owner had consented to his having the orange and according to *Lawrence* 1971, HL (by analogy with s. 2(1)(b)), this would negative dishonesty. This is a better argument than s. 2(1)(a) would provide because Percy is unlikely to believe that he is legally entitled (i.e., as of right) to have the orange except in the context of the owner's consenting. Since theft is a crime of specific intent (*Ruse* v *Read* 1949 and Lord Simon in *Majewski*), Percy must be acquitted even though his lack of *mens rea* was due to intoxication.

Criminal damage

13. Percy, in his intoxicated state, destroys property belonging to another and since criminal damage is a crime of basic intent (*Caldwell* 1981, HL), there is no need to worry about proving *mens rea* at least if Percy is charged with '**recklessly**' destroying the orange. (Even if he is charged only with '**intentionally**' destroying it, so that lack of such intention might, on one view of *Caldwell*, lead to acquittal, in this case Percy would appear to have the necessary intention to destroy the orange.) For the same reason, it is no use pleading automatism. However, Percy can escape conviction by pleading that his destruction of the orange was not 'without lawful excuse' because he had a 'lawful excuse' under s. 5(2) of the Criminal Damage Act 1971. This provides that D has a lawful excuse if he believes that the owner has consented to the destruction and s. 5(3) expressly provides that the belief does not have to be justified or reasonable. Percy would seem to have this belief. Does it matter that it is caused by voluntary intoxication? According to *Jaggard* v *Dickinson* 1980, DC, the *Majewski* principle does

not apply to express statutory defences such as this (even if the crime is basic intent) and if the relevant belief is honestly held, it matters not that it is attributable to intoxication. This creates yet another anomaly and illogicality in the treatment of intoxication but it means that Percy does not commit criminal damage. The Law Commission's proposal to overturn *Jaggard* v *Dickinson* has yet to be implemented.

Question 9.1

A fire broke out in an office block trapping the workers on the top floor of a five-storey building. The flames and fumes prevented them from either getting onto the roof or being able to use the stairs. The fire brigade had, however, managed to get a ladder to a window of the top floor and workers were being carried down to safety.

There were still ten more to save when Graham, who had climbed out onto the window ledge became paralysed with fear. He refused either to descend the ladder or to return to the now smoke-filled room, despite the pleas of Helen, who was next in line to escape. The firefighter, Isabel, at the top of the ladder, said to Helen 'If you don't push him off you will all die.' Helen then shoved Graham off the ledge and he fell to his death. She and three more office workers managed to escape down the ladder, but five had become overcome with the fumes and died.

Discuss the criminal liability, if any, of Helen for the **murder** of Graham.

Indicative Answer to 9.1

1. The question specifies the offence required for discussion and therefore no credit is given for discussion of other offences. Liability turns on issues of *mens rea* and the defences of necessity and duress of circumstances. Since the law is not particularly clear on these issues, there is scope for differing arguments and interpretations and credit would be given for evidence of wider research and appreciation of alternative possibilities.

Murder

2. Murder is the unlawful killing of another human being with malice aforethought. G's death was clearly the direct result of H's shove

and there is no difficulty in establishing that H both factually and legally caused it. (Do not be tempted to waste words on discussing the intricacies of causation where there is obviously no problem.)

3. The *mens rea* requires an intention to kill or cause grievous bodily harm (GBH) (*Moloney*) and your discussion should centre on the meaning of 'intention'. It is highly unlikely that H was aiming to kill or injure G. No doubt she would have been delighted to find that he had escaped injury. It follows that the only possibility of establishing the mens rea for murder is by utilising the '*Woollin* principle' which extends the concept of intention to some non-purpose cases.

4. The prosecution in *Woollin* accepted that D did not aim to kill or injure his baby and therefore conviction could only be possible if there existed a form of intention not based on aim or purpose. The House of Lords implicitly assumed that there was such a 'non-purpose' type of intention and at some points in the judgment appeared to define it **positively** as where death or GBH was virtually certain to result and D appreciated this. However, the ultimate adoption of a modified *Nedrick* direction means that the ratio of the decision falls short of designating foresight of virtual certainty **as itself** a form of intention. Rather, foresight of virtual certainty is the minimum condition for allowing a jury to **find** intention in non-purpose cases. Whether or not they do so is entirely a matter for their discretion in any given case. This latter interpretation of *Woollin* was adopted by the Court of Appeal in *Matthews and Alleyne* although the majority in the civil case of *Re A (Conjoined Twins)* seemed to adopt the former view. Note that there is no guidance as to when a jury should find intention in foresight of virtual certainty cases, and when not. Equally there is no explanation of the nature of this non-purpose state of mind and how it differs from foresight of virtual certainty itself. The truth is that the House has abdicated its responsibility to define fully the *mens rea* for murder and has left an area of discretion where the jury can effectively please themselves. Thus the door is opened for the jury to refuse to find intention in cases they regard as 'deserving' even though they are satisfied that D realised that death or GBH was virtually certain to result.

5. A number of medical cases support this idea by invoking the notion of 'double effect' whereby D aims to produce a beneficial consequence but knows the practically inevitable effect will be to produce a parallel bad effect (e.g., death). D is held to intend only the 'good' consequence but it seems that he has to be following accepted and acceptable practice (i.e., proper medical treatment in the best interests of the patient) for this stance to be taken (see *Gillick* v *W. Norfolk Area Health Authority*; *Moor*). However, this view seems to base the existence of intention on the interpretation and evaluation of D's motive which should properly be categorised as an issue of defence (justification or excuse). It would make intention a far too fluid and uncertain concept. The Court of Appeal in the important case of *Re A (Conjoined Twins)* refused to countenance the doctrine of double effect where the bad effect was felt by a party (the non-viable twin) who derived no benefit from the good effect. Since in our case G received no benefit from the good effect, it seems that the doctrine is of no help to H.

6. However, *Woollin* is not dependent on 'double effect' principles and it is possible that a jury might exercise their discretion to refuse to find intention in a case like this if our suggested interpretation of the ratio is correct. The majority in *Re A* considered that the *Woollin* principle meant that the doctors would intend the non-viable twin's death which they knew to be the inevitable result of performing the operation to separate the twins. (The remaining judge, Walker LJ, applied *Gillick* to hold that the bona fide exercise of their clinical judgment would negate the doctors' criminal intent.) If the majority's view were applied to our case, H would be held to have an intent to kill or cause GBH and thus the *mens rea* for murder. GBH was a virtually certain result of falling five storeys and the only feasible inference is that H foresaw that. However, the majority's view seems to presuppose that D's foresight of virtual certainty **was itself** intention (i.e., our first, rejected interpretation of *Woollin*) but our suggested ratio of *Woollin* (endorsed by *Matthews and Alleyne*) denies this and holds that a finding of intention in foresight of virtual certainty cases is left to the undefined discretion of the jury. It may be that this is just the kind of case where a jury would decline to find intention but nobody could be sure until the jury had pronounced in the actual case! This illustrates how unsatisfactory is the law's failure to define intention fully and to allow issues which are

properly matters of defence (excusing or justifying factors) to intrude upon and distort basic concepts defining prima facie liability.

Defences

7. Assuming that H is found to have the *mens rea* for murder, two possible defences suggest themselves, duress of circumstances and necessity.

Duress of circumstances

8. On the face of it, this established, excusatory defence fits this situation very well. H's will is overborne by the imperative of the circumstances. She is coerced by a fear of imminent death. She feels compelled to commit the 'crime' as the only way of avoiding death in a situation where a person of reasonable firmness might easily have acted in the same way. Unfortunately, the House of Lords in *Howe* has categorically held that the defence of duress is **never** available to a charge of murder. This kind of situation illustrates that the rule is too draconian and rigid. It is true that, at the time, the House was referring only to traditional duress by threats since duress of circumstances had not yet been 'invented', but, given its assimilation to duress by threats, there seems no reason to doubt that the same restriction will be applied to duress of circumstances. The Court of Appeal, obiter, in *Pommell* and *Abdul-Hussain* certainly thought so. It would be anomalous not to have the same rule for both forms of duress.

Necessity

9. Whereas duress is a claim that immediate danger of death or serious injury means that compliance with the law cannot reasonably be expected, necessity is a claim that a higher, competing value takes precedence over compliance with the law. The higher value to be achieved **justifies** the commission of the 'crime'. It is the right thing to do. That a general defence of necessity exists can no longer be doubted after the House of Lords' decisions in *F* v *West Berkshire Health Authority* and *R* v *Bournewood Community and Mental Health NHS Trust*. The doubt surrounds its scope and the conditions required for a successful plea. It is possible that it is confined to situations of medical intervention by qualified medical practitioners leaving all other 'necessity' situations to be brought under the head of duress of circumstances. That seems to be the currently

favoured view of the Court of Appeal (*Shayler*; *Quayle*) but the facts of our case illustrate why it would be unfortunate to confine the true necessity defence to being an exceptional, doctor's defence. It is submitted that the Court of Appeal's stance cannot be supported.

10. One immediate obstacle to a successful plea is the case of *Dudley and Stephens* which, in the eyes of the House of Lords in *Howe*, decided that the defence of necessity was not available on a charge of murder. Of course, the view in *Howe* was obiter since it concerned a case of duress by threats and it is possible to argue that *Dudley* was not a true necessity situation in that it was no more necessary for the cabin boy to be killed than any of the survivors. Unlike for duress, it could be said, therefore, that there is no clear, binding authority ruling out necessity in murder cases. Indeed a majority of the Court of Appeal in *Re A* decided that it was available in the very unusual circumstances of that case. For Brooke LJ, the key difference was that the innocent person who would die for the greater good was not the product of the defendant's choice as in *Dudley*, but had been 'self-designated for a very early death'. The **only** way to save the viable twin was to kill the non-viable twin. It might also be pointed out that the non-viable twin's dependence on the viable twin meant that the former was the **source** of the latter's difficulties whereas the innocent cabin boy in *Dudley* was no threat to his fellow crew and had nothing to do with their difficulties. Walker LJ agreed on the necessity point but, having found that the doctors would lack the necessary *mens rea* for murder, found it unnecessary to utilise the defence. One further difference also applicable in our case was that the defendants in *Dudley* were **aiming** to kill the cabin boy when they wielded the knife whereas it was not the doctors' purpose to kill the non-viable twin nor H's to kill G.

11. A similar distinction could be made in our case because again the victim 'chooses himself' and is the very source of the difficulty. As Smith & Hogan put it (p. 251), G was preventing H and the others 'from going where they had a right and most urgent need to go. He was, unwittingly, imperilling their lives.' The conditions adopted by Brooke LJ from *Stephen's Digest of Criminal Law* (1889) are clearly satisfied in our case: (a) H's action is needed to avoid the 'inevitable and irreparable evil' of several deaths; (b) H did no

more than was 'reasonably necessary' to achieve her purpose of saving herself and the others; and (c) the death caused was not 'disproportionate' to the several lives saved. (In this connection, it might be argued that the victim's position was not made significantly worse by H's action in that he was about to perish anyway *cf. Re A* where there was essentially no hope for the non-viable twin whatever happened.) Objectively (confirmed by the on the spot 'expert' judgement of the firefighter), it was the right thing to do and justified. It is one of those rare instances where interference with the bodily integrity—even their right to life—can be justified by necessity. *Re A* should be applied not *Dudley and Stephens*. It appears from *Re A* that, even though the innocent victim's life is at stake, his right to life under Art. 2 of the ECHR is not infringed. The failure in the Article to express a necessity exception does not matter because the Article only applies to cases where D's **purpose** is to kill and not *Woollin* non-purpose intention cases.

Conclusion

12. It would seem likely that H would escape conviction. Either the jury would refuse to 'find' intention from her foresight of virtual certainty or the courts would allow, in these very special circumstances clearly distinguishable from *Dudley*, a defence of necessity.

Question 9.2

Coward is of a rather nervous disposition and is in awe of Bully, who lives with him and has ill-treated him over a long period of time. One night Bully comes home from the pub after having had a violent argument with Hard. Bully tells Coward to 'burn out' Hard's house the next night 'because Hard will be away and the house empty'. In fact, Bully well knows that Hard will not be away and hopes that Hard will be seriously hurt.

Coward refuses but Bully threatens to 'spoil your good looks forever' and to reveal to Coward's employer that Coward is homosexual. Faced with these threats, Coward decides to set fire to Hard's house and does so in the dead of the next night, believing the house to be empty. The fire severely damages the house and its contents and Hard suffers serious burns and injuries in jumping through a glass window to escape.

Hard is taken unconscious to hospital where Dr Finlay gives him a life-saving blood transfusion despite protests from Hard's family that Hard is a Jehovah's Witness and would conscientiously object to any blood transfusion. When Hard recovers consciousness he is very angry with Dr Finlay for having given him the transfusion without permission.

Discuss the criminal liability, if any, of:

1. Coward for causing criminal damage by fire (arson) to Hard's property contrary to s. 1(1) and s. 1(3) of the Criminal Damage Act 1971.
2. Bully for causing grievous bodily harm to Hard with intent to do so contrary to s. 18 of the Offences Against the Person Act 1861.
3. Dr Finlay for assault occasioning actual bodily harm to Hard contrary to s. 47 of the Offences Against the Person Act 1861. You are required to assume that the blood transfusion did cause actual bodily harm to Hard.

Indicative Answer to 9.2

1. This question illustrates the importance of reading the rubric (i.e., the examiner's instructions) at the end of the question. Instead of leaving it to you to identify the offences which may have been committed by each of the protagonists, it defines and limits the discussion to one specified offence for each of the main characters. There is no point in discussing any other possible offences since the examiner has by design made such discussion irrelevant. No marks will be gained and valuable time will be lost.

Coward's liability

2. The first task would be to set out the statutory definition of criminal damage under s. 1(1) of the Criminal Damage Act 1971. The *actus reus* of destroying or damaging property belonging to another is clearly present and little time needs to be spent on establishing this or going into elaborate explanations of what constitutes 'damage' or 'property'. Equally there is no question of any circumstances suggesting a 'lawful excuse' so that it is unnecessary to dwell on that concept. It is evident that Coward deliberately set fire to the house and must have aimed to cause some damage to another's property. It follows that a simple statement of what is the mens rea (intention to

destroy or damage another's property or recklessness thereto) and why it is clear that Coward has it is all that is needed.

3. What is clear is that Coward seems to be acting under the pressure of threats and this is your 'signpost' to consider the defence of duress. Set out the basic requirements for a successful plea of duress: (i) threats (or what he reasonably believed to be threats) of death or serious injury; (ii) aimed at making Coward commit the 'crime' he did; and (iii) which actually impelled him to commit that 'crime' because he feared, with good reason, that the threats would otherwise be carried out; and (iv) which were such that a sober person of reasonable firmness might have succumbed to the threats and committed the crime (*Graham; Howe*). The task then is to elaborate on these elements using the case law to arrive at a statement of legal principle which is then applied to the given facts to conclude whether it can be established. Obviously you have to orient the discussion to those matters raised by the problem facts.

4. The courts have consistently emphasised that the defence cannot succeed unless death or serious harm is threatened (e.g., *DPP for NI* v *Lynch*; *Howe*). However, *Valderama-Vega* holds that lesser threats can be taken into account cumulatively with threats of death or serious harm provided D would not have committed the crime but for the latter threats. Here the threat to spoil Coward's good looks seems to constitute a threat of serious harm and the threat to disclose his homosexuality would be taken into account as adding to the duress so long as the threats of violence were a significant cause of the crime's commission.

5. It is evident that Bully's objective was to get Coward to commit the crime of arson ('the nominated offence') so that we are concerned with duress by threats rather than duress of circumstances (*Cole*). Further, there seems little doubt that Coward, in the light of his own timidity and the history of his relationship with Bully, genuinely and with good cause feared that the threats were serious and was actually impelled to commit the crime because of the threats of violence ('faced with these threats, Coward . . . '). The House of Lords in *Hasan* rejected the Court of Appeal case of *Martin (David)* [2000] 2 Cr App R 42 which contradicted the requirement laid down in *Graham* that D must have 'good cause to fear' that

the threats will be carried out. Therefore, Coward's belief that they would be carried out must be based on reasonable grounds. That should be no problem given the history of ill-treatment suffered at the hands of Bully.

6. The objective limb requires Coward's compulsion to be judged against the yardstick of the ordinary person of reasonable firmness—'an average member of the public; not a hero necessarily, not a coward, just an average person' (*Horne*). As with the analogous test in the defence of provocation, this calls into question what, if any, of Coward's characteristics should be given to the hypothetical ordinary person in judging how the latter might react to the threats. It appears that the ordinary person would be given Coward's age and sex and any other characteristics which might affect the gravity of the threat on Coward **but not** temperamental characteristics which bear on Coward's general ability to resist threats (*Horne*; *Hegarty*) unless these constitute a 'recognised medical impairment or psychiatric condition' (*Bowen*; *Antar*). It would seem that Coward's 'nervous disposition' falls into the last category so that it would be ignored for this purpose. Nonetheless, *Emery* (accepted as correct in *Hegarty*) suggests that the ordinary person would have to be regarded as having been subjected to the same history of ill-treatment and abuse as Coward. Thus the ordinary person originally of reasonable firmness may likewise have been cowed by persistent, violent abuse so as to be less able to resist the threats. However, *Bowen* suggests that the abuse must have led to 'recognised mental illness or psychiatric condition' before it can be taken into account. Presumably the ordinary person's resistance would also be influenced by the nature of the crime involved. They would be more likely to succumb to threats where the crime was, say, against property than if it involved serious violence against the person. Here Coward thinks there is no danger to persons but, although the point has yet to be decided, it may be that the test would be based on whether a reasonable person would have believed that the house was empty and that there was no danger to persons. It might depend on what checks Coward made to be sure the house was empty.

7. It is difficult to come to any firm conclusion on the facts but it is conceivable that Coward could satisfy the two-stage test for duress. However, a further difficulty for him is the

requirement to take advantage of any reasonably safe avenue of escape open to him prior to the commission of the crime (*Hasan; Gill; Hudson and Taylor*). On the face of it, Coward could have gone to the police instead of setting fire to the house. The fact that Coward lived with Bully and was under his domination would be factors for the jury to consider and they might conclude that effective protection by the police would not be possible long term (see *Hudson and Taylor*). However, *Hudson and Taylor* was criticised by the House of Lords in *Hasan* who thought that, unless the retribution for non-compliance with the threat would follow 'immediately or almost immediately', it would be very difficult to establish that there was no reasonable alternative but to commit the crime. That would suggest that unless the crime was to be committed straight away with no time to avoid it, the defence would be unlikely to succeed. That would be incredibly restrictive of the defence and would make it difficult for Coward to succeed here.

8. Unless the prosecution was able to convince the jury beyond reasonable doubt that Coward did not satisfy the requirements for duress, he would be acquitted of the criminal damage charge.

Bully's liability

[The issues raised by this part of the problem are covered in **Chapter 14** not **Chapter 9** and you should postpone consideration until you have studied **Chapter 14**.]

9. It is obvious that Bully has not physically performed the actions immediately causing harm to Hard and that would suggest that any liability would have to be as an accessory to a crime perpetrated by Coward. The difficulty is that Coward does not commit the only crime you are asked to consider, s. 18 of the Offences Against the Person Act 1861. In regard to the *actus reus*, Hard clearly suffers grievous bodily harm ('serious burns and injuries'—*Saunders*). Coward's setting fire to the house is the direct cause of the burns (probably themselves GBH) and Hard's action in jumping out of the window to escape would not break the chain of causation being reasonably foreseeable in the circumstances (*Roberts*). Thus all the resultant injuries would be caused by Coward. However, Coward believes the house to be empty and therefore does not possess either an intention to do GBH or an intention to resist the lawful

apprehension or detainer of any person. It follows that he does not commit a s. 18 offence. (Even if he had the *mens rea*, there would be a possible defence of duress as discussed above.)

10. Because of the derivative nature of accessorial liability, it is a fundamental principle that the principal offence was actually perpetrated by another. If the offence is not perpetrated, D cannot aid, abet, counsel or procure it (*Thornton* v *Mitchell*; *Loukes*). However, the courts have developed a number of exceptions to this principle. Thus if the perpetrator has a defence, say, of duress, his non-commission of the crime would not prevent the duressor from conviction as an accessory to it (*Bourne*). More recently the case of *Millward* has for the first time clearly extended the exceptions to embrace situations where the perpetrator does not commit the principal offence due to a lack of the requisite *mens rea*. For the exception to apply, it is essential that the perpetrator causes the *actus reus* of the principal offence (*Loukes*) and, in this case, as demonstrated above, Coward did. Although not decided by the courts, it is possible that the rule will be confined to accessories who procure the principal offence. All the cases, *Millward, Wheelhouse* and *DPP* v *K and B*, which have applied the principle to secure conviction have been 'procuring' cases. 'Procure', according to *Attorney-General's Reference (No. 1 of 1975)*, means 'to produce by endeavour'. It must be D's purpose that the perpetrator should commit the offence (or in the exceptional case under consideration, the actus reus of the offence) and D's conduct must bring about or cause its commission. The question here indicates that it was Bully's threats that led Coward to do the acts which caused the grievous bodily harm and that it was Bully's intention that such harm should be caused to Hard ('Bully…hopes that Hard will be seriously hurt'). On the *Millward* principle, therefore, Bully could be convicted of procuring the s. 18 offence.

11. An alternative route to conviction might be the innocent agency principle. The courts sometimes regard D as the perpetrator of the crime notwithstanding that another physically performs the *actus reus* of the crime. They seem prepared to do this where the physical performer is duped by D and does not have the *mens rea* for the crime. On the basis of *Cogan and Leak*, it could be argued that Coward's lack of *mens rea* in respect of the s. 18 offence would make him Bully's

innocent agent so that his actions in causing GBH would be regarded as Bully's actions. The view that Coward is Hard's innocent agent would be reinforced by the fact that the actions are forced on him by Hard's duress so that his acts are not the voluntary intervention of a human being and do not break the chain of causation between Hard's conduct and the resulting GBH. Since Bully clearly intended GBH to Hard, he could be convicted as the perpetrator or principal of the s. 18 offence.

Dr Finlay's liability

12. Section 47 requires an assault occasioning actual bodily harm. Here the question tells you to assume that Finlay caused actual bodily harm so that no discussion of that is needed. In terms of 'assault', you should explain that this is used in its general sense to embrace either technical assault or battery. Battery involves an intentional or reckless application of unlawful force to the victim's body and it is obvious that Finlay intentionally used force (no particular violence is needed) on Hard's body to administer the blood transfusion. The only issue is whether the force used in these circumstances is lawful.

13. Clearly Hard did not consent to the treatment as he was unconscious. Finlay's best hope would seem to lie in the defences of necessity or duress of circumstances. This might render his application of force lawful. The House of Lords in two civil cases, *F* v *West Berkshire Health Authority* and *Airedale NHS Trust* v *Bland*, has accepted that where a patient has made no decision and is incapable of making a decision about treatment which is urgently necessary (presumably to prevent death or serious injury) and which a reasonable doctor acting in the best interests of the patient might give, will not constitute a battery or other offence against the person. *Re T* takes an even more generous view in stating that it is the duty of doctors (and therefore presumably cannot involve them in criminal liability) to treat the patient in whatever way they consider, in the exercise of their clinical judgment, to be in the patient's best interests. Two of the judges further stated that the patient's next of kin or relatives do not have the right to refuse treatment (or consent to it) on behalf of an incapable patient. This was also the unanimous view of the Court of Appeal in the conjoined twins case of *Re A (Children)*.

14. In this situation, Finlay would seem not to commit the offence unless it could be established that Hard had made a clear decision before he became unconscious to refuse a blood transfusion in a life-threatening situation. Thus if Hard carried a card making such a wish clear (as do some religious objectors including the patient in the Canadian case of *Malette* v *Shulman*), Finlay would be bound to respect those wishes even if it was a matter of life and death. The law values a person's personal autonomy more highly than the imperative to preserve life and health. However, it would seem insufficient that Hard is known to Finlay to be a Jehovah's Witness whose creed forbids such treatment. Hard may not adhere to that particular tenet and, where there is any doubt as to what Hard would wish, Finlay cannot be faulted criminally for choosing to do what is necessary to keep the patient alive, even if this turns out to have been contrary to what the patient would have wanted. Indeed it could well be that Finlay would be under a legal duty to treat in this way. According to *Re T*, the protests of Hard's relatives would make no difference to Finlay's criminal liability.

15. Interestingly the situation would also fall within the parameters of the tests for the defence of duress of circumstances. Using the formulation in *Martin*, Finlay was 'impelled to act as he did, because as a result of what he reasonably believed to be the situation, he had good cause to fear that otherwise death or serious bodily harm would result;' and 'a sober person of reasonable firmness, sharing the characteristics of' Finlay (e.g., a doctor with his expertise) might have 'responded to that situation by acting as' Finlay did.

16. It would seem that Finlay would be acquitted unless the evidence proved that Hard had made an unequivocal choice not to have a blood transfusion even if this would cause his death. The evidence appearing in the question falls short of this.

Question 10.1

Discuss the criminal liability of Flash for **theft**, if any, in each of the following situations—

(a) Flash, an animal rights activist, broke into a research laboratory and released several dogs which were being forced to smoke cigarettes as part of a medical research project.

(b) Flash drove into a self-service petrol station, filled up with petrol and drove off without paying.

(c) Flash rented a car for one week from a car hire company. After four days, he decided to sell the car and pocket the proceeds. He drove it over to the local car auction and was standing in the queue to enter it into the auction, when he was arrested by the police.

Indicative Answer to 10.1

Introduction

1. The question is expressly confined to the offence of theft and therefore no marks are awarded for discussion of any other offence. **Stick to the question asked even though you think that there are more appropriate and obvious offences applicable to the situation**. Since it features in all three situations, it would be appropriate to give the basic statutory definition of theft in s. 1 of the Theft Act 1968. However, it would be a mistake to elaborate this definition generally, divorced from the context of the three situations. By discussing each element in the context of the concrete situation, you will find it much easier to ensure focus on what is relevant to the question. If the same point comes up in succeeding situations, you can just refer back to the previous discussion.

Situation (a)

2. The *actus reus* of theft is: 'appropriates property belonging to another'. There is no doubt that domesticated animals such as dogs constitute 'personal property' within the definition in s. 4(1). There is no question of these dogs being 'wild animals' so that s. 4(4) has no application. Since 'appropriates' has been interpreted by the House of Lords in *Morris*, *Gomez* and *Hinks* to mean an assumption of **any** of the rights of an owner, any physical handling of the dogs must be an appropriation. Even if they are not touched but merely released from the cages, it is likely that the courts would construe this as assuming a right of the owner. Obviously, at the time of the appropriations, the dogs 'belong to another' on all three of the alternatives given in s. 5(1)—they are in the 'possession' and also the 'control' of the owner of the laboratory, who has 'a proprietary right or interest' in them as their owner.

3. The *mens rea* is more difficult. If F's plan was that the dogs would be taken away and found new homes, there is no doubt that F intended to permanently deprive the research lab. However, if his intention was simply to publicise the way the dogs were treated and he anticipated that the dogs would soon be rounded up and returned to the lab, he would seem to lack an intention to permanently deprive, thus negating theft. The question would then arise as to whether s. 6(1) might apply to **deem** him to have such an intention. It would have to be established that he intended to treat the dogs as his own to dispose of regardless of the owner's rights. Arguably, this would be the case but possibly only if the dogs were to be let loose in circumstances where there was a significant risk that they might not be found by the owner.

4. The heart of the question is whether F acted 'dishonestly'. Section 2(1) of the Theft Act 1968 lists three situations where a person is **definitely not** dishonest but none seems to apply here. Even if F believed he had a **moral** right to take the dogs, it is unlikely that he believed he had a **legal** right to them as required by s. 2(1)(a). Neither s. 2(1)(b) nor s. 2(1)(c) is applicable here. It follows that the issue of dishonesty will be resolved in accordance with the definitions and tests developed in the case law. According to *Feely*, this is a question of fact for the jury who must judge it by the standards of 'ordinary, decent people'. After some inconsistent decisions, the test was modified by the Court of Appeal in *Ghosh* in situations where D claims that he did not regard his actions as dishonest. It is very likely that D would make such a claim here. The jury would first have to consider whether, having regard to D's subjective thoughts, beliefs and intentions, ordinary, law-abiding citizens would regard the conduct as dishonest. It is likely that this objective limb would be satisfied though, because each case is a question of fact for the jury, one could never be certain. The jury might have a big majority of animal lovers who thought the treatment of the dogs disgraceful and the actions of F entirely justified. Assuming the jury were to take the orthodox view that to deprive someone of his property which was being put to lawful use, however unpalatable that use might be, was dishonest, they would have to apply the second limb of the *Ghosh* test: did F realise that reasonable and honest people would regard his actions as

dishonest? It could well be the case that F believed that all 'ordinary, decent people' would applaud his actions, not condemn them as dishonest. It would seem that the more passionate and, indeed, extreme one's beliefs, the more likely one is to escape under the second limb of the *Ghosh* test! It seems that the issue turns on whether the prosecution could establish beyond reasonable doubt that F knew that people generally would regard him as dishonest. It should finally be noted that it is irrelevant that F does not act for gain or for his own benefit (s. 1(2)). He probably would be guilty of theft but it is not by any means certain.

Situation (b)

5. It is clear that the petrol is personal property within s. 4(1). When F operates the pump, he assumes a right of the owner over the petrol by taking control and possession of it. Thus he appropriates it. Whilst the petrol is in the pump, it clearly belongs to another. The station owner owns, possesses and controls it. However, it appears from *Edwards* v *Ddin*, that when the petrol is delivered into F's tank, the ownership, possession and control of it passes exclusively to F. Under s. 17 of the Sale of Goods Act 1979, ownership passes when the parties intend it to and, where this is unclear, s. 18 lays down rules to be applied in order to ascertain that intention. *Edwards* v *Ddin* holds that the parties' intention in a petrol station transaction is to pass ownership when the petrol is poured into the tank and 'irretrievably mixed' with the petrol already in the tank. The moment of appropriation seems therefore to be coincident with the transfer of ownership etc. to F. The implication of *Lawrence* v *MPC* and *Hinks* is that this is an appropriation of property belonging to another.

6. The key question therefore is whether F has the *mens rea* when he pours the petrol into the tank. There is no doubt that his intention is to permanently deprive the garage of its petrol—he intends to consume it. If he has no intention to pay from the outset, he must be dishonest at the moment of appropriation and commit theft. None of the provisions in s. 2 is applicable to this situation so that the *Feely* and *Ghosh* tests will apply. By the standards of ordinary, decent people, a simple intention to avoid payment would surely make F dishonest and render him guilty of theft. It was so held by the Court of Appeal in

McHugh (1976), a case on all fours with the situation posited.

7. On the other hand, if F initially intended to pay and was not acting dishonestly, he could not be guilty of theft when he filled up with petrol. He would not 'dishonestly' appropriate. If he subsequently became dishonest by deliberately deciding not to pay, he would 'appropriate' the petrol when he drove off. Section 3(1) specifically provides that where D 'has come by the property without stealing it [e.g., has 'honestly' appropriated it], any later assumption of a right to it by keeping or dealing with it as owner' amounts to an appropriation. If F was not initially dishonest, he came by the property without stealing it and, by driving off, he keeps it and deals with as owner. However, it is clear from *Edwards* v *Ddin* that such an appropriation would not be of property 'belonging to another' and could not be theft. At the time F dishonestly appropriates, he has exclusive possession and control and is the only person with any proprietary right or interest in it because the ownership had previously passed to him by virtue of the transaction, notwithstanding non-payment.

Situation (c)

8. There is no doubt that, as with all chattels, the car is personal property within s. 4(1). When F takes the car from the hire company, he assumes a right of the owner—the right to possess and control it for a week. The fact that it is with the consent of the owner makes no difference (*Gomez*; *Hinks*). At the moment of appropriation, the car belongs to another, the hire company which possesses, controls and owns it. In fact, the car always belongs to the company even after it parts with possession and control because it retains throughout a proprietary right or interest (i.e., the ownership) in the car. It follows that an appropriation at any point in time must be of property belonging to another.

9. If, at the time of hiring, F had never intended to return the car at the end of the hiring period, he would certainly be dishonest under the tests in *Feely* and *Ghosh* previously discussed. Section 2 would have no application and ordinary decent people would regard it as dishonest to intend to deceive and defraud the company in this way. No doubt F would also regard it as dishonest or at least realise that reasonable and honest people would. It would be on all fours with *Atakpu*. In

Atakpu, there was an intention to permanently deprive because the accused planned to disguise the identity of the vehicles by forging new documentation, repainting, etc. If F intended to sell the vehicle undisguised, he might argue that since he knew the car would eventually be traced and returned to the hire company, he did not intend to permanently deprive. In that case, the courts would apply s. 6(1) to deem him to have an intent to permanently deprive because, in purporting to sell the car, he intended to treat it 'as his own to dispose of regardless of' the company's rights. Consequently if he was dishonest at the outset, he would commit theft the moment he picked it up and it would not matter that he subsequently changed his mind and returned it at the end of the hire period.

10. However, the question implies that F only became dishonest when he decided to sell the car four days into the hire period. His initial appropriation was honest and therefore not theft. Thus it is necessary to find a fresh appropriation of property belonging to another occurring at a time when he was dishonest. According to s. 3, where F has come by the property without stealing it, a later assumption of a right to the car by keeping or dealing with it as owner will do. Clearly if F had actually sold the car or even just entered it for sale, he would have been dealing with it as owner. *Pitham and Hehl* held that simply to offer goods for sale was an appropriation.

11. Nonetheless, here, F had not yet offered it for sale. He was on the way to do so but, at the time of arrest, he had done nothing that he was not entitled to do under the hiring contract. The key question is whether this could be described as 'keeping or dealing with it as owner' as seems to be required by s. 3(1) before 'a later assumption' amounts to an appropriation. A mere **decision** to assume an owner's right is not itself an assumption of that right. Professor Smith argues that when a company hires out the car, it divides up the proprietary rights in the car between itself and the hirer. When the hirer drives anywhere in, say, the UK during the hire period, he is not assuming any rights of the owner but simply exercising the right to use the car which, for the week of the hire, is vested in him, not the company. One could reinforce this argument by saying that, so long as F is not departing from the terms of the hire, he cannot be 'keeping it as owner' or 'dealing with it as owner'. The difficulty with the argument is that *Hinks* (HL) recently held that a

person can steal property by receiving it as a fully valid gift. If receiving what is given to you so that you become the unchallengeable owner of it under the civil law is an appropriation, why is not continuing to use the car that has been hired to you? The distinction which might be made is that, in *Hinks*, D was dishonest at the outset so that the latter part of s. 3(1) ('later assumption of rights') had no relevance. Where dishonesty occurs only after the initial appropriation, the wording of s. 3(1) appears to require some action of D which indicates that he is actually keeping or dealing with the property as owner, not just preparing to do that. It is by no means clear that the courts would follow Smith's argument and the distinction suggested but that will determine whether F has committed theft or not. They might well take the simplistic view evident in *Gomez* and *Hinks* and hold that once F decided to sell, he was henceforth 'keeping it as owner' even though this may not yet have manifested itself in any overt wrongful usage or dealing.

Question 10.2

Twitch, a keen bird-watching student, orders a pair of binoculars from Kwikmail plc, a mail order company which guarantees same day despatch of all orders sent with payment. Twitch sends with his order a cheque for the appropriate amount, notwithstanding that he knows there is no money in his bank account.

Two days later Twitch receives the binoculars from Kwikmail plc. After trying out the binoculars Twitch decides they are not suitable for his purpose and sells them to Crow.

The next day Twitch receives a letter from Kwikmail plc informing him that his bank has refused to pay the cheque and demanding the return of the binoculars.

Discuss the criminal liability, if any, of Twitch for **theft**.

Would your answer differ if the letter from Kwikmail plc demanding the return of the binoculars had been received before Crow bought the binoculars?

Indicative Answer to 10.2

1. Theft questions always seem to create problems for students and it is essential to adopt a systematic approach examining each element of the

definition of theft in turn. This is a particularly difficult question.

2. By s. 1(1) of the Theft Act 1968, D commits theft if he 'dishonestly appropriates property belonging to another with the intention of permanently depriving the other of it'. For the *actus reus* D must appropriate property which at the moment of appropriation belongs to another. Under s. 4(1), 'property' includes all personal property and it is clear that the binoculars are property within this definition. It is equally clear that at the start of the transaction they 'belong to another', Kwikmail plc, which has a 'proprietary right or interest in it' as well as 'possession or control of it' (s. 5(1)). However, when the binoculars are despatched, it would appear that they cease to be in the possession or control of Kwikmail (though it is sometimes argued that the Royal Mail is simply the agent of the sender) and it is possible that Kwikmail, at that point, transfers the ownership to Twitch so that it ceases to have any 'proprietary right or interest' in them. If this is so, at some point in the transaction, the binoculars cease to belong to another and belong exclusively to Twitch.

3. In such a case, the crucial question is whether any dishonest appropriation occurs before or only after the transfer of ownership. If it is the latter, the dishonest appropriation is **not** of property belonging to another and therefore not theft unless the extending provisions in s. 5(2)–(4) deem it to 'belong to another'. Does the ownership transfer to Twitch and if so, when? The rules of civil law provide that ownership passes if and when the parties to the transaction intend it to. This might be expressed in the terms of the contract, e.g., Kwikmail may have stipulated that ownership should not transfer until cheques have been cashed and full payment received. More often nothing is said and it is left to the courts to deduce the parties' intention from the nature of the transaction. Thus they have held that in a petrol station transaction, the intention is to transfer ownership of the petrol as it goes into the customer's tank (*Edwards* v *Ddin*), whereas in a normal shop or supermarket sale the intention is to pass ownership in the goods only when payment is made (*Davies* v *Leighton*). If the parties' intention cannot be ascertained, the matter is governed by s. 18 of the Sale of Goods Act 1979 which would here provide that ownership in the binoculars would pass when they were

'unconditionally appropriated' to the sale to Twitch. Presumably this would at the latest be when they were posted to Twitch. Therefore unless the courts were to apply *Davies* v *Leighton* and imply an intention not to pass ownership until unconditional payment, the ownership would pass to Twitch on posting.

4. Did Twitch appropriate the binoculars and if so, when? Section 3(1) defines 'appropriates' as 'any assumption of the rights of the owner'. This has been interpreted in the broadest possible way by the House of Lords. *Morris* held that the phrase meant the assumption of **any one** of the owner's rights and was, in this respect, approved, obiter, by *Gomez*. It appears from *Gomez* (adopting *Lawrence* v *MPC* and disapproving *Morris* on this point) that the fact that the owner consents to D assuming his rights does not prevent there being an appropriation. Twitch would thus appropriate the binoculars on receipt notwithstanding that Kwikmail had 'presented' him with ownership and possession. This is reinforced by the House of Lords' decision in *Hinks* where even receipt of a fully valid gift was held to be an appropriation. The difficulty is that, as indicated in the preceding paragraph, this appropriation may not be of property belonging to another and so not theft. Of course, if ownership did not transfer to Twitch, his appropriation would clearly be of property belonging to another since Kwikmail would retain its 'proprietary right or interest' throughout.

5. Is there any earlier appropriation? It is certainly possible to appropriate property without any physical dealing with it (*Pitham and Hehl*). In the civil case of *Dobson* v *General Accident Insurance Corporation plc* D agreed to buy a ring over the telephone. Parker LJ thought that, even if the ownership passed as soon as the contract to buy was concluded on the telephone without D having been near the ring, 'the result would be that the making of the contract constituted the appropriation. It was by that act that the rogue assumed the rights of an owner and at that time the property did belong to the plaintiff.' If this is correct, Twitch would by analogy appropriate at the very moment the transfer of ownership occurred on the posting of the goods and *Lawrence* v *MPC* and *Hinks* establish that where the appropriation and transfer of ownership are coincident, there is an appropriation of property belonging to another. *Gomez* did not consider

the *Dobson* point but, given the tenor of the judgments, it would probably have approved Parker LJ's view. Again the precise point is not considered in *Hinks* though a possible interpretation is that receipt of ownership is itself an appropriation.

6. If that view is wrong and there is no appropriation until the binoculars are delivered to Twitch, can s. 5(4) be utilised to deem the property still to belong to Kwikmail even if the ownership has passed to Twitch? It is clear that Twitch got the binoculars as a result of Kwikmail's mistake that the cheque would be met. The key question is whether he 'is under an obligation to make restoration (in whole or in part) of the property or its proceeds or of the value thereof'. Obligation means a **legal** not a mere moral obligation (*Gilks*). It would appear that, even if Twitch was dishonest, there is a valid contract which is voidable for misrepresentation. However, unless and until the contract is avoided (i.e., rescinded) by Kwikmail, Twitch is under no obligation to 'restore' the binoculars to Kwikmail. It could be argued that, if he is acting dishonestly, his fraudulent misrepresentation amounts to the tort of deceit and puts him under an immediate obligation to restore the **value** of the binoculars, in which case s. 5(4) would apply irrespective of whether Kwikmail rescinds the contract. That argument has never been considered by the courts. In this case, provided Crow was an innocent purchaser for value, the sale to him would destroy Kwikmail's right to rescind and its letter demanding the return of the binoculars would have come too late to effect rescission and impose an obligation to restore the binoculars. Therefore if rescission is necessary before an obligation arises in these circumstances, s. 5(4) would not assist the prosecution.

7. If Kwikmail's letter of rescission had been received by Twitch prior to the sale to Crow, it would have been effective to avoid the mail order contract and immediately put Twitch under an obligation to restore the binoculars to Kwikmail. At the moment of rescission, the binoculars would once more 'belong to another'—Kwikmail—by virtue of s. 5(4). In fact, it is questionable whether s. 5(4) is needed because if the contract is rescinded, the ownership in the goods reverts to the seller who would then have 'a proprietary right or interest' in them within s. 5(1)! Either way, any dishonest

appropriation subsequent to the rescission would be of property belonging to another. Section 3(1) specifically provides that where D 'has come by the property (innocently or not) without stealing it, any later assumption of a right to it by keeping or dealing with it as owner' is an appropriation. Clearly in 'selling' the binoculars, Twitch is dealing with them as owner and thus appropriating property which at that time once more 'belongs to another'.

8. The final pieces in the jigsaw are whether, at the time he appropriated property belonging to Kwikmail, Twitch acted dishonestly and with an intention to permanently deprive Kwikmail of the binoculars. There being no evidence to the contrary, it is plain that, when he ordered the binoculars, Twitch intended to keep them and permanently deprive Kwikmail of them and equally when he sold them to Crow. There is no need to have recourse to s. 6.

9. Dishonesty is more difficult. None of the situations defined in s. 2(1) seems applicable and Twitch's conduct must be judged in accordance with the general tests laid down by the case law, notably *Feely* and *Ghosh*. The matter is ultimately a question of fact for the jury who must, however, 'apply the current standards of ordinary decent people' (*Feely*). *Ghosh* adds that D must also realise that ordinary people would regard the conduct as dishonest. If D knew that the bank would dishonour the cheque, there can be little doubt that his conduct would be dishonest. Equally if he was convinced that the bank would honour the cheque (e.g., agreed overdraft, credit of salary expected), he would not be dishonest when he ordered the goods. If he realised there was a significant risk that the cheque would not be honoured, it is likely, on the basis of *McIvor*, that he would be dishonest in deliberately taking a risk that Kwikmail might not get paid.

10. If he was not initially dishonest, it would seem that he could not be convicted of theft. If he was initially dishonest, it would seem that he could be convicted of theft only if Parker LJ's suggestion in *Dobson* was adopted.

11. In the alternative scenario where Kwikmail rescinds the contract **before** the sale to Crow, Twitch would be guilty of theft where he was dishonest initially, even if Parker LJ's suggestion is incorrect, because of his later appropriation after rescission (see above). If he was not dishonest initially, he might escape liability thanks

to the operation of s. 3(2). If Twitch acted 'in good faith' in connection with the transfer for value, s. 3(2) provides that any later assumption of rights he believed himself to be acquiring on the transfer cannot be theft. Therefore, if he believed the cheque would be met, even a dishonest dealing with Kwikmail's property after he has discovered that the cheque has bounced and the contract has been rescinded, cannot be theft.

Question 12.1

Cain, who is short of money, decides on a plan to take his father's video recorder and sell it. Having supposedly gone to the cinema one evening, Cain secretly returns home knowing that his parents would by then have gone out to play bingo.

He enters the house, takes the video recorder and drives with it to a public house where he persuades the barmaid, Phoebe, to buy it for £50.

Subsequently Phoebe overhears a policeman, investigating the recorder's disappearance, questioning the landlord of the public house about whether anyone had been trying to sell a recorder in his pub.

Phoebe, then suspecting for the first time that the recorder she had bought might be the one to which the policeman was referring, sells it for £50 to Aesop.

Discuss the criminal liability, if any, of Cain and Phoebe.

Indicative Answer to 12.1

Cain's liability

Theft

1. Theft is committed by someone who dishonestly appropriates property belonging to another with the intention of permanently depriving the other of it (s. 1 of the Theft Act 1968). According to s. 3(1), 'any assumption of the rights of an owner amounts to an appropriation'. When Cain takes the video, he clearly assumes the rights of the owner, his father, and appropriates the video. The video is personal property and therefore within the definition of 'property' under s. 4(1). The property at all times belongs to another under s. 5(1) since Cain's father has 'a proprietary right or interest' in it throughout. It seems that, at the moment of

appropriation, Cain intended that his father should be permanently deprived of the video because his plan was to sell it to raise money. There is little doubt that his actions would be found to be dishonest by a jury. He did not have any of the beliefs defined as negativing dishonesty by s. 2 and using the general case law test set out in *Feely* 1973, CA, it would be dishonest according to 'the standards of ordinary decent people'. It would seem unnecessary to invoke the *Ghosh* test because Cain would likewise surely regard it as dishonest himself. If by some chance, this were not so, he would surely realise that people generally would regard it as dishonest which would be enough to establish dishonesty (*Ghosh* 1982, CA). The conclusion is that he would certainly be guilty of theft.

Burglary

2. Burglary takes two forms but both require proof that D entered a building or part of a building as a trespasser. The crucial issue in this case is whether Cain entered the house 'as a trespasser'. The facts of the question do not state who owns the house and it is possible that Cain is the owner in which case there could be no question of his being a trespasser. Burglary would be ruled out. However, the more likely scenario is that the house belongs to his parents and that suggests an analogy with *Jones and Smith* 1976, CA, where the situation was similar. D had impliedly been given by his father a general permission to enter his father's home. D claimed that this extended to any purpose D might have. However, the Court of Appeal rejected that claim and held that, however general the permission, it could not extend to entry for the purposes of theft. D had entered his father's home as a trespasser. It may be possible to distinguish *Jones and Smith* on the basis that D did not there live in his father's house whereas here it is described as Cain's 'home'. It appears therefore that Cain lived there with his parents. In *Collins* 1972, CA, a girl living with her parents was held to have authority to give permission to a stranger to enter their home (even though it may well be that the parents would have disapproved of the purpose of that entry—sexual intercourse with their daughter). If this is correct, it would seem strange if any entry by a member of the family was itself a trespass. It is submitted that it should not be held to be a trespass even in a case like the instant, there being no policy reason to extend

the scope of burglary to cover such a situation. Where D is living at the premises, it lacks the quality of an 'invasion' of the property against which it is the proper role of burglary to protect.

3. However, if the courts refused to distinguish *Jones and Smith*, there would be a further requirement of *mens rea* in relation to being a trespasser. *Collins* held that D must know he is or (recklessness) might be a trespasser. As *Jones and Smith* put it, in a case like this, D must enter 'knowing he is entering in excess of the permission... or being reckless as to whether he is... Providing the facts are known to the accused which enable him to realise that he is acting in excess of the permission given or that he is acting recklessly as to whether he exceeds that permission, then that is sufficient for the jury to decide that he is in fact a trespasser.' It is debatable whether Cain, in this case would realise that he might be **entering** as a trespasser.

4. If he did knowingly or recklessly enter as a trespasser, he would commit burglary under s. 9(1)(a) immediately he entered because he had an intent to steal within the building. Equally he would commit burglary under s. 9(1)(b) immediately he appropriated, and thus stole, the video in the building. Since, as Cain well knows, the building is a 'dwelling', a conviction for burglary would carry here a higher maximum sentence by virtue of s. 9(3)(a).

Phoebe's liability

Handling stolen goods

5. By s. 22 of the Theft Act 1968 'a person handles stolen goods if (otherwise than in the course of the stealing) knowing or believing them to be stolen goods he dishonestly receives the goods, dishonestly undertakes or assists in their retention, removal, disposal or realisation by or for the benefit of another person, or if he arranges to do so.' When Phoebe took possession of the video on buying it, she clearly 'received' it outside the course of the initial stealing (which ended long before Cain reached the pub). As established above, Cain clearly stole the video which was therefore 'stolen goods' (s. 24). Although she caused the *actus reus* of handling, it is clear that she lacked the *mens rea* for, at that stage, she neither knew nor believed the video to be stolen nor was she dishonest. Her suspicions were aroused only later when she overheard the policeman.

6. Would she commit the offence when she sold the video to Aesop? It is clear that, otherwise than in the course of the initial stealing, she 'undertook the realisation' of the stolen video since 'realisation' is 'exchanging goods for money' (*Bloxham* 1982, HL). However, this must be done 'by or for the benefit of another'. The realisation was done **by** Phoebe not another and *Bloxham* holds that it would only be done 'for the benefit of' someone other than the seller if the seller was acting as the other's agent in the transaction. It is not enough that another—for example, the buyer—incidentally benefits from D's realisation. The same would apply to a charge of 'undertaking the disposal'.

7. Even if the *actus reus* was present, Phoebe may lack the appropriate *mens rea*. She must know or believe that the goods are stolen and be acting dishonestly. She does not appear to have actual knowledge that the video is stolen: she is not 'told by someone with first-hand knowledge' (*Hall* 1985, CA). She suspects that the video is stolen but time and time again the Court of Appeal has stressed that believing the goods **might be** stolen (suspicion) is not the same as believing the goods **are** stolen and it is the latter that is required (*Griffiths* 1974, CA). According to *Forsyth* 1997, CA, 'belief is the mental acceptance of a fact as true or existing' and seems to require that Phoebe had no significant doubt that the video was stolen. Even a belief that the video is probably stolen is not in itself enough (*Reader* 1977, CA). It is doubtful if Phoebe has a sufficiently positive belief. However, it would seem that simple suspicion that the goods are stolen would render her dishonest, but dishonesty is only one element of the *mens rea*.

Theft

8. Since Phoebe does not appear to be guilty of handling, can she be convicted of theft? Section 3(1) of the Theft Act 1968 provides that where D has 'come by the property (innocently or not) without stealing it, any later assumption of a right to it by keeping or dealing with it as owner' is an appropriation. It is clear that Phoebe's selling of the video is such a later assumption and would appear to satisfy the remaining ingredients of theft. However, she would be protected from liability by s. 3(2) which provides that a later assumption of rights which a purchaser for value in good faith believed herself to be acquiring in

her purchase cannot, 'by reason of any defect in the transferor's [Cain's here] title, amount to theft of the property.'

Fraud

9. Perhaps the best chance of conviction lies with an offence under s. 1 of the Fraud Act 2006. This can be committed by the simple means of making a 'false representation' (s. 2). It appears that Phoebe impliedly represented to Aesop that she was entitled to sell the video. She therefore made a representation of fact by conduct, expressly covered by s. 2(3). That representation was 'untrue or misleading' and Phoebe knew that it was 'or might be untrue or misleading' as required by s. 2(2) because she realised that the video might be stolen. The final requirements relate to *mens rea*. Phoebe must (a) make the false representation **dishonestly** and (b) **intend** by making the representation (i) to make a gain for herself or another or (ii) to cause loss to another or expose another to a risk of loss (s. 2(1)). It seems that she did intend to make a gain for herself by enabling the sale of the property and that her actions would be viewed as dishonest. Notice that, unlike under the replaced offence of obtaining property by deception, there is no need to prove that Aesop was fooled by this representation. Even if he assumed the video was stolen, Phoebe could still be convicted of fraud. (This assumes that she did not disclose the fact to Aesop because in that case she would obviously not be making any representation that it was hers to sell.) It is also necessary to point out that, by virtue of *Gomez* 1993, HL, she would also commit theft of the money, notwithstanding that Aesop presented her with the ownership.

Cain and handling

10. Cain could not be guilty of handling stolen goods because his undertaking of the video's retention and subsequent realisation and disposal was not 'by or for the benefit of another' (see 6 above).

Question 14.1

Stan and Ollie decide to steal antiques from Lord Wooster's country mansion. Stan buys a gun from Winchester, who knows Stan to be a violent criminal. Before the raid, Ollie discovers that Stan intends to take a gun and he tells Stan that he is not going ahead. Stan threatens to inform Ollie's wife of the affair Ollie is having with another woman unless Ollie participates. Ollie goes ahead because of these threats but obtains from Stan a promise that, should they encounter anyone, he will not use the gun except to frighten.

The two break into the mansion. As they are leaving the house, they are challenged by Jeeves, Lord Wooster's butler. Stan pulls out his gun and deliberately shoots Jeeves dead. Ollie shouts, 'That's another fine mess you've got me into, Stan' and they rush to escape.

Discuss the criminal liability, if any, of Stan, Ollie and Winchester for the death of Jeeves.

Indicative Answer to 14.1

Introduction

1. This question again illustrates the importance of reading the rubric which limits the discussion to liability for Jeeves' death. The simplest approach is to deal with each character in turn starting with the principal offender.

Stan's liability

2. The obvious possibility is murder and this should alert you to avoid a detailed discussion of the offence. The question tells you that Stan 'deliberately shoots Jeeves dead'. Thus there is no difficulty in establishing that he caused death and equally that he intended to kill or at least cause grievous bodily harm (*Moloney*). There is absolutely no need to get involved in detail about the meaning of 'intention' or 'causation.' You can conclude very quickly that Stan is guilty of murder.

Ollie's liability

3. It is clear that Stan and Ollie embark on a joint unlawful enterprise with 'a shared common intention' to burgle Wooster's mansion (*Petters and Parfitt*). Both will be liable for any crimes committed by the other which are within the scope of the common purpose. In view of Ollie's stipulation that the gun should be used only to frighten, Stan's deliberate shooting of Jeeves is clearly outside the scope of the common design and a deliberate departure from it. Unfortunately for Ollie this does not necessarily mean that he

escapes liability for murder. It appears that if he foresaw the murder 'as a possible incident of the common unlawful enterprise and...with such foresight...participated in the enterprise', he would be an accessory to and guilty of murder. This principle was recently put beyond any doubt by the House of Lords in the consolidated appeals of *Powell*; *English*. Thus if Ollie realised there was a possibility that Stan might renege on his promise not to use the gun other than to frighten and, if necessary, use it to shoot someone with the *mens rea* for murder (i.e., intending to kill or cause GBH), then the act of shooting with intent to kill or cause GBH and the consequent death will be regarded as the responsibility of all knowing participants. It is impossible to say whether Ollie realised this but if he knew the gun was loaded with live ammunition, a jury would be likely to conclude he did contemplate the possibility and find him guilty of murder.

4. If Ollie did not contemplate the possibility of shooting with the *mens rea* for murder or 'genuinely dismissed it as altogether [a] negligible' risk (*Powell*), he would not be guilty of murder but would he be guilty of manslaughter? On principle, he should not because Stan's act of intentionally shooting to kill or cause GBH was a deliberate departure from the common purpose and neither authorised nor foreseen by Ollie (*Davies* v *DPP*; *Wan and Chan*). There is a line of Court of Appeal cases including *Reid* and *Stewart and Schofield* which would dispute this principle and argue that a jury would be entitled to conclude as a matter of fact that Stan's acts were still within the 'course' of the joint enterprise notwithstanding that Ollie did not even contemplate the possibility of killing with the *mens rea* for murder! If this were so, Ollie would be convicted of manslaughter on the basis that he contemplated the possibility of an 'accidental' killing by an unlawful and dangerous act (using a loaded gun to frighten). However, it is difficult to see how an act deliberately going against what has been agreed as the common design and not foreseen could be within the scope of the joint enterprise. It is submitted that, in the terms of *Powell*, shooting with intent to kill or cause GBH is 'fundamentally different' to using even a loaded gun merely to threaten without shooting, so that Ollie would have no liability for the death if he contemplated only the latter. Oddly neither *Wan and Chan* nor *Stewart and Schofield* was

referred to in *Powell*. The cases of *Gilmour*, *Day* and *D* provide little help to the prosecution for they are clearly distinguishable in that Ollie did not here contemplate the 'very deed' which was done. He did not envisage that Stan might deliberately fire the gun. As was emphasised in *Attorney-General's Reference (No. 3 of 2004)*, if the act done (shooting to kill) was fundamentally different from any act contemplated as a significant possibility by Ollie (using the gun to frighten—even to the point of firing it to frighten), Ollie is not responsible for the death.

Winchester's liability

5. It appears that Winchester is not a participant in the joint enterprise because he lacks the shared common purpose of Stan and Ollie to burgle the mansion (*Petters and Parfitt*). It follows that the ordinary principles of accessorial liability govern his position and none of the special extending rules (if any!) applicable to joint enterprise affect him (though it is debatable whether that makes any difference to his liability on these facts).

6. Did Winchester aid, abet, counsel or procure the murder of Jeeves by Stan so as to make him liable for murder by virtue of s. 8 of the Accessories and Abettors Act 1861? 'Aiding' requires that the accessory gives assistance to the perpetrator to commit the crime. It is well established that this includes the provision before the crime of an article for use in the crime (*NCB* v *Gamble*). The supply of the gun by Winchester would constitute the *actus reus* and 'aid' the murder by Stan.

7. A major obstacle to Winchester's liability is establishing that he had the requisite *mens rea*. Although the *mens rea* is often stated to be an intention to assist the commission of the crime, it does not seem to be necessary to establish that the accessory desired the crime to be committed with his assistance. 'Even though he regretted the plan [to commit the crime] or indeed was horrified by it', he would have the *mens rea* if he intended to do the acts of assistance knowing that they were capable of assisting the perpetrator to commit the crime (*DPP for NI* v *Lynch*; *NCB* v *Gamble*). Although there are some authorities which run counter to this suggesting that the accessory must want the offence to be committed to be liable (*Fretwell*; *Gillick* v *West Norfolk Area Health Authority*), it is submitted that they do not

currently represent the law. *Fretwell* is a nineteenth-century case and *Gillick* a civil case dealing primarily with other issues. The recent Court of Appeal case of *Bryce* does insist on the necessity for 'an intention to assist (and not to hinder or obstruct) the perpetrator in acts which the accessory knows are steps taken by the perpetrator towards the commission of the offence.' It is not clear what precisely this means but it probably only makes a difference where an accessory does the acts with a positive intention to hinder or obstruct the perpetrator in his commission of the crime. In any event, it appears that Winchester, even if he is indifferent to what Stan does with the gun and is motivated purely by monetary gain, does not intend to hinder the crime and, if he knows what Stan is planning (see below), he intentionally assists him in acts (going armed) which he 'knows are steps taken … towards the commission of the crime'.

8. Winchester also needs *mens rea* in relation to Stan's crime. If Winchester were a participant in the joint enterprise, that would mean that he must be aware of the possibility that Stan might shoot with an intent to kill or cause GBH. *Powell* did not discuss the position of accessories who, like Winchester, were not participants in a joint enterprise and left it unclear as to whether mere contemplation by them of the possibility of murder at the time of giving assistance would suffice for conviction. Some authorities suggested that foresight of mere possibility suffices (*J.F. Alford Transport Ltd*; *Carter* v *Richardson*) whilst others suggested that, as a minimum, D must foresee or, at least, believe that the principal **will** (as opposed to **may**) perform the *actus reus* with the requisite *mens rea* (*Bainbridge*). Although it could be said to widen the scope of liability to an unacceptable degree, it is submitted that the courts now would require proof only that Winchester foresaw that Stan **might** shoot someone with intent to kill or cause GBH, for him to be an accessory to the murder that took place. This was the line taken by the Court of Appeal in *Reardon* and now *Bryce*. In that respect the rule for joint enterprise participants applies equally to all accessories.

9. If Winchester thought only that Stan might accidentally kill when using the gun to frighten, it is possible that the courts might convict of manslaughter even though Stan was guilty of murder (though again there is a lack of certainty as to how the rules applied differ, if at all, from the joint enterprise principles enunciated in *Powell*). However, the probable outcome would be that shooting with murderous intent would be classed as fundamentally different from an 'accidental' shooting (even where the discharge of the gun was deliberate) so that Winchester would not be responsible at all for the killing. It must be said that the decision on whether an act is fundamentally different is a question for the jury in each individual case and it could not be said with certainty what they would find in a case like this (*Attorney-General's Reference (No. 3 of 2004)*; *D*).

10. It is clear from *Bainbridge* and *DPP for NI* v *Maxwell* that it is not necessary for Winchester to have knowledge of the precise details of the crime, e.g., when, where or even the identity of the victim. Although knowledge that some criminal conduct is planned is insufficient, as long as he knows the type of crime to be committed or contemplates the crime committed as one of several possible crimes, he will be liable. Only if he contemplated at the time he supplied the gun that Stan might well murder someone with it, could Winchester be an accessory to murder.

Question 15.1

Assume that Parliament has recently made it an offence 'to use or permit to be used any land for the conduct of any car boot sale without a licence'.

Crooks Limited, a company which specialises in car boot sales, instructs Sharp, its area manager, to organise a sale on Lord Fauntleroy's land. Sharp reaches agreement with Lord Fauntleroy and applies to the local authority for a licence.

As the date approaches, Sharp telephones the local authority and is told by Duff, a clerk in the relevant department, that the licence for the sale has been granted but that owing to staff shortages it may not be possible to get a letter of confirmation to him in time. Duff assures him that he need not worry because the sale is licensed. In fact Duff has made a mistake and the local authority has refused a licence for the sale.

The sale goes ahead with Sharp thinking that a licence has been granted.

Discuss the criminal liability, if any, of Crooks Limited and Sharp for 'using the land for a car boot sale without a licence', Lord Fauntleroy for 'permitting it to be so used' and of Duff for aiding and abetting Sharp.

Indicative Answer to 15.1

Sharp's liability

1. It appears that Sharp, the actual organiser, physically 'uses' the land for the unlicensed car boot sale and there seems no doubt that the *actus reus* is present. Sharp, however, genuinely and, quite possibly, reasonably believes the sale to be licensed and so exhibits no *mens rea* or even negligence in relation to that element of the *actus reus*. He could, therefore, be guilty only if the offence was held to be strict liability in relation to the sale being 'without a licence'.

2. The statute is stated to be recent and it is assumed that there is no previous case law interpreting the provision. Since fundamentally the court is endeavouring to ascertain the will of the legislature as expressed in the words used in the statute, one might expect that if there is no reference to *mens rea* in the words, the conclusion would be that Parliament's intention was to dispense with it. However, it is clear from *Sweet* v *Parsley* 1969, HL and more recently *B* v *DPP* 2000, HL that there is in such cases always a presumption that Parliament nonetheless intended *mens rea* to be required. According to the Privy Council in *Gammon (Hong Kong) Ltd* v *Attorney-General of Hong Kong* 1984 rejecting statements to the contrary in *Champ* 1982, CA, this presumption applies even to offences which are regulatory in nature as opposed to 'truly criminal'. Despite this, it is undoubtedly the case that the courts will be much more willing to find the presumption rebutted where the offence is regulatory or quasi-criminal rather than truly criminal.

3. How should this offence be classified? Regulatory offences 'are not criminal in any real sense, but are acts which in the public interest are prohibited under a penalty' (*Sherras* v *de Rutzen* 1895, approved by the House of Lords in *Alphacell Ltd* v *Woodward* 1972). Such offences tend to regulate a particular activity, often carried on for commercial profit, which involves risk to public health, safety or welfare and in which citizens or companies have a choice whether or not to participate. The provision in question seems clearly of this type and it follows that

the presumption of *mens rea* is likely to be quite easily rebutted.

4. The courts would examine closely the statutory context for any clues as to Parliament's intention. For instance, if other offences created by other sections or subsections of the statute expressly contained *mens rea* words, this would tend to suggest they were intentionally omitted from the offence in issue (*Pharmaceutical Society of Great Britain* v *Storkwain Ltd* 1985, HL) though this is certainly not conclusive (*B* v *DPP*). Equally the court may gain assistance from interpretations of precursor legislation or analogous statutes in other areas using a similar formula. 'Using' offences have often been held to be strict liability (see, e.g., *James & Son Ltd* v *Smee* 1954, DC). In general, the heavier the penalty available, the more reluctant the courts will be to impose strict liability. In this case, there is little information about the statutory context and it is impossible to be certain which way the court would decide. Although *B* v *DPP* stressed that the presumption of *mens rea* could be displaced only if it was a 'necessary implication' that that was what Parliament intended, looking at the general run of cases since *Sweet* v *Parsley*, the court might well feel justified in imposing strict liability to promote observance of the regulation. Even since *B* v *DPP*, the Court of Appeal has not shown any less inclination to find strict liability in relation to regulatory offences, even where these carry a penalty of up to two years' imprisonment (*Muhamad*; *Matudi*). *Muhamad* proposed a slightly different test arguing that the strength of the presumption of *mens rea* varies from strong to weak according to the seriousness of the offence, in terms of penalty and stigma. Obviously the question gives little information on the various factors which might influence their decision so that it is impossible to come to any categorical conclusion. If it was not held to be strict liability, Sharp would be not guilty.

5. If it was held to be strict liability, Sharp would seem to be liable. Is it a defence to have relied (let us assume, reasonably) on the advice of Duff, the Council employee? The Privy Council in *Yip Chiu-Cheung* v *R* 1994 held that the Government (and presumably *a fortiori* a local council/official) has no power to authorise a breach of the law. Equally there is no question of the state, whose official's conduct or erroneous advice causes D to commit an offence, being 'estopped'

from prosecuting the offence (*Cambridgeshire and Isle of Ely County Council* v *Rust* 1972, DC). Sharp would thus be convicted.

Duff's liability

6. If Sharp is not guilty, then Duff would not be an accessory because there would be no principal offence to aid and abet. If the offence is one of strict liability and Sharp is guilty, it is clear that Duff's erroneous advice would have encouraged the offence's commission in fact. Duff would therefore have caused the *actus reus* of aiding, abetting, counselling or procuring. However, he would appear to lack the necessary *mens rea* of an intention to encourage the commission of the offence knowing 'the essential matters which constitute that offence. He need not actually know an offence has been committed, because he may not know that the facts constitute an offence and ignorance of the law is not a defence' (*Johnson* v *Youden* 1950, DC). The 'essential matters' mean all the elements of the *actus reus* and in this case that means knowledge that the sale has no licence. This applies even to an offence of strict liability. Since Duff, albeit negligently, believes a licence has been granted, he cannot be convicted as an accessory to Sharp's offence. The case is on all fours with *Callow* v *Tillstone* 1900 where a vet who negligently certified tainted meat as sound did not aid and abet the butcher (who quite properly relied on his advice) to commit the strict liability offence of exposing unsound meat for sale, because the vet did not know it was unsound.

Crooks Ltd's liability

Personal liability

7. A limited company is a separate person in law distinct from the humans who work for it and manage it. It can be held criminally liable for most offences in situations where it is itself deemed to have physically performed the *actus reus* of the offence with any requisite *mens rea*. This will only occur in respect of the acts and state of mind of certain senior controlling officers of the company who are 'identified' with the company and regarded as the embodiment of the company. Their acts are the company's acts; their state of mind the company's state of mind. It is clear from *Tesco Supermarkets Ltd* v *Nattrass* 1971,

HL that only very senior management will be viewed as the 'directing mind and will' of the company and it would appear that Sharp is unlikely to be sufficiently senior or have sufficient executive discretion to be identified with the company in this way. His acts in 'using' the land would not therefore be the company's acts and the company would not be personally liable. However, this does not preclude it from being vicariously liable for Sharp's acts.

8. Doubt has been cast on the universal applicability of the identification principle by the Privy Council in *Meridian Global Funds Management Asia Ltd* v *Securities Commission*. Their view was that the courts can and sometimes must 'fashion a special rule of attribution … tailored as it always must be to the terms and policies' of the particular offence. If that view were taken here, it might well be decided that the actions of a person with authority within the company structure to enter into the contract to use the land would be attributed to the company whether or not he represented the 'directing mind and will' of the company. Sharp might well be such a person in this case so that recourse to vicarious liability would be unnecessary.

Vicarious liability

9. The two main ways in which a person may be vicariously liable where another has physically performed the *actus reus* are under (a) the delegation principle and (b) the extensive construction principle. Although the delegation principle is well established, the courts have in recent years been reluctant to extend its scope. It is unlikely to be found that Crooks Ltd has delegated to Sharp in this case, assuming, as in the *Tesco* case, there is in place a proper system of supervision and management of Sharp and fellow employees (*Vane* v *Yiannopolous* 1964, HL). A far more likely avenue to vicarious liability is the extensive construction principle where the courts stretch the meaning of the main verb defining the offence so as to attribute an act physically performed by an employee to his employer (*Coppen* v *Moore (No. 2)* 1898). A number of offences employing the word 'use' have been extensively construed in this way (see, e.g., *Griffiths* v *Studebakers Ltd* 1924). It is submitted that the employee Sharp's physical use of the land in the course of his employment would be regarded as use by the employer, Crooks Ltd (*cf. National Rivers' Authority* v *Alfred McAlpine*

Homes East Ltd 1994, DC). It should be pointed out that under the extensive construction principle only the *actus reus* can be imputed to the employer in this way, not the employee's state of mind. It follows that, unlike the delegation principle, it can only operate if the offence in question is one of strict liability requiring no *mens rea*. As indicated above, it is quite possible that this offence would be held to be strict liability making Sharp personally liable and Crooks Ltd vicariously liable.

Lord Fauntleroy's liability

10. It appears that Lord Fauntleroy is unaware that the sale does not have a licence. The general (but not invariable) approach of the courts to offences of 'permitting' is to hold that *mens rea* is implicit. Permitting is a conscious action requiring knowledge of the happening of what is alleged to be permitted. In *James & Son Ltd* v *Smee* 1954, DC, D could not be convicted of 'permitting' a lorry to be used with defective brakes when it was unaware of the defect. More recently, the Divisional Court in *DPP* v *Kellet* 1994 was 'tentatively' of the view that D could not 'allow' a dangerous dog to be in a public place whilst unmuzzled unless she knew the dog was able to get out of the house in that state. Although there are some authorities to the contrary, e.g., *Lyons* v *May* 1947; *Chief Constable of Norfolk* v *Fisher* 1992, DC (both cases of 'permitting' a vehicle to be used whilst uninsured), it is submitted that the better view is that Lord Fauntleroy could not be convicted of 'permitting' his land to be used for the unlicensed sale unless he was aware there was (or at the very least might be) no licence.

11. It is submitted that the ambiguous House of Lords' decision in *Vehicle Inspectorate* v *Nuttall* 1999 should not undermine this conclusion because two judges thought 'permitting' offences would always require a fault element of **at least** recklessness, i.e., realising the use might be unlicensed or not caring whether it was or not. Assuming Lord Fauntleroy honestly believed there was a licence, he would not exhibit the necessary fault. It is true that two judges thought that, in **some** 'permitting' offences, it could go as low as negligence, i.e., an **unreasonable** belief would not negate the requisite fault. However, the final judge purported to agree with both the opposing views! In addition it is probable that the courts would construe this particular 'permitting'

offence in its strict sense of 'authorising' which would require either knowledge or subjective recklessness as to the **unlicensed** use. The better view remains that recklessness in the sense of realisation of the risk of there being no licence would be required.

Question 16.1

Esme married Osama in 1997. In 2003, Osama left Esme and travelled to Iraq to fight on behalf of a militant organisation which was opposing an American-led coalition. The organisation's forces suffered many casualties under sustained aerial bombardment.

Ayub, who had also fought for the organisation in Iraq but who hated Osama, found his way back to England. He told Esme and his friend, Rashid, who he knew had always loved Esme, that he had witnessed Osama's death during a bombing raid, although he knew that Osama had been captured alive by American forces. Rashid, believing Osama was dead, comforted Esme and eventually both he and Ayub persuaded her to 'marry' him. Esme and Rashid arrived at the Registry Office and the Registrar had just begun the ceremony of 'marriage' when Osama's brother arrived with the news that Osama was alive and in American captivity. The ceremony was abandoned.

Discuss the criminal liability, if any, of (a) Esme for attempted bigamy and (b) Ayub, Rashid and Esme for conspiracy to commit bigamy.

Section 57 of the Offences Against the Person Act 1861 defines bigamy and provides:

> Whosoever, being married, shall marry any other person during the life of the former husband or wife...shall be guilty of felony...Provided, that nothing in this section contained shall extend...to any person marrying a second time whose husband or wife shall have been continually absent from such person for the space of seven years then last past, and shall not have been known by such person to be living within that time...

Indicative Answer to 16.1

Esme's liability for attempt

1. The inchoate offence of attempt requires proof of both an *actus reus* and a *mens rea*. The *actus*

reus necessitates that D did 'an act which is more than merely preparatory to the commission of the offence' (s. 1(1) of the Criminal Attempts Act 1981). No guidance is given by the Act on when mere preparation ends and the *actus reus* of attempt begins. It is a question of fact for the jury to decide in each case though the trial judge can rule that the acts in question are not, as a matter of law, reasonably capable of amounting to an attempt (s. 4(3) of the 1981 Act). Such elucidation as there is must be gleaned from an examination of the case law.

2. It is reasonably clear that if D has done the last act dependent on him to secure the commission of the crime, he has performed the *actus reus* of attempt. Equally the fact that he has not, does not preclude an attempt. *Gullefer*, an authority for both of those propositions, requires D to have 'embarked upon the crime proper [or] the actual commission of the offence'. In the more homely phrase, D must have been 'on the job'. According to the Court of Appeal in *Geddes* and *Tosti*, the test is whether D 'has done an act which shows that he has actually tried to commit the offence . . . or whether he has only got ready or put himself in a position or equipped himself to do so.'

3. In the instant case, although Esme had not performed the last act dependent on her (saying, 'I do'), she is likely to be viewed by a jury as having been 'on the job' and embarked on the crime proper when the ceremony began. The facts can be distinguished from *Campbell* where there could be no attempt to rob a Post Office unless D had entered that Post Office and unlike *Geddes* she was not simply lying in wait. The 'job' had started. It is submitted that Esme had gone beyond 'mere preparation' and committed the *actus reus* of the attempt to commit bigamy.

4. The *mens rea* required for an attempted conviction is an 'intent to commit an offence' contrary to s. 57 of the Offences Against the Person Act 1861. At first sight this would seem to require that Esme's aim or purpose was to marry bigamously. This seems to imply that she knew or at least believed that all the circumstances prescribed by the *actus reus* were present. Since she was convinced of Osama's demise, her purpose would seem to have been to marry whilst free to do so. Her intent was to do acts which did not

constitute the offence and she would therefore lack the requisite *mens rea* for the attempt. On principle, it should not matter that the full offence requires a lesser *mens rea* or even no *mens rea* in relation to some or all of the elements of the *actus reus*. Thus in the case, if Esme had completed the marriage ceremony, she might well have committed bigamy notwithstanding that she genuinely believed Osama to be dead. According to *Tolson* and *Gould*, only if D's belief that she is free to marry is based on reasonable grounds would it negate liability for bigamy. It could well be the case that it is not reasonable to rely on the testimony of one person, Ayub, however plausible.

5. The strict view that attempt always requires D to aim to do the prohibited acts with full knowledge of all of those circumstances forming part of the *actus reus*, whatever the completed offence requires, was rejected by the Court of Appeal in *Khan*. It was held that the *mens rea* for attempted rape was the same as the *mens rea* for actual rape, namely an intent to have sexual intercourse knowing or being reckless as to the fact that the woman does not consent. It does not have to be D's purpose to have intercourse with a non-consenting woman ('knowing' she does not consent) but rather with a woman who might not be consenting ('being reckless' that she does not consent). [Note the ingredients of rape have been significantly altered by s.1 of the Sexual Offences Act 2003.] *Khan* at least required subjective recklessness as to (i.e., awareness of) the relevant circumstance. *Attorney-General's Reference (No. 3 of 1992)*, perhaps unwittingly, extends the principle to offences which require only negligence or even no fault (i.e., strict liability) in relation to the vital circumstance. D 'must be in one of the states of mind required for the commission of the full offence and did [sic] his best . . . to supply what was missing from the completion of the offence.' If this is applied to Esme's situation, she would simply require (i) whatever state of mind suffices for the full offence and (ii) an intention to supply the physical element missing from the complete offence. If she **unreasonably** believes Osama is dead, she would be guilty of attempt under that rule. In relation to (i) she intends to go through the second ceremony without reasonably believing that she is free to marry. That would

suffice as the *mens rea* for the full offence. Of course, if her belief is **reasonable**, she would not have the state of mind required for the full offence (*Tolson*). In relation to (ii), the missing physical element from the offence is the going through the ceremony of 'marriage' (because if that were done all the elements of the *actus reus* of bigamy would be present—Esme is still married) and Esme intends to supply it. Whether this principle will be applied in the future remains to be seen but it would be an unwelcome extension of the scope of attempt and run counter to the Law Commission's formulation. It is not sensible to say that Esme is attempting to commit bigamy in these circumstances whether or not her belief in Osama's death is reasonable.

The liability of the parties for conspiracy

6. Statutory conspiracy is in essence an agreement by two or more parties to commit a crime and is committed as soon as the agreement is concluded irrespective of what, if anything, is actually done in pursuance of it. It is clear from s. 2(1) of the Criminal Law Act 1977 that 'an intended victim' of an offence cannot be guilty of conspiring to commit it. It is unlikely that Esme here is such 'an intended victim' because that term is probably reserved for those whom the offence is designed to protect. Since she alone would be the alleged bigamist, it is difficult to see how she could be the 'intended victim'. If she were, it follows from s. 2(2) that Rashid could not be convicted of conspiracy either, if the only other party to the plan was Esme, the 'intended victim'. The position of Ayub would therefore be crucial to Ron's liability.

7. According to s. 1(1) Rashid, Esme and Ayub (or any two of them, assuming Esme is not an 'intended victim') must have agreed that 'a course of conduct shall be pursued which, if the agreement is carried out in accordance with their intentions...will necessarily amount to or involve the commission of' bigamy by any or all of them. There are several difficulties in the way of satisfying this definition. Firstly, although 'course of conduct' must sensibly include not only the physical acts agreed to be performed but also any consequences intended to result from those acts, it appears from s. 1(2) that it only

includes those circumstances that the parties 'intend or know...will exist at the time when the conduct constituting the offence is to take place.' The problem here is that, in contrast to Ayub, neither Esme nor Rashid 'intends or knows' or even believes that Esme will still be married at the time of the ceremony. On the contrary they believe that she will be free to marry. Therefore the course of conduct agreed is not the 'marriage' of someone already married and so will not necessarily result in the commission of the offence if carried out in accordance with their intentions. The fact that the completed crime does not require *mens rea* in respect of Esme's marital status is irrelevant to conspiracy (*Harmer* and *Ali* disapproving *Sakavickas*).

8. Although Ayub clearly did 'know' (which presumably includes 'believe') that Esme would still be married, he would not be guilty of conspiracy either. Before *Anderson*, HL, it was thought that there had to be at least two parties to the agreement who intended it to be carried through in the circumstances making it criminal, otherwise no offence would result from carrying out their **mutual** intentions. Here there is no **mutual** intention for a **bigamous** union. However, *Anderson* asserts that it is unnecessary to prove 'an intention on the part of each conspirator that the criminal offence...should in fact be committed.' The House of Lords did not indicate whether this principle would apply where only one or even none of the parties to the agreement intended it to be carried out in the circumstances of criminality but it is submitted that the courts would confine *Anderson* to situations where at least two parties to the agreement are intent on carrying it out even if others are not. This is made more likely by the Privy Council's decision in *Yip Chiu-Cheung* v *R* which seems inconsistent with *Anderson*. In the Privy Council's view, 'The crime of conspiracy requires an agreement between two or more persons to commit an unlawful act with the intention of carrying it out. It is the intention to carry out the crime that constitutes the necessary *mens rea* for the offence.' Although the latter case concerned a common law conspiracy and is in any event persuasive only, it is submitted that it should and would be applied to statutory conspiracy at least in the situation arising here where there is only one person intending the agreement to be carried

out in circumstances of criminality. It would follow that conspiracy would be ruled out for all three on this ground unless *Anderson* were extended to cover this situation. Put simply, what Ayub intends to be carried out is quite different from what Esme and Rashid intend to be carried out.

9. In conclusion, it is submitted that, on these facts, none of the parties commits any conspiracy.

■ INDEX

A

Abandoned property, theft 295
Abetting 424–5
Absolute offences *see* **State of affairs offences**
Abstracting electricity 364
Accessories
  actus reus
    abetting 424–5
    aiding 423–5
    assisting after offence 427–34
    counselling 424–5
    procuring 424–5
  as victims 451
  entrapment 453–5
  mens rea 434–41
  perpetrators
    different crimes 431
    perpetrator has defence 432
    perpetrator lacks *mens rea* 432–4
    perpetrators exempt 431
  withdrawal 451–3
Accomplices *see* **Accessories**
Acts 22–3
Actual bodily harm
  actus reus 106–8
  mens rea 108–9
  reform proposals 109
Actus reus
  see also **Causation**
  accessories
    abetting 424–5
    aiding 423–5
    assisting after offence 427–34
    counselling 424–5
    procuring 424–5
  acts 22–3
  actual bodily harm 106–8
  assault 88–91
  assault by penetration 129
  attempts 480–5
  automatism 208
  battery 92–4
  blackmail 373–6
  causing persons to engage in sexual activity without consent 133

circumstances 20–1
coincidence with *mens rea* 43–4
consequences 19–20
criminal damage 388–94
elements 19
fraud
  by abuse of position 341–2
  by failure to disclose information 339–40
  by false representation 332–6
  making off without payment 347–50
  obtaining services dishonestly 344–5
grievous bodily harm 110–14
handling stolen goods 379–86
homicide 140–3
incitement 511–13
mistake 226–8
not sufficient alone 18
omissions
  assumption of responsibility 25–7
  common law duty 24
  contract 28–9
  dangerous situations created by defendant 28–9
  extent of liability 23–4
  family relationships 25
  medical treatment 27–8
  statutory provisions 23–4
overview 17–18
perpetrators 420–2
rape 123–7
removal of articles from public places 362–3
sexual assault 130–2
state of affairs offences 29
statutory conspiracy 495–6
summary 45–6
theft
  appropriation 277–90
  'belonging to another' 294–305
  obligation to retain and deal in a particular way 305–8
  property 291–4 308–10
voluntary conduct 21–2

wounding with intent 116
Age *see* **Children**
Agent provocateur 453–5
Aggravated offences
  burglary 371–3
  criminal damage 395–7
  taking a conveyance without consent 361–2
Aiding 423–5
Animals, theft 294
Appeals 5–7
Appropriation
  bank accounts 287–9
  cheques 287–9
  companies 290
  consent 279–81
  dishonesty 297–9
  indefeasible ownership 281–3
  innocent acquisition 286–7
  instantaneous or continuing 283–4
  later assumption of rights 285
  meaning 277–8
  physical interference 287
Arson 398
Assault
  see also **Actual bodily harm;**
    Grievous bodily harm;
    Sexual offences;
    Wounding with intent
  actus reus 88–91
  mens rea 91–2
Assisting after offence 427–34
Assumption of responsibility, liability for omissions 25–7
Attempts
  actus reus 480–5
  mens rea 485–9
  scope 479–80
  summary 515–16
Automatism
  insanity 210–11
  loss of control 208–10
  reform proposals 215
  self-induced 213–15
  specific intent 211–13
  summary 242–3
  voluntary act 208

B

Bank accounts
appropriation 287–9
theft 308–10
Basic intent 63
drugs 219–20
intoxication 219–20
Battery
actus reus 92–4
consent 96–104
mens rea 104–6
necessity 95–6
parental chastisement 94–5
reform proposals 106
self-defence 94
unlawful force 94
Belief *see* **Knowledge and belief**
Blackmail
actus reus 373–6
mens rea 376–8
summary 400–1
Borrowing, theft 316–17
Buildings, burglary 369–70
Burden of proof
diminished
responsibility 170–1
general principles 8–12
insanity 203–4
Burglary
aggravated 371–3
buildings 369–70
entry 365–6
mens rea 370–1
scope 364–5
summary 399–400
trespassers 366–9

C

Capacity
children 195–6
summary 205–6
Causation
abnormal conditions 38–40
actual bodily harm 107
egg-shell skull principle 38–40
factual causation 31
fraud 327–8
homicide 142
intervening events
general principles 33–4
natural events 34
involuntary manslaughter 177
legal causation 31–2

reform proposals 42
scope 30
substantial and operational
cause 40–2
substantial effect 32–3
summary 46
third party intervention
general principles 34–5
involuntary acts 36–7
medical treatment 37
regulatory offences 35–6
substantial and operational
cause 37
victim's own actions 37–8
**Causing persons to engage in
sexual activity without
consent** 133
Chastisement 84–5
Cheques
appropriation 287–9
theft 308–10, 320
Children
capacity 195–6
consent to battery 97
parental chastisement 94–5
rape 123–4
sexual offences 195–6
victims under sixteen 134
victims under thirteen 134
Circumstances
actus reus 20–1
attempts 486–8
duress 259–63, 271–2
intention 75
knowledge and belief 75–6
mens rea 49
negligence 77–8
recklessness 76–7
subjectivity 75
Common assault *see* **Assault**
Common law duties *see*
**Assumption of
responsibility**
Companies
appropriation 290
corporate liability
conceptual problems 474–5
directors and executives
473–4
exceptions 469–70
identification principle 466–9
scope 464–6
Conduct *see* **Actus reus**
Consent
appropriation 279–81

assault by penetration 129
battery 96–104
causing persons to engage in
sexual activity without
consent 133
criminal damage 391
dishonesty 311
drugs 221–2
grievous bodily
harm 113–14
intoxication 221–2
medical treatment 264–5
rape
actus reus 123–4
mens rea 128–9
reasonable mistake 230–2
taking a conveyance without
aggravated 361–2
definitions 357–60
mens rea 360–1
Consequences
actus reus 19–20
attempts 485–6
Conspiracy
see also **Joint enterprises**
acquittal of
co-conspirators 494
agreements 492–4
common law
defrauding 503–7
morality and decency 508–9
rationale 509–10
scope 491–2
statutory offence
course of conduct 495–6
impossibility 501
intention 496–501
territorial jurisdiction 501–2
summary 516–17
Contract
liability for omissions 28–9
Conveyances *see* **Taking a
conveyance without**
Corporate liability
conceptual problems 474–5
directors and executives 473–4
exceptions 469–70
identification principle 466–9
scope 464–6
summary 476
Counselling 424–5
Crime
classification of offences 4
defined 2
reform proposals 12–14

role of substantive law 2–4
summary 15
Criminal damage
actus reus 388–94
mens rea 394
summary 402

D

Decency, common law
conspiracy 508–9
Deception *see* **Fraud**
Deception offences
rape 125
Defences
automatism
insanity 210–11
loss of control 208–10
reform proposals 215
self-induced 213–15
specific intent 211–13
summary 242–3
voluntary act 208
capacity
children 195–6
summary 206
consent 100
diminished responsibility
abnormality of mind 167–8
burden of proof 170–1
defined 166–7
reform proposals 171–2
specified causes 168–9
substantial impairment
169–70
drugs
basic intent 219–20
basic rules 216
insanity 216
scope 215–16
specific intent 217–18
summary 243–4
duress
of circumstances 259–63,
271–2
flow chart 272
overview 247–9
by threats 249–50, 271
insanity
burden of proof 203
defined 198–203
mens rea 203
reform proposals 204–5
scope and rationale 196–7
summary 205–6

summary trials 203
intoxication
basic intent 219–20
basic rules 216
insanity 216
scope 215–16
specific intent 217–18
summary 243–4
marital coercion 269
mens rea 208
mistake
actus reus 226–8
as to civil law 232
as to criminal law 232–3
effects 230
negligence crimes 228–9
reasonable belief of consent
or duress 230–2
strict liability 229–30
summary 244
necessity
balance of harm 263–4
general defence 267–8
limited application 268–9
medical treatment 264–5
murder 265–7
overview 247–9
statutory exclusions 268
summary 272
negligence 74
overview 193–5
perpetrators and
accessories 432
provocation
mistake 152
momentary loss of
control 150, 152–5
reform proposals 164–6
requirements 150–64
self-induced 152
self-defence
mistake 240–1
property 238–9
reasonable force 234–8
reform proposals 242
scope and effect 239–40
summary 244–5
superior orders 270
Delegation principle, vicarious
liability 463–4
Diminished responsibility
abnormality of
mind 167–8
burden of proof 170–1
defined 166–7

reform proposals 171–2
specified causes 168–9
substantial impairment 169–70
Directors, personal liability 473–4
Dishonesty
appropriation 297–9
fraud by false
representation 338–9
handling stolen goods 381–2
mens rea 80
mistake 299–304
theft 310–16
Doctors *see* **Medical treatment**
Drugs
automatism 213–15
basic intent 219–20
consent 221–2
defences
basic intent 219–20
basic rules 216
insanity 216
scope 215–16
specific intent 217–18
duress 221–2
medical treatment 223–4
non-dangerous drug
taking 224–5
provocation 160–2, 221–2
reform proposals 225–6
self-defence 220–1
specific intent 217–18
summary 243–4
Duress
see also **Blackmail**
by threats
association with
criminals 256–7
death or serious injury 253–4
escape opportunities 254–5
imminent danger 255–6
murder 257–9
standard test 250–3
summary 271
third parties 254
causing persons to engage in
sexual activity without
consent 133
of circumstances 259–63,
271–2
consent to battery 97–8
drugs 221–2
flow chart 273
intoxication 221–2
marital coercion 269
overview 247–9

rape 124
reasonable mistake 230–2
superior orders 270

E
Egg-shell skull principle 38–40
Electricity (abstracting) 364
Employees, corporate
    liability 464–6
Entrapment 453–5
Equitable interests, theft 296–7
Executives, personal
    liability 473–4
**Extensive construction
    principle,** vicarious
    liability 460–3

F
Family relationships
    liability for omissions 25
    marital coercion 269
    parental chastisement 94–5
Fault *see Mens rea*
Firearms, aggravated
        burglary 371–3
Force, robbery 355–7
Foresight, joint enterprises 443–4,
        445–6
Fraud
    by abuse of position
        actus reus 341–2
        mens rea 342
    by failure to disclose information
        actus reus 339–40
        mens rea 340
    by false representation
        actus reus 332–6
        mens rea 336–9
    consent to battery 98–100
    conspiracy 503–7
    making off without
        payment
        actus reus 347–50
        mens rea 350–1
    obtaining services
        dishonestly 343–7
    recent reform 325
    summary
        new offences 352–4
        repealed offences 351–2
    summary of old law
        causation 327–8
        concept of deception 326–7

defects in law 331
overlapping offences 326
specific offences 328–31

G
Grievous bodily harm
    actus reus 110–14
    consent 113–14
    intention for murder 148–9
    mens rea 115
    reform proposals 116

H
Handling stolen goods
    actus reus 379–86
    mens rea 386–8
    summary 401
Homicide
    actus reus 140–3
    causation 142
    infanticide 105
    involuntary manslaughter
        corporate liability 470–3
        gross negligence 173–80
        reckless manslaughter 180–1
        scope 172–3
        summary 191
        unlawful acts 181–9
    murder
        mens rea 143–9
        sentencing 142–3
        summary 189–90
    scope 139–40
    unlawful killing 140–1
    victims 141–2
    voluntary manslaughter
        diminished
            responsibility 166–72
        provocation 150–66
        scope 149–50
        suicide pacts 172
        summary 190–1
Human body, theft 292–3
Human rights
    burden of proof 8–9
    entrapment 454

I
Identification principle,
        corporate liability 466–9
Impossibility
    attempts 489–90
    incitement 514–15

statutory conspiracy 501
Inchoate offences
    attempts
        actus reus 480–5
        mens rea 485–9
        scope 479–80
        summary 515–16
    conspiracy
        acquittal of co-
            conspirators 494
        agreements 492–4
        defrauding 503–7
        morality and decency 508–9
        rationale 509–10
        scope 491–2
        statutory offence 495–502
        summary 516–17
    incitement
        actus reus 511–13
        impossibility 514–15
        mens rea 513–14
        summary 517
    scope and rationale 477–8
Incitement
    actus reus 511–13
    impossibility 514–15
    mens rea 513–14
    summary 517
Infanticide 105
Innocent agents 422
Insanity
    see also **Diminished
        responsibility**
    automatism 210–11
    burden of proof 203–4
    defined
        defect of reason 201
        disease of mind 198–201
        knowing nature and quality
            of act 202–3
        medical diagnosis
            distinguished 198
    drugs 216
    intoxication 216
    mens rea 203
    reform proposals 204–5
    scope and rationale 196–7
    summary 205–6
    summary trials 203
Intangibles, theft 292
Intention
    accessories 434–41
    actual bodily harm 108–9
    assault 91
    attempts 488–9

automatism 211–13
basic intent 63
battery 104–6
blackmail 376–8
certain outcome of prohibited
    act 52–4
circumstances 75
grievous bodily harm 115
involuntary manslaughter 172
motive compared 58–62
murder 143–9
offences other than
    murder 58
probable outcome of prohibited
    act 48–51
rape 127–8
sexual assault 130–2
specific intent 63
state of mind 50
statutory conspiracy 496–501
theft
    borrowing 316–17
    cheques 320
    conditional deprivation 321
    conditional transfers 319
    disposal as owner 317–19
    permanent deprivation 316
ulterior intent 62
unlawful act
    manslaughter 181–2
wounding with intent 116–17
Intervening events
general principles 33–4
natural events 34
third parties
    general principles 34–5
    involuntary acts 36–7
    medical treatment 37
    regulatory offences 35–6
    substantial and operational
        cause 37
    victim's own actions 37–8
Intoxication
automatism 213–15
basic intent 219–20
consent 221–2
defences
    basic intent 219–20
    basic rules 216
    insanity 216
    scope 215–16
    specific intent 217–18
duress 221–2
non-dangerous drug
    taking 224–5

provocation 160–2, 221–2
reform proposals 225–6
self-defence 220–1
specific intent 217–18
spiked drinks 223–4
statutory defences 221–2
summary 243–4
Involuntary acts
see also **Automatism**
third party intervention 36–7
Involuntary manslaughter
causation 177
corporate liability 470–3
duty of care 177
gross negligence 173–80
objectively gross breach 177–80
reckless manslaughter 180–1
scope 172–3
summary 191
unlawful acts
    causation 185–7
    dangerous acts 184–5
    directed at another 187–8
    intention 181–2
    reform proposals 188
    unlawfulness 182–4

J

Joint enterprises
see also **Conspiracy**
accidental departure from
        common purpose 449–51
assistance and encouragement
        beforehand 444
deliberate departure from
        common purpose 442–3
foresight 443–4
lesser offences 446–9
murder 443–4
unforeseen acts 445–6
Jurisdiction
statutory conspiracy 501–2
Justification

K

Knowledge and belief
accessories 434–41
circumstances 75–6
dishonesty 310–11

L

Land, theft 293

M

Malice
mens rea 79
murder 143–4
transferred 82–3
Malicious wounding *see*
        Grievous bodily harm
Manslaughter *see* also
        **Involuntary
        manslaughter; Voluntary
        manslaughter**
corporate liability 470–3
Marital coercion 269
Medical treatment
consent 264–5
consent to battery 96–7
intoxication 223–4
liability for omissions 27–8
necessity 264–5
third party intervention 37
Menaces, blackmail 375–6
Mens rea
accessories 434–41
actual bodily harm 108–9
aggravated criminal
        damage 396–7
assault 91–2
assault by penetration 129
attempts 485–9
automatism 211–13
battery 104–6
blackmail 376–8
burglary 371–3
causing persons to engage in
        sexual activity without
        consent 133
circumstances 74–5
coincidence with *actus
        reus* 43–4
conspiracy to defraud 506–7
corporate liability 468
criminal damage 394
defences generally 208
delegation principle 463
dishonesty 80
fault 79
fraud
    by abuse of position 342
    by failure to disclose
        information 340
    by false representation
        336–9
    making off without
        payment 350–1

obtaining services
    dishonestly 345–6
grievous bodily harm 115
handling stolen goods 386–8
incitement 513–14
indifference 78–9
insanity 203
intention 50–2
    basic intent 63
    certain outcome of
        prohibited act 52–4
    circumstances 75
    conceptual issues 50–2
    motive irrelevant 58–62
    offences other than
        murder 58
    probable outcome of
        prohibited act 54–8
    specific intent 63
    ulterior intent 62
knowledge and belief
    circumstances 75–6
malice 79
    transferred 82–3
mistake 80–2
murder 143–9
negligence
    circumstances 77–8
    recklessness distinguished 74
    scope 72–4
    strict liability 74
objectivity 75
perpetrators and
    accessories 432–4
rape 127–9
recklessness
    circumstances 76–7
    meaning 63–4
    negligence distinguished 74
    objectivity 66–71
    reform proposals 71
    subjectivity 65–6, 71–2
    unjustifiable risk taking 64–5
removal of articles from public
    places 363
sexual assault 130–2
state of mind 47–50
strict liability 406–8
subjectivity
    circumstances 74–5
summary 84–6
taking a conveyance without
    consent 360–1
theft
    dishonesty 310–16

intention to permanently
    deprive 316–21
wilfulness 76
wounding with intent 116–17
Mental incapacity
    see also **Diminished
        responsibility**
    consent to battery 97
    rape 123–4
Mistake
    actus reus 226–8
    battery 105
    as to civil law 232
    as to criminal law 232–3
    effects 230
    mens rea 82–3
    negligence crimes 228–9
    provocation 152
    reasonable belief of consent or
        duress 230–2
    self-defence 240–1
    strict liability 229–30
    summary 244
    theft 299–304
M'Naghten **Rules** *see* **Insanity**
Money, theft 291, 308–10
Morality, common law
    conspiracy 508–9
Motive
    intention compared 58–62
    sexual assault 130–2
Murder
    duress by threats 257–9
    intention
        certain outcome of
            prohibited act 52–4
        probable outcome of
            prohibited act 54–8
    joint enterprises 443–4
    mens rea 143–9
    necessity 266
    sentencing 142–3
    summary 189–90

N

Natural events 34
Necessity
    see also **Duress**
    balance of harm 263–4
    battery 95–6
    general defence 267–8
    limited application 268–9
    medical treatment 264–5
    murder 265–7

statutory exclusions 268
summary 272
Negligence
    circumstances 77–8
    defences 74
    involuntary
        manslaughter 173–80
    mistake 228–9
    recklessness distinguished 74
    scope 72–4
    state of mind 50
    strict liability 74, 414–15

O

Objectivity
    circumstances 75
    involuntary
        manslaughter 177–80
    mens rea 49–50
    provocation 155–64
    recklessness 66–71
Offences, classification 4
Offences against property
    abstracting electricity 364
    arson 398
    blackmail
        actus reus 373–6
        mens rea 376–8
        summary 400–1
    burglary
        aggravated 371–3
        buildings 369–70
        entry 365–6
        mens rea 370–1
        scope 364–5
        summary 399–400
        trespassers 366–9
    criminal damage
        actus reus 388–94
        aggravated 395–7
        mens rea 394
        summary 402
    fraud
        by abuse of position 340–2
        by failure to disclose
            information 339–40
        by false representation
            332–9
        making off without
            payment 347–51
        miscellaneous offences
            342–3
        obtaining services
            dishonestly 343–7

overview of new
offences 331–2
recent reform 325
summary 351–4
summary of old law 326–31
grievous bodily harm
consent 113–14
handling stolen goods
actus reus 379–86
mens rea 386–8
summary 401
removal of articles from public
places
actus reus 362–3
mens rea 363
robbery 355–7
summary 399
scope 275–6
taking a conveyance without
summary 399
taking a conveyance without
consent
aggravated 361–2
definitions 357–60
mens rea 360–1
theft 276–324
Offences against the person
see also **Homicide; Sexual
offences**
actual bodily harm
actus reus 106–8
mens rea 108–9
reform proposals 109
assault
actus reus 88–91
mens rea 91–2
battery
actus reus 92–4
consent 96–104
mens rea 104–6
necessity 95–6
parental chastisement 94–5
reform proposals 106
self-defence 94
unlawful force 94
common assault 88
grievous bodily harm
actus reus 109
mens rea 115
reform proposals 116
reform proposals 117–18
scope 87–8
summary 118–20
wounding with intent
actus reus 116

mens rea 116–17
reform proposals 117
Offensive weapons, aggravated
burglary 371–3
Omissions
assumption of
responsibility 25–7
battery 93–4
common law duty 24
contract 28–9
dangerous situations created by
defendant 28–9
extent of liability 23
family relationships 25
medical treatment 27–8
statutory provisions 23–4

P

Parental chastisement 94–5
Pecuniary advantages *see*
**Obtaining pecuniary
advantage** by deception
Perpetrators
accessories
different crimes 431
perpetrator has defence 432
perpetrator lacks *mens
rea* 432–4
perpetrators exempt 431
importance of
identification 420–2
Personal property, theft 291
Presumptions
rape 124–7
strict liability 406–8
Principals *see* **Perpetrators**
Procuring 424–5
Property
see also **Offences against
property**
cheques 308–10
human body 292–3
intangibles 292
land 293
money 291, 308–10
personal property 291
protection 389–90
real property 291
self-defence 238–9
things in action 291–2
wild animals 294
Provocation
drugs 221–2
intoxication 221–2

mistake 152
momentary loss of control 150,
152–5
reform proposals 164–6
requirements 150–64
self-induced 152
Public decency, common law
conspiracy 430–2
Public places *see* **Removal of
articles from public
places**
Public policy, consent to
battery 100–2
Punishment
murder 142–3
strict liability 415–16

R

Rape
see also **Assault by
penetration**
actus reus 123–7
mens rea 127–9
Real property, theft 291
Receiving, stolen goods 382–3
Recklessness
actual bodily harm 108–9
assault 91
automatism 214
battery 104–6
circumstances 76–7
grievous bodily harm 115
involuntary
manslaughter 180–1
meaning 63–4
negligence distinguished 74
objectivity 66–71
rape 128
reform proposals 71
state of mind 50
subjectivity 51, 65–6, 71–2
unjustifiable risk taking 64–5
Reform proposals
actual bodily harm 96
automatism 215
battery 106
causation 42
criminal law 12–14
diminished responsibility
171–2
drugs 225–6
duress of circumstances 263
fraud 325
grievous bodily harm 116

intoxication 225–6
offences against the
      person 117–18
provocation 164–6
recklessness 71
secondary participation 455
self-defence 242
sentencing for murder 142–3
unlawful acts 188
vicarious liability 464
wounding with intent 117
Regulatory offences
strict liability 408–11
third party intervention
      35–6
**Removal of articles from
      public places**
actus reus 362–3
mens rea 363
Reverse burdens of proof 9–12
Robbery 355–7, 399

S
Sadomasochism, consent to
      battery 102–3
Secondary participation
accessories
      actus reus 423–34
      as victims 451
      entrapment 453–5
      mens rea 434–41
      withdrawal 451–3
companies 470–3
innocent agents 422
joint enterprises
      accidental departure from
            common purpose 449–51
      assistance and
            encouragement
            beforehand 444
      deliberate departure from
            common purpose 442–3
      foresight 443–4
      lesser offences 446–9
      murder 443–4
      unforeseen acts 445–6
perpetrators 420–2
reform proposals 455
scope 419–20
summary 456–8
Self-defence
battery 94
drugs 220–1
intoxication 220–1

mistake 240–1
property 238–9
reasonable force 234–8
reform proposals 242
scope and effect 239–40
summary 244–5
Sentencing
murder 142–3
strict liability 415–16
Services *see* **Obtaining services
      by deception**
Sexual offences
assault by penetration 129
causing persons to engage in
      sexual activity without
      consent 133
children 195–6
      victims under sixteen 134
      victims under thirteen 134
consent to battery 96
corporate liability 469
rape
      actus reus 123–7
      mens rea 127–9
scope 121–2
sexual assault
      actus reus 130–2
summary 135–7
Specific intent
basic intent distinguished 63
drugs 217–18
intoxication 217–18
Sports, consent to
      battery 103–4
Standard of proof 12
State of affairs offences
general principles 29
strict liability
      distinguished 403–4
Statutory offences
conspiracy 495–502
vicarious liability 462
Strict liability
absolute offences
      distinguished 403–4
delegation principle 463
development 405
judicial inconsistency 406
justification 416–17
mistake 229–30
negligence 74
presumption of *mens
      rea* 406–8
punishment 415–16
purpose 416

rationale 416–17
regulatory offences 408–11
statutory context 411–15
summary 417
Subjectivity
automatism 214
circumstances 74–5
mens rea 49–50
provocation 152–5
reckless manslaughter 181
recklessness 51, 65–6, 71–2
Suicide pacts 172
Superior orders 270

T
**Taking a conveyance without
      consent**
aggravated 361–2
definitions 357–60
mens rea 360–1
summary 399
Territorial jurisdiction,
      statutory conspiracy
      501–2
Theft
actus reus
      appropriation 277–90
      'belonging to another'
            294–305
      property 291–4, 308–10
general observations 276–7
handling stolen
      goods 379–86
mens rea
      dishonesty 310–16
      intention to permanently
            deprive 316–21
robbery 355–7
summary 322–4
Things in action, theft 291–2
Third parties
duress by threats 254
intervening events
      general principles 34–5
      involuntary acts 36–7
      medical treatment 37
      regulatory offences 35–6
      substantial and operational
            cause 37
provocation 151–2
Threats
see also **Duress**
assault 91
duress

association with
    criminals 256–7
death or serious injury
    253–4
escape opportunities
    254–5
imminent danger 255–6
murder 257–9
standard test 250–3
third parties 254
robbery 355–7
Transferred malice 82–3
Trespassers, burglary 366–9
Trust property, theft 308

U

Unlawful act manslaughter
causation 185–7
dangerous acts 184–5
directed at another 187–8
intention 181–2
unlawfulness 182–4
Unlawful acts
reform proposals 188
Unlawful killing 140–1

V

Vicarious liability
common law offences 461
delegation principle 463–4
extensive construction
    principle 460–3
reform proposals 464
scope 460
statutory offences 462
summary 476
Victims
accessories 451
homicide 141–2
third party intervention
    37–8
Violence, assault 89–90
Voluntary conduct 21–2
Voluntary manslaughter
diminished responsibility
    abnormality of
        mind 167–8
    burden of proof 170–1
    defined 166–7
    reform proposals 171–2
    specified causes 168–9

substantial impairment
    169–70
provocation
    mistake 152
    momentary loss of
        control 150, 152–5
    reform proposals 164–6
    requirements 150–64
    self-induced 152
suicide pacts 172
summary 190–1

W

Weapons, aggravated
    burglary 371–3
Wild animals, theft 294
Wilfulness, *mens rea* 76
Words, assault 90–1
Wounding
grievous bodily
    harm 112
with intent
    actus reus 116
    mens rea 116–17
    reform proposals 117